State Trooper Exam

14th Edition

ARCO

THOMSON LEARNING™

Australia • Canada • Mexico • Singapore • Spain • United Kingdom • United States

ARCO

THOMSON LEARNING ™

An ARCO Book

ARCO is a registered trademark of Thomson Learning, Inc., and is used herein under license by Peterson's.

About Peterson's

Founded in 1966, Peterson's, a division of Thomson Learning, is the nation's largest and most respected provider of lifelong learning resources, both in print and online. The Education Supersite℠ at www.petersons.com—the Internet's most heavily traveled education resource—has searchable databases and interactive tools for contacting U.S.-accredited institutions and programs. In addition, Peterson's delivers unmatched financial aid resources and test-preparation tools. Peterson's serves more than 100 million education consumers annually.

Peterson's is a division of Thomson Learning, one of the world's largest providers of lifelong learning. Thomson Learning serves the needs of individuals, learning institutions, and corporations with products and services for both traditional and distributed learning. Headquartered in Stamford, Connecticut, with offices worldwide, Thomson Learning is a division of The Thomson Corporation (www.thomson.com), one of the world's leading e-information and solutions companies in the business, professional, and education marketplaces. For more information, visit www.thomsonlearning.com.

For more information, contact Peterson's, 2000 Lenox Drive, Lawrenceville, NJ 08648; 800-338-3282; or find us on the World Wide Web at: www.petersons.com/about

An American BookWorks Corporation Project

ISBN 0-7689-0701-2

Printed in the United States of America

10 9 8 7 6 5 4 3 2 1   03 02 01

CONTENTS

PART FIVE: CAREER INFORMATION RESOURCES

WHAT THIS BOOK WILL DO FOR YOU

Arco Publishing has followed testing trends and methods ever since the firm was founded in 1937. We *specialize* in books that prepare people for tests. Based on this experience, we have prepared the best possible book to help *you* score high.

To write this book we carefully analyzed every detail surrounding the forthcoming examinations. Since there is such variation in exams, we cannot predict exactly what your exam will be like. *However*, after studying many announcements and many exams, we have written this book to prepare you for the most probable question types. The instructional chapters will prepare you for questions that you are likely to face. The model exams, while they are not actual exams, will give you excellent practice and preparation for your state trooper exam. Other features of this book include details about:

- the job itself

- official and unofficial announcements concerning the examination

- all the previous examinations, although many not available to the public

- related examinations

- technical literature that explains and forecasts the examination

CAN YOU PREPARE YOURSELF FOR YOUR TEST?

You want to pass this test. That's why you bought this book. Used correctly, your "self-tutor" will show you what to expect and will give you a speedy brush-up on the subjects tested in your exam. Some of these are subjects not taught in schools at all. Even if your study time is very limited, you should:

- become familiar with the type of examination you will have

- improve your general examination-taking skill

- improve your skill in analyzing and answering questions involving reasoning, judgment, comparison, and evaluation

- improve your speed and skill in reading and understanding what you read — an important part of your ability to learn and an important part of most tests

This book will help you in the following ways:

Present every type of question you will get on the actual test. This will make you at ease with the test format.

Find your weaknesses. Once you know what subjects you're weak in, you can get right to work and concentrate on those areas. This kind of selective study yields maximum test results.

Give you confidence *now.* It will build your self-confidence while you are preparing for the test. As you proceed, it will prevent the kind of test anxiety that causes low test scores.

Stress the multiple-choice type of question because that's the kind you'll have on your test. You must not be satisfied with merely knowing the correct answer for each question. You must find out why the other choices are incorrect. This will help you remember a lot you thought you had forgotten.

After testing yourself, you may find that you are weak in a particular area. You should concentrate on improving your skills by using the specific practice sections in this book that apply to you.

HOW DO I USE THIS BOOK?

If you already know what type of career you wish to pursue, this book will help you prepare for any of the major exams. If you don't know what type of job you'd like to apply for, this book will also help you. Not only will you be able to prepare for your exam, but you will also find information here about various types of careers, and perhaps it will narrow down your choices. This book offers you an overview of the world of civil service; a brief introduction to federal, state, and city employers and their hiring requirements; and in-depth descriptions of a number of widely used examinations.

PART ONE

There are five parts to this book. Part One covers the major employment sectors: federal, state, municipal (city), and private industry careers. There's more than enough for everyone here. Each sector has its own requirements and tests. However, as you will see, there are certain types of questions that will appear on most of these exams, regardless of the type of test you will take.

Also in this section is important information on test-taking techniques. This will give you guidelines to help you prepare for the actual test. Feeling anxious before you take a test is a normal reaction. We provide you with tips on feeling relaxed and comfortable with your exam so you can get a great test score.

PART TWO

Part Two is an overview of the various types of careers available. If you haven't already been in the field, you will be surprised by the number of different job opportunities there are as well as the varied jobs within an area. For example, did you know that there are almost 2,000 different job titles just within the United States Postal Service? This is just *one* federal agency.

If you are beginning your career or job shopping at this time, you should read this section carefully. It will help introduce you to the different jobs and the many opportunities that await you. We hope you will be inspired and excited and will be motivated to apply for, study for, and land one of those jobs. If this section helps you narrow your area of interest, you can then concentrate on the exams that will help you prepare for the job you want. If you are still wide open, give equal attention to each exam.

PART THREE

That leads us into Part Three of this book. In this section, we detail test-types and requirements. We've also given you a review section so that you can practice on a variety of different question types. We suggest you go through this chapter to get an idea of where your strengths lie and what weaknesses you'll have to deal with on the actual test.

We've also provided you with a variety of different types of tests that you will encounter in almost any job you apply for in the civil service, since there are certain basics that need to be covered. For example, in most tests, you will be asked to understand vocabulary and the use of grammar. Some tests will test your memory abilities and your ability for recall. Can you alphabetize easily and quickly? That's an area also covered on many of these tests.

PART FOUR

In Part Four, there are either real examinations, (official sample examinations) or others are model examinations closely patterned on the actual exams. Timing, level of difficulty, question styles, and scoring methods all conform closely to the examinations for which they are meant to prepare. And a special feature of this book is that all the correct answers are explained.

When you do take the sample exams, try to set aside the full measure of time to take the exam at one sitting. Time yourself accurately (a stopwatch or a kitchen timer will work well) and stop working when the time is up. If you have not completed all of the questions when the time expires, stop anyway. Check your answers against the provided correct answers and score your paper. Then continue with the remaining questions to get in all the practice you can. Carefully study all the answer explanations, even those for questions that you answered correctly. By reading all of the explanations, you can gain greater insight into methods of answering questions and the reasoning behind the correct choices.

One very important suggestion: We strongly believe that regardless of the test that you think you're planning to take—or the career path you want to follow—try to take *all* of the exams in this book. It may seem like a lot of extra work, but you never know where you may end up. You may think you're interested in a job with the local city government, and end up instead in a private company. Or the exam you were hoping to take is not being given for another year, but some other test is being given next month. It is always better to be prepared.

PART FIVE

Finally, Part Five contains civil service career information resources. Here you will find out how to go about looking for available jobs, as well as important addresses, phone numbers, and Internet Web sites that will help you pursue your career in civil service.

The most important thing is to *use* this book. By going through all of the sections and reading them, reviewing question types, and taking the practice exams, you will be using what you learned here to the best of your ability to succeed in your intended career path.

PART ONE

So You Want to Work for The Government

Government service is one of the nation's largest sources of employment. About one in every six employed persons in the United States is in some form of civilian government service. Of those government employees, five out of six workers are employed by state or local governments, and the remainder work for the federal government.

As you can see, government employees represent a significant portion of the nation's work force. They work in large cities, small towns, and remote and isolated places such as lighthouses and forest ranger stations, and a small number of federal employees work overseas. In this chapter, we will outline the various types of careers that are available in the federal, state, and local governments.

WHERE THE JOBS ARE: FEDERAL CIVILIAN EMPLOYMENT

The federal government is the nation's largest employer. It employs almost 3 million civilian workers in the United States and an additional 130,000 civilian workers—half of them U.S. citizens—in U.S. territories and foreign countries. The headquarters of most government departments and agencies are in the Washington, D.C., area, but only one out of eight federal employees works there.

Federal employees work in occupations that represent nearly every kind of job in private employment as well as some unique to the federal government such as regulatory inspectors, foreign service officers, and Internal Revenue agents. Most federal employees work for the executive branch of the government.

The executive branch includes the Office of the President, the cabinet departments, and about 100 independent agencies, commissions, and boards. This branch is responsible for activities such as administering federal laws, handling international relations, conserving natural resources, treating and rehabilitating disabled veterans, delivering the mail, conducting scientific research, maintaining the flow of supplies to the armed forces, and administering other programs to promote the health and welfare of the people of the United States.

The Department of Defense, which includes the Departments of the Army, Navy, and Air Force, is the largest department. It employs about one million civilian workers. The Departments of Agriculture, Health and Human Services, and the Treasury are also big employers. The two largest independent agencies are the U.S. Postal Service and the Veterans Administration.

There is also federal civilian employment available in the legislative branch, which includes Congress, the Government Printing Office, the General Accounting Office, and the Library of Congress. The judicial branch, the smallest employer, hires people for work within the court system.

WHITE-COLLAR OCCUPATIONS

Because of its wide range of responsibilities, the federal government employs white-collar workers in a great many occupational fields. About one of four of these are administrative and clerical workers.

General clerical workers are employed in all federal departments and agencies. These include office machine operators, secretaries, stenographers, clerk-typists, mail- and file-clerks, telephone operators, and workers in computer and related occupations. In addition, there are the half million postal clerks and mail carriers.

Many government workers are employed in engineering and related fields. The engineers represent virtually every branch and specialty of engineering. There are large numbers of technicians in areas such as engineering, electronics, surveying, and drafting. Nearly two-thirds of all engineers are in the Department of Defense.

Of the more than 120,000 workers employed in accounting and budgeting work, 35,000 are professional accountants or Internal Revenue officers. Among technician and administrative occupations are accounting technicians, tax accounting technicians, and budget administrators. There are also large numbers of clerks in specialized accounting work. Accounting workers are employed throughout the government, particularly in the Departments of Defense and the Treasury and in the General Accounting Office.

Many federal employees work in hospitals or in medical, dental, and public health activities. Three out of five are either professional nurses or nursing assistants. Other professional occupations in this field include physicians, dieticians, technologists, and physical therapists. Technician and aide jobs include medical technicians, medical laboratory aides, and dental assistants. Employees in this field work primarily for the Veterans Administration; others work for the Departments of Defense and Health and Human Services.

Other government workers are engaged in administrative work related to private business and industry. They arrange and monitor contracts with the private sector and purchase goods and services needed by the federal government. Administrative occupations include contract and procurement specialists, production control specialists, and Internal Revenue officers. Two out of three of these workers are employed by the Departments of Defense and Treasury.

Another large group works in jobs concerned with the purchase, cataloging, storage, and distribution of supplies for the federal government. This field includes many managerial and administrative positions such as supply management officers, purchasing officers, and inventory management specialists, as well as large numbers of specialized clerical positions. Most of these jobs are in the Department of Defense.

Throughout the federal government, many people are employed in the field of law. They fill professional positions, such as attorneys or law clerks, and administrative positions, such as passport and visa examiners or tax law specialists. There also are many clerical positions that involve examining claims.

The social sciences also employ many government employees. Economists are employed throughout the government; psychologists and social workers work primarily for the Veterans Administration; and foreign affairs and international relations specialists, for the Department of State. One third of the workers in this field are social insurance administrators employed largely in the Department of Health and Human Services.

About 50,000 biological and agricultural science workers are employed by the federal government, mostly in the Departments of Agriculture and Interior. Many of these work in forestry and soil conservation activities. Others administer farm assistance programs. The largest number are employed as biologists, forest and range fire controllers, soil conservationists, and forestry technicians.

The federal government employs another 50,000 people in investigative and inspection work. Large numbers of these are engaged in criminal investigation and health regulatory inspections, mostly in the Departments of Treasury, Justice, and Agriculture.

Physical sciences is another area of government employment. Three out of four workers in the physical sciences are employed by the Departments of Defense, Interior, and Commerce. Professional workers include chemists, physicists, meteorologists, cartographers, and geologists. Aides and technicians include physical science technicians, meteorological technicians, and cartography technicians.

And in the mathematics field are professional mathematicians and statisticians and mathematics technicians and statistical clerks. They are employed primarily by the Departments of Defense, Agriculture, Commerce, and Health and Human Services.

Entrance requirements for white-collar jobs vary widely. A college degree in a specified field or equivalent work experience is usually required for professional occupations such as physicists and engineers.

Entrants into administrative and managerial occupations usually are not required to have knowledge of a specialized field, but must instead indicate a potential for future development by having a degree from a 4-year college or responsible job experience. They usually begin as trainees and learn their duties on the job. Typical jobs in this group are budget analysts, claims examiners, purchasing specialists, administrative assistants, and personnel specialists.

Technician, clerical, and aide-assistant jobs have entry-level positions for people with a high school education or the equivalent. For many of these positions, no previous experience or training is required. The entry level position is usually that of trainee. Persons who have junior college or technical school training or those who have specialized skills may enter these occupations at higher levels. Typical jobs are engineering technicians, supply clerks, clerk-typists, and nursing assistants.

BLUE-COLLAR OCCUPATIONS

Blue-collar occupations—craft, operative, laborer, and some service jobs—provide full-time employment for more than half a million federal workers. The Department of Defense employs about three fourths of these workers in establishments such as naval shipyards, arsenals, and the Air or Army depots as well as on construction, harbor, flood control, irrigation, or reclamation projects. Others work for the Veterans Administration, U.S. Postal Service, General Services Administration, Department of the Interior, and Tennessee Valley Authority.

The largest single blue-collar group consists of manual laborers. Large numbers also are employed in machine tool and metal work, motor vehicle operation, warehousing, and food preparation and serving. The federal government employs a wide variety of individuals in maintenance and repair work, such as electrical and electronic equipment installation and repair, and in vehicle and industrial equipment maintenance and repair. All these fields require a range of skill levels and include a variety of occupations comparable to the private sector.

Although the federal government employs blue-collar workers in many different fields, about half are concentrated in a small number of occupations. The largest group, the skilled mechanics, works as air-conditioning, aircraft, automobile, truck, electronics, sheet-metal, and general maintenance mechanics. Another large number of craft workers is employed as painters, pipefitters, carpenters, electricians, and machinists. A similar number serves as warehouse workers, truck drivers, and general laborers. An additional group of workers is employed as janitors and food service workers.

ENTRANCE REQUIREMENTS

Persons with previous training in a skilled trade may apply for a position with the federal government at the journey level. Those with no previous training may apply for appointment to one of several apprenticeship programs. Apprenticeship programs generally last four years; trainees receive both classroom and on-the-job training. After completing this training, a person is eligible for a position at the journey level. There are also a number of positions which require little or no prior training or experience, including janitors, maintenance workers, messengers, and many others.

THE MERIT SYSTEM

More than nine out of ten jobs in the federal government are under a merit system. The Civil Service Act, administered by the U.S. Office of Personnel Management, covers six out of ten federal titles. This act was passed by Congress to ensure that federal employees are hired on the basis of individual merit and fitness. It provides for competitive examinations and the selection of new employees from among the most qualified applicants.

Some federal jobs are exempt from civil service requirements either by law or by action of the Office of Personnel Management. However, most of these positions are covered by separate merit systems of other agencies such as the Foreign Service of the Department of State, the Federal Bureau of Investigation, the Nuclear Regulatory Commission, and the Tennessee Valley Authority.

EARNINGS, ADVANCEMENT, AND WORKING CONDITIONS

Most federal civilian employees are paid according to one of three major pay systems: the **General Pay Schedule,** the **Wage System,** or the **Postal Service Schedule.**

GENERAL PAY SCHEDULE

More than half of all federal workers are paid under the General Schedule (GS), a pay scale for workers in professional, administrative, technical, and clerical jobs, and for workers such as guards and messengers. General Schedule jobs are classified by the U.S. Office of Personnel Management in one of fifteen grades, according to the difficulty of duties and responsibilities and the knowledge, experience, and skills required of the workers. GS pay rates are set by Congress and apply to government workers nationwide. They are reviewed annually to see whether they are comparable with salaries in private industry. They are generally subject to upwards adjustment for very high-cost-of-living regions. In low-cost areas, the GS pay scale may exceed that of most private-sector workers.

Most employees receive within-grade pay increases at one-, two-, or three-year intervals if their work is acceptable. Within-grade increases may also be given in recognition of high-quality service. Some managers and supervisors receive increases based on their job performance rather than on time in grade.

High school graduates who have no related work experience usually start in GS-2 jobs, but some who have special skills begin at grade GS-3. Graduates of 2-year colleges and technical schools often can begin at the GS-4 level. Most people with bachelor's degrees appointed to professional and administrative jobs such as statisticians, economists, writers and editors, budget analysts, accountants, and physicists, can enter at grades GS-5 or GS-7, depending on experience and academic record. Those who have a master's degree or Ph.D. or the equivalent education or experience may enter at the GS-9 or GS-11 level. Advancement to higher grades generally depends upon ability, work performance, and openings in jobs at higher grade levels.

FEDERAL WAGE SYSTEM

About one quarter of federal civilian workers are paid according to the Federal Wage System. Under this system, craft, service, and manual workers are paid hourly rates established on the basis of "prevailing" rates paid by private employers for similar work in the same locations. As a result, the federal government wage rate for an occupation varies by locality. This commitment to meeting the local wage scale allows the federal wage earner to bring home a weekly paycheck comparable to that which he or she would earn in the private sector and to enjoy the benefits and security of a government job at the same time. The federal wage earner has the best of all possible worlds in this regard.

Federal government employees work a standard 40-hour week. Employees who are required to work overtime may receive premium rates for the additional time or compensatory time off at a later date. Most employees work eight hours a day, five days a week, Monday through Friday, but in some cases, the nature of the work requires a different workweek. Annual earnings for most full-time federal workers are not affected by seasonal factors.

Federal employees earn 13 days of annual (vacation) leave each year during their first three years of service; 20 days each year until the end of 15 years; after 15 years, 26 days each year. Workers who are members of military reserve organizations also are granted up to 15 days of paid military leave a year for training purposes. A federal worker who is laid off, though federal layoffs are uncommon, is entitled to unemployment compensation similar to that provided for employees in private industry.

Other benefits available to most federal employees include: a contributory retirement system, optional participation in low-cost group life and health insurance programs which are partly supported by the government (as the employer), and training programs to develop maximum job proficiency and help workers achieve their highest potential. These training programs may be conducted in government facilities or in private educational facilities at government expense.

GENERAL SCHEDULE
(Range of Salaries)

Effective as of January 1, 2001

GS Rating	Low	High
1	$14,244	$17,819
2	16,015	20,156
3	17,474	22,712
4	19,616	25,502
5	21,957	28,535
6	24,463	31,798
7	27,185	35,339
8	30,107	39,143
9	33,254	43,226
10	36,621	47,610
11	40,236	52,305
12	48,223	62,686
13	57,345	74,553
14	67,765	88,096
15	79,710	103,623

WHERE THE JOBS ARE: STATE AND LOCAL GOVERNMENTS

State and local governments provide a very large and expanding source of job opportunities in a wide variety of occupational fields. About fifteen million people work for state and local government agencies; nearly three fourths of these work in units of local government such as counties, municipalities, towns, and school districts. The job distribution varies greatly from that in federal government service. Defense, international relations and commerce, immigration, and mail delivery are virtually non-existent in state and local governments. On the other hand, there is great emphasis on education, health, social services, transportation, construction, and sanitation.

EDUCATIONAL SERVICES

About one half of all jobs in state and local government are in educational services. Educational employees work in public schools, colleges, and various extension services. About half of all education workers are instructional personnel. School systems, colleges, and universities also employ administrative personnel, librarians, guidance counselors, nurses, dieticians, clerks, and maintenance workers.

HEALTH SERVICES

The next largest field of state and local government employment is health services. Those employed in health and hospital work include physicians, nurses, medical laboratory technicians, dieticians, kitchen and laundry workers, and hospital attendants. Social services make up another aspect of health and welfare. Unfortunately, the need for welfare and human services has been increasing greatly. As the need grows, the opportunities for social workers and their affiliated administrative and support staff also grows.

GOVERNMENT CONTROL/FINANCIAL ACTIVITIES

Another million workers work in the areas of general governmental control and financial activities. These include chief executives and their staffs, legislative representatives, and persons employed in the administration of justice, tax enforcement and other financial work, and general administration. These functions require the services of individuals such as lawyers, judges and other court officers, city managers, property assessors, budget analysts, stenographers, and clerks.

STREETS AND HIGHWAYS

The movement of people is of great concern to both state and local governments. Street and highway construction and maintenance are of major importance. Highway workers include civil engineers, surveyors, operators of construction machinery and equipment, truck drivers, concrete finishers, carpenters, construction laborers, and, where appropriate, snow removers. Toll collectors are relatively few in number, but they too are state or county employees or employees of independent authorities of the states or counties. Mass transportation within municipalities and between the cities and their outlying suburbs is also the province of local government. Maintaining vehicles, roadbeds and signaling systems, and staffing the vehicles themselves, requires a large and varied work force.

POLICE AND FIRE PROTECTION SERVICES

Police and fire protection is another large field of employment. Along with uniformed officers, these services include extensive administrative, clerical, maintenance, and custodial personnel.

MISCELLANEOUS STATE AND LOCAL OCCUPATIONS

Other state and local government employees work in a wide variety of activities, including local utilities (water in most areas, electricity in some); natural resources; parks and recreation; sanitation; corrections; local libraries; sewage disposal; and housing and urban renewal. These activities require workers in diverse occupations such as economists, electrical engineers, electricians, pipefitters, clerks, foresters, and bus drivers.

CLERICAL, ADMINISTRATIVE, MAINTENANCE, AND CUSTODIAL WORKERS

A large percentage of employment in most government agencies is made up of clerical, administrative, maintenance, and custodial workers. Among the workers involved in these activities are word processors, secretaries, data processors, computer specialists, office managers, fiscal and budget administrators, bookkeepers, accountants, carpenters, painters, plumbers, guards, and janitors. The list is endless.

Most positions in state and local governments are filled by residents of the state or locality. Many localities have residency requirements. Exceptions are generally made for persons with skills that are in special demand.

EARNINGS

Job conditions and earnings of state and local government employees vary widely, depending upon occupation and locality. Salary differences from state to state and even within some states tend to reflect differences in the general wage level and cost of living in the various localities.

As with the federal government, a majority of state and local government positions are filled through some type of formal civil service test; that is, personnel are hired and promoted on the basis of merit. State and local government workers have the same protections as federal government workers: they cannot be refused employment because of their race; they cannot be denied promotion because someone else made a greater political contribution; and they cannot be fired because the boss's son needs a job. Jobs tend to be classified according to job description and pegged to a salary schedule that is based upon the job classifications. Periodic performance reviews also are standard expectations. Nearly every group of employees has some sort of union or organization, but the functions and powers of these units vary greatly.

Since states and local entities are independent, the benefits packages they offer their employees can be quite different. Most state and local government employees are covered by retirement systems or by the federal social security program. Most have some sort of health coverage. They usually work a standard week of 40 hours or less with overtime pay or compensatory time benefits for additional hours of work.

PREPARING YOURSELF FOR THE CIVIL SERVICE EXAMINATION

Most federal, state, and municipal units have recruitment procedures for filling civil service positions. They have developed a number of methods to make job opportunities known. Places where such information may be obtained include:

1. The offices of the State Employment Services. There are almost two thousand throughout the country. These offices are administered by the state in which they are located, with the financial assistance of the federal government. You will find the address of the one nearest you in your telephone book.

2. Your state Civil Service Commission. Address your inquiry to the capital city of your state.

3. Your city Civil Service Commission. It is sometimes called by another name, such as the Department of Personnel, but you will be able to identify it in your telephone directory under the listing of city departments.

4. Your municipal building and your local library.

5. Complete listings are carried by such newspapers as *The Chief-Leader* (published in New York City), as well as by other city and state-wide publications devoted to civil service employees. Many local newspapers run a section on regional civil service news.

6. State and local agencies looking for competent employees will contact schools, professional societies, veterans organizations, unions, and trade associations.

7. School boards and boards of education, which employ the greatest proportion of all state and local personnel, should be asked directly for information about job openings.

You will find more in-depth information at the end of this book.

THE FORMAT OF THE JOB ANNOUNCEMENT

When a position is open and a civil service examination is to be given for it, a job announcement is drawn up. This generally contains everything an applicant has to know about the job.

The announcement begins with the job title and salary. A typical announcement then describes the work, the location of the position, the education and experience requirements, the kind of examination to be given, and the system of rating. It may also have something to say about veteran preference and the age limit. It tells which application form is to be filled out, where to get the form, and where and when to file it.

Study the job announcement carefully. It will answer many of your questions and help you decide whether you like the position and are qualified for it. We have included sample job announcements in a later chapter.

There is no point in applying for a position and taking the examination if you do not want to work where the job is. The job may be in your community or hundreds of miles away at the other end of the state. If you are not willing to work where the job is, study other announcements that will give you an opportunity to work in a place of your choice. A civil service job close to your home has an additional advantage since local residents usually receive preference in appointments.

The words **Optional Fields**—sometimes just the word **Options**—may appear on the front page of the announcement. You then have a choice to apply for that particular position in which you are especially interested. This is because the duties of various positions are quite different even though they bear the same broad title. A public relations clerk, for example, does different work from a payroll clerk, although they are considered broadly in the same general area.

Not every announcement has options. But whether or not it has them, the precise duties are described in detail, usually under the heading, **Description of Work.** Make sure that these duties come within the range of your experience and ability.

Most job requirements give a **deadline for filing** an application. Others bear the words **No Closing Date** at the top of the first page; this means that applications will be accepted until the needs of the agency are met. In some cases a public notice is issued when a certain number of applications has been received. No application mailed past the deadline date will be considered.

Every announcement has a detailed section on **education and experience requirements** for the particular job and for the optional fields. Make sure that in both education and experience you meet the minimum qualifications. If you do not meet the given standards for one job, there may be others open where you stand a better chance of making the grade.

If the job announcement does not mention **veteran preference,** it would be wise to inquire if there is such a provision in your state or municipality. There may be none or it may be limited to disabled veterans. In some jurisdictions, surviving spouses of disabled veterans are given preference. All such information can be obtained through the agency that issues the job announcement.

Applicants may be denied examinations and eligible candidates may be denied appointments for any of the following reasons:

- intentional false statements

- deception or fraud in examination or appointment

- use of intoxicating beverages to the extent that ability to perform the duties of the position is impaired

- criminal, infamous, dishonest, immoral, or notoriously disgraceful conduct

The announcement describes the **kind of test** given for the particular position. Please pay special attention to this section. It tells what areas are to be covered in the written test and lists the specific subjects on which questions will be asked. Sometimes sample questions are given.

Usually the announcement states whether the examination is to be **assembled** or **unassembled.** In an assembled examination applicants assemble in the same place at the same time to take a written or performance test. The unassembled examination is one where an applicant does not take a test; instead, he or she is rated on his or her education and experience and whatever records of past achievement the applicant is asked to provide.

In the competitive examination all applicants for a position compete with each other; the better the mark, the better the chance of being appointed. Also, competitive examinations are given to determine desirability for promotion among employees.

Civil service written tests are rated on a scale of 100, with 70 usually as the passing mark.

FILLING OUT THE APPLICATION FORM

Having studied the job announcement and having decided that you want the position and are qualified for it, your next step is to get an application form. The job announcement tells you where to send for it.

On the whole, civil service application forms differ little from state to state and locality to locality. The questions that have been worked out after years of experimentation are simple and direct, designed to elicit a maximal amount of information about you.

Many prospective civil service employees have failed to get a job because of slipshod, erroneous, incomplete, misleading, or untruthful answers. Give the application serious attention, for it is the first important step toward getting the job you want.

Here, along with some helpful comments, are the questions usually asked on the average application form, although not necessarily in this order.

- **Name of examination or kind of position applied for.** This information appears in large type on the first page of the job announcement.

- **Optional job** (if mentioned in the announcement). If you wish to apply for an option, simply copy the title from the announcement. If you are not interested in an option, write *None*.

- **Primary place of employment applied for.** The location of the position was probably contained in the announcement. You must consider whether you want to work there. The announcement may list more than one location where the job is open. If you would accept employment in any of the places, list them all; otherwise list the specific place or places where you would be willing to work.

- **Name and address.** Give in full, including your middle name if you have one, and your maiden name as well if you are a married woman.

- **Home and office phones.** If none, write *None*.

- **Legal or voting residence.** The state in which you vote is the one you list here.

- **Height without shoes, weight, sex.** Answer accurately.

- **Date of birth.** Give the exact day, month, and year.

- **Lowest grade or pay you will accept.** Although the salary is clearly stated in the job announcement, there may be a quicker opening in the same occupation but carrying less responsibility and thus a lower basic entrance salary. You will not be considered for a job paying less than the amount you give in answer to this question.

- **Will you accept temporary employment if offered you for (a) one month or less, (b) one to four months, (c) four to twelve months?** Temporary positions come up frequently and it is important to know whether you are available.

- **Will you accept less than full-time employment?** Part-time work comes up now and then. Consider whether you want to accept such a position while waiting for a full-time appointment.

- **Were you in active military service in the Armed Forces of the United States?** Veterans' preference, if given, is usually limited to active service during the following periods: 12/7/41–12/31/46; 6/27/50–1/31/55; 6/1/63–5/7/75; 6/1/83–12/1/87; 10/23/83–11/21/83; 12/20/89–1/3/90; 8/2/90 to end of Persian Gulf hostilities.

- **Do you claim disabled veterans credit?** If you do, you have to show proof of a war-incurred disability compensable by at least 10 percent. This is done through certification by the Veterans Administration.

- **Special qualifications and skills.** Even though not directly related to the position for which you are applying, information about licenses and certificates obtained for teacher, pilot, registered nurse, and so on, is requested. List your experience in the use of machines and equipment and whatever other skills you have acquired. Also list published writings, public speaking experience, membership in professional societies, and honors and fellowships received.

- **Education.** List your entire educational history, including all diplomas, degrees, and special courses taken in any accredited or armed forces school. Also give your credits toward a college or a graduate degree.

- **References.** The names of people who can give information about you, with their occupations and business and home address, are often requested.

- **Your health.** Questions are asked concerning your medical record. You are expected to have the physical and psychological capacity to perform the job for which you are applying. Standards vary, of course, depending on the requirements of the position. A physical handicap usually will not bar an applicant from a job he can perform adequately unless the safety of the public is involved.

- **Work history.** Considerable space is allotted on the form for the applicant to tell about all his past employment. Examiners check all such answers closely. Do not embellish or falsify your record. If you were ever fired, say so. It is better for you to state this openly than for the examiners to find out the truth from your former employer.

On the following pages are samples of a New York City Application for Examination and a state application from Louisiana.

WHY PEOPLE CHOOSE GOVERNMENT SERVICE

There are many similarities between work in the private sector and work for the government. Within each occupation, the similarities of the daily duties far outweigh the differences in employers. Regardless of the nature of the employer—government, private business, nonprofit organization—typists type; doctors heal; teachers teach; electricians install wiring.

As was mentioned at the beginning of this chapter, one in six of employed persons in the United States is in government service. The five in six persons who are employed by nongovernmental employers all hope for just compensation for their work, for promotions when merited, and for fair and equal treatment with reference to their coworkers. They all hope that they will not be discriminated against for any non-job-related reasons, that they will not be fired capriciously, and that their opinions and suggestions will be taken seriously. In the great majority of cases, these expectations will be met.

But, in the private sector, there are no guarantees of employment practices. In government service these guarantees are a matter of policy and law. Each governmental jurisdiction has its own body of rules and procedures. In other words, not all government service is alike. The Federal Civil Service does serve as a model for all other governmental units.

NEW YORK CITY APPLICATION FOR EXAMINATION

DEPARTMENT OF CITYWIDE ADMINISTRATIVE SERVICES
DIVISION OF CITYWIDE PERSONNEL SERVICES
1 Centre Street, 14th floor
New York, NY 10007

APPLICATION FOR EXAMINATION

(Directions for completing this application are on the *back* of this form. Additional information is on the Special Circumstances Sheet)

Download this form on-line: nyc.gov/html/dcas

FOLLOW DIRECTIONS ON BACK
Fill in all requested information clearly, accurately, and completely.

The City will only process applications with complete, correct, legible information which are accompanied by correct payment or waiver documentation.

All unprocessed applications will be returned to the applicant.

1. EXAM #:

Check One:
☐ Open Competitive
☐ Promotion

2. EXAM TITLE:

3. SOCIAL SECURITY NUMBER:

4. LAST NAME:

5. FIRST NAME:

6. MIDDLE INITIAL:

7. MAILING ADDRESS:

8. APT. #:

9. CITY OR TOWN:

10. STATE:

11. ZIP CODE:

12. PHONE:

13. OTHER NAMES USED IN CITY SERVICE:

14. RACE/ETHNICITY (Check One):
☐ White
☐ American Indian/ Alaskan Native
☐ Black
☐ Asian/Pacific Islander
☐ Hispanic

15. SEX (Check One):
☐ Male
☐ Female

Questions 14 & 15:
Discrimination on the basis of sex, sexual orientation, race, creed, color, age, disability status, veteran status or religious observance is prohibited by law. The City of New York is an equal opportunity employer. The identifying information requested on this form is to be used to determine the representation of protected groups among applicants. This information is voluntary and will not be made available to individuals making hiring decisions.

16. ARE YOU EMPLOYED BY THE HEALTH AND HOSPITALS CORPORATION? (Check One)   ☐ YES   ☐ NO

17. CHECK ALL BOXES THAT APPLY TO YOU: (Directions for this section are found on the "Special Circumstances" Sheet)
☐ I AM A SABBATH OBSERVER AND WILL REQUEST AN ALTERNATE TEST DATE (Verification required. See Item A on Special Circumstances Sheet)
☐ I HAVE A DISABILITY AND WILL REQUEST SPECIAL ACCOMMODATIONS (Verification required. See item B on Special Circumstances Sheet)
☐ I CLAIM VETERANS' CREDIT (For qualifications see item C on Special Circumstances Sheet)
☐ I CLAIM DISABLED VETERANS' CREDIT (For qualifications see item C on Special Circumstances Sheet)

18. Your Signature: _____   Date: _____

STATE OF LOUISIANA APPLICATION—page 1

SF10
(Page 1)
REV. 1/97

STATE PRE-EMPLOYMENT APPLICATION

STATE OF LOUISIANA
DEPARTMENT OF CIVIL SERVICE
P.O. Box 94111, Capitol Station
Baton Rouge, Louisiana 70804-9111

AN EQUAL OPPORTUNITY EMPLOYER

FOR OFFICE USE

Special _____
Promo _____
Action(s) _____

Session _____

Data Entry Completed _____

1. TEST LOCATION-Check only one.

Baton Rouge (3) (Weekday) ☐   New Orleans (6) (Weekday) ☐   Lafayette (4) (Sat. only) ☐   Shreveport (7) (Sat. only) ☐

New Orleans (12) (Saturday) ☐   Lake Charles (5) (Sat. only) ☐   West Monroe (8) (Sat. only) ☐

2. Enter Name and Complete Address below.

3. Parish of Residence

4. Are you 18 or older? ☐ Yes ☐ No

5. Other names ever used on SF-10

NAME - First   Middle   Last

Mailing Address

City   State   Zip Code

6. Social Security Number (For identification purpose)

Work Telephone No.

Home Telephone No.

L A S T → P R I N T   F I R S T   N A M E → M I D D L E

7. REGISTER TITLE(S) APPLIED FOR	FOR OFFICE USE					ADDITIONAL TITLES	FOR OFFICE USE				
	SER	CD	REJ	GRD	TR		SER	CD	REJ	GRD	TR

JS No.

V.P.

S.R.

ALL TITLES LISTED ABOVE MUST HAVE THE SAME SERIES NO.

8. JOB LOCATION AVAILABILITY - IMPORTANT: Read Item 9 on the Instruction Page before completing this item. Mark at least one (1), but no more than twenty (20) parishes.

01 Acadia	09 Caddo	17 E. Baton Rouge	25 Jackson	33 Madison	41 Red River	49 St. Landry	57 Vermillion
02 Allen	10 Calcasieu	18 E. Carroll	26 Jefferson	34 Morehouse	42 Richland	50 St. Martin	58 Vernon
03 Ascension	11 Caldwell	19 E. Feliciana	27 Jeff Davis	35 Natchitoches	43 Sabine	51 St. Mary	59 Washington
04	12 Cameron	20 Evangeline	28 Lafayette	36 Orleans	44 St. Bernard	52 St. Tammany	60 Webster
05 Avoyelles	13 Catahoula	21 Franklin	29 Lafourche	37 Ouachita	45 St. Charles	53 Tangipahoa	61 W. Baton Rouge
06 Beauregard	14 Claiborne	22 Grant	30 LaSalle	38 Plaquemines	46 St. Helena	54 Tensas	62 W. Carroll
07 Bienville	15 Concordia	23 Iberia	31 Lincoln	39 Pte. Coupee	47 St. James	55 Terrebonne	63 W. Feliciana
08 Bossier	16 DeSoto	24 Iberville	32 Livingston	40 Rapides	48 St. John	56 Union	64 Winn

9. ☐ Permanent ☐ Temporary—Type of employment you will accept

NOTE: Most Temporary Appointments are 3 - 12 months

10. ☐ YES ☐ NO   Do you possess a valid driver's license?

11. ☐ YES ☐ NO   Do you possess a valid commercial driver's license?

12. ☐ YES ☐ NO   Are you currently holding or running for an elective public office?

13. ☐ YES ☐ NO   Have you ever been on probation or sentenced to jail/prison as a result of a felony conviction or guilty plea?

14. ☐ YES ☐ NO   Have you ever been fired from a job or resigned to avoid dismissal?

NOTE: If answers to Items 13 and/or 14 are "YES", you MUST complete Item 24 on Page 2 of this application

15. ☐ YES ☐ NO   Are you claiming Veteran's Preference points on this application? (If "YES", see Item 20 on Page 2.)

The following information is collected to complete Equal Opportunity Reports required by law. You ARE NOT LEGALLY OBLIGATED to provide this information.

16. RACIAL/ETHNIC GROUP   **16A.** DATE OF BIRTH   **17.** SEX ☐ Male ☐ Female

I HAVE READ THE FOLLOWING STATEMENTS CAREFULLY BEFORE SIGNING THIS APPLICATION:

18. Date   Social Security No. (for verification)

19. Signature of Applicant

AUTHORITY TO RELEASE INFORMATION: I consent to the release of information concerning my capacity and/or all aspects of prior job performance by employers, educational institutions, law enforcement agencies, and other individuals and agencies to duly accredited investigators, personnel technicians, and other authorized employees of the state government for the purpose of determining my eligibility and suitability for employment.

I certify that all statements made on this application and any attached papers are true and complete to the best of my knowledge. I understand that information on this application may be subject to investigation and verification and that any misrepresentation or material omission may cause my application to be rejected, my name to be removed from the eligible register and/or subject me to dismissal from state service.

STATE OF LOUISIANA APPLICATION—page 2

20. ACTIVE MILITARY SERVICE/VETERAN'S PREFERENCE

See Item 10 on the Instruction Page to determine your eligibility for Veteran's Preference. If you are a first-time applicant or if you are claiming Veteran's Preference for the first time, required PROOF MUST BE ATTACHED to this application to have preference points added to your score.

List the dates (month and year) and branch for all ACTIVE DUTY military service. Was this service performed on an active, full-time basis with full pay and allowances? (Check YES or NO for each period of service.)

FROM	TO	BRANCH OF SERVICE	YES	NO

List all GRADES held and dates of each grade. Begin with the highest grade. IMPORTANT: Use E-, O-, or WO-grade.

FROM	TO	GRADE HELD	FROM	TO	GRADE HELD

21. TRAINING AND EDUCATION

Have you received a high school diploma or equivalency certificate?

☐ YES   Date received _____

☐ NO   Highest grade completed _____

A. LIST *BUSINESS OR* TECHNICAL COLLEGES ATTENDED	NAME/LOCATION OF SCHOOL	Dates Attended (Month & Year) FROM — TO	Did You Graduate? YES — NO	TITLE OF PROGRAM	CLOCK HOURS PER WEEK

List any accounting practice sets completed: _____

B. LIST COLLEGES OR UNIVERSITIES ATTENDED (Include graduate or professional schools)	NAME OF COLLEGE OR UNIVERSITY/ CITY AND STATE	Dates Attended (Month & Year) FROM — TO	Total Credit Hours Earned Semester — Quarter	Type of Degree Earned	Major Field of Study	Date Degree Received (Month & Yr.)

C. MAJOR SUBJECTS	CHIEF UNDERGRADUATE SUBJECTS (Show Major on Line 1.)	Total Credit Hours Earned Semester — Quarter	CHIEF GRADUATE SUBJECTS (Show Major on Line 1.)	Total Credit Hours Earned Semester or Qtr.
1				
2				
3				

22. LICENSES AND CERTIFICATION

23. TYPING SPEED

List any job-related licenses or certificates that you have (CPA, lawyer, registered nurse, etc.)

	TYPE OF LICENSE OR CERTIFICATE (Specify Which One)	DATE ORIGINALLY LICENSED/ CERTIFIED	EXPIRATION DATE	NAME AND ADDRESS OF LICENSING OR CERTIFYING AGENCY
1				
2				

WPM _____

DICTATION SPEED

WPM _____

24. Explain a "YES" answer to Items 13 and/or 14 here. A "YES" ANSWER WILL NOT NECESSARILY BAR YOU FROM STATE EMPLOYMENT. WE WILL CONSIDER THE DATE, FACTS, AND CIRCUMSTANCES OF EACH INDIVIDUAL CASE. For Item 13, give the law enforcement authority (city police, sherrif, FBI, etc.), the offense, date of offense, place, and disposition of case.

_____

_____

Name _____

STATE OF LOUISIANA APPLICATION—page 3

Name _____

25.   WORK EXPERIENCE — <u>IMPORTANT</u>: Read Item 11 of Instruction Page carefully before completing these items. List all jobs and activities including military service, part-time employment, self-employment, and volunteer work. BEGIN with your FIRST job in Block A; END with your MOST RECENT or PRESENT job.

A EMPLOYER/COMPANY NAME	KIND OF BUSINESS	
STREET ADDRESS	YOUR OFFICIAL JOB TITLE	
CITY AND STATE	BEGINNING SALARY	ENDING SALARY
DATES OF EMPLOYMENT (MO/DA/YR) / AVERAGE HOURS WORKED PER WEEK	REASON FOR LEAVING	NO. OF EMPLOYEES YOU DIRECTLY SUPERVISED
FROM / TO		
NAME/TITLE OF YOUR SUPERVISOR)	LIST JOB TITLES OF EMPLOYEES YOU DIRECTLY SUPERVISED	
NAME/TITLE OF PERSON WHO CAN VERIFY THIS EMPLOYMENT (IF OTHER THAN SUPERVISOR)		

DUTIES: List the major duties involved with job and give an approximate percentage of time spent on each duty.

% OF TIME	MAJOR DUTIES
100%	

B EMPLOYER/COMPANY NAME	KIND OF BUSINESS	
STREET ADDRESS	YOUR OFFICIAL JOB TITLE	
CITY AND STATE	BEGINNING SALARY	ENDING SALARY
DATES OF EMPLOYMENT (MO/DA/YR) / AVERAGE HOURS WORKED PER WEEK	REASON FOR LEAVING	NO. OF EMPLOYEES YOU DIRECTLY SUPERVISED
FROM / TO		
NAME/TITLE OF YOUR SUPERVISOR)	LIST JOB TITLES OF EMPLOYEES YOU DIRECTLY SUPERVISED	
NAME/TITLE OF PERSON WHO CAN VERIFY THIS EMPLOYMENT (IF OTHER THAN SUPERVISOR)		

DUTIES: List the major duties involved with job and give an approximate percentage of time spent on each duty.

% OF TIME	MAJOR DUTIES

STATE OF LOUISIANA APPLICATION—page 4

100%

USE REVERSE SIDE OF THIS PAGE IF ADDITIONAL SPACE REQUIRED FOR WORK EXPERIENCE

Name _____

25. WORK EXPERIENCE (Continued)

C

EMPLOYER/COMPANY NAME	KIND OF BUSINESS	
STREET ADDRESS	YOUR OFFICIAL JOB TITLE	
CITY AND STATE	BEGINNING SALARY	ENDING SALARY
DATES OF EMPLOYMENT (MO/DA/YR) / AVERAGE HOURS WORKED PER WEEK	REASON FOR LEAVING	NO. OF EMPLOYEES YOU DIRECTLY SUPERVISED
FROM / TO		
NAME/TITLE OF YOUR SUPERVISOR	LIST JOB TITLES OF EMPLOYEES YOU DIRECTLY SUPERVISED	
NAME/TITLE OF PERSON WHO CAN VERIFY THIS EMPLOYMENT (IF OTHER THAN SUPERVISOR)		

DUTIES: List the major duties involved with job and give an approximate percentage of time spent on each duty.

% OF TIME	MAJOR DUTIES

100%

D

EMPLOYER/COMPANY NAME	KIND OF BUSINESS	
STREET ADDRESS	YOUR OFFICIAL JOB TITLE	
CITY AND STATE	BEGINNING SALARY	ENDING SALARY
DATES OF EMPLOYMENT (MO/DA/YR) / AVERAGE HOURS WORKED PER WEEK	REASON FOR LEAVING	NO. OF EMPLOYEES YOU DIRECTLY SUPERVISED
FROM / TO		
NAME/TITLE OF YOUR SUPERVISOR)	LIST JOB TITLES OF EMPLOYEES YOU DIRECTLY SUPERVISED	
NAME/TITLE OF PERSON WHO CAN VERIFY THIS EMPLOYMENT (IF OTHER THAN SUPERVISOR)		

DUTIES: List the major duties involved with job and give an approximate percentage of time spent on each duty.

% OF TIME	MAJOR DUTIES

TEST-TAKING TECHNIQUES

Many factors enter into a test score. The most important factor should be ability to answer the questions, which in turn indicates the ability to learn and perform the duties of the job. Assuming that you have this ability, knowing what to expect on the exam and familiarity with techniques of effective test taking should give you the confidence you need to do your best on the exam.

There is no quick substitute for long-term study and development of your skills and abilities to prepare you for doing well on tests. However, there are some steps you can take to help you do the very best that you are prepared to do. Some of these steps are done before the test, and some are followed when you are taking the test. Knowing these steps is often called being "test-wise." Following these steps may help you feel more confident as you take the actual test.

"Test-wiseness" is a general term which simply means being familiar with some good procedures to follow when getting ready for and taking a test. The procedures fall into four major areas: (1) being prepared, (2) avoiding careless errors, (3) managing your time, and (4) guessing.

BE PREPARED

Don't make the test harder than it has to be by not preparing yourself. You are taking a very important step in preparation by reading this book and taking the sample tests which are included. This will help you to become familiar with the tests and the kinds of questions you will have to answer.

As you use this book, read the sample questions and directions for taking the test carefully. Then, when you take the sample tests, time yourself as you will be timed in the real test.

As you are working on the sample questions, don't look at the correct answers before you try to answer them on your own. This can fool you into thinking you understand a question when you really don't. Try it on your own first, then compare your answer with the one given. Remember, in a sample test, you are your own grader; you don't gain anything by pretending to understand something you really don't.

On the examination day assigned to you, allow the test itself to be the main attraction of the day. Do not squeeze it in between other activities. Be sure to bring admission card, identification, and pencils, as instructed. Prepare these the night before so that you are not flustered by a last-minute search. Arrive rested, relaxed, and on time. In fact, plan to arrive a little bit early. Leave plenty of time for traffic tie-ups or other complications that might upset you and interfere with your test performance.

In the test room, the examiner will hand out forms for you to fill out. He or she will give you the instructions that you must follow in taking the examination. The examiner will tell you how to fill in the grids on the forms. Time limits and timing signals will be explained. If you do not understand any of the examiner's instructions, ASK QUESTIONS. It would be ridiculous to score less than your best because of poor communication.

At the examination, you must follow instructions exactly. Fill in the grids on the forms carefully and accurately. Misgridding may lead to loss of veteran's credits to which you may be entitled or misaddressing of your test results. Do not begin until you are told to begin. Stop as soon as the examiner tells you to stop. Do not turn pages until you are told to do so. Do not go back to parts you have already completed. Any infraction of the rules is considered cheating. If you cheat, your test paper will not be scored, and you will not be eligible for appointment.

The answer sheet for most multiple-choice exams is machine scored. You cannot give any explanations to the machine, so you must fill out the answer sheet clearly and correctly.

HOW TO MARK YOUR ANSWER SHEET

1. Blacken your answer space firmly and completely. ● is the only correct way to mark the answer sheet. ◐, ✖, ⊘, and ⊘ are all unacceptable. The machine might not read them at all.

2. Mark only one answer for each question. If you mark more than one answer, you will be considered wrong, even if one of the answers is correct.

3. If you change your mind, you must erase your mark. Attempting to cross out an incorrect answer like this ✖ will not work. You must erase any incorrect answer completely. An incomplete erasure might be read as a second answer.

4. All of your answering should be in the form of blackened spaces. The machine cannot read English. Do not write any notes in the margins.

5. MOST IMPORTANT: Answer each question in the right place. Question 1 must be answered in space 1; question 52 in space 52. If you should skip an answer space and mark a series of answers in the wrong places, you must erase all those answers and do the questions over, marking your answers in the proper places. You cannot afford to use the limited time in this way. Therefore, as you answer each question, look at its number and check that you are marking your answer in the space with the same number.

6. For the typing tests, type steadily and carefully. Just don't rush, since that's when the errors occur. Keep in mind that each error subtracts 1 wpm from your final score.

AVOID CARELESS ERRORS

Don't reduce your score by making careless mistakes. Always read the instructions for each test section carefully, even when you think you already know what the directions are. It's why we stress throughout this book that it's important to fully understand the directions for these different question-types before you go into the actual exam. It will not only reduce errors, but it will save you time—time you will need for the questions.

What if you don't understand the directions? You will have risked getting the answers wrong for a whole test section. As an example, vocabulary questions can sometimes test synonyms (words which have similar meanings), and sometimes test antonyms (words with opposite meanings). You can easily see how a mistake in understanding in this case could make a whole set of answers incorrect.

If you have time, reread any complicated instructions after you do the first few questions to check that you really do understand them. Of course, whenever you are allowed to, ask the examiner to clarify anything you don't understand.

Other careless mistakes affect only the response to particular questions. This often happens with arithmetic questions, but can happen with other questions as well. This type of error, called a "response error," usually stems from a momentary lapse of concentration.

Example

The question reads: "The capital of Massachusetts is …." The answer is (D) Boston, and you mark (B) because "B" is the first letter of the word "Boston."

Example

The question reads: "8 - 5 = …." The answer is (A) 3, but you mark (C) thinking "third letter."

A common error in reading comprehension questions is bringing your own information into the subject. For example, you may encounter a passage that discusses a subject you know something about. While this can make the passage easier to read, it can also tempt you to rely on your own knowledge about the subject. You must rely on information within the passage for your answers—in fact, sometimes the "wrong answer" for the questions are based on true information about the subject not given in the passage. Since the test-makers are testing your reading ability, rather than your general knowledge of the subject, an answer based on information not contained in the passage is considered incorrect.

MANAGE YOUR TIME

Before you begin, take a moment to plan your progress through the test. Although you are usually not expected to finish all of the questions given on a test, you should at least get an idea of how much time you should spend on each question in order to answer them all. For example, if there are 60 questions to answer and you have 30 minutes, you will have about one-half minute to spend on each question.

Keep track of the time on your watch or the room clock, but do not fixate on the time remaining. Your task is to answer questions. Do not spend too much time on any one question. If you find yourself stuck, do not take the puzzler as a personal challenge. Either guess and mark the question in the question booklet or skip the question entirely, marking the question as a skip and taking care to skip the answer space on the answer sheet. If there is time at the end of the exam or exam part, you can return and give marked questions another try.

MULTIPLE-CHOICE QUESTIONS

Almost all of the tests given on civil service exams are multiple-choice format. This means that you normally have four or five answer choices. But it's not something that should be overwhelming. There is a basic technique to answering these types of questions. Once you've understood this technique, it will make your test-taking far less stressful.

First, there should only be one correct answer. Since these tests have been given time and again, and the test-developers have a sense of which questions work and which questions don't work, it will be rare that your choices will be ambiguous. They may be complex, and somewhat confusing, but there will still be only one right answer.

The first step is to look at the question, without looking at the answer choices. Now select the correct answer. That may sound somewhat simplistic, but it's usually the case that your first choice is the correct one. If you go back and change it, redo it again and again, it's more likely that you'll end up with the wrong answer. Thus, follow your instinct. Once you have come up with the answer, look at the answer choices. If your answer is one of the choices, you're probably correct. It's not 100 percent infallible, but it's a strong possibility that you've selected the right answer.

With math questions you should first solve the problem. If your answer is among the choices, you're probably correct. Don't ignore things like the proper function signs (adding, subtracting, multiplying, and dividing), negative and positive numbers, and so on.

But suppose you don't know the correct answer. You then use the "process of elimination." It's a time-honored technique for test-takers. There is always one correct answer. There is usually one answer choice that is totally incorrect—a "distracter." If you look at that choice and it seems highly unlikely, then eliminate it. Depending on the number of choices (four or five), you've just cut down the number of choices to make. Now weigh the other choices. They may seem incorrect or they may be correct. If they seem incorrect, eliminate them. You've now increased your odds at getting the correct answer.

In the end, you may be left with only two choices. At that point, it's just a matter of guessing. But with only two choices left, you now have a 50 percent chance of getting it right. With four choices, you only have a 25 percent chance, and with five choices, only a 20 percent chance at guessing correctly. That's why the process of elimination is important.

SHOULD YOU GUESS?

You may be wondering whether or not it is wise to guess when you are not sure of an answer (even if you've reduced the odds to 50 percent) or whether it is better to skip the question when you are not certain. The wisdom of guessing depends on the scoring method for the particular examination part. If the scoring is "rights only," that is, one point for each correct answer and no subtraction for wrong answers, then by all means you should guess. Read the question and all of the answer choices carefully. Eliminate those answer choices that you are certain are wrong. Then guess from among the remaining choices. You cannot gain a point if you leave the answer space blank; you may gain a point with an educated guess or even with a lucky guess. In fact, it is foolish to leave any spaces blank on a test that counts "rights only." If it appears that you are about to run out of time before completing such an exam, mark all the remaining blanks with the same letter. According to the law of averages, you should get some portion of those questions right.

If the scoring method is *rights minus wrongs*, such as the address checking test found on Postal Clerk Exam 470, DO NOT GUESS. A wrong answer counts heavily against you. On this type of test, do not rush to fill answer spaces randomly at the end. Work as quickly as possible while concentrating on accuracy. Keep working carefully until time is called. Then stop and leave the remaining answer spaces blank.

In guessing the answers to multiple-choice questions, take a second to eliminate those answers that are obviously wrong, then quickly consider and guess from the remaining choices. The fewer choices from which you guess, the better the odds of guessing correctly. Once you have decided to make a guess, be it an educated guess or a wild stab, do it right away and move on; don't keep thinking about it and wasting time. You should always mark the test questions at which you guess so that you can return later.

For those questions that are scored by subtracting a fraction of a point for each wrong answer, the decision as to whether or not to guess is really up to you.

A correct answer gives you one point; a skipped space gives you nothing at all, but costs you nothing except the chance of getting the answer right; a wrong answer costs you 1/4 point. If you are really uncomfortable with guessing, you may skip a question, BUT you must then remember to skip its answer space as well. The risk of losing your place if you skip questions is so great that we advise you to guess even if you are not sure of the answer. Our suggestion is that you answer every question in order, even if you have to guess. It is better to lose a few 1/4 points for wrong guesses than to lose valuable seconds figuring where you started marking answers in the wrong place, erasing, and re-marking answers. On the other hand, do not mark random answers at the end. Work steadily until time is up.

One of the questions you should ask in the testing room is what scoring method will be used on your particular exam. You can then guide your guessing procedure accordingly.

SCORING

If your exam is a short-answer exam such as those often used by companies in the private sector, your answers will be graded by a personnel officer trained in grading test questions. If you blackened spaces on the separate answer sheet accompanying a multiple-choice exam, your answer sheet will be machine scanned or will be hand scored using a punched card stencil. Then a raw score will be calculated using the scoring formula that applies to that test or test portion—rights only, rights minus wrongs, or rights minus a fraction of wrongs. Raw scores on test parts are then added together for a total raw score.

A raw score is not a final score. The raw score is not the score that finds its way onto an eligibility list. The civil service testing authority, Postal Service, or other testing body converts raw scores to a scaled score according to an unpublicized formula of its own. The scaling formula allows for slight differences in difficulty of questions from one form of the exam to another and allows for equating the scores of all candidates. Regardless of the number of questions and possible different weights of different parts of the exam, most civil service clerical test scores are reported on a scale of 1 to 10. The entire process of conversion from raw to scaled score is confidential information. The score you receive is not your number right, is not your raw score, and, despite being on a scale of 1 to 100, is not a percentage. It is a scaled score. If you are entitled to veterans' service points, these are added to your passing scaled score to boost your rank on the eligibility list. Veterans' points are added only to passing scores. A failing score cannot be brought to passing level by adding veterans' points. The score earned plus veterans' service points, if any, is the score that finds its place on the rank order eligibility list. Highest scores go to the top of the list.

Test-Taking Tips

1. Get to the test center early. Make sure you give yourself plenty of extra time to get there, park your car, if necessary, and even grab a cup of coffee before the test.

2. Listen to the test monitors and follow their instructions carefully.

3. Read every word of the instructions. Read every word of every question.

4. Mark your answers by completely darkening the answer space of your choice. Do not use the test paper to work out your answers.

5. Mark only ONE answer for each question, even if you think that more than one answer is correct. You must choose only one. If you mark more than one answer, the scoring machine will consider you wrong.

6. If you change your mind, erase completely. Leave no doubt as to which answer you mean.

7. If your exam permits you to use scratch paper or the margins of the test booklet for figuring, don't forget to mark the answer on the answer sheet. Only the answer sheet is scored.

8. Check often to be sure that the question number matches the answer space, that you have not skipped a space by mistake.

9. Guess according to the guessing suggestions we have made.

10. Stay alert. Be careful not to mark a wrong answer just because you were not concentrating.

11. Do not panic. If you cannot finish any part before time is up, do not worry. If you are accurate, you can do well even without finishing. It is even possible to earn a scaled score of 100 without entirely finishing an exam part if you are very accurate. At any rate, do not let your performance on any one part affect your performance on any other part.

12. Check and recheck, time permitting. If you finish any part before time is up, use the remaining time to check that each question is answered in the right space and that there is only one answer for each question. Return to the difficult questions and rethink them.

PART TWO

What Kind of Work Will You Be Doing?

STATE POLICE OFFICER

DUTIES OF THE JOB

State police officers provide police services to the public by patrolling state and interstate high-ways, turnpikes, and freeways and by enforcing motor vehicle and criminal laws. Powers of the state police vary widely among the states. Some forces have full police powers throughout the state, while others are restricted to highway patrol and traffic regulation. Regardless of these variations, the officers perform a vital service in ensuring the safety of all citizens. The following are typical work activities of state police officers.

In most cases, state police units are organized into posts or troops within specified geographic areas. Each troop or post is housed in a headquarters building that contains a communications center, barracks, lockup, crime laboratory, pistol range, and motor pool. The workday begins at the headquarters location, where state police officers report daily for roll call, inspection, and duty assignment. The vast majority of these officers use specially equipped patrol cars in performing their assignments, but there are a small number on special duty who use motorcycles or fly helicopters or light fixed-wing aircraft. When patrolling assigned sectors, state police officers carefully observe conditions, strictly enforce motor vehicle codes and criminal laws, watch for traffic violations, and issue warnings or citations to offenders. Where justified, arrests are made for violations of motor vehicle regulations and safe driving practices, and offenders are escorted to headquarters for detainment.

Other duties include monitoring traffic to detect vehicles reported as stolen and arresting drivers whose ownership credentials are lacking or questionable. Often, state police officers provide assistance to motorists on the highway or furnish road information and directions to drivers, and they may give details about restaurants, lodging, or tourist attractions in the area. At accident scenes, or where vehicles are disabled, state police officers radio for emergency equipment, such as ambulances or towing vehicles, and give first aid to injured parties until help arrives. They prevent further accidents, damage, or injuries by directing traffic around the accident, using road flares at night, and by removing debris and vehicles from the roadway. They investigate the causes of each accident and prepare detailed written reports, which include such information as the names and addresses of parties involved, scale drawings of the scene, road and weather conditions at the time of the accident, description of damage, and estimated speed of the vehicle or vehicles involved in the accident. This report is legal evidence that the officer may be called upon to present in court.

State police officers are also responsible for providing help to victims of fires, floods, or other disasters and for controlling traffic in such circumstances. In some states, job duties include weighing commercial vehicles, stopping vehicles for a spot check of drivers' licenses, and conducting driver training sessions in public schools. State police officers may also test applicants for drivers' licenses, inspect motor vehicles for safety, and, on occasion, serve as escorts for parades, military convoys, and funeral processions.

In many states, besides being involved with highway activities, state police officers have responsibilities similar to those of municipal and county police, particularly in areas that do not have local police forces. In such cases, these activities include investigation of burglaries, robberies, assaults, domestic disturbances, drug traffic, and liquor violations; taking part in roadblocks to apprehend suspects or escaped criminals; and helping city and county police agencies in cases of riot or civil disturbance. They seize and arrest lawbreakers using physical force and/or firearms when the situation warrants, patrol business and residential areas, and check security of buildings in the district. Some state police officers are given special training and serve as radio dispatchers, instructors at police academies, or pilots of police aircraft. They also may work with canine and mounted units or may be assigned to protect governors and legislators. All state police officers are required to prepare written reports of their work activities and to maintain accurate records, and they may be called upon to testify in court proceedings.

Once a candidate has completed recruit school and is confirmed as a state trooper, there are a number of opportunities that are available. For example, in the state of Michigan, they offer:

- Aviation

- Canine Handler

- Complaint Investigation

- Criminal Investigation

- DARE Officer

- Emergency Support Team Member

- Lab Officer

- Motorcycle Detail

- Recruit School Instructor

- Recruiter

- Traffic Enforcement

- Underwater Recovery Team Member

- Youth Services Officer

After five years of service as a qualified trooper, they offer the following opportunities for advancement:

- Sergeant Shift Commander

- Accident Reconstructionist

- Detective Sergeant

- Fire Marshall Division

WORKING CONDITIONS

The conditions under which state police officers work vary according to assignment. For the most part, they work outdoors in all types of weather while patrolling highways and roads in their sectors. Officers work alone or with a partner and, because of the nature of their duties, do not receive direct supervision. They do, however, stay in constant touch with their communications centers to report to superior officers and to receive new or revised orders. Since the state police operate around the clock, officers are subject to rotating shifts, usually consisting of a five-day, 40-hour workweek, including weekends and holidays. In addition, they are on call at all times and may work for extended periods during emergencies. *Certain aspects of this work are dangerous.* State police officers risk serious injury or death from high speed pursuits and during the apprehension of criminals who may be armed and dangerous.

Fringe benefits that state police officers receive usually include paid vacation, sick leave, and holidays; overtime pay; life, medical, and disability insurance; uniform allowances; a tuition-refund program; and retirement pension.

TRAINING AND PROMOTION OPPORTUNITIES

As is the case with nearly all law enforcement positions, prospective state police officers do not achieve permanent status until they have successfully completed the probationary period that follows training. Probation may last from six months to a year, depending on the state. During the probationary period, the new officer gets valuable experience at the side of a veteran officer.

Advancement opportunities in state police agencies are based on merit, and promotional examinations are scheduled periodically. All qualified personnel can compete for promotional opportunities. The first level of advancement is to Sergeant. Thereafter, qualified officers may advance through experience and education to the positions of First Sergeant, Lieutenant, Captain, Major, Inspector, Deputy Superintendent, and Superintendent.

HOW TO QUALIFY

Candidates for the position of state police officer are selected according to civil service regulations that vary from state to state. Generally, applicants must be U.S. citizens between the ages of 21 and 35 at the time of appointment; service in the military may be deducted from the candidate's chronological age in meeting this requirement. As a rule, most state police agencies demand completion of high school or its equivalent, but persons with college training have a distinct advantage. In many states a certain number of college credits is required. Secondary and postsecondary courses considered useful in preparing for this work include government, English, psychology, geography, American history, physics, chemistry, and foreign languages. It is necessary to receive a passing mark on a written civil service examination as well as a qualifying rating on an interview conducted by a police board of examiners. The board evaluates candidates for such factors as verbal communication skills, tact, physical appearance, and the ability to exercise sound judgment. Each applicant must pass a comprehensive medical examination, and some state police agencies require candidates to undergo psychological and psychiatric testing to determine emotional stability and suitability for this work. In addition to meeting the physical requirements (including standards of height, weight, and vision), applicants are given performance tests designed to measure strength, agility, and stamina. A thorough background investigation is also made to determine general character, honesty, past history, and overall suitability for the job. Finally, possession of a valid driver's license is necessary prior to employment by the state police agency.

Candidates who meet all of the entry requirements of the state police agency are placed on a certified civil service list of eligibles and are selected from this list as vacancies occur. The annual number of openings for this work varies within each state and is dependent on such factors as budget limitations and legislative actions.

When a number of vacancies occur or appear to be imminent, a group of prospective state police officers is selected from the civil service list. These recruits enter training school on a probationary basis. They must complete an intensive training program of approximately twelve to sixteen weeks. Instruction is given in a variety of subjects, such as criminal law; state motor vehicle codes; laws of evidence, arrest, search, and seizure; methods of patrol, surveillance, and communications; arrest, search, and seizure procedures; accident prevention and traffic control; crime prevention and criminal investigation methods; police ethics; pursuit and defensive driving; armed and unarmed defense tactics; use of various types of firearms; physical conditioning; safety education; first aid; community relations; photography; written and oral communications; and agency rules and regulations. Candidates who successfully conclude this training are assigned to duty on a probationary basis for a period ranging from six months to one year or longer, depending on the state's policy. They work with experienced troopers until they are skillful enough to function independently, and they receive permanent employment status after completing a probationary period.

Some police agencies have cadet programs for high school graduates under the age of 21 who are interested in a law enforcement career. They work as civilian employees performing nonenforcement duties but also receive instruction in the various facets of police work. Some of these cadets attend colleges offering programs in law enforcement and criminal justice as preparation for a police career. Cadets who successfully complete this program may receive an appointment as state police officer upon reaching the age of 21.

TRAITS OF A STATE POLICE OFFICER

State police work differs from city police work only in the proportion of time spent at various duties. State police officers deal with traffic control and with helping motorists in distress. The traffic accidents to which state police are called tend to include more vehicles and more damage to persons and property. High-speed traffic presents problems quite different from heavy-congestion traffic. State police are more likely to deal with hijacking, drug traffic, and smuggling and are less likely to deal with domestic violence and burglary. The emphasis of the work may be different, but the traits desired in a police officer are the same regardless of the duties or the location.

1. *The police officer must be intelligent.* First of all, the recruit must be intelligent enough to make it through the police academy or whatever training program that the particular department offers. The recruit must be able to read well in order to comprehend written materials, must have good listening skills, and must remember what she has been taught. The recruit must be able to synthesize material, that is, be able to learn rules and then be able to apply them to hypothetical or actual situations. Remembering information is not enough. The candidate must convince the examiners that he or she can understand, interpret, and apply information in the field. The intelligent police officer can separate what is important from what is less important, can make quick judgments, and can express herself well in speech and in writing. Most police departments begin the applicant screening process with a written test. Written tests require a minimum of administrative time. They can be administered to a large number of applicants at one sitting. Applicants who do not score well on the written test are dropped from consideration. There is no reason to spend time administering medical exams, physical performance tests, psychological exams, or interviews to candidates who do not demonstrate the intelligence to learn the job and to serve as effective police officers.

2. *The police officer must be healthy and physically strong and agile.* Police work is physically taxing. The officer must be able to spend many hours on his feet or on the road, to move quickly, to see and hear accurately, and to lift, move, or carry, as the emergency requires. Obviously, an officer who is often·ill or who cannot perform all physical activities adequately is not acceptable. Police departments have strict medical standards; they hire only recruits in excellent health. A great many medical conditions that are not severe enough to interfere with everyday life or with most occupations are disqualifying for the police officer. Likewise, police departments have carefully devised physical performance tests of strength, speed, and agility. The applicant who cannot qualify on the tests does not show great promise for success as a police officer. Medical and physical screenings are important hurdles in the selection process.

3. *The police officer must be emotionally stable.* A police officer carries a gun. Obviously, anyone who is armed must be even-tempered, well-adjusted, and impartial. When it comes to dealing with firearms, there is no room for error. It is vital that the officer not become excited or fire too soon. The police officer must be able to size up a situation without fear or prejudice, then act appropriately. The police officer cannot be ruled by anger; at the same time, the officer

cannot hesitate when prompt action is required. Police brutality, insult, and behavior on the basis of preconceived opinions have no place anywhere in the police force. Choosing the most stable recruits from among the applicants is one of the more difficult tasks for those in charge of hiring. Applicants who have done well on the written exam and who have passed the medical examinations and physical fitness tests must often submit to psychological examinations. Psychological examinations are not always satisfactory, but police departments must rely on them to eliminate those candidates who appear to be less than perfectly well-adjusted and stable. Because psychological testing tends to be inexact, the test results are often confirmed through interviews. Through a psychological test (often more than one) and interviews, each applicant who has reached this stage of the screening process must prove the stability required for responsible behavior in the police role.

4. *The police officer must be honest.* The person charged with upholding the law must have a clean record as a law-abiding citizen. Youthful infractions of the law must be few, of a minor nature, and explainable. Character flaws are unacceptable in any law enforcement officer. Every applicant must undergo a thorough background check before appointment to the training academy. Beyond merely acting with integrity, the prospective officer must demonstrate the sensitivity to avoid giving any appearance of impropriety. The interviewers are looking for the recruit who projects upright behavior as he or she performs according to the rules.

5. *The police officer must be self-confident and tactful.* These personality aspects are the final refinements upon which hiring decisions are based. These judgments are based upon interviews. The police officer must have the self-confidence to make quick decisions and to stick with them. Unwavering decisions and firm actions are vital in maintaining control. Tactful, gentle, but firm: these are the hallmarks of the effective, successful police officer. The interviewer hopes to choose the applicants who best display these qualities in a fine, delicate balance. The judgment cannot be entirely objective, but the interviewer does his or her best. The police officer candidate, in turn, can make a conscious effort to impress the interviewer as a tactful, thoughtful person who can communicate and take over effectively under pressure.

SAMPLE OFFICIAL ANNOUNCEMENTS

STATE TROOPER

JOB ELEMENTS

To perform the duties of a State Trooper, you must have good judgment, thoroughness, conscientiousness, common sense, motivation, and enthusiasm for the job. You must be dependable and willing to get involved. You must be able to assume responsibility; make decisions, often under pressure; work without supervision; take orders; function in physical danger; act under pressure; communicate well; and combine physical and mental resources.

DUTIES AND RESPONSIBILITIES

As a State Trooper, you will use these characteristics to perform duties involving patrol investigation, station duties, maintenance activities, and special assignments:

- In the course of your *patrol duties* you will direct traffic; assist lost, stranded, or disabled motorists; approach motorists concerning routine or nonroutine violations; and make arrests. You may be called upon to control crowds and support other Troopers in stress situations. Other patrol duties will include inspecting and safeguarding property, responding to bank alarms, chasing violators on foot, and checking buildings at night for break-ins.

- When you perform *investigative duties,* your work will include interviewing complainants and witnesses; aiding people injured in highway, home, and industrial accidents; handling fatal accident and crime scenes; responding to complaints involving vicious animals; using deadly physical force or firearms; interrogating suspects; and executing search and arrest warrants.

▨ There are times when you will be expected to carry out *desk work*. You will send and receive radio and teletype messages, make entries in station records, and respond to telephone inquiries concerning weather and road conditions, locations, law, or other topics. You will also prepare written memoranda and reports.

▨ You will be required to maintain a *good personal appearance*. Your equipment, uniforms, and vehicle must be properly cared for. You also will assist in keeping your station clean and orderly.

▨ In the course of your career, you may be assigned to *special work*. These assignments may be varied and may include securing major disaster areas, policing areas during natural disasters, participating in community public relations programs, escorting VIPs presenting speeches or lectures, scuba diving, and recruit training or counseling. When the work schedule or special duty require, you will work weekends, holidays, irregular hours, overtime, and in inclement weather.

HOW TO APPLY

Application blanks are available at all state police stations. Candidates may also obtain the forms by mail.

You must file a completed written application in order to be eligible to take the written examination. You will then be advised of the time and place of the written examination and provided with an admission ticket to the test location most convenient to you.

Following is a typical application for employment—this one is from the state of West Virginia. However, please be aware that most applications are similar in the type of information they require.

DPS 1

Revised 1-98

WEST VIRGINIA STATE TROOPER
EMPLOYMENT APPLICATION
- EQUAL OPPORTUNITY EMPLOYER -

West Virginia State Police Personnel Office
725 Jefferson Road
South Charleston, WV 25309-1698
(304) 746-2117

INSTRUCTIONS: TYPE or PRINT LEGIBLY IN INK to complete application. Be certain to fill in all spaces on this application form, specify not applicable (n/a) if necessary. IF ANY INFORMATION IS MISSING YOUR APPLICATION MAY BE REJECTED. All information will be treated confidentially. USE ATTACHMENTS WHERE NECESSARY. An Informational Brochure is available at any local state police detachment or by writing to the above address.
It is the policy of the West Virginia State Police to be fair and equitable in all its relations with its employees and applicants for employment without regard to race, color, religion, ancestry, marital status or disability.

NAME: _____
　　　　　　　LAST　　　　　　　JR/SR　　　　　　　FIRST　　　　　　　MIDDLE
List other name(s) that may be pertinent to checking previous employment and educational records:

_____

SOCIAL SECURITY # _____/_____/_____　　DRIVER'S LICENSE # _____/_____
　　　　　　　　　　　　　　　　　　　　　　　　　　　　　　　STATE　　NUMBER

CURRENT ADDRESS: _____
　　　　　　　　　　STREET　　　　　　CITY　　　COUNTY　　　STATE　　ZIP CODE

HOME TELEPHONE# (_____)_____-_____　　OTHER PHONE# (_____)_____-_____

List ALL previous home addresses (attach additional sheets if necessary):

_____
_____

EDUCATION

NAME AND LOCATION	YEARS COMPLETED	DID YOU GRADUATE?	DIPLOMA OR DEGREE
HIGH SCHOOL			
COLLEGE			
OTHER			

MILITARY

Have you ever served in any branch of the armed forces?　　　　　　　　　　　YES [　] NO [　]
Have you ever been discharged from the armed forces
under conditions other than honorable? (excluding a medical discharge)　　　YES [　] NO [　]
If yes, explain: _____
If applicable, List any Military information below (include military reserve) and attach MILITARY FORM DD214 (MUST include CHARACTER OF SERVICE):

BRANCH OF ARMED SERVICES	FROM	TO	RANK OR GRADE
	/　／	/　／	
	/　／	/　／	

EMPLOYMENT HISTORY

List ALL areas of employment (could result in ELIMINATION if not inclusive). List all periods of unemployment. DO NOT list Military Service as employment. Attach additional sheets if necessary.

FROM	TO	EMPLOYER		TELEPHONE
JOB TITLE		ADDRESS		
IMMEDIATE SUPERVISOR		TYPE OF BUSINESS		
SALARY		SUMMARIZE THE NATURE OF WORK PERFORMED AND RESPONSIBILITIES		

FROM	TO	PAST EMPLOYER		TELEPHONE
JOB TITLE		ADDRESS		
IMMEDIATE SUPERVISOR		TYPE OF BUSINESS		
SALARY		SUMMARIZE THE NATURE OF WORK PERFORMED AND RESPONSIBILITIES		
REASON FOR LEAVING				

FROM	TO	PAST EMPLOYER		TELEPHONE
JOB TITLE		ADDRESS		
IMMEDIATE SUPERVISOR		TYPE OF BUSINESS		
SALARY		SUMMARIZE THE NATURE OF WORK PERFORMED AND RESPONSIBILITIES		
REASON FOR LEAVING				

SKILLS AND QUALIFICATIONS

Summarize any training, skills, licenses and/or certificates you possess which you feel will be beneficial to you in this position:

_____
_____
_____

REFERENCES

Give the NAME, ADDRESS, TELEPHONE AND OCCUPATION of five (5) reliable persons who have known you a greater part of your life. DO NOT LIST RELATIVES, FELLOW EMPLOYEES, FORMER OR PRESENT EMPLOYERS.

NAME AND HOME ADDRESS				YEARS KNOWN	TELEPHONE #
Name	Occupation				(_____) _____ - _____ Area Code
Street	City	State	Zip		
Name	Occupation				(_____) _____ - _____ Area Code
Street	City	State	Zip		
Name	Occupation				(_____) _____ - _____ Area Code
Street	City	State	Zip		
Name	Occupation				(_____) _____ - _____ Area Code
Street	City	State	Zip		
Name	Occupation				(_____) _____ - _____ Area Code
Street	City	State	Zip		

Q & A

Are you legally authorized to work in the United States?	YES [ ] NO [ ]
Have you ever held a position of trust, such as handling money or confidential material?	YES [ ] NO [ ]
Have you had a valid driver's license for two (2) years prior to the date of this application?	YES [ ] NO [ ]
Has your driver's license ever been revoked or suspended?	YES [ ] NO [ ]

If yes, explain: _____

Have you ever been convicted of a misdemeanor crime?	YES [ ] NO [ ]

If yes, explain: _____

Have you ever been convicted for domestic violence?	YES [ ] NO [ ]
Have you ever been convicted of a felony crime?	YES [ ] NO [ ]
Have you ever been convicted of a traffic violation? (Include moving and non-moving offenses.)	YES [ ] NO [ ]

If yes, explain: _____

Are you currently using illegal drugs?	YES [ ] NO [ ]
Do you drink alcoholic beverages?	YES [ ] NO [ ]
Have you applied for the position of police officer at another agency?	YES [ ] NO [ ]

If yes, where: _____

Have you ever been employed by the West Virginia State Police?	YES [ ] NO [ ]
Have you previously tested for the position of West Virginia State Trooper?	YES [ ] NO [ ]
Have you previously applied for employment with the West Virginia State Police?	YES [ ] NO [ ]

If you checked YES to any of the questions pertaining to a previous application with the WVSP please give details:

_____

Before a person is selected for enlistment entries made in his/her application are verified and a careful and complete character investigation is conducted. You may use this space to explain any irregularities that may be disclosed by our investigations:

_____

CERTIFICATION

I attest to the accuracy and truthfulness of the information provided and that any misstatement of material facts will be grounds for disqualifying me from further consideration in the selection process, or, if hired, grounds for discharge. I further understand that consideration for employment is conditioned upon the results of a reference-check, and that the state police is authorized to investigate all statements made by me on the application, to contact former employers and references and to advise contacted persons that they may respond to questions. I hereby release all such persons from any liability of damage resulting from such information.

I understand that nothing contained in this employment application or in the granting of an interview is intended to create an employment contract between the West Virginia State Police and myself for either employment or for the providing of any benefit. No promises regarding employment have been made to me, and I understand that no such promise or guarantee is binding upon the West Virginia State Police unless made in writing. If an employment relationship is established, I understand that I have the right to terminate my employment at any time and the West Virginia State Police retains the same right.

I understand that prior to being offered employment with the West Virginia State Police I may be requested to take an employment examination. In the event I have a disability which will affect my ability to take the test, I will so inform the West Virginia State Police prior to the administration of the test in order for a reasonable accommodation to be made. Requested accommodations may include accessible testing sites, modified testing conditions and accessible testing formats. The West Virginia State Police reserves the right to require medical documentation concerning the need for these accommodations.

I understand that if employed, policies and rules which are issued are not conditions of employment and that the employer may revise policies or procedures, in whole or in part, at any time.

I understand that this application will be retained for one year upon receipt, or after taking action on the application, whichever is later, after which time I would have to re-apply in accordance with established West Virginia State Police Procedures.

_____   ___/___/_____
Applicant Signature (BLUE INK Please)   Date

DOCUMENTS REQUIRED FOR PROOF OF QUALIFICATIONS

Submit copies only of the following:

- BIRTH CERTIFICATE (Hospital Certificate UNACCEPTABLE) Court House or Vital Statistics certificate only
  Applicants who are 20 years of age at the onset of testing are permitted to test provided he/she will be 21 years of age by target date of enlistment
- HIGH SCHOOL DIPLOMA or G.E.D. (Transcripts UNACCEPTABLE) however, an *original letter signed* by High School principal or counselor, on school letterhead certifying graduation *IS* acceptable

EXAMINATION LOCATIONS

Examinations are usually conducted in the state capital and most large cities. Exact locations can be found on the latest announcements.

GENERAL INFORMATION

The number of candidates selected for appointment will depend on budget allocations. All appointments are probationary for a minimum period of one year following completion of the Academy Basic Course.

EXAMINATION PROCEDURES

The selection process has been developed through analysis of the Trooper position. The complete selection process consists of six phases: Written Examination, Physical Performance Test, Medical Examination, Preemployment Interview, Psychological Examination, and an extensive Background Investigation that will include a polygraph test. The process is job related and competitive in nature and is designed to determine a candidate's potential for successful performance as a State Trooper. No prior police experience is required.

Candidates are ranked in order of composite scores determined after completion of the written examination plus any applicable veteran's credit. Candidates remain on the continuous eligible list for a maximum period of four years from the date of the most recent eligibility list to which their name is posted, unless otherwise deemed to be ineligible (e.g., overage). The eligible list is continually updated by adding the names of those applicants who subsequently pass future written examinations, based on the scores they achieve. Examinations are given periodically. Candidates may retake an examination no earlier than one year from their latest examination date; however, only the *latest* score achieved by an individual on any one examination is retained and posted to the continuous eligible list. As new Trooper positions are authorized, sufficient candidates from the eligible list is notified to appear for processing through the remaining phases of the testing procedure.

The Physical Performance Test measures the candidate's ability to combine mental and physical resources. The candidate must perform physical tests that are evaluated on a pass-fail basis. A detailed description of the Physical Performance Test is provided to the candidates when they are notified to appear for processing at Division Headquarters.

Those candidates successfully passing this phase is also given a Preemployment Interview. This interview serves to acquaint the candidate with the job of Trooper and enables the State Police to develop information that assists in completion of the background investigation.

The Psychological Examination consists of written tests completed by the candidate and a follow-up interview with a psychologist.

CHARACTER AND FITNESS

Each potential appointee is the subject of a thorough background investigation, including a polygraph examination, to help determine character and fitness and also to verify information provided by the applicant. Applicants must authorize access to educational, financial, employment, criminal history, and mental health records. Family, neighbors, associates, and others are interviewed. Derogatory information is evaluated and may result in disqualification. Candidates who receive a satisfactory evaluation on the background investigation and meet all other administrative requirements are considered eligible for appointment.

ADMINISTRATIVE REQUIREMENTS

In addition to completing the competitive examinations successfully, a candidate must meet administrative standards established by the Division of State Police:

MINIMUM AGE

All candidates must be at least 20 years old on the date of examination and at least 21 years old on the date of appointment.

MAXIMUM AGE

Candidates without allowable military service must not have reached their 29th birthday on date of appointment. Candidates with active military duty, as defined in Section 243 of the Military Law, may use allowable service time to extend the age limit proportionately, up to a maximum of six years.

EDUCATION

Candidates must have graduated from a senior high school or possess a State High School Equivalency Diploma prior to appointment. Military GED Certificates must be converted to State High School Equivalency Diplomas before appointment. In addition, all candidates must have completed a minimum of 60 credit hours at an accredited college or university at time of application. The Division may waive up to 30 credit hours *only* for individuals who:

   a.   have an Honorable Discharge from the United States Military after serving at least two full years of active duty. A DD-214 (showing type of discharge) must be submitted with application.

   NOTE: Individuals who are currently on active duty may apply without submitting a DD-214, providing they have completed at least two full years.

   OR

   b.   have completed a certified Basic Police Officer Training Course approved by or equivalent to a course approved by the Municipal Police Training Council. A certificate of completion of training must be submitted with application.

   NOTE: A certified Peace Officer Training Course does NOT satisfy this requirement.

RESIDENCE

Only citizens of the United States are eligible to take the examination. State law requires that any person appointed as a Trooper must be a resident of the state on the date of appointment and must maintain such residency for as long as employment continues.

DRIVER'S LICENSE

Candidates must have a current valid state driver's license on the date of appointment.

CRIMINAL RECORD

Any felony conviction is an automatic disqualification. Conviction for any other crimes and offenses is subject to evaluation during a background investigation.

MEDICAL FITNESS

Sound health and physical condition are required of all candidates since the physical activities of the job often demand extreme exertion in emergency situations. A medical examination is given prior to appointment, during which vision, hearing, weight, dental condition, and general fitness are determined. Visual acuity can be not worse than 20/40 in each eye uncorrected and must be correctable to 20/20. Color deficiency is disqualifying. There is no minimum or maximum height standard. Weight must be in proportion to height and build. Candidates must conform to weight standards for appointment. Potential appointees may be required to provide blood or urine samples for analysis to determine use of dangerous or illegal drugs. Any medical problems deemed by the Division Physician to be disqualifying for service as a Trooper shall be grounds for rejection.

   On unannounced occasions while in the State Police Academy Basic School and during the probationary period following graduation from the Basic School, appointees MAY be required to provide urine samples for analysis to determine the presence of illegal drugs (including marijuana) and controlled substances. Confirmed positive tests are grounds for discharge from employment.

STATE TRAFFIC OFFICER CADET

DEFINITION
Under close supervision, a Cadet participates in a basic traffic law enforcement training program in order to learn the work of a State Traffic Officer and does other related work as required.

JOB CHARACTERISTICS
The class of State Traffic Officer Cadets must successfully complete all academy courses, including academic classes, physical training, vehicle operation, and use of weapons, in order to move to the class of State Traffic Officer. Failure in the Cadet class to qualify for movement to the class of State Traffic Officer within the prescribed training period is cause for termination.

TYPICAL TASKS
The cadet in training receives instruction in the interpretation and application of the Vehicle Code and other laws affecting the operation of vehicles on public highways; receives instruction in basic criminal investigation processes and techniques, including police ethics, witness interrogation, and collection of evidence; participates in firearms training; participates in the Emergency Vehicle Operations Course, which includes skid training, high-speed pursuit, defensive driving, and emergency driving; receives classroom instruction in enforcement psychology, enforcement tactics, effective writing, and effective speaking; learns radio operation and methods of traffic control; and participates in a physical training program.

MINIMUM QUALIFICATIONS

- Education: Equivalent to completion of the twelfth grade

- Knowledge and ability to: Learn rules and regulations; think clearly and logically and apply general rules to specific situations; observe and record events accurately and completely; operate or learn to operate a motorcycle; analyze situations accurately, think and act quickly in emergencies, and adopt an effective course of action; follow oral and written directions; write legibly, spell correctly, and prepare understandable reports

- Special personal characteristics: Interest in law enforcement work; willingness to work throughout the state, at night, and at unusual hours; willingness to work under strict discipline; willingness to operate or learn to operate a motorcycle; satisfactory record as a law-abiding citizen; tact; reliability; communication skills; officer-like bearing; keenness of observation; neat personal appearance

- Special physical characteristics: Good health, sound physical condition; freedom from any physical or mental condition that would interfere with the full performance of the essential duties of a State Traffic Officer; effective use of both hands; strength, endurance, and agility; normal hearing; normal visual function and visual acuity, not less than 20/40 in each eye without correction and corrected to 20/20 in each eye; normal color vision as assessed by the Farnsworth-Munsell D-15 test. Wearing an X-Chrome lens during vision testing is prohibited; height not more than 6'6"; weight proportional to age and height

- Age limits for participation in examination: 20–31 years

- Minimum age for appointment: 21 years

- Felony disqualification: Existing law provides that persons convicted of a felony are disqualified from employment as peace officers. Such persons are not eligible to compete for, or be appointed to, positions in this class.

■ Citizenship requirement: Existing law provides that no person who is not a U.S. citizen shall be appointed as a member of the Highway Patrol. Persons who are not citizens may compete in examinations for this class, but must show proof of citizenship before appointment can be made.

■ Additional desirable qualifications: Education beyond the twelfth grade.

DEPARTMENT OF CIVIL SERVICE STATE POLICE TROOPER I EXAMINATION PROCESS

GENERAL INFORMATION

The State Police Trooper I Employment List is established through a competitive examination process. This is an entry-level job classification.

The Departments of State Police and Civil Service are under a federal court order that stipulates hiring goals in regard to minorities and females for the State Police Trooper Training Schools. In order to ensure compliance with the federal court consent decree, the Department of Civil Service must maintain adequate sex/race representation on the Trooper Employment List. Adequate sex/race representation may require expedited processing of applications from members of minority groups and females.

Positions in this job classification are located throughout the state.

Names of applicants who successfully complete the examination process are combined with those on the current Employment List for the class.

When job vacancies occur, they are filled from the list. The Employment List is continuously updated by adding the names of those applicants who subsequently pass the examination, based on the score they achieved. Passing the test and having your name placed on the Employment List does not mean that you will be offered employment in this job classification. Appointment to this job classification is dictated by departmental work force needs. Applicants who are appointed to positions must successfully complete one year of probationary training, which includes sixteen weeks of State Police Trooper Training School conducted at the State Police Training Academy. An employee is in pay status during the training period.

POLICY ON TAKING THE EXAMINATION AGAIN

Candidates may retake an examination and receive a new score. However, the Bureau of Selection policy requires that only the *latest* passing score achieved by an individual on any one examination is retained on Department of Civil Service records for that examination.

CONDITIONS OF EMPLOYMENT

The employee is required to work on a rotating shift basis, to be available for duty 24 hours a day, to work on state and national holidays, and to work and drive in inclement weather. The employee is subject to transfer on a temporary or permanent basis anywhere in the state. The employee must carry firearms and may be required to use them in the line of duty. The employee must maintain the capability to perform strenuous tasks requiring muscular strength and cardiovascular endurance.

REALLOCATION

After completion of one year of satisfactory service at the entry-level classification, the employee is appointed to the position of State Police Trooper II. Should an employee fail to meet the requirements for the position, the employee is separated from the job.

EXAMPLES OF WORK

First-year employees receive training in the knowledge and skills required to function independently as law enforcement officers. The employee is initially assigned to residence in the State Police Trooper Training School for approximately sixteen weeks, where she completes a basic police training curriculum of law enforcement course work and physical training. Upon graduation from school, the employee is assigned to a State Police post as a probationary trooper. In the company of an experienced trooper, the employee patrols an area to detect or prevent traffic and criminal law violations, investigates complaints of law violations, and provides a variety of related services to the general public.

MINIMUM QUALIFICATIONS:

Citizenship
A citizen of the United States at the time of the written test

Residence
A resident of the state for at least one year immediately prior to taking the written examination or for four years between the ages of 17 and 35 years. State residents in the armed forces and students attending colleges or universities out of state for the past school year are considered as meeting this requirement.

Age
At least 21 years of age at the time of the written examination and less than 36 years of age as of the date of hire,

Education
Graduation from high school or General Education Development (GED) Test scores meeting Department of Education standards. (GED tests must have been taken at an official GED center. A standard score of 35 or above on each of the five tests *and* an average of 45 for the five tests must have been attained. GED results should be submitted at the time of application if they are not already on file with Civil Service.)

Driver's License
Possession of a valid operator's or chauffeur's license without restrictions applying to time, area, special mechanical control devices, or conditions (except corrective lenses).

Vision
At least 20/40 vision in each eye without lenses, corrected to 20/20 with lenses prior to appointment to a Training School. (Some states, like New Jersey, will accept vision corrected to 20/30, preferably using soft lenses.) Must have adequate color and depth perception and a visual field of no less than 70 degrees in the horizontal meridian in each eye. Must have normal vertical and lateral muscle balance.

Hearing
Must have normal hearing in both ears. Hearing deficiency, if any, must not exceed 25 decibels (L.S.O.) in either ear in frequency ranges 500, 1000, 2000, 3000 cycles. Deficiencies in higher frequency ranges (4000–6000 cycles) must not exceed an average of 40 decibels.

Convictions of Law Violations or Civil Infractions
Conviction may serve as a basis for disqualification. The applicant's total record is evaluated. The pattern of law violations, the seriousness, the surrounding circumstances, number, and recency are considered. The convictions noted below are cause for automatic disqualification:

1. Conviction of a felony

2. Lost driving privilege through suspension or revocation of license due to an unsatisfactory driving record as defined by the state's driver's license point system

   EXCEPTION: Those who maintain a driving record free of license suspension or revocation and moving violation convictions or civil infraction determinations in the two years previous to taking the written examination through appointment to a training school are accepted.

In the four years previous to taking the written examination through appointment to a training school:

3. Conviction of driving while license was suspended or revoked

4. Conviction of driving while under the influence of alcohol or drugs (includes driving while ability impaired)

5. Two or more convictions of reckless driving

In the two years previous to taking the written examination through appointment to a training school:

6. Accumulation of eight or more points on the driving record

7. Conviction or civil infraction determination of three or more moving violations

8. A record of two or more traffic accidents, each resulting in a moving violation conviction or civil infraction determination

SELECTION PROCESS

Written Examination

A written test containing multiple-choice and true-false questions pertaining to accuracy of observation and memory and ability to read and comprehend reports, manuals, and laws determines 40 percent of the final score.

The written test is administered by the Department of Civil Service at various examination centers throughout the state.

Background Investigation

Applicants who pass the written test may be scheduled to participate in the remainder of the examination process (oral appraisal), based on departmental work force needs. The candidates are subjected to a thorough background investigation designed to assist in measuring suitability for police work. The background investigation includes fingerprinting and a vision test. Evidence of unsuitability may serve as a basis for disqualification from the oral appraisal examination process. Applicants who are disqualified receive notification of the disqualification by mail.

Oral Appraisal Examination

Applicants who pass the background investigation are scheduled for the oral appraisal examination in which a board of examiners assesses their communication skills and personal fitness. Questions asked by the oral board pertain to the applicant's background investigation and employment objectives. The oral appraisal examination determines 60 percent of the final score.

Medical Examination

Applicants who are called to a training school must pass a medical examination. The applicant's physical condition must be adequate for performance of the work as determined by an examining physician. A hearing test, blood test, urinalysis, and blood pressure examination are included. The applicant must be free from any chronic diseases, organic or functional conditions, or physical defects that may tend to impair efficient performance of a Trooper's duties. Failure to meet medical standards results in removal from the Employment List for this job classification. Correction of a medical deficiency may result in a return to the Employment List.

Physical Performance Test

Prior to their hiring, applicants are called to the Training School for a physical performance test. Failure to meet required standards results in rejection of the applicant for the Training School.

There are six test parts designed to assess: strength to push, pull, drag, and lift; cardiorespiratory endurance for strenuous work and running; and abdominal strength and spine flexibility to avoid low back pain, problems of strains, loss of mobility, and agility.

The physical performance test consists of the following:

1. **Push-ups:** This is a standard push-up where the back and legs are kept straight. The event starts in the up position and the count occurs when the applicant returns to the up position after having touched an audible beeper on the mat with his/her chest. The applicant is to do as many push-ups as possible in 60 seconds.

2. **Grip:** Using a hand grip dynamometer, the applicant squeezes the meter while keeping the arm extended parallel to the leg. Both right and left grips are tested and recorded in kilograms of pressure.

3. **Obstacle Course:** The total distance for this obstacle course is 90 feet, and it is run for time. The applicant runs 20 feet crawls 6 feet through a $2\frac{1}{2}$-foot high simulated tunnel, runs 20 feet, and climbs a 6-foot 6-inch burner with footholds and handholds. The applicant then runs 20 feet to and around a set of pylons, then back to the barrier, which has footholds and handholds on it. After climbing the barrier a second time, the applicant runs 4 feet to the stop position.

4. **165-Pound Drag:** The applicant drags a 165-pound life-form dummy 30 feet for time. The dummy is gripped in the armpits and dragged backwards.

5. **95-Pound Carry:** The applicant lifts a 95-pound bag, which has handholds, runs with it 30 feet, and places it on a 32-inch platform for time.

6. $\frac{1}{2}$**-Mile Shuttle Run:** The applicant runs between two pylons placed 88 feet apart for a total of 15 round trips for time.

Examinees are encouraged to practice ahead of time for the physical performance test.

All physical tests, and especially the half-mile run, are aided by conditioning ahead of time. Physical training for law enforcement positions requires that new hires be physically fit when they are hired. The physical performance test screens for minimal levels of physical fitness required for State Police Trooper I.

It is very important that applicants adequately prepare themselves to pass the physical performance test. It is recommended that applicants consult a medical doctor before attempting the physical performance skills.

ANNUAL MAINTENANCE PROGRAM

Annually, after initial hiring, State Police Troopers may participate in an evaluation of physical fitness consisting of:

1. **Push-Up Test:** Fifteen push-ups in 60 seconds.

2. **Chin-Up Test:** Five chin-ups in a continuous manner, palms toward body, with full arm extension between each one.

3. **One-Mile Continuous Run Test:** Run 1 mile in less than 9 minutes.

4. **Bent-Knee Sit-Up Test:** 30 bent-knee sit-ups in 90 seconds.

5. **Seated Stretch Test:** Sit on the floor with legs together and knees straight and stretch forward as far as possible. Fingertips must extend to ankles within 6 inches of the heel.

STATE POLICE TROOPER TRAINEE

The State Police are now recruiting able men and women from all walks of life for the position of State Police Trooper Trainee. The selection process begins with a written examination and continues over the following months with several interviews and investigations. At the end of this multiphase process, a select group of candidates qualifies to begin the physically demanding training program. This select group reflects the commitment of the State Police to affirmative action–equal employment opportunity goals.

QUALIFICATIONS

Candidates for entry-level Trooper Trainee appointments must:

1. be at least 18 years old by the date of appointment;

2. be U.S. citizens by the date of appointment;

3. be in general good health and have sufficient strength, stamina, and agility as required for the duties of the position;

4. have good education and/or work record and excellent moral character;

5. and have normal hearing and normal color vision and depth perception, with no marked muscle imbalance. Distant and near visual acuity without vision correction devices shall not be less than 20/40 in either eye with binocular visual acuity of not less than 20/30. Distant and near vision must be correctable to 20/20.

In addition, prior to graduation from the Academy Training Program, successful candidates are required to obtain and retain a current, valid state motor vehicle operator's license and establish residence in the state.

THE WRITTEN EXAM

When the completed application is received, the candidate is scheduled for the examination. The exact time and place is sent about 10 days before that date. The exam includes questions to assess the candidate's ability to observe and remember details, to analyze facts and make decisions, to reason logically, and to understand and communicate written and oral instructions as well as questions about the candidate's interests. There is no makeup exam. To be eligible to go on in the selection process, each phase must be passed. However, because of the large number of applicants, passing one phase may not automatically qualify a candidate for the next.

PHYSICAL ASSESSMENT

This phase is intended to give an overall measurement of a candidate's physical fitness and preparation for State Police Academy training. Blood pressure and vision are measured, and candidates must fall within required levels to continue in the process, which includes:

1. a 1.5-mile run measuring cardiovascular efficiency;

2. push-ups measuring shoulder muscular endurance;

3. sit-ups measuring abdominal and hip flex or muscle strength;

4. an agility run measuring quickness, speed, and balance;

5. a vertical jump measuring leg muscle strength and explosiveness;

6. a sit and reach test measuring thigh and back muscle extensiveness;

7. a grip test measuring wrist and forger muscle strength;

8. and a measure of body fat composition.

ORAL INTERVIEW

A panel of State Police officers interviews each candidate to measure his/her judgment, motivation for police work, ability to deal effectively with the public, and oral communication ability. A writing sample is also required and evaluated for written communication ability.

POLYGRAPH AND BACKGROUND INVESTIGATIONS

Candidates successful up to this point in the process undergo a polygraph examination and thorough background investigation. A psychological evaluation may also be performed. Only those candidates with good education and/or work records and excellent moral character are chosen.

MEDICAL EXAM

Candidates reaching this point in the process are given a thorough medical evaluation to include eyes, ears, blood, and heart as well as other tests. All candidates must meet the minimum acceptable standards in each area. Successful completion of all phases of the selection process means that they are eligible to be considered for final appointment as a Trooper Trainee.

STATE POLICE TRAINING PROGRAM

Candidates selected as State Police Trooper Trainees enter the physically and mentally demanding training program at the State Police Academy. The program lasts up to six months and includes classroom instruction and physical conditioning. It requires them to live at the academy Monday through Friday. After graduation from the program, Trooper Trainees are assigned to one of the State Police Troops throughout the state for a probationary period and on-the-job training.

BASIS QUALIFICATION AND REQUIREMENTS FOR EMPLOYMENT AS A HIGHWAY PATROL TROOPER

1. **Age:** Minimum—21 years as of date of application

2. **Height:** Maximum—6'6" (without shoes)

3. **Weight:** Maximum—240 pounds (Weight must be commensurate with height and body frame.)

4. **Physical Condition:** Must be in excellent physical condition with no obvious condition that would impair performance of patrol duties

5. **Education:** Applicant must have graduated from an accredited high school or hold an approved General Education Development Certificate; college- or university-level education is desired

6. **Citizenship:** Must be a citizen of the U.S. and must have resided in the state for twelve months immediately preceding date of application; military service in the state qualifies

7. **Criminal History:** Must not have pled guilty, entered a plea of no contest, or have been convicted of any crime other than a minor misdemeanor; must not, during the three years preceding the date of his/her application, have been convicted of a traffic offense that required suspension or revocation of driving privileges; must not have accumulated more than eight points against his/her driving record during the preceding three years

8. **Former Employment:** Must, if a former patrol member, complete all patrol pre-employment requirements, including recompletion of Patrol Basic School

9. **Acceptance of Conditions and Benefits:** Must be willing to live and work in any section of the state and to be transferred at the discretion of the Patrol Commander

10. **Vision Requirements:** Must have 20/20 vision in each eye; uncorrected vision of no more than 20/40 in each eye is acceptable if corrected with lens; must not be color blind or affected by night blindness; must pass depth-perception test

11. **Agility Test:** Must be able to perform an agility test according to standards approved by the Patrol Medical Services Director

12. **Written Test:** Must pass a specific aptitude test battery and a reading comprehension/writing skills examination; must also take an examination that measures attitudes desired for law enforcement officers

13. **Background Investigation:** Must satisfactorily pass a thorough background investigation, including a check of state and Federal Bureau of Investigation records

14. **Applicant Review Board:** Applicants must be interviewed by the Patrol's Applicant Review Board

15. **Physical Examination:** Must meet physical standards set by the Patrol Medical Services Director

16. **Acceptance by Patrol Commander:** Must be accepted by the Patrol Commander to attend the Patrol Basic School

17. **Completion of Training:** Must successfully complete the Patrol Basic School

TRAINING AND ADVANCEMENT

This section provides essential information about the field in which you will be working. It gives you details concerning your chosen specialty, what you can look forward to in the future, and points up how desirable and interesting your job can be. When you know more about your job, you'll be more inclined to struggle and study for it.

NATURE OF THE WORK

The laws and regulations that govern the use of our nation's roadways are designed to ensure the safety of all citizens. State Troopers patrol our highways and enforce these laws.

State Troopers issue traffic tickets to motorists who violate the law. At the scene of an accident, they direct traffic; give first aid; call for emergency equipment, including ambulances; and write reports to be used in determining the cause of the accident.

In addition, State Troopers provide services to motorists on the highways. For example, they radio for road service for drivers in mechanical trouble, direct tourists to their destination, or give information about lodging, restaurants, and tourist attractions

State Troopers also provide traffic assistance and control during road repairs, fires, and other emergencies as well as for special occurrences, such as parades and sports events. They sometimes check the weight of commercial vehicles, conduct driver examinations, and give information on highway safety to the public.

In addition to highway responsibilities, State Troopers may investigate crimes, particularly in a police force. They sometimes help city or county police catch lawbreakers and control civil disturbances. State Highway Patrols, however, normally are restricted to vehicle and traffic matters.

Some Troopers work with special State Police units, such as the mounted police, canine corps, and marine patrols. Others instruct trainees in State Police Schools, pilot police aircraft, or specialize in fingerprint classification or chemical and microscopic analysis of criminal evidence.

State Troopers also write reports and maintain police records. Some Troopers, including division or bureau chiefs responsible for training or investigation and those who command police operations in an assigned area, have administrative duties.

TRAINING, OTHER QUALIFICATIONS, AND ADVANCEMENT

State Civil Service regulations govern the appointment of State Troopers. All candidates must be citizens of the U.S. Other entry requirements vary, but most states require that applicants have a high school education or an equivalent combination of education and experience and be at least 21 years old.

Troopers must pass a competitive examination and meet physical and personal qualifications. Physical requirements include standards of height, weight, and eyesight. Tests of strength and agility often are required. Because honesty and a sense of responsibility are important in police work, an applicant's character and background are investigated.

Although State Troopers work independently, they must perform their duties in line with department rules. They should want to serve the public, and be willing to work outdoors in all types of weather.

In all states, recruits enter a formal training program for several months. They receive classroom instruction in state laws and jurisdictions, and they study procedures for accident investigation, patrol, and traffic control. Recruits learn to use guns, defend themselves from attack, handle an automobile at high speeds, and give first aid. After gaining experience, some Troopers take advanced training in police science, administration, law enforcement, or criminology. Classes are held at community colleges, colleges and universities, or at special police institutions, such as the National Academy of the Federal Bureau of Investigation.

High school and college courses in English, government, psychology, sociology, American history, and physics help in preparing for a police career. Physical education and sports are useful for developing stamina and agility. Completion of a driver education course and training received in military police school also are assets.

State Trooper recruits serve a probationary period ranging from six months to three years. After a specified length of time, Troopers become eligible for promotion. Most states have merit promotion systems that require Troopers to pass a competitive examination to qualify for the next higher rank. Although the organization of police forces varies by state, the typical avenue of advancement is from private to corporal to sergeant to first sergeant to lieutenant and then to captain. State Troopers who show administrative ability may be promoted to higher-level jobs, such as commissioner or director.

In some states, high school graduates may enter the State Police as cadets. These paid civilian employees of the police organization attend classes to learn various aspects of police work and are assigned nonenforcement duties. Cadets who qualify may be appointed to the State Police force at age 21.

EMPLOYMENT OUTLOOK

State Trooper employment is expected to grow at a much faster rate than other occupations. Although most jobs will result from this growth, some openings will be created as Troopers retire, die, or leave the occupation for other reasons. As job openings are filled from the ranks of available applicants, the increased interest of women in police work will result in greater employment of women for patrol duties.

Although some Troopers will be needed in criminal investigation and other non-highway functions, the greatest demand will be for Troopers to work in highway patrol. Motorcycles, campers, and other recreational vehicles will continue to add to the nation's traffic flow and require additional officers to ensure the safety of highway users.

Because law enforcement work is becoming more complex, specialists will be needed in crime laboratories and electronic data processing centers to develop administrative and criminal information systems. However, in many departments, these jobs will be filled by civilian employees rather than uniformed officers.

EARNINGS AND WORKING CONDITIONS

Although starting salaries are normally higher in the West and lower in the South, State Troopers on the average earn about 1.5 times as much as nonsupervisory workers in private industry, except farming.

State Troopers generally receive regular increases, based on experience and performance, until a specified maximum is reached.

State Police agencies usually provide Troopers with uniforms, firearms, and other necessary equipment, or give special allowances for their purchase.

In many states, the scheduled workweek for State Troopers is 40 hours. Although the workweek is longer in some states, hours over 40 are being reduced. Since police protection must be provided around the clock, some officers are on duty over weekends, on holidays, and at night. State Troopers also are subject to emergency calls at any time.

State Troopers usually are covered by liberal pension plans. Paid vacations, sick leave, and medical and life insurance plans frequently are provided.

The work of State Troopers is sometimes dangerous. They always run the risk of an automobile accident while pursuing speeding motorists or fleeing criminals. Troopers also face the risk of injury while apprehending criminals or controlling disorders.

SOURCES OF ADDITIONAL INFORMATION

Information about specific entrance requirements may be obtained from State Civil Service commissions or State Police headquarters, usually located in each state capital.

JOB ELEMENT SELF-APPRAISAL FORM

Every state has different application forms and different application procedures. The Self-Appraisal Form below is part of the application packet of one state. You may or may not find yourself filling out something similar. Now that you have read sample announcements and job descriptions from a variety of states, try filling out this self-appraisal form to see how you "fit."

Please Fill out This Section:

NAME (PRINT) _____
                            LAST   FIRST   MIDDLE
ADDRESS_____

This Form Is to Be Completed and Returned With Your Application

The Job Element Self-Appraisal Form consists of questions about many of the personal qualities and behaviors that are important in performing the job of a State Trooper. The items have been identified by a thorough study of current job requirements. The information may help you in determining whether you are interested in the job and have some of the needed qualifications.

Directions

You are asked to respond to every question on this form in a direct and honest manner. While your answers to this form will not be scored, you should be aware that many of your answers may be checked in later phases of the examination process. For example, requirements in terms of agility and strength will be checked on the physical performance test.

You may not have had the opportunity to perform all the job demands listed on this form. On such questions, you will have to make your best judgment as to whether you would be able to meet the demands. If you think that you probably will be able to perform the job demand, give the appropriate answer. On the other hand, if you think you probably won't be able to do so, answer accordingly. If you are unsure, try performing the job demand before answering the question.

Answer "Yes" or "No" to each of the following questions.

1. Do you have the ability to drive:

    (a)   on expressways and limited-access highways, such as interstate highways, thruways, or turnpikes? _____
    (b)   in city areas? _____
    (c)   in suburban areas? _____

2. Are you able to:

    (a)   drive at night for extended periods of time? _____
    (b)   drive a car for long periods of time under adverse weather conditions? _____
    (c)   quickly transfer your foot from the gas pedal to the brake pedal of a car in an emergency? _____

3. While driving a car, can you move your head from side to side without moving your body? _____

4. If you were driving a full-sized sedan without aids or adaptive devices:
   (a) are you tall enough to see over the steering wheel without assuming a body position that would make safe operation of the car difficult? _____
   (b) could you reach all the hand controls, switches, and levers on the dashboard without assuming a body position that would make safe operation of the car difficult? _____

5. Are your legs long enough to reach the gas and brake pedals in a full-sized sedan without the aid of any devices? _____

6. Under normal conditions, do you experience motion sickness while riding in:
   (a) cars? _____
   (b) boats? _____
   (c) planes? _____

7. If you were driving a police car on the way to an emergency, could you maneuver your way through moving traffic using the flashing red lights and siren? _____

8. Are you tall enough to see over the roof of a full-sized sedan (car height approximately five feet)? _____

9. Are your arms long enough to hold an Ithaca Model 37 pump-action shotgun level at shoulder height? _____

10. Can you meet these physical requirements:
    (a) climb over a fence 4 feet high? _____
    (b) hurdle over an obstacle 3 feet high? _____
    (c) scale a wall 4 feet high? _____
    (d) climb to the top of a ladder 20 feet high? _____
    (e) enter a window from the top of a ladder? _____
    (f) climb, unaided, into a window 5 feet above the ground? _____
    (g) climb lengthwise over a full-sized sedan? _____
    (h) pass through an opening 3 feet by 3 feet? _____
    (i) pull a 120-lb. object off the road? _____
    (j) lift a 90-lb. weight from ground to waist level and place it in the rear of a station wagon? _____
    (k) change a car tire, including removal and tightening of lug nuts from a car wheel? _____
    (l) remove and replace the spare tire from the trunk of a car? _____
    (m) maintain your balance, for example, riding a bicycle? _____
    (n) work without regular meal times? _____
    (o) use a pry bar to force open a car door? _____

11. (a) Are you missing any fingers, toes, arms, or legs? _____
    If you answer "yes," then complete section b of this question.
    (b) If so, do you feel that you could still perform the job of a Trooper? _____

12. Can you accurately copy names, addresses, and a long series of numbers and letters as required in filling out a traffic ticket? _____

13. Can you add, subtract, multiply, and divide accurately? _____

14. Are you able to copy information accurately from a driver's license and vehicle registration? _____

15. Do you have the mental and physical abilities needed to make an arrest? _____

16. If a police situation required it, could you use a nightstick to poke or hit someone? _____

17. Could you use a gun to kill an injured or vicious animal at close range? _____

18. If you were a Trooper, could you direct traffic? _____

19. In an emergency situation, could you take the responsibility of directing motorists to drive in the wrong traffic lanes or in a direction that they had not intended to drive? _____

20. Can you learn how to use a two-way radio? _____

21. Are you now or have you been in the military service? _____

    If you answer "yes," then complete section b of this question.
    (b) Are you willing to sign a waiver to permit examination of your military records and/or discharge papers? _____

22. Are you able to:

    (a) run 1/2 mile (2,640 feet)? _____
    (b) work outdoors in inclement weather for extended periods of time? _____

23. Do you:

    (a) have sufficient strength in each hand to control a .357 magnum handgun (a powerful weapon with considerable recoil)? _____
    (b) have sufficient strength to control a shotgun during rapid fire? _____

24. Have you had any compensation claims for injury connected with your employment, including military service, within the past ten years? _____

    (If "yes," explain.)

25. Have you ever been discharged or forced or requested to resign from a job? _____

    (If "yes," explain.)

26. Are you now or have you ever been employed in or compensated for any unlawful activity? _____

    (If "yes," explain.)

27. Do you have:

    (a) frequent and uncontrollable need for sleep? _____
    (b) any speech defects that would interfere with your ability to communicate orally? _____
    (c) any mental or emotional problems that would prevent you from functioning under physical or emotional pressure? _____
    (d) any addiction to unlawful drugs? _____
    (e) any alcohol addiction? _____
    (f) any major physical disabilities? _____
    (g) excessive concern about your health? _____

28. Are you afraid of the dark? _____

29. Are you generally in good health? _____

30. Are you able to maintain your emotional stability without the use of drugs? _____

31. Do you have good peripheral (side) vision? _____

32. Can you focus your eyes quickly on objects at various distances away from you? _____

33. Are you able to distinguish different colors, such as in the clothing of suspects or the exterior of automobiles? _____

34. Can you read a state license plate in the daylight at a distance of 40 feet? _____

35. Can you move both eyes in the same direction at the same time? _____

36. Can you observe merging traffic while driving? _____

37. When blinded by oncoming headlights at night, are you able to recover from the glare quickly enough to maintain control of your vehicle? _____

38. (a)   Do you wear prescribed glasses? _____

    If you answer "yes," then complete sections b through e of this question.
    If your glasses were broken or removed, could you:
    (b)   drive a car? _____
    (c)   physically defend yourself in hand-to-hand combat? _____
    (d)   effectively use a handgun at 15 yards? _____
    (e)   chase a fleeing person across a field? _____

39. Could you hear and understand a normal radio transmission while on patrol? _____

40. Police officers often have to conduct investigations or make arrests involving members of the opposite sex. Would you be afraid to conduct such investigations or make arrests involving members of the opposite sex? _____

41. Are you willing to:

    (a)   physically defend yourself? _____
    (b)   inflict physical injury on someone, under proper circumstances, when acting in defense of another person? _____

42. Are you aware of the need for safety when handling firearms? _____

43. Are you afraid to handle or shoot firearms? _____

44. Could you withstand boredom, such as driving for a long period at night with no other activity, or watching a specific location for 8 hours without relief? _____

45. Are you honest? _____

46. Can you resist a bribe? _____

47. Can you resist the temptation to accept gratuities, for example, special discounts or free meals? _____

48. Can you distinguish between right and wrong? _____

49. Could you remember your work schedule if the hours were changed from week to week? _____

50. Would you be willing to give up your right to strike in a labor-management dispute as a condition of State Police employment? _____

51. A State Trooper must learn law, legal procedures, interpersonal skills, and investigative procedures. Would you be willing to learn:

(a) how to develop information about the criminal elements in a patrol area? _____

(b) how to make a crime scene search? _____

(c) how to respond to armed robberies? _____

(d) the criteria by which evidence is admitted in a trial? _____

(e) how to plan an investigation? _____

(f) how to interview a person, obtain the desired information, and reduce it to writing? _____

(g) how to recognize and preserve evidence? _____

(h) how to use the Criminal Procedure Law, Penal Law, and Vehicle and Traffic Law? _____

(i) about the Criminal Justice System? _____

(j) how to determine reasonable grounds for an arrest? _____

(k) how to develop criminal informants? _____

(l) how to become a leader and assume responsibility? _____

(m) how much force to use in a given situation? _____

(n) how to identify the symptoms of drug abuse? _____

(o) how to react correctly to a dangerous situation? _____

(p) how to work on your own without supervision? _____

(q) how to maintain your composure on the witness stand? _____

(r) how to recognize and deal with an agitator in a crowd? _____

(s) how to cross-examine a witness at a trial when acting as a prosecutor for your own arrests? _____

(t) how to shoot a revolver and shotgun accurately? _____

(u) proper circumstances under which you can take a human life? _____

(v) emergency removal of a child from a dangerous family situation? _____

(w) distinctions between grades of crime? _____

(x) stop and frisk procedures? _____

(y) regulations regarding reciprocity between states (for example, vehicles, weights, and measures)? _____

PART THREE

Preparing for the Civil Service Exams

THE WRITTEN EXAMINATION

Step one in the screening process is nearly always the written examination. Police departments want to avoid any possible accusation of favoritism or prejudice in hiring, so they invariably use written examinations to screen out unqualified candidates. The written examination is, in almost all cases, a multiple-choice examination. Multiple choice assures objectivity. If the questions are well designed, each question has only one right answer. Such exams are easy to score and are generally considered to be fair. The unique feature of entry-level examinations is that they do not presuppose any knowledge. The applicant taking a state police officer entry exam is not expected to know police rules, regulations, or procedures. On the other hand, the candidate is expected to reason and even think like a police officer. Questions that evaluate the candidate's thinking and reasoning processes include all the necessary information with which to reason. This means that police officer exams tend to include many lists of rules and procedures. They often include long excerpts from manuals and rulebooks. The test taker must read and understand the rules that are the basis for each judgment or reasoning question and then must think through the best answer.

READING-BASED QUESTIONS

By now you should have gathered that much of the measure of police intelligence is based upon how well you read and what you do with that which you read. Reading-based questions include questions of fact to be extracted directly from reading passages, questions of inference from reading passages, questions that require a choice of actions based upon rules and a fact situation, and questions of judgment of the behavior of others, again, based upon both rules and a fact situation. They may also probe your ability to interpret and judge from what you read by presenting a series of definitions and descriptions of situations and then asking you to classify the situations based on the fact situations.

Since reading-based questions of one form or another constitute the bulk of all police exams, we have devoted a full chapter in this book to preparing you for these questions.

PRACTICAL JUDGMENT QUESTIONS

Closely related to reading-based questions are questions of practical police judgment. These are questions that present you with a fact situation and require you to make a spot decision for appropriate action in that situation. The judgment questions do not presuppose knowledge of the proper police action. Your answer should be based upon good judgment and common sense.

However, some familiarity with "police thinking" should stand you in good stead with these questions. The good judgment that you demonstrate in police practical judgment questions should predict the same good judgment in actual police situations.

There are also those questions that test your sensitivity to specific problems, such as the questions based on stories or descriptions by various witnesses that require you to identify a specific problem.

OBSERVATION AND MEMORY QUESTIONS

The intelligent police officer reads well, is able to choose a course of action on the basis of knowledge from reading, and can make good judgments in both emergency and non-emergency situations. He or she must also be a keen observer with a good memory. Observation with instant forgetting is totally useless. Observation and memory questions, which appear on many, though by no means all, police officer exams, serve to identify those recruits who are wide awake and know what to watch for. In a way, they also are a test of judgment, for the test-taker must be able to decide what to focus on. Obviously, no one can notice and remember every detail of a scene or event. The intelligent observer can choose what is most important and commit it to memory. The test situation is not, of course, the same as real life. If your exam does not include this type of question, it is because your police department considers observation and memory questions on a written test to be too artificial to be truly predictive. Since this type of question does appear frequently, we have included a chapter for instruction and practice. The information will prove useful whether or not you must answer observation and memory questions on your exam; you will certainly need to sharpen these skills in order to perform your state police duties.

VISUALIZATION

Similar to the memorization-type of questions, the visualization questions ask that you look at a scene or picture and imagine what the objects or people would look like after they have been, somehow, changed. A car may change its color. A person might change his hair, wear sunglasses, or grow a beard. It also involves getting to a particular place from a different direction.

GRAMMAR AND EFFECTIVE EXPRESSION QUESTIONS

Another important line of questioning on police entrance exams has to do with grammar and effective expression. The reason for these questions is obvious. A police officer must communicate in both speech and in writing; his or her message must come across clearly and accurately. All important information must be included, and it must be stated in logical order. There must be no opportunity for misinterpretation or misunderstanding. Police recruits should present their best language skills along with their other qualifications. Grammar and effective expression are, of course, also related to reading. The person who has done extensive reading should be aware of ways to best express information in a clear and orderly fashion. We will not attempt to teach grammar at this late stage. Your logical thinking and your eye for what "looks right" will have to see you through. However, we can forewarn you of various forms that grammar and effective expression questions may take and how to approach them.

Your exam may offer you four sentences and ask you to choose the sentence that is wrong with respect to grammar or English usage. This type of question can prove quite difficult. Often two or even three sentences appear to be wrong. Draw upon your school training. Try the sentences aloud (very softly). You may have to weed out the sentences that you are sure are correct, then guess from among the remaining ones.

Another approach is to offer you four sentences, often all attempting to give the same information, and to ask you which one is best. This is a little easier. Concentrate on the literal reading of each sentence. Be sure that the one you choose says what you think it means.

Other exams may ask your advice in rephrasing an awkward sentence or in repositioning a sentence or paragraph for more reasonable presentation.

A common effective expression question gives a series of sentences in random order. You must choose the logical progression of steps—what happened first, next, and so on.

WRITTEN COMPREHENSION

Related to the effective expression question is written comprehension, a type of question that presents a list of facts, then asks you to include all these facts in a statement of one or two sentences. You must take care to include all the facts and to express them in an unambiguous way. Read each choice literally to catch word orders that may make the meaning incorrect or even ridiculous. Check the list of facts often to ensure that all facts are presented clearly and appropriately in the statement.

In addition, there are questions about what information is important to include in a written statement or report. This type of question relies on judgment as well as on knowing the best way of expressing information. Put yourself in the position of the person receiving and having to act on the information. What would be most useful? What do you need to know? In what order would you find the information most helpful?

READING MAPS AND ORIENTATION

Except in cases of extreme emergency, police officers are required to obey all traffic laws. The police officer who goes to the scene of an accident by entering a one-way street in the wrong direction is likely to create another accident. On the other hand, time may be of the essence. A victim may have injuries that require immediate attention. An officer may have to choose the most efficient legal way to get there. Map/Orientation questions on police exams involve a combination of reading, logical thinking, and common sense. The police candidate can learn how to use maps effectively while undergoing training; however, the applicant who comes with a well-developed skill will be able to spend more time getting specialized police training. Concentrate on map questions on your exam. Read carefully. Put yourself in the driver's seat, and follow all instructions. Do not hesitate to turn the test booklet as needed to maintain your sense of direction.

FILLING OUT FORMS

Police officers must fill out forms and must read and follow them. A few state police exams include questions based upon a form, instructions for filling out the form, and a fact situation. There is no trick to these questions. Read carefully. Be especially alert to instructions that read, "fill in blank 3 only if such and such" or "leave number 7 blank unless this and that both apply." Exclusionary and inclusive words present the keys in answering many form questions.

MISCELLANEOUS QUESTIONS

There are a variety of miscellaneous questions that appear on isolated state police qualification exams. Some or all of them may occur on yours. If they are included, they tend not to comprise a significant part of the exam. These questions include arithmetic, synonyms, verbal analogies, spelling, and various types of coding questions. In addition, there may be some questions that require deductive reasoning. You will be given a list of items or categories, and you must be able to classify them or interpret them with respect to the given situation.

Read directions carefully, then do your best with these.

Model Examination I includes a variety of different chart and table interpretation and coding questions that have appeared on recent examinations. These questions should serve as your introduction to a line of questioning that is increasing in popularity among examiners.

Throughout the Model Examinations in Part IV of this book, you will find almost every type of question that will appear on your actual test. However, the memorization and visualization questions may require additional effort on your part. And of course, without strong reading-comprehension skills, it may be difficult to do well on this exam. Therefore, it is worth your while to spend some time reviewing the material in the chapter that follows, as well as taking the model exams. Create code words for yourself in order to help you memorize pictures. Read over the directions carefully for each type of question so that you won't have to waste time rereading them several times on the exam in order to understand them.

HOW TO SHARPEN READING COMPREHENSION SKILLS

State Trooper candidates must be able to read quickly and carefully and with comprehension. The two essential ingredients for successful performance on reading tests are speed and comprehension. This chapter will explain the different kinds of comprehension questions and provide reading passages that will help to sharpen your skills. For the best results, follow the simple steps below:

1. Read the section "Planning a Strategy" to learn about the different kinds of reading comprehension questions.

2. Read the section "Reading: Quick Tips" to pick up valuable information on how to increase your reading speed and how to use the principles of paragraph construction to improve your comprehension.

3. Review the section "Sample Questions with Full Explanations." This section contains the kinds of reading comprehension questions most likely to appear on your examination. Each question is fully explained with reasons for discarding incorrect choices and justifications for the correct answers.

4. You can practice what you have learned in this chapter with the questions in the following chapter. The chapter contains forty-seven reading comprehension questions taken from actual examinations.

PLANNING A STRATEGY

HINTS

1. Read the passage quickly but carefully enough to get the main idea and major supporting details.

2. Read each question and decide which kind it is. Always consider each possible answer before making a choice.

3. Eliminate obviously wrong responses immediately. If possible, check confusing answer choices in the passage text.

The reading comprehension questions on your examination will usually be one of three kinds. Sample questions of each kind follow.

MAIN IDEA

The question, whether an act repugnant to the Constitution can become the law of the land, is a question deeply interesting to the United States; but, happily, not of an intricacy proportioned to its interest. It seems only necessary to recognize certain principles, supposed to have been long and well established, to decide it. That the people have an original right to establish, for their future government, such principles as, in their opinion, shall be most conducive to their own happiness, is the basis on which the whole American fabric has been erected. The exercise of this original right is a very great exertion; nor can it, nor ought it to, be frequently repeated. The principles, therefore, so established, are deemed fundamental; and as the authority from which they proceed is supreme, and can seldom act, they are designed to be permanent.

The best title for the paragraph would be
(A) "Principles of the Constitution."
(B) "The Root of Constitutional Change."
(C) "Only People Can Change the Constitution."
(D) "Methods of Constitutional Change."

This selection deals with the basis for possible changes in the Constitution. Therefore, the correct answer is choice (B).

DETAILS

"Another explanation of the persistence of the criminal is found in the existence of criminality or near-criminality in the general society." Which statement is the *least* consistent with the statement in this question?

(A) Not all criminals are apprehended and sentenced for their crimes.
(B) Advertisements of many commodities are often fraudulent in their claims.
(C) The reformation of the offender would be much simpler if society contained more persons of the near criminal type.
(D) Many business concerns are willing to purchase stolen goods.

Choice (C) is in direct opposition to the quotation. It is therefore least consistent with the quotation.

INFERENCE

An inference is a conclusion made from something that is implied. The answer to an inference question will not be found in the passage and is therefore the most difficult type of reading comprehension question to answer. You must read carefully and think logically in order to draw the correct conclusion from the information given. The following is an example of an inference question.

The facts, as we see them, on drug use and the dangerous behavior caused by drugs are that some people get into trouble while using drugs, and some of those drug users are dangerous to others. Sometimes a drug is a necessary element in order for a person to commit a crime, although it may not be the cause of his or her criminality. On the other hand, the use of a drug sometimes seems to be the only convenient excuse by means of which the observer can account for the undesirable behavior.

The author apparently feels that
(A) the use of drugs always results in crime.
(B) drugs and crime are only sometimes related.
(C) drug use does not always cause crime.
(D) drugs are usually an element in accidents and suicides.

The author states that drugs are sometimes a necessary element in a crime, but at other times are just an excuse for criminal behavior. Therefore, choice (B) is the correct answer.

READING: QUICK TIPS

■ **Main ideas** are the most important thoughts in a paragraph or selection. The main idea is often stated in a topic sentence.

■ **Supporting details** are the major thoughts used to explain and expand the main idea.

■ **Skimming** is a speed-reading technique that is used to extract the main idea and supporting details from a selection.

■ **Scanning** is the method used to locate specific information in a selection.

For speed and accuracy in reading and answering comprehension questions, practice and use these skimming and scanning techniques.

TO ANSWER MAIN IDEA AND INFERENCE QUESTIONS:

1. Use your index finger as a guide and a pacer. Read the selection through quickly.

2   As you move your finger across each line, concentrate on looking at three or four word phrases, not at one word at a time. Try not to "say" the words in your mind as you go.

3. Follow your finger only with your eyes, not with your whole head.

4. Your purpose is to locate the topic sentence, the main idea, and the major supporting details. This information should enable you to answer most main idea and inference questions.

TO ANSWER DETAIL QUESTIONS:

1. Take a key word from the question you want to answer and "lock" it in your mind.

2. Using your index finger as a guide, scan the lines for that word.

3. *Do not read when you scan*! You are simply looking for the key word.

4. When you find the word, *stop*! The answer to your question will usually be in the same sentence.

5. Read the entire sentence carefully before choosing an answer.

The most important ingredients in successful reading performance are accuracy and speed. Both require lots of practice. The tips you have just read should noticeably improve your accuracy and speed if you practice them conscientiously.

SAMPLE QUESTIONS WITH FULL EXPLANATIONS

Answer questions 1 through 5 on the basis of the information given in the following passage. Circle the letter of the answer you choose.

If we are to study crime in its widest social setting, we will find a variety of conduct that, although criminal in the legal sense, is not offensive to the moral conscience of a considerable number of persons. Traffic violations, for example, do not brand the offender as guilty of moral offense. In fact, the recipient of a traffic ticket is usually simply the subject of some good-natured joking by friends. Although there may be indignation among certain groups of citizens against gambling and liquor law violations, these activities are often tolerated, if not openly supported, by the more numerous residents of the community. Indeed, certain social and service clubs regularly conduct gambling games and lotteries for the purpose of raising funds. Some communities regard violations involving the sale of liquor with little concern in order to profit from increased license fees and taxes paid by dealers. The thousand and one forms of political graft and corruption that infest our urban centers only occasionally arouse public condemnation and official action.

1. According to the passage, all types of illegal conduct are

   (A) condemned by all elements of the community.
   (B) considered a moral offense, although some are tolerated by a few citizens.
   (C) violations of the law, but some are acceptable to certain elements of the community.
   (D) found in a social setting and therefore not punishable by law.

2. According to the passage, traffic violations are generally considered by society to be

   (A) crimes requiring the maximum penalty set by the law.
   (B) more serious than violations of the liquor laws.
   (C) offenses against the morals of the community.
   (D) relatively minor offenses requiring minimum punishment.

3. According to the passage, a lottery conducted for the purpose of raising funds for a church

   (A) is considered a serious violation of the law.
   (B) may be tolerated by a community that has laws against gambling.
   (C) may be conducted under special laws demanded by the more numerous residents of a community.
   (D) arouses indignation in most communities.

4. On the basis of the passage, the most likely reaction in the community to a police raid on a gambling casino would be

   (A) more an attitude of indifference than interest in the raid.
   (B) general approval of the raid.
   (C) condemnation of the raid by most people.
   (D) demand for further action, since this raid is not sufficient to end gambling.

5. The one of the following that best describes the central thought of this passage and would be most suitable as a title would be

   (A) "Crime and the Police."
   (B) "Public Condemnation of Graft and Corruption."
   (C) "Gambling Is Not Always a Vicious Business."
   (D) "Public Attitude toward Law Violations."

Answer questions 6 through 8 on the basis of the information given in the following passage.

The law enforcement agency is one of the most important agencies in the field of juvenile delinquency prevention. This is so, however, not because of the social work connected with this problem, for this is not a police matter, but because the officers are usually the first to come in contact with the delinquent. The manner of arrest and detention makes a deep impression on the delinquent and affects his or her lifelong attitude toward society and toward the law. The juvenile court is perhaps the most important agency in this work. Contrary to general opinion, however, it is not primarily concerned with putting children into correctional schools. The main purpose of the juvenile court is to save the child and to develop his or her emotional makeup so that he or she can grow up to be a decent and well-balanced citizen. The system of probation is the means by which the court seeks to accomplish these goals.

6. According to the passage, police work is an important part of a program to prevent juvenile delinquency because

   (A) social work is no longer considered important in juvenile delinquency prevention.
   (B) police officers are the first to have contact with the delinquent.
   (C) police officers jail the offender in order to be able to change his or her attitude toward society and the law.
   (D) it is the first step in placing the delinquent in jail.

7. According to the passage, the chief purpose of the juvenile court is to

   (A) punish the child for the offense.
   (B) select a suitable correctional school for the delinquent.
   (C) use available means to help the delinquent become a better person.
   (D) provide psychiatric care for the delinquent.

8. According to the passage, the juvenile court directs the development of delinquents under its care chiefly by

   (A) placing the child under probation.
   (B) sending the child to a correctional school.
   (C) keeping the delinquent in prison.
   (D) returning the child to his or her home.

9. "Prostitution is a crime, but one meets it at every corner." The clearest implication of this statement is

   (A) some laws are ignored.
   (B) prostitution is a serious offense.

    (C)   the principal purpose of any law is to catch a lawbreaker.

    (D)   prostitution is quite uncommon.

10. "Discipline should be education; instead it is little more than application of the theory of spanking to adults." This means most nearly that

    (A)   whipping is a good way to handle a man who beats his wife.

    (B)   a thieving banker should be imprisoned for life.

    (C)   those who commit crimes exhibit a marked lack of self-control.

    (D)   reeducation is really a kind of discipline.

11. "Crimes against the person are apt to be more spectacular than other types of crime and, consequently, space is accorded them in the public press out of proportion to their actual frequency." This means most nearly that

    (A)   there has been a notable increase in crimes against the person.

    (B)   the newspapers pay more attention to robberies than to cases of fraud.

    (C)   the newspapers pay no attention to crimes against property.

    (D)   crimes against property are not as serious as crimes against the person.

ANSWER KEY—READING COMPREHENSION

1.	C	5.	D	9.	A
2.	D	6.	B	10.	D
3.	B	7.	C	11.	B
4.	A	8.	A		

EXPLANATORY ANSWERS—READING COMPREHENSION

1.   **The correct answer is (C).**

(A) Not true; the passage indicates that certain violations of laws are more or less accepted by the citizenry, e.g., traffic violations, liquor laws, etc.

(B) Not true; the passage indicates that traffic violators are usually not deemed guilty of a moral offense.

(C) Exactly what the passage implies; this choice is correct.

(D) Nothing in the passage indicates that this is true.

2.   **The correct answer is (D).**

(A) Nothing in the passage indicates this. In fact, traffic violators are usually only subjected to good-natured joking by their friends.

(B) The implication in the passage is that violators of liquor laws are probably frowned upon more than traffic violators.

(C) The passage states exactly the opposite.

(D) This is the exact inference of the passage and is the correct choice.

3.   **The correct answer is (B).**

(A) There is nothing in the passage to indicate this.

(B) This is the correct choice as supported by the contents of the passage.

(C) There is nothing in the passage to support this choice.

(D) The passage supports the opposite point of view.

4.   **The correct answer is (A).**

(A) This is the correct choice.

(B) Not correct; the community, in general, would not approve of a raid on an activity that it favors.

(C) Not correct; the community's reaction would be that the police could better busy themselves on other areas of crime prevention.

(D) There is nothing in the passage to support this choice.

5. **The correct answer is (D)**

(A) Not suitable; this title is too broad. The passage deals specifically with certain kinds of crime.

(B) The passage makes the point that the public does not always condemn crime and corruption.

(C) This title is too narrow since other crimes are discussed in addition to gambling.

(D) The correct choice; this title describes the main focus of the passage.

6. **The correct answer is (B).**

(A) The passage states exactly the opposite; social work is a very important part of any juvenile delinquency program.

(B) The correct choice; a police officer's attitude during this initial encounter is of great importance.

(C) Not true; in fact, the passage states that probation is preferred to accomplish these goals.

(D) Not true; the passage emphasizes that the solution to the problem is not placing the delinquent in a jail or correctional school but helping to modify his or her attitudes by means of a probation program.

7. **The correct answer is (C).**

(A) The passage stresses reform rather than punishment.

(B) The passage states that the chief purpose of the juvenile court is to change the attitude of the juvenile offender, not to institutionalize him or her.

(C) This is the implication of the passage and therefore the correct choice.

(D) Psychiatric care is not mentioned directly, although it may be implied in the passage. In any case, it is neither a main means of reformation nor the chief purpose of the juvenile court.

8. **The correct answer is (A).**

(A) The correct choice; refer to the last sentence of the passage.

(B) The juvenile court prefers probation as a means of effecting change in delinquents.

(C) Not true; the final sentence makes it quite clear that probation is preferred.

(D) Not true; this is never mentioned in the passage. The home may be the source of the problem.

9. **The correct answer is (A).**

(A) This is the correct choice. If prostitution is prevalent, it must mean that the law that prohibits it is usually ignored.

(B) Not correct; there is nothing in this quotation to indicate that this is true.

(C) Not correct; the implication of the quotation is that prostitution and other victimless crimes are sometimes ignored by law enforcement officials.

(D) Not correct; the opposite is true according to this quotation.

10. **The correct answer is (D).**

(A) Not correct; the quotation refers to the *theory* of the spanking, not to actual physical punishment.

(B) Not correct; nothing in the quotation supports this implication.

(C) Not correct; self-control is not specifically mentioned or implied in this quotation.

(D) The correct choice; proper discipline will change the attitudes of offenders.

11. **The correct answer is (B).**

(A) Not correct; the quotation does not say that this is so.

(B) The correct choice; the implication is that newspaper readers find robbery stories more interesting.

(C) Not correct; the quotation does not state that crimes against property are completely ignored.

(D) Not correct; the quotation does not deal with the seriousness accorded to specific crimes.

PRACTICE WITH READING COMPREHENSION QUESTIONS

1. "The force reconciling and coordinating all human conflicts and directing people in the harmonious accomplishments of their work is the supervisor. To deal with people successfully, the first one a supervisor must learn to work with is him- or herself." According to the quotation, which of the following conclusions is the most accurate?

   (A) Human conflicts are not the basic lack in harmonious accomplishment.
   (B) A supervisor should attempt to reconcile all the different views subordinates may have.
   (C) A supervisor who understands him- or herself is in a good position to deal with others successfully.
   (D) The reconciling force in human conflicts is the ability to deal with people successfully.

2. "Law must be stable and yet it cannot stand still" means most nearly that

   (A) law is a fixed body of subject matter.
   (B) law must adapt itself to changing conditions.
   (C) law is a poor substitute for justice.
   (D) the true administration of justice is the firmest pillar of good government.

3. "The treatment to be given the offender cannot alter the fact of the offense; but we can take measures to reduce the chance of similar acts occurring in the future. We should banish the criminal, not in order to exact revenge nor directly to encourage reform, but to deter that person and others from further illegal attacks on society." According to the quotation, prisoners should be punished in order to

   (A) alter the nature of their offenses.
   (B) banish them from society.
   (C) deter them and others from similar illegal attacks on society.
   (D) directly encourage reform.

4. "On the other hand, the treatment of prisoners on a basis of direct reform is foredoomed to failure. Neither honest persons nor criminals will tolerate a bald proposition from anyone to alter their characters or habits, least of all if we attempt to gain such a change by a system of coercion." According to this quotation, criminals

   (A) are incorrigible.
   (B) are incapable of being coerced.
   (C) are not likely to turn into law-abiding citizens.
   (D) possess very firm characters.

5. "A moment's reflection will show that it is never possible to determine the exact amount of blame to be attached to the individual criminal. How can we ascertain how much is due to inheritance, how much to early environment, how much to other matters over which the offender has had no control whatsoever?" According to this quotation, criminals

   (A) cannot be held to account for their crimes.
   (B) cannot be blamed for their crimes.
   (C) are variously motivated in committing crimes, and it is senseless to assume that we can know how much blame to attach to a particular violator of the law.
   (D) can blame their misdeeds on their early environment.

6. "While much thought has been devoted to the question of how to build walls high enough to keep persons temporarily in prison, we have devoted very little attention to the treatment necessary to enable them to come out permanently cured, inclined to be friends rather than enemies of their law-abiding fellow citizens." According to this quotation, much thought has been devoted to the problem of prisons as

   (A) vengeful agencies.
   (B) efficient custodial agencies.
   (C) efficient sanatoria.
   (D) places from which society's friends might issue.

7. "There has been a tragic failure on the part of the home, the school, the church, industry, and every other social agency to adjust the incompetent individual to his or her proper sphere and to impart to him or her wholesome principles of proper living. The failure is finally shunted onto the prison in one last desperate effort to make the person over. Theoretically, the church, the school, and the college have a clean page in the mind of the pupil upon which to make their impressions, but the prison school faces the tremendous task of obliterating many erroneous and corrupt notions before it can secure a clean page upon which to write." According to this statement, the prison has as pupils

   (A) those persons with which society's educational institutions have been able to do nothing.
   (B) those who have failed in business and the arts.
   (C) those who have scoffed at God.
   (D) those who have learned nothing from the outside world.

8. "Community organizations most often include persons whose behavior is unconventional in relation to generally accepted social definitions, if such persons wield substantial influence with the residents." The inference one can most validly draw from this statement is that

   (A) influential persons are often likely to be unconventional.
   (B) the success of a community organization depends largely on the democratic processes employed by it.
   (C) a gang leader may sometimes be an acceptable recruit for a community organization.
   (D) the unconventional behavior of a local barkeeper may often become acceptable to the community.

9. "Essential to the prevention and early treatment of delinquency is the discovery of potential or incipient cases. Finding them is not as difficult as making assistance available and acceptable to them and their families." On the basis of this statement, it is most accurate to state that

    (A)   the families of delinquents are largely responsible for their behavior.
    (B)   "an ounce of prevention is worth more than a pound of cure."
    (C)   potential for criminality is readily discernible.
    (D)   the family of a delinquent may often reject a recommended plan for therapy.

10. "The safeguard of democracy is education. The education of youth during a limited period of more or less compulsory attendance at school does not suffice. The educative process is a lifelong one." The statement most consistent with this quotation is that

    (A)   school is not the only institution that can contribute to the education of the population.
    (B)   all democratic peoples are educated.
    (C)   the entire population should be required to go to school throughout life.
    (D)   if compulsory education were not required, the educative process would be more effective.

11. "The state police officer's art consists of applying and enforcing a multitude of laws and ordinances in such degree or proportion and in such manner that the greatest degree of social protection will be secured. The degree of enforcement and method of application will vary with each neighborhood and community." According to this statement,

    (A)   each neighborhood or community must judge for itself to what extent the law is to be enforced.
    (B)   a police officer should only enforce those laws that are designed to give the greatest degree of social protection.
    (C)   the manner and intensity of law enforcement is not necessarily the same in all communities.
    (D)   all laws and ordinances must be enforced in a community with the same degree of intensity.

12. "Police control in the sense of regulating the details of police operations involves such matters as the technical means for organizing the available personnel so that competent police leadership, when secured, can operate effectively. It is concerned not so much with the extent to which popular controls can be trusted to guide and direct the course of police protection as with the administrative relationships that should exist among the component parts of the police organism." According to this statement, police control is

    (A)   solely a matter of proper personnel assignment.
    (B)   the means employed to guide and direct the course of police protection.
    (C)   principally concerned with the administrative relationships among units of a police organization.
    (D)   the sum total of means employed in rendering police protection.

13. "As a rule, state police officers, through service and experience, are familiar with the duties and the methods and means required to perform them. Yet, left to themselves, their aggregate effort would disintegrate and the vital work of preserving the peace would never be accomplished." According to this statement, which is the most accurate of the following conclusions?

    (A)   Police officers are sufficiently familiar with their duties as to need no supervision.
    (B)   Working together for a common purpose is not efficient without supervision.
    (C)   Police officers are familiar with the methods of performing their duties because of rules.
    (D)   Preserving the peace is so vital that it can never be said to be completed.

Answer questions 14 through 16 on the basis of the information given in the following passage.

Criminal science is largely the science of identification. Progress in this field has been marked and sometimes very spectacular because new techniques, instruments, and facts flow continuously from the scientists. But the crime laboratories are understaffed; trade secrets still prevail; and inaccurate conclusions are often the result. Moreover, modern gadgets cannot substitute for the skilled, intelligent investigator; he or she must be their master.

14. According to this passage, criminal science

(A) excludes the field of investigation.
(B) is primarily interested in establishing identity.
(C) is based on the equipment used in crime laboratories.
(D) uses techniques different from those used in other sciences.

15. Advances in criminal science have been, according to the passage,

(A) extremely limited.
(B) slow but steady.
(C) unusually reliable.
(D) outstanding.

16. A problem that has not been overcome completely in crime work is, according to the passage,

(A) unskilled investigators.
(B) the expense of new equipment and techniques.
(C) an insufficient number of personnel in crime laboratories.
(D) inaccurate equipment used in laboratories.

17. "The large number of fatal motor vehicle accidents renders necessary the organization of special units in the police department to cope with the technical problems encountered in such investigations." The generalization that can be inferred most directly from this statement is that

(A) the number of fatal motor vehicle accidents is large.
(B) technical problems require specialists.
(C) many police problems require special handling.
(D) many police officers are specialists.

18. "While the safe burglar can ply his or her trade the year round, the loft burglar has more seasonal activities, since only at certain periods of the year is a substantial amount of valuable merchandise stored in lofts." The generalization that this statement best illustrates is that

(A) nothing is ever completely safe from a thief.
(B) there are safe burglars and loft burglars.
(C) some types of burglary are seasonal.
(D) the safe burglar considers safecracking a trade.

Questions 19 through 22 relate to the report of an accident. In Part A, you are given the regulations governing filling out the report form. In Part B, you are given the completed report, which you will use to answer the questions that follow.

Part A

1. A report form will be filled out for each person injured.

2. Be brief but do not omit any information that can help the department reduce the number of accidents. If necessary, use more than one form.

3. Under Details, enter all important facts not reported elsewhere on the form that may be pertinent to the completeness of the report, such as: the specific traffic violation, if any; whether the injured person was crossing not at the intersection or against the lights; the direction the vehicle was proceeding and if making a right or left turn; attending surgeon; etc. If the officer is an eyewitness, he or she should be able to determine the cause of the accident.

Part B

Injured Person: John C. Witherspoon
Sex: Male
Age: 52
Address: 2110 Fairwell Road
Place of Occurrence: 72nd Street and Broadway
Date: 3/12/95
Accident: Yes
Number of Persons Involved: 12
Time: 10 a.m.
Nature of Injury: Right forearm fractured
Struck by: Vehicle 3
Drivers Involved: Vehicle 1: Helmut Baldman, 11 Far Street, Lic. 2831, owner
                     Vehicle 2: John Dunn, 106 Near Avenue, Lic. 1072, owner
                     Vehicle 3: Robert Payne, 32 Open Road, Lic. 666, owner

Details: (1) Vehicle 1 came out of 72nd Street just as the lights along 72nd Street were changing to green west. (2) Vehicle 2 proceeding north along Broadway and continued across the intersection as the lights in his direction turned red. (3) Vehicle 1 collided with Vehicle 2, turning said vehicle over and throwing it into the path of Vehicle 3, which was going east along 72nd Street. (4) This had manifold results: other vehicles were struck; a hydrant was obliterated; several pedestrians were injured; there was considerable property damage; and the three riders in the cars involved were killed. (5) This was a very tragic accident.

19. Of the following critical evaluations of the report, the most correct is that it is a
    (A) good report; it gives a graphic description of the accident.
    (B) bad report; the damage to the car is not given in detail.
    (C) bad report; it does not indicate, in detail, the cause of Witherspoon's injury.
    (D) good report; it is very brief.

20. Of the following, the report indicates most clearly
    (A) the driver at fault.
    (B) that Witherspoon was a pedestrian.
    (C) the names of all the drivers involved.
    (D) that some city property was damaged.

21. Of the following, the report indicates least clearly
    (A) the time of the accident.
    (B) the direction in which Baldman was driving.
    (C) how the accident might have been avoided.
    (D) the number of persons involved.

22. From the report, as submitted, it is most reasonable to infer that
    (A) Baldman was at fault.
    (B) the information is too hazy to determine the guilty person.
    (C) Dunn was at fault.
    (D) something was wrong with the light system.

Answer questions 23 through 26 on the basis of the information given in the following passage.

When a vehicle has been disabled in a tunnel, the officer on patrol in this zone shall press the emergency truck light button. In the fast lane, red lights will go on throughout the tunnel. The yellow zone light will go on at each signal control station throughout the tunnel and will flash the number of the zone in which the stoppage has occurred. A red flashing pilot light will appear only at the signal control station at which the emergency truck button was pressed. The emergency garage will receive an audible and visual signal indicating the signal control station at which the emergency truck button was pressed. The garage officer shall acknowledge receipt of the signal by pressing the acknowledgement button. This will cause the pilot light at the operated signal control station in the tunnel to cease flashing and to remain steady. It is an answer to the officer at the operated signal control station that the emergency truck is responding to the call.

23. According to this passage, when the emergency truck light button is pressed
    (A) amber lights will go on in every lane throughout. the tunnel.
    (B) emergency signal lights will go on only in the lane in which the disabled vehicle is located.
    (C) red lights will go on in the fast lane throughout the tunnel.
    (D) pilot lights at all signal control stations will turn amber.

24. According to this passage, the number of the zone in which the stoppage has occurred is flashed
    (A) immediately after all the lights in the tunnel turn red.
    (B) by the yellow zone light at each signal control station.
    (C) by the emergency truck at the point of stoppage.
    (D) by the emergency garage.

25. According to the passage, an officer near the disabled vehicle will know that the emergency tow truck is coming when
    (A) the pilot light at the operated signal control station appears and flashes red.
    (B) an audible signal is heard in the tunnel.
    (C) the zone light at the operated signal control station turns red.
    (D) the pilot light at the operated signal control station becomes steady.

26. Under the system described in the passage, it would be correct to come to the conclusion that
    (A) officers at all signal control stations are expected to acknowledge that they have received the stoppage signal.
    (B) officers at all signal control stations will know where the stoppage has occurred.
    (C) all traffic in both lanes of that side of the tunnel in which the stoppage has occurred must stop until the emergency truck has arrived.
    (D) there are two emergency garages, each able to respond to the stoppage in traffic going in one particular direction.

Answer questions 27 through 29 on the basis of the information given in the following passage.

The use of a roadblock is simply an adaptation of the military concept of encirclement to police practices. Successful operation of a road block plan depends almost entirely on the amount of advance study and planning given to such operations. A thorough and detailed examination of the roads and terrain under the jurisdiction of a given police agency should be made with the locations of the roadblock pinpointed in advance. The first principle to be borne in mind in the location of each roadblock is the time element. Its location must be at a point beyond which the fugitive could not possibly have traveled in the time elapsed from the commission of the crime to the arrival of the officers at the roadblock.

27. According to the passage,
    (A) military operations have made extensive use of roadblocks.
    (B) the military concept of encirclement is an adaptation of police use of roadblocks.
    (C) the technique of encirclement has been widely used by military forces.
    (D) a roadblock is generally more effective than encirclement.

28. According to the passage,
    (A) advance study and planning are of minor importance in the success of roadblock operations.
    (B) a thorough and detailed examination of all roads within a radius of 50 miles should precede the determination of a roadblock location.
    (C) consideration of terrain features is important in planning the location of roadblocks.
    (D) a roadblock operation can seldom be successfully undertaken by a single police agency.

29. According to the passage,
    (A) the factor of time is the sole consideration in the location of a roadblock.
    (B) the maximum speed possible in the method of escape is of major importance in roadblock location.
    (C) the time the officers arrive at the site of a proposed roadblock is of little importance.
    (D) a roadblock should be sited as close to the scene of the crime as the terrain will permit.

Answer questions 30 through 32 on the basis of the information given in the following passage.

A number of crimes, such as robbery, assault, rape, certain forms of theft, and burglary, are high visibility crimes in that it is apparent to all concerned that they are criminal acts prior to or at the time they are committed. In contrast to these, check forgeries, especially those committed by first offenders, have low visibility. There is little in the criminal act or in the interaction between the check passer and the person cashing the check to identify it as a crime. Closely related to this special quality of the forgery crime is the fact that, while it is formally defined and treated as a felonious or "infamous" crime, it is informally held by the legally untrained public to be a relatively harmless form of crime.

30. According to the passage, crimes of "high visibility"
    (A) are immediately recognized as crime by the victims.
    (B) take place in public view.
    (C) always involve violence or the threat of violence.
    (D) are usually committed after dark.

31. According to the passage,

    (A) the public regards check forgery as a minor crime.
    (B) the law regards check forgery as a minor crime.
    (C) the law distinguishes between check forgery and other forgery.
    (D) it is easier to spot inexperienced check forgers than other criminals.

32. As used in this passage, an "infamous" crime is

    (A) a crime attracting great attention from the public.
    (B) more serious than a felony.
    (C) a felony.
    (D) more or less serious than a felony depending upon the surrounding circumstances.

Answer questions 33 and 34 on the basis of the information given in the following passage.

The racketeer is primarily concerned with business affairs, legitimate or otherwise, and preferably those that are close to the margin of legitimacy. The racketeer gets the best opportunities from business organizations that meet the need of large sections of the public for goods or services that are defined as illegitimate by the same public, such as prostitution, gambling, illicit drugs, or liquor. In contrast to the thief, the racketeer and the establishments controlled deliver goods and services for the money received.

33. It can be deduced from the passage that suppression of racketeers is difficult because

    (A) victims of racketeers are not guilty of violating the law.
    (B) racketeers are generally engaged in fully legitimate enterprises.
    (C) many people want services that are not obtainable through legitimate sources.
    (D) laws prohibiting gambling and prostitution are unenforceable.

34. According to the passage, racketeering, unlike theft, involves

    (A) objects of value.
    (B) payment for goods received.
    (C) organized gangs.
    (D) unlawful activities.

35. "In examining the scene of a homicide, one should not only look for the usual, standard traces—fingerprints, footprints, etc.—but should also have eyes open for details which at first glance may not seem to have any connection with the crime." The most logical inference to be drawn from this statement is that

    (A) in general, standard traces are not important.
    (B) sometimes one should not look for footprints.
    (C) usually only the standard traces are important.
    (D) one cannot tell in advance what will be important.

Answer questions 36 and 37 on the basis of the information given in the following passage.

If a motor vehicle fails to pass inspection, the owner will be given a rejection notice by the inspection station. Repairs must be made within ten days after this notice is issued. It is not necessary to have the required adjustment or repairs made at the station where the inspection occurred. The vehicle may be taken to any other garage. Reinspection after repairs may be made at any official inspection station, not necessarily the same station that made the initial inspection. The registration of any motor vehicle for which an inspection sticker has not been obtained as required, or which is not repaired and inspected within ten days after inspection indicates defects, is subject to suspension. A vehicle cannot be used on public highways while its registration is under suspension.

36. According to the passage, the owner of a car that does not pass inspection must

(A) have repairs made at the same station that rejected the car.

(B) take the car to another station and have it reinspected.

(C) have repairs made anywhere and then have the car reinspected.

(D) not use the car on a public highway until the necessary repairs have been made.

37. According to the passage, the one of the following that may be cause for suspension of the registration of a vehicle is that

(A) an inspection sticker was issued before the rejection notice had been in force for ten days.

(B) it was not reinspected by the station that rejected it originally.

(C) it was not reinspected either by the station that rejected it originally or by the garage that made the repairs.

(D) it has not had defective parts repaired within ten days after inspection.

38. A statute states: "A person who steals an article worth less than $100 where no aggravating circumstances accompany the act is guilty of petit larceny. If the article is worth $100 or more, it may be larceny second degree." If all you know is that Edward Smith stole an article worth $100, it may be reasonably be said that

(A) Smith is guilty of petit larceny.

(B) Smith is guilty of larceny second degree.

(C) Smith is guilty of neither petit larceny nor larceny second degree.

(D) precisely what charge will be placed against Smith is uncertain.

Answer questions 39 through 41 on the basis of the information given in the following passage.

The City Police Department will accept for investigation no report of a person missing from his residence if such residence is located outside of the city. The person reporting the same will be advised to report such fact to the police department of the locality where the missing person lives, which will, if necessary, communicate officially with the City Police Department. However, a report will be accepted of a person who is missing from a temporary residence in the city, but the person making the report will be instructed to make a report also to the police department of the locality where the missing person lives.

39. According to the passage, a report to the City Police Department of a missing person whose permanent residence is outside of the city will

(A) always be investigated provided that a report is also made to local police authorities.

(B) never be investigated unless requested officially by local police authorities.

(C) be investigated in cases of temporary residence in the city, but a report should always be made to local police authorities.

(D) always be investigated and a report will be made to the local police authorities by the City Police Department.

40. Of the following, the most likely reason for the procedure described in the passage is that

(A) nonresidents are not entitled to free police service from the city.

(B) local police authorities would resent interference in their jurisdiction.

(C) local police authorities sometimes try to unload their problems on the City Police Department.

(D) local authorities may be better able to conduct an investigation.

41. Mr. Smith of Oldtown and Mr. Jones of Newtown have an appointment in the city, but Mr. Jones doesn't appear. Mr. Smith, after trying repeatedly to phone Mr. Jones the next day, believes that something has happened to him. According to the passage, Mr. Smith should apply to the police of

    (A) Oldtown.
    (B) Newtown.
    (C) Newtown and the city.
    (D) Oldtown and the city.

42. A Police Department rule reads as follows: "A Deputy Commissioner acting as Police Commissioner shall carry out the order of the Police Commissioner, previously given, and such orders shall not, except in cases of extreme emergency, be countermanded." This means most nearly that, except in cases of extreme emergency,

    (A) the orders given by a Deputy Commissioner acting as Police Commissioner may not be revoked.
    (B) a Deputy Commissioner acting as Police Commissioner should not revoke orders previously given by the Police Commissioner.
    (C) a Deputy Commissioner acting as Police Commissioner is vested with the same authority to issue orders as the Police Commissioner.
    (D) only a Deputy Commissioner acting as Police Commissioner may issue orders in the absence of the Police Commissioner.

43. "A crime is an act committed or omitted in violation of a public law either forbidding or commanding it." This statement implies most nearly that

    (A) crimes can be omitted.
    (B) a forbidding act, if omitted, is a crime.
    (C) an act of omission may be criminal.
    (D) to commit an act not commanded is criminal.

44. "He who by command, counsel, or assistance procures another to commit a crime is, in morals and in law, as culpable as the visible actor himself, for the reason that the criminal act, whichever it may be, is imputable to the person who conceived it and set the forces in motion for its actual accomplishment." Of the following, the most accurate inference from this statement is that

    (A) a criminal act does not have to be committed for a crime to be committed.
    (B) acting as counselor for a criminal is a crime.
    (C) the mere counseling of a criminal act can never be a crime if no criminal act is committed.
    (D) a person acting only as an adviser may be guilty of committing a criminal act.

45. "A felony is a crime punishable by death or imprisonment in a state prison, and any other crime is a misdemeanor." According to this quotation, the decisive distinction between felony and misdemeanor is the

    (A) degree of criminality.
    (B) type of crime.
    (C) place of incarceration.
    (D) judicial jurisdiction.

Answer questions 46 and 47 on the basis of the information given in the following passage.

If the second or third felony is such that, upon a first conviction, the offender would be punished by imprisonment for any term less than his or her natural life, then such person must be sentenced to imprisonment for an indeterminate term, the minimum of which shall be not less than one half of the longest term prescribed upon a first conviction, and the maximum of which shall be not longer than twice such longest term; provided, however, that the minimum sentence imposed hereunder upon such second or third felony offender shall in no case be less than five years; except that where the maximum punishment for a second or third felony offender hereunder is five years or less, the minimum sentence must be not less than two years.

46. According to this passage, a person who has a second felony conviction shall receive as a sentence for that second felony an indeterminate term

    (A) not less than twice the minimum term prescribed upon a first conviction as a maximum.
    (B) not less than one-half the maximum term of the first conviction as a minimum.
    (C) not more than twice the minimum term prescribed upon a first conviction as a minimum.
    (D) with a maximum of not more than twice the longest term prescribed for a first conviction for this crime.

47. According to the passage, if the term for this crime for a first offender is up to three years, the possible indeterminate term for this crime as a second or third felony shall have a

    (A) minimum of not more than two years.
    (B) maximum of not more than five years.
    (C) minimum of not less than one and one-half years.
    (D) maximum of not less than six years.

ANSWER KEY—READING COMPREHENSION

1.	C	13.	B	25.	D	37.	D
2.	B	14.	B	26.	B	38.	D
3.	C	15.	D	27.	C	39.	C
4.	C	16.	C	28.	C	40.	D
5.	C	17.	B	29.	B	41.	B
6.	B	18.	C	30.	A	42.	B
7.	A	19.	C	31.	A	43.	C
8.	C	20.	C	32.	C	44.	D
9.	D	21.	C	33.	C	45.	C
10.	A	22.	B	34.	B	46.	D
11.	C	23.	C	35.	D	47.	C
12.	C	24.	B	36.	C		

OBSERVATION AND MEMORY

To function effectively, a state police officer must possess a keen memory for details. He or she must be on constant alert for physical characteristics that will help to identify key people, places, or things, thereby leading to the apprehension of a criminal or to the solution of a criminal investigation.

Most people have distinguishing features that are difficult to disguise: the contour of the face; the size, shape, and position of the ears; the shape of the mouth; and the color of the eyes. Any of these may be sufficient for an officer to detect an individual wanted for criminal activities. On the other hand, the color or style of an individual's hair or the first impression of his or her face may change drastically with the addition of a wig, mustache, or beard. Therefore, the police officer must focus attention on those physical features that cannot be changed easily and that might serve as the basis of a positive identification of that person at some time in the future.

Observation is not limited to the act of seeing. In addition, the officer must learn to recognize and recall distinctive features of people, places, and things. An official record in the memorandum book may serve as a refresher for the facts stored in the officer's mental record. The officer should be aware of the people who frequent his or her post and of the surrounding buildings and stores on that post, so that important details may be brought to bear in a case when necessary. An officer without a keen sense of recall cannot perform his or her duties effectively.

Because state police departments all over the country recognize the importance of a good memory for details and a good sense of recall in the officer's job, examinations for the position frequently contain sections that evaluate these skills. To best sharpen your memory and sense of recall, you must practice using these skills. You need only walk around your neighborhood and observe. Keep your eyes open to everything you see. Later try to recall details of buildings or people that you saw. Remember, your environment is your study aid. Virtually any place you go, you can practice observing and recalling details.

POLICE OBSERVATION OF PERSONS, PLACES, AND THINGS

The state police officer must be thoroughly observant at all times. The nonobservant officer is soon found out by the criminal element, who will take advantage of this deficiency to commit crimes on the officer's post. Good observation is a matter of training and knowledge. A state police officer may have perfect eyesight, yet be blind when it comes to observing matters calling for police action.

Many dangerous criminals have been arrested due to a state police officer's keen observation. An officer should observe the customary activities on his or her post as well as the people who live in or frequent it so that the officer can quickly spot a stranger or an unusual activity. Some places will call for more observation than others: banks, jewelry stores, taverns, service stations, and any place where crime is likely to occur or where the criminal element may gather.

An essential element in observation is the ability to remember details. Officers should practice observation by giving themselves such tests as describing a man or woman encountered casually or trying to remember details on a billboard. The identification of persons, places, and things depends on accurate observation. Many witnesses testify inaccurately in court because they failed to observe properly at the time of the incident's occurrence. A failure of this kind is *inexcusable* on the part of an officer.

POLICE OBSERVATION OUTLINE

I. DEFINITION

Observation may be defined as

A. the act, ability, or practice of taking notice.

B. the act of seeing or fixing the mind on anything.

C. the act of drawing a mental picture of what has been seen.

II. OBSERVATION BY A STATE POLICE OFFICER

A. As stated in the definition, observation means first noticing things and second remembering what was noticed. So a police officer should know how to observe if he or she is to be effective in performing police work.

B. Essentially, observation by a police officer is the control of his or her senses to note and record in his or her mind accurately any occurrence, person, place, thing, or condition that is or may be related to the performance of the officer's duty.

C. The basis of observation is the proper use of the five senses, namely: sight, hearing, smell, taste, and touch.

1. Sight is used in noting the actions and appearance of persons, places, and things.

2. Hearing is used in listening to what is said and listening for noises and sounds that may indicate the need for police action.

3. Smell is used to notice odors, such as gas, liquor, gasoline, dead bodies, etc.

4. Taste is used in identifying liquids as sweet, salty, sour, etc.

5. Touch is used in feeling for pulse, temperature, etc.

Note: Psychologists have estimated that roughly 85 percent of our knowledge is obtained through the sense of sight, 12 percent through the sense of hearing, and the remaining 3 percent through the senses of smell, touch, and taste combined. The reliability of all sense information is considered to be the same. The combination of sight and hearing is the most useful and productive in observation.

D. The senses are of little value unless they are used and directed by intelligence.

E. Random reflection is also of little value. We must note consciously all things in relation to our duty. We must refer our observations to our knowledge of laws, places, people, and conditions.

F. Our senses must be quick to seek out criminal characteristics in those we meet, or lawless possibilities in any situation, and to note that which is unusual.

G. We should be on the alert for emergencies in order to prevent them or to control them properly.

H.   We must develop our memory.

I.   We must study all situations and conditions closely so as to be able to render an accurate report to a higher authority when required.

III. NECESSITY FOR POLICE OBSERVATION

A nonobservant state trooper is a poor trooper. Proper police work is greatly dependent on a trooper's power of observation. The following is a list of situations that depend on good observation in police work.

A.   **Noting Suspicious Persons.** A state police officer who becomes familiar with the type of people usually on his or her post will quickly notice a stranger, and if he or she knows how criminals act and pays attention to those he or she sees, the officer will note those acting suspiciously.

B.   **Preventing Crimes.** Observation of places where lights are ordinarily left burning at night, of when business places usually open and close, and of those who do business on his or her post will prevent many burglaries and robberies.

C.   **Saving Lives.** A state police officer noting the odor of poisonous or explosive gases and dangerous conditions will aid in this respect.

D.   **Controlling Emergencies.** Noting where the trouble lies is the first step in the proper control of the ordinary emergency.

E.   **Securing Evidence.** Many a case is ruined because the police officer overlooked evidence of clues.

F.   **Reporting to Superiors.** Proper police administration is greatly dependent on complete and accurate reports. Observation is essential to such completeness.

G.   **Recovering Stolen Property.** Stolen cars, particularly, are recovered by the officer who pays attention to license numbers, descriptions, and alarms.

H.   **Detecting Criminals.** The police officer who notes something special or unusual about a person, a car, or the modus operandi of a criminal is of great value in locating criminal suspects.

IV. GENERAL OBSERVATIONS BY STATE POLICE OFFICERS

A.   Persons

1.   The Individual

     (a) Facial expression
     (b) Complexion
     (c) Scars
     (d) Physique; carriage
     (e) Gait
     (f) Actions
     (g) Manner of dress
     (h) Tone of voice
     (i) Physical deformities; eccentricities
     (j) Occupation

2. The Group

   (a) Character of the gathering
   (b) Manner of the gathering
   (c) Individual members of the group
   (d) Language of the group; criminal jargon, etc.
   (e) Locale of the gathering
   (f) Time of day or night

B. Places

1. The Neighborhood

   (a) Social or economic level
   (b) Neighborhood esprit de corps
   (c) Likelihood of, or temptation to, crime, etc.

2. The Street

   (a) Children
   (b) Obstructions
   (c) Health conditions

3. The Buildings

   (a) Locations
   (b) Uses
   (c) Occupants; residents; storekeepers; janitors; doormen; etc.
   (d) Licenses
   (e) Signs

C. Things

1. Vehicles

   (a) Uses
   (b) Location
   (c) Occupants
   (d) Licenses

V. SPECIFIC OBSERVATIONS BY STATE POLICE OFFICERS

A. Persons

1. With criminal records

2. On probation or parole

3. Acting suspiciously

4. Associating with criminals or suspicious persons

5. Living in idleness

6. Hanging about pool parlors, dance halls, cabarets, cellar clubs, etc.

7. Without any visible means of support

8. Loitering in hallways, entering or leaving buildings, ringing bells, etc.

9. Loitering in the vicinity of banks, jewelry stores, railroad and bus stations, near trucks carrying valuable merchandise, etc.

10. Entering or leaving pawn shops, junk shops, secondhand stores

11. Showing an inclination to engage patrol officers in conversations, especially in high crime districts at night

B. Places

1. Licensed premises

2. Disorderly houses

3. All-night restaurants, social clubs, discos, nightclubs, etc.

4. Suspicious places and premises where known criminals congregate

5. Premises suspected of housing unlawful practices, such as gambling, vice, prostitution, etc.

6. Business places such as ,jewelry stores, banks, check cashing stores, loft buildings, garages, hackstands, etc.

C. Things

1. Automobiles, especially those in which the occupants are acting suspiciously

2. Automobiles standing at the curb with the motor :running

3. Automobiles stopped in front of banks, financial institutions, etc.

4. Taxicabs and hacks

5. Various classes of business
    (a) Time of opening and closing
    (b) Who opens and who closes such business places
    (c) Location of safes, cash registers, and valuable merchandise

VI. UNDESIRABLE OR DEFECTIVE OBSERVATIONS

A. **Haste**. Combine deliberation with observation. Proceed methodically; omit no details. Remember that patchwork is useless.

B. **Prejudice**. See all things equally. Avoid personal and biased points of view that destroy the real observations.

C. **Absentmindedness**. Avoid daydreaming. No one is on duty while his or her observational faculties—the senses—are off duty.

D. **Carelessness**. Failure to observe and note persons, places, things, and incidents results in fewer arrests, fewer convictions, and an increase in crime.

E. **Exaggeration**. See a thing as it is without enlarging its importance.

F. **Emotion**. The reactions of hope, fear, love, hate, or other strong feelings result in a loss of intelligent thinking, power to observe, and sense of proportion.

VII. QUALITIES OF AN OBSERVANT POLICE OFFICER

A. Faithful in the performance of his or her duties

B. Zealous in his or her work.

C. Unwearying in his or her devotion to the public need and to the civic ideal of which he or she is the personal embodiment

D. Good memory

E. Alertness

F. Knowledge of law, places, persons, etc.

G. Intelligence

H. Suspicion

I. Ambition

J. Attention to details

VIII. RESPONSIBILITY OF A POLICE OFFICER IN THE MATTER OF POLICE OBSERVATION

A. Improve his or her observational faculties by constantly exercising them. Thus, the officer should look at persons, places, and things while patrolling a post, describing them mentally and fixing their details in his or her mind. On returning back to the same post, the officer should check the accuracy of the observations.

B. Associate his or her observations with some line of police duty. Relevance to police work is the major consideration in the association of a police officer's observations. The main objects of police observation are to save time and effort, solve crimes more efficiently, and prepare effective evidence for presentation in court.

1. A police officer should learn to associate a certain kind of scar with a certain kind of weapon; a certain kind of gait and mannerism with the drug addict; a vehicle parked outside a jewelry store with the motor running with robbery.

2. In observing a person whom the police officer suspects of committing crime, the police officer should associate observation of the following general illustrations.

   (a) A guilty person will try to act overly natural, but, in many instances, will make a wrong move that will cause his or her arrest.
   (b) Those who are about to commit a crime usually look about. Sometimes they will walk into hallways and then walk out boldly.
   (c) The reward of careful observations and association of observations is the making of good arrests.

C. A police officer should classify his or her observations. This merely puts the observations into an orderly grouping to aid recall. A police officer who fulfills his or her responsibility in good observation will classify his or her observations into such divisions as health, sanitation, traffic, business, etc.

D. A police officer should review and remember his or her observations. Old impressions are reviewed in the light of new impressions. New impressions are reviewed in the light of old impressions. In this way, the observational faculties are sharpened and the power of retention is perfected. The finest kind of observation is a waste of time if, at the moment of need, the faculty to remember fails.

IX. MAXIMS OF POLICE OBSERVATION

A. Observe sanely and sensibly.

B. Always be suspicious.

C. Do not look for trouble.

D. Look out for trouble.

E. Take nothing for granted.

X. MEMORY AS A PART OF OBSERVATION

As already stated, memory is an essential part of observation. To note a condition and then to forget it is of little use in police work. It is essential, therefore, that police officers train their memories.

Things are best remembered by association with some other thing that we know or have experienced in the past. Thus, when we note something, we should try to associate it with something we already know. Association is easier when what we know is of recent origin or if it was something that made a deep impression on us.

XI. MISTAKES IN OBSERVATION

A. **Memory**. Much of what we see or hear is frequently supplied by our memory. Thus, if we read a printed page, we often don't notice a misprint because we suppose the words are spelled correctly.

B. **Imagination**. Imagination of what we see is often regarded as an observation. Thus, children left in a dark room often "see" things that don't exist except in the imagination.

C. **Illusion**. The eye is often deceived. Thus, if we look at a stick partly under water, it seems to be bent although it actually isn't.

D. **Rapidity of Action**. If something occurs rapidly, we often fail to notice all details and often supply these details from past experiences.

E. **Emotional Stress**. Under stress of emotion, excitement, etc., we often see things that never happened. This has been proven time and again by questioning witnesses on stated situations.

F. **Prejudice**. What we see is often colored by what we want to see or expect to see. If we want our side to win, we see only the good features and often disparage those of the other side.

XII. TESTING RELIABILITY OF OBSERVATION

We can test the reliability of an observation by referring to:

A. Circumstances at the time

B. Whether the observation was made carelessly or deliberately and calmly

C. State of mind of the observer

D. Type of mind of the observer

E. Eyesight, etc., of the observer

F. Time between observation and recording it

G. Subject matter observed

H. Whether fact regarded as having been observed is consistent with known facts and physical laws

XIII. HOW TO DESCRIBE PERSONS AND PROPERTY WANTED

A. Importance

1. A description of persons or property wanted by a police department is of little or no value unless it is *distinctive*. Remember that such descriptions must be relied upon by other police officers for recognition and identification of the wanted person or property.

2. When a criminal flees after the commission of a crime, his or her chance of escape will be greatly reduced by an accurate description immediately broadcast to all police officers in that area through a general alarm or all points bulletin (APB).

3. Therefore, the original police investigator must be certain to obtain distinctive descriptions since many other officers must work from such descriptions.

4. The data for obtaining descriptions is particularly important for detectives, and it is equally applicable to members of the uniformed branch of a police department. Review the following lists for important points to cover in your description.

B. Description of Persons Wanted, such as an Escaped Criminal or Missing Person

1. Sex

2. Color

3. National Origin

4. Occupation

5. Age

6. Height

7. Weight

8. Build (stout or very stout, medium, slim; stooped or square shouldered)

9. Complexion (florid, sallow, pale, fair, dark)

10. Hair (color, thick or thin, bald or partly bald, curly, kinky, wavy, how cut or parted)

11. Eyes and Eyebrows (color, eyes bulgy or small, eyebrows bushy or meeting, any peculiarities)

12. Nose (small or large, pug, hooked or straight)

13. Whiskers (color, Vandyke, straight, rounded, goatee, chin whiskers, side whiskers)

14. Mustache (color, short, stubby, long, pointed ends, turned-up ends, Kaiser style)

15. Chin (small, large, square, dimpled, double)

16. Face (long, round, square, peg-top, fat, thin)

17. Neck (long, short, thick, thin)

18. Lips (thick, thin)

19. Mouth (large, small; drooping or upturned at corners)

20. Ears (small, large; close to or sticking out from head)

21. Forehead (high, low, sloping, bulging, straight, wrinkled)

22. Distinctive Marks (scars, moles, missing fingers or teeth, gold teeth, tattoos, lameness, bow legs, pigeon toes, knock knees, cauliflower ears, pockmarks)

23. Peculiarities (twitching of features, rapid or slow gait, eyeglasses, cane, stuttering, gruff or effeminate voice)

24. Clothes (hat and shoes—color and style; suit—color, cut, maker's name; shirt and collar—style and color, make; tie—style and color; neat or careless dresser)

25. Jewelry (kind, where worn)

26. Where likely to be found (residence, former residences, places frequented or hangouts, where employed, addresses of relatives)

27. Personal Associates (friends who might know of movements of wanted person or with whom wanted person would be most likely to communicate)

28. Habits (heavy drinker or smoker; drug user; gambler; frequenter of theaters, dance halls, taverns, race tracks, or casinos)

29. Personal possessions (licenses, union cards, club memberships, credit cards, social security card, etc.

C. Property Wanted

1. Watches (kind of metal; description of case, movement and numbers; type-pocket or wrist; initials; inscriptions; value; man's or woman's)

2. Rings (kind of metal; man's or woman's; setting; kind and number of stones; weight; maker's name; initials or other marks; value)

3. Chains (kind of metal; length; weight; kind of link or style; value)

4. Earrings or Studs (kind of metal; style; screw-backed or pierced; size and number of stones; value)

5. Miscellaneous Jewelry (kind of article; kind of metal or material; kind and number of stones; design; initials; inscriptions; maker's name; value)

6. Antiques and Works of Art (kind of article; material; design; size; shape; carved, engraved, inlaid; age; value)

7. Handbags, Suitcases, etc. (kind of article; material; size; color; shape; maker's name; contents; initials; peculiar marks; value)

8. Clothing (kind of article; material; style; color; shape; maker's name; labels; marks; value)

9. Furs (kind of article; kind of fur; size, color; value)

10. Animals (kind; size; color; distinctive markings; age; sex)

11. Trucks and Wagons (type; shape; color; distinctive marks; size; contents)

12. Motorcycles (make; year of model; number of cylinders; manufacturer's number; make of saddle; make and condition of tires; position of speedometer; horn; front and rear lights; distinctive marks; license number)

13. Bicycles (make; color; type; number; kind of brake and saddle; number of speeds)

14. Typewriters (kind; serial and model numbers)

15. Automobiles (license number; make and year; kind of body and description of appearance; motor number; changes or repairs; exterior injuries; kind of wheels; size, make, and condition of tires; what precautions were taken to prevent theft of car: doors locked, alarm, etc.)

16. Table Silverware (kind of article; solid silver or plated; heavy or lightweight; maker's name; design, such as plain, beaded, flower, formal, animal; initials, inscriptions, or monograms; value)

17. Miscellaneous Gold and Silver Goods (kind of article; kind of material; plated or solid; size; maker's name; design; number of pieces, if a set; initials, inscriptions, or monograms; plain, chased, etched, or engraved; open or solid pattern; value)

18. Television Sets, Stereo Equipment, Video Recorders, Cameras, Computers, etc. (serial number; make; model; size; other identifying markings; value)

D. Description of Escaping Automobiles

1. License number

2. Make and model of car

3. Number of passengers and their descriptions

4. Direction taken

5. Kind of body

6. Color

7. Size

8. Shape and location of ventilators of hood

9. Shape of mudguards

10. Type, shape, and location of lights

11. Tail light position

12. Hub caps

13. Type of wheels

14. Damage such as broken lights, missing hub cap, dents, etc.

15. Rear view—Note the presence of anything such as a tire carrier, tool box, gas tank, baggage rack, bumper, etc.

OBSERVATION AND MEMORY QUIZZES

OBSERVATION QUIZ 1

This exercise measures your ability to observe and recognize the basic differences and similarities in the faces of people. Many alleged criminals being sought by the police disguise their facial features to make it difficult for the police to apprehend them. Aside from surgery, there are many things that the wanted person can do to make recognition difficult. The addition and removal of beards and mustaches, or even change in hair color or hair style, are relatively easy to accomplish. Tinted contact lenses, now very common, can alter the color of eyes. However, there are some features that an individual cannot change easily. These are the features a police officer should concentrate on when attempting to identify a wanted person: the size, shape, and position of the ears; the shape of the jaw. The shape of the nose and the jaw are difficult to change without surgery. The police officer should also recognize that the wanted male with a distinctive jaw would likely try to disguise that feature by growing a beard.

Directions: Answer the following ten questions by selecting the face, labeled (A), (B), (C), or (D), that is most likely to be the same as that of the suspect on the left. You are to assume that no surgery has taken place since the sketch of the suspect was made. Only observation and recognition are factors in this exercise. Do not try to memorize features of these faces. Circle the letter of the face you choose. Explanations follow the last questions.

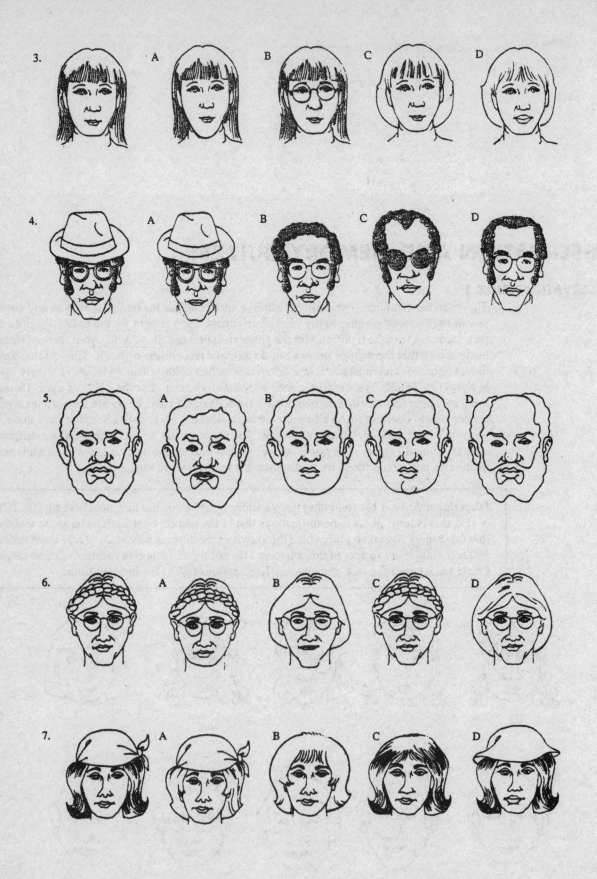

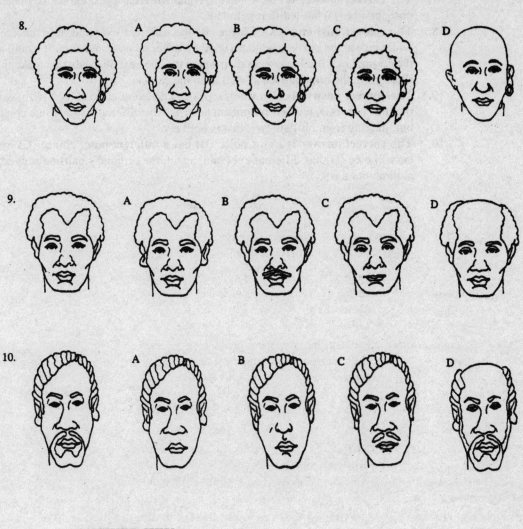

ANSWER KEY

1. D	4. D	7. B	10. A
2. B	5. C	8. A	
3. C	6. D	9. B	

EXPLANATORY ANSWERS

1. **The correct answer is (D).** Choice (A) has different nose; choices (B) and (C) have different chins.
2. **The correct answer is (B).** Choice (A) has a longer face; choice (C) has a fuller face with different chin; choice (D) has a different nose.
3. **The correct answer is (C).** Choice (A) has a longer face; choice (B) has dark eyes; choice (D) has much fuller lips.
4. **The correct answer is (D).** Choice (A) has thinner lips; choice (B) has a different nose; choice (C) has different ears.
5. **The correct answer is (C).** Choice (A) has a different mouth; choice (B) has a different nose; choice (D) has different eyes.
6. **The correct answer is (D).** Choice (A) has a different chin; choice (B) has a different mouth; choice (C) has different eyes.

7. **The correct answer is (B).** Choice (A) has different eyes; choice (C) has a different nose; choice (D) has a different mouth.

8. **The correct answer is (A).** Choice (B) has different eyes and nose; choice (C) has a wider face at the jaw line; choice (D) has a different nose and chin. It would appear that the original face has larger eyes than any of the choices. Be aware that makeup can create illusions in the original face as well as in the choices.

9. **The correct answer is (B).** Choice (A) has different ears; choice (C) has a different mouth; choice (D) has less prominent nostrils. The difference in hairline could be a wig, but, judging from his hairstyle, that is unlikely.

10. **The correct answer is (A).** Choice (B) has a different nose; choice (C) has different ears; choice (D) has different eyes and, again, the original's hairline suggests that it is natural, not a wig.

OBSERVATION QUIZ 2

Directions: Answer the following questions on the basis of the following sketches. The first face on top is a sketch of an alleged criminal based on witnesses' descriptions at the crime scene. One of the four sketches below represents the way the suspect might look after changing his or her appearance. Assume that NO surgery has been done on the suspect's face. Circle the letter of the face you choose.

(A)   (C)

(B)   (D)

(A)

(C)

(B)

(D)

(A)

(C)

(B)

(D)

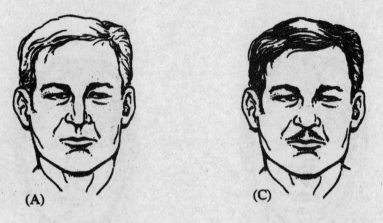

(A)

(C)

(B)

(D)

(A)

(C)

(B)

(D)

ANSWER KEY

1. B	2. B	3. D	4. C	5. B

EXPLANATORY ANSWERS

1. **The correct answer is (B).** The suspect in choice (A) has larger eyes; the suspect in choice (C) has different ears; the suspect in choice (D) has a fuller face.

2. **The correct answer is (B).** The suspect in choice (A) has a smaller nose; the suspect in choice (C) has a fuller face and fuller lips; the suspect in choice (D) has lighter eyes and thinner lips.

3. **The correct answer is (D).** The suspect in choice (A) has a different nose; the suspect in choice (B) has different ears; the suspect in choice (C) has an entirely different head and face shape.

4. **The correct answer is (C).** The suspect in choice (A) has a much finer nose; the suspect in choice (B) has a narrower jaw structure; the suspect in choice (D) has different ears.

5. **The correct answer is (B).** The suspect in choice (A) has a smaller nose; the suspect in choice (C) has lighter eyes and a wider mouth; the suspect in choice (D) has a fuller face and thinner lips.

MEMORY QUIZ 1

MEMORY BOOKLET

> **Directions:** You will be given 10 minutes to study the six "Wanted Posters" below. Try to remember as many details as you can. You may not take any notes during this time.

Wanted for Assault

Name: John Markham
Age: 27
Height: 5' 11"
Weight: 215 lbs.
Race: Black
Hair color: black
Eye color: brown
Complexion: dark
Identifying marks: eagle tattoo on back of right hand; very hard of hearing
Suspect is a former boxer. He favors brass knuckles as his weapon.

Wanted for Rape

Name: Arthur Lee
Age: 19
Height: 5'7"
Weight: 180 lbs.
Race: Asian
Hair color: black
Eye color: brown
Complexion: medium
Identifying marks: none
Suspect carries a pearl-handled knife with an 8-inch curved blade. He tends to attack victims in subway passageways.

Wanted for Armed Robbery

Name: Antonio Gomez
Age: 31
Height: 5'6"
Weight: 160 lbs.
Race: Hispanic
Hair color: brown
Eye color: brown
Complexion: medium
Identifying marks: missing last finger of right hand; tattoo on back says "Mother"; tattoo on left biceps says "Linda"; tattoo on right biceps says "Carmen"
Suspect was seen leaving the scene in a stolen yellow 1987 Corvette. He carries a gun and must be considered dangerous.

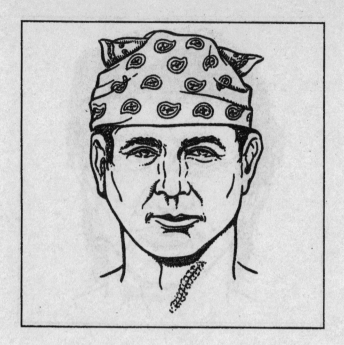

Wanted for Car Theft

Name: Robert Miller
Age: 24
Height: 6'3"
Weight: 230 lbs.
Race: White
Hair color: brown
Eye color: blue
Complexion: light
Identifying marks: tracheotomy scar at base of neck; tattoo of dragon on right upper arm
Suspect chain smokes unfiltered cigarettes. He always wears a red head scarf.

Wanted for Murder

Name: Janet Walker
Age: 39
Height: 5' 10"
Weight: 148 lbs.
Race: Black
Hair color: black
Eye color: black
Complexion: dark
Identifying marks: large hairy mole on upper left thigh; stutters badly
Suspect has frequently been arrested for prostitution. She often wears multiple ear and nose rings.

Wanted for Arson

Name: Margaret Pickford
Age: 42
Height: 5'2"
Weight: 103 lbs.
Race: White
Hair color: red
Eye color: green
Complexion: light
Identifying marks: known heroin addict with track marks on forearms; walks with decided limp because left leg is shorter than right
Suspect has a child in foster care in Astoria. She usually carries two large shopping bags.

MEMORY QUESTIONS

> **Directions:** Answer the following questions on the basis of the information given on the "Wanted Posters" that you just studied. Circle the letter of the answer you choose.

1. Which of the following suspects may have committed a crime in order to support a drug habit?

    (A)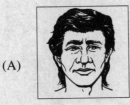

    (B)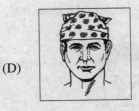

    (C)

    (D)

2. Which one of the following is missing a finger? The suspect wanted for

    (A) rape.
    (B) assault.
    (C) murder.
    (D) armed robbery.

3. Which of the suspects is most likely to be found in the subway?

    (A) John Markham
    (B) Margaret Pickford
    (C) Arthur Lee
    (D) Robert Miller

4. Which of these suspects has a dragon tattoo?

(A)

(B)

(C)

(D)

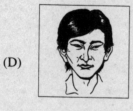

5. Which is an identifying mark of this suspect?

(A) Deafness
(B) A large mole
(C) A tattoo that reads "Mother"
(D) Needle tracks

6. Which of the following is considered to be the most dangerous?

(A)

(B)

(C)

(D)

7. Which of these suspects is known to be a parent?

(A) The suspect who stutters
(B) The former boxer
(C) The smoker
(D) The suspect who limps

8. Which of these suspects escaped the scene of the crime in a stolen car?

(A)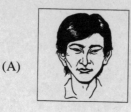

(B)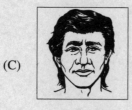

(C)

(D)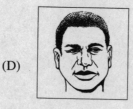

9. Which of these suspects would have the hardest time running from the police?
   (A) The heroin addict
   (B) The suspect who is nearly deaf
   (C) The suspect who wears lots of jewelry
   (D) The suspect with brass knuckles in his pocket

10. Which of these suspects is wanted for rape?

(A)

(B)

(C)

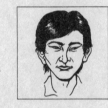

(D)

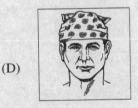

ANSWER KEY

1. B	4. A	7. D	9. A
2. D	5. B	8. C	10. C
3. C	6. B		

EXPLANATORY ANSWERS

1. **The correct answer is (B).** Margaret Pickford is a known heroin addict.
2. **The correct answer is (D).** Antonio Gomez is wanted for armed robbery. He is missing the last finger of his right hand.
3. **The correct answer is (C).** Arthur Lee often attacks his victims in subway passageways.
4. **The correct answer is (A).** Robert Miller has a tattoo of a dragon on his right upper arm.
5. **The correct answer is (B).** Janet Walker has a large hairy mole on her upper left thigh.
6. **The correct answer is (B).** Antonio Gomez carries a gun. Arthur Lee carries a wicked looking knife, but Lee is not offered among the choices.
7. **The correct answer is (D).** Margaret Pickford, who walks with a limp because her left leg is shorter than her right, has a child in foster care so obviously is a parent.

8. **The correct answer is (C).** Antonio Gomez escaped from the scene of a recent armed robbery in a stolen yellow 1987 Corvette.

9. **The correct answer is (A).** Margaret Pickford, who is a drug addict, has a severe limp caused by one leg being shorter than the other, so she would have a hard time running from police.

10. **The correct answer is (C).** Arthur Lee is wanted for rape.

MEMORY QUIZ 2

> **Directions**: You will have ten minutes to read and study the following description of a police action. Then you must answer 15 questions based on this incident without referring back to the description.

Police Officers Brown and Reid are on patrol in a radio car on a Saturday afternoon in the fall. They receive a radio message that a burglary is in progress on the fifth floor of a seven-floor building on the corner of 7th Street and Main. They immediately proceed to that location to investigate and take appropriate action.

The police officers are familiar with the location, and they know that the Fine Jewelry Company occupies the entire fifth floor of the building. They are also aware that the owner, who is not in the office on weekends, often leaves large amounts of gold in his office safe. The officers, upon arrival at the scene, lock their radio car and proceed to look for the building superintendent in order to get into the building. The superintendent states that he has not seen or heard anything unusual, although he admits that he did leave the premises for approximately one hour to have lunch. The officers start for the fifth floor, using the main elevator. As they reach that floor and open the door, they hear noises followed by the sound of the freight elevator door in the rear of the building closing and the elevator descending. They quickly run through the open door of the Fine Jewelry Company and observe that the office safe is open and empty. The officers then proceed to the rear of the building and use the rear staircase to reach the ground floor. They open the rear door and go out onto the street where they observe four individuals running up the street, crossing at the corner. At that point, the police officers get a clear view of the suspects. There are three males and one female. One of the males appears to be white, one is obviously Hispanic, and the other male is African American. The female is white.

The white male is bearded. He is dressed in blue jeans, white sneakers, and a red and blue jacket. He is carrying a white duffel bag on his shoulder. The Hispanic male limps slightly and has a large dark mustache. He is wearing brown pants, a green shirt, and brown shoes. He is carrying a blue duffel bag on his shoulder. The African-American male is clean-shaven, wearing black pants, a white shirt, a green cap, and black shoes. He is carrying what appears to be a toolbox. The white female is carrying a sawed-off shotgun, has long brown hair, and is wearing white jeans, a blue blouse, and blue sneakers. She has a red kerchief around her neck.

The officers chase the suspects for two blocks without being able to catch them. At that point, the suspects separate. The white and black males quickly get into a black 1983 Chevrolet station wagon with Connecticut license plates with the letters AWK on them and drive away. The Hispanic male and the white female get away in an old light blue Dodge van. The van has a prominent CB antenna on top and large yellow streaks running along the doors on both sides. There is a large dent on the right rear fender and the van bears New Jersey license plates, which the officers are unable to read.

The station wagon turns left and enters the expressway headed towards Connecticut. The van makes a right turn and proceeds in the direction of the tunnel headed for New Jersey.

The officers quickly return to their radio car to report what has happened.

Do not refer back to the passage while answering these questions. Circle the letter of your choice.

1. The officers were able to read the following letters from the license plates on the station wagon:

    (A) WAX
    (B) EWK
    (C) AUK
    (D) AWK

2. The van used by the suspects had a dented

    (A) left front fender.
    (B) right front fender.
    (C) right rear fender.
    (D) left rear fender.

3. The officers observed that the van was headed in the direction of

    (A) Long Island.
    (B) Pennsylvania.
    (C) New Jersey.
    (D) Connecticut.

4. The best description of the female suspect's hair is

    (A) short and light in color.
    (B) long and light in color.
    (C) short and dark in color.
    (D) long and dark in color.

5. The suspect who was wearing a white shirt is the

    (A) white male.
    (B) Hispanic male.
    (C) African-American male.
    (D) white female.

6. The suspect who wore white jeans is the

    (A) white male.
    (B) Hispanic male.
    (C) African-American male.
    (D) white female.

7. The Hispanic male suspect carried a duffel bag of what color?

    (A) Yellow
    (B) Red
    (C) Blue
    (D) Brown

8. Of the following, the best description of the shoes worn by the Hispanic suspect is

    (A) white sneakers.
    (B) black shoes.
    (C) black boots.
    (D) brown shoes.

9. The suspect who was carrying the white duffel bag was the

    (A) white female.
    (B) African-American male.
    (C) Hispanic male.
    (D) white male.

10. The suspect who was carrying the shotgun was the

    (A) white female.
    (B) African-American male.
    (C) Hispanic male.
    (D) white male.

11. The green cap was worn by the

    (A) white female.
    (B) African-American male.
    (C) Hispanic male.
    (D) white male.

12. The suspect who limped when he or she ran was the

    (A) white female.
    (B) African-American male.
    (C) Hispanic male.
    (D) white male.

13. Of the following, the best description of the station wagon used by the suspects is a

    (A) 1983 black Chevrolet: station wagon.
    (B) 1981 blue Ford.
    (C) 1981 green Dodge.
    (D) 1986 red Ford.

14. The best description of the suspects who used the station wagon to depart is

    (A) an African-American male and a white female.
    (B) an African-American male and a white male.
    (C) a white female and a Hispanic male.
    (D) an African-American male and a Hispanic male.

15. The van's license plates were from which of the following states?

    (A) New York
    (B) Delaware
    (C) New Jersey
    (D) Connecticut

ANSWER KEY
Observation and Memory

1. D	5. C	9. D	13. A
2. C	6. D	10. A	14. B
3. C	7. C	11. B	15. C
4. D	8. D	12. C	

EXPLANATORY ANSWERS
If you answered any of these questions incorrectly, the fault may lie either in the care with which you read the description or with your memory of the facts. For ease in locating the source of your errors, we refer you to the source of the information in the passage.

1. **The correct answer is (D).** Fourth paragraph, third sentence.
2. **The correct answer is (C).** Fourth paragraph, last sentence.
3. **The correct answer is (C).** Fifth paragraph, second sentence.
4. **The correct answer is (D).** Third paragraph, next-to-last sentence.

5. **The correct answer is (C).** Third paragraph, seventh sentence.
6. **The correct answer is (D).** Third paragraph, next-to-last sentence.
7. **The correct answer is (C).** Third paragraph, sixth sentence.
8. **The correct answer is (D).** Third paragraph, fifth sentence.
9. **The correct answer is (D).** Third paragraph, third sentence.
10. **The correct answer is (A).** Third paragraph, next-to-last sentence.
11. **The correct answer is (B).** Third paragraph, seventh sentence.
12. **The correct answer is (C).** Third paragraph, fourth sentence.
13. **The correct answer is (A).** Fourth paragraph, third sentence.
14. **The correct answer is (B).** Fourth paragraph, third sentence.
15. **The correct answer is (C).** Fourth paragraph, third sentence.

POLICE JUDGMENT QUIZZER

ABOUT THE POLICE JUDGMENT QUIZZER

Early police officer examinations were a strange mixture of questions covering municipal government, municipal geography, spelling, grammar, and first aid—everything, in fact, that every person should know something about, but very little specific to measuring the ability of future police officers to do their job well. As testing methods matured and examiners gained experience in mass testing, they determined that the best measure of a good police officer is a measure of his or her judgment in actual police situations. So the emphasis shifted from factual to actual exams. "Let the questions supply the facts," the examiners reasoned, "and let the aspiring police officers display their judgment in choosing the correct answers."

WHAT WOULD YOU DO IF . . .

This is the essential form of the practical question on police officer exams. Assume you are a police officer. Here is a given situation. How would you respond to it? This is a very subtle and efficient method of testing. Questions are often based on actual patrol situations. What would you do if you saw a woman walking down the street dressed only in a sheet and leading a doe on a leash? Arrest her? On what charge? Take the doe to an animal shelter? Take the woman to a doctor? Ask her for her phone number? It actually happened. What would you do?

TEST-TAKING STRATEGY FOR PRACTICAL JUDGMENT QUESTIONS

Police applicants are placed in a peculiar position by practical judgment questions in that the correct answers for these questions are influenced by actual police department procedures. As an applicant taking the exam, you are not expected to know the police department's policies or procedures. Yet, test makers often assume that police departmental policies or procedures are just common sense. To do really well on practical judgment questions, you need something more than common sense. You need a good understanding of ordinary police department policies and procedures as they apply to routine patrol situations. This is the reason why close relatives of police officers tend to earn high scores on the police officer exam. Their familiarity with "police language" and "police thinking" stands them in good stead when they must choose the correct answers to police practical judgment questions.

   This chapter will familiarize you with many of the "common sense" ideas that underlie police practical judgment questions. The chapter will serve as "your brother the police officer," teaching you to think like a patrol officer. By the time you have finished studying this material, you will be thinking like a patrol officer. You will then be prepared to score high on your police officer exam.

The Police Role

To start with, you must understand the role of a police officer. This role varies according to size, location, and philosophy of the police department. State police find that their role encompasses major problems like traffic pileups and serious accidents as well as the more routine problems of stranded motorists. Small-town police find that they have a broad role in maintaining public safety and assuring law and order. Big-city police tend to have a more narrow role, because in big cities other agencies take on primary responsibility for certain tasks: medics handle health situations beyond emergency first-aid; traffic department personnel deal with many traffic situations; social workers handle many crises concerning the elderly, children, and the mentally ill. Part of your preparation for your own exam should be acquiring some familiarity with the ordinary role of police officers in the department to which you are applying.

With this information in mind, you must follow one basic rule when answering police practical judgment questions: fulfill the police role and only the police role. This means:

1. Be professional. Avoid emotional responses, show of bias, or incurring any kind of indebtedness to persons on your beat.

2. Avoid all roles other than the police role, e.g., parent, physician, tradesman, private security, etc. Sometimes you may find it hard to draw the line, such as that between giving emergency first aid and the role of the medic. In an emergency where time is pressing, the police officer must provide assistance to people to the full extent of his or her competence. Where more time is available, leave doubtful roles to others.

3. Fulfill the police role of assisting endangered people 24 hours a day. Be prepared to assist in keeping the peace at any time and to take the initiative in urgent situations. Fulfilling the police role does not necessarily mean making arrests when there is no great need to do so. In practical judgment questions, think of the police role as one of keeping the peace rather than one of making arrests, especially in the off-duty situation.

4. Avoid even the slightest appearance of corruption. Maintain police integrity. Avoid all partiality. Do not accept gifts or favors. Do not refer business to any particular businessman, company, or professional person.

Police Priorities

A hierarchy is an arrangement of things according to their importance. Something near the top of a hierarchy is more important than something near the bottom of the hierarchy. Basically it is an arrangement of things or activities according to their priorities.

There are five basic functions in police work. These have a definite hierarchical order. If an officer finds him- or herself in a situation in which several of these functions must be done, the officer should consider the hierarchical order, or order of priorities, and act in accordance with each function in that order.

1. **Assist endangered people.** Essentially this means assisting

    a. seriously injured persons.
    b. physically endangered persons (e.g., victims of a crime in progress, drowning persons, etc.).

2. **Keep the peace.** Calm any major disorder. Prevent tumult, aggression, or destruction of property.

3. **Enforce the law.** Where no actual harm to persons or property is threatened, peacekeeping and maintaining order may be adequate. Where there is unlawful injury or loss, arrest may be necessary in addition to the restoring of order.

4. **Assist people who are not immediately endangered but who need help.** This means assisting

    a. physically or mentally needy persons: children; the elderly; the handicapped; the homeless; and persons who appear to be sick, mentally ill, or intoxicated.

    b. crime victims, lost persons, and stranded persons.

5. **Maintain order on the beat.** This involves

    a. investigating suspicious persons or circumstances. Something is suspicious if it is unusual for the time or the place or the persons involved.

    b. regulating the use of streets and sidewalks for safety and for the efficient flow of traffic.

    c. knowing the beat. You must be familiar with the physical features of the beat, you must be aware of routine events, and you must develop positive contacts with the people on the beat.

    d. making recommendations that will improve safety or flow of traffic in the area. Remember to stay "professional" by recommending only activities, not particular products or businesses.

The Principle of Use of Minimum Necessary Force

Many police practical judgment questions concern the possible use of force. Police officers are empowered to use force, even deadly force, under certain circumstances. In general, common sense should rule judgments about the use of force. There are some basic principles that are part of "common sense."

A police officer should always handle problems with the minimum amount of force necessary to resolve the problem. Never use more force than the problem deserves. Obviously, a police officer should not shoot somebody for failing to show identification, even if the person is being unreasonably stubborn. A police officer's action should not cause greater harm than the problem the officer is trying to resolve. In other words, a problem should not be handled in such a way as to create an even bigger problem.

When a police officer is evaluating the gravity of a situation to determine how much force is necessary (or when a candidate is making this choice in an examination), the officer must consider the physical setting, the actual actions and the apparent intentions of the people involved, and the intent of the law. Differences in physical settings require differences in policies and regulations. Big-city police departments, for example, practically never permit police officers to fire warning shots, to shoot at moving vehicles, or to shoot at people on public streets. It is assumed that such shooting would endanger innocent bystanders. On the other hand, state police departments often do allow warning shots, shooting at moving vehicles, and even shooting at people on the road, because they assume a highway setting without any innocent bystanders in the line of fire.

The Value Hierarchy

Occasionally a police officer has to make a quick decision in a situation that involves value conflicts. For example, it may be necessary to chose between risking injury to a hostage or letting a dangerous criminal escape. Such a decision involves a value judgment. An officer makes the decision based on the order of priorities.

If a police department's hierarchy of values is spelled out clearly, officers are assisted in making rapid and proper judgments. Police exam candidates can rely on the same list of priorities. The list below is the value hierarchy that has been the basis for practical judgment questions on police officer exams for many years. In order of priority:

1. Protection of life and limb

2. Obeying orders in an emergency situation

3. Protection of property

4. Obeying orders in a non-emergency situation

5. Maintaining the assigned role

6. Efficiency in getting the job done

7. Avoiding blame or earning praise or respect

Use the hierarchy of values in making decisions. If a situation presents a conflict of values, always choose the value that is highest on the list. Here are three examples:

Example 1. You are assigned to stay in a particular spot during an emergency situation, but by leaving that spot you will save a life. You are justified in shooting to save a life, priority (1), rather than obeying orders, priority (2). The understanding is, of course, that leaving your spot will not result in other lives being lost. "Protecting life and limb" is your number one priority, the highest value in the police hierarchy of values.

Example 2. You are assigned to watch a prisoner, and a fellow officer is assigned to write up the arrest report. Stay in your own role even if you are more skilled than the other officer at writing up arrest reports. The conflict is between carrying out an assigned duty, priority (5), and getting a job done efficiently, priority (6). Choose the highest priority.

Example 3. You are patrolling alone at night, and you come across a business that has been burglarized, with the front door smashed in. At this hour, you are expected to be making a routine check of illegal parking on a certain street. The police department might be criticized by residents if the illegal parking is not addressed, but the store is likely to be further burglarized if you leave this spot. Stay where you are and protect the property, priority (3), rather than carrying out your assigned illegal parking patrol, priority (5), or concerning yourself with criticism of the department, priority (7). Always choose the highest value.

Please note that no value is given to the officer's personal gains or benefits or reputation. Personal consideration is never a good reason for doing anything so far as a civil service exam question is concerned.

As the hierarchy of values suggests, the best reason for any action is the protection of life and limb. If safety is a real issue in the fact pattern of the question, then safety is the number one priority in choosing the answer. Sometimes there is no real issue of safety. In such a case, the next value assumes the greatest importance. If there is an emergency situation and you have been given specific orders, your priority is to carry out those orders. If not, the next priority is the protection of property. Property includes public property and police department property as well as private property. If there are no threats to property, you are expected to carry out routine, nonemergency orders and to fulfill your assigned duties. Doing what you were told to do and carrying out your routine assignments as a police officer take priority over efficiency. A police force is a highly organized bureaucracy. The organization functions best as a whole if each person does just his or her own assigned job.

Read each question carefully. Is there really something in the question situation to indicate that there is an issue of life and limb at stake? Would a proposed answer based on efficiency really be possible and efficient? Be realistic. Unless told otherwise, assume that the officer is an ordinary police officer and not a sharpshooter or a trained firefighter.

When all other reasoning fails you, answer to the Chief. In other words, the Chief of Police is testing you for your job. If you are faced with a difficult choice in making a decision, imagine that the question is being asked you personally by the Chief of Police. Give the answer the Chief would want you to give.

ANSWERING THE QUESTIONS

This quizzer contains questions that have actually appeared on examinations for entry-level law enforcement positions conducted over a considerable number of years. The questions have been carefully screened for current relevancy.

Answering these questions will accomplish much in preparing you to do your best on the examination. Ideally, you can consider yourself well prepared if, on the day of the examination, you are thinking like a police officer. This quizzer will help you get in that frame of mind. Most of the questions found here concern incidents that a police officer may encounter on a daily basis.

The position of police officer is unique in that, although it is an entry-level position, it involves a great deal of responsibility and requires the ability to make reliable on-the-spot decisions. Therefore, accurate judgment is perhaps the most important qualification of the police officer. In order to make accurate police decisions, the officer must thoroughly understand the duties of the position and the police officer's role in society.

By the time you finish the Police Judgment Quizzer, you no doubt will be thinking like a police officer, and you thus will be well on your way towards earning that high examination score.

Choose the best answer to each question from among the four suggested answers. Circle the letter of your answer choice. Following the answer key is a full explanation of the police reasoning behind each correct answer choice.

1. An off-duty police officer was seated in a restaurant when two men entered, drew guns, and robbed the cashier. The officer made no attempt to prevent the robbery or apprehend the criminals. Later he justified his conduct by stating that an officer, when off duty, is a private citizen with the same duties and rights of all private citizens. The officer's conduct was

   (A) wrong; a police officer must act to prevent crimes and apprehend criminals at all times.
   (B) right; the police officer was out of uniform at the time of the robbery.
   (C) wrong; he should have obtained the necessary information and descriptions after the robbers left.
   (D) right; it would have been foolhardy for him to intervene when outnumbered by armed robbers.

2. While you are on traffic duty, a middle-aged man crossing the street cries out with pain, presses his hand to his chest, and stands perfectly still. You suspect that he may have suffered a heart attack. You should

   (A) help him cross the street quickly in order to prevent his being hit by moving traffic.
   (B) permit him to lie down flat in the street while you divert traffic.
   (C) ask him for the name of his doctor so that you can summon him.
   (D) request a cab to take him to the nearest hospital for immediate treatment.

3. Assume that you have been assigned to a traffic post at a busy intersection. A car bearing out-of-state license plates is about to turn into a one-way street going in the opposite direction. You should blow your whistle and stop the car. You should then

   (A) hand out a summons to the driver in order to make an example of him, since out-of-town drivers notoriously disregard our traffic regulations.
   (B) pay no attention to him and let him continue in the proper direction.
   (C) ask him to pull over to the curb and advise him to get a copy of the latest New York City traffic regulations.
   (D) call his attention to the fact that he was violating a traffic regulation and permit him to continue in the proper direction.

4. You have been assigned to a patrol post in the park during the winter months. You hear the cries of a boy who has fallen through the ice. The first thing you should do is to

(A) rush to the nearest telephone and call an ambulance.
(B) call upon a passerby to summon additional police officers.
(C) rush to the spot from which the cries came and try to save the boy.
(D) rush to the spot from which the cries came and question the boy concerning his identity so that you can summon his parents.

5. While you are patrolling your post, you find a flashlight and a screwdriver lying near a closed bar and grill. You also notice some jimmy marks on the door. You should

(A) continue patrolling your post after noting in your memorandum book what you have seen.
(B) arrest any persons standing in the vicinity.
(C) determine whether the bar has been robbed.
(D) telephone the owner of the bar and grill to relate what you have seen outside the door.

6. While patrolling a post late Saturday night, a police officer notices a well-dressed man break a car window with a rock, open the front door, and enter the car. He is followed into the car by a female companion. Of the following, the most essential action for the officer to take is to

(A) point a gun at the car, enter the car, and order the man to drive to the station house to explain his actions.
(B) approach the car and ask the man why it was necessary to break the car window.
(C) take down the license number of the car and note the description of both the man and the woman in the event that the car is later reported as stolen.
(D) request proof of ownership of the car from the man.

7. Assume that a police officer is assigned to duty in a radio patrol car. The situation in which it would be *least* advisable for the officer to use the siren to help clear traffic when answering a call is when a report has come in that

(A) a man is involved in an argument with a cleaning store proprietor.
(B) a man is holding up a liquor store.
(C) two cars have crashed, resulting in loss of life.
(D) two gangs of juveniles are engaged in a street fight.

8. Police officers are instructed to pay particular attention to anyone apparently making repairs to an auto parked in the street. The most important reason for this rule is that

(A) the person making the repairs may be stealing the auto.
(B) the person making the repairs may be obstructing traffic.
(C) working on autos is prohibited on certain streets.
(D) many people injure themselves while working on autos.

9. Inspections of critical points on a post are purposely made at irregular intervals to

(A) permit leaving the post when arrests are necessary.
(B) make it difficult for wrongdoers to anticipate the inspections.
(C) allow for delays due to unusual occurrences at other points.
(D) simplify the scheduling of lunch reliefs and rest periods.

10. Suppose that, in the course of your duties, you are called to the scene of a disturbance in which some 7 or 8 people are involved. Of the following, the action most likely to end the disturbance quickly and effectively is for you to

(A) divide the disorderly group immediately into three approximately equal sections.
(B) take the nearest person promptly into custody and remove that person from the scene.

    (C)   announce your authority and call for order in a firm and decisive manner.

    (D)   question a bystander in detail about the reasons for the disorder.

11. A newly appointed officer of a uniformed force may least reasonably expect an immediate supervising officer to

    (A)   help him or her avoid errors.

    (B)   give him or her specific instructions.

    (C)   check on the progress he or she is making.

    (D)   make all necessary decisions for him or her.

12. In lecturing on the law of arrest, an instructor remarked: "To go beyond is as bad as to fall short." The one of the following that most nearly expresses the same thing is

    (A)   never undertake the impossible.

    (B)   extremes are not desirable.

    (C)   look before you leap.

    (D)   too much success is dangerous.

13. In addressing a class, an instructor remarked: "Carelessness and failure are twins." The one of the following that most nearly expresses the same thing is

    (A)   negligence seldom accompanies success.

    (B)   incomplete work is careless work.

    (C)   conscientious work is never attended by failure.

    (D)   a conscientious person never makes mistakes.

14. The primary function of a police department is

    (A)   the prevention of crime.

    (B)   the efficiency and discipline of its members.

    (C)   to preserve property values.

    (D)   to minimize conflicts.

15. Law enforcement officials receive badges with numbers on them so that

    (A)   their personalities may be submerged.

    (B)   they may be more easily identified.

    (C)   they may be spied upon.

    (D)   their movements may be kept under constant control.

16. The best attitude for an officer to take is to

    (A)   be constantly on the alert.

    (B)   be hostile.

    (C)   vary watchfulness with the apparent necessity for it.

    (D)   regard tact as the most effective weapon for handling any degree of disorder.

17. An officer receives instructions from his supervisor that he does not fully understand. For the officer to ask for a further explanation would be

    (A)   good; chiefly because his supervisor will be impressed with his interest in his work

    (B)   poor; chiefly because the supervisor's time will be needlessly wasted.

    (C)   good; chiefly because proper performance depends on full understanding of the work to be done.

    (D)   poor; chiefly because officers should be able to think for themselves.

18. Which of the following statements concerning the behavior of law enforcement officers is most accurate?

    (A) A show of confident assurance on the part of a law enforcement officer will make it possible to cover a shortage of knowledge in any given duty.

    (B) In ordinary cases, when a newly appointed officer does not know what to do, it is always better to do too much than to do too little.

    (C) It is not advisable for officers to recommend the employment of certain attorneys for individuals taken into custody.

    (D) A prisoner who is morose and refuses to talk will need less watching by an officer than one who is suicidal.

19. Which one of the following is the most probable reason for the considerably increasing proportion of serious crimes committed by women?

    (A) The increasing proportion of women in the population

    (B) The increasing number of crime gangs in operation

    (C) The success of women in achieving social equality with men

    (D) The increasing number of crime stories in the movies and on television

20. It frequently happens that a major crime of an unusual nature is followed almost immediately by an epidemic of several crimes, in widely scattered locations, with elements similar to the first crime. Of the following, the most likely explanation for this situation is that

    (A) the same criminal is likely to commit the same type of crime.

    (B) a gang of criminals will operate in several areas simultaneously.

    (C) newspaper publicity on a major crime is apt to influence other would-be criminals.

    (D) the same causes that are responsible for the first crime are also responsible for the others.

21. "A member of the department shall not indulge in intoxicants while in uniform. A member of the department, not required to wear a uniform, and a uniformed member, while out of uniform, shall not indulge in intoxicants to an extent unfitting him or her for duty." It follows that a

    (A) member off duty, not in uniform, may drink intoxicants to any degree desired.

    (B) member on duty, not in uniform, may drink intoxicants.

    (C) member on duty, in uniform, may drink intoxicants.

    (D) uniformed member, in civilian clothes, may not drink intoxicants.

22. The reason police officers have greater authority than private citizens in making arrests is

    (A) to protect citizens against needless arrest.

    (B) to ensure a fair trial.

    (C) that they have greater knowledge of the law.

    (D) that they are in better physical shape.

23. A police officer stationed along the route of a parade has been ordered not to allow cars to cross the route while the parade is in progress. An ambulance driver on an emergency run attempts to drive an ambulance across the route while the parade is passing. Under these circumstances, the officer should

    (A) ask the driver to wait while the officer calls headquarters and obtains a decision.

    (B) stop the parade long enough to permit the ambulance to cross the street.

    (C) direct the ambulance driver to the shortest detour available, which will add at least 10 minutes to the run.

    (D) hold up the ambulance in accordance with the order.

24. Which of the following is the most accurate statement concerning the proper attitude of a police officer towards persons in his or her custody?

    (A) Ignore any serious problems of those in custody, if they have no bearing on the charges preferred.
    (B) Do not inform the person who has been arrested of the reason for the arrest.
    (C) Do not permit a person in custody to give vent to feelings at any time.
    (D) Watch a brooding or silent person more carefully than one who loudly threatens suicide.

25. When approaching a suspect to make an arrest, it is least important for the police officer to guard against the possibility that the suspect may

    (A) be diseased.
    (B) have a gun.
    (C) use physical force.
    (D) run away.

26. "In any uniformed service, strict discipline is essential." Of the following, the best justification for requiring that subordinates follow the orders of superior officers without delay is that

    (A) not all orders can be carried out quickly.
    (B) it is more important that an order be obeyed accurately than promptly.
    (C) prompt obedience makes for efficient action in emergencies.
    (D) some superior officers are too strict.

27. In submitting a report of an unusual arrest or other unusual occurrence, the first paragraph of the report should contain

    (A) a brief outline of what occurred.
    (B) your conclusions and recommendations.
    (C) the authority and reason for the investigation of the arrest or occurrence.
    (D) complete and accurate answers to the questions who, what, where, when, why, and how.

28. A police officer in civilian clothes appearing as a witness in a court must wear his or her shield over the left breast. This procedure

    (A) helps the officer in reporting for duty promptly if called.
    (B) impresses the judge.
    (C) identifies the witness as a police officer.
    (D) preserves order.

29. According to the police manual, when circumstances permit, not more than one prisoner shall be confined in a cell. Of the following, the most important reason for this regulation is to

    (A) ensure reasonable privacy for the prisoners.
    (B) minimize the development of troublesome situations.
    (C) protect the civil rights of the prisoners.
    (D) separate the hardened from the less-hardened criminals.

30. A motorist who has been stopped by an officer for speeding acts rudely. He hints about his personal connections with high officials in the state government and demands the officer's name and shield number. The officer should

    (A) ask the motorist why he wants the information and give it only if the answer is satisfactory.
    (B) give both name and shield number without comment.
    (C) ignore the request since both name and shield number will appear on the summons the officer will issue.
    (D) give name and shield number but increase the charges against the motorist.

31. "Driver 1 claimed that the collision occurred because, as he approached the intersection, Driver 2 started to make a left turn suddenly and at a high speed, even though the light had been red for 15 to 20 seconds." Suppose that you have been assigned to make a report on this accident. The position of the vehicles after the accident is indicated in the diagram below. The point in each case indicates the front of the vehicle. On the basis of this diagram, the best reason for concluding that Driver 1's statement is false is that

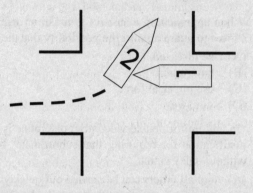

(A) Driver 2's car is beyond the center of the intersection.
(B) Driver 2's car is making the turn on the proper side of the road.
(C) Driver 1's car is beyond the sidewalk line.
(D) Driver 1's car is on the right-hand side of the road.

32. While patrolling a bridge approach road alone in a radio car, you are signaled to stop by a private car traveling in the opposite direction. The driver tells you that he was robbed by two men in a sedan ahead of him. Your car cannot cross the concrete safety-strip to get into the other lane. Of the following, the best course of action for you to take is to

(A) tell the driver you cannot cross to his lane and ask him to report the matter.
(B) leave your car where it is, cross over to the private car, and use it to pursue the suspects.
(C) notify headquarters over your radio.
(D) make a U-turn in your car and chase the suspect vehicle on the wrong side of the parkway.

33. It is suggested that an officer should keep all persons away from the area of an accident until an investigation has been completed. This suggested procedure is

(A) good; witnesses will be more likely to agree on a single story.
(B) bad; such action blocks traffic flow and causes congestion.
(C) good; objects of possible use as evidence will be protected from damage or loss.
(D) bad; the flow of normal traffic provides an opportunity for an investigator to determine the cause of the accident.

34. Before permitting automobiles involved in an accident to depart, a police officer should take certain measures. Of the following, it is least important that the officer make certain that

(A) both drivers are properly licensed.
(B) the automobiles are in safe operating condition.
(C) the drivers have exchanged names and license numbers.
(D) he or she obtains the names and addresses of drivers and witnesses.

35. A radio motor patrol team arrives on the scene a few minutes after a pedestrian has been killed by a hit-and-run driver. After obtaining a description of the car, the first action the officer should take is to

    (A) radio a description of the fleeing car to precinct headquarters.
    (B) try to overtake the fleeing car.
    (C) obtain complete statements from everyone at the scene.
    (D) inspect the site of the accident for clues.

36. It has been claimed that a person who commits a crime sometimes has an unconscious wish to be punished, which is caused by strong unconscious feelings of guilt. Of the following actions by a criminal, the one that may be partly due to an unconscious desire for punishment is

    (A) claiming that he or she doesn't know anything about the crime when questioned by the police.
    (B) running away from the state where the crime was committed.
    (C) revisiting the place where the crime was committed.
    (D) taking care not to leave any clues at the scene of the crime.

37. Which of the following statements about fingerprints is least accurate?

    (A) The value of fingerprints left at the scene of the crime does not vary with the distinctness of the fingerprint impressions.
    (B) It is of value to fingerprint a person with an abnormal number of fingers.
    (C) Fingerprints of different persons have never been found to be alike.
    (D) The prime value of fingerprints lies in their effectiveness in identifying people.

38. According to a police manual, the delivery for laboratory examination of any article required as evidence must be made by the member of the force finding or coming into the possession of such evidence. Of the following, the most likely reason for this procedure is that it

    (A) assists in the establishment of the authenticity of the evidence.
    (B) encourages a more careful search of the crime scene for all physical evidence that may be related to the crime.
    (C) ensures that the evidence will be properly marked or tagged for future identification.
    (D) prevents the undue delay that might result from a delivery through official channels.

39. You are watching a great number of people leave a ball game. Of the persons described below, the one whom it would be easiest to spot would be

    (A) female; age 15; height 5'6"; weight 140 lbs.; long straight black hair
    (B) male; age 50; height 5'8"; weight 150 lbs.; missing toe on right foot
    (C) male; age 60; height 5'7"; weight 170 lbs.; all false teeth
    (D) male; age 25; height 6'3"; weight 220 lbs.; pockmarked

40. You are preparing a description of a woman to be broadcast. Of the following characteristics, the one that would be of most value to an officer driving a squad car is

    (A) wanted for murder.
    (B) age 45 years.
    (C) height 6'1".
    (D) smokes very heavily.

41. Assume that on a hot summer day you are stationed on the grass at the south bank of a busy parkway looking at southbound traffic for a light blue 1974 Ford two-door sedan. If traffic is very heavy, which of the following additional pieces of information would be most helpful to you in identifying the car?

    (A) All chrome is missing from the left side of the car.
    (B) There is a bullet hole in the left front window.
    (C) The paint on the right side of the car is somewhat faded.
    (D) The front bumper is missing.

42. You are watching a great number of people leave a sports arena after a boxing match. Of the characteristics listed below, the one that would be of greatest value to you in spotting a man wanted by the department is

    (A) height: 5'3"; weight: 200 lbs.
    (B) eyes: brown; hair: black, wavy; complexion: sallow.
    (C) that he frequents bars and grills and customarily associates with females.
    (D) scars: thin 1/2" scar on left upper lip; tattoos: on right forearm—"Pinto."

43. "Social Security cards are not acceptable proof of identification for police purposes." Of the following, the most important reason for this rule is that the Social Security card

    (A) is easily obtained.
    (B) states on its face "for Social Security purposes—not for identification."
    (C) is frequently lost.
    (D) does not contain a photograph, description, or fingerprints of the person.

44. On patrol you come upon 2 drivers in dispute over which of them has the right to park in a certain parking space. For you to settle this dispute would be

    (A) appropriate; it shows a willingness to be helpful.
    (B) inappropriate; it is not within the scope of your duty.
    (C) appropriate; it would satisfy at least one claimant to the parking space.
    (D) inappropriate; there is no specific regulation you could cite to explain your decision.

45. "The 4 witnesses to the bank robbery, including the bank president and the cashier, were left together for 1 hour in the president's office at the bank before they were questioned." This kind of procedure is

    (A) desirable and considerate as there is no point in treating respectable citizens as criminals.
    (B) unwise as it permits undue pressure to be brought upon some of the witnesses.
    (C) unwise as it permits an exchange of actual and imagined details that may result in invalid testimony.
    (D) wise as it keeps the witnesses all in one place.

46. Suppose that you are questioning witnesses to a hit-and-run accident. Of the following, the information that will probably be least valuable for the purpose of sending out an alarm for the hit-and-run automobile is the

    (A) direction that the automobile took after the accident.
    (B) number of occupants in the automobile at the time of the accident.
    (C) speed at which the automobile was moving when it struck the victim.
    (D) part of the automobile that struck the victim of the accident.

47. The marks left on a bullet by a gun barrel are different from those left by any other gun barrel. This fact is most useful in directly identifying the

    (A) direction from which a shot was fired.
    (B) person who fired a particular gun.

(C) gun from which a bullet was fired.

(D) bullet that caused a fatal wound.

48. Uniformed officers are constantly urged to consider every revolver loaded until proven otherwise. Of the following, the best justification for this recommendation is that

(A) no time is lost when use of the revolver is required.

(B) there are many accidents involving apparently empty revolvers.

(C) less danger is involved when facing armed criminals.

(D) ammunition deteriorates unless replaced periodically.

49. A police officer should fire a pistol

(A) only as a last resort.

(B) at no time.

(C) primarily to inspire fear.

(D) to impress upon citizens the need for respect.

50. Assume that you are driving a police car, equipped with a two-way radio, along an isolated section of the parkway at 3 a.m. You note that the headlights of a car pulled to the side of the road are blinking rapidly. When you stop to investigate, the driver of the car informs you that he was just forced to the side of the road by two men in a green station wagon who robbed him of a large amount of cash and jewelry at gunpoint and then sped away. Your first consideration in this situation should be to

(A) drive rapidly along the parkway in the direction taken by the criminals in an effort to apprehend them before they escape.

(B) question the driver carefully, looking for inconsistencies indicating that he made up the whole story.

(C) obtain a complete listing and identification of all materials lost.

(D) notify your superior to have the parkway exits watched for a car answering the description of the getaway car.

51. When the bodies of two women were found stabbed in an inner room of an apartment, it was first believed that it was a case of mutual homicide. Of the following clues found at the scene, the one that indicates that it was more likely a case of murder by a third party is the fact that

(A) the door to the apartment was found locked.

(B) there were bloodstains on the outer door of the apartment.

(C) there was a switchblade knife in each body.

(D) no money could be found in the room where the bodies were.

52. "The questioning of witnesses is often much less truth-revealing than are physical clues found at the scene of the crime." Of the following, the chief justification for this statement is that

(A) most witnesses rarely tell the truth.

(B) physical clues are always present if examination is thorough.

(C) questioning of witnesses must be supported by other evidence.

(D) the memory of witnesses is often unreliable.

53. Jones, who is suspected of having committed a crime of homicide at 8:30 p.m. in the building where he lives, claims that he could not have committed the act because he worked overtime until 8:00 p.m. In order to prove that Jones actually could not have committed the act in question, it is most important to know

(A) how long it takes to get from Jones's building to Jones's place of work.

(B) if there are any witnesses to that fact that Jones worked overtime.

(C) Jones's reputation in the community.

(D) what kind of work Jones does.

54. In a recent case of suicide, the body was found slumped in a chair and no revolver, knife, or razor was found in the room. Of the following, the most reasonable hypothesis from the data given is that

(A) the person had taken some poison.
(B) the person had hanged himself.
(C) the person had died as a result of a heart attack.
(D) the murderer had taken the weapon.

55. Suppose that a 7-year-old boy was kidnapped as he was returning home from a playground at dusk. The following day, his parents received an anonymous letter that told them the child was well and designated a close friend of the family, who was known to be very fond of the boy, as an intermediary to arrange payment of a ransom. On the basis of these data only, we may most reasonably assume that

(A) the friend kidnapped the boy.
(B) the friend was probably an accessory in the kidnapping.
(C) further investigation is necessary to determine the identity of the kidnapper.
(D) the boy is dead.

56. A representative group of young criminals in a certain state was found to be normal in intelligence, but 86 percent were behind from one to six grades in school. The best inference from these data is that

(A) lack of intelligence is highly correlated with delinquency.
(B) criminals should be removed from the school system.
(C) educational maladjustments are closely associated with delinquency.
(D) the usual rate at which criminals progress educationally represents the limit of their learning powers.

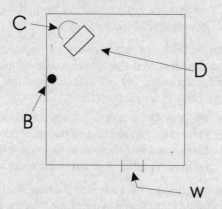

57. Assume that you are investigating a case of reported suicide. You find the deceased sitting in a chair, sprawled over his desk, a revolver still clutched in his right hand. In your examination of the room, you find that the window is partly open. Only one bullet has been fired from the revolver. The bullet has lodged in the wall. Assume that the diagram above is a scale drawing of the scene. D indicates the desk, C indicates the chair, W indicates the window, and B indicates the bullet. Of the following, which indicates most strongly that the deceased did not commit suicide?

(A) The distance between the desk and the bullet hole
(B) The relative position of the bullet hole and the chair
(C) The fact that the window was partly open
(D) The relative position of the desk and the window

58. The proprietor of a tavern summons a police officer and turns over a loaded revolver that was found in one of the tavern's booths. The least appropriate action for the officer to take is to

    (A) unload the gun and place it in an inside pocket.
    (B) determine exactly when the revolver was found.
    (C) obtain the names or descriptions of the persons who occupied the booth before the revolver was found.
    (D) question the proprietor very closely concerning the matter.

59. Assume that you have stopped a 1988 Dodge four-door sedan that you suspect is a car reported as stolen the day before. The items of information that would be most useful in determining whether or not this is the stolen car is that

    (A) the stolen car's license number was QA2356; this car's license number is U21375.
    (B) the stolen car's engine number was AB6231; this car's engine number is CS2315.
    (C) the windshield of the stolen car was not cracked; this car's windshield is cracked.
    (D) the stolen car had whitewall tires; this car does not have whitewall tires.

60. In some states, statutes forbid the payment of ransom to kidnappers. Such statutes are

    (A) actually in violation of the due process of law clause of the federal constitution.
    (B) necessary to encourage kidnappers to return the kidnapped person unharmed.
    (C) harmful because kidnapping is encouraged by such legislation.
    (D) examples of laws that protect society although sometimes working hardships on individuals.

ANSWER KEY

1. A	16. A	31. A	46. C
2. A	17. C	32. C	47. C
3. D	18. C	33. C	48. B
4. C	19. C	34. C	49. A
5. C	20. C	35. A	50. 'D
6. D	21. B	36. C	51. B
7. A	22. C	37. A	52. D
8. A	23. B	38. A	53. A
9. B	24. D	39. D	54. A
10. C	25. A	40. C	55. C
11. D	26. C	41. D	56. C
12. B	27. A	42. A	57. B
13. A	28. C	43. D	58. A
14. A	29. B	44. B	59. B
15. B	30. B	45. C	60. D

EXPLANATORY ANSWERS

1. **The correct answer is (A).** A police officer is always a police officer, even when not officially on duty. Off-duty status does not relieve a police officer from fulfilling the police role.

2. **The correct answer is (A).** The first thing to do is to protect the man's life by escorting him out of danger. Securing medical assistance should follow.

3. **The correct answer is (D).** Obviously, going the wrong way on a one-way street creates a dangerous situation for many people. By stopping the driver, you have averted the danger. The out-of-towner has not actually committed a violation, he was just about to. It would be wise to point out to him exactly how one-way streets are marked in your town.

4. **The correct answer is (C).** Drowning occurs very quickly. Try to rescue the boy.

5. **The correct answer is (C).** Anything unusual should be investigated as soon as possible. The first thing to do is to determine whether or not a burglary has occurred. Then the premises should be secured and the owner notified. If the premises were not entered, they should be kept under surveillance in case the burglar returns.

6. **The correct answer is (D).** You can assume that these people are up to no good. The quickest way to find this out is to ask for registration papers, for proof of ownership. If the keys were simply locked inside the car, the owner should readily clear up your suspicion. If ownership cannot be proved, arrest is indicated.

7. **The correct answer is (A).** An argument in a cleaning store is not an emergency situation. There is no need to disrupt traffic nor to create alarm. On the other hand, the situation could lead to blows so the officer should stop in to try to calm the tempers.

8. **The correct answer is (A).** The owner may indeed be caring for his or her car, in which case the owner can prove ownership. An open hood can also be a sign of car theft by means of jump start or of battery theft in progress.

9. **The correct answer is (B).** A pattern of regular inspections gives fair notice to prospective wrongdoers as to when no one will be looking.

10. **The correct answer is (C).** Seven or eight people do not constitute an unruly crowd. The appearance of a person of authority demanding order should end the disturbance.

11. **The correct answer is (D).** A newly appointed officer assumes some responsibility immediately. The supervising officer will give guidance but will not make all decisions.

12. **The correct answer is (B).** Common sense. Extremes are not desirable. You must respect the rights of the innocent even as you make sure to arrest the guilty.

13. **The correct answer is (A).** The careless person is not likely to succeed; the negligent person will probably fail.

14. **The correct answer is (A).** You have four choices. Of these, crime prevention is the primary function of a police department.

15. **The correct answer is (B).** Police badges serve as identification of the police officers.

16. **The correct answer is (A).** The police officer must be alert at all times.

17. **The correct answer is (C).** The officer must understand what he or she is to do in order to do it. Watch out for distracting answers like that offered by choice (A). Self-interest is never the reason for doing anything when taking a civil service exam.

18. **The correct answer is (C).** Remember not to step out of the police officer's role. The police officer must never recommend individuals, not even a choice of individuals. The most the police officer may do is recommend that the individual contact the local Bar Association or consult directories in a library.

19. **The correct answer is (C).** Criminal behavior is not exempt from the struggle for equality.

20. **The correct answer is (C).** This phenomenon is called "copycat crime." It is an unfortunate but unavoidable consequence of a free press.

21. **The correct answer is (B).** This question requires careful reading and interpreting rather than judgment. A member on duty but not in uniform may drink intoxicants but not to an extent to make him or her unfit for duty. Judgment enters into the situation in that the officer must judge at what point to stop drinking.

22. **The correct answer is (C).** Police officers are trained in the law and in the law of arrest. They are better able to judge when arrest is called for.

23. **The correct answer is (B).** The police officer's first priority is to save lives. An ambulance on an emergency run is on a mission to save a life. Lifesaving supersedes all other orders.

24. **The correct answer is (D).** If you do not really know the answer to this question, you can reach it by a process of elimination. Choice (A) is incorrect because a medical problem cannot be ignored; choice (B) is incorrect because the person must be informed of the reason for arrest; choice (C) is incorrect because the person is certainly allowed to speak and to express feelings. Choice (D) is your best choice. While all suicide threats must be taken seriously, the person newly taken into custody may well be blustering. Suicide in custody is a serious problem. The silent, brooding, distressed prisoner must be carefully watched.

25. **The correct answer is (A).** Even in this age of AIDS, the officer must be least concerned with diseases the suspect may carry. The officer must be more concerned with the possibility that the suspect will use a gun or physical force to resist arrest or that he or she will try to flee.

26. **The correct answer is (C).** Your superiors have the advantage of years of training and experience. Their judgment is quicker, and they must be obeyed without question at the site of an emergency.

27. **The correct answer is (A).** An introductory statement describing the occurrence establishes the framework on which to hang details and conclusions.

28. **The correct answer is (C).** The police badge is an identifying emblem. The police officer who serves as a witness must be identified as such.

29. **The correct answer is (B).** Pure common sense. Overcrowding leads to friction. Furthermore, prisoners in constant proximity have more opportunity to plan trouble together.

30. **The correct answer is (B).** It is true that the officer's name and shield number will appear on the summons, but there is no harm in giving these to the motorist. Professional behavior requires that the summons be given without further discussion.

31. **The correct answer is (A).** You do not need to have had training in investigation of traffic accidents to recognize from the diagram that car 2 is too far beyond the center of the intersection to have been attempting a left turn. Driver 1 is trying to cover himself with a false statement about Driver 2.

32. **The correct answer is (C).** You have a radio. Use it. The alleged robbers should be pursued promptly and safely.

33. **The correct answer is (C).** Access to the area of an accident should be limited to those who are attending to the injured. Beyond lifesaving, the first priority is to preserve evidence. Inconvenience to the public is a later consideration.

34. **The correct answer is (C).** The police role at the scene of a property-damage accident is to be certain that both drivers are licensed drivers and are authorized to drive the vehicles, that the automobiles are safe to operate on the public roadway, and that information has been obtained for police files as to those involved in the accident and witnesses. It is not the role of the police officer to be concerned with the parties' arrangements to collect damages from one another.

35. **The correct answer is (A).** A hit-and-run driver must be pursued and apprehended as quickly as possible. The efficient way to intercept the hit-and-run car is to radio a description of the car to precinct headquarters for instant broadcast to patrol cars in the vicinity.

36. **The correct answer is (C).** The person with an unconscious wish to be punished, also known as a "death wish," will draw attention to him- or herself with respect to the crime. Revisiting the crime scene is a common means of doing this. The other choices represent efforts to avoid detection and punishment.

37. **The correct answer is (A).** Read carefully. *The least accurate* format of the question makes it tricky to answer. Choices (B), (C), and (D) make correct, positive statements.

Choice (A) makes a wrong statement. The value of fingerprints left at the scene of the crime does vary with the distinctness of the fingerprint impressions. Clearer fingerprints are more valuable.

38. **The correct answer is (A).** In general, the fewer people who handle a piece of evidence, the fewer things can go wrong. Personal delivery of the evidence makes for less hearsay. Choice (C) is incorrect because of the strong word "ensures." Evidence can still be mismarked even with personal delivery and initially correct information.

39. **The correct answer is (D).** Choices (B) and (C) are of no use whatsoever. Watching people leave a ball game, you have no way of knowing who is missing a toe or who has false teeth. Choice (A) describes a very typical young girl. Choice (D) is a big man who stands out in a crowd, and his pockmarked face is further visible identification.

40. **The correct answer is (C).** Common sense. How many 6'1" women do you see roaming the streets?

41. **The correct answer is (D).** As the car is coming towards you, the most useful information is that the front bumper is missing. A bullet hole would be too small to see in a moving car on a busy highway.

42. **The correct answer is (A).** A 5'3" man weighing 200 lbs. is obese. He should be relatively easy to spot if you are alerted to watch for him. All these identification judgment questions are meant to test your judgment as to what you would report if other officers were to search on the basis of your descriptions.

43. **The correct answer is (D).** A Social Security card is not acceptable proof of identification for any purpose because it does not identify. The Social Security card contains neither picture nor descriptive text of any sort.

44. **The correct answer is (B).** Obviously, each driver is convinced that he or she has the right to the space. Any information that either one gives to you is biased. You may attempt to cool tempers, but it is not within your scope of duty to allot the space.

45. **The correct answer is (C).** You want the personal recollection of each individual witness, not the consensus of a committee.

46. **The correct answer is (C).** The speed at which an automobile was traveling when it hit a victim may affect the extent of damage to the vehicle, but it is the least valuable information from among the choices. The direction in which the automobile fled can direct the chase; the number of occupants helps with identification; the part of the automobile that struck the victim may be distinctively damaged.

47. **The correct answer is (C).** Markings on a bullet left by a gun barrel serve the same purpose as fingerprints. Since they are unique, they effectively identify the gun from which the bullet was fired.

48. **The correct answer is (B).** Common sense. Read the newspapers for confirmation.

49. **The correct answer is (A).** Of course, there are police regulations concerning the firing of guns. Common sense dictates that the officer has a pistol to use if necessary, but that there must be a very good reason to use that gun.

50. **The correct answer is (D).** You can't catch the robbers yourself; they have already gone too far. On the other hand, you must not allow them to exit the parkway while you are questioning the victim. Radio to have the exits monitored. A limited-access parkway offers possibilities that are absent on city streets for interception of thieves.

51. **The correct answer is (B).** The blood on the door bears investigation. It was likely left by the murderer at exit.

52. **The correct answer is (D).** Unfortunately, observation is often incomplete and memory may fill in the gaps or even distort the facts.

53. **The correct answer is (A).** The first question to be raised is the amount of time taken to travel from Jones's place of work to his home. If it is determined that it does indeed take longer than one-half hour, then Jones must supply proof that he really was working at 8 p.m. If the distance can be covered in less than a one-half hour, whether or not Jones was really working at 8 p.m. is irrelevant.

54. **The correct answer is (A).** Read carefully. The question describes a suicide, thereby eliminating choices (C) and (D). A body slumped in a chair is not consistent with hanging.

55. **The correct answer is (C).** With these facts, the only certainty is that further investigation is warranted on an urgent basis.

56. **The correct answer is (C).** A person who is normal in intelligence but is below grade level in school is educationally maladjusted. The fact that 86 percent of delinquents appear to be normally intelligent but below grade level points to a close association of educational maladjustment with delinquency. With this information, we can describe a correlation but not a causal relationship. The data do not indicate that educational maladjustment causes delinquency nor that delinquency leads to educational maladjustment, only that they are related.

57. **The correct answer is (B).** For the deceased to have committed suicide with the bullet lodged as indicated, the shot would have had to come from a revolver in his left hand. The revolver is in his right hand.

58. **The correct answer is (A).** This is unintelligent handling of evidence. Fingerprints and ballistics evidence may be destroyed. It would be wise to close off the booth to the public so as to safeguard possible clues, such as match covers, bits of paper with notes on them, and fingerprints on drinking glasses.

59. **The correct answer is (B).** Comparison of engine numbers is usually the determining factor in establishing whether or not a car is indeed the stolen one in question. Engine numbers are changed only with great difficulty; it is most unlikely that this would be accomplished in one day. This 1988 Dodge is probably not the car that was reported stolen. License plates and tires are easily changed and cannot serve as positive identification of stolen cars. A stolen car can easily acquire a cracked windshield.

60. **The correct answer is (D).** This is a situation in which individual interests must be subverted for the common good. The individual family wants its kidnapped member back at any price. However, allowing kidnappers to profit from kidnapping encourages other kidnappers. The principle is the same as the principle of not negotiating with terrorists. Wrongdoers must not achieve their goals through their wrongdoing. Hopefully, prospective kidnappers who know that they will fail in their attempt to collect ransom will be discouraged from kidnapping.

COMPASS DIRECTION QUIZ

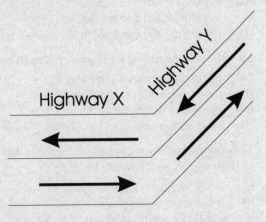

1. Highway Y comes down to join Highway X at the direction of

   (A) southwest.
   (B) northeast.
   (C) southeast.
   (D) east.

2. A vehicle traveling on Highway Y and entering Highway X would then be traveling

   (A) northeast.
   (B) east.
   (C) southwest.
   (D) west.

3. A vehicle traveling east on Highway X would enter Highway Y and then be traveling

   (A) southwest.
   (B) northeast.
   (C) southeast.
   (D) east.

4. Highway X comes in to join Highway Y while traffic is moving in the direction of

   (A) north.
   (B) south.
   (C) northeast.
   (D) west.

5. A motorist traveling southwest on Highway Y would have to make the following turn to continue his trip:
   (A) Right lane east on Highway Y
   (B) Left lane east on Highway Y
   (C) Right lane west on Highway X
   (D) Left lane south on Highway X

6. Highway X and Highway Y are said to have a junction at
   (A) an acute angle.
   (B) an obtuse angle.
   (C) a right angle.
   (D) a direct intersection.

7. Although a car traveling east on Highway X would enter Highway Y for continuous travel, its direction would change
   (A) toward the left and north.
   (B) toward the left and west.
   (C) toward the left and northeast.
   (D) toward the right and south.

8. Motorists traveling east on Highway X must enter Highway Y and then
   (A) travel northwest on Highway Y.
   (B) travel northeast on Highway Y.
   (C) move east on Highway X.
   (D) None of the above

9. The one of the following vehicle movements that would not be permitted at the junction of Highways X and Y would be
   (A) a left turn from Highway X to Y.
   (B) a U-turn at the junction.
   (C) a right turn from Highway Y to X.
   (D) a left turn from Highway X into a lane traveling in the same direction.

10. Assume that a cautionary yellow light is in place at each traffic lane. The purpose of the light would be to prevent
    (A) speeding cars from crossing traffic lanes and continuing into opposite directional traffic.
    (B) slow-moving cars from continuing their pace as they turn from Highways Y to X.
    (C) normal-moving cars from continuing at their current speed.
    (D) slow-moving cars from continuing their pace as they turn from Highways X to Y.

ANSWER KEY—COMPASS DIRECTIONS

1. A	4. C	7. C	9. B
2. D	5. C	8. B	10. A
3. B	6. B		

PART FOUR

Model Examinations

MODEL EXAMINATION 1: ANSWER SHEET

1. Ⓐ Ⓑ Ⓒ Ⓓ	21. Ⓐ Ⓑ Ⓒ Ⓓ	41. Ⓐ Ⓑ Ⓒ Ⓓ	61. Ⓐ Ⓑ Ⓒ Ⓓ	81. Ⓐ Ⓑ Ⓒ Ⓓ
2. Ⓐ Ⓑ Ⓒ Ⓓ	22. Ⓐ Ⓑ Ⓒ Ⓓ	42. Ⓐ Ⓑ Ⓒ Ⓓ	62. Ⓐ Ⓑ Ⓒ Ⓓ	82. Ⓐ Ⓑ Ⓒ Ⓓ
3. Ⓐ Ⓑ Ⓒ Ⓓ	23. Ⓐ Ⓑ Ⓒ Ⓓ	43. Ⓐ Ⓑ Ⓒ Ⓓ	63. Ⓐ Ⓑ Ⓒ Ⓓ	83. Ⓐ Ⓑ Ⓒ Ⓓ
4. Ⓐ Ⓑ Ⓒ Ⓓ	24. Ⓐ Ⓑ Ⓒ Ⓓ	44. Ⓐ Ⓑ Ⓒ Ⓓ	64. Ⓐ Ⓑ Ⓒ Ⓓ	84. Ⓐ Ⓑ Ⓒ Ⓓ
5. Ⓐ Ⓑ Ⓒ Ⓓ	25. Ⓐ Ⓑ Ⓒ Ⓓ	45. Ⓐ Ⓑ Ⓒ Ⓓ	65. Ⓐ Ⓑ Ⓒ Ⓓ	85. Ⓐ Ⓑ Ⓒ Ⓓ
6. Ⓐ Ⓑ Ⓒ Ⓓ	26. Ⓐ Ⓑ Ⓒ Ⓓ	46. Ⓐ Ⓑ Ⓒ Ⓓ	66. Ⓐ Ⓑ Ⓒ Ⓓ	86. Ⓐ Ⓑ Ⓒ Ⓓ
7. Ⓐ Ⓑ Ⓒ Ⓓ	27. Ⓐ Ⓑ Ⓒ Ⓓ	47. Ⓐ Ⓑ Ⓒ Ⓓ	67. Ⓐ Ⓑ Ⓒ Ⓓ	87. Ⓐ Ⓑ Ⓒ Ⓓ
8. Ⓐ Ⓑ Ⓒ Ⓓ	28. Ⓐ Ⓑ Ⓒ Ⓓ	48. Ⓐ Ⓑ Ⓒ Ⓓ	68. Ⓐ Ⓑ Ⓒ Ⓓ	88. Ⓐ Ⓑ Ⓒ Ⓓ
9. Ⓐ Ⓑ Ⓒ Ⓓ	29. Ⓐ Ⓑ Ⓒ Ⓓ	49. Ⓐ Ⓑ Ⓒ Ⓓ	69. Ⓐ Ⓑ Ⓒ Ⓓ	89. Ⓐ Ⓑ Ⓒ Ⓓ
10. Ⓐ Ⓑ Ⓒ Ⓓ	30. Ⓐ Ⓑ Ⓒ Ⓓ	50. Ⓐ Ⓑ Ⓒ Ⓓ	70. Ⓐ Ⓑ Ⓒ Ⓓ	90. Ⓐ Ⓑ Ⓒ Ⓓ
11. Ⓐ Ⓑ Ⓒ Ⓓ	31. Ⓐ Ⓑ Ⓒ Ⓓ	51. Ⓐ Ⓑ Ⓒ Ⓓ	71. Ⓐ Ⓑ Ⓒ Ⓓ	91. Ⓐ Ⓑ Ⓒ Ⓓ
12. Ⓐ Ⓑ Ⓒ Ⓓ	32. Ⓐ Ⓑ Ⓒ Ⓓ	52. Ⓐ Ⓑ Ⓒ Ⓓ	72. Ⓐ Ⓑ Ⓒ Ⓓ	92. Ⓐ Ⓑ Ⓒ Ⓓ
13. Ⓐ Ⓑ Ⓒ Ⓓ	33. Ⓐ Ⓑ Ⓒ Ⓓ	53. Ⓐ Ⓑ Ⓒ Ⓓ	73. Ⓐ Ⓑ Ⓒ Ⓓ	93. Ⓐ Ⓑ Ⓒ Ⓓ
14. Ⓐ Ⓑ Ⓒ Ⓓ	34. Ⓐ Ⓑ Ⓒ Ⓓ	54. Ⓐ Ⓑ Ⓒ Ⓓ	74. Ⓐ Ⓑ Ⓒ Ⓓ	94. Ⓐ Ⓑ Ⓒ Ⓓ
15. Ⓐ Ⓑ Ⓒ Ⓓ	35. Ⓐ Ⓑ Ⓒ Ⓓ	55. Ⓐ Ⓑ Ⓒ Ⓓ	75. Ⓐ Ⓑ Ⓒ Ⓓ	95. Ⓐ Ⓑ Ⓒ Ⓓ
16. Ⓐ Ⓑ Ⓒ Ⓓ	36. Ⓐ Ⓑ Ⓒ Ⓓ	56. Ⓐ Ⓑ Ⓒ Ⓓ	76. Ⓐ Ⓑ Ⓒ Ⓓ	96. Ⓐ Ⓑ Ⓒ Ⓓ
17. Ⓐ Ⓑ Ⓒ Ⓓ	37. Ⓐ Ⓑ Ⓒ Ⓓ	57. Ⓐ Ⓑ Ⓒ Ⓓ	77. Ⓐ Ⓑ Ⓒ Ⓓ	97. Ⓐ Ⓑ Ⓒ Ⓓ
18. Ⓐ Ⓑ Ⓒ Ⓓ	38. Ⓐ Ⓑ Ⓒ Ⓓ	58. Ⓐ Ⓑ Ⓒ Ⓓ	78. Ⓐ Ⓑ Ⓒ Ⓓ	98. Ⓐ Ⓑ Ⓒ Ⓓ
19. Ⓐ Ⓑ Ⓒ Ⓓ	39. Ⓐ Ⓑ Ⓒ Ⓓ	59. Ⓐ Ⓑ Ⓒ Ⓓ	79. Ⓐ Ⓑ Ⓒ Ⓓ	99. Ⓐ Ⓑ Ⓒ Ⓓ
20. Ⓐ Ⓑ Ⓒ Ⓓ	40. Ⓐ Ⓑ Ⓒ Ⓓ	60. Ⓐ Ⓑ Ⓒ Ⓓ	80. Ⓐ Ⓑ Ⓒ Ⓓ	100. Ⓐ Ⓑ Ⓒ Ⓓ

MODEL EXAMINATION 1

TIME: 4 HOURS-100 QUESTIONS

> **Directions:** Each question numbered 1 through 100 has four possible answers lettered A, B, C, and D. Select the correct answer and darken its letter on your answer sheet.

1. You are driving east on Sunrise Highway. You make a U-turn to pursue a suspect, then make a left turn. In what direction are you now heading?

    (A) North
    (B) South
    (C) East
    (D) West

2. You are driving south. You make a right turn to get to an accident scene and pass a military convoy traveling the opposite way. In what direction is the convoy headed?

    (A) North
    (B) South
    (C) East
    (D) West

3. You are traveling north on State Highway 12. At the junction of State 12 and County Road 113, you turn and proceed west on County 113. At the next stop sign, you stop and yield the right of way to a car crossing County 113 and entering the intersection from your right. The car is traveling

    (A) north.
    (B) south.
    (C) east.
    (D) west.

4. You are pursuing a car that was just involved in a hit-and-run accident and is now speeding north on High Street. In an attempt to lose you, the car turns left, then left, then left again. As the fleeing car goes through a red light, it is hit in the right side by a car legally entering the intersection. The car that hits the fugitive car is traveling

    (A) north.
    (B) south.
    (C) east.
    (D) west.

5. As you are patrolling the southbound highway, you see smoke billowing from an area to your right. In order to investigate the source of the smoke, you should turn into the next exit to the

    (A) north.
    (B) south.
    (C) east.
    (D) west.

6. You are traveling in a southwesterly direction on the parkway, and traffic is merging into your lane from the left. The merging traffic is traveling

    (A) north.
    (B) south.
    (C) east.
    (D) west.

7. If you travel west one block on Grand Street, turn left onto North Street for one block, then turn right onto River Road for just one block, right again for one block on Church Street, and then take a left, you will be headed

   (A) west on Grand Street.
   (B) north on North Street.
   (C) east on Grand Street.
   (D) west on River Road.

Answer questions 8 through 17 by choosing the most grammatical and precise sentence.

8. (A) If he would have answered the detective honestly, he would not have been arrested.
   (B) If he had answered the detective honestly, he would not have been arrested.
   (C) He would not of been arrested if he had answered the detective honestly.
   (D) If he'd answered the detective honestly, he wouldn't of been arrested.

9. (A) There are some people which don't know how to be happy.
   (B) Some people can't be happy in no way.
   (C) There are some people who don't know how to be happy.
   (D) There are some people whom simply can't find happiness.

10. (A) Picking the cartridge up off the floor, the officer placed it on the counter.
    (B) The officer placed the cartridge on the counter after picking it up off the floor.
    (C) Picking the cartridge off of the floor, it was the officer who placed it on the counter.
    (D) The officer placed the cartridge on the counter and picked it up from the floor.

11. (A) If you talk right, people will know you are in possession of a good education.
    (B) If you speak good, people will know that your education is good.
    (C) By talking real good, you show how good your education is.
    (D) If you speak correctly, people will know that you are well educated.

12. (A) The suspect said he had done nothing wrong.
    (B) The suspect said he hadn't done nothing wrong.
    (C) The suspect says he ain't done anything wrong.
    (D) The suspect says he done nothing wrong.

13. (A) In order to watch his favorite team play, 40 miles it was that he drove.
    (B) He drove 40 miles in order to watch his favorite team play.
    (C) He drove, in order to watch his favorite team play, 40 miles.
    (D) His favorite team was playing, and he drove 40 miles in order to watch them play.

14. (A) Sergeant Miller, every morning at breakfast, the paper she likes to read.
    (B) At breakfast every morning it is the paper that Sergeant Miller likes to read.
    (C) At breakfast, reading the paper is what Sergeant Miller likes to do every morning.
    (D) Sergeant Miller likes to read the paper every morning at breakfast.

15. (A) If Trooper Howard had joined our barracks sooner, she might of made Sergeant by now.
    (B) If Trooper Howard would have joined our barracks sooner, she could of become a Sergeant already.
    (C) If Trooper Howard had joined our barracks sooner, she might be a Sergeant today.
    (D) If Trooper Howard joined our barracks sooner, she would be a Sergeant now.

16. (A) Entering the room, a strange mark on the floor attracted the officer's attention.
    (B) The officer entered the room and attracted the attention of a strange mark on the floor.
    (C) The officer's attention was attracted by a strange mark on the floor entering the room.
    (D) As the officer entered the room, his attention was attracted by a strange mark on the floor.

17. (A) The door opens, and in walk Captain Gomez and Officer Hua.
    (B) The door opens, and in walked Captain Gomez and Officer Hua.
    (C) The door opened, and in walk Captain Gomez and Officer Hua.
    (D) The door opened, and in walks Captain Gomez and Officer Hua.

18. The speed limit on the bridge is 35 mph, but Henry Smith crosses doing 42 mph. By what percent is he exceeding the speed limit?

    (A) 7%
    (B) 17%
    (C) 20%
    (D) 22%

19. The supply sergeant is filling out requisition forms and requests your ammunition needs for the next four months. Last month you used 270 rounds, including those needed for target practice. Assuming that you will be using about the same amount per month, how much ammunition should you request?

    (A) 880 rounds
    (B) 980 rounds
    (C) 1080 rounds
    (D) 1180 rounds

20. At 6:15 a.m. on a fog-bound morning, seven passenger cars, two vans, three tractor-trailers, and a bus pile up in a chain-reaction collision on the thruway. At 6:19 a.m. the first patrol car arrives on the scene and immediately radios for assistance. By 6:33 a.m. three ambulances, two fire engines, five tow trucks, and eight additional patrol cars have arrived. Between 6:33 a.m. and 7:15 a.m. three of the tow trucks hook up to damaged cars and remove them from the scene. How many vehicles remain at the accident site at 7:15 a.m.?

    (A) 32
    (B) 26
    (C) 25
    (D) 20

21. State Patrol Barracks C, home base to twenty patrol cars, is responsible for patrolling 235 miles of thruway and the surrounding vicinity. One Thursday morning, three cars were out of service for maintenance and repairs and four cars were assigned to off-highway duties. If all remaining cars were assigned equal territories, approximately how many miles of thruway did each car patrol?

    (A) 12
    (B) 17
    (C) 18
    (D) 19.5

22. The average gasoline usage of a patrol car in highway service is 28 miles per gallon. Officer Prince took out a car with a full tank of gas and an odometer reading of 4,682 and returned it with an odometer reading of 5,067. Approximately how many gallons of gasoline did Officer Prince use?

    (A) 28
    (B) 13.65
    (C) 12.85
    (D) 13.75

23. State troopers are permitted to place two in-state personal telephone calls per day at no charge. Excess phone calls are charged to the trooper at the rate of $0.50 each for the first two calls and $0.75 for each additional call. Out-of-state calls are billed at telephone company rates. Officer Zappa has been conducting family business by telephone during his break period. One day Officer Zappa made a long-distance call for which the charge was $2.35. His total telephone bill for that day was $5.60. How many telephone calls did Officer Zappa make that day?

    (A) 8
    (B) 7
    (C) 9
    (D) 6

24. Two troopers left the barracks at 3:00 p.m. Officer Tolski drove north maintaining an average speed of 42 mph. Officer Hara drove south at a steady speed of 38 mph. How many miles apart were the troopers at 4:30 p.m.?

    (A) 6
    (B) 80
    (C) 120
    (D) 150

25. A trooper left Barracks A at 9:15 a.m. and arrived at Barracks C at 2:45 p.m. How long did the trip take this trooper?

    (A) 6 hours 30 minutes
    (B) 5 hours 30 minutes
    (C) 5 hours 15 minutes
    (D) 4 hours 45 minutes

26. A large group of demonstrators has gathered at a construction site to protest alleged discriminatory practices in hiring. The captain has dispatched 24 officers to avert a potential riot. No sooner have the officers arrived at the site when a call comes over the radio requesting that 5 officers report to a serious accident 7 miles to the north. Shortly afterwards 3 officers are requested to control traffic at an intersection at which the traffic signal has malfunctioned. At the construction site, a worker is suddenly injured by a swinging boom, and 2 officers take the injured worker to the hospital in their patrol car. Then the captain arrives to survey the situation. What is the total number of law enforcers on hand to avert a riot?

    (A) 14
    (B) 15
    (C) 21
    (D) 22

27. Cars in police service receive very hard use and must be serviced every 3,000 miles or sooner. Officer Lindner's vehicle was last serviced at 8,782 miles. Officer Lindner drives an average of 140 miles a day, and his odometer currently reads 10,461. Within how many more working days must Officer Lindner bring in the car for servicing?

    (A) 14
    (B) 8
    (C) 10
    (D) 9

28. Officer Cohen's personal car was using 12 gallons of gasoline to travel 240 miles. Officer Cohen took the car to the mechanic for a tune-up and carburetor adjustment. After this service, Officer Cohen discovered that the car used only 80 percent as much gasoline as before. How many miles can Officer Cohen now drive with 12 gallons of gasoline?

    (A) 320
    (B) 280
    (C) 300
    (D) 342

29. The schedule of speeding penalties is as follows:

10% to 14% over the speed limit	$25
15% to 19% over the speed limit	$35
20% to 24% over the speed limit	$50
25% to 29% over the speed limit	$70
30% to 34% over the speed limit	$100
35% to 39% over the speed limit	$125
40% to 44% over the speed limit	$150
More than 44% over the speed limit	$200

    In a 40 mph zone, Officer David gave one ticket each to drivers clocked at 45 mph, 48 mph, and 53 mph and two tickets to drivers clocked at 60 mph and 58 mph, respectively. Later that day, while working in a 55 mph zone, Officer David gave two tickets to drivers traveling at 64 mph, one ticket to a driver clocked at 71.5 mph, and one ticket to a speeder doing 85 mph. If all ticketed drivers plead or are proven guilty, what is the total of fines to be collected from Officer David's tickets?

    (A) $945
    (B) $845
    (C) $910
    (D) $810

Questions 30 through 35 are based on the personnel chart below.

PERSONNEL CHART

Name	Sex	SS Number	Date of Birth	Date Hired	Position	Supervisor
Hail, C.B.	M	123-45-6789	5/7/57	1/2/90	cook	Hood, R.B.
Hale, T.J.	F	083-68-1218	6/12/60	4/1/88	trooper	Dale, A.A.
Hales, N.A.	F	221-91-0031	4/28/53	5/10/74	property clerk	Tuck, F.R.
Hall, F.X.	M	118-22-5410	1/9/48	6/6/76	custodian	Hood, R.B.
Hals, F.T.	F	630-98-1234	12/21/64	11/23/85	sergeant	Allen, G.
Hill, R.L.	F	562-76-7977	9/30/30	10/4/86	security	Tuck, F.R.
Hill, P.C.	M	987-40-3939	10/14/41	9/2/72	mechanic	John, L.T.
Hilly, J.G.	M	406-18-6238	7/2/73	4/8/94	trooper	Dale, A.A.

30. Which person is supervised by F.R. Tuck?

    (A) P.C. Hill
    (B) F.X. Hall
    (C) N.A. Hales
    (D) T.J. Hale

31. The job held by the oldest person is

    (A) mechanic.
    (B) security.
    (C) cook.
    (D) trooper.

32. The oldest trooper was born on

    (A) 9/30/30
    (B) 12/21/64
    (C) 7/2/73
    (D) 6/12/60

33. The person who has been employed here for the longest time is

    (A) P. C. Hill.
    (B) C. B. Hail.
    (C) R. L. Hill.
    (D) F. X. Hall.

34. F. T. Hals's social security number is

    (A) 630-89-1234
    (B) 118-22-5410
    (C) 118-22-5401
    (D) 630-98-1234

35. The person whose social security number is 987-40-3939 is a

    (A) cook.
    (B) trooper.
    (C) security guard.
    (D) mechanic.

Questions 36 through 41 are based on the work schedule below.

WORK SCHEDULE

	Sun	Mon	Tues	Wed	Thurs	Fri	Sat
Group 1	South Quadrant	training	West Quadrant	off	South Quadrant	off	East Quadrant
Group 2	East Quadrant	off	training	North Quadrant	West Quadrant	West Quadrant	off
Group 3	North Quadrant	West Quadrant	off	West Quadrant	off	training	North Quadrant

Group 1
Supervisor: Jose Primo
Mary Clark
James McDonald
Thoru Moro
Akeel Morris
Training at: 146 Butler Road
Training supervisor: Gregor Ozmanian

Group 2
Supervisor: Steve Chen
Robert Park
Linda LaRue
Barbara Benson
Marvin Cohen

Group 3
Supervisor: Jane Shulz
Clifford Rose
Gino Abate
Ben Trotsky
Charles O'Day

JULY

Sun	Mon	Tues	Wed	Thurs	Fri	Sat
				1	2	3
4	5	6	7	8	9	10
11	12	13	14	15	16	17
18	19	20	21	22	23	24
25	26	27	28	29	30	31

36. Where is Gino Abate working on July 21?

(A) North Quadrant
(B) 146 Butler Road
(C) West Quadrant
(D) Not working

37. A person who will be working in only two quadrants during the month of July is

(A) Linda LaRue.
(B) Jane Shulz.
(C) Thorn Moro.
(D) Gregor Ozmanian.

38. On what date will Akeel Morris report for training?

(A) July 2
(B) July 4
(C) July 19
(D) July 22

39. The supervisor of the group that will work in the south quadrant on July 15 is

    (A) Jose Primo.
    (B) Jane Shulz.
    (C) Mary Clark.
    (D) Gregor Ozmanian.

40. A person who will be off on July 25 is

    (A) Steven Chen.
    (B) Charles O'Day.
    (C) Gregor Ozmanian.
    (D) Robert Park.

41. Which group will work in the west quadrant on July 11?

    (A) Group 1
    (B) Group 2
    (C) Group 3
    (D) Cannot be determined

Questions 42 through 46 are based on the daily arrest report below:

Area	Arresting Officer	Burglary	Murder	Arson	Assault	Total
Arch	Sgt. Tomas	X			X	2
Cove	Sgt. Blau		X		X	2
Dale	Sgt. Paik	X			X	2
Hill	Sgt. Leary			X		1
Wall	Sgt. Rossi	X		X		2
	Total	3	1	2	3	9

Those arrested today are: D. Tramp, A. Wilson, E. Brown, M. Allen, L. King, J. Harris, B. Davis, S. Grant, G. Evans.

■   M. Allen lives in Dale.

■   E. Brown was arrested in her home vicinity.

■   S. Grant was arrested by Sgt.. Tomas.

■   D. Tramp was arrested for murder.

■   J. Harris and E. Brown are roommates. Sgt. Leary arrested only male suspects.

■   No person arrested by Sgt. Paik lives in the area in which the arrest took place.

■   Sgt. Rossi did not arrest any residents of Arch.

■   L. King is a juvenile.

■   Wilson was carrying a fur jacket and silver candlesticks in a pillowcase when arrested.

■   E. Brown lives in Arch.

■   G. Evans is on probation stemming from prior conviction for assaulting his wife.

42. The person who could NOT have been arrested by Sgt. Leary is

    (A) G. Evans.
    (B) L. King.
    (C) J. Harris.
    (D) Cannot be determined from information given

43. Which of these suspects could Sgt. Paik have arrested?

    (A) M. Allen
    (B) B. Davis
    (C) D. Tramp
    (D) E. Brown

44. The person who might have been arrested by Sgt. Rossi on suspicion of arson is

    (A) J. Harris.
    (B) A. Wilson.
    (C) L. King.
    (D) S. Grant.

45. D. Tramp was arrested by

    (A) Sgt. Blau.
    (B) Sgt. Paik.
    (C) Sgt. Tomas.
    (D) Cannot be determined from information given

46. Sgt. Leary arrested M. Allen on a charge of

    (A) burglary.
    (B) arson.
    (C) murder.
    (D) Cannot be determined from information given

In the diagrams for questions 47 and 48, symbols are used to represent vehicles, pedestrians, animals, and their movements.

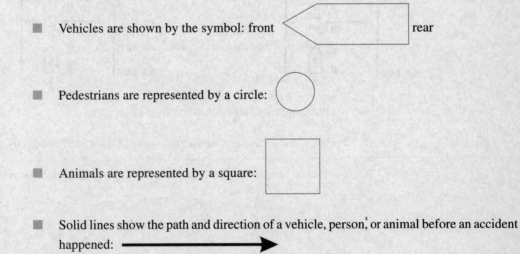

■ Vehicles are shown by the symbol: front   rear

■ Pedestrians are represented by a circle:

■ Animals are represented by a square:

■ Solid lines show the path and direction of a vehicle, person, or animal before an accident happened:

■ Dotted lines show the path and direction of a vehicle, person, or animal after an accident happened:

47. Car 1 was driving north on State Road 112 when a deer crossing the road from the left of the car ran into the roadway directly in front of the car. Car 1 glanced off the rear end of the deer and swerved to the left. Car 2, proceeding south on State Road 112, swerved to its right to avoid a head-on collision with Car 1 and stopped in the underbrush off the shoulder. Which of the four diagrams below best represents the accident described?

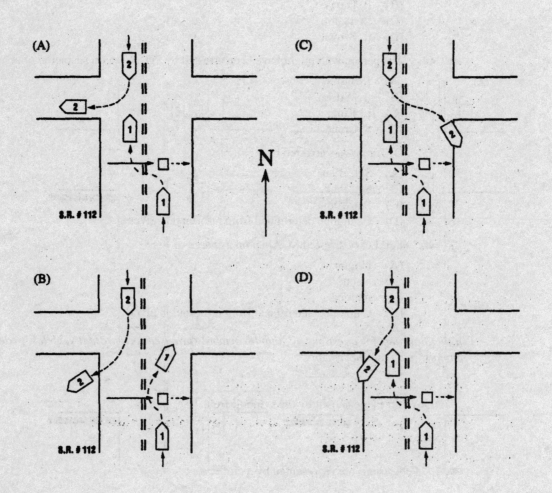

48. Officer Wood was standing beside a radar-equipped patrol car on the west shoulder of southbound I-95 and observed the following: Car 1 was proceeding south on I-95 in accordance with the posted speed limit. Car 2, approaching I-95 from the east on Hilton Crossway and signaling for a left turn, came to a full stop at the intersection. Car 3, directly behind Car 2, was signaling for a right turn and not paying attention. Car 3 hit Car 2 from behind. Car 2 swerved into the northbound roadway so as to avoid a collision in the southbound direction. Which of the four diagrams below best represents the accident observed by Officer Wood?

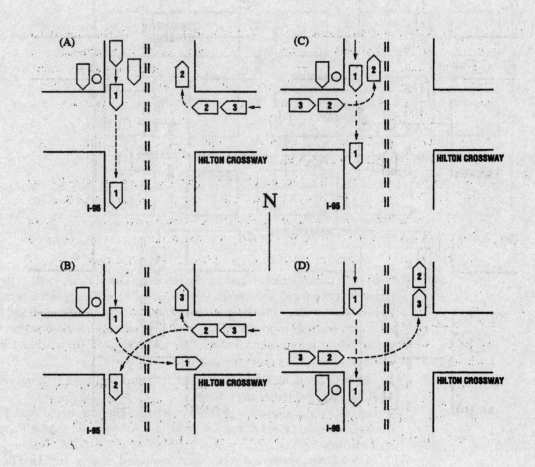

Use the map below to answer questions 49 and 50. The flow of traffic is indicated by the arrows. If there is only one arrow shown, then traffic flows only in the direction indicated by the arrow. If there are two arrows shown, then traffic flows in both directions. You must follow the flow of traffic.

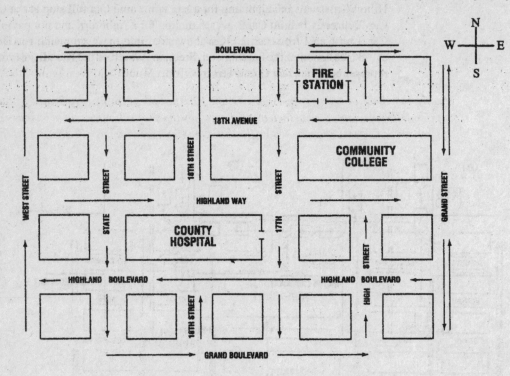

49. You have just come into town and are driving along Grand Boulevard. At the corner of Grand Boulevard and State Street, you notice a woman sitting on the curb holding a handkerchief to a very bloody face. You inquire as to what happened, and she tells you that she carelessly tripped and fell. The injury probably looks worse than it is, but you place her in your patrol car and drive her to the hospital. The quickest legal route to take to the emergency room entrance on 17th Street is

(A) east on Grand Boulevard to High Street, left onto High Street, right onto Highland Boulevard, and right onto 17th Street.

(B) east on Grand Boulevard to High Street, left onto High Street, right onto Highland Way, left onto Grand Street, left onto 18th Avenue, and then left again onto 17th Street.

(C) east on Grand Boulevard to Highland Boulevard, west on Highland Boulevard to Highland Way, east on Highland Way, and south on 17th Street to the emergency room.

(D) east on Grand Boulevard to Grand Street, left onto Grand Street, then a left turn onto 18th Avenue, and south on 17th Street.

50. As you leave the hospital, your radio crackles with information about a demonstration in front of the 18th Avenue entrance of the fire station. A noisy group of citizens is protesting poor fire protection in the North End of town. You must report to the scene of the demonstration to be certain it does not get out of hand. The quickest legal route is

(A) south on 17th Street and make a left onto Highland Boulevard, then north on West Street to Highland Way, then right onto Highland Way to 18th Street, then north on 18th Street to Grand Boulevard, east on Grand Boulevard to Grand Street, and right onto 18th Avenue.

(B)   south on 17th Street to Grand Boulevard, left onto Grand Boulevard to Grand Street, north on Grand Street to 18th Avenue, and then left onto 18th Avenue.

(C)   exit the hospital and go left on 17th Street to Highland Way, follow Highland Way east to Grand Street, then turn north onto Grand Street for one block, and left onto 18th Avenue.

(D)   south on 17th Street to Highland Boulevard, go west on Highland Boulevard to 18th Street, then north on 18th Street to Boulevard, right on Boulevard to Grand Street, south on Grand Street to 18th Avenue, and west onto 18th Avenue.

Use the map below to answer questions 51 and 52. The flow of traffic is indicated by the arrows. If there is only one arrow shown, then traffic flows only in the direction indicated by the arrow. If there are two arrows shown, then the traffic flows in both directions. You must follow the traffic flow.

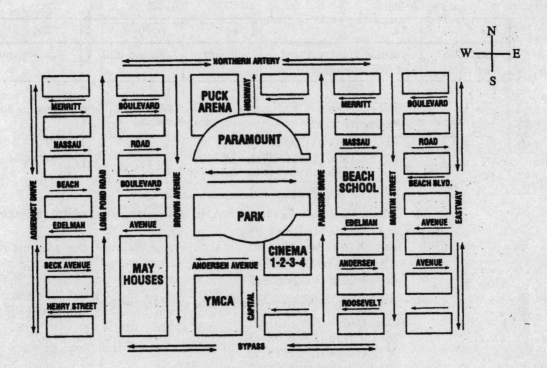

51.   You have been asked to give a highway-safety talk to the students at Beach School. Entering town on Capital Highway, the best way for you to get to the school is to

(A)   turn west on Andersen Avenue and go to Long Pond Road, then turn right onto Long Pond Road to Beach Boulevard, and turn right to go through the park to the Beach School.

(B)   go east on Roosevelt to Parkside Drive, then turn left onto Parkside Drive and continue to Beach School.

(C)   turn left onto Andersen Avenue, then turn left to go south on Brown Avenue, then right for one block on Bypass, right again onto Long Pond Road to Beach Boulevard, and right onto Beach Boulevard for the ride through the park to Beach School.

(D)   turn west on Andersen Avenue to Brown Avenue, south on Brown Avenue to Bypass, east on Bypass to Eastway, north on Eastway to Beach Boulevard, and left onto Beach Boulevard to Beach School.

52. You are helping to direct traffic at the hockey game at Puck Arena when word comes over your radio of a patron with a gun at the movie house. You must get to Cinema 1-2-3-4 as quickly as possible without endangering lives by traveling against traffic. Your best route is to

    (A) go east on Merritt Boulevard to Martin Street, south on Martin Street to Edelman, and turn right onto Edelman Avenue to the movie house.
    (B) go south on Brown Avenue to Andersen Avenue, then turn left onto Andersen Avenue to Cinema 1-2-3-4.
    (C) take Capital Highway through the park to Cinema 1-2-3-4.
    (D) take Brown Avenue south to the Bypass, turn left onto Bypass for one block, and left onto Capital to the movie house.

Questions 53 through 58 are based on driver's license personal identification numbers as explained below.

G	14	69	042969	7486
first letter last name	position in the alphabet of first letter, first name	height	date of birth	random numbers

53. Robert Stone was in elementary school in 1943. Which of the following could be his license number?

    (A) R 1971 981334 56818
    (B) S 1868 122132 90756
    (C) S 2059 030336 58734
    (D) S 1874 092043 71212

54. Which of the people with the following ID numbers would be easiest to pick out in a crowd?

    (A) T 1386 110765 67727
    (B) A 0263 043071 09791
    (C) Z 2469 090941 12345
    (D) F 2058 101828 62262

55. Which of the following could NOT be a real ID number?

    (A) C 0648 020955 31652
    (B) E 1160 120929 68517
    (C) H 0366 023049 68712
    (D) 0 1568 070915 63480

56. Of the following, who is most likely to have special restrictions on his or her driver's license?

    (A) 11040 103050 77134
    (B) K 1460 061972 84356
    (C) D 0863 010377 95604
    (D) M 1370 082246 74569

57. Which of the following is least likely to be a driver's license ID number?

    (A) A 2172 052411 54367
    (B) P 1568 041943 84685
    (C) K 1048 092888 65823
    (D) T 2366 123179 65125

58. Which one of the following is Donato Panetta's driver's license number?

    (A) D 1690 032456 88610
    (B) P 0369 062763 54769
    (C) P 0426 082695 44126
    (D) P 0459 102030 65241

Questions 59 through 64 are based on roadside mile markers as explained below.

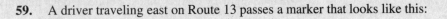

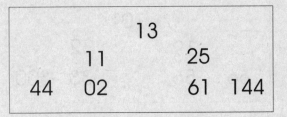

country designator code ⸺ 08   138 ⸺ mile number (in direction traveled

next intersecting route ⸺ 22   39   46   308 ⸺ distance to other end of highway

       code for point at   code for point at end
       beginning of highway   of highway

59.   A driver traveling east on Route 13 passes a marker that looks like this:

> 13
>
> 11   25
>
> 44   02   61   144

He makes a right turn onto Route 44 and proceeds to drive 6 more miles. The next marker he passes could look like

(A)
> 13
>
> 11   28
>
> 44   02   61   144

(B)
> 44
>
> 11   16
>
> 13   12   76   210

(C)
> 44
>
> 11   112
>
> 06   63   08   92

(D)
> 44
>
> 11   86
>
> 44   10   19   103

60. A highway traveler passes a road marker that looks like this:

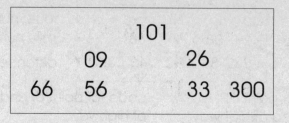

The next highway marker that she notices looks like this:

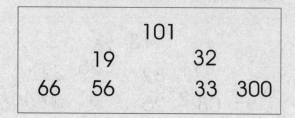

This marker indicates that

(A) the traveler has turned onto another highway.
(B) the route number has changed.
(C) the traveler has gone 10 miles since the last marker she noticed.
(D) the traveler has crossed a county line.

61. A trooper patrolling an assigned sector passes a route marker that looks like this:

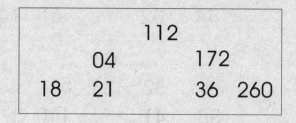

Thirty minutes later, the marker the trooper passes looks like this:

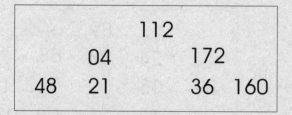

Indications are that the trooper

(A) has made a U-turn.
(B) has exceeded the speed limit in the line of duty.
(C) is now on a cloverleaf.
(D) has changed highways.

62. A motorist passes a roadside marker that looks like this:

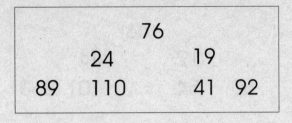

As the motorist continues his trip, he makes a number of turns. Which of the following roadside markers might this motorist now pass?

(A)

```
            76
      32          22
   08   25          41   96
```

(B)

```
           113
      24          53
   66   81          05   123
```

(C)

```
            08
      32          56
   38   41          110   379
```

(D)

```
            89
      24          88
   89   05          94   100
```

63. A state highway officer passes a marker that looks like this:

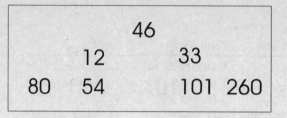

One hour later, the same officer passes a marker that looks like this:

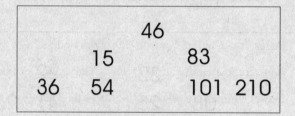

We can be certain that the officer

(A) traveled at least 60 miles.
(B) crossed at least three county lines.
(C) made a number of U-turns.
(D) crossed more than one intersection.

64. A highway patrol car passed a marker that looked like this:

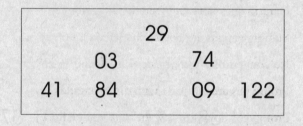

Some time later this same car passed a marker that looked like this:

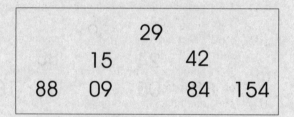

This car definitely did NOT

(A) cross a county line.
(B) travel at least 32 miles.
(C) make a single right turn.
(D) make a U-turn.

Questions 65 through 70 are based on vehicle identification numbers as explained below.

Year	Engine Size	Plant Made	Style	Day Assembled	Shift	Individual Identifying numbers
A-1988	A-3.7 *l*	1-Dearborn, MI	A-2dr sedan	1-Mon	L-1st	
B-1989	B-3.15 *l*	2-Gary, IN	B-4dr sedan	2-Tues	M-2nd	
C-1990	C-3.9 *l*	3-Detroit #1	C-3dr hatchback	3-Wed	N-3rd	
D-1991	D-3.9 *l* diesel	4-Detroit #2	D-station wagon	4-Thurs		
E-1992	E-3.39 *l*	5-Toledo, OH	E-convertible	5-Fri		
F-1993	F-3.45 *l*	6-Flint, MI	F-5dr van	6-Sat		
G-1994		7-Ontario				
H-prototype						

■ Pacers and Canters come in 2dr or 4dr sedans.

■ Vans are made only at the Ontario, Gary, and Detroit #1 plants.

■ Diesel engines are assembled only in the Detroit plants.

■ Convertibles do not have diesel engines.

■ Vans are made only with 3.7 *l* and 3.9 *l* engines.

■ Vans use gasoline or diesel fuel.

■ Only sedans are assembled on the third shift.

■ There is no third shift on Saturday.

■ Ontario does not manufacture 3.45 *l* engines.

■ Station wagons are not assembled on Saturday.

■ No convertibles were made in 1988 and 1989.

■ Prototypes are all made with diesel engines.

■ Prototypes do not follow the above guidelines.

65. The vehicle with ID#DC5C4MN2X438 is a

(A) 1991 sedan with a 3.9 *l* engine assembled in Toledo during the third shift on a Thursday.

(B) 1991 Pacer hatchback with a 3.9 *l* engine assembled in Detroit during the second shift on a Friday.

(C) 1991 hatchback with a 3.9 *l* engine assembled in Toledo during the second shift on a Thursday.

(D) 1991 hatchback prototype with a 3.9 *l* diesel engine assembled in Toledo during the second shift on a Thursday.

66. A 1994 station wagon with a 3.45 *l* engine could be identified by which one of the following serial numbers?

    (A) GF6D3L1H5T07
    (B) GFID6MP9684B
    (C) HF7D21U674RS
    (D) GF4D2N2M9064

67. The vehicle with ID#BF1A63F732RZ is a

    (A) 1989 2dr convertible with a 3.45 *l* engine made in Dearborn on a Friday third shift.
    (B) 1989 2dr Canter with a 3.45 *l* engine made in Dearborn on a Friday third shift.
    (C) 1990 2dr Pacer with a 3.39 *l* engine made in Dearborn on a Saturday third shift.
    (D) prototype 1989 Pacer with a 3.9 *l* diesel engine made in Dearborn on a Friday second shift.

68. Which of the following serial numbers identifies a prototype 1994 convertible?

    (A) GH3F2L9Y14R7
    (B) HE4F6N2P8VB5
    (C) HD6E4MI17X22
    (D) HD3E1M60G916

69. The vehicle identified by serial number EC4B5NKJ0273 could be

    (A) a diesel-powered Pacer.
    (B) a prototype Canter.
    (C) a 2dr convertible.
    (D) a 4dr Pacer.

70. Which of the following serial numbers identifies a van?

    (A) FA7E2L5P7UY6
    (B) CD2E1M7RE123
    (C) DC5E4N00748B
    (D) GA2E6N5HJ864

Questions 71 through 73 are based on the following rules for use of the community room at Barracks B.

Now that our new training facility has been completed and we are no longer pressed for space, Barracks B is offering the use of the old common room to the people of the region we serve. This use, of course, will be governed by certain rules and conditions.

Availability: The common room is reserved for the exclusive personal use of troopers assigned to Barracks B on Monday and Wednesday between 6:00 p.m. and 8:00 p.m., on Saturday between 10:00 a.m. and 3:30 p.m. unless specifically relinquished by the troopers in residence, and on Sunday from 4:00 p.m. on. The common room is available for use by recognized community groups on Monday and Tuesday from 9:00 a.m. to 2:00 p.m., on Friday from 10:00 a.m. to 11:3O a.m. and from 1:00 p.m. to 4:00 p.m. Weekend use of the common room by members of the community is limited to Saturday from 6:00 p.m. to 11:00 p.m. and Sunday from 10:00 a.m. to 2:00 p.m. At all other times the common room is to be left vacant or occupied by scheduled activities within the barracks.

Procedure for use of the facility by members of Barracks B: A trooper who wishes to reserve the common room for a private purpose may do so by applying to the superintendent in writing at least twenty days before the date requested. The application must describe the nature of the activity, the number of people expected, and any special facilities that will be needed (chairs, food service, extra lighting, booths, etc.). A $25 charge for cleanup will be deducted from the trooper's paycheck on the payday following the event. If a group of troopers wishes to reserve the common room for a special group event, this $25 charge must be paid in advance of the event from money contributed by members to the group.

Procedure for application by members of the public: The recognized leader of a community group must submit a signed application in writing at least twenty days before the date requested. The application must state the general nature of the function, the number of persons expected to attend, and the special facilities required. A community group must post a refundable bond in the sum of $100 at the time permission for use is granted. Routine cost of cleanup is $25, payable by money order on the date of the event. Should cleanup costs exceed this sum, the excess will be deducted before the bond money is returned. An individual citizen may reserve the common room for a personal function subject to the same rules except that a cancellation fee of $50 will apply as well.

Priority: Within the day and time restrictions outlined above, the application with the earliest date of filing will receive priority. In case of applications for the same date that are filed on the same date, priority is as follows: (1) members of Barracks B; (2) youth groups; (3) senior citizen groups; (4) civic groups; (5) social groups.

Other rules:

1. Under no circumstances may the common room be used between the hours of 11:00 p.m. and 8:00 a.m.
2. The maximum legal occupancy of the common room is 138 people.
3. No group or individual may reserve the common room for use on a regular basis, nor may any such group or individual reserve the common room for more than two functions in any month.
4. Any group disrupting the regular activities of the barracks will be denied future use of the facilities.

71. Who might be using the common room on Thursday afternoon at 4:00?

(A) A quilting group consisting of 18 elderly women
(B) A Girl Scout troop having its regular weekly meeting
(C) An off-duty trooper in a penny-ante poker game
(D) A local physician teaching an advanced CPR class to 10 troopers

72. Which request for use of the common room is most likely to be granted?

(A) On March 15 Officer Carroll requests use of the common room on Sunday, April 1, from 11:00 a.m. to 2:00 p.m. for a christening party with 80 guests.

(B) On March 3 the Boy Scouts request use of the common room on Saturday, March 31, from 6:00 p.m. to 10:00 p.m., and on Sunday, April 1, from 10:00 a.m. to 2:00 p.m., for a bazaar with an estimated total attendance of 300 people coming and going over the two-day span of time.

(C) On March 3 a senior citizen group requests use of the common room on Sunday, April 1, from 10:00 a.m. to 2:00 p.m. for a tax clinic to be attended by about 40 people in all.

(D) On March 3 the Eton Squares, a local dance club, requests use of the common room for a square dance on Saturday, March 31, from 6:00 p.m. to 11:00 p.m., with expected attendance of about 75 people.

73. Officer Barone will be married on June 14. His fellow officers decide to throw a bachelor's party in Barone's honor in the common room on Sunday, June 9. On May 1, a group of Barone's trooper friends, led by Officer Yamato, approach the superintendent to apply for use of the common room Sunday, June 9, from 7:00 p.m. to 11:00 p.m. Their application states that approximately 15 troopers and 15 friends from the community will attend and that the group will supply food, drink, and music but will need tables, chairs, and a microphone. The superintendent grants this request and tells Officer Yamato that

(A) he will have $25 deducted from the first paycheck following June 14.

(B) he must post $100 bond and give the superintendent $25 within the next few weeks.

(C) he should collect a total of $25 from the participating troopers and pay this sum over to the superintendent before June 9.

(D) there will be no charge if the troopers clean up after themselves, but if the event is canceled there will be a $50 fee.

Questions 74 through 76 are based on the following rules for the use of a college gym.

Since budgetary constraints have halted construction of the gym and pool at our new state police barracks, the superintendent of the barracks has made special arrangements with Elmtop Community College for use of college athletic facilities at specified times and subject to certain restrictions.

Locker room: The locker room and showers are available to our troopers at any time that the swimming pool is available for our use. For any other use of the college facilities—gym, weight room, outdoor track—troopers are asked not to overtax college facilities but rather to use shower and changing facilities at the barracks and to travel between campus and barracks in exercise clothing.

Swimming pool: The swimming pool is reserved for our exclusive use from 6:00 a.m. to 7:30 a.m. on Monday, Tuesday, and Saturday and from 8:30 p.m. to 10:00 p.m. on Friday. In addition, upon presentation of trooper identification, troopers may be admitted at no charge to the general public swim session from 7:30 a.m. to 9:00 a.m. on Tuesday and Thursday, from 8:00 p.m. to 9:30 p.m. on Monday and Wednesday, and from 9:00 a.m. to 11:00 a.m. on Saturdays. Sundays from 4:00 p.m. to 6:00 p.m. there is a "women-only" swim period at which women troopers are welcome. Likewise, the "men-only" swim period on Sundays from 1:00 p.m. to 3:00 p.m. is open to men troopers.

Weight room: The weight room is "ours" between the hours of 5:30 a.m. and 7:30 a.m. every morning except Wednesday and Friday.

Gym: We have use of the gym for individual purposes or for organized group activities (see barracks bulletin board for schedule of organized games) every morning at the same times that we have use of the weight room and on Saturday between 1:00 p.m. and 3:00 p.m.

Track: The track is available for use by the general public at any time that it is not specifically reserved for use by a college group. College use changes each semester; a schedule is posted on the bulletin board in each college locker room. As a general rule, the track is available every day before 9:00 a.m. and after 8:00 p.m. Lighting at the track makes this an attractive exercise option at these uncrowded hours.

74. Women troopers may use the facilities from

(A) 6:00 a.m. to 9:00 a.m. on Tuesday and from 4:00 p.m. to 6:00 p.m. on Sunday.

(B) 8:30 p.m. to 10:00 p.m. on Friday and from 1:00 p.m. to 6:00 p.m. on Sunday.

(C) 7:30 a.m. to 9:00 a.m. on Tuesday and from 5:30 a.m. to 7:00 a.m. on Thursday.

(D) 6:00 a.m. to 7:30 a.m. on Monday, from 3:00 p.m. to 5: 30 p.m. on Saturday, and on Thursday after 8:00 p.m.

75. What athletic activity is occurring at the college on Wednesday evening?

 (A) Troopers' weight lifting
 (B) Women's swim
 (C) Free swim for the general public
 (D) Trooper's volleyball tournament in the gym

76. On Thursday at 6:00 a.m., a trooper could be engaging in any of these activities EXCEPT

 (A) working out with weights.
 (B) shooting foul shots.
 (C) trying to break the 3-minute mile.
 (D) swimming laps.

Answer questions 77 through 79 on the basis of the information in the following paragraph.

All automotive accidents, no matter how slight, are to be reported to the Safety Division by the employee involved on Accident Report Form 5-23 in duplicate. When the accident is of such a nature that it requires the filling out of the State Motor Vehicle Report Form MV-104, this form is also prepared by the employee in duplicate and sent to the Safety Division for comparison with the Form 5-23. The Safety Division forwards both copies of Form MV-104 to the Corporation Counsel, who sends one copy to the State Bureau of Motor Vehicles. When the information on the Form S-23 indicates that the employee may be at fault, an investigation is made by the Safety Division. If this investigation shows that the employee was at fault, the employee's dispatcher is asked to file a complaint on Form D-11. The foreman of mechanics prepares a damage report on Form D-8 and an estimate of the cost of repairs on Form D-9. The dispatcher's complaint, the damage report, the repair estimate, and the employee's previous accident record are sent to the Safety Division, where they are studied together with the accident report. The Safety Division then recommends whether or not disciplinary action should be taken against the employee.

77. According to the paragraph, the forwarding of Form MV-104 to the State Bureau of Motor Vehicles is done by the

 (A) Corporation Counsel.
 (B) dispatcher.
 (C) employee involved in the accident.
 (D) Safety Division.

78. According to the paragraph, the Safety Division investigates an automotive accident if the

 (A) accident is serious enough to be reported to the State Bureau of Motor Vehicles.
 (B) dispatcher files a complaint.
 (C) employee appears to have been at fault.
 (D) employee's previous accident record is poor.

79. Of the forms mentioned in the paragraph, the dispatcher is responsible for preparing the

 (A) accident report form.
 (B) complaint form.
 (C) damage report.
 (D) estimate of cost of repairs.

Answer questions 80 through 82 on the basis of the information in the following passage.

Society's historical approach to criminals can be conveniently summarized as a succession of three Rs: revenge, restraint, and reformation. Revenge was the primary response prior to the first revolution in penology in the eighteenth and nineteenth centuries. During that revolution, revenge was replaced by an emphasis upon restraint. When the second revolution occurred in the late nineteenth and twentieth centuries, reformation became an important objective. Attention was focused upon the mental and emotional makeup of the offender, and efforts were made to alter these primary sources of difficulty.

We have now entered yet another revolution in which a fourth concept has been added to the list of Rs: reintegration. This has come about because students of corrections feel that a singular focus upon reforming the offender is inadequate. Successful rehabilitation is a two-sided coin that includes reformation on one side and reintegration on the other.

It can be argued that this third revolution is premature. Society itself is still very ambivalent about the offender. It has never really replaced all vestiges of revenge or restraint but has merely supplemented them. Thus, although it is unwilling to kill or lock up all offenders permanently, it is also unwilling to give full support to the search for alternatives.

80. According to the passage, revolutions against accepted treatment of criminals have resulted in all of the following approaches to handling criminals EXCEPT

(A) revenge.
(B) restraint.
(C) reformation.
(D) reintegration.

81. According to the passage, the second revolution directed particular attention to

(A) preparing the offender for his or her return to society.
(B) making the pain of punishment exceed the pleasure of crime.
(C) exploring the inner feelings of the offender.
(D) restraining the offender from continuing a life of crime.

82. The author of the passage suggests that the latest revolution will

(A) fail and the cycle will begin again with revenge or restraint.
(B) be the last revolution.
(C) not work unless society's correctional goals can be defined.
(D) succumb to political and economic pressures.

Answer questions 83 through 85 on the basis of the information in the following paragraph.

The practice of occasionally adulterating marijuana complicates analysis of the effects of marijuana use in noncontrolled settings. Behavioral changes that are attributed to marijuana may actually derive from the adulterants or from the interaction of tetrahydrocannabinols and adulterants. Similarly, in today's society marijuana is often used simultaneously or sequentially with other psychoactive drugs. When drug interactions occur, the simultaneous presence of two or more drugs in the body can exert effects that are more than those that would result from the simple addition of the effects of each drug used separately. Thus, the total behavioral response may be greater than the sum of its parts. For example, if a given dose of marijuana induced 2 units of perceptual distortion and a certain dose of LSD given alone induced 2 units of perceptual distortion, the simultaneous administration of these doses of marijuana and LSD may induce not 4 but 5 units of perceptual distortion.

83. According to the paragraph, the concurrent presence of two drugs in the body can

    (A) compound the effects of both drugs.
    (B) reduce perceptual distortion.
    (C) simulate psychotic symptoms.
    (D) be highly toxic.

84. On the basis of the paragraph, it is most reasonable to assume that tetrahydrocannabinols are

    (A) habit-forming substances.
    (B) components of marijuana.
    (C) similar to quinine or milk-sugar.
    (D) used as adulterants.

85. Based on the paragraph, it is most reasonable to state that marijuana is

    (A) most affected by adulterants when used as a psychoactive drug.
    (B) erroneously considered to be less harmful than other drugs.
    (C) frequently used in conjunction with other mind-affecting drugs
    (D) occasionally used as an adjunct to LSD in order to reduce bad reactions

For questions 86 through 88, arrange the five sentences into a logical sequence to create your own coherent story.

86. 1. A man crawled across the sand.
    2. A man saw a pool of water in the distance.
    3. A man ran out of gas crossing the desert.
    4. A helicopter pilot spotted a body sprawled in the sand.
    5. A family sent out an alarm for a missing person.

    (A) 3-4-1-2-5
    (B) 5-3-2-1-4
    (C) 3-2-1-5-4
    (D) 4-5-3-2-1

87. 1. Acreage is destroyed.
    2. An airplane sprays the fields.
    3. A crop is planted.
    4. A person is assigned a task.
    5. Seedlings sprout.

    (A) 4-5-2-1-3
    (B) 3-4-5-1-2
    (C) 2-4-3-5-1
    (D) 3-5-4-2-1

88. 1. A person came to investigate.
    2. Witnesses were questioned.
    3. A large crate was missing.
    4. A dog barked.
    5. A green van was sought.

    (A) 5-1-3-2-4
    (B) 4-1-3-2-5
    (C) 4-3-2-5-1
    (D) 3-1-2-5-4

For questions 89 through 96, complete the sentence.

89. The body that was found in the woods smelled so bad that the trooper knew _____.

    (A) it must have been lying there for many days.
    (B) it must have laid there many days.
    (C) it must of lain there for many days.
    (D) it must have layed there for many days.

90. Our training supervisor has more patience _____.

    (A) than any officer on the force.
    (B) then any other training officer in the whole entire place.
    (C) than any training supervisor I ever had on any job.
    (D) than any other officer here.

91. Perhaps we could keep details of our getting lost as a secret _____.

    (A) among you and me.
    (B) between you and I.
    (C) between you and me.
    (D) among the two of us.

92. By May 1, each trooper is expected to hand in _____.

    (A) a schedule of when they want to take vacation.
    (B) his preferred vacation schedule.
    (C) their vacation plans.
    (D) a detailed plan of when they would like to have a vacation.

93. An assignment sometimes handed out as a reward is that of delivering bus-safety lectures to _____ groups.

    (A) childrens
    (B) children's
    (C) childrens'
    (D) childrens's

94. The officer was willing to _____ all of the new working conditions _____ the shift rotation schedule.

    (A) except . . . accept
    (B) accept . . . accept
    (C) accept . . . except
    (D) except . . . except

95. It is bad _____ that _____ of the patrol cars will be out of service when they are needed so badly to control holiday weekend traffic.

    (A) too . . . to
    (B) to . . . two
    (C) too . . . too
    (D) too . . . two

96. _____ should listen to the weather forecast so that _____ may anticipate a heavy snowstorm.

    (A) People . . . one
    (B) One . . . they
    (C) One . . . he
    (D) We . . . one

For questions 97 through 100, choose the best statement of the underlined portion.

97. The suspect fleeing the scene of the crime with a bloody knife in his hand was seized and arrested. While the suspect was in custody, his clothing was searched and one-half ounce of heroin was found in his pockets. <u>The suspect complained that the police did not have a search warrant though the Court will say that a person in custody has no right to expect a privileged privacy of his things.</u>

   (A) The suspect complained that the police did not have a search warrant, but the Court ruled that a person in custody has a diminished expectation of privacy.
   (B) The suspect complained that he had no right of privacy in custody because the police did not have a Court search warrant.
   (C) The Court said that a suspect who complains about his privacy has no right to expect a search warrant in custody.
   (D) Correct as written.

98. Frank questioned the witness about the car that she had seen speeding from the scene. The witness said that the car looked like one of those things you see in war pictures, but it was red. <u>Frank says to the sergeant that the suspect was probably driving a red Jeep.</u>

   (A) The suspect was probably escaping in a red Jeep is what the sergeant hears from Frank.
   (B) The sergeant is being told by Frank that the witness is thinking that she probably saw a red Jeep driving away.
   (C) Frank then told the sergeant that a red Jeep was observed leaving the scene.
   (D) Correct as written.

99. Officers Reiner and Orsini were investigating a report of a man with a gun at the mile 3,580 scenic overlook. They approached a man who seemed to fit the description they were given and asked for identification. <u>Officer Orsini then frisked the man and felt an object in the man's pocket that might have been suspicious.</u>

   (A) Officer Orsini frisks the man and feels an object that makes him very suspicious.
   (B) When Officer Orsini frisked the man, he felt an object that raised his suspicions.
   (C) Then Officer Orsini took to frisking the man and feeling a suspicious feeling object.
   (D) Correct as written.

100. The suspect crashed through a roadblock and was placed under arrest for reckless driving. In the police car, she quickly swallowed the contents of a plastic pouch that she pulled from her pocket. <u>The troopers then drove her directly to a hospital to have her stomach pumped so that they could learn what she had swallowed.</u>

   (A) So the troopers had to take her to the hospital and pump out her stomach so that they could get back for her that what she swallowed.
   (B) The troopers took her to a hospital and arrested her when they pumped out of her stomach what she swallowed.
   (C) So then the troopers have to take her to the hospital and have her stomach pumped so they can arrest her.
   (D) Correct as written.

MODEL EXAMINATION 1: ANSWERS AND EXPLANATIONS

ANSWERS

1.	B	21.	C	41.	D	61.	A	81.	C
2.	C	22.	D	42.	D	62.	B	82.	C
3.	B	23.	A	43.	B	63.	D	83.	A
4.	A	24.	C	44.	C	64.	C	84.	B
5.	D	25.	B	45.	A	65.	C	85.	C
6.	D	26.	B	46.	B	66.	A	86.	C
7.	A	27.	D	47.	D	67.	B	87.	D
8.	B	28.	C	48.	A	68.	D	88.	B
9.	C	29.	A	49.	D	69.	D	89.	A
10.	B	30.	C	50.	B	70.	A	90.	D
11.	D	31.	B	51.	C	71.	D	91.	C
12.	A	32.	D	52.	D	72.	B	92.	B
13.	B	33.	A	53.	B	73.	C	93.	B
14.	D	34.	D	54.	A	74.	A	94.	C
15.	C	35.	D	55.	C	75.	C	95.	D
16.	D	36.	C	56.	A	76.	D	96.	C
17.	A	37.	B	57.	C	77.	A	97.	A
18.	C	38.	C	58.	D	78.	C	98.	C
19.	C	39.	A	59.	C	79.	B	99.	B
20.	B	40.	C	60.	D	80.	A	100.	D

EXPLANATIONS

1. **The correct answer is (B).** If you are driving east and make a U-turn, you will be heading west. A left turn when driving west heads you south.

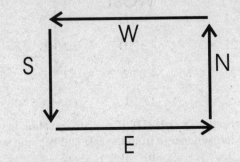

2. **The correct answer is (C).** If you are driving south and make a right turn, you will be heading west. The convoy going in the other direction is going east.

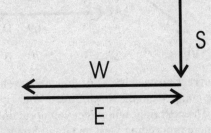

3. **The correct answer is (B).** If you are traveling west, a car approaching from your right is traveling south.

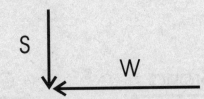

4. **The correct answer is (A).** The car is traveling north. With the first left turn, it is traveling west; with the second left, south; with the third left, east. If the car is headed east, then its right side faces to the south, and the car that hits it is traveling north.

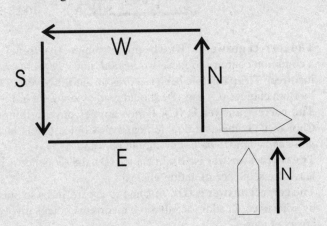

5. **The correct answer is (D).** If you are traveling south, west is on your right.

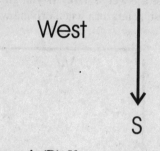

6. **The correct answer is (D).** If you are traveling in a southwesterly direction, the merge on your left is a merge from the east and is going west.

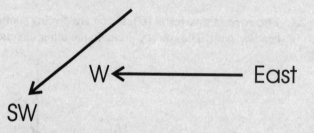

7. **The correct answer is (A).** If you are traveling west on Grand Street and turn left, you will be going south on North Street. Your right turn will have you going west on River Road. The next right will direct you north on Church Street. The next left will have you once more proceeding west on Grand Street.

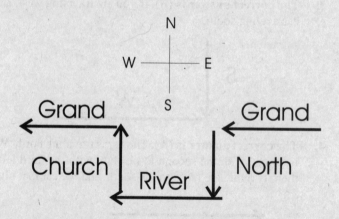

8. **The correct answer is (B).** The proper subjunctive form (the form used for a wish or for a condition contrary to fact) is *if he had*, not *if he would have*. Therefore, choice (A) is incorrect. The participle been requires an auxiliary verb. *Of* is not an auxiliary verb; *had* is. Both choices (C) and (D) should read "would not have been."

9. **The correct answer is (C).** *Which* applies only to things, so choice (A) is incorrect. Choice (B) contains a double negative. Choice (D) is incorrect because the subject of *don't know how to be happy* should be *who*.

10. **The correct answer is (B).** In choice (D), the sequence is reversed. Choices (A) and (C) leave the sequence of action unclear.

11. **The correct answer is (D).** *Talk* and *speak* are verbs so must be modified by adverbs, not by adjectives. In addition, all three incorrect choices involve pretentious construction or errors of tense.

12. **The correct answer is (A).** Choice (B) involves a double negative. In choice (C), *ain't* is an unacceptable word. Choice (D) requires an auxiliary verb; it could also be stated using a simple past tense, as in, "he did nothing wrong."

13. **The correct answer is (B).** Simple is best. Both choices (A) and (C) are awkward, unwieldy constructions. Choice (D) introduces disagreement of noun and pronoun. "Team" is a singular noun even though it includes a number of individuals; the correct pronoun is "it."

14. **The correct answer is (D).** All other choices are awkward.

15. **The correct answer is (C).** The incorrect answers all involve problems with the auxiliary verb.

16. **The correct answer is (D).** Who entered the room? Whose attention was attracted? Only choice (D) makes it clear.

17. **The correct answer is (A).** The opening of the door and the entry of the captain and officer happen at the same time. All other choices mix present and past tenses.

18. **The correct answer is (C).** $42 - 35 = 7$; he is exceeding the speed limit by 7 mph; $7 \div 35 = .20$; 7 is 20% of 35.

19. **The correct answer is (C).** $270 \times 4 = 1080$

20. **The correct answer is (B).** 7 cars + 2 vans + 3 trucks + 1 bus = 13 vehicles involved in the accident; 1 patrol car + 3 ambulances + 2 fire engines + 5 tow trucks + 8 patrol cars = 19 rescue vehicles; $13 + 19 = 32$ vehicles at the scene. 3 tow trucks remove 3 damaged vehicles = 6 vehicles leave. $32 - 6 = 26$ vehicles remain.

21. **The correct answer is (C).** 3 out of service + 4 with other duties = 7 not patrolling. $20 - 7 = 13$ available to patrol. $235 \div 13 = 18$ miles patrolled by each.

22. **The correct answer is (D).** $5,067 - 4,682 = 385$ miles driven. $385 \div 28 = 13.75$ gal.

23. **The correct answer is (A).** $\$2.35 + \$1.00 = \$3.35$ for one long distance plus two in-state calls. $\$5.60 - \$3.35 = \$2.25 \div .75 =$ three more in-state calls. $1 + 2 + 3 = 6 + 2$ free calls = 8 calls in all.

24. **The correct answer is (C).** 42 mph x 1.5 hrs. = 63 miles to the north; 38 mph x 1.5 hrs. = 57 miles to the south; $63 + 57 = 120$ miles apart.

25. **The correct answer is (B).** 9:15 a.m. to noon = 12:00 – 9:15 = 11:60 – 9:15 = 2 hrs. 45 min. Noon to 2:45 p.m. = 2 hrs. 45 min; 2 hrs. 45 min. + 2 hrs. 45 min. = 4 hrs. 90 min. = 5 hrs. 30 min.

26. **The correct answer is (B).** 24 – 5 to the accident – 3 to direct traffic – 2 to the hospital = 14 + 1 captain = 15 officers on hand.

27. **The correct answer is (D).** $8,782 + 3,000 = 11,782$ by which reading car must be serviced. $11,782 - 10,461 = 1,321$ miles Lindner may drive. $1,321 \div 140 = 9.44$ average working days to reach servicing mileage. Car may drive no more than 3,000 miles between servicing, so must be brought in within 9 days.

28. **The correct answer is (C).** 240 miles ÷ 12 gal. = 20 mpg original mileage. 80% of 12 gal. = 12 x .80 = 9.6 gal. 240 miles ÷ 9.6 = 25 mpg; 12 gal. x 25 mpg = 300 miles per 12 gal.

29. **The correct answer is (A).** Calculate percentage over the speed limit by subtracting the speed limit from the speed driven and dividing the difference by the speed limit. Thus, 45 mph in a 40 mph zone is: $45 - 40 = 5$; $5 \div 40 = 12.5\%$. Similarly, 48 mph is 20% over the 40 mph limit, 53 mph is 33.5% over, and both 58 mph and 60 mph are more than 44% over the 40 mph limit. 64 mph is 16.36% over the 55 mph limit (and there were two such tickets), 71.5 mph is 30% over the 55 mph limit, and 85 mph is 54.5% over the 55 mph limit. Totaling up all the speeders and their fines:

1 car exceeding by 12.5%	=	$25
2 cars exceeding by 16.36%	=	$70 ($35 each)
1 car exceeding by 20%	=	$50
1 car exceeding by 30%	=	$100
1 car exceeding by 33.5%	=	$100
3 cars more than 44% over	=	600 ($200 each)
Total fines	=	$945

30. **The correct answer is (C).** N.A. Hales is supervised by F.R. Tuck.
31. **The correct answer is (B).** The oldest employee, R.L. Hill, was born 9/30/30. R.L. Hill is security.
32. **The correct answer is (D).** The oldest trooper, T.J. Bale, was born 6/12/60.
33. **The correct answer is (A).** The person longest employed is the mechanic, P.C. Hill, who was hired 9/2/72.
34. **The correct answer is (D).** F.T. Hals's social security number is 630-98-1234.
35. **The correct answer is (D).** The mechanic's social security number is 987-40-3939.
36. **The correct answer is (C).** July 21 is a Wednesday, and Gino Abate is in group 3. On Wednesday group 3 is in the west quadrant.
37. **The correct answer is (B).** During July group 3 will work in only the north and west quadrants. Jane Shulz is supervisor of group 3.
38. **The correct answer is (C).** Akeel Morris is in group 1 and group 1 reports for training on Monday. July 19 is a Monday.
39. **The correct answer is (A).** July 15 is a Thursday. Group 1 works in the south quadrant on Thursday. The supervisor of group 1 is Jose Primo.
40. **The correct answer is (C).** July 25 is a Sunday. Since Gregor Ozmanian is the training supervisor and no groups are scheduled for training on Sunday, Ozmanian will have the day off.
41. **The correct answer is (D).** July 11 is a Sunday. This particular work schedule does not specify what group is working in the west quadrant on Sunday in July.
42. **The correct answer is (D).** The only restrictive information given with regard to Sgt. Leary is that Leary arrested only male suspects. G. Evans beats his wife, so he is definitely male and might have been arrested by Leary. L. King is a juvenile, gender unspecified. J. Harris is roommate of E. Brown, who is female, but J. Hams may well be a man. Sgt. Leary could have arrested any of these; we can't tell.
43. **The correct answer is (B).** Eliminate: Sgt. Paik arrested no resident of the district of arrest; M. Allen lives in Dale where Paik worked. D. Tramp was arrested for murder. E. Brown was arrested in her home vicinity, which is Arch. There is no reason why Sgt. Paik might not have arrested B. Davis.
44. **The correct answer is (C).** Eliminate: Sgt. Rossi did not arrest any residents of Arch; as roommate of E. Brown who lives in Arch, J. Harris lives in Arch. A. Wilson was carrying a pillowcase containing a fur jacket and silver candlesticks when arrested, most likely for burglary rather than arson. S. Grant was arrested by Sgt. Tomas. There is no reason why Sgt. Rossi might not have arrested L. King on suspicion of arson.
45. **The correct answer is (A).** D. Tramp was arrested for murder. The only arrest for murder on this date was made by Sgt. Blau.
46. **The correct answer is (B).** Sgt. Leary made only one arrest on this date, and the arrest was for arson. It is stated that Sgt. Leary arrested M. Allen, so the charge against Allen must have been arson.
47. **The correct answer is (D).** Mentally hop into the cars and follow the narrative.
48. **The correct answer is (A).** Put yourself into Officer Wood's place and follow the story carefully.

49. **The correct answer is (D).** Choice (A) cannot be correct because 17th Street is one-way southbound. Choice (B) is perfectly legal but includes some extra corner-turns, which make it not the "best" route. Choice (C) is impossible from the outset because Grand Boulevard never intersects Highland Boulevard. Do not waste time looking at the rest of a proposed route once you have found the point at which it become impossible.

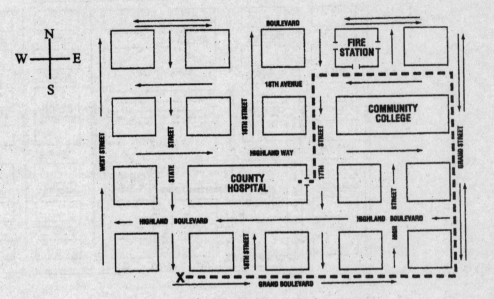

50. **The correct answer is (B).** Choice (A) is entirely legal, but it is unnecessarily long and roundabout. Choice (C) starts out going north on a one-way southbound street. Choice (D) is physically impossible because the hospital intervenes, making it impossible to go from Highland Boulevard to Boulevard on 18th Street.

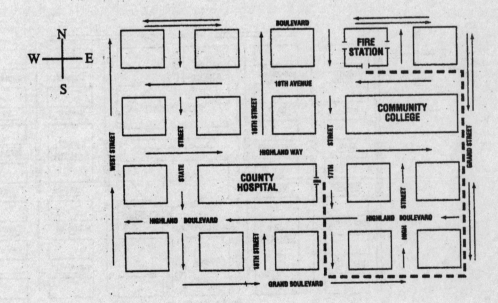

51. **The correct answer is (C).** Choice (A) is impossible because Andersen Avenue does not go through to Long Pond Road. Choice (B) involves going the wrong way on one-way Roosevelt. Choice (D) is not illegal, but is a much longer route than that recommended in choice (C).

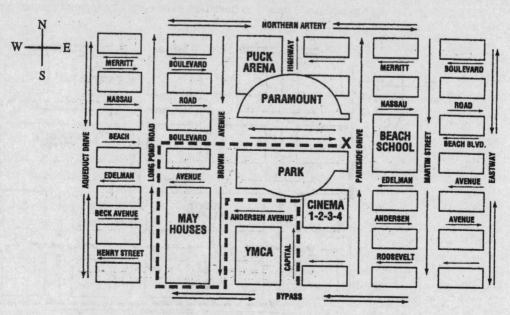

52. **The correct answer is (D).** Choice (A) is incorrect because Merritt Boulevard is a two-way street only on the west side of Puck Arena; from Puck Arena one cannot go east on Merritt Boulevard. Andersen Avenue between Brown Avenue and Cinema 1-2-3-4 is a west-bound street making choice (B) incorrect. As for choice (C), Capital Highway does not go through the park.

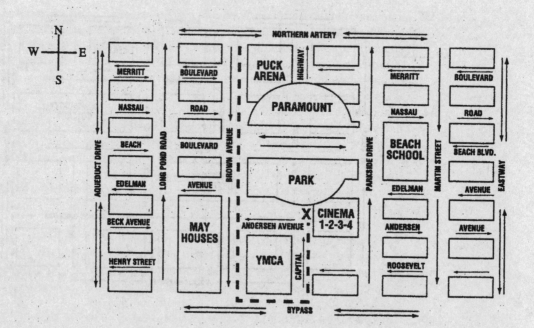

53. **The correct answer is (B).** Choices (A) and (C) both miscode Robert Stone's name. Choice (D) offers 1943 as a birth year; a person born that year could not have been in elementary school.

54. **The correct answer is (A).** Eighty-six inches is 7 ft. 2 in. This tall person should stand out in a crowd.

55. **The correct answer is (C).** No one can have a birthdate of February 30.

56. **The correct answer is (A).** Forty inches is 3 ft. 4. in. A person of this height must have a specially equipped automobile.

57. **The correct answer is (C).** A person born in 1988 is too young to have a driver's license; a person born in 1888 is too old.

58. **The correct answer is (D).** Choice (A) reverses first and last names; the height of 7 ft. 6 in. is unusual but not impossible. In choice (B), the letter "D" is miscoded. In choice (C) the year '95 must refer to 1995 because the person is only 2 ft. 2 in. tall; a person born in 1895 could still have a driver's license, but a person born in 1995 is too young.

59. **The correct answer is (C).** The driver has turned onto Route 44, so the top center number must be 44; eliminate choice (A). The driver does not make a U-turn, so the next intersecting route cannot be the Route 13 from which he has just turned; eliminate choice (B). Route 44 cannot intersect itself, so choice (D) cannot be correct.

60. **The correct answer is (D).** The number that designates the county has changed; the traveler has crossed a county line. The number that indicates distance traveled along the highway has increased by 6 while the number that indicates distance remaining along this highway has decreased by 6; the traveler has driven 6 miles.

61. **The correct answer is (A).** The trooper has made a U-turn. The trooper is still on Route 112, but the order of the locations between which mileage is calculated has been reversed. Distance is now being calculated from locality 36 to locality 21, whereas on the earlier marker it was calculated from locality 21 to locality 36.

62. **The correct answer is (B).** If he had made a number of turns and returned to Route 76, the beginning and end points of Route 76 would still be the same, so eliminate choice (A). In choice (C) the route on which the motorist is traveling runs between the same two cities as the original route, but the distance between them is vastly greater; this cannot be. A highway cannot intersect itself, as in choice (D).

63. **The correct answer is (D).** We can be certain only that the officer traveled 50 miles, so eliminate choice (A). We know for certain only that the officer crossed at least one county line; county lines do not run in order. The officer may have made any number of U-turns, but we have no way of knowing. The officer is traveling in the same direction on the same highway, but the next intersection has a different number, so the officer must at least have crossed Route 80.

64. **The correct answer is (C).** Answer this question by simple elimination. The car definitely did cross a county line, travel at least 32 miles, and make a U-turn. One right turn could not head the car in the opposite direction on the same highway.

65. **The correct answer is (C).** Just follow along letter for letter and number for number to find the only possible answer meeting all requirements.

66. **The correct answer is (A).** Neither choice (B) nor choice (D) is possible because station wagons are not assembled on Saturdays or on third shifts. Choice (C) is impossible because prototypes must have diesel engines.

67. **The correct answer is (B).** The first letter, B, identifies a 1989 model; the fourth letter, A, identifies this 1989 car as a 2dr sedan, either a Pacer or a Canter.

68. **The correct answer is (D).** The year of a prototype is irrelevant, so eliminate choice (A). All prototypes have diesel engines, so eliminate choice (B). Diesels are made only in Detroit, so eliminate choice (C).

69. **The correct answer is (D).** This car is a 4dr sedan, not a prototype, with a 3.91 gasoline engine.

70. **The correct answer is (A).** Eliminate choice (B) because diesel engines are not made in Gary. Eliminate choice (C) because vans are not made in Toledo. Eliminate choice (D) because vans are not assembled on Saturday or on third shifts.

71. **The correct answer is (D).** The Thursday slot at 4:00 p.m. is a time for the common room to be left vacant or to be used by scheduled trooper activities. A. CPR class clearly is a scheduled use. Choice (B) is also wrong because use of the common room for regular weekly meetings is not permitted.

72. **The correct answer is (B).** If Officer Carroll had asked at least twenty days in advance, he would have gotten the common room for his christening, but he waited too long. In the order of priorities, youth groups take precedence over senior citizens and social groups. Since the Boy Scouts' application covered both dates requested at the same time by other legitimate groups, the Boy Scouts preempted both the seniors' tax clinic and the square dance.

73. **The correct answer is (C).** A single trooper requesting the use of the common room may have the cleanup fee deducted from a paycheck, but a group should take up a collection and pay in advance of the event. The bond is required only of outside groups, and no one is exempt from the cleanup fee.

74. **The correct answer is (A).** Women troopers may use the locker room any time they may use the pool. Trooper swim is from 6:00 a.m. to 7:30 a.m. on Tuesday, running into free general swim from 7:30 a.m. to 9:00 a.m. Women troopers may also swim at the "women-only" session from 4:00 p.m. to 6:00 p.m. on Sunday. 1:00 p.m. to 3:00 p.m. on Sunday is "men only." The general swim on Thursday does not begin until 7:30 a.m. There is no swim for which troopers are eligible after 8:00 p.m. on Thursday.

75. **The correct answer is (C).** Wednesday from 8:00 p.m. to 9:30 p.m. is free swim for the general public. Troopers never have access to weight room or gym in the evening.

76. **The correct answer is (D).** The pool is not open to troopers at 6:00 a.m. on Thursday. The gym, weight room, and track are all available.

77. **The correct answer is (A).** The employee sends two copies of Form MV-104 to the Safety Division, which sends both copies to the Corporation Counsel. The Corporation Counsel, in turn, sends one copy to the State Bureau of Motor Vehicles.

78. **The correct answer is (C).** The Safety Division investigates only when the employee appears to have been at fault.

79. **The correct answer is (B).** The dispatcher files the complaint form, Form D-11. The accident report form is filed by the employee, and both the damage report and the estimate of cost of repairs are filed by the foreman of mechanics.

80. **The correct answer is (A).** Revenge was the approach prior to the first revolution.

81. **The correct answer is (C).** The second revolution focused attention upon the mental and emotional makeup of the offender, that is, the offender's inner feelings.

82. **The correct answer is (C).** If society is still ambivalent about the offender, society's correctional goals are not fully defined. Hence, the third revolution may be premature.

83. **The correct answer is (A).** "The simultaneous presence of two or more drugs in the body can exert effects that are more than would result from the simple addition of the effect of each drug used separately."

84. **The correct answer is (B).** Adulterants interact with tetrahydrocannabinols, so tetrahydrocannabinols must be components of marijuana.

85. **The correct answer is (C).** The whole point of the passage is to discuss the problems created by the practice of using marijuana along with other mind-affecting drugs.

86. **The correct answer is (C).** 3-2-1-5-4

    The story must begin with the man's running out of gas as he drove across the desert. Getting out of his car, he was deluded by a mirage; he thought he saw water in the distance. He began walking toward the illusory water, eventually becoming so dehydrated that he fell to his knees and crawled. When his family finally missed him, they sent out an alarm and a highway patrol search helicopter was dispatched. By the time the helicopter pilot spotted him, it was too late.

87. **The correct answer is (D).** 3-5-4-2-1

    A crop of a substance that is grown to produce illegal drugs (probably marijuana) is planted. Seedlings sprout. At this point someone recognizes the growing crop and alerts the state police. The captain assigns a pilot the task of eliminating this crop. The pilot flies over the fields spraying them with a substance that is toxic to the plants, thereby destroying the acreage.

88. **The correct answer is (B).** 4-1-3-2-5

    A dog, presumably a watch dog, barked. The dog's barking alerted a man, probably a watchman, to investigate. The watchman discovered that a large crate was missing. Clearly the dog's barking was in response to a burglary. Upon questioning, a witness mentioned seeing a green van at the site, so a green van was sought.

89. **The correct answer is (A).** *Laid* is a form of the verb *to lay*, but what we need here is a form of the verb *to lie*. The requisite auxiliary verb is *have*, not *of. Layed* is an altogether incorrect form.

90. **The correct answer is (D).** Since the training supervisor is already on the force, the comparison must be completed by making it clear that the supervisor has more patience that *any other*. Choice (B) answers this problem but is wordy and redundant.

91. **The correct answer is (C).** Since we are only two, the correct term is *between* rather than among. Between is a preposition that must be followed by the objective *me*.

92. **The correct answer is (B).** Each trooper is one person; the pronoun must be singular.

93. **The correct answer is (B).** *Children* is a plural noun that forms the possessive by adding "apostrophe *s*."

94. **The correct answer is (C).** *Accept* means "agree to." *Except* means "but."

95. **The correct answer is (D).** *Too* means "extremely." *Two* stands for the number 2. *To* refers to "going toward," which does not apply in this sentence.

96. **The correct answer is (C).** In order to maintain parallelism within the sentence, both blanks must be filled with words of the same number. In choices (A) and (D), the first word is plural and the second is singular. In choice (B), the first word is singular and the second is plural. In choice (C), both *one* and *he* are singular.

97. **The correct answer is (A).** Read carefully. None of the other choices really makes sense.

98. **The correct answer is (C).** The first two sentences of the paragraph are written in the past tense. The third sentence must continue in the past tense.

99. **The correct answer is (B).** In the original, the object itself was feeling suspicious. Obviously, it is the trooper who felt suspicious, not the object. Choice (A) shifts into the present tense. (C) is too colloquial and is poorly written.

100. **The correct answer is (D).** The troopers had already arrested the woman, so you can eliminate choices (B) and (C) without considering any mistakes other than simple sequence of events. choice (A) is grammatically incorrect (that what); the stated purpose is also not reasonable in context with the first two sentences.

MODEL EXAMINATION 2: ANSWER SHEET

1. Ⓐ Ⓑ Ⓒ Ⓓ   21. Ⓐ Ⓑ Ⓒ Ⓓ   41. Ⓐ Ⓑ Ⓒ Ⓓ   61. Ⓐ Ⓑ Ⓒ Ⓓ   81. Ⓐ Ⓑ Ⓒ Ⓓ
2. Ⓐ Ⓑ Ⓒ Ⓓ   22. Ⓐ Ⓑ Ⓒ Ⓓ   42. Ⓐ Ⓑ Ⓒ Ⓓ   62. Ⓐ Ⓑ Ⓒ Ⓓ   82. Ⓐ Ⓑ Ⓒ Ⓓ
3. Ⓐ Ⓑ Ⓒ Ⓓ   23. Ⓐ Ⓑ Ⓒ Ⓓ   43. Ⓐ Ⓑ Ⓒ Ⓓ   63. Ⓐ Ⓑ Ⓒ Ⓓ   83. Ⓐ Ⓑ Ⓒ Ⓓ
4. Ⓐ Ⓑ Ⓒ Ⓓ   24. Ⓐ Ⓑ Ⓒ Ⓓ   44. Ⓐ Ⓑ Ⓒ Ⓓ   64. Ⓐ Ⓑ Ⓒ Ⓓ   84. Ⓐ Ⓑ Ⓒ Ⓓ
5. Ⓐ Ⓑ Ⓒ Ⓓ   25. Ⓐ Ⓑ Ⓒ Ⓓ   45. Ⓐ Ⓑ Ⓒ Ⓓ   65. Ⓐ Ⓑ Ⓒ Ⓓ   85. Ⓐ Ⓑ Ⓒ Ⓓ
6. Ⓐ Ⓑ Ⓒ Ⓓ   26. Ⓐ Ⓑ Ⓒ Ⓓ   46. Ⓐ Ⓑ Ⓒ Ⓓ   66. Ⓐ Ⓑ Ⓒ Ⓓ   86. Ⓐ Ⓑ Ⓒ Ⓓ
7. Ⓐ Ⓑ Ⓒ Ⓓ   27. Ⓐ Ⓑ Ⓒ Ⓓ   47. Ⓐ Ⓑ Ⓒ Ⓓ   67. Ⓐ Ⓑ Ⓒ Ⓓ   87. Ⓐ Ⓑ Ⓒ Ⓓ
8. Ⓐ Ⓑ Ⓒ Ⓓ   28. Ⓐ Ⓑ Ⓒ Ⓓ   48. Ⓐ Ⓑ Ⓒ Ⓓ   68. Ⓐ Ⓑ Ⓒ Ⓓ   88. Ⓐ Ⓑ Ⓒ Ⓓ
9. Ⓐ Ⓑ Ⓒ Ⓓ   29. Ⓐ Ⓑ Ⓒ Ⓓ   49. Ⓐ Ⓑ Ⓒ Ⓓ   69. Ⓐ Ⓑ Ⓒ Ⓓ   89. Ⓐ Ⓑ Ⓒ Ⓓ
10. Ⓐ Ⓑ Ⓒ Ⓓ   30. Ⓐ Ⓑ Ⓒ Ⓓ   50. Ⓐ Ⓑ Ⓒ Ⓓ   70. Ⓐ Ⓑ Ⓒ Ⓓ   90. Ⓐ Ⓑ Ⓒ Ⓓ
11. Ⓐ Ⓑ Ⓒ Ⓓ   31. Ⓐ Ⓑ Ⓒ Ⓓ   51. Ⓐ Ⓑ Ⓒ Ⓓ   71. Ⓐ Ⓑ Ⓒ Ⓓ   91. Ⓐ Ⓑ Ⓒ Ⓓ
12. Ⓐ Ⓑ Ⓒ Ⓓ   32. Ⓐ Ⓑ Ⓒ Ⓓ   52. Ⓐ Ⓑ Ⓒ Ⓓ   72. Ⓐ Ⓑ Ⓒ Ⓓ   92. Ⓐ Ⓑ Ⓒ Ⓓ
13. Ⓐ Ⓑ Ⓒ Ⓓ   33. Ⓐ Ⓑ Ⓒ Ⓓ   53. Ⓐ Ⓑ Ⓒ Ⓓ   73. Ⓐ Ⓑ Ⓒ Ⓓ   93. Ⓐ Ⓑ Ⓒ Ⓓ
14. Ⓐ Ⓑ Ⓒ Ⓓ   34. Ⓐ Ⓑ Ⓒ Ⓓ   54. Ⓐ Ⓑ Ⓒ Ⓓ   74. Ⓐ Ⓑ Ⓒ Ⓓ   94. Ⓐ Ⓑ Ⓒ Ⓓ
15. Ⓐ Ⓑ Ⓒ Ⓓ   35. Ⓐ Ⓑ Ⓒ Ⓓ   55. Ⓐ Ⓑ Ⓒ Ⓓ   75. Ⓐ Ⓑ Ⓒ Ⓓ   95. Ⓐ Ⓑ Ⓒ Ⓓ
16. Ⓐ Ⓑ Ⓒ Ⓓ   36. Ⓐ Ⓑ Ⓒ Ⓓ   56. Ⓐ Ⓑ Ⓒ Ⓓ   76. Ⓐ Ⓑ Ⓒ Ⓓ   96. Ⓐ Ⓑ Ⓒ Ⓓ
17. Ⓐ Ⓑ Ⓒ Ⓓ   37. Ⓐ Ⓑ Ⓒ Ⓓ   57. Ⓐ Ⓑ Ⓒ Ⓓ   77. Ⓐ Ⓑ Ⓒ Ⓓ   97. Ⓐ Ⓑ Ⓒ Ⓓ
18. Ⓐ Ⓑ Ⓒ Ⓓ   38. Ⓐ Ⓑ Ⓒ Ⓓ   58. Ⓐ Ⓑ Ⓒ Ⓓ   78. Ⓐ Ⓑ Ⓒ Ⓓ   98. Ⓐ Ⓑ Ⓒ Ⓓ
19. Ⓐ Ⓑ Ⓒ Ⓓ   39. Ⓐ Ⓑ Ⓒ Ⓓ   59. Ⓐ Ⓑ Ⓒ Ⓓ   79. Ⓐ Ⓑ Ⓒ Ⓓ   99. Ⓐ Ⓑ Ⓒ Ⓓ
20. Ⓐ Ⓑ Ⓒ Ⓓ   40. Ⓐ Ⓑ Ⓒ Ⓓ   60. Ⓐ Ⓑ Ⓒ Ⓓ   80. Ⓐ Ⓑ Ⓒ Ⓓ   100. Ⓐ Ⓑ Ⓒ Ⓓ

MODEL EXAMINATION 2

MEMORY BOOKLET

> **Directions:** You will be given 10 minutes to study the scene that follows and to try to notice and remember as many details as you can. You may not take any notes during this time.

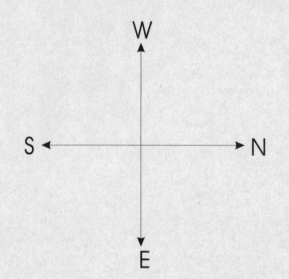

MODEL EXAMINATION 2

TEST QUESTION BOOKLET

TIME: 3 HOURS—100 QUESTIONS

> **Directions**: Now that the Memory Booklets have been collected, you have 3 hours in which to answer the test questions. Questions 1 to 10 are based on the scene that you just studied. Answer these questions first. Then proceed directly to the remaining 90 questions. Choose the best answer to each question and mark its letter on your answer sheet.

Answer questions 1 through 10 on the basis of the scene in the memory booklet.

1. The car that is on fire is

    (A)   on the southbound shoulder.
    (B)   upended.
    (C)   partly off the road.
    (D)   the private car closest to the ambulance.

2. How many people appear to be seriously injured?

    (A)   None
    (B)   Two
    (C)   Four
    (D)   Six

3. The people in the right-hand southbound lane who are not state troopers are

    (A)   sitting in the roadway.
    (B)   looking at the accident scene.
    (C)   standing on the shoulder.
    (D)   standing in the roadway.

4. The fire engine is

    (A)   approaching from the north.
    (B)   putting out the fire.
    (C)   crossing the divider.
    (D)   in front of the ambulance.

5. The number of state troopers on the scene who have gotten out of their cars is

    (A)   3
    (B)   5
    (C)   6
    (D)   7

6. The passenger car that is not in the roadway is

    (A)   on fire.
    (B)   on the divider.
    (C)   touching another car.
    (D)   upside down.

7. The vehicles in the left lane, southbound are

    (A)   a fire engine and a police car.
    (B)   two passenger cars.
    (C)   a fire engine, a police car, and two passenger cars.
    (D)   a police car and two passenger cars.

8. What are the people on the divider side doing?
   (A) They are sitting.
   (B) They are standing.
   (C) Some are sitting, some are standing.
   (D) There are no people on the divider.

9. This accident happened
   (A) at night.
   (B) at high noon.
   (C) in the afternoon.
   (D) in the morning.

10. Among the southbound cars are
    (A) a tanker truck, a bus, and three motorcycles.
    (B) a large double trailer, a tanker truck, and two motorcycles.
    (C) a tow truck, a car transport, a large double trailer, and a tanker truck.
    (D) two large trailer trucks, a tanker truck, and a motorcycle.

Questions 11 and 12 are based on the following scenario.

You are a highway patrol officer traveling north in the right lane on Route 75 at 50 mph. You have driven exactly 5 miles when a speeding car passes on your left, swerves around you, and speeds right on intersecting County Road 34. You broadcast alerts to the police departments of towns near which Road 34 passes, turn to follow, and accelerate to 90 mph in pursuit of the speeding car. Fifteen minutes later the cloud of dust that you have been following turns to the right, loses control, and smashes into a tree. You are at the scene of the accident in seconds.

11. In what direction was the speeding car traveling when it lost control?
    (A) North
    (B) South
    (C) East
    (D) West

12. About how many miles have you driven in pursuit?
    (A) 15
    (B) 20
    (C) 24
    (D) 28

Questions 13 and 14 are based on the following procedure.
When making a highway stop for any reason, highway patrol officers must take the following steps in the prescribed order:

1. Request the operator's driver's license and registration certificate.

2. Compare picture and information on license with the operator at the wheel.

3. Compare information on the registration with vehicle and with operator information.

4. If operator is not owner, ask for explanation.

5. Scan interior of car for suspicious objects or occupants.

6. Ask operator to step out of car; pat for weapons; conduct sobriety test by asking operator to walk straight line.

7. For routine violation by sober driver, issue summons.

8. If outcome of any step is unsatisfactory, request backup assistance to take operator into custody.

13. State Highway Patrol Officer Hellman traveling east notices a westbound car with one headlight burned out. Officer Hellman makes a U-turn, overtakes the offending car, and pulls it over. Hellman asks the operator for license and registration. The operator is a 17-year-old young man and the license he presents is clearly his. The registration is in the name of a woman with a different surname. Officer Hellman asks for an explanation, and the young man says that the car belongs to his mother who is remarried. Officer Hellman should now

    (A) issue a summons because the car has only one headlight
    (B) ask the driver to step out of the car to test his sobriety
    (C) scan the interior of the car for suspicious objects
    (D) call for backup so the young man can be taken into custody for driving a car not his own

14. State Trooper Malone follows a car that is weaving back and forth over two lanes and even over the double yellow line. Malone then signals that the car should pull to the side. When the driver rolls down the window, Trooper Malone is struck with the strong odor of marijuana from the smoke-filled car. The three passengers in the car are all smoking. Trooper Malone asks the driver to step out of the car to prove that he is not high on drugs.

    This action by Malone is
    (A) correct; the driver was operating the car as if he were drunk.
    (B) incorrect; Malone should have called for assistance to take the driver and marijuana-smoking passengers into custody.
    (C) correct; the suspicious objects and passengers in the car were obvious.
    (D) incorrect; he should have first asked to see driver's license and registration.

15. Taxes are deducted each pay period from the amount of salaries or wages, including payments for overtime, that is paid to law enforcement personnel in excess of the withholding exemptions allowed under the Internal Revenue Act. The amount of tax to be withheld from each payment of wages to any employee will be determined from the current official table of pay and withholding exemptions to be found on page 32 of the employee manual.

    The paragraph best supports the statement that salaries of law enforcement personnel
    (A) do not include overtime.
    (B) are determined by provisions of the Internal Revenue Act.
    (C) are paid from tax revenues.
    (D) are subject to tax deductions.

16. A state police officer attempting to extract information from a witness should not ask questions that can be answered by a "yes" or "no." An officer is interviewing a witness to a car accident that resulted in serious injury to two people. The officer has reason to believe that the car involved went through an intersection against the light. Of the following, the proper question for the officer to ask the witness would be:

    (A) Did you see the car go through a red light?
    (B) Can you recall if the light turned red before the car went through the intersection?
    (C) What color was the light at the time the car went through the intersection?
    (D) Was the light red when the car went through the intersection?

17. State Trooper Cato has just assisted the victim of a hit-and-run accident. He has seen the victim safely removed by ambulance, has broadcast a description of the vehicle, and has made these notes in his memo book:

Location: intersection of Route 3 and Main Street
Occurrence: hit-and-run accident
Victim: elderly black woman, unconscious
Witness: Mary Clark of 323 North State Road
Vehicle: red sports car with Nevada license plates
Response by: Highland Hospital ambulance #l; driver: Barry Brown; EMT: Bill Briggs

Trooper Cato must file a report about this incident as part of his daily activity log. Which of the following expresses the information most clearly, accurately, and completely?

(A) A red sports car from Nevada killed an old black lady in front of Mary Clark of 323 North State Road. Barry Brown and Bill Briggs picked her up in ambulance #l.

(B) Mary Clark of 323 North State Road reported that an elderly black woman was hit by a red sports car at the intersection of Main Street and Route 3. Ambulance #1 with Barry Brown driving and Bill Briggs, EMT, responded and took the unconscious victim to Highland Hospital.

(C) An old black woman was hit by Mary Clark in a red sports car from Nevada at 323 North State Road. Highland Hospital ambulance #1 took her away with Barry Brown and Bill Briggs in attendance.

(D) Mary Clark was hit by an elderly black woman at the intersection of Route 3 and Main Street. The red sports car was from Nevada, and the ambulance was Highland Hospital #1 driven by Barry Brown and Bill. Briggs.

18. The service plaza serving both directions on the thruway is on the east shoulder of the northbound lanes. A car traveling southbound may gain entry to this service plaza by making a right turn onto a feeder road that loops around, crosses the highway, and merges with the cars on the feeder entered by cars making a right turn from the northbound lanes. Cars wishing to park in the lot of the service plaza proceed straight ahead from the feeder into the lot. Cars that need gasoline make a left turn before the entrance to the parking lot and then a right turn into the gasoline service lines. When a car that had been traveling southbound arrives at a gasoline pump, in what direction is it facing?

(A) North
(B) South
(C) East
(D) West

19. Detectives assigned to investigate violent crimes with no obvious motive and no apparent witnesses must direct their whole effort toward success in their work. If they wish to succeed in such investigations, their work will be by no means easy, smooth, or peaceful; on the contrary, they will have to devote themselves completely and continuously to a task that requires all their ability.

The paragraph best supports the statement that an investigator's success depends most upon

(A) persistence in the face of difficulty.
(B) training and experience.
(C) superior ability.
(D) ambition to advance rapidly in rank.

20. A state trooper should not ask leading questions, that is, questions that suggest the answer that the officer desires. A state trooper arrives at the scene of an accident that involved a red car and a green car. It would be proper for the officer to ask a witness to the accident:

    (A) "You observed the red car hit the green car, didn't you?"
    (B) "Did you see the green car hit the red car?"
    (C) "The red car caused the accident, didn't it?"
    (D) "Just what caused the accident between the red car and the green car?"

21. Toll charges on a certain toll road are roughly calculated on the basis of two cents per mile per axle. A ten-wheeler that enters the toll road at mile 75 and exits at mile 130 will pay a total toll of

    (A) $1.10
    (B) $2.20
    (C) $3.30
    (D) $5.50

22. State Police Officer Rescigno is investigating a shoe store break-in at the Eastview Mall. The break-in evidently had occurred during the previous night. She compiles the following information:

    Location: Manny's Shoes and Boots, first floor, west wing, Eastview Mall
    Incident: burglary
    Date of event: night of Tuesday, May 3 to Wednesday, May 4
    Time of event: between 9:40 p.m. and 8:15 a.m.
    Reporter: Manny Monroe, owner, of 350 Main Street, East Hills
    Damage: broken window; empty cash register

    Officer Rescigno must write a report of this incident for follow-up. Which of the following expresses the information most clearly, accurately, and completely?

    (A) Manny Monroe of 350 Main Street, East Hills, reports that his Manny's Shoes and Boots located at Eastview Mall on the first floor of the west wing was broken into between 9:40 p.m., May 3, and 8:15 a.m., May 4. Contents of the cash register are missing.
    (B) Manny Monroe had a burglary between closing on May 3 and opening May 4. He got a broken window and they emptied the cash register and took his money.
    (C) Manny's Shoes and Boots on the first floor of the west wing of Eastview Mall had a burglary at night on May 3rd. They broke a window and took the money.
    (D) Manny's Shoes and Boots was burgled through a broken window on the first floor of Eastview Mall's west wing during the night May 3–4. The burglars took everything out of the cash register. Mr. Monroe lives at 350 Main Street, East Hills, and keeps the store open from 8:15 a.m. to 9:40 p.m.

23. Highway Patrol Officer Patel answers a motorist's request for directions by telling the motorist to: "Proceed south, as you are now headed, for two blocks; turn right at the traffic light and, at the next intersection, turn right again. Immediately after you see a gas station on your right, make a left turn and go one block. The post office is in the strip mall on your left." In what direction will the car be traveling when the motorist reaches his destination?

    (A) North
    (B) South
    (C) East
    (D) West

24. State troopers often respond to the scene of traffic accidents involving two vehicles. In situations in which one of the drivers involved in the accident has left the scene before the arrival of a trooper, the responding trooper must use the following procedures in the order given:

   1. Question the driver of the remaining vehicle as to the license plate number of the vehicle that fled.

   a. If the complete license plate number is known, call Vehicle Inquiry Section to determine name and address of owner.

   b. Write down name and address of owner of vehicle that fled.

   c. Give name and address of owner of vehicle that fled to driver remaining at scene of accident.

   2. Obtain from driver remaining at scene all details of accident, including description of vehicle that fled.

   3. Call Stolen Vehicle Desk.

   4. Prepare Complaint Form in duplicate.

State Trooper Yoshida has arrived at the scene of a traffic accident involving two cars. One of the drivers fled the scene immediately after the impact, but the driver of the remaining vehicle, Myra Lamonica, did notice that the last three digits of the license plate were 7-9-7, and she gives this information to Trooper Yoshida. Which one of the following actions should Trooper Yoshida take next?

(A) Call the Vehicle Inquiry Section to determine name and address of owner.
(B) Call the Stolen Vehicle Desk.
(C) Write down the name and address of Myra Lamonica.
(D) Ask Lamonica for a description of the other car and for details of the accident.

25. Of the following, the most grammatical and precise sentence is:

(A) Speed limits do not know about road and weather conditions so you should not always be guided by them.
(B) Consider road and weather conditions and modify your driving speed accordingly.
(C) Road and weather conditions can change speed limits.
(D) Driving at the posted speed limit should be slowed down by bad road and weather conditions.

Answer questions 26 and 27 ors the basis of the following procedure.
When speaking to a traffic violator, a highway patrol officer should adhere to the following:

1. Use the words "Sir" or "Ma'am" until you get to know the name of the violator; then the use of Mr. Jones or Ms. Smith is proper.

2. Advise the driver of the violation he or she has committed.

3. Do not argue with the motorist.

4. Be impersonal in your conversation; do not mention yourself.

5. Do not be critical of the motorist

26. Officer Thomas stops a motorist for speeding. The officer approaches the car, and the driver says, "I haven't done anything wrong. Why did you stop me?" An appropriate reply from Officer Thomas would be

(A) "I stopped you for speeding."
(B) "Buddy, you were speeding to a fire."

(C) "Sir, you were exceeding the speed limit."

(D) "Sir, I know exactly how fast you were going. You were speeding."

27. Officer Provo stops a motorist because of erratic driving on a busy highway. The motorist had come close to hitting several cars. The motorist extends his license to the officer, who notes his name as being William Doran. The motorist asks the officer why he was stopped, declaring that he was not driving too fast. Officer Provo calmly says, "Mr. Doran, you are a lousy driver." Officer Provo's statement to the motorist is

(A) improper; the officer should first ask the motorist how much he has had to drink.

(B) proper; the officer is being truthful.

(C) improper; the officer is criticizing the motorist.

(D) proper; the officer is using the motorist's name respectfully.

28. Choose the most logical order of the sentences to create a coherent story.

1. The officer asked the witness if his brother had been drinking.
2. The witness angrily replied that his brother was sober.
3. A highway patrol officer on the scene was interviewing the witness to a serious car accident.
4. The accident had resulted in the death of the witness's brother, driver of one of the vehicles.

(A) 3-4-1-2

(B) 3-1-2-4

(C) 4-3-1-2

(D) 1-2-3-4

29. State troopers must be trained in the safe and efficient operation of motor vehicles. Principles and techniques are thoroughly explained in the classroom before students are allowed to participate in the actual performance of practical exercises. Under close supervision and guidance, the students train until they recognize their personal limitations as well as limitations of the vehicle. The training curriculum should include courses in: highway response, defensive driving, skid control, transportation of prisoners, pursuit driving, evasive maneuver driving techniques, and accident investigation.

The paragraph best supports the statement that

(A) it is important for police officers to understand the principles of motor vehicle operation.

(B) the training curriculum is specific to the special requirements of police driving.

(C) state troopers have personal limitations so must be closely supervised.

(D) vehicle maintenance is an important part of police driver training.

30. A highway patrol officer pulls into a gas station at an easy-off/easy-on location parallel to the highway and discovers a holdup in progress. When he identifies himself as a law officer, the robber takes off at high speed and reenters the highway. The officer gives chase. They proceed west on the highway for 3 miles. Then they make a right turn off the highway onto a secondary road for another mile and a half, and then turn left onto a dirt road. Driving at high speed on the dirt road, the holdup man's car develops a flat tire. The man jumps out of the driver's seat and runs directly into the woods. The highway patrol officer follows on foot, but loses sight of his suspect. The officer then turns around and runs back to his car to radio for assistance. In what direction is he running?

(A) North

(B) South

(C) East

(D) West

31. State Police Officer vanNess on routine highway patrol on the Cross River Bridge notices a car pulled to the side of the bridge with the driver's door open, motor running, and no one inside. She quickly radios for help and jumps from her patrol car. She finds a young Hispanic man clinging to the underside of the bridge, grabs him by both hands, and waits for backup. Officer vanNess attempts to question and reason with the man, but the man speaks no English. Before backups arrive, another motorist pulls up and asks if he can be of assistance. The motorist, while not fluent, knows enough Spanish to keep the man engaged until assistance arrives. Officer vanNess jots the following notes in her memo book:

    Location: mid-span, southbound shoulder, Cross River Bridge
    Time: 3:40 p.m.
    Event: threatened suicide
    Description: 23-year-old Hispanic male, slight build, about 5 ft. 8 in., primary language Spanish, wearing denim cutoffs, gray tank top, and canvas sneakers. Name not revealed. Individual's wife just left him, taking baby.
    Assisting bystander: James Hogan of 381 Baird Boulevard, North City, CT

    Having transported the individual to the county hospital, Officer vanNess must prepare a report to enter into her activity record and to transmit to psychiatrists who will examine and treat the threatened suicide. Which of the following expresses the information most clearly, accurately, and completely?

    (A) A 23-year-old Hispanic male whose wife left him speaking Spanish tried to jump off the Cross River Bridge at 3:40 p.m. James Hogan talked him out of it wearing denim cutoffs, gray tank top, and canvas sneakers.

    (B) A 23-year-old Spanish-speaking male wearing denim cutoffs, gray tank top, and canvas sneakers is 5 ft. 8 in. and has a slight build. His wife and baby left him and he won't tell us his name. He wanted to jump off the Cross River Bridge but James Hogan told him not to at 381 Baird Boulevard, North City, CT.

    (C) At 3:40 p.m., James Hogan and I convinced an unidentified 23-year-old Hispanic male, about 5 ft. 8 in., slightly built, and wearing denim cutoffs, gray tank top, and canvas sneakers, not to jump from the middle of the Cross River Bridge.

    (D) At 3:40 p.m., an unidentified 23-year-old Hispanic male, about 5 ft. 8 in., slightly built, wearing denim cutoffs, gray tank top, and canvas sneakers, threatened to jump from the south side of the Cross River Bridge. A Spanish-speaking motorist, James Hogan of 381 Baird Boulevard, North City, CT, learned that his wife had just left him and stopped him from jumping.

32. State troopers assigned to patrol in a radio car are instructed to adhere to the following rules concerning the use of the police radios in patrol cars:
    1. The use of the radio is to be restricted to performance of duty only.
    2. All conversations should be to the point and as short as possible.
    3. Names of people are not to be used.
    4. All conversations should begin by identifying the vehicle by number.
    5. A message received is to be acknowledged by "ten-four."

    State Troopers Abel and Flynn apprehend two men in the act of stealing a stereo tape and disc player from a car in a service area parking lot. They place the men in their car—car 14—and radio in a report of the activity. Which one of the following messages would conform to the procedure specified?

    (A) "Officers Abel and Flynn, car one-four, proceeding to barracks number 3 with two prisoners."

    (B) "Car one-four, proceeding to barracks number 3 with two prisoners."

    (C)   "Car one-four, Troopers Abel and Flynn, proceeding to barracks number 3 with two prisoners, ten-four."

    (D)   "Car one-four proceeding to barracks number 3 with prisoners Bossey and Warren; ten-four."

33. Of the following, the most grammatical and precise sentence is:

    (A)   In arresting and detention of suspects, a trooper has to give advice about Miranda rights.

    (B)   Constitutional rights like Miranda warnings are advice given by arresting officers.

    (C)   A suspect being arrested or detained must be given a Miranda warning, that is, must be advised of his or her constitutional rights.

    (D)   A trooper must give the suspect their Miranda warning and tell them they have constitutional rights before anyone can be arrested.

34. Choose the most logical order of the sentences to create a coherent story.

    1.   Everyone entering the elevators for the upper floors of the municipal building must pass through a metal detector.

    2.   The man was not permitted to take the exam.

    3.   As the man approached the elevator, the alarm began to sound.

    4.   A sign in the lobby read, "All applicants for the state trooper exam must check their weapons."

    (A)   1-3-4-2

    (B)   4-3-1-2

    (C)   1-4-2-3

    (D)   4-1-3-2

35. An assumption commonly made in regard to the reliability of testimony is that when a number of persons report the same matter, those details upon which there is an agreement may generally be considered substantiated. Experiments have shown, however, that there is a tendency for the same errors to appear in the testimony of different individuals, and that, apart from any collusion, agreement of testimony is no proof of dependability.

This paragraph suggests that

    (A)   if the testimony of a group of people is in substantial agreement, it cannot be ruled out that those witnesses have not all made the same mistake.

    (B)   if details of the testimony are true, all witnesses will agree to it.

    (C)   if most witnesses do not independently attest to the same facts, the facts cannot be true.

    (D)   unless there is collusion, it is impossible for a number of persons to give the same report.

36. State Police Officer Waksman, cruising in an unmarked car on Main Street in Littleton, answers an alert on the car radio and begins to follow two robbery suspects. The suspects go south for two blocks, then turn left for two blocks, then make another left turn for one more block. At this point, the suspects sense that they are being followed. They hurriedly make a left turn, travel two more blocks, and then make a right turn. In what direction are the suspects now headed?

    (A)   North

    (B)   South

    (C)   East

    (D)   West

37. A black Ford Escort pulled up at the tollbooth, and the driver pointed a gun at the toll collector and demanded money. The frightened toll collector tossed a sack of tokens at the gunman. The driver was thrown off guard by the weight of the sack hurled at him and sped off without demanding bills. State Trooper Prensky, responding to the booth, learned that the sack had contained 50 rolls of $3.50 tokens. Each roll is made up of 10 tokens. What was the value of the sack of tokens?

    (A) $35.00
    (B) $175.00
    (C) $500.00
    (D) $1750.00

38. State Police Officer Thomases, on patrol in an unincorporated village policed by her barracks, notices an elderly gentleman wandering aimlessly in the elementary schoolyard. The man tells Officer Thomases that he thinks that his name is Bob and that he was a student at this school but was kidnapped by aliens in a flying saucer and just escaped. Officer Thomases puts the man in her car and broadcasts the following alert to her sergeant and to officers in other patrol cars:

    Incident: lost, disoriented adult
    Location: schoolyard of Central Consolidated Elementary School
    Description: white male; about 80; 5 ft. 7 in.; weight 150; thin gray hair; blue eyes; wearing gray pants, white shirt, and green windbreaker; "Bob"

    Which of the following expresses the information most clearly, accurately, and completely?

    (A) An old man who might be Bob says that he was left in front of Central Consolidated School by aliens who kidnapped him. He is about 5 ft. 7 in., weighs about 150 lbs., and has thin gray hair and blue eyes. He is wearing gray pants, white shirt, and a windbreaker.

    (B) Bob is an old man who was kidnapped by aliens and returned to the schoolyard at Central Consolidated Elementary where he used to go to school. He is confused wearing gray pants, a white shirt, and a green windbreaker. He has gray hair and blue eyes and is average size.

    (C) A confused white man, about 80, was found in the schoolyard of Central Consolidated Elementary. The man is about 5'7", weighing about 150 lbs., with thin gray hair and blue eyes. He is wearing gray pants, white shirt, and a windbreaker and is uncertain of his name and address.

    (D) A man with thin gray hair and blue eyes wearing gray pants, a white shirt, and a green windbreaker says he is Bob who was left by aliens in the schoolyard at Central Consolidated where he used to go to school before they kidnapped him. He is 5 ft. 7 in. and weighs 150 lbs.

Answer questions 39 and 40 on the basis of the following procedure.

1. When a suspect in custody requests medical attention or is in apparent need of it, the officer should arrange for the suspect to be promptly examined by a doctor.

2. In the event that a suspect in custody is in need of medical treatment, the officer should notify a supervisor immediately so that an ambulance can be summoned. Suspects who are drug addicts and who are in need of treatment for their addiction should be taken to a hospital by a radio car.

3. Under no circumstances should an officer prescribe any medication for a suspect in custody.

4. An officer should not attempt to diagnose a suspect's illness or injury and should not attempt to treat the suspect except in a situation where first aid is required. First aid should be administered promptly.

39. Bill Adams, a suspect well known to police because of his long record, is in custody when he claims that he has a severe headache as a result of being badly beaten. There are no apparent signs of a physical injury, but the suspect is demanding medical attention.

The state police officer in charge of Bill Adams should

(A) consider the suspect's long record before deciding to call a doctor.
(B) see that Bill Adams is promptly examined by a doctor.
(C) give the suspect two aspirins.
(D) ignore the suspect's request for medical attention since there are no apparent physical injuries.

40. It is a hot summer day, and Trooper Domonkos has in his custody a suspect who is a drug addict. The suspect opens his shirt to reveal a large unhealed wound that is obviously infected. Trooper Domonkos suggests to the suspect that he call a doctor in to examine him, but the suspect refuses, saying the wound is of no consequence. In this instance, Trooper Domonkos should

(A) request that his supervisor call an ambulance.
(B) closely examine the wound in order to evaluate its severity.
(C) adhere to the suspect's wishes and do nothing about the matter.
(D) take the suspect at once to a hospital in a radio car.

Questions 41 through 46 are based on the personnel chart below.

PERSONNEL CHART

Name	Sex	SS Number	D.O.B.	Date Hired	Position	Supervisor
Cain, G.C.	M	112-22-8765	4/8/48	5/12/73	sergeant	Barton, H.
Cane, P.T.	M	221-63-5432	9/21/56	10/10/80	custodian	Frank, L.T.
Canes, L.D.	F	868-91-0870	12/9/70	6/22/96	dispatcher	Holmes, R.G.
Coan, R., Jr.	M	555-06-9892	5/16/39	12/5/79	mechanic	Frank, L.T.
Coen, B.B.	F	342-78-1234	1/25/63	8/18/81	cook	Smith, A.X.
Cone, A.R.	F	630-12-7654	1/21/68	3/30/91	trooper	Cain, G.C.
Cone, F.J.	F	366-42-4759	11/3/72	5/7/95	trooper	Cain, G.C.
Cope, E.M.	M	633-41-8076	3/6/63	9/13/87	paramedic	Holmes, R.G.

41. Which person is supervised by A.N. Smith?

(A) G.C. Cain
(B) A.R. Cone
(C) B.B. Coen
(D) R. Coan Jr.

42. The job held by the oldest person is

(A) sergeant.
(B) dispatcher.
(C) mechanic.
(D) custodian.

43. The person whose social security number is 633-41-8076 is a

(A) dispatcher.
(B) paramedic.
(C) custodian.
(D) trooper.

44. The social security number of the person who has been employed here for the longest time is

(A) 221-63-5432
(B) 555-06-8982
(C) 212-22-8765
(D) 112-22-8765

45. The oldest trooper was born on

(A) 1/21/68
(B) 1/25/63
(C) 5/7/95
(D) 11/3/72

46. A.F. Cone's social security number is

(A) 630-12-7554
(B) 630-12-7564
(C) 630-12-7654
(D) 630-12-7645

Answer questions 47 and 48 on the basis of the following Employee Leave Regulations.

As a full-time permanent state employee under the Career and Salary Plan, Trooper Fogarty earns an "annual leave allowance." This consists of a certain number of days off a year with pay and may be used for vacation, for personal business, or for observing religious holidays. During his first eight years of state service, he will earn an "annual leave allowance" of twenty days a year (an average of 1-2/3 days off a month). After he has finished eight full years of state employment, he will begin earning an additional five days off a year. His "annual leave allowance" will then be twenty-five days a year and will remain at this level for seven full years. He will begin earning an additional two days off a year after he has completed a total of fifteen years of state employment.

A "sick leave allowance" of one day a month is also given to Trooper Fogarty, but it can be used only in case of actual illness. When Fogarty returns to work after using "sick leave allowance," he must have a doctor's note if the absence is for a total of more than three days, but he may also be required to show a doctor's note for absences of one, two, or three days.

47. According to the preceding passage, Trooper Fogarty's "annual leave allowance" consists of a certain number of days off a year that he

(A) does not get paid for.
(B) should use if he is sick.
(C) may use for personal business.
(D) may not use for observing religious holidays.

48. According to the preceding passage, when he uses "sick leave allowance," Trooper Fogarty may be required to show a doctor's note

(A) even if his absence is for only one day
(B) only if his absence is for more than two days
(C) only if his absence is for more than three days
(D) only if his absence is for three days or more

49. Choose the most logical order of the sentences to create a coherent story.

1. There was a turnpike crash between two trucks, one of which overturned.
2. One highway patrol officer called for an ambulance for the driver of the overturned truck, who appeared to be seriously injured.

3. Cartons of cigarettes, some burst open, were scattered all over the highway.

4. Another highway patrol officer noticed that the federal tax stamps on the cigarettes were counterfeit.

(A) 1-2-3-4
(B) 1-3-2-4
(C) 3-1-2-4
(D) 3-2-4-1

50. Choose the most grammatical and precise statement.

(A) Without prior authorization, personal telephone calls are prohibited by on-duty state police officers.

(B) State police officers without prior authorization on duty are prohibited from making personal telephone calls.

(C) State police officers are prohibited from making personal telephone calls while on duty without prior authorization.

(D) State police officers without prior authorization are prohibited from making personal telephone calls while on duty.

Questions 51 through 56 ore based on the work schedules below.

WORK SCHEDULE

	Sun	Mon	Tues	Wed	Thurs	Fri	Sat
Group 1	South Quadrant	West Quadrant	training	off	West Quadrant	South Quadrant	off
Group 2	East Quadrant	training	off	North Quadrant	South Quadrant	off	West Quadrant
Group 3	North Quadrant	off	South Quadrant	East Quadrant	off	training	North Quadrant

Group 1
Supervisor: Mark Cross
Traci Baron
Evan Luwisch
Janice Payson
Warren Correa
Training at: 9848 State Road
Training supervisor: Herbert Talmini

Group 2
Supervisor: Mary Gelb
Scott McKeon
Demearia Kougios
Bruce Nelson
Marina Drabek

Group 3
Supervisor: Andy Mao
Ramon Martinez
Horace Logan
Kathy Choong
David Cotino

SEPTEMBER

Sun	Mon	Tues	Wed	Thurs	Fri	Sat
	1	2	3	4	5	
6	7	8	9	10	11	12
13	14	15	16	17	18	19
20	21	22	23	24	25	26
27	28	29	30			

51. Where is Bruce Nelson working on September 17?

(A) 9848 State Road
(B) South Quadrant
(C) Not working
(D) East Quadrant

52. On what date will Kathy Choong report for training?

    (A) September 18
    (B) September 3
    (C) September 1
    (D) September 28

53. A person who will be working in all four quadrants during the month of September is

    (A) Mark Cross.
    (B) Ramon Martinez.
    (C) Demetria Kougios.
    (D) Herbert Talmini.

54. The supervisor of the group that will work in the East Quadrant on September 9 is

    (A) Herbert Talmini.
    (B) Mark Cross.
    (C) Andy Mao.
    (D) Cannot be determined.

55. A person who will be off on September 24 is

    (A) Evan Luwisch.
    (B) Marina Drabek.
    (C) Mark Cross.
    (D) Herbert Talmini.

56. Which group will work in the North Quadrant on September 18?

    (A) Group 1
    (B) Group 2
    (C) Group 3
    (D) Cannot be determined

57. Choose the most grammatical and precise sentence.

    (A) On account of the prediction that there would be heavy snow, it was required of the troopers that they put chains on their cars.
    (B) Due to the fact that it was due to snow heavily, troopers were told to put on chains.
    (C) Because heavy snow was predicted, troopers were directed to use tire chains.
    (D) The forecasters said that it was going to snow hard which led the troopers to put chains on their tires.

58. The civil service commission shall designate a qualified trainer to administer the physical fitness screening test to determine the underlying physiological capacity of a candidate to learn and perform the essential jolt functions of an entry-level state police officer. Such a test shall be administered prior to the making of a conditional offer of employment and shall be administered to the candidate prior to the post-offer medical examination to be conducted by a qualified physician or practitioner unless the civil service commission can demonstrate that it could not reasonably conduct such a screening test at the pre-offer stage of employment. The paragraph best supports the statement that

(A) physical fitness screening is the first step in the hiring process for state police officers.

(B) an applicant may be offered employment before physical fitness screening if the civil service commission could not conduct this screening before the offer was made.

(C) the purpose of physical fitness screening is to determine if the candidate will be able to pass the medical examination.

(D) the medical examination is administered by a qualified trainer or practitioner.

59. Prior to the administration of the test by the qualified trainer, the civil service commission may ask the candidate to assume legal responsibility and release such commission of liability for injuries resulting from any physical or mental disorders. In addition, the commission may furnish such candidate with a description of the physical fitness screening test and require certification from the candidate's physician that he or she is physically capable of participating in the physical fitness screening test. If the commission requests such certification from one candidate, it must request such certification from all candidates.

The paragraph best supports the statement that

(A) the physical fitness test causes injuries to persons with physical or mental disorders.

(B) the civil service commission is not liable for injuries to state police candidates.

(C) all candidates must be treated equally with respect to certifying fitness for the fitness test.

(D) persons with physical or mental disorders must be furnished with a description of the physical fitness screening test.

60. If a candidate is unable to perform an element of the test, the civil service commission may provide for an alternative element to be substituted, which, in the judgment of such commission, will render a demonstrably valid assessment of the individual's physiological capacity for the particular factor to be measured.

The paragraph best supports the statement that

(A) the civil service commission may offer substitute tasks to measure fitness if a candidate has failed to pass on one of the established measures.

(B) individuals may offer substitute tasks to prove their fitness if unable to adequately perform on a designated element.

(C) candidates are offered second chances to prove their fitness for employment.

(D) an alternative may be offered for only one element of the test.

Answer questions 61 and 62 on the basis of the drawing below. This drawing shows parts of the magazine of a police revolver and the order in which these parts fit together.

61. The part that is NOT a part of the magazine is

(A)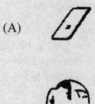

(B)

(C)

(D)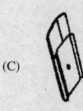

62. The part that goes between 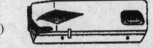 and 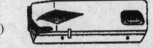 is

(A)

(B)

(C)

(D)

63. State Highway Patrol Officer Zildgian has just issued a summons to a driver and has obtained the following information:

Time of Occurrence: 6:08 a.m.
Place of Occurrence: U.S. Highway 202 at milepost 74
Offense: illegal U-turn
Driver: Malcolm Brooks, age 29
Address of Driver: 76 Shady Lane, Martinsburgh

Officer Zildgian is making an entry in his daily activity log regarding the incident. Which of the following conveys the information most clearly, accurately, and completely?

(A) Malcolm Brooks, age 29, made a U-turn at 76 Shady Lane. I arrested him.
(B) At 6:08 a.m. I stopped 29-year-old Malcolm Brooks of 76 Shady Land, Martinsburgh, for making an illegal U-turn on Highway 202 at mile 74 and gave him a summons.
(C) 29-year-old Malcolm Brooks made an illegal U-turn on Highway 202 at 76 Shady Lane. This happened early this morning, and I gave him a summons.
(D) When Malcolm Brooks, age 29, made an illegal U-turn on Highway 202 at milepost 74, I gave him a summons at 76 Shady Lane, Martinsburgh, at 6:08 a.m.

64. Highway patrol officers occasionally discover vehicles that appear to have been abandoned along the roadside. An officer coming upon such a vehicle should do the following:

1. Make a memo book entry describing the vehicle and the location at which the vehicle was found.
2. Notify the barracks desk officer and request a registration check.
3. Check registration and vehicle identification number against stolen automobile files.
4. Arrange for removal of vehicle.
5. Notify owner.

Highway Patrol Officer Boersma notices a badly battered and partially stripped red Camaro unattended along the shoulder abutting a highway entrance ramp. Officer Boersma makes a memo book entry, notifies the barracks desk officer, and requests a registration check. Next, Officer Boersma should

(A) arrange for removal of the vehicle before it is hit by entering traffic.
(B) notify the owner.
(C) check the stolen automobile files.
(D) write a complete report.

Answer questions 65 through 67 on the basis of the following map. The flow of traffic is indi-
cated by the arrows. You must follow the flow of traffic.

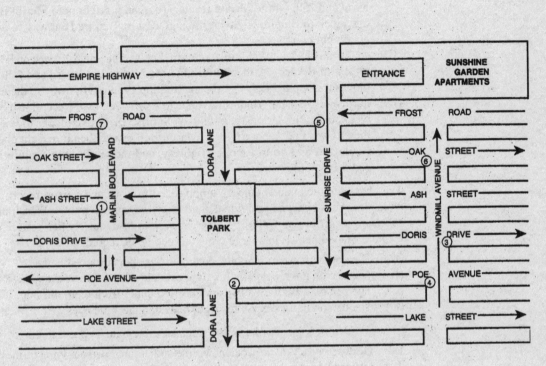

65. If you are located at point (1) and travel north three blocks, then turn east and travel
one block, then turn south and travel five blocks, then turn west and travel one block,
you will be closest to point

   (A) 2
   (B) 3
   (C) 5
   (D) 7

66. You are located at Marlin Boulevard and Ash Street while patrolling in the town
depicted on the map portion and receive a call to respond to the corner of Doris Drive
and Windmill Avenue. Which of the following is the most direct route for you to take
in your patrol car, making sure to obey all traffic regulations?

   (A) Travel two blocks south on Marlin Boulevard to Poe Avenue, then three blocks
        east to Windmill Avenue, then north one block to Doris Drive.
   (B) Travel three blocks north on Marlin Boulevard to Empire Highway, then one
        block east to Sunrise Drive, then two blocks south to Dora Lane, then one
        block east to Windmill Avenue, then two blocks to Doris Drive.
   (C) Travel two blocks north on Marlin Boulevard to Frost Road, then three blocks
        east to Windmill Avenue, then three blocks south to Doris Drive.
   (D) Travel one block north on Marlin Boulevard to Oak Street, then east two blocks
        to Sunrise Drive, then south two blocks to Doris Drive, then east one block to
        Windmill Avenue.

67. The call to Doris Drive and Windmill Avenue turns out to be a false alarm, but your patrol car radio suddenly alerts you to a disturbance in the entry courtyard of the Sunshine Garden Apartments. You must get to the site of the disturbance in the quickest legal way. You should drive:

    (A) north three blocks on Windmill Avenue to Frost Road, then turn left onto Frost Road and go one block to Sunrise Drive, then turn right and go one block on Sunrise Drive to the entrance.

    (B) north three blocks on Windmill Avenue to Frost Road, then turn left onto Frost Road and follow it to Marlin Boulevard, then go right onto Marlin Boulevard one block to Empire Highway, then go east on Empire Highway to the garden apartment complex.

    (C) south one block on Windmill Avenue to Poe Avenue, then go west on Poe Avenue to Marlin Boulevard, then turn right onto Marlin Boulevard and follow it five blocks to Empire Highway, then go east on Empire Highway to the entrance.

    (D) north one block on Windmill Avenue to Ash Street, then west on Ash Street one block to Sunrise Drive, then south on Sunrise Drive two blocks to Poe Avenue, then follow Poe Avenue west to Marlin Boulevard, then turn right onto Marlin Boulevard and go to Empire Highway, and turn right onto Empire Highway and drive to the entry.

68. The characteristics that should be emphasized in a wanted person report are those which most easily set an individual apart from the general public. Which one of the following descriptions would be of greatest help to a state police officer trying to locate a wanted person in a large crowd of people on a cold winter day?

    (A) The person is wearing a blue coat, and has short-cropped hair.
    (B) The person has a patch on his right eye and a long thin scar on his left cheek.
    (C) The person talks with a lisp and has two upper front teeth missing.
    (D) The person has a scar on his right knee and has blue eyes.

69. Choose the most logical order of the sentences to create a coherent story.

    1. He observed a vehicle accident with several injured persons lying on the roadway.
    2. Officer Wolchock immediately requested that two ambulances be dispatched to the scene.
    3. Highway Patrol Officer Wolchock on vehicle patrol was traveling on a local freeway.
    4. Prompt action was taken to establish traffic control to protect the injured parties from further injury.

    (A) 3-1-4-2
    (B) 1-3-4-2
    (C) 3-1-2-4
    (D) 1-3-2-4

70. Choose the most grammatical and precise sentence.

    (A) Johnny Carabitsis come out of the store and says to Trooper Milligan that he seen the victim fall to the ground and then two white guys search the victim and run off.

    (B) Johnny Carabitsis exited the store he had been in and informed Trooper Milligan that he observed that the victim fell to the ground being searched by a pair of white males running away after searching his body and clothing.

    (C) Exiting the store, Johnny Carabitsis told what he saw to Trooper Milligan that the victim fell down and the two white men searched him and the two white men ran away.

    (D) Johnny Carabitsis came out of the store and told Trooper Milligan that he had seen the victim fall down and that two white men had searched the victim and had then run off.

In the diagrams for questions 71 and 72, symbols are used to represent vehicles, pedestrians, animals, and their movements.

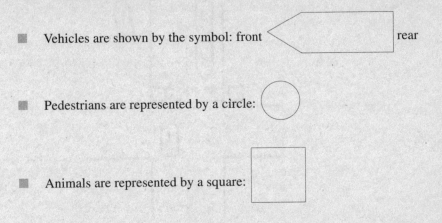

■ Vehicles are shown by the symbol: front   rear

■ Pedestrians are represented by a circle:

■ Animals are represented by a square:

■ Solid lines show the path and direction of a vehicle, person, or animal before an accident happened: ⟶

■ Broken lines show the path and direction of a vehicle, person, or animal after an accident happened: ⇢

71. Car 1 was driving north on County Road #3; car 2 was driving south on the same road. The two cars were nearly abreast when a squirrel began to cross the roadway from west to east. Car 1 swerved onto the right shoulder to avoid hitting the squirrel. Just past the middle of the roadway, the squirrel changed its mind, turned around, and began to scamper back across the road from east to west. Car 2 slammed on its brakes. Car 3, unable to see the road in front of car 2 and therefore unaware of any reason for car 2 to stop suddenly, rear-ended car 2. Which of the four diagrams below best represents the accident described?

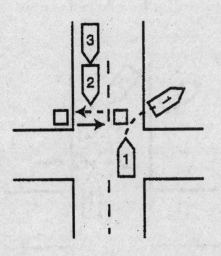

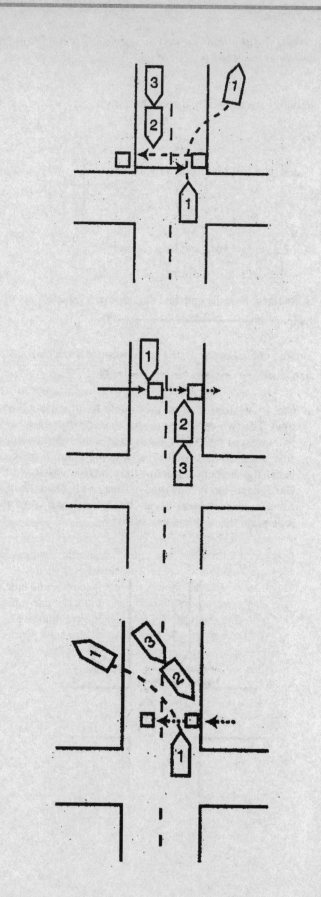

72. The diagram below represents a highway accident. Which of the narratives following the diagram best describes the accident depicted?

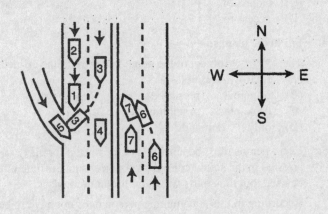

(A) Car 1, car 2, and car 3 were all driving southbound in the right lane of a divided highway when car 5 cut in from the right and smashed into car 3. Traffic in the left lane and northbound traffic were unaffected.

(B) Car 6, traveling in the right lane, northbound, attempted to illegally pass car 7 on the right causing car 7 to jump the divider and forcing car 3 from the left lane to the right lane of southbound traffic. Car 3 then hit car 5, which was entering the highway from an entrance ramp, and car 3, in turn, was hit by car 1. Car 2 stopped in time and didn't hit anyone.

(C) Car 1 and car 2 were traveling southbound in the right lane of a divided highway and were passed by car 3 in the left lane. Car 3 then impatiently cut into the right lane in front of car 1, hitting car 5, which was entering the highway from an entrance ramp on the right. Meanwhile car 6, distracted by rubbernecking, veered from the right lane of the northbound roadway onto the left lane, hitting car 7 and pushing car 7 up onto the divider.

(D) Car 4, traveling slowly in the left southbound lane of a divided highway, caused car 3 to cut into the right lane and to hit car 1. Car 1 then hit car 5, which was entering the highway from an entrance ramp. Car 7, northbound, attempting a U-turn into the southbound lanes, got hung up on the divider and was hit by car 6, which was entering the left lane of the northbound roadway.

73. Fill in the blank:

The Freedom of Information Act gives private citizens _____ government files.
(A) excess to
(B) access from
(C) excess of
(D) access to

74. Fill in the blanks:

The _____ object of the penal law is to define crime and _____ punishments.
(A) final . . . declare
(B) principal . . . prescribe
(C) principle . . . proclaim
(D) only . . . demand

75. Every person must be informed of the reason for his or her arrest unless that person is arrested in the actual commission of a crime. Sufficient force to effect the arrest may be used, but the courts frown on brutal methods.

According to this statement, a person does not have to be informed of the reason for his or her arrest if
(A) brutal force was not used in effecting it.
(B) the courts will later free the defendant.
(C) the person arrested knows force will be used if necessary.
(D) the reason for the arrest is clearly evident from the circumstances.

Answer questions 76 through 84 solely on the basis of the following information. Read the passage thoroughly and review the Report of Arrest form before attempting to answer the questions.

State Police Officer Chris Hazarika passing by an in-town all-night convenience store late at night hears a male voice shouting for help. Officer Hazarika enters the store through the front door where he is met by the franchise owner, Barry Nielsen, who tells the officer that he has just been robbed by a tall, slim, young, white man who can still be seen running in the distance. The officer chases after the youth who climbs into a light blue two-door Toyota bearing the New York license plate X45-2CP. The car fails to start, and Officer Hazarika catches up to it and arrests its occupant in front of 72 Lenox Street. From crime to arrest, barely 5 minutes of time have elapsed. The officer then takes the prisoner to the state police substation located in the village hall. There it is determined that the prisoner's legal name is Peter Bright, that he lives alone in apartment S at 72 Camptown Road in the nearby town of Libertyville, and his telephone number is 841-9708. Bright's nickname is "Fatso," and he is single. He was born in Rochester, NY, on April 15, 1969, and his Social Security number is 987-06-5432. Bright is employed by the Springwater Bottling Company, 276 High Street, Libertyville. An arrest record is completed and is assigned the number 18431.

Nielsen arrives at the state police substation and is able to describe the incident in detail. He states that at approximately 10:30 p.m. on August 14, 1996, a young, slim, white man entered his store. He approximated the weight of the man to be 145 lbs. and his height to be 5 ft. 11 in. The man had brown hair and eyes. Nielsen said he went to wait on the man who suddenly pointed a knife at Nielsen and said, "Give me all your money, or else." Nielsen noticed that the man had a red and blue tattoo of the head of an Indian Chief on his right forearm. Nielsen picked up an empty soda bottle from the counter and threw it at the man, hitting him in the chest. The man turned and ran out of the store, heading south on Lenox Street. Nielsen then headed for the door, yelling for help.

Nielsen was born on June 17, 1957, and he lives with his wife at 694 Judson Drive in Mount Lawrence. His business address is 26 Lenox Street, Mount Lawrence. His home telephone number is 336-6787 and his business phone number is 336-4234.

76. Which one of the following dates should be entered in the box numbered (1)?

    (A) April 15, 1969
    (B) August 14, 1996
    (C) August 15, 1996
    (D) April 14, 1969

77. Which one of the following times should be placed in the box numbered (2)?

    (A) 10:25 p.m.
    (B) l0:30 p.m.
    (C) l0:35 p.m.
    (D) 10:45 p.m.

78. Which one of the following should be placed in the box numbered (7)?

    (A) April 15, 1996, 10:30 p.m.
    (B) August 14, 1996, 10:25 p.m.
    (C) June 17, 1996, 10:35 p.m.
    (D) August 14, 1996, 10:30 p.m.

REPORT OF ARREST

ARREST INFORMATION	(1) Date of arrest	(2) Time of arrest	(3) Place of arrest	(4) Station	(5) Arrest number

DESCRIPTION OF INCIDENT	(6) Prisoner's weapon (description)		(7) Date and time
	(8) Prisoner's auto (color, year, make, model, license plate number, state)		
	(9) Type of business	(10) Location of incident (be specific)	

DESCRIPTION OF PRISONER	(11) Last name First name Middle initial			(12) Date of birth		
	(13) Sex	(14) Race	(15) Eyes	(16) Hair	(17) Weight	(18) Height	(19) Age
	(20) Address City State		(21) Apt. no.	(22) Home phone number		
	(23) Citizenship Citizen ☐ Non-Citizen ☐		(24) Place of birth	(25) Marital status		
	(26) Social Security number	(27) Where employed (company and address)				
	(28) Nickname	(29) Scars, tattoos (describe fully and give location)				

DESCRIPTION OF COMPLAINANT	(30) Last name First name Middle initial		(31) Date of birth
	Telephone Numbers (32) Business (33) Home	(34) Address City State	

79. Which of the following should be entered in the box numbered (6)?

(A) Knife
(B) Bottle
(C) Gun
(D) Ax

80. Of the following, which one should be entered in the box numbered (8)?

(A) Light blue, 1993 two-door Toyota., X45-2CP, New York
(B) Light blue, two-door Toyota, X45-C2P, New York
(C) Light blue, two-door Nissan, X45-2PC, New York
(D) Light blue, two-door Toyota, X45-2CP, New York

81. Which of the following should be entered in the box numbered (12)?

(A) June 17, 1957
(B) April 15, 1969
(C) June 17, 1969
(D) August 14, 1957

82. Of the following, which should be entered in the box numbered (27)?

(A) Springwater Bottling Company, 267 High Street, Libertyville
(B) Springwater Bottling Company, 26 Lenox Street, Mount Lawrence
(C) Springwater Bottling Company, 276 High Street, Libertyville
(D) Springwater Bottling Company, 276 High Street, Mount Lawrence

83. Of the following, which one should be entered in the box numbered (34)?

(A) 964 Judson Drive, Mount Lawrence
(B) 72 Camptown Road, Libertyville
(C) 694 Judson Drive, Libertyville
(D) 694 Judson Drive, Mount Lawrence

84. Of the following, which one should be entered in the box numbered (32)?

(A) 336-9767
(B) 336-6787
(C) 336-4234
(D) 841-9708

Answer question 85 on the basis of the information below.

Under the Penal Law, a highway patrol officer is a peace officer. A peace officer is charged with keeping the peace whether officially on duty or not and whether in uniform or not. A peace officer must attempt to prevent crime from occurring, must attempt to stop crime in progress, and must attempt to assist crime victims.

85. Highway Patrol Officer Mahoney has completed his day's tour of duty and is on his way home. He has just parked his car in his usual space, three blocks from his home, when he comes upon a woman screaming that her purse has just been snatched. Officer Mahoney begins to chase the perpetrator, who is still visible running up the street. The purse snatcher suddenly turns, shoots, and kills Officer Mahoney. Highway Patrol Officer Mahoney's widow files to collect "death-in-the-line-of-duty" benefits. Mrs. Mahoney's request is

(A) proper; Officer Mahoney was murdered in cold blood.
(B) improper; Mahoney was off duty when he was killed.
(C) proper; it is the duty of peace officers to assist victims of crimes in progress.
(D) improper; Mahoney deliberately put himself in unnecessary danger.

Answer questions 86 through 88 on the basis of the following procedure.

The final step in an accident investigation is the making out of the report. In the case of a traffic accident, the officer should go right from the scene to his or her office to write up the report. However, if a person was injured in the accident and taken to a hospital, the officer should visit the victim there before going to the office to prepare a report. This personal visit to the injured person does not mean that the officer must make a physical examination, but the officer should make an effort to obtain a statement from the injured person or persons. If this is not possible, information should be obtained from the attending physician as to the extent of the injury. In any event, without fail, the name of the physician should be secured and the report should state the name of the physician and the fact that the physician told the officer that, at a certain stated time on a certain stated date, the injuries were of such and such a nature. If the injured person dies before the officer arrives at the hospital, it may be necessary to take the responsible person into custody at once.

86. When a person has been injured in a traffic accident, the one of the following actions that it is necessary for the officer to take in connection with the accident report is to

(A) prepare the report immediately after the accident and then go to the hospital to speak to the victim.

(B) do his or her utmost to verify the victim's story prior to preparing the official report of the accident.

(C) be sure to include the victim's statement in the report in every case.

(D) try to get the victim's version of the accident prior to preparing the report.

87. When one of the persons injured in a motor vehicle accident dies, the above procedure provides that

(A) if the injured person is already dead when the officer appears at the scene of the accident, the officer must immediately take the responsible person into custody.

(B) if the injured person dies after arrival at the hospital, the officer must either arrest the responsible person or get a statement from him or her.

(C) if the injured person dies in the hospital prior to the officer's arrival there, the officer may have to immediately arrest the responsible person.

(D) the officer may refrain from arresting the responsible person, but only if the responsible person is also seriously injured.

88. When someone has been injured in a collision between two automobiles and is given medical treatment shortly thereafter by a physician, the one of the following actions that the officer must take with regard to the physician is to

(A) obtain the physician's name and diagnosis of the injuries, regardless of the place where treatment was given.

(B) obtain the physician's approval of the portion of the report relating to the injured person and the treatment given prior to and after arrival at the hospital.

(C) obtain physician's name, opinion of the extent of the person's injuries, and signed statement regarding the treatment the physician gave the injured person.

(D) set a certain stated time on a certain stated date for interviewing physician, unless physician is an attending physician in a hospital.

89. Choose the most logical order of the sentences to create a coherent story.

1. Security staff are now checking packages being carried by employees into the state office building.

2. This checking resulted in discovery and confiscation of a revolver on December 18.

3. The suspect stated that he carried it to keep it away from his children.

4. The weapon was turned over to state police officers for further investigation.

(A) 2-3-4-1
(B) 1-2-3-4
(C) 4-3-1-2
(D) 4-3-2-1

90. Fill in the blanks:

If the interviewer does not _____ the witness, it is better to proceed _____ permitting the witness to know that _____ statements are being doubted.

(A) understand . . . quickly . . . his
(B) like . . . cautiously . . . their
(C) believe . . . cautiously . . . its
(D) believe . . . without . . . his

Questions 91 through 96 are based on the following explanation of the coding on a state motor vehicle operator's license

H12027005087110199905

H	12	02	70	050871	101999	05
first letter, last name	position in alphabet of first letter, first name	gender	height	date of birth	expiration date	county

91. Which of the following is Martha Goldstein's license number?

(A) M070262122365122339703
(B) G13026808177511149710
(C) G30259110893060669801
(D) M13016309247909249608

92. John Jacobson graduated from junior high school in 1950. Which of the following could be his license number?

(A) J100174071236005169911
(B) J10016812313112020004
(C) J10016109285009289608
(D) J10027001244404259715

93. Which of the people with the following license numbers would be easiest to pick out in a crowd?

(A) P26017212122903309801
(B) B03025302294005059906
(C) F11027604257005229911
(D) G22016910197208279709

94. Which of the following could NOT be a real driver's license number?

(A) A18015711234506260003
(B) K05027006197312299914
(C) T20036408287209079806
(D) W05016601108004269903

95. Which of the following is least likely to be a driver's license number?

(A) X01028210197710199909
(B) V26015607265709249805
(C) L11016108287809079707
(D) Y19016305159009189813

96. Of the following, who is most likely to have special restrictions on his or her driver's license?

    (A) 0070265032543111159701
    (B) H20013807265809129907
    (C) P22017004306604329811
    (D) T09026511277210199904

97. Choose the most grammatical and precise statement:

    (A) The traffic light being red, the intersection should not be entered by a driver.
    (B) A driver with a traffic light turning red should not enter the intersection.
    (C) A driver making the observation that the traffic light at the intersection is about to turn red should refrain from entering that intersection until it is red no more.
    (D) If the light at the intersection is red, a driver should not enter the intersection.

98. On the basis of a tip from a reliable informer, State Police Officer Carey has verified the location of a cocaine processing factory. He has made a number of notes in his memo book and must now write a report and request search warrant and backups before actually raiding the establishment. These are Officer Carey's notes:

    Date: Monday, November 4
    Location: 481 West Martini Parkway, Apt. 4-R
    Activity: processing and packaging cocaine for street sale
    Time of activity: 9:00 p.m. to 3:00 a.m.
    Persons involved: at least five unidentified males, one female
    Basis of request: tip from reliable paid informant, John Doe, and personal observation of activity from undercover post

    Which of the following expresses this information most clearly, accurately, and completely?

    (A) On the basis of informant, John Doe, I observed 5 men and 1 woman carrying on drug-related activity at 481 West Martini Parkway, Apt. 4-R, between 9:00 p.m. and 3:00 a.m. I would like a search warrant and assistance to follow this information.
    (B) Five men and one woman are packing cocaine at 481 West Martini Parkway, Apt. 4-R from 9 to 3 on November 4. John Doe and I want to raid the premises.
    (C) According to John Doe, 5 men and 1 woman pack cocaine from 9:00 p.m. to 3:00 a.m. on November 4 at Apt. 4.-R, 481 West Martini Parkway. I saw them.
    (D) Five men, one of them is John Doe, and one woman went into 481 West Martini Parkway, Apt. 4-R on November 4 from 9:00 a.m. to 3:00 p.m. to do drugs. I saw them and want a search warrant to raid the place.

99. Highway Patrol Officer Clements left Barracks #2 and began driving south on I-95. As Officer Clements cruised along at the posted 55 mph speed limit, her car was passed by a red sports car doing 75 mph. Officer Clements turned on her flashing lights and siren and gave chase. The speeding car exited the highway on a southwest ramp. At the end of the ramp, the car turned right onto State Route 201 running parallel to the interstate. When the driver of the car realized that the state police car was still in hot pursuit, he made a quick U-turn on Route 201. Three miles later, the sports car turned right onto County Road 680 and, at the next intersection, collided with a car crossing from its right. In what direction was the unfortunate car traveling when it was hit by the red car?

    (A) North
    (B) South
    (C) East
    (D) West

100. Suppose that 10% of those who commit serious crimes are convicted and that 15% of those convicted are sentenced for more than three years. The percentage of those committing serious crimes who are sentenced for more than three years is

(A) 15%
(B) 1.5%
(C) 0.15%
(D) 0.015%

MODEL EXAMINATION 2: ANSWERS AND EXPLANATIONS

ANSWERS

1. C	21. C	41. C	61. B	81. B
2. B	22. A	42. C	62. D	82. A
3. B	23. D	43. B	63. B	83. D
4. A	24. D	44. D	64. C	84. C
5. C	25. B	45. A	65. A	85. C
6. D	26. C	46. C	66. D	86. D
7. A	27. C	47. C	67. B	87. C
8. D	28. A	48. A	68. B	88. A
9. C	29. B	49. B	69. C	89. B
10. B	30. A	50. D	70. D	90. D
11. B	31. D	51. B	71. A	91. B
12. C	32. B	52. A	72. C	92. A
13. C	33. C	53. C	73. D	93. C
14. D	34. D	54. C	74. B	94. C
15. D	35. A	55. D	75. D	95. D
16. C	36. A	56. D	76. B	96. B
17. B	37. D	57. C	77. C	97. D
18. C	38. C	58. B	78. D	98. A
19. A	39. B	59. C	79. A	99. B
20. D	40. A	60. A	80. D	100. B

EXPLANATIONS

1. **The correct answer is (C).** The car that is on fire is right side up, partly in the right-hand lane and partly on the shoulder.

2. **The correct answer is (B).** There are two people lying in the roadway. It is reasonable to assume that these victims are seriously hurt. Those who are sitting and standing are probably not seriously hurt.

3. **The correct answer is (B).** The right-hand southbound lane consists of bumper-to-bumper traffic. The people who are stuck in this traffic are rubbernecking, that is, they are looking at the accident.

4. **The correct answer is (A).** The fire engine is in the left lane, southbound. It is approaching from the north.

5. **The correct answer is (C).** Two troopers are near the people lying in the roadway; two are on the shoulder near the seated victims; one is talking to the group of four standing off on the shoulder; and one is in the roadway near the broadside car.

6. **The correct answer is (D).** The passenger car that is entirely on the shoulder is upside down.

7. **The correct answer is (A).** In the left lane southbound is a fire engine about to cross to the northbound side, followed by a police car.

8. **The correct answer is (D).** There are no people on the divider.

9. **The correct answer is (C).** All the shadows are to the east of the vehicles, bushes, and people. If the shadows are to the east, the sun is in the west, and it is afternoon.

10. **The correct answer is (B).** Stuck among the cars in the southbound direction are a large double trailer, a tanker truck, and two motorcycles.

11. **The correct answer is (B).**

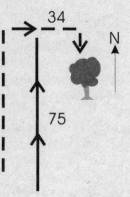

12. **The correct answer is (C).** Driving at 90 mph for 15 minutes, you have driven 22_ miles, closest to 24. The 5 miles you drove before the car passed you were not miles driven in pursuit. Read questions carefully.

13. **The correct answer is (C).** All steps must be taken in the required order. Officer Hellman must next scan the interior of the car for suspicious occupants or objects. Then Hellman must pat down the operator for weapons and check for sobriety. Only after these steps are taken should the summons be issued for the burned-out headlight violation.

14. **The correct answer is (D).** Remember, the steps must be taken in order. First comes the check of driver's license and registration.

15. **The correct answer is (D).** The paragraph tells us that the payroll department complies with IRS regulations in withholding taxes from salaries and wages. The IRS determines the tax, not the salaries.

16. **The correct answer is (C).** All other choices can be answered by "yes" or "no."

17. **The correct answer is (B).** Choice (A) is an overstatement; the lady was not necessarily killed. Choice (C) gets it all wrong; Mary Clark was the witness, not the driver. Choice (C) also incorrectly places the location of the accident at Mary Clark's residence. Choice (D) has the location right, but confuses the people involved.

18. **The correct answer is (C).** Southbound cars make a loop and join northbound cars to enter the service plaza.

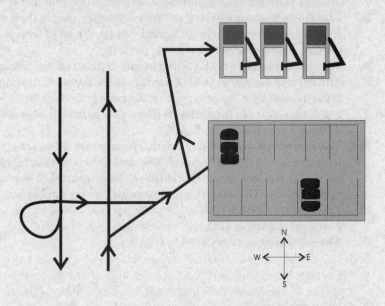

19. **The correct answer is (A).** By saying that investigators must devote themselves completely though the work may not be easy, smooth, or peaceful, the paragraph is saying that they must be persistent in the face of difficulty.
20. **The correct answer is (D).** All other choices are leading questions.
21. **The correct answer is (C).** The truck travels 130 - 75 = 55 miles.
    A ten-wheeler has three axles. At 2 cents per mile per axle, the truck must pay 3 x .02 or 6 cents per mile. 55 x $ .06 = $3.30.
22. **The correct answer is (A).** Choice (D) does include all of the necessary information, but choice (A) is more clearly written.
23. **The correct answer is (D).**

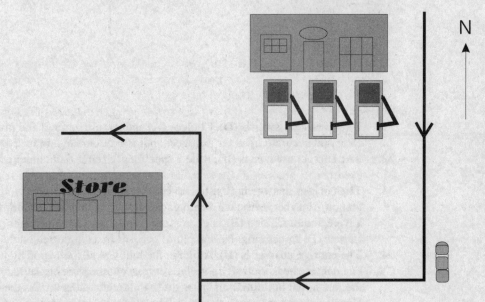

24. **The correct answer is (D).** The complete license number of the vehicle that fled is not known, so the name and address of its owner cannot be immediately determined. Trooper Yoshida must get as much information as possible from the remaining driver.

25. **The correct answer is (B).** All four sentences do get their messages across, but the sentence that addresses the driver and tells the driver what to do is clearly best. The other choices do not have appropriate subjects.

26. **The correct answer is (C).** Refer to rules 1 and 2 of the procedure.

27. **The correct answer is (C).** Officer Provo is indeed addressing the driver properly, but Provo is otherwise out of order because he is criticizing the driver's ability (Rule 5) and not advising him of his violation (Rule 2). There is no mention in the question that the driver may have been drinking.

28. **The correct answer is (A).** A highway patrol officer on the scene was interviewing the witness of a serious car accident. The accident had resulted in the death of the witness's brother, driver of one of the vehicles. The officer asked the witness if his brother had been drinking. The witness angrily replied that his brother was sober.

29. **The correct answer is (B).** The paragraph lists some of the specialized courses in the police driving curriculum.

30. **The correct answer is (A).**

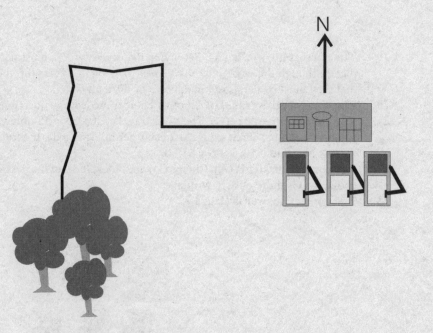

31. **The correct answer is (D).** Choices (A) and (B) are garbled and incorrect. Choice (C) is clear and accurate in so far as it goes, but is incomplete and inadequate.

32. **The correct answer is (B).** Rule 3 specifically states that names of people are not to be used.

33. **The correct answer is (C).** In choice (A), a parallel structure would be "arrest and detention." Further, Miranda warnings are advice in themselves, not something to receive advice about. Choice (B) is even more imprecise. Constitutional rights are not advice. Choice (D) mixes singular and plural persons in a single sentence.

34. **The correct answer is (D).** A sign in the lobby read, "All applicants for the state trooper exam must check their weapons." Everyone entering the elevators for the upper floors of the municipal building must pass through a metal detector. As the man approached the elevator, the alarm began to sound. The man was not permitted to take the exam.

35. **The correct answer is (A).** Just as *agreement of testimony is no proof of dependability*, so agreement of testimony is no proof of undependability; they all can make the same mistake either way.

36. **The correct answer is (A).** Put yourself in the driver's seat, pencil in hand, and turn the paper as needed to be certain of right and left from the driver's point of view.

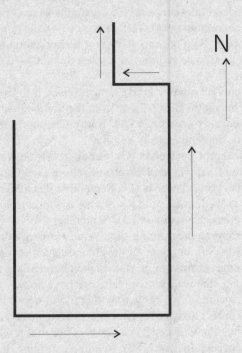

37. **The correct answer is (D).** The value of each roll is $3.50 x 10 = $35.00
    50 rolls @ $35 = $35.00 x 50 = $1750.00

38. **The correct answer is (C).** Choices (B) and (D) both report the alien kidnapping as fact. Choice (A) reports that the old man was dropped off at the school, but not necessarily that he was found there. Choice (C) is the most clear and accurate of the reports even though it omits the color of the windbreaker. In the case of unidentified persons, the color of clothing is important.

39. **The correct answer is (B).** Rule 1. When a suspect requests medical attention, the officer should arrange for the suspect to be promptly examined by a doctor. An officer should never assume the responsibility of deciding whether or not a suspect requires the services of a doctor.

40. **The correct answer is (A).** Rule 2 governs. It is apparent that the suspect requires medical attention even though there is no emergency. Medical attention is required for the suspect's wound, not for his drug addiction; therefore an ambulance should be called.

41. **The correct answer is (C).** A.N. Smith supervises B.B. Coen

42. **The correct answer is (C).** R. Coan Jr., who was born in 1939, is a mechanic.

43. **The correct answer is (B).** E.M. Cope's social security number is 633-41-8076. Cope is a paramedic.

44. **The correct answer is (D).** Sergeant G.C. Cain was hired on 5/12/73. His social security number is 112-22-8765.

45. **The correct answer is (A).** Of the two troopers, the one who was born earlier is older. A.F. Cone, who was born 1/21/68, is older than F.J. Cone, whose birthdate is 11/3/72.

46. **The correct answer is (C).** Beware of reversed numbers. Read carefully.

47. **The correct answer is (C).** The second sentence lists the permissible uses of annual leave allowance.

48. **The correct answer is (A).** According to the last sentence of the paragraph, he *may* be required to show a doctor's note for absences of one, two, or three days.

49. **The correct answer is (B).** There was a turnpike crash between two trucks, one of which overturned. Cartons of cigarettes, some burst open, were scattered all over the highway. One highway patrol officer called for an ambulance for the driver of the overturned truck, who appeared to be seriously injured. Another highway patrol officer noticed that the federal tax stamps on the cigarettes were counterfeit.

50. **The correct answer is (D).** In choice (A), the police officers prohibit the telephone calls. In choice (B) it appears that prior authorization must be obtained while the officers are on duty. Choice (C) makes it seem that the officers actually need prior authorization to go on duty.

51. **The correct answer is (B).** Bruce Nelson is in Group 2, and September 17 is a Thursday. On Thursdays, Group 2 works in the South Quadrant.

52. **The correct answer is (A).** Kathy Choong is in Group 3. Group 3 takes training on Friday. September 18 is a Friday.

53. **The correct answer is (C).** Group 2 will be working in all four quadrants during the month of September. Demetria Kougios is in Group 2.

54. **The correct answer is (C).** September 9 is a Wednesday. Group 3 works in East Quadrant on Wednesday, and Andy Mao is supervisor of Group 3.

55. **The correct answer is (D).** September 24 is a Thursday. No training is scheduled for Thursday, so the training supervisor, Herbert Talmini, has the day off. Group 3 also has Thursday off, but none of the choices is a member of that group.

56. **The correct answer is (D).** September 18 is a Friday. From the portion of the work schedule that we are given here, we have no way of knowing which group will work the north quadrant; we know only that it will not be one of the three groups described here.

57. **The correct answer is (C).** Choices (A) and (D) are wordy, childish formulations of the information. Choice (B) is incorrect because a sentence must never begin with due to.

58. **The correct answer is (B).** Reading carefully, the physical fitness screening test comes prior to the conditional offer of employment. It is reasonable to assume that there is a basis for the conditional offer, most likely a written test. Choice (A) is therefore incorrect. Choice (C) is ridiculous. As for choice (D), the physical fitness test is administered by a qualified trainer; the medical examination by a physician or qualified practitioner. Choice (B) is a correct interpretation of the second sentence.

59. **The correct answer is (C).** This is exactly what the last sentence says.

60. **The correct answer is (A).** This is a very generous provision, accurately restated.

61. **The correct answer is (B).**

62. **The correct answer is (D).**

63. **The correct answer is (B).** Choice (A) is incomplete; choice (C) is incomplete and inaccurate as to location of the violation; choice (D) is inaccurate as to where the summons was presented and residence of the violator.

64. **The correct answer is (C).** After step 2 comes step 3.

65. The correct answer is (A).

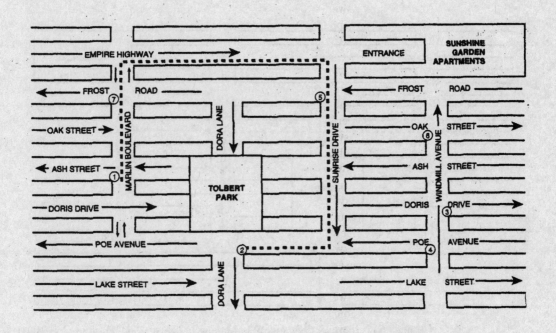

66. The correct answer is (D).

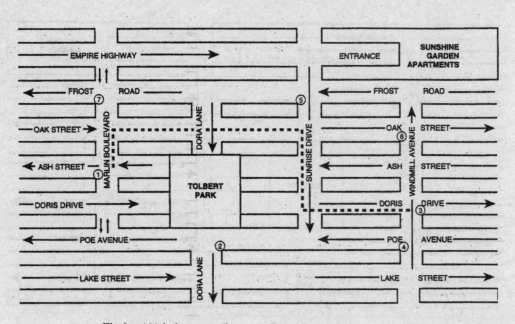

Choice (A) is incorrect because Poe Avenue is one-way westbound; choice (B) is impossible because Sunrise Drive and Dora Lane are parallel streets; choice (C) is incorrect because Frost Road is one-way westbound.

67.   **The correct answer is (B).**

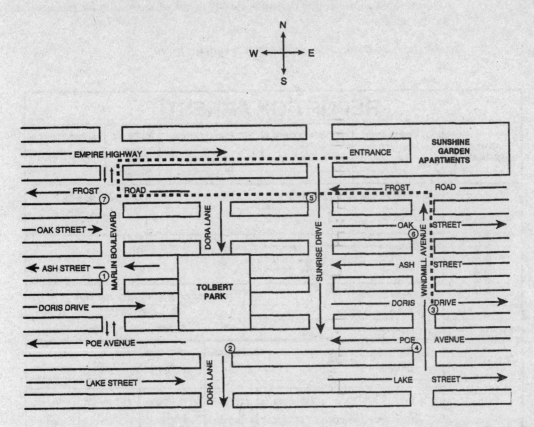

Choice (A) is incorrect because you cannot turn right from Frost Road onto Sunrise Drive without going the wrong way on a one-way street; choice (C) is incorrect because Windmill Avenue is one-way northbound; choice (D) is legal but is an unnecessarily long route.

68.   **The correct answer is (B).** The eye patch makes for good identification because very few people wear them. The long, thin scar on the cheek would be highly visible as well. Points of identification must be distinctive or unusual, visible, and not readily subject to change.

69.   **The correct answer is (C).** Highway Patrol Officer Wolchock on vehicle patrol was traveling on a local freeway. He observed a vehicle accident with several injured persons lying on the roadway. Officer Wolchock immediately requested that two ambulances be dispatched to the scene. Prompt action was taken to establish traffic control to protect the injured parties from further injury.

70.   **The correct answer is (D).** Choice (A) plays havoc with verbs in terms of both number and tense; in choice (B) the ground is being searched; choice (C) is a childish, run-on sentence.

71.   **The correct answer is (A).** Choice (B) does not describe this accident because the squirrel makes it all the way across the road before changing its mind; choice (C) has the cars traveling in the wrong directions and the squirrel going only one way; choice (D) sends the cars swerving in the wrong directions as well as placing the squirrel incorrectly.

72.   **The correct answer is (C).**

73.   **The correct answer is (D).** *Excess* means too much. *Access* is a right or a means of getting; therefore *to* is the correct preposition.

74.   **The correct answer is (B).** All laws to some degree specify procedures and discuss exceptions and alternatives; therefore neither choices (A) nor (D) is a good answer. Choice (C) is incorrect because the word meaning *primary* or *chief* is *principal*. Having filled the first blank, the second blank is properly filled with choice (B). The penal law prescribes punishment for the crimes it has defined. *Demand* and *declare* are too strong; *proclaim* is an inappropriate word choice.

75. **The correct answer is (D).** Obviously, if the person is arrested in the actual act of performing the crime, that person is clearly aware of the reason for the arrest and need not be informed.

For questions 76 through 84, refer to the completed form.

REPORT OF ARREST

ARREST INFORMATION	(1) Date of arrest Aug. 14, 1996	(2) Time of arrest 10:45 P.M.	(3) Place of arrest in front of 72 Lenox St. Mt. Lawrence	(4) Station village hall Substation	(5) Arrest number 18431

DESCRIPTION OF INCIDENT

(6) Prisoner's weapon (description) Knife		(7) Date and time Aug. 14, 1996 10:30 P.M.

(8) Prisoner's auto (color, year, make, model, license plate number, state)
light blue, 2-door Toyota Corolla, 1991
New York X45-2CP

(9) Type of business Convenience store	(10) Location of incident (be specific) 26 Lenox Street Mount Lawrence

DESCRIPTION OF PRISONER

(11) Last name Bright	First name Peter	Middle initial NMI	(12) Date of birth April 15, 1969

(13) Sex M	(14) Race W	(15) Eyes brown	(16) Hair brown	(17) Weight 145lb.	(18) Height 5'11"	(19) Age 27

(20) Address 72 Camptown Rd.	City Libertyville,	State NY	(21) Apt. no. 5	(22) Home phone number 841-9708

(23) Citizenship Citizen ☒ Non-Citizen ☐	(24) Place of birth Rochester, NY	(25) Marital status Single

(26) Social Security number 987-06-5432	(27) Where employed (company and address) Springwater Bottling Company 276 High Street, Libertyville, NY

(28) Nickname Fatso	(29) Scars, tattoos (describe fully and give location) Red and blue tattoo, head of Indian Chief, right forearm

DESCRIPTION OF COMPLAINANT

(30) Last name Nielsen	First name Barry	Middle initial NMI	(31) Date of birth June 17, 1957

Telephone Numbers		(34) Address City State
(32) Business 356-4254	(33) Home 356-6787	694 Judson Drive Mount Lawrence, NY

85. **The correct answer is (C).** According to the excerpt from the Penal Law, Officer Mahoney was indeed performing his duty when he was killed.

86. **The correct answer is (D).** Prior to writing the report, the officer should try to obtain a statement from the injured person or persons; that is, the officer should try to get the victim's version of the accident prior to preparing the report.

87. **The correct answer is (C).** This is a restatement of the last sentence.

88. **The correct answer is (A).** This answer is made clear in the next to the last sentence.

89. **The correct answer is (B).** Security staff are now checking packages being carried by employees into the state office building. This checking resulted in discovery and confiscation of a revolver on December 18. The suspect stated that he carried it to keep it away from his children. The weapon was turned over to state police officers for further investigation.

90. **The correct answer is (D).** Start with the first word. You can eliminate choice (B) immediately. Liking or not liking a witness should be irrelevant to an interview. At choice (A), the first word is possible, so you should look at the second. It makes no sense for the interviewer to proceed quickly if he or she is having trouble understanding the witness. Choice (C) can be eliminated on two counts. For one, a witness is not an *it*. Proceeding cautiously in the face of disbelief would make sense if the sentence did not continue. However permitting the witness to know that his or her statements are being doubted does not lead to a fruitful interview. Read the sentence carefully, using the words from choice (D) to verify that choice (D) is indeed best.

91. **The correct answer is (B).** In light of Martha Goldstein's name, only choices (B) and (C) are correctly coded. The code at choice (C) gives '93 as a birth year. A person born in 1893 is most unlikely to still be driving; one born in 1993 cannot possibly be doing so.

92. **The correct answer is (A).** A person graduating from junior high school in 1950 would have been born in the middle 1930s. 1936 is a very reasonable birth year for John Jacobson.

93. **The correct answer is (C).** A 6 ft. 4 in. woman stands head and shoulders above the crowd.

94. **The correct answer is (C).** There are only two options for gender.

95. **The correct answer is (D).** A person born in the year '90, no matter which century, is unlikely to have a driver's license.

96. **The correct answer is (B).** This individual is 3 ft. 2 in. in height. He needs a specially equipped car, and his license must specify that he is restricted to driving a car especially designed for one his size.

97. **The correct answer is (D).** Both choices (A) and (B) are awkwardly stated. Choice (C) is grammatical but verbose.

98. **The correct answer is (A).** Choice (B) is unclear as to the time frame in which the activity has gone on and may continue. Choice (B) also involves the informant in enforcement; this is obviously irregular. Choice (C) also neglects the ongoing nature of the activity and overstates the officer's current knowledge. Choice (D) misidentifies John Doe.

99. **The correct answer is (B).**

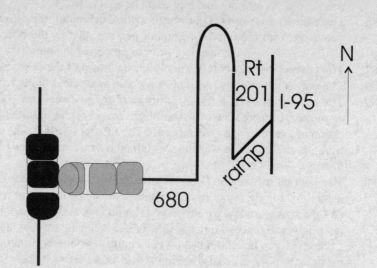

100. **The correct answer is (B).** 15% of 10% = .15 x .10 = 0.015 = 1.5%

MODEL EXAMINATION 3: ANSWER SHEET

1. Ⓐ Ⓑ Ⓒ Ⓓ   21. Ⓐ Ⓑ Ⓒ Ⓓ   41. Ⓐ Ⓑ Ⓒ Ⓓ   61. Ⓐ Ⓑ Ⓒ Ⓓ   81. Ⓐ Ⓑ Ⓒ Ⓓ

2. Ⓐ Ⓑ Ⓒ Ⓓ   22. Ⓐ Ⓑ Ⓒ Ⓓ   42. Ⓐ Ⓑ Ⓒ Ⓓ   62. Ⓐ Ⓑ Ⓒ Ⓓ   82. Ⓐ Ⓑ Ⓒ Ⓓ

3. Ⓐ Ⓑ Ⓒ Ⓓ   23. Ⓐ Ⓑ Ⓒ Ⓓ   43. Ⓐ Ⓑ Ⓒ Ⓓ   63. Ⓐ Ⓑ Ⓒ Ⓓ   83. Ⓐ Ⓑ Ⓒ Ⓓ

4. Ⓐ Ⓑ Ⓒ Ⓓ   24. Ⓐ Ⓑ Ⓒ Ⓓ   44. Ⓐ Ⓑ Ⓒ Ⓓ   64. Ⓐ Ⓑ Ⓒ Ⓓ   84. Ⓐ Ⓑ Ⓒ Ⓓ

5. Ⓐ Ⓑ Ⓒ Ⓓ   25. Ⓐ Ⓑ Ⓒ Ⓓ   45. Ⓐ Ⓑ Ⓒ Ⓓ   65. Ⓐ Ⓑ Ⓒ Ⓓ   85. Ⓐ Ⓑ Ⓒ Ⓓ

6. Ⓐ Ⓑ Ⓒ Ⓓ   26. Ⓐ Ⓑ Ⓒ Ⓓ   46. Ⓐ Ⓑ Ⓒ Ⓓ   66. Ⓐ Ⓑ Ⓒ Ⓓ   86. Ⓐ Ⓑ Ⓒ Ⓓ

7. Ⓐ Ⓑ Ⓒ Ⓓ   27. Ⓐ Ⓑ Ⓒ Ⓓ   47. Ⓐ Ⓑ Ⓒ Ⓓ   67. Ⓐ Ⓑ Ⓒ Ⓓ   87. Ⓐ Ⓑ Ⓒ Ⓓ

8. Ⓐ Ⓑ Ⓒ Ⓓ   28. Ⓐ Ⓑ Ⓒ Ⓓ   48. Ⓐ Ⓑ Ⓒ Ⓓ   68. Ⓐ Ⓑ Ⓒ Ⓓ   88. Ⓐ Ⓑ Ⓒ Ⓓ

9. Ⓐ Ⓑ Ⓒ Ⓓ   29. Ⓐ Ⓑ Ⓒ Ⓓ   49. Ⓐ Ⓑ Ⓒ Ⓓ   69. Ⓐ Ⓑ Ⓒ Ⓓ   89. Ⓐ Ⓑ Ⓒ Ⓓ

10. Ⓐ Ⓑ Ⓒ Ⓓ   30. Ⓐ Ⓑ Ⓒ Ⓓ   50. Ⓐ Ⓑ Ⓒ Ⓓ   70. Ⓐ Ⓑ Ⓒ Ⓓ   90. Ⓐ Ⓑ Ⓒ Ⓓ

11. Ⓐ Ⓑ Ⓒ Ⓓ   31. Ⓐ Ⓑ Ⓒ Ⓓ   51. Ⓐ Ⓑ Ⓒ Ⓓ   71. Ⓐ Ⓑ Ⓒ Ⓓ   91. Ⓐ Ⓑ Ⓒ Ⓓ

12. Ⓐ Ⓑ Ⓒ Ⓓ   32. Ⓐ Ⓑ Ⓒ Ⓓ   52. Ⓐ Ⓑ Ⓒ Ⓓ   72. Ⓐ Ⓑ Ⓒ Ⓓ   92. Ⓐ Ⓑ Ⓒ Ⓓ

13. Ⓐ Ⓑ Ⓒ Ⓓ   33. Ⓐ Ⓑ Ⓒ Ⓓ   53. Ⓐ Ⓑ Ⓒ Ⓓ   73. Ⓐ Ⓑ Ⓒ Ⓓ   93. Ⓐ Ⓑ Ⓒ Ⓓ

14. Ⓐ Ⓑ Ⓒ Ⓓ   34. Ⓐ Ⓑ Ⓒ Ⓓ   54. Ⓐ Ⓑ Ⓒ Ⓓ   74. Ⓐ Ⓑ Ⓒ Ⓓ   94. Ⓐ Ⓑ Ⓒ Ⓓ

15. Ⓐ Ⓑ Ⓒ Ⓓ   35. Ⓐ Ⓑ Ⓒ Ⓓ   55. Ⓐ Ⓑ Ⓒ Ⓓ   75. Ⓐ Ⓑ Ⓒ Ⓓ   95. Ⓐ Ⓑ Ⓒ Ⓓ

16. Ⓐ Ⓑ Ⓒ Ⓓ   36. Ⓐ Ⓑ Ⓒ Ⓓ   56. Ⓐ Ⓑ Ⓒ Ⓓ   76. Ⓐ Ⓑ Ⓒ Ⓓ   96. Ⓐ Ⓑ Ⓒ Ⓓ

17. Ⓐ Ⓑ Ⓒ Ⓓ   37. Ⓐ Ⓑ Ⓒ Ⓓ   57. Ⓐ Ⓑ Ⓒ Ⓓ   77. Ⓐ Ⓑ Ⓒ Ⓓ   97. Ⓐ Ⓑ Ⓒ Ⓓ

18. Ⓐ Ⓑ Ⓒ Ⓓ   38. Ⓐ Ⓑ Ⓒ Ⓓ   58. Ⓐ Ⓑ Ⓒ Ⓓ   78. Ⓐ Ⓑ Ⓒ Ⓓ   98. Ⓐ Ⓑ Ⓒ Ⓓ

19. Ⓐ Ⓑ Ⓒ Ⓓ   39. Ⓐ Ⓑ Ⓒ Ⓓ   59. Ⓐ Ⓑ Ⓒ Ⓓ   79. Ⓐ Ⓑ Ⓒ Ⓓ   99. Ⓐ Ⓑ Ⓒ Ⓓ

20. Ⓐ Ⓑ Ⓒ Ⓓ   40. Ⓐ Ⓑ Ⓒ Ⓓ   60. Ⓐ Ⓑ Ⓒ Ⓓ   80. Ⓐ Ⓑ Ⓒ Ⓓ   100. Ⓐ Ⓑ Ⓒ Ⓓ

MODEL EXAMINATION 3

TIME: 3½ HOURS—100 QUESTIONS

> **Directions:** Each question numbered 1 through 100 has four possible choices lettered A, B, C, and D. You are to select the answer that you deem to be correct.

1. Suppose that, while on patrol late at night, you find a woman lying in the road, apparently the victim of a hit-and-run driver. She seems to be injured seriously, but you wish to ask her one or two questions in order to help locate the hit-and-run car. Of the following, which is the best question to ask?

   (A) In what direction did the car go?
   (B) What time did it happen?
   (C) What kind of car was it?
   (D) How many persons were in the car?

2. "Driver 1 claimed that the collision occurred because, as he approached the intersection, Driver 2 started to make a left turn suddenly and at high speed, even though the light had been red against him for 15 or 20 seconds." Suppose that you have been assigned to make a report on this accident. The position of the vehicles after the accident is indicated in the figure; the point in each case indicates the front of the vehicle. On the basis of this sketch, the best reason for concluding that Driver 1's statement is false is that

   (A) Driver 2's car is beyond the center of the intersection.
   (B) Driver 2's car is making the turn on the proper side of the road.
   (C) Driver 1's car is beyond the sidewalk line.
   (D) Driver 1's car is on the right-hand side of the road.

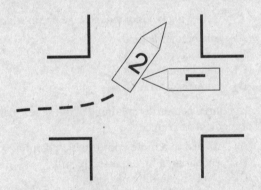

3. "If possible, the principal witnesses, especially the most trustworthy ones, should be heard before the suspect is interrogated." The most valid reason for this procedure is that

   (A) the investigator will tend to be more adequately informed when questioning the suspect.
   (B) waiting to be questioned increases the pressure on the subject.
   (C) trustworthy witnesses tend to become untrustworthy if kept waiting.
   (D) all witnesses should be heard before the suspect.

4. A state trooper must be observant of people he or she encounters while patrolling an assigned post. This attribute is most useful in law enforcement in the

   (A) detection and apprehension of criminals.
   (B) fostering of good public relations.
   (C) maintenance of a state of alertness in the state trooper.
   (D) preparation of a state trooper for promotion.

5. You are on your way to report for an assignment when you see two men fighting on the street. For you to attempt to stop the fight would be

   (A) unjustified; it is none of your business.
   (B) justified; a fight between individuals may turn into a riot.
   (C) unjustified; you may get hurt with the result that you will not be able to report for duty.
   (D) justified; as a peace officer it is your duty to see that the public peace is kept.

6. While patrolling your post you notice several people in two groups entering an old abandoned house by means of the rear entrance. The best action to take would be to

   (A) call headquarters notifying your superior of the occurrences.
   (B) ignore the situation.
   (C) enter the house, gun drawn.
   (D) note the occurrence by an entry in your memorandum book.

7. "On a dark background bloodstains are often difficult to recognize. When searching for bloodstains in such cases, one should use a flashlight, even in the daytime." Of the following, the best reason for this procedure is that

   (A) it is important to get as much light as possible.
   (B) the contrast around the edges of the light is great.
   (C) artificial light may make differentiation between the blood and the background possible.
   (D) the movement of the flashlight will cause a moving reflection.

8. Of the following kinds of wounds, the one in which there is the least danger of infection is

   (A) an abraded wound.
   (B) a puncture wound.
   (C) a lacerated wound.
   (D) an incised wound.

9. An injured person complaining about severe pains in his back should, pending arrival of medical assistance, be

   (A) moved to a more comfortable position.
   (B) encouraged to lie perfectly still.
   (C) put in a standing position.
   (D) seated in a straight-back chair.

10. One of the following deserves your primary attention when administering first aid to an injured person pending arrival of medical assistance. It is

    (A) a broken arm.
    (B) severe bleeding.
    (C) an irregular heartbeat.
    (D) a state of hysteria.

11. Which of the following statements made by a prisoner would be called an alibi?

    (A) "He struck me first."
    (B) "I didn't intend to hurt him."

(C) "I was miles away from there at the time."

(D) "I don't remember what happened."

12. A person who, after the commission of a crime, conceals the offender with the intent that the latter may escape from arrest and trial, is called

(A) an accessory.

(B) an accomplice.

(C) a confederate.

(D) an associate.

13. A sworn statement of fact is called

(A) an affidavit.

(B) an oath.

(C) an acknowledgment.

(D) a subpoena.

14. Among the following, the signature cards of a bank might be employed as a means of verifying an individual's

(A) character.

(B) identity.

(C) financial status.

(D) employment.

15. An accomplice is

(A) one who, after full knowledge that a felony has been committed, conceals same from law officers.

(B) one who is liable to prosecution for the same offense with which the defendant on trial has been charged.

(C) one who harbors a person charged with or convicted of a felony.

(D) a person who has knowledge of a given act.

In answering questions 16 through 22, make use of the following statement: "A description of persons or properly wanted by this department which is to be given to the police force through the medium of a general alarm, if not distinctive, is of no value."

16. You are watching a great number of people leave a ball game. Of the persons who are described below, the one whom it would be easiest to spot would be

(A) female; age 15; height 5'6"; weight 130 lbs.; long straight black hair.

(B) female; age 35; height 5'4"; weight 150 lbs.; wears glasses.

(C) male; age 60; height 5'7"; weight 170 lbs.; all false teeth.

(D) male; age 25; height 6'3"; weight 220 lbs.; pockmarked.

17. You are preparing a woman's description to be broadcast. Of the following characteristics, the one that would be of most value to the driver of a squad car is

(A) frequents movie theaters.

(B) age 45 years.

(C) height 6'1".

(D) smokes very heavily.

18. Under the portrait pane system of identification, of the following the most important part of a description of a person is the

(A) dress, since it is the most noticeable.

(B) ears, since no two are alike.

(C) eyes, since they cannot be altered.

(D) nose, since it is most distinctive.

19. Assume that on a hot summer day you are stationed on the grass at the south bank of a busy parkway looking at eastbound traffic for a light blue Ford two-door sedan. If traffic is very heavy, the one of the following additional pieces of information that would be most helpful to you in identifying the car is that

   (A) all of the chrome is missing from the left side of the car.
   (B) there is a bullet hole in the left front window.
   (C) the paint on the right side of the car is somewhat faded.
   (D) the front bumper is missing.

20. Assume that you have stopped a Dodge four-door sedan that you suspect is a car that was reported as stolen the day before. The one of the following items of information that would be of greatest value in determining whether this is the stolen car is that

   (A) the stolen car's license plate number was QA2356; this car's license number is U21375.
   (B) the stolen car's engine number was AB6231; this car's engine number is CS2315.

   (C) the windshield of the stolen car was not cracked; this car's windshield is cracked.
   (D) the stolen car had no dents; this car has numerous dents.

21. You are watching a great number of people leave a sports arena after a boxing match. Of the characteristics listed below, the one that would be of greatest value to you in spotting a man wanted by the department is

   (A) Height 5'3"; Weight 200 lbs.
   (B) Eyes: brown; Hair: black, wavy; Complexion: sallow
   (C) Mustache: when last seen in August, he wore a small black mustache
   (D) Scars: thin 1/2" scar on left upper lip; Tattoos: on right forearm-"Pinto"

22. The only personal description the police have of a particular criminal was made several years ago. Of the following, the item in the description that will be most useful in identifying him at the present time is the

   (A) color of his eyes.
   (B) color of his hair.
   (C) number of teeth.
   (D) weight.

23. "Photographs of suspected persons should not be shown to a witness if the criminal himself can be arrested and placed on view for identification." The above recommendation is

   (A) inadvisable; this procedure might subject the witness to future retribution by suspect.
   (B) advisable; a photograph cannot be used for identification purposes with the same degree of certainty as the suspect in person.
   (C) inadvisable; the appearance of the subject may have changed since the commission of the crime.
   (D) advisable; photography as an art has not achieved an acceptable degree of perfection.

24. Stationed at a busy highway, you are given the description of a vehicle that has been stolen. Of the following characteristics, the one that will permit you to eliminate most easily a large number of vehicles is

   (A) no spare tire.
   (B) make-Buick, two-door sedan.
   (C) color-black.
   (D) tires 750 x16, white walled.

25. If a sick or injured woman to whom a male trooper is rendering aid is unknown and the trooper has reason to believe that her clothing contains a means of identification, the trooper should

    (A) immediately search the clothing for such identification and remove any identification found therein.

    (B) send for a female trooper to search the clothing for such identification.

    (C) ask any female present to search the clothing for such identification.

    (D) accompany her to the hospital and there seek the necessary information from hospital authorities.

26. Which of the following means of avoiding identification would be most likely to meet with success?

    (A) Growing a beard

    (B) Shaving off the beard if there was one originally

    (C) Burning the fingers so as to remove the fingerprints

    (D) Changing the features by facial surgery

27. In asking a witness to a crime to identify a suspect, it is common practice to place the suspect with a group of persons and ask the witness to pick out the person in question. Of the following, the best reason for this practice is that it will

    (A) make the identification more reliable than if the witness were shown the suspect alone.

    (B) protect the witness against reprisals.

    (C) make sure that the witness is telling the truth.

    (D) help select other participants in the crime at the same time.

28. "Social security cards are not acceptable proof of identification for police purposes." Of the following, the most important reason for this rule is that the social security card

    (A) is easily obtained.

    (B) states on its face "for social security purposes—not for identification."

    (C) is frequently lost.

    (D) does not contain a photograph, description, or fingerprints of the person.

29. Of the following facts about a criminal, the one that would be of most value in apprehending and identifying the criminal would be that he

    (A) drives a black Chevrolet sedan with chrome license plate holders.

    (B) invariably uses a .38-caliber Colt blue-steel revolver with walnut stock and regulation front sight.

    (C) talks with a French accent and frequently stutters.

    (D) usually wears three-button single-breasted "Ivy League" suits and white oxford cloth button-down collar shirts.

30. The investigator is tracing a fugitive suspect. Which of the following means of identification is the suspect least able to suppress?

    (A) He suffers from spastic paralysis.

    (B) His picture is available for identification.

    (C) He is a habitual frequenter of a certain type of restaurant.

    (D) He is a rabid baseball fan.

31. The least accurate characterization of crime is that it

    (A) consists of an overt act and, in most cases, of a culpable intent.

    (B) is an act prohibited by a group with the power to enforce observation.

    (C) may be either an act of omission or commission.

    (D) is an act that, generally of an illegal nature, is quite possibly legal in its essence.

32. The most effective method of crime prevention is in general

    (A) severe punishment of malefactors.
    (B) probation.
    (C) psychiatric examination of offenders.
    (D) eradication of causal factors.

33. Of the following, the one that is reason for believing prevention of criminal behavior to be superior to the cure of criminals as a method for handling crime problems is that with the adoption of prevention programs it is most probable that

    (A) less money will be spent on jails and prisons.
    (B) more money will be spent on preventive programs.
    (C) the "born" criminal will exhibit criminal behavior anyway.
    (D) less money will have to be spent on such matters as recreational programs, housing, and the like.

34. If it is assumed that all criminals believe in no legal restraints, then

    (A) all persons who are not criminals believe in legal restraint.
    (B) any person who believes in no legal restraints is a criminal.
    (C) any person who does not believe in no legal restraints is not a criminal.
    (D) there would be no criminals if there were no legal restraints.

35. "It is an undeniable fact that people are not born criminals." Of the following, the chief implication of the above statement is that

    (A) the youth who is a juvenile delinquent becomes the adult who violates the law.
    (B) violations of the law are usually due to a combination of environmental factors.
    (C) most crimes are committed by adults.
    (D) criminals are not easily detected.

Use the cross compass below to answer questions 36 through 40.

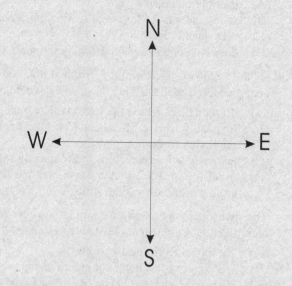

36. A state trooper driving east makes a left turn and then a right turn. He would thereafter be traveling

    (A) north.
    (B) east.
    (C) south.
    (D) west.

37. A state trooper driving north makes a left turn and then a second left turn. He would thereafter be traveling

    (A) north.
    (B) east.
    (C) south.
    (D) west.

38. A state trooper driving west makes a right turn and then a left turn. He would thereafter be traveling

    (A) north.
    (B) east.
    (C) south.
    (D) west.

39. A state trooper driving north crosses from a highway right onto a dirt road across a field traveling diagonally. He would be traveling

    (A) north by northeast.
    (B) north by northwest.
    (C) west by southwest.
    (D) east by northeast.

40. A state trooper traveling west on a limited access highway makes a right-hand exit at a "cloverleaf" intersection and heads down the exit ramp to a lower roadway crossing underneath the highway. If she continues in the same direction without crossing the lower roadway, she would be traveling

    (A) north.
    (B) south.
    (C) east.
    (D) west.

Answer questions 41 through 45 on the basis of the passage below and the Accident Report form shown below.

At approximately 5:00 p.m. on a foggy, rainy afternoon, Trooper Ressa arrived at the scene of an accident a few minutes after it occurred. On the basis of his observations, and from the statements of the persons involved in the accident, he decided that the accident happened this way: Mr. Goldsmith was driving his car east on Tenth Street. Tenth is a straight, one-way street that runs downhill as one goes from west to east. At the intersection of Tenth Street and Pacific Highway, Mr. Goldsmith came to a full stop for a red light. When the light turned green, he started downhill and immediately struck Mr. Bates, a 43-year-old high school teacher who was jogging north on Pacific. Mr. Bates was not seriously injured and admitted that he had been careless in crossing the intersection.

Trooper Ressa filled out an Accident Report form, similar to that which is shown above.

41. Under the section, *Vehicle in Collision With*, Officer Ressa should have checked the box for

    (A) Pedestrian.
    (B) Other Vehicle.
    (C) Fixed Object.
    (D) Other.

42. The box that he should have checked under *Type of Traffic Control* is

    (A) Flashing Light.
    (B) Other.
    (C) Signal Light in Operation.
    (D) Stop Sign.

43. Under *Character of Road*, Officer Ressa should have checked the box for

    (A) Curve Approaching Hilltop.
    (B) Straight Approaching Hilltop.
    (C) Straight on Hill.
    (D) Curve on Hill.

44. The box that he should have checked under *Action of Pedestrian at Intersection* is

    (A) Crossing Against Signal.
    (B) Crossing, No Signal.
    (C) Crossing With Signal.
    (D) Crossing Diagonally.

ACCIDENT REPORT

Date_____   Time_____   Location of Accident_____

Vehicle in Collision With

☐ Pedestrian   ☐ Motorcycle
☐ Other Vehicle   ☐ Fixed Object
☐ Train   ☐ Bicycle
☐ Animal   ☐ Other

Type of Traffic Control

☐ Police Officer   ☐ Stop Sign
☐ Signal Light in Operation   ☐ Yield Sign
☐ Signal Light Not in Operation ☐ Other
☐ Flashing Light   ☐ None

Character of Road

☐ Straight and Level   ☐ Curve and Level
☐ Straight On Hill   ☐ Curve On Hill
☐ Straight Approaching Hilltop   ☐ Curve Approaching Hilltop

Action of Pedestrian at Intersection

☐ Crossing With Signal   ☐ Crossing Diagonally
☐ Crossing Against Signal   ☐ Crossing, No Signal

Action of Vehicle at Time of Accident

☐ Going Straight Ahead   ☐ Making U-Turn
☐ Overtaking   ☐ Backing Up
☐ Making Right Turn   ☐ Starting from Parking
☐ Making Left Turn   ☐ Slowing or Stopping
☐ Parked

45. He should have checked which box under *Action of Vehicle at Time of Accident*?

(A) Starting from Parking
(B) Slowing or Stopping
(C) Going Straight Ahead
(D) Overtaking

46. During the year when July 4th falls on a Monday, the first day of June would have fallen on

(A) Tuesday.
(B) Wednesday.
(C) Thursday.
(D) Friday.

47. A state trooper, before testifying in court, notes from his memo book that he made an arrest on April 15. If he were asked to testify in court as to the day of the week that the arrest took place he could do so by

(A) determining the number of days from Good Friday.
(B) determining the number of days from the second Wednesday of the month.
(C) counting back from his last payday.
(D) determining the day that the month began.

48. If the last of November occurs on a Wednesday, November 1st will have fallen on

(A) Monday.
(B) Tuesday.
(C) Thursday.
(D) Saturday.

49. During 1987, the one of the following months that could not have contained five Mondays was

(A) January.
(B) February.
(C) March.
(D) April.

50. A state trooper, while completing his report of an altercation between two motorists, should know that during a year when the first of May falls on a Friday, the incident, which occurred on April 15, happened on

(A) Monday.
(B) Tuesday.
(C) Wednesday.
(D) Thursday.

51. A Highway Patrol car follows for 25 miles a car driven by a suspect in a crime. The suspect then veers off the road and hides. The patrol car passes the hiding place and goes 7 miles further in pursuit before the troopers realize their quarry has eluded them. They then turn around and retrace their route until the 25-mile intersection. According to this story, the troopers have traveled

(A) 39 miles and the suspect 25 miles.
(B) 25 miles and the suspect 39 miles.
(C) 25 miles and the suspect 25 miles.
(D) 32 miles and the suspect 25 miles.

52. On a road map the scale of miles reads 1 inch = 50 miles. In order to find the mileage between two towns that are three inches apart on this map and to allow for a return trip, the trooper would have to

    (A) multiply by 3.
    (B) multiply by 50 and then double the mileage.
    (C) multiply by 3 and divide by 2.
    (D) measure off the distance in inches, divide by 3, and multiply by 2.

53. A Highway Patrol car travels 60 miles per hour for 10 minutes and then decreases its speed to 40 miles per hour for the next 30 minutes. How many miles would the patrol car have traveled?

    (A) 10 miles
    (B) 20 miles
    (C) 30 miles
    (D) 40 miles

54. Having chased a suspect's car for 20 minutes at 75 miles per hour, a Highway Patrol car increases its speed to 90 mph for 10 minutes. How many miles has the patrol car given chase?

    (A) 15 miles
    (B) 25 miles
    (C) 40 miles
    (D) 55 miles

55. A state trooper approaches an intersection and follows the directional signs "right turn to Cobblestone" for 20 miles. He then turns right again and drives for 30 miles. At this point he stops, studies his map, and then decides to return to his original starting point. Upon his return he will have traveled

    (A) 50 miles.
    (B) 100 miles.
    (C) 70 miles.
    (D) 80 miles.

56. A state trooper is on patrol on a four-lane divided highway during a rainstorm. He approaches a bridge over a creek and discovers that the eastbound portion has broken off and fallen into the creek. The creek is swollen, the water level is very high, and the current is swift. Of the following, the first action the trooper should take is to

    (A) stop traffic in both directions of the highway.
    (B) radio his supervisor to report this condition and to ask for help.
    (C) go down to the creek to examine conditions closely.
    (D) call the nearest local sheriff.

57. A four-lane divided highway is intersected by a two-lane road. The standard red-yellow-green signal lights are at this intersection. A left turn is permitted from the center lane on the yellow signal light. If the car turns left on a green signal, this action would be

    (A) correct, if no traffic is coming from the other direction.
    (B) incorrect, since the yellow signal is not showing.
    (C) correct, since there is no danger involved.
    (D) incorrect, since left turns at this kind of intersection are always hazardous.

58. A state trooper is patrolling a divided highway and drives on one part where the lights are out. The only illumination is moonlight. Upon driving through this part, he reports the conditions to his superior. He is advised that the lights cannot be turned on for the next few hours due to a local power failure. This condition is best described as

    (A) hazardous; oncoming traffic may have bright headlights that are momentarily blinding.
    (B) not hazardous; moonlight is sufficient for driving on the highway.
    (C) very hazardous; highway lighting is essential for night driving.
    (D) somewhat hazardous; lighting from car headlights is generally sufficient for night driving.

59. In lonely, uninhabited stretches of road the trooper may come upon a motorist with a disabled car. Either a flat tire or a dead battery are the most frequent causes of such disabled cars. Upon observing the situation described above, the first action for the trooper to take is to

    (A) use his radio to report the occurrence and ask for assistance but continue on patrol.
    (B) stop to help the motorist in trouble.
    (C) stop only to help change a tire but not to diagnose mechanical difficulties.
    (D) place a white cloth on the radio antenna of the disabled car and stand there in case another motorist drives by to avoid accidents.

60. Large volumes of traffic at major highway intersections, particularly after dawn and sunset, are major causes of highway congestion and lead to accidents. A state trooper assigned to highway patrol in areas including such intersections should

    (A) maintain surveillance of such intersections during periods of heavy traffic.
    (B) avoid such intersections so as not to get caught in traffic and prevent continued patrol duties of the rest of the route.
    (C) approach such intersections only when assistance is requested by a motorist.
    (D) None of the above.

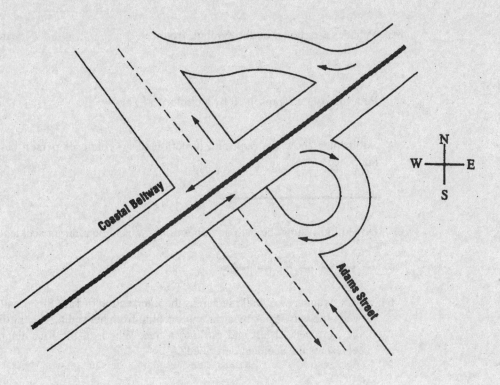

The above map for questions 61 through 63 illustrates two exit ramps from Coastal Beltway, a median divided highway on to Adams Street, a local street.

61. A car traveling southwest on the Coastal Beltway exits to Adams Street. It can then proceed only

(A) northwest.
(B) southeast.
(C) northeast.
(D) southwest.

62. A car traveling northeast on the Coastal Beltway exits to Adams Street. It can then proceed only

(A) northwest.
(B) southeast.
(C) northeast.
(D) southwest.

63. A car traveling northwest on Adams Street desires to enter Coastal Beltway. The one of the following that is correct is that

(A) the car can enter traveling northeast.
(B) it can make a U-turn and enter the Coastal Beltway.
(C) the car cannot enter the Coastal Beltway at this junction.
(D) it can exit Adams Street by traveling southeast.

In the diagrams for questions 64 and 65, symbols are used to represent vehicles and pedestrians and their movements.

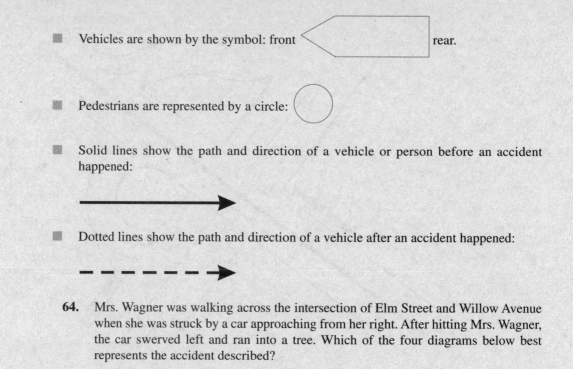

- Vehicles are shown by the symbol: front   rear.

- Pedestrians are represented by a circle:

- Solid lines show the path and direction of a vehicle or person before an accident happened:

- Dotted lines show the path and direction of a vehicle after an accident happened:

64. Mrs. Wagner was walking across the intersection of Elm Street and Willow Avenue when she was struck by a car approaching from her right. After hitting Mrs. Wagner, the car swerved left and ran into a tree. Which of the four diagrams below best represents the accident described?

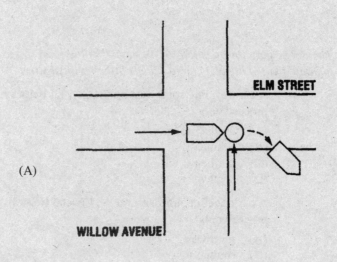

(A)

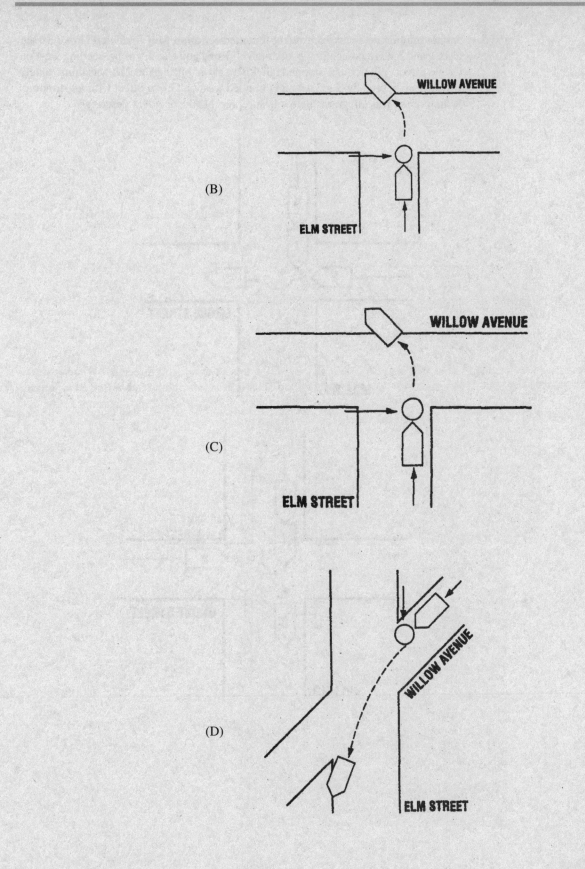

65. An automobile accident occurred at the intersection of Mill Road and Grove Street. Cars 1 and 3 were proceeding south on Mill Road and Car 2 was proceeding west on Grove Street. When Car 1 stopped quickly to avoid hitting Car 2, it was immediately struck from behind by Car 3. Car 2 continued west on Grove Street without stopping. Which of the four diagrams below best represents the accident described?

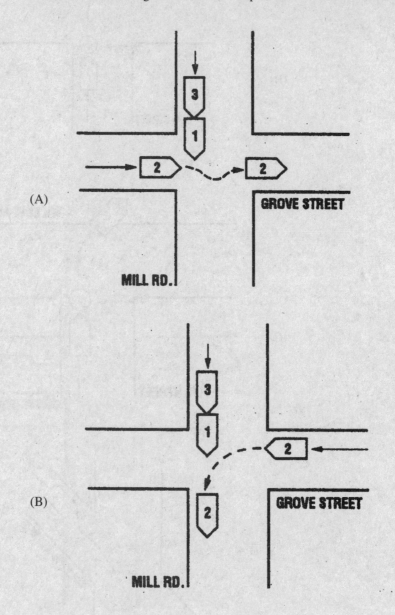

(A)

(B)

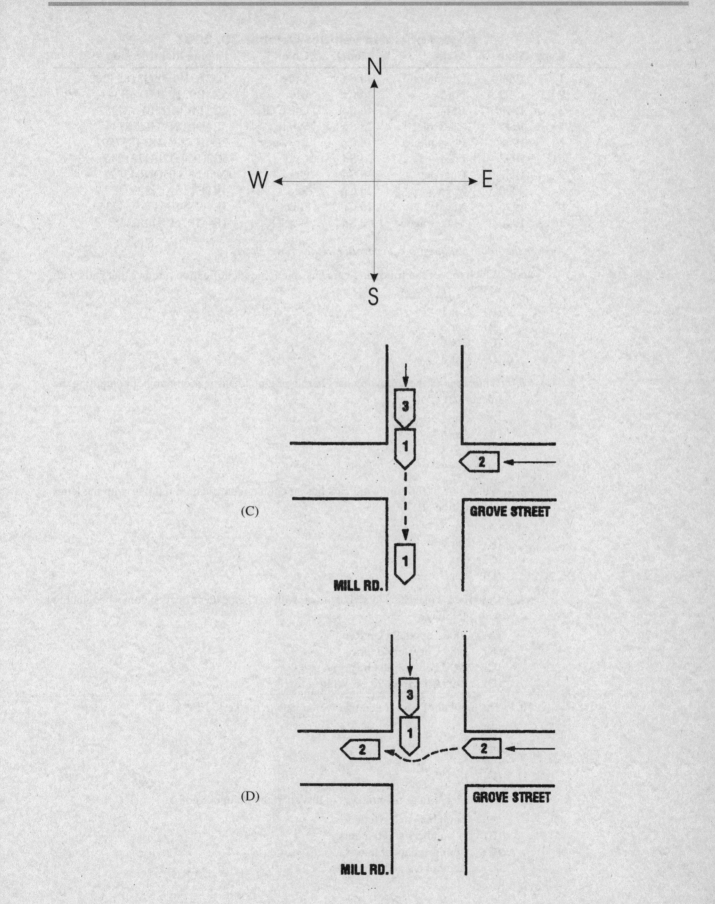

Report of stolen vehicles October 30, 2001

Car#	Year	Make	Model	Color	Engine Identification #
1	1998	Oldsmobile	4d Sd	Gray	1G3AJ19E4EG318532
2	1992	Ford	2d Cp	Blue	5X4B021C4CT46B341
3	1999	BMW	4d Sd	Olive Green	2C3TW15H5BF524352
4	1995	Chevrolet	2d Sd	White	3B4DL12F3HI256734
5	1988	Plymouth	4d Cp	Brown	2D7HT37G4KM837591
6	1992	Ford	2d Sd	Gray	5E2CK45J2LO721845
7	1989	Chrysler	4d Sd	Gray	7J5LN08T5DN643721
8	2000	Toyota	2d Cp	Red	4K8ET15AINS297127
9	1996	Mazda	2d Cp	Blue	7L4FX54B6TW934235
10	1990	Volkswagen	4d Sd	Black	1F4MP76LF40J63251

Answer the following questions according to the above chart.

66. Which one of the following cars has an engine identification number that ends with "45"?

(A) Car 1
(B) Car 3
(C) Car 6
(D) Car 8

67. Which one of the following cars has an engine identification number containing the integer "21"?

(A) Car 2
(B) Car 5
(C) Car 8
(D) Car 9

68. Which one of the following cars has an engine identification number with the letter combination "FX"?

(A) Car 3
(B) Car 4
(C) Car 6
(D) Car 9

69. Describe the make and model of the car with an engine identification number beginning with "4K8ET."

(A) 2000 Toyota 2d Cp Red
(B) 1989 Chrysler 4d Gray
(C) 1992 Ford 2d Sd Gray
(D) 1995 Chevrolet 2d Sd White

70. The number of cars stolen that were made in the period 1992–96 is

(A) 1
(B) 2
(C) 3
(D) 4

71. Engine identification numbers in this chart are composed of

(A) 8 numbers and 9 letters.
(B) 11 numbers and 6 letters.
(C) 6 numbers and 9 letters.
(D) 12 numbers and 4 letters.

72. Which of the following cars has an engine identification number that ends with "721"?

(A) Car 2
(B) Car 5
(C) Car 7
(D) Car 9

73. Which of the following cars has an engine identification number containing the letter combination "DN"?

(A) Car 1
(B) Car 3
(C) Car 6
(D) Car 7

74. Which of the following cars has an engine identification number containing the combination "HT37"?

(A) Car 1
(B) Car 3
(C) Car 5
(D) Car 7

75. Which of the following cars has an engine identification number containing the integer "15"?

(A) Car 1
(B) Car 3
(C) Car 5
(D) Car 7

Directions: Each selection is followed by a number of questions based upon the information given in the selection. Read the selection carefully; then read each questions carefully before marking your answer.

Selection for questions 76 through 79.

A summons is an official statement ordering a person to appear in court. In traffic violation situations, summonses are used when arrests need not be made. The main reason for traffic summonses is to deter motorists from repeating the same traffic violation. Occasionally motorists may make unintentional driving errors and sometimes they are unaware of the correct driving regulation. In cases such as these, the policy is to have the officer verbally inform the motorist of the violation and warn him or her against repeating it. The purpose of this practice is not to limit the number of summonses, but rather to prevent the issuing of summonses when the violation is not due to deliberate intent or to inexcusable negligence.

76. According to the preceding passage, the principal reason for issuing traffic summonses is to

(A) discourage motorists from violating these laws again.
(B) increase the money collected by the city.
(C) put traffic violators in prison.
(D) have them serve as substitutes for police officers.

77. The reason a verbal warning may sometimes be substituted for a summons is to

    (A) limit the number of summonses.
    (B) distinguish between excusable and inexcusable violations.
    (C) provide harsher penalties for deliberate intent than for inexcusable negligence.
    (D) decrease the caseload in the courts.

78. The author of the preceding passage feels that someone who violated a traffic regulation because he or she did not know about the regulation should be

    (A) put under arrest.
    (B) fined less money.
    (C) given a summons.
    (D) told not to do it again.

79. Using the distinctions made by the author of the preceding passage, the one of the following motorists to whom it would be most desirable to issue a summons is the one who exceeded the speed limit because he or she

    (A) did not know the speed limit.
    (B) was late for an important business appointment.
    (C) speeded to avoid being hit by another car.
    (D) had a speedometer that was not working properly.

Selection for questions 80 and 81.

All members of the police force must recognize that the people, through their representatives, hire and pay the police and that, as in any other employment, a proper employer-employee relationship must exist. Police officers must understand that the essence of a correct police attitude is a willingness to serve, but at the same time, they should distinguish between service and servility, between courtesy and softness. They must be firm but also courteous, avoiding even an appearance of rudeness. They should develop a position that is friendly and unbiased, pleasant and sympathetic in their relations with the general public, but firm and impersonal on occasions calling for regulation and control. Police officers should understand that their primary purpose is to prevent violations, not to arrest people. They should recognize the line of demarcation between a police function and passing judgment, which is a court function. On the other side, a public that cooperates with the police, that supports them in their efforts, and that observes laws and regulations may be said to have a desirable attitude.

80. In accordance with this paragraph, the proper attitude for a police officer to take is

    (A) to be pleasant and sympathetic at all times.
    (B) to be friendly, firm, and impartial.
    (C) to be stern and severe in meting out justice to all.
    (D) to avoid being rude, except in cases where the public is uncooperative.

81. Assume that an officer is assigned by his superior officer to a busy traffic intersection and is warned to be on the lookout for motorists who skip the light or who are speeding. According to this paragraph, it would be proper for the officer in this assignment to

    (A) give a summons to every motorist whose car was crossing when the light changed.
    (B) hide behind a truck and wait for drivers who violate traffic laws.
    (C) select at random motorists who seem to be impatient and lecture them sternly on traffic safety.
    (D) stand on post in order to deter violations and give offenders a summons or a warning as required.

Selection for questions 82 and 83.

Proper firearms training is one phase of law enforcement that cannot be ignored. No part of the training of a police officer is more important or more valuable. The officer's life and often the lives of his fellow officers depend directly upon his skill with the weapon he is carrying. Proficiency with the revolver is not attained exclusively by the volume of ammunition used and the number of hours spent on the firing line. Supervised practice and the use of training aids and techniques help make a proficient shooter. It is essential to have a good firing range where new officers are trained and older personnel practice in scheduled firearms sessions. The fundamental points to be stressed are grip, stance, breathing, sight alignment, and trigger squeeze. Coordination of thought, vision, and motion must be achieved before the officer gains confidence in his shooting ability. Attaining this ability will make the student a better officer and enhance his value to the force.

82. A police officer will gain confidence in his shooting ability only after he has

    (A) spent the required number of hours on the firing line.

    (B) been given sufficient supervised practice.

    (C) learned the five fundamental points.

    (D) learned to coordinate revolver movement with his sight and thought.

83. Proper training in the use of firearms is one aspect of law enforcement that must be given serious consideration chiefly because it is the

    (A) most useful and essential single factor in the training of a police officer.

    (B) one phase of police officer training that stresses mental and physical coordination.

    (C) costliest aspect of police officer training, involving considerable expense for the ammunition used in target practice.

    (D) most difficult part of police officer training, involving the expenditure of many hours on the firing line.

Selection for questions 84 through 87.

Because of the importance of preserving physical evidence, the officer should not enter a scene of a crime if it can be examined visually from one position and if no other pressing duty requires his presence there. There are some responsibilities, however, that take precedence over preservation of evidence. Some examples are as follows: rescue work, disarming dangerous persons, and quelling a disturbance. The officer should learn how to accomplish these more visual tasks while at the same time preserving as much evidence as possible. If he finds it necessary to enter upon the scene, he should quickly study the place of entry to learn if any evidence will suffer by his contact; then he should determine the routes to use in walking to the spot where his presence is required. Every place where a foot will fall or where a hand or other part of his body will touch should be examined with the eye. Objects should not be touched or moved unless there is a definite and compelling reason. For identification of most items of physical evidence at the initial investigation it is seldom necessary to touch or move them.

84. The one of the following titles that is the most appropriate for the above paragraph is

    (A) "Determining the Order of Tasks at the Scene of a Crime."

    (B) "The Principal Reasons for Preserving Evidence at the Scene of a Crime."

    (C) "Precautions to Take at the Scene of a Crime."

    (D) "Evidence to be Examined at the Scene of a Crime."

85. When an officer feels that it is essential for him to enter the immediate area where a crime has been committed, he should

    (A) quickly but carefully glance around to determine whether his entering the area will damage any evidence present.

    (B) remove all objects of evidence from his predetermined route in order to avoid stepping on them.

    (C) carefully replace any object immediately if it is moved or touched by his hands or any other part of his body.

    (D) use only the usual place of entry to the scene in order to avoid disturbing any possible clues left on rear doors and windows.

86. The one of the following that is the least urgent duty of an officer who has just reported to the scene of a crime is to

    (A) disarm the hysterical victim of the crime who is wildly waving a loaded gun in all directions.

    (B) give first aid to a possible suspect who has been injured while attempting to leave the scene of the crime.

    (C) prevent observers from attacking and injuring the persons suspected of having committed the crime.

    (D) preserve from damage or destruction any evidence necessary for the proper prosecution of the case against the criminals.

87. An officer has just reported to the scene of a crime in response to a phone call. The best of the following actions for him to take with respect to objects of physical evidence present at the scene is to

    (A) make no attempt to enter the crime scene if his entry will disturb any vital physical evidence.

    (B) map out the shortest straight path to follow in walking to the spot where the most physical evidence may be found.

    (C) move such objects of physical evidence as are necessary to enable him to assist the wounded victim of the crime.

    (D) quickly examine all objects of physical evidence in order to determine which objects may be touched and which may not.

Selection for questions 88 through 91.

Our system of criminal justice fails to reduce crime. If police, courts, and prisons functioned at the most effective level possible, they would not substantially or permanently reduce crime while conditions that breed crime persist. Mere words of prohibition, with force and the threat of force their only sanction, cannot shape human conduct in mass society.

As turbulence, doubt, and anxiety cause fear to increase, fear in turn seeks repression as a source of safety. But the result of repression is more turbulence and more crime. In frustration over the failure of law enforcement to control crime, new, quick, and cheap methods by which police and courts and prisons might be made effective are sought amid desperate hope and rising hatred. A public that believes the police alone are responsible for crime control, and therefore no other effort is needed, will vest any power in the police force that promises safety where fear of crime is great. But there is no such power.

Excessive reliance on the criminal justice system is extremely dangerous because it separates the people from the government. It is the one clear avenue to irreconcilable division in America. It puts government institutions in which people must have confidence in direct confrontation with dynamics they cannot control. When the system is abusive, society itself is unfair; government demeans human dignity. There then follows a contest of cunning between the people and the state that the state can never win.

88. The one of the following titles that most nearly expresses the main thought of this passage is

    (A) "The Need for Additional Police Power"
    (B) "Frustrated Law Enforcement"
    (C) "Police, Courts, and Prisons—A Balancing of Power"
    (D) "The Problem of Crime Control"

89. Based solely on this passage, which of the following statements is most correct?

    (A) Increasing fear is a direct result of repression.
    (B) Repression is a direct result of increasing turbulence and crime.
    (C) Turbulence, doubt, and anxiety are a direct cause of more crime.
    (D) Repression is both a result of increasing fear and a cause of greater turbulence.

90. According to this passage, the desire for improvements in the system of criminal justice in response to increasing crime

    (A) stems largely from a failure to appreciate the actual cost of crime to the community.
    (B) is not likely to result in greater safety for the public.
    (C) will result in a lack of confidence in the police.
    (D) is caused by the resentment that is felt by certain groups in our society.

91. When the author of this passage states that excessive reliance on the system of criminal justice is dangerous, he or she implies that

    (A) citizens will not accept restraints imposed by the police.
    (B) division in America is a result of undue emphasis upon the rights of the individual.
    (C) government institutions would be asked to perform an impossible task.
    (D) police cause distrust by their failure to enforce the law diligently.

Directions: Each problem in this section involves a certain amount of logical reasoning and thinking on your part, along with the usual simple computations. Read each problem carefully and choose the correct answer from the four choices that follow.

---

92. If the average cost of sweeping a square foot of a city street is $7.50, the cost of sweeping 100 square feet is

    (A) $75.00
    (B) $7,500.00
    (C) $750.00
    (D) $700.00

93. If a Sanitation Department scow is towed at the rate of 3 miles an hour, it will need how many hours to go 28 miles?

    (A) 10 hrs. 30 mins.
    (B) 12 hrs.
    (C) 9 hrs. 20 min.
    (D) 9 hrs. 15 min.

94. If a truck is 60 feet away from a sanitation worker, it is how many feet nearer to him than a truck that is 100 feet away?

    (A) 60 ft.
    (B) 40 ft.
    (C) 50 ft.
    (D) 20 ft.

95. A clerk divided his 35-hour workweek as follows: 1/5 of his time in sorting mail; 1/2 of his time in filing letters; and 1/7 of his time in reception work. The rest of his time was devoted to messenger work. The percentage of time spent on messenger work by the clerk during the week was most nearly

(A) 6%
(B) 10%
(C) 14%
(D) 16%

96. Twelve clerks are assigned to enter certain data on index cards. This number of clerks could perform the task in eighteen days. After these clerks have worked on this assignment for 6 days, 4 more clerks are added to the staff to do this work. Assuming that all the clerks work at the same rate of speed, the entire task, instead of taking 18 days, will be performed in

(A) 9 days.
(B) 12 days.
(C) 17 days.
(D) 15 days.

97. Six gross of special pencils were purchased for use in a city department. If the pencils were used at the rate of twenty-four a week, the maximum number of weeks that the six gross of pencils would last is

(A) 6 weeks.
(B) 12 weeks.
(C) 24 weeks.
(D) 36 weeks.

98. A man worked 30 days. He paid 2/5 of his earnings for room and board, then had $1,440. What was his daily wage?

(A) $95.00
(B) $80.00
(C) $85.00
(D) $110.00

99. After gaining 50% on his original capital, a man had capital of $18,000. Find the original capital.

(A) $12,200.00
(B) $13,100.00
(C) $12,000.00
(D) $12,025.00

100. A cog wheel having 8 cogs plays into another cog wheel having 24 cogs. When the small wheel has made 42 revolutions, how many has the larger wheel made?

(A) 14
(B) 20
(C) 16
(D) 10

MODEL EXAMINATION 3: ANSWERS AND EXPLANATIONS

ANSWERS

1. C	21. A	41. A	61. A	81. D
2. C	22. A	42. C	62. A	82. D
3. A	23. B	43. C	63. C	83. A
4. A	24. C	44. A	64. B	84. C
5. D	25. D	45. C	65. D	85. A
6. A	26. D	46. B	66. C	86. D
7. C	27. A	47. D	67. A	87. C
8. D	28. D	48. B	68. D	88. D
9. B	29. C	49. B	69. A	89. D
10. B	30. A	50. C	70. D	90. B
11. C	31. D	51. A	71. B	91. C
12. A	32. D	52. B	72. C	92. C
13. A	33. A	53. C	73. D	93. C
14. B	34. C	54. C	74. C	94. B
15. A	35. B	55. B	75. B	95. D
16. D	36. B	56. B	76. A	96. D
17. C	37. C	57. A	77. B	97. D
18. B	38. D	58. D	78. D	98. B
19. D	39. A	59. A	79. B	99. C
20. B	40. B	60. A	80. B	100. A

EXPLANATIONS

1. **The correct answer is (C).** This response to the question would be most useful in locating the vehicle.
2. **The correct answer is (C).** Self-explanatory in the illustration.
3. **The correct answer is (A).** The information supplied by the witnesses would form the basis for the main part of the interrogation.
4. **The correct answer is (A).** This ability will enable troopers to apprehend wanted criminals they may encounter while on patrol.
5. **The correct answer is (D).** A state trooper is always on duty, even on off-hours. If the trooper encounters an incident that is in violation of a law or is a disturbance of the peace, he or she should intercede just as if the incident were taking place while the trooper was on active duty.
6. **The correct answer is (A).** This is a suspicious incident worthy of your attention. But since there are several people involved, you will be able to do little alone. Your superior will be able to provide the assistance necessary.
7. **The correct answer is (C).** Self-explanatory.
8. **The correct answer is (D).** The wound is clean. There are no rough edges where infection can breed.
9. **The correct answer is (B).** It is imperative that an individual with a back injury not be moved without professional assistance.
10. **The correct answer is (B).** Loss of a good deal of blood can lead to a loss of life.
11. **The correct answer is (C).** An alibi is supposed to support the accused's plea that he or she did not commit the crime in question.
12. **The correct answer is (A).** An accessory is a person who, even if not present when the crime is committed, is involved either before or after the perpetration of a felony.
13. **The correct answer is (A).** The answer is self-explanatory. Acknowledgment: A formal declaration before a competent authority or the official certificate of such a declaration. Oath: A solemn assertion or promise, with the invocation of God, to be a witness of the truth of what one says. Subpoena: A judicial writ requiring a person to appear as a witness at a specified time and place, under penalty of default.
14. **The correct answer is (B).** There is no reference to character on a bank's signature card, nor is there any financial information there. Places of employment are not kept current.
15. **The correct answer is (A).** An individual may be deemed to be an "accomplice" under these circumstances.
16. **The correct answer is (D).** The pockmarks are distinctive. Not very many people have them. All of the other physical qualities can apply to many people.
17. **The correct answer is (C).** Not very many females are that tall. Again, the features in the other choices can and do apply to many females.
18. **The correct answer is (B).** No two ears are exactly alike.
19. **The correct answer is (D).** Not many cars are on the road with their front bumper missing. This will make this vehicle distinctive and easily spotted.
20. **The correct answer is (B).** The number of an automobile engine is not easily changed, so in all likelihood this is not the stolen car, especially since only one day has passed. License plates can be substituted easily, a windshield can be readily cracked, and dents can be made to avoid identification of the vehicle.
21. **The correct answer is (A).** There are not many men around who weigh that much; therefore this man would tend to stand out. The identifications in choices (B) and (C) are quite common. The thin scar on the upper left lip would be difficult to recognize, and the tattoo would not be easily visible.
22. **The correct answer is (A).** The color of the eyes cannot be changed. Hair color is easily changed, teeth could have been lost or replaced in the interim, and of course the weight of a person is subject to change over a period of time.
23. **The correct answer is (B).** The answer is self-explanatory.

24. **The correct answer is (C).** On a busy highway, tire size and spare would be impossible to determine. Make of car is also difficult to screen quickly. Color is obvious, and many cars are not black.

25. **The correct answer is (D).** To avoid a future embarrassing situation, a male trooper should avoid searching a female. Since this is a sick or injured female and there is no danger of a concealed weapon, the course of action in choice (D) would be best.

26. **The correct answer is (D).** The burning of the fingers indicated in choice (C) would only call attention to the attempt. Facial surgery might be more successful.

27. **The correct answer is (A).** This is commonly known as a "lineup."

28. **The correct answer is (D).** Social Security cards do not bear any information that specifically identifies the individuals carrying them.

29. **The correct answer is (C).** A very small number of people stutter, and a stutterer with a French accent is unusual indeed.

30. **The correct answer is (A).** This type of disorder is marked by spasmodic uncontrolled physical movements.

31. **The correct answer is (D).** This is an incorrect statement; therefore it should be selected.

32. **The correct answer is (D).** If you do away with the reasons that people become criminals, you will probably do away with most crime.

33. **The correct answer is (A).** If a program of crime prevention is successful, there will be less need for correctional institutions.

34. **The correct answer is (C).** All criminals believe in "no legal restraints." Therefore, if a person does not believe in "no legal restraints," that person cannot be a criminal.

35. **The correct answer is (B).** Most authorities support the theory that individuals are strongly influenced by their environment and that if that environment is conducive to criminal behavior, criminal tendencies may result.

36. **The correct answer is (B).** Review this diagram.

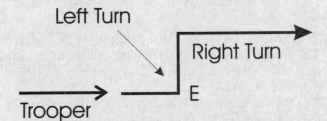

The right turn reverses direction of the left turn and keeps the trooper in the same direction as when he started.

37. **The correct answer is (C).** Unlike question 36, this trooper, in making a second left, goes in the opposite direction from that in which he or she started.

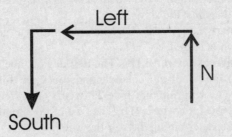

38. **The correct answer is (D).** This is the same result as question 36, except that the original direction is westward. Nevertheless, he finishes up in the same direction.

39.   **The correct answer is (A).**

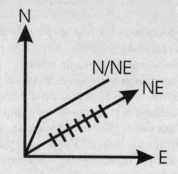

Of the choices given, choice (A) is the most correct. (The tracked line is shown for guidance only.)

40.   **The correct answer is (B).**

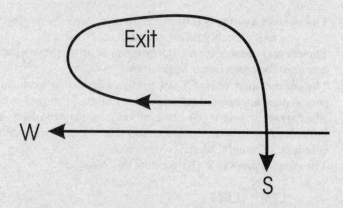

In a cloverleaf intersection, this is the path of the trooper.

41.   **The correct answer is (A).** From the statements of the parties involved and from his own observations of the scene, it is clear that the vehicle was in a collision with Mr. Bates, a pedestrian.

42.   **The correct answer is (C).** According to the trooper's findings, the signal light had turned green when Mr. Goldsmith started downhill.

43.   **The correct answer is (C).** According to the account, Tenth Street, on which Mr. Goldsmith was traveling, is a straight, one-way street that runs downhill as one goes from west to east.

44.   **The correct answer is (A).** According to the account, the signal light had turned green for Mr. Goldsmith when Mr. Bates was crossing on Pacific. Therefore, Bates must have crossed against the signal.

45.   **The correct answer is (C).** Mr. Goldsmith was going downhill on Tenth Street when the accident occurred.

46.   **The correct answer is (B).** The first day of June will be the same day of the week as the 29th of June (look at a calendar and you'll see this). Count backward from Monday, July 4, and you will find that June 29 occurs on a Wednesday.

47.   **The correct answer is (D).** The first of the month is by far the most reasonable starting point for determining days of the week.

48.   **The correct answer is (B).** Use the same method as in question 46, above.

49.   **The correct answer is (B).** 1987 was not a leap year, so February was exactly four weeks long and could not have contained five Mondays.

50.   **The correct answer is (C).** Use the same method as in question 46, above.

51. **The correct answer is (A).** 25 miles + 7 miles + 7 miles = 39. Suspect has only traveled 25 miles.

52. **The correct answer is (B).** The answer is self-explanatory.

53. **The correct answer is (C).** 60 mph for 10 minutes = 10 miles
40 mph for 30 minutes = 20 miles
Total = 30 miles

54. **The correct answer is (C).** 75 mph for 20 minutes $= \dfrac{20}{60} \times 75 = 25$ miles
90 mph for 10 minutes $= \dfrac{10}{60} \times 90 = 15$ miles
Total = 40 miles

55. **The correct answer is (B).** Assuming that he turned around and retraced his route, the trooper traveled 100 miles.

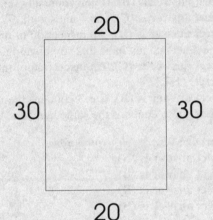

56. **The correct answer is (B).** A single trooper cannot stop traffic in both directions at the same time. He should stop eastbound traffic and radio for help right away.

57. **The correct answer is (A).** Since left turns are permitted, they are permitted on green. Left on yellow is permitted, not required.

58. **The correct answer is (D).** Ordinarily headlights are adequate for night driving on a highway. Lights were probably installed on this stretch for a reason, so their absence can create some problem. Choice (A) is true but has no relation to street lighting.

59. **The correct answer is (A).** Part of the trooper's job is to locate motorists in distress. If he stays with this one car, others may be stranded even longer. It is sufficient to radio for help and then to continue on patrol.

60. **The correct answer is (A).** A primary part of the patrol function is maintaining surveillance (observation). Choices (B) and (C) would be a means of avoiding the responsibilities of highway patrol. There is no other principle of patrol other than choice (A), so choice (D) is incorrect.

61. **The correct answer is (A).** Placing the cross compass over the map, the student will see that a vehicle traveling southwest following the arrow into the exit to Adams Street will then go northwest.

62. **The correct answer is (A).** The vehicle traveling northeast and exiting first turns toward the southeast but must enter Adams Street going northwest.

63. **The correct answer is (C).** An examination of the map shows no entrances (only exits) from the Beltway. Therefore, choice (C) is the only answer. The map does not indicate any exits after this junction. Therefore, choice (D) is wrong.

64. **The correct answer is (B).** Put yourself in Mrs. Wagner's place. The right and left directions will be apparent.

65. **The correct answer is (D).** Answer is apparent from the maps.
The table for questions 66 through 75 requires an ability to read numbers in detail. If you check the table, you will find the answer to each question.

66. **The correct answer is (C).** Car 6 has an engine number that ends with "45." The others don't end with this number.

67. **The correct answer is (A).** Car 2 has an engine number that contains the number " 21." The other choices don't and therefore choice (A) is the only answer. Car 8 also contains the number, but is not one of the choices. Make sure you read the questions carefully.

68. **The correct answer is (D).** Car 9 has the letter combination "FX" near the beginning of the number. Cars 3, 4, and 6 have no such letters anywhere in their engine numbers.

69. **The correct answer is (A).** An inspection of the table shows that Car 8 has the engine number called for by the question.

70. **The correct answer is (D).** Cars 2, 4, 6, and 9 were made between 1992 and 1996.

71. **The correct answer is (B).** If you count any set, you will find 11 numbers and 6 letters.

72. **The correct answer is (C).** Car 7 ends with "721." The others end differently.

73. **The correct answer is (D).** An inspection of the table shows that Car 7 has the letters "DN." The others do not have this combination.

74. **The correct answer is (C).** An inspection of the table shows that Car 5 has the letters and numerals "HT37."

75. **The correct answer is (B).** Car 3 contains the integer "15" in its engine identification number. Car 8 also contains the same numbers, but is not one of the choices.

Answers 76 through 91 are self-explanatory.

76. **The correct answer is (A).**
77. **The correct answer is (B).**
78. **The correct answer is (D).**
79. **The correct answer is (B).**
80. **The correct answer is (B).**
81. **The correct answer is (D).**
82. **The correct answer is (D).**
83. **The correct answer is (A).**
84. **The correct answer is (C).**
85. **The correct answer is (A).**
86. **The correct answer is (D).**
87. **The correct answer is (C).**
88. **The correct answer is (D).**
89. **The correct answer is (D).**
90. **The correct answer is (B).**
91. **The correct answer is (C).**
92. **The correct answer is (C).** To multiply by 100, move the decimal point two places to the right. $7.50 x 100 = $750.00

93. **The correct answer is (C).** $28 \div 3 = 9\frac{1}{3}$
($\frac{1}{3}$ of 60 minutes is 20 minutes.)

94. **The correct answer is (B).** $100 - 60 = 40$

95. **The correct answer is (D).** $\frac{1}{5} = 20\%$

$$\frac{1}{7} = 14\frac{2}{7}\%$$

$$+\frac{1}{2} = 50\%$$

$$100\% \quad 84\frac{2}{7}$$

$$100\%$$

$$-84\frac{2}{7}$$

$$15\frac{5}{7}\% \text{ (most nearly 15\%)}$$

96. **The correct answer is (D).**

Clerks		Days	
12	×	18	= 216
12	×	6	= 72
216	−	72	= 144

Now work from 144:

16	×	9	= 144
144	÷	16	= 9
9	+	6	= 15 (answer)

97. **The correct answer is (D).** A gross is 144.
$144 \times 6 = 864$
$864 \div 24 = 36$

98. **The correct answer is (B).** $\quad \frac{3}{5} = 1,440$

$$\frac{1}{5} = 480$$

$$\frac{5}{5} = 2,400$$

$$2,400 \div 30 = \$80.00$$

99. **The correct answer is (C).** $\$18,000 = 150\%$
$\$12,000 = 100\%$ (original capital)

100. **The correct answer is (A).** $\quad \frac{8}{24} = \frac{1}{3}$

$$\frac{1}{3} \times 42 = 14$$

MODEL EXAMINATION 4: ANSWER SHEET

1. Ⓐ Ⓑ Ⓒ Ⓓ   21. Ⓐ Ⓑ Ⓒ Ⓓ   41. Ⓐ Ⓑ Ⓒ Ⓓ   61. Ⓐ Ⓑ Ⓒ Ⓓ   81. Ⓐ Ⓑ Ⓒ Ⓓ
2. Ⓐ Ⓑ Ⓒ Ⓓ   22. Ⓐ Ⓑ Ⓒ Ⓓ   42. Ⓐ Ⓑ Ⓒ Ⓓ   62. Ⓐ Ⓑ Ⓒ Ⓓ   82. Ⓐ Ⓑ Ⓒ Ⓓ
3. Ⓐ Ⓑ Ⓒ Ⓓ   23. Ⓐ Ⓑ Ⓒ Ⓓ   43. Ⓐ Ⓑ Ⓒ Ⓓ   63. Ⓐ Ⓑ Ⓒ Ⓓ   83. Ⓐ Ⓑ Ⓒ Ⓓ
4. Ⓐ Ⓑ Ⓒ Ⓓ   24. Ⓐ Ⓑ Ⓒ Ⓓ   44. Ⓐ Ⓑ Ⓒ Ⓓ   64. Ⓐ Ⓑ Ⓒ Ⓓ   84. Ⓐ Ⓑ Ⓒ Ⓓ
5. Ⓐ Ⓑ Ⓒ Ⓓ   25. Ⓐ Ⓑ Ⓒ Ⓓ   45. Ⓐ Ⓑ Ⓒ Ⓓ   65. Ⓐ Ⓑ Ⓒ Ⓓ   85. Ⓐ Ⓑ Ⓒ Ⓓ
6. Ⓐ Ⓑ Ⓒ Ⓓ   26. Ⓐ Ⓑ Ⓒ Ⓓ   46. Ⓐ Ⓑ Ⓒ Ⓓ   66. Ⓐ Ⓑ Ⓒ Ⓓ   86. Ⓐ Ⓑ Ⓒ Ⓓ
7. Ⓐ Ⓑ Ⓒ Ⓓ   27. Ⓐ Ⓑ Ⓒ Ⓓ   47. Ⓐ Ⓑ Ⓒ Ⓓ   67. Ⓐ Ⓑ Ⓒ Ⓓ   87. Ⓐ Ⓑ Ⓒ Ⓓ
8. Ⓐ Ⓑ Ⓒ Ⓓ   28. Ⓐ Ⓑ Ⓒ Ⓓ   48. Ⓐ Ⓑ Ⓒ Ⓓ   68. Ⓐ Ⓑ Ⓒ Ⓓ   88. Ⓐ Ⓑ Ⓒ Ⓓ
9. Ⓐ Ⓑ Ⓒ Ⓓ   29. Ⓐ Ⓑ Ⓒ Ⓓ   49. Ⓐ Ⓑ Ⓒ Ⓓ   69. Ⓐ Ⓑ Ⓒ Ⓓ   89. Ⓐ Ⓑ Ⓒ Ⓓ
10. Ⓐ Ⓑ Ⓒ Ⓓ   30. Ⓐ Ⓑ Ⓒ Ⓓ   50. Ⓐ Ⓑ Ⓒ Ⓓ   70. Ⓐ Ⓑ Ⓒ Ⓓ   90. Ⓐ Ⓑ Ⓒ Ⓓ
11. Ⓐ Ⓑ Ⓒ Ⓓ   31. Ⓐ Ⓑ Ⓒ Ⓓ   51. Ⓐ Ⓑ Ⓒ Ⓓ   71. Ⓐ Ⓑ Ⓒ Ⓓ   91. Ⓐ Ⓑ Ⓒ Ⓓ
12. Ⓐ Ⓑ Ⓒ Ⓓ   32. Ⓐ Ⓑ Ⓒ Ⓓ   52. Ⓐ Ⓑ Ⓒ Ⓓ   72. Ⓐ Ⓑ Ⓒ Ⓓ   92. Ⓐ Ⓑ Ⓒ Ⓓ
13. Ⓐ Ⓑ Ⓒ Ⓓ   33. Ⓐ Ⓑ Ⓒ Ⓓ   53. Ⓐ Ⓑ Ⓒ Ⓓ   73. Ⓐ Ⓑ Ⓒ Ⓓ   93. Ⓐ Ⓑ Ⓒ Ⓓ
14. Ⓐ Ⓑ Ⓒ Ⓓ   34. Ⓐ Ⓑ Ⓒ Ⓓ   54. Ⓐ Ⓑ Ⓒ Ⓓ   74. Ⓐ Ⓑ Ⓒ Ⓓ   94. Ⓐ Ⓑ Ⓒ Ⓓ
15. Ⓐ Ⓑ Ⓒ Ⓓ   35. Ⓐ Ⓑ Ⓒ Ⓓ   55. Ⓐ Ⓑ Ⓒ Ⓓ   75. Ⓐ Ⓑ Ⓒ Ⓓ   95. Ⓐ Ⓑ Ⓒ Ⓓ
16. Ⓐ Ⓑ Ⓒ Ⓓ   36. Ⓐ Ⓑ Ⓒ Ⓓ   56. Ⓐ Ⓑ Ⓒ Ⓓ   76. Ⓐ Ⓑ Ⓒ Ⓓ   96. Ⓐ Ⓑ Ⓒ Ⓓ
17. Ⓐ Ⓑ Ⓒ Ⓓ   37. Ⓐ Ⓑ Ⓒ Ⓓ   57. Ⓐ Ⓑ Ⓒ Ⓓ   77. Ⓐ Ⓑ Ⓒ Ⓓ   97. Ⓐ Ⓑ Ⓒ Ⓓ
18. Ⓐ Ⓑ Ⓒ Ⓓ   38. Ⓐ Ⓑ Ⓒ Ⓓ   58. Ⓐ Ⓑ Ⓒ Ⓓ   78. Ⓐ Ⓑ Ⓒ Ⓓ   98. Ⓐ Ⓑ Ⓒ Ⓓ
19. Ⓐ Ⓑ Ⓒ Ⓓ   39. Ⓐ Ⓑ Ⓒ Ⓓ   59. Ⓐ Ⓑ Ⓒ Ⓓ   79. Ⓐ Ⓑ Ⓒ Ⓓ   99. Ⓐ Ⓑ Ⓒ Ⓓ
20. Ⓐ Ⓑ Ⓒ Ⓓ   40. Ⓐ Ⓑ Ⓒ Ⓓ   60. Ⓐ Ⓑ Ⓒ Ⓓ   80. Ⓐ Ⓑ Ⓒ Ⓓ   100. Ⓐ Ⓑ Ⓒ Ⓓ

MODEL EXAMINATION 4

TIME: $3\frac{1}{2}$ HOURS—100 QUESTIONS

Directions: Each question has four suggested answers, lettered (A), (B), (C), and (D). Decide which one is the best answer, and, on the sample answer sheet, locate the question number and darken the area corresponding to your answer choice.

Questions 1 through 15 are to be answered on the basis of the description of the police action that follows. You will have ten minutes to read and study the description. Then you will have to answer the 15 questions about the incident without referring back to the description of the incident.

State Police Officers Smith and Jones were working a midnight to 8 a.m. tour of duty. It was a Saturday morning in the month of July and the weather was clear. At about 4:30 a.m., they received a radio call reporting a burglary in progress at 777 Seventh Street, the address of an appliance store.

Upon their arrival at the scene, the troopers could not find any evidence of a break-in. However, as they continued their investigation, they heard noises coming from the rear of the building. As they raced to the rear of the building, they saw 4 people alighting from the roof, by way of a ladder, and climbing over a fence that leads to the rear of a warehouse. The troopers climbed over the fence and observed 2 of the people running into an alleyway on the west side of the warehouse and the other 2 people running into a parking lot on the east side of the warehouse.

Smith, using a walkie-talkie, called for assistance and proceeded to give chase after the 2 persons who entered the alley. The description of these 2 individuals was as follows: One was a white male with long blond hair, wearing light pants, a blue shirt, and white sneakers, and carrying what appeared to be a portable TV set. The other was also a white male, with short dark hair, wearing dungarees, a white T-shirt, and cowboy boots, and carrying what appeared to be a portable cassette-stereo-radio.

Jones continued to give chase to the 2 individuals who had entered the parking lot. The description of these 2 individuals was as follows: one was a Hispanic male with long dark hair, wearing dark pants, a yellow shirt, and dark shoes, and carrying what appeared to be a video recorder. The other was an African-American male with a bald head, wearing dungarees, a white T-shirt, and white sneakers, and carrying what appeared to be a baseball bat and portable TV set.

As Smith emerged from the alley onto the sidewalk, he again observed the 2 individuals he had been chasing. They were entering a dark blue Chevrolet with license plates beginning with the letters AKG. The vehicle drove west on Seventh Street. The male with the long blond hair appeared to be driving.

As Jones reached the parking lot, he observed the two individuals he was pursuing speed off in a white station wagon, heading west on Seventh Street. The license plates could not be discerned. Officer Jones found a broken portable TV set in the parking lot.

Smith broadcast this additional information, and both officers then quickly returned to their radio car to conduct a search of the area.

Do not refer back to the description while answering questions 1 through 15.

1. Officers Smith and Jones responded to a "burglary in progress" call at approximately
   - (A) midnight.
   - (B) 8:00 a.m.
   - (C) 4:30 p.m.
   - (D) 4:30 a.m.

2. The suspects in the burglary gained entrance to the store by
   - (A) breaking a front window.
   - (B) breaking a rear window .
   - (C) breaking in from an adjoining warehouse.
   - (D) using a ladder to get to the roof.

3. The suspects, when fleeing from the burglary
   - (A) all ran into an alleyway.
   - (B) all ran into a parking lot.
   - (C) all ran into a warehouse.
   - (D) went in different directions.

4. The white male with the long blond hair was carrying what appeared to be a
   - (A) portable TV set.
   - (B) portable cassette-stereo-radio.
   - (C) video recorder.
   - (D) portable cassette player.

5. The Hispanic male was carrying what appeared to be a
   - (A) video recorder.
   - (B) portable cassette-stereo-radio.
   - (C) portable TV set.
   - (D) portable cassette player.

6. The white male with the short hair was carrying what appeared to be a
   - (A) portable TV set.
   - (B) portable cassette-stereo-radio.
   - (C) video recorder.
   - (D) portable cassette player.

7. The suspect wearing cowboy boots was the
   - (A) white male with long blond hair.
   - (B) African-American male.
   - (C) Hispanic male.
   - (D) white male with short hair.

8. The suspect wearing light pants and a blue shirt was the
   - (A) African-American male.
   - (B) white male with long blond hair.
   - (C) Hispanic male.
   - (D) white male with short hair.

9. The suspect wearing dark pants and a yellow shirt was the
   - (A) white male with long blond hair.
   - (B) African-American male.
   - (C) white male with short hair.
   - (D) Hispanic male.

10. When the suspects were fleeing, the two white males entered a
    - (A) blue station wagon with unknown license plates.
    - (B) white station wagon with license plates beginning with the letters AKG.

(C) blue Chevrolet with license plates beginning with the letters AKG.

(D) white Chevrolet with unknown license plates.

11. From reading the description of the incident, one could assume

(A) that Seventh Street is one-way westbound.

(B) that Seventh Street is a two-way street.

(C) that Seventh Street is one-way eastbound.

(D) none of the above.

12. Upon entering the parking lot, Jones found a broken portable TV set that had apparently been dropped by the

(A) white male with blond hair.

(B) white male with dark hair.

(C) African-American male.

(D) Hispanic male.

13. The black male was

(A) bald and wearing dark pants, a yellow shirt, and dark shoes.

(B) bald and wearing dungarees, a white T-shirt, and white sneakers.

(C) wearing dungarees, a white T-shirt, and cowboy boots and had dark hair.

(D) bald and wearing light pants and a blue shirt.

14. The suspect who was carrying the baseball bat was also carrying what appeared to be a

(A) portable TV set.

(B) video recorder.

(C) portable cassette-stereo-radio.

(D) portable cassette player.

15. A description of the suspects was broadcast to other police units so that they could assist in searching the area. This was done by

(A) both Jones and Smith as they both had walkie-talkies.

(B) Trooper Jones as he had a walkie-talkie.

(C) Trooper Smith as he had a walkie-talkie.

(D) both troopers upon returning to their radio car.

16. In the investigation of a homicide case, it is desirable to have photographs taken of the body in its original condition and position. Of the following, the best reason for this practice is that the photographs

(A) show the motive for the homicide and thus indicate likely suspects

(B) indicate if the corpse has been moved in any way

(C) form a permanent record of the body and the scene of the crime

(D) reveal the specific method used in committing the homicide

17. A state trooper hears two shots fired and proceeds in the direction of the shots. He comes upon an intoxicated man who is angrily screaming at a woman. The trooper notices that the handle of a pistol is protruding from the man's pocket and orders him to surrender the pistol. The man apparently ignores the order and continues screaming at the woman. For the trooper now to fire a warning shot over the man's head would be

(A) bad; it is quite possible that the man is so intoxicated that he did not clearly hear or understand the trooper's order.

(B) bad; the trooper should realize that an intoxicated person is not entirely responsible for his actions.

(C) good; the warning shot will impress the man with the seriousness of the situation.

(D) good; since the man had already fired twice, the trooper should take no further chances.

18. The practice of writing down confessions while a suspect is being questioned is
    - (A) bad, chiefly because the time taken to put a confession into written form may prove to be a waste of time since it may later be declared to be inadmissible as evidence in court.
    - (B) bad, chiefly because this may cause the suspect to withhold information when he or she knows that the confession is being recorded.
    - (C) good, chiefly because the suspect cannot claim at a later date that the information was obtained by force.
    - (D) good, chiefly because the suspect is thereby given more time to gather his or her thoughts and give the information wanted by the police.

19. An escaped prisoner has been wounded and is lying flat on his stomach with his head turned to one side. The one of the following directions from which a state trooper should approach the prisoner in order to make it most difficult for the prisoner to fire quickly and accurately at the police officer is from the side
    - (A) directly behind the prisoner's head.
    - (B) facing the top of the prisoner's head.
    - (C) facing the prisoner's face.
    - (D) facing the prisoner's heels.

20. A gas main explosion has caused some property damage. Examination by an emergency repair crew clearly indicates that no further explosions will occur. Nevertheless, rumors are circulating that more explosions and greater damage are going to occur. This situation has resulted in a high degree of fear among local residents. The best of the following actions for a state trooper on duty at the scene to take first would be to
    - (A) ignore the rumors since they are false and no real danger exists.
    - (B) inform the people of the true circumstances of the emergency.
    - (C) question several people at the scene in an attempt to determine the source of the rumors.
    - (D) order everyone to leave the area quickly and in an orderly fashion.

21. A state trooper finds a young child wandering about a residential neighborhood. After unsuccessfully questioning the child as to the location of his home, the trooper phones police headquarters and is informed that no child meeting the description given by the officer has been reported missing. The officer decides to make inquiries about the child in the immediate area before taking any other action. The action is advisable chiefly because
    - (A) the child's parents probably know of his whereabouts since no report of the missing child has been received at headquarters.
    - (B) the child has probably been away from home only a short time since no report of the missing child has been received at headquarters.
    - (C) the child is less likely to become emotionally disturbed if he remains in his own neighborhood.
    - (D) young children, when lost, never wander more than a short distance from home.

22. While a trooper in plain clothes is following and watching a suspect in a homicide case, the trooper becomes convinced that the suspect realizes he is being watched. The suspect's identity is known to the police, but he is also known to have changed his place of residence frequently during the past few months. The trooper does not have sufficient evidence to arrest the suspect at this time. Of the following, the best action for the trooper to take is to

(A) approach the suspect, inform him that he is being followed, and demand an explanation of his suspicious past conduct.

(B) continue to follow the suspect until an opportunity is presented for the officer to telephone for a replacement.

(C) continue to follow the suspect since he will probably commit an illegal act eventually.

(D) discontinue following the suspect and attempt to gain evidence by other means.

23. Probationary State Police Officers A and B are given a special assignment by the sergeant. Officer B does not fully understand some of the instructions given by the sergeant concerning the carrying out of the assignment. Of the following, it would be best for Officer B to

(A) proceed with those parts of the assignment he understands and ask for an explanation from the sergeant when he can go no further.

(B) observe Officer A's work carefully in order to determine how the assignment is to be carried out.

(C) ask the sergeant to explain that portion of the instructions that he does not fully understand before starting the assignment.

(D) suggest to Officer A that he supervise the operation since he probably understands the sergeant's instruction better.

24. A state police officer responds at night to a telephone complaint that a prowler has been observed at a particular location. The officer arrives at the location and notices someone who appears to fit the description of the prowler that was previously given by the complainant. In approaching the individual, it would be best for the police officer to

(A) consider this individual to be a potentially dangerous criminal.

(B) avoid taking any precautionary measures since there is no way of knowing whether any offense has been committed.

(C) consider that this individual is probably harmless and is only a "Peeping Tom."

(D) fire a warning shot over the man's head.

25. A state police officer has been asked by a merchant on his post to recommend the best make of burglar alarm for his store. The chief reason why the police officer should not make any specific recommendation is that

(A) he does not have enough technical knowledge of the operation of burglar alarms.

(B) the merchant may interpret the officer's recommendation as an official police department endorsement.

(C) such a recommendation would imply that the police are incapable of protecting the merchant's property.

(D) he is not likely to know the prices of the various makes and models available.

26. Two state police officers in a radio patrol car stop a car that they recognize as having been reported stolen. The police officers immediately separate the 2 occupants of the car and proceed to question them apart from each other. Of the following, the most important reason for questioning them separately is to

(A) give each suspect an opportunity to admit guilt out of the presence of the other suspect.

(B) prevent the suspects from agreeing on an explanation of their presence in the car.

(C) prevent the errors that may arise when attempting to record in a notebook two separate statements being made at the same time.

(D) determine which of the two suspects actually planned the theft of the car.

27. A state trooper is informed by the manager of a supermarket that an object that appears to be a homemade bomb has been discovered in his market. His first action should be to

(A) go to the market and make sure that everyone leaves it immediately.
(B) go to the market, examine the bomb, and then decide what action should be taken .
(C) question the manager in detail in an effort to determine whether this really is a bomb.
(D) telephone the bomb squad for instructions as to how the bomb should be rendered harmless.

28. The most reasonable advice that a state police officer can give to a merchant who asks what he should do if he receives a telephone call from a person he doesn't recognize regarding an alleged emergency at his store after ordinary business hours is that the merchant should go to the store and, if officers are not at the scene, he should

(A) continue past the store and call the police for assistance.
(B) continue past the store, and return and enter it if there doesn't appear to be an emergency.
(C) enter the store and ascertain whether the alleged emergency exists.
(D) enter the store only if there is no one apparently loitering in the vicinity.

29. Whenever a crime has been committed, the criminal has disturbed the surroundings in one way or another by his or her presence. The least valid deduction for the police to make from this statement is that

(A) clues are thus present at all crime scenes.
(B) even the slightest search at crime scenes will turn up conclusive evidence.
(C) the greater the number of criminals involved in a crime, the greater the number of clues likely to be available.
(D) the completely clueless crime is rarely encountered in police work.

30. An off-duty state police officer was seated in a restaurant when two men entered, drew guns, and robbed the cashier. The officer made no attempt to prevent the robbery or to apprehend the criminals. Later he justified his conduct by stating that an officer, when off duty, is a private citizen with the same duties and rights of all private citizens. The officer's conduct was

(A) wrong; a police officer must act to prevent crimes and apprehend criminals at all times.
(B) right; the police officer was out of uniform at the time of the robbery.
(C) wrong; he should have obtained the necessary information and descriptions after the robbers left.
(D) right; it would have been foolhardy for him to intervene when outnumbered by armed robbers.

31. A state police officer is the first one to arrive at the scene of a murder. The suspect offers to make a statement concerning the crime. The police officer refuses to accept the statement. The officer's action is

(A) good; interrogation of suspects should be performed by experienced detectives.
(B) poor; the suspect may later change his mind and refuse to make any statement.
(C) good; the officer will be too busy maintaining order at the scene to be able to accept the statement.
(D) poor; a statement made by the suspect would quickly solve the crime.

Answer questions 32 through 41 on the basis of the following legal definitions.

BURGLARY is committed when a person enters a building to commit a crime therein.

LARCENY is committed when a person wrongfully takes, obtains, or withholds the property of another.

ROBBERY is the forcible stealing of property. If a person, while committing a larceny, uses or threatens the immediate use of force, the crime changes from larceny to robbery.

SEXUAL ABUSE is committed when a person subjects another person to sexual contact without the second person's consent or when a person has sexual contact with another person less than 17 years of age. (A person less than 17 years of age cannot legally consent to any sexual conduct.) "Sexual contact" may be defined as touching the sexual or other intimate parts of a person to achieve sexual gratification.

SEXUAL MISCONDUCT is committed when a male has sexual intercourse with a consenting female who is at least 13 years of age but less than 17 years of age.

HARASSMENT is committed when a person intends to harass, annoy, or alarm another person and does so by striking, shoving, kicking, or otherwise subjecting the other person to physical contact.

ASSAULT is committed when a person unlawfully causes a physical injury to another person.

32. James Kelly enters the home of Mary Smith with the intention of taking Mary's portable TV set. While Kelly is in the apartment, Mary wakes up and attempts to retrieve her TV set from Kelly. Kelly punches Mary in the face and flees with the TV set. Kelly can be charged with

   (A) burglary and larceny.
   (B) burglary only.
   (C) robbery and larceny.
   (D) burglary and robbery.

33. John Brown enters a department store with the intention of doing some shopping. Brown has a .38 caliber revolver in his coat pocket and also has a criminal conviction for armed robbery. As he passes the jewelry counter, he notices an expensive watch lying on the showcase. He checks to see if anyone is watching him, and, when he feels that he is not being observed, he slips the watch into his pocket and leaves the store. Brown could be charged with

   (A) larceny.
   (B) burglary and larceny.
   (C) burglary and robbery.
   (D) robbery.

34. Tom Murphy enters a crowded subway car. He positions himself behind a woman and starts to touch her buttocks with his hand. The woman becomes very annoyed and starts to move away. As she does so, Murphy reaches into her pocketbook and removes $10. He then exits the train at the next station. Murphy could be charged with

   (A) robbery, larceny, and sexual misconduct
   (B) burglary, robbery, and sexual abuse
   (C) burglary, larceny, and sexual misconduct
   (D) larceny and sexual abuse

35. Ed Saunders entered the apartment of Jane Robers with the intent to sexually abuse her. However, Robers was not at home and Saunders left the apartment. Saunders could be charged with

    (A) sexual abuse.
    (B) sexual misconduct.
    (C) burglary.
    (D) none of the above, as a crime did not take place because Robers was not at home.

36. Frank Taylor entered the apartment of his 16-year-old girlfriend, Doris, to have sexual intercourse with her. Doris consented to this sexual conduct and they engaged in intercourse. Taylor could be charged with

    (A) burglary.
    (B) sexual misconduct.
    (C) both burglary and sexual misconduct.
    (D) no crime as Doris consented to the activity.

37. Brian Jones asks his 17-year-old girlfriend, Mary, if she would like to go to a motel and have sexual intercourse. She agrees and they go to the motel. Jones could be charged with

    (A) burglary.
    (B) sexual misconduct.
    (C) both burglary and sexual misconduct.
    (D) no crime, as she consented to the activity.

38. Bill is at a party at Joan's house. An argument ensues between two of the guests. Bill overhears Helen make a derogatory comment about him. He walks up to Helen and demands she "apologize or else." Helen refuses to apologize; Bill slaps her in the face and then rushes from the apartment. Bill could be charged with

    (A) assault.
    (B) burglary and assault.
    (C) harassment.
    (D) burglary and harassment.

39. Joe is on his way to work. He is in a very bad mood. As he enters the warehouse where he works, he slips and falls to the floor. This only escalates his foul mood. As he is getting up, he sees a fellow worker who had made some unkind remarks to him two days before. Joe picks up a piece of board that is lying on the floor, walks up to the other worker, and hits him across the arm. This causes the other worker to suffer a broken arm. Joe could be charged with

    (A) assault.
    (B) burglary and assault.
    (C) harassment.
    (D) none of the above, as Joe was emotionally upset.

40. Jim enters a school through a rear window at 2:00 a.m. He wants to take a movie projector that he knows is kept in a specific room. He enters the room, takes the projector, and starts to leave when he is confronted by a security guard. The guard attempts to grab Jim; however, Jim slips away. As a guard again attempts to apprehend him, Jim swings the projector, striking the guard in the face. The guard falls to the floor unconscious and suffers a broken nose. Jim could be charged with

    (A) burglary, larceny, and robbery.
    (B) robbery, larceny, and assault.
    (C) burglary, larceny, and assault.
    (D) burglary, robbery, and assault.

41. Sue invites Tom to her apartment for dinner. After dinner, Tom decides that he would like to have a sexual encounter with Sue. She attempts to discourage his advances. Tom then proceeds to hold her down on the couch and to fondle her breasts and touch her private parts. When Sue starts to scream, Tom rushes from the apartment. Tom could be charged with

    (A) burglary and sexual abuse.
    (B) burglary and sexual misconduct.
    (C) sexual abuse.
    (D) no crime, as Sue invited him to her apartment.

42. It is important that the police give proper attention to the investigation of apparently minor, as well as major, complaints made by citizens. Of the following, the one that is the most valid reason for doing so is that

    (A) minor complaints may be of great importance in the mind of the complainant.
    (B) minor complaints are more readily disposed.
    (C) minor complaints may be an indication of a serious police problem.
    (D) police efficiency is determined by the attitude shown towards citizen complaints.

43. Hearsay evidence may be defined as testimony by one person that another person told him or her about a criminal act that that other person had witnessed. Hearsay evidence is usually not admissible in a criminal trial mainly because

    (A) hearsay evidence is consistently biased and deliberately distorted.
    (B) hearsay evidence is usually not relevant to the issues of the case.
    (C) such evidence is usually distorted by both the original witness and the person to whom the observations were stated.
    (D) the actual witness to the criminal act is not being examined under oath.

44. "Arrests should not be given too much weight in the appraisal of a police officer's performance since a large number of arrests does not necessarily indicate that a good police job is being done." This statement is

    (A) true; factors other than the number of arrests made must also be considered in judging police effectiveness
    (B) false; the basic job of the police is to suppress crime and the surest measure of this is the number of arrests made
    (C) true; arrest figures are not indicative in any way of a police officer's efficiency
    (D) false; although some police officers are in a better position to make arrests than others, the law of averages should operate to even this out

45. "Arson is a particularly troublesome crime for the police." Of the following statements, the one that is the most important reason why this is so is that

    (A) arsonists usually seek the protection of darkness for their crimes.
    (B) arson occurs so infrequently that the police lack a definite approach for combating it.
    (C) important evidence is frequently destroyed by the fire itself.
    (D) witnesses find it difficult to distinguish arsonists from other criminals.

46. "Undoubtedly, the police have an important contribution to make to the welfare of youth." Of the following, the principal reason for this is that

    (A) effectiveness is a result of experience, and the police have had the longest experience in youth work.
    (B) no other agency can make use of the criminal aspects of the law as effectively as the police.
    (C) the police are in a strategic position to observe children actually or potentially delinquent and the conditions contributing thereto.
    (D) welfare agencies lack an understanding of the problems of youth.

47. An apparently senile man informs a police officer that he is returning from a visit to his daughter and that he is unable to find his way back home because he has forgotten his address. Of the following courses of action, the first one that should be taken by the officer is to

   (A) question the man in an effort to establish his identity.
   (B) request the police missing persons section to describe any person recently reported as missing.
   (C) suggest that the man return to his daughter for travel directions to his home.
   (D) telephone a description of the man to the precinct station house.

48. The one of the following that is the most accurate statement concerning the proper attitude of a state trooper toward persons in his or her custody is that the officer should

   (A) ignore any serious problems of those in custody if they have no bearing on the charges preferred
   (B) not inform the person who has been arrested of the reason for the arrest
   (C) not permit a person in custody to give vent to feelings at any time
   (D) watch a brooding or silent person more carefully than one who noisily threatens suicide

49. A pawnshop dealer has submitted to the police an accurate and complete description of a wristwatch that he recently purchased from a customer. The one of the following factors that would be most important in determining whether this wristwatch was stolen is the

   (A) degree of investigative perseverance demonstrated by the police.
   (B) exactness of police records describing stolen property.
   (C) honesty and neighborhood reputation of the pawnbroker.
   (D) time interval between the purchase of the wristwatch by the pawnbroker and the report made to the police.

50. A police officer at the scene of a serious vehicular accident requests 2 witnesses to the accident not to speak to each other until each one has given a statement to the officer concerning the accident. The most likely reason for this request by the police officer is that if the witnesses were allowed to speak to each other at this time they might

   (A) become involved in a violent quarrel over what actually happened.
   (B) change their opinion so that identical statements to the police would result.
   (C) discuss the possibility of a bribe offer to either of them by one of the operators involved in the accident.
   (D) have their original views of the accident somewhat altered by hearing each other's view of the accident.

51. "Tests have shown that sound waves set up by a siren have a greater intensity ahead than at either side or at the rear of a police car." On the basis of this quotation, it would be most reasonable for the operator of a police car, when responding to the scene of an emergency and using the siren, to expect that a motorist approaching an intersection from

   (A) a side street may not stop his vehicle as soon as a more distant motorist directly ahead of the police car.
   (B) directly ahead may not stop his vehicle as soon as a more distant motorist approaching from the rear of the police car.
   (C) directly ahead may not stop his vehicle as soon as a more distant motorist approaching from the side of the police car.
   (D) the rear of the police car may stop this vehicle before the less distant motorist approaching from a side street.

52. A police officer is guarding the entrance of an apartment in which a homicide occurred. While awaiting the arrival of the detectives assigned to the case, the officer is approached by a newspaper reporter who asks to be admitted. The police officer refuses to admit the reporter. The officer's action is

    (A) wrong; the police should cooperate with the press.
    (B) right; the reporter might unintentionally destroy evidence if admitted.
    (C) wrong; experienced newspaper reporters can be trusted to act intelligently in situations such as this.
    (D) right; this reporter should not be given an advantage over other reports.

53. A phone call is received at police headquarters indicating that a burglary is now taking place in a large loft building. Several radio motor patrol teams are dispatched to the scene. In order to prevent the escape of the burglars, the two police officers arriving first at the building, knowing that there is at least one entrance on each of the four sides of the building, should first

    (A) station themselves at diagonally opposite corners outside of the building.
    (B) enter the building and proceed to search for the criminals.
    (C) station themselves at the most likely exit from the building.
    (D) enter the building and remain on the ground floor, attempting to keep all stairways under observation.

54. Soon after being appointed a police officer, you decide that some of the rules and regulations of the police department are unwise. It would be best for you to

    (A) carry out these rules and regulations regardless of your opinion.
    (B) make any changes that you decide are necessary.
    (C) not do your job until some changes are made.
    (D) disregard these rules and regulations and use your own good judgment.

55. In most cases, a written report about a serious accident is better than an oral report, mainly because a written report

    (A) includes more of the facts.
    (B) can be referred to later.
    (C) takes less time to prepare.
    (D) is more accurate.

56. Officers assigned to regular posts for an extended period of time should try to establish friendly relations with the people in the area. For officers to follow this procedure is generally

    (A) advisable, mainly because the officers will be more likely to get the cooperation of the residents when needed.
    (B) inadvisable, mainly because it will take the officers' attention away from their regular duties.
    (C) advisable, mainly because it will help officers to impress their superior officers.
    (D) inadvisable, mainly because the people may be encouraged to take advantage of this friendliness to commit minor violations.

Assume that a police officer at a certain location is equipped with a two-way radio to keep him in constant touch with his security headquarters. Radio messages and replies are given in code form, as follows:

Radio Code for Type of Situation   J P M F B
Radio Code for Action to Be Taken   o r a z q
Radio Response for Action Taken   1 2 3 4 5

Assume that each of the above capital letters is the radio code for a particular type of situation, that the small letter below each capital letter is the radio code for the action a police officer is directed to take, and that the number directly below each small letter is the radio response the police officer should make to indicate what action was actually taken.

Directions: In each of the following questions, 57 through 62, the code letter for the action directed (column 2) and code number for the action taken (column 3) should correspond to the capital letters in column 1.

    If only column 2 is different from column 1, mark your answer (A).
    If only column 3 is different from column 1, mark your answer (B).
    If both column 2 and column 3 are different from column 1, mark your answer (C).
    If both columns 2 and 3 are the same as column 1, mark your answer (D).

SAMPLE QUESTION:

Column 1	Column 2	Column 3
JPFMB	orzaq	12453

The code letters in column 2 are correct, but the numbers "53" in column 3 should be " 35." Therefore, the correct answer is (B).

	Column 1	Column 2	Column 3
57.	PBFJM	rqzoa	25413
58.	MPFBJ	zrqoa	32541
59.	JBFPM.	oqzra	15432
60.	BJPMF	qaroz	51234
61.	PJFMB	rozaq	21435
62.	FJBMP	zoqra	41532

Answer questions 63 through 71 solely on the basis of the following narrative and assistance report. The report contains 20 numbered boxes. First read the narrative and the information given concerning the form and then study the form thoroughly before answering the questions.

    A state trooper is required to prepare an assistance report whenever an occurrence that requires that a person receive medical aid or assistance comes to the trooper's attention. However, if a person is sick at his or her own residence, an assistance report is not required. The officer then need only make a logbook entry.

    It was 9:30 a.m., Sunday, June 14. State Troopers Whelan and Murphy of the 2nd Precinct, riding in patrol car 1294, received a radio call of an injury at the northwest corner of Seventh Avenue and 83rd Street. The location of the injury was within the confines of the 3rd Precinct; however, the 3rd Precinct did not have any cars available to respond.

Upon arriving at the scene, Whelan and Murphy found a white male, approximately 28 years of age, lying on the sidewalk. The man was bleeding moderately from a cut on the forehead. When questioned by the officers, the man identified himself as John Mandello, and he stated that someone ran up behind him and pushed him to the ground, causing him to strike his head on the sidewalk. The person who pushed him to the ground also took a wallet containing $100 from his rear left pocket. Trooper Whelan informed Mr. Mandello that an ambulance was on the way. Mr. Mandello stated that he would take care of the injury himself and did not want any medical assistance.

Trooper Whelan canceled the ambulance and proceeded to take the information to be included in the report. As he was doing so, he noticed that the corner traffic light was not working.

Just as Whelan was finished getting the information, he and Trooper Murphy heard what sounded like brakes screeching and cars colliding. The two ran around the corner and saw a car on the southeast corner sidewalk of 82nd Street and Seventh Avenue. They also observed a van, lying on its side, in the intersection of 82nd Street and Seventh Avenue. Murphy ran back to his car and put in a call for an additional car to handle traffic conditions. The accident had occurred within the confines of the Village of Monroe.

Whelan checked the car that was on the sidewalk. The car, after colliding with the van, apparently mounted the sidewalk and went through the front windows of a men's clothing store, setting off the burglar alarm. The driver was lying on the front seat with moderate bleeding from a cut on his head and had what appeared to be a broken arm. The driver of the car was identified as Joe Serrano, a white male, 29 years of age, residing at 384 Lincoln Place.

Murphy went to the van and, with the help of several passersby, pulled the driver out. The driver was unconscious. A search of the unconscious van driver's wallet identified him as Juan Rodriguez, a Hispanic male, 24 years of age, residing at 98 Fourth Avenue.

An ambulance from Washington Hospital arrived at the scene. The ambulance attendant, John Francis, administered first aid to both drivers, who were then removed to Washington Hospital.

Further investigation produced 2 witnesses to the accident. The first witness was Mary Randolph of 876 First Avenue; the second was Helen Sweeney of 684 Broadway. The witnesses stated to Trooper Whelan that the traffic light at the intersection of 82nd Street and Seventh Avenue was not working.

Mr. Thomas Serrano of 384 Lincoln Place, Apt. 4E, phone 287-8777, was notified that his brother, Joe, was admitted to Washington Hospital. The admission number for Joe Serrano was 18764.

No friends or relatives of Juan Rodriguez could be notified that he was admitted to Washington Hospital. His admission number was 18763.

Box #1 will indicate the date that the report is being prepared. If the occurrence happened on a date that is different from the date of the report, the date of occurrence will be listed under "Remarks," box #17. The reasons for the delay in reporting the incident will also be noted under "Remarks," box #17.

Box #8 will give the specific location of the occurrence, i.e., 374 First Street, Apt. 1D; Front of 374 First Street on sidewalk; NW corner of 86th Street and First Avenue.

Box #39 will indicate, to the best of your knowledge, the illness or injury sustained, i.e., cut on forehead, dizziness, etc. The official doctor's or hospital's diagnosis, if available, will be listed under "Remarks," box #17.

Box #10 will list the precinct of the site of the incident and the precinct report number. Check the appropriate circumstance in box #11.

ASSISTANCE REPORT

1. Date	2. Last name First name M.I.	3. Age	4. Sex	5. Color

6. Time **7. Residence (including street address, apt. # & Zip Code)**

8. Location of occurrence (including street address, apt. # & Zip Code)

9. Illness or injury   **10. Precinct and report number**

11. Check:

    sick   mentally ill

    injured   dead

12. Taken to: Name of

    hospital   (   )

    morgue   (   )

13. Admission number   **14. Name of doctor or ambulance attendant**

15. Person notified   Relationship

16. Witnesses

17. Remarks

18. Additional required reports (Check appropriate boxes, if any)

    Crime report   Morgue report

    Vehicle accident report   Street injury report

19. Other agency notifications

20. Reporting Officer

Rank   Name   Number   Precinct

Check the appropriate disposition in box #12. If a person is treated at his or her home and is not removed to another location, no report is required. If a person is removed to a hospital or morgue, check the appropriate box and list the name of the hospital or morgue. If the person refuses medical assistance, write "refused assistance" in box #12.   If a person is treated at another location other than his or her home and is not removed to a hospital or morgue, state such facts under "Remarks," box #17.

The hospital admission number is listed in box #13 only if a relative or a friend cannot be notified that the person is being admitted to the hospital.

Box #14 will indicate the name of the doctor or ambulance attendant who treated the individual.

Box #15 will list the name and address of the friend or relative who was notified of the person's admission to the hospital. The relationship of the person notified to the person admitted will also be listed, i.e., friend, wife, brother, etc.

Box #16 will indicate the names and addresses of any witnesses.

Box #17 will contain a short description of the incident.

In box #18, check the appropriate box for any additional forms that may be needed. Check crime report if medical assistance was made necessary as a result of a criminal act. Check vehicle accident report if the incident involved a motor vehicle accident. Check morgue report if the individual involved dies. Check street injury report if the person was injured as a result of a defect in a street or sidewalk.

Box #19 will list the names of any other city agencies that may have to be notified, i.e., Traffic Department—damaged or broken traffic or street lights; Department of Highways—potholes in the street or broken sidewalks; Department of Water Supply—broken or damaged fire hydrants or water mains, etc.

Box #20 will contain the rank, name, and command of the Police Officer making the report.

Questions 63 through 66 are to be answered solely on the basis of the information relating to the case of John Mandello.

63. An assistance report

(A) would not be required because Mr. Mandello refused medical assistance.

(B) would not be required; only a police officer's log entry would be necessary.

(C) would be required, and the precinct that would be listed in box #10 would be the 2nd Precinct.

(D) would be required, and the precinct number that would be listed in box #20 would be the 2nd Precinct.

64. In box #9, the trooper would

(A) enter the official hospital diagnosis when it became available.

(B) enter the description of the illness or injury in his own words.

(C) make a reference to see box #17, "Remarks," for the official diagnosis.

(D) enter "refused medical assistance."

65. In box #18, the trooper would check the boxes for

(A) street injury report, because Mr. Mandello was injured when his head struck the sidewalk.

(B) street injury report, because the injury was incurred when Mr. Mandelo's head struck the sidewalk, and crime report, because he was apparently the victim of a robbery.

(C) crime report only.

(D) No additional report would be required because Mr. Mandello refused medical assistance.

66. In box #19, the trooper would

    (A) enter Traffic Department.

    (B) enter Department of Highways.

    (C) enter both Traffic Department and Department of Highways.

    (D) make no entry as no additional agency would have to be notified.

Answer questions 67 through 71 based on the information given regarding Joe Serrano and Juan Rodriguez.

67. Box #13 would be

    (A) filled in only in the case of Mr. Serrano.

    (B) filled in only in the case of Mr. Rodriguez.

    (C) filled in, in the cases of both Mr. Serrano and Mr. Rodriguez.

    (D) left blank in both cases.

68. The official hospital diagnoses of Mr. Serrano's injuries were a laceration of the forehead and a fracture of the right arm. This information would

    (A) be listed in box #17, "Remarks."

    (B) be listed in box #9, "Illness or Injury."

    (C) be listed in box #14 next to the doctor's name.

    (D) not be listed in the report.

69. In box #18, the additional report(s) that would be required is (are)

    (A) a crime report.

    (B) a street injury report.

    (C) a vehicle accident report.

    (D) a vehicle accident report and a crime report.

70. Based on the information given by the witnesses, box #19 would contain the names of which other agency or agencies?

    (A) Traffic Department

    (B) Traffic Department and Department of Highway

    (C) Department of Highway

    (D) Building Department

71. In preparing the assistance report

    (A) the caption "Sick" would be checked in box #11.

    (B) the relationship of the person notified in the case of Mr. Serrano would be "father" and would be entered in box #15.

    (C) the location of the occurrence would be the intersection of 83rd Street and Seventh Avenue and would be entered in box #8.

    (D) the name John Francis would be entered in box #14.

Answer questions 72 through 75 on the basis of the information given in the following passage.

The public often believes that the main job of a uniformed officer is to enforce laws simply by arresting people. In reality, however, many of the situations that an officer deals with do not call for the use of the power of arrest. In the first place, an officer spends much of his or her time preventing crimes from happening by spotting potential violations or suspicious behavior and taking action to prevent illegal acts. In the second place, many of the situations in which officers are called on for assistance involve elements such as personal arguments, husband and wife quarrels, noisy juveniles, or emotionally disturbed persons. The majority of these problems do not result in arrests and convictions, and often they do not even involve illegal behavior. In the third place, even in situations where there seems to be good reason to make an arrest, an officer may have to exercise very good judgment. There are times when making an arrest too soon could touch off a riot, or could result in the detention of a minor offender while major offenders escape, or could cut short the gathering of necessary on-the-scene evidence.

72. The passage implies that most citizens
    (A) will start to riot if they see an arrest being made.
    (B) appreciate the work that law enforcement officers do.
    (C) do not realize that making arrests is only a small part of law enforcement.
    (D) never call for assistance unless they are involved in a personal argument or a husband and wife quarrel.

73. According to the passage, one way in which law enforcement officers can prevent crimes from happening is by
    (A) arresting suspicious characters.
    (B) letting minor offenders go free.
    (C) taking action on potential violations.
    (D) refusing to get involved in husband and wife fights.

74. According to the passage, which of the following statements is not true of situations involving emotionally disturbed persons?
    (A) It is a waste of time to call on law enforcement officers for assistance in such situations.
    (B) Such situations may not involve illegal behavior.
    (C) Such situations often do not result in arrests.
    (D) Citizens often turn to law enforcement officers for help in such situations.

75. The last sentence in the passage mentions "detention of minor offenders." Of the following, which best explains the meaning of the word "detention" as used here?
    (A) Sentencing someone
    (B) Indicting someone
    (C) Calling someone before a grand jury
    (D) Arresting someone

Answer questions 76 through 79 on the basis of the information given in the following passage.

Automobile tire tracks found at the scene of a crime constitute an important link in the chain of physical evidence. In many cases, these are the only clues available. In some areas, unpaved ground adjoins the highway or paved streets. A suspect will often park his or her car off the paved portion of the street when committing a crime, sometimes leaving excellent tire tracks. Comparison of the tire track impressions with the tires is possible only when the vehicle has been found. However, the initial problem facing the police is the task of determining what kind of car probably made the impressions found at the scene of the crime. If the make, model, and year of the car that made the impressions can be determined, it is obvious that the task of elimination is greatly lessened.

76. The one of the following that is the most appropriate title for this passage is
    (A) "The Use of Automobiles in the Commission of Crimes."
    (B) "The Use of Tire Tracks in Police Work."
    (C) "The Capture of Criminals by Scientific Police Work."
    (D) "The Positive Identification of Criminals Through Their Cars."

77. When searching for clear signs left by the car used in the commission of a crime, the most likely place for the police to look would be on the

(A) highway adjoining unpaved streets.
(B) highway adjacent to paved streets.
(C) paved streets adjacent to a highway.
(D) unpaved ground adjacent to a highway.

78. Automobile tire tracks found at the scene of a crime are of value as evidence in that they are

(A) generally sufficient to trap and convict a suspect.
(B) the most important link in the chain of physical evidence.
(C) often the only evidence at hand.
(D) circumstantial rather than direct.

79. The primary reason that the police try to determine the make, model, and year of the car involved in the commission of a crime is to

(A) compare the tire tracks left at the scene of the crime with the type of tires used on cars of that make.
(B) determine if the mud on the tires of the suspected car matches the mud in the unpaved road near the scene of the crime.
(C) reduce, to a large extent, the amount of work involved in determining the particular car used in the commission of a crime.
(D) alert the police patrol forces to question the occupants of all automobiles of this type.

Answer questions 80 through 83 on the basis of the information given in the following passage.

When stopping vehicles on highways to check for suspects or fugitives, the police use an automobile roadblock whenever possible. This consists of three cars placed in prearranged positions. Car 1 is parked across the left lane of the roadway with the front diagonally facing toward the center line. Car 2 is parked across the right lane, with the front of the vehicle also toward the center line, in a position perpendicular to car 1 and appropriately 20 feet to the rear. Continuing another 20 feet to the rear along the highway, car 3 is parked in an identical manner to car 1. The width of the highway determines the angle or position in which the autos should be placed. In addition to the regular roadblock signs, and the use of flares at night only, there is an officer located at both the entrance and exit to direct and control traffic from both directions. This type of roadblock forces all approaching autos to reduce speed and zigzag around the police cars. Officers standing behind the parked cars can most safely and carefully view all passing motorists. Once a suspect is inside the block, it becomes extremely difficult to crash out.

80. Of the following, the most appropriate title for this passage is

(A) "The Construction of an Escape-Proof Roadblock."
(B) "Regulation of Automobile Traffic Through a Police Roadblock."
(C) "Safety Precautions Necessary in Making an Automobile Roadblock."
(D) "Structure of a Roadblock to Detain Suspects or Fugitives."

81. When setting up a three-car roadblock, the relative positions of the cars should be such that

(A) the front of car 1 is placed diagonally to the center line and facing car 3.
(B) car 3 is placed parallel to the center line, and its front faces the right side of the road.
(C) car 2 is placed about 20 feet from car 1, and its front faces the left side of the road.
(D) car 3 is parallel to and about 20 feet away from car 1.

82. Officers can observe occupants of all cars passing through the roadblock with greatest safety when

   (A) warning flares are lighted to illuminate the area sufficiently at night.
   (B) warning signs are put up at each end of the roadblock.
   (C) they are stationed at both the exit and the entrance of the roadblock.
   (D) they take up positions behind cars in the roadblock.

83. The type of automobile roadblock described in the passage is of value in police work because

   (A) a suspect is unable to escape its confines by using force.
   (B) it is frequently used to capture suspects, with no danger to police officers.
   (C) it requires only two officers to set up and operate.
   (D) vehicular traffic within its confines is controlled as to speed and direction.

Answer questions 84 through 86 on the basis of the information given in the following passage.

When police officers search for a stolen car, they first check for the color of the car, then for the make, model, year, body damage, and, finally, the license number. The first five checks can be made from almost any angle, while the recognition of the license number is often not immediately apparent. The serial number and motor number, though less likely to be changed than the easily substituted license number, cannot be observed in initial detection of the stolen car.

84. According to the passage, the one of the following features that is least readily observed in checking for a stolen car in moving traffic is the

   (A) license number.
   (B) serial number.
   (C) model.
   (D) make.

85. The feature of a car that cannot be determined from most angles of observation is the

   (A) make.
   (B) model.
   (C) year.
   (D) license number.

86. Of the following, the feature of a stolen car that is most likely to be altered by a car thief shortly after the car is stolen is the

   (A) license number.
   (B) motor number.
   (C) color.
   (D) minor body damage.

Answer questions 87 and 88 on the basis of the information given in the following passage.

A survey has shown that crime prevention work is most successful if the officers are assigned on rotating shifts to provide around-the-clock coverage. An officer may work for days at a time and then be switched to nights. The prime object of the night work is to enable the officer to spot conditions inviting burglars. Complete lack of, or faulty locations of, night lights and other conditions that may invite burglars, which might go unnoticed during the daylight hours, can be located and corrected more readily through night work. Night work also enables the officer to check local hangouts of teenagers, such as where a teenage dance is held every Friday night. Detectives also join patrol officers cruising in radio patrol cars to check on teenagers loitering late at night and to spot-check local bars for teenagers.

87. The most important purpose of assigning officers to night shifts is to make it possible for them to
   (A) correct conditions that may not be readily noticed during the day.
   (B) discover the location of and replace missing and faulty night lights.
   (C) locate criminal hangouts.
   (D) notice things at night that cannot be noticed during the daytime.

88. The type of shifting of officers that best prevents crime is to have
   (A) day-shift officers rotated to night work.
   (B) rotating shifts provide sufficient officers for coverage 24 hours daily.
   (C) an officer work around the clock on a 24-hour basis as police needs arise.
   (D) rotating shifts to give officers varied experience.

Answer questions 89 through 91 on the basis of the information given in the following passage.

In addition to making the preliminary investigation of crimes, police patrol officers should serve as eyes, ears, and legs for the detective division. The patrol division may be used for surveillance, to serve warrants and bring in suspects and witnesses, and to perform a number of routine tasks for the detectives that will increase the time available for tasks that require their special skills and facilities. It is to the advantage of individual detectives, as well as of the detective division, to have patrol officers working in this manner. More cases are cleared by arrest, and a greater proportion of stolen property is recovered when, in addition to the detective regularly assigned, a number of patrol officers also work on the case. Detectives may stimulate the interest and participation of patrol officers by keeping them informed of the presence, identity or description, hangouts, associates, vehicles, and method of operation of each criminal known to be in the community.

89. According to this passage, a patrol officer should
   (A) assist the detective in certain routine functions.
   (B) be considered for assignment as a detective on the basis of patrol performance.
   (C) leave the scene once a detective arrives.
   (D) perform as many of the detective's duties as time permits.

90. According to this passage, patrol officers should aid detectives by
   (A) accepting from detectives assignments that give promise of recovering stolen property.
   (B) making arrests of witnesses for the detectives' interrogation.
   (C) performing all special investigative work for detectives.
   (D) producing for questioning individuals who may aid the detectives in the investigation.

91. According to this passage, detectives can keep patrol officers interested by

(A) ascertaining that patrol officers are doing investigative work properly.
(B) having patrol officers directly under their supervision during an investigation.
(C) informing patrol officers of the value of their efforts in crime prevention.
(D) supplying the patrol officers with information regarding known criminals in the community.

Answer questions 92 and 93 on the basis of the information given in the following passage.

The medical examiner may contribute valuable data to the investigator of fires that cause fatalities. By careful examination of the bodies of any victims, the examiner not only establishes cause of death, but may also furnish, in many instances, answers to questions relating to the identity of the victim and the source and origin of the fire. The medical examiner is of greatest value to law enforcement agencies because he or she is able to determine the exact cause of death through an examination of tissue of the apparent arson victims. Thorough study of a burned body or even of parts of a burned body will frequently yield information that will help to clarify problems confronting the arson investigator and the police.

92. According to the passage, the most important task of the medical examiner in the investigation of arson is to obtain information concerning the

(A) identity of arsonists.
(B) cause of death.
(C) identity of victims.
(D) source and origin of fires.

93. The central thought of the passage is that the medical examiner aids in the solution of crimes of arson when

(A) a person is burned to death.
(B) identity of the arsonist is unknown.
(C) the cause of the fires is unknown.
(D) trained investigators are not available.

Directions: Each of the following sentences may or may not be correct as written. Below each sentence you will find four different ways of writing the italicized part. If you think the sentence is correct as written, choose answer A, which is always the same as the italicized part. If you think one of the other choices makes a better sentence, mark the letter of your choice.

---

94. Edna burst into the room shouting, *"Why was Marilyn and he* permitted to go?"

(A) was Marilyn and he
(B) was Marilyn and him
(C) was Marilyn and his
(D) were Marilyn and he

95. The teacher, *with all her students, was* late for the train

(A) with all her students, was
(B) with all her students was
(C) with all her students, were
(D) with all her students; was

96. Watching the takeoff, the small boy waved his arms *as if he were a plane himself.*

- (A) as if he were a plane himself.
- (B) as if he was a plane himself.
- (C) like he was a plane hisself.
- (D) like he was a plane himself.

97. How much *has fuel costs raised* during the past year?

- (A) has fuel costs raised
- (B) have fuel costs raised
- (C) has fuel costs risen
- (D) have fuel costs risen

98. *It was all so different than I expected.*

- (A) It was all so different than I expected.
- (B) It was all so different from what I expected.
- (C) It was all different and not expected.
- (D) It was all different than what I had expected.

99. Some gardeners put dead leaves or straw between the rows of seedlings so that the ground doesn't dry out and *you don't have to weed as much.*

- (A) you don't have to weed as much.
- (B) they don't have to weed as much.
- (C) they don't have weeding as much as before.
- (D) your weeding is less.

100. *Pat went to Jones Beach with his girlfriend wearing a blue and white bathing suit.*

- (A) Pat went to Jones Beach with his girlfriend wearing a blue and white bathing suit.
- (B) Pat went to Jones Beach, wearing a blue and white bathing suit, with his girlfriend.
- (C) Pat, wearing a blue and white bathing suit, went to Jones Beach with his girlfriend.
- (D) To Jones Beach, wearing a blue and white bathing suit, went Pat with his girlfriend.

MODEL EXAMINATION 4: ANSWERS AND EXPLANATIONS

ANSWERS

1.	D	21.	B	41.	C	61.	D	81.	C
2.	D	22.	B	42.	C	62.	A	82.	D
3.	D	23.	C	43.	D	63.	D	83.	D
4.	A	24.	A	44.	A	64.	B	84.	B
5.	A	25.	B	45.	C	65.	C	85.	D
6.	B	26.	B	46.	C	66.	A	86.	A
7.	D	27.	A	47.	A	67.	B	87.	D
8.	B	28.	A	48.	D	68.	A	88.	B
9.	D	29.	B	49.	B	69.	C	89.	A
10.	C	30.	A	50.	D	70.	A	90.	D
11.	D	31.	B	51.	A	71.	D	91.	D
12.	C	32.	D	52.	B	72.	C	92.	B
13.	B	33.	A	53.	A	73.	C	93.	A
14.	A	34.	D	54.	A	74.	A	94.	D
15.	C	35.	C	55.	B	75.	D	95.	A
16.	C	36.	C	56.	A	76.	B	96.	A
17.	A	37.	D	57.	D	77.	D	97.	D
18.	B	38.	C	58.	C	78.	C	98.	B
19.	A	39.	A	59.	B	79.	C	99.	B
20.	B	40.	D	60.	A	80.	D	100.	C

EXPLANATIONS

1. **The correct answer is (D).** Refer to the third sentence of the description.
2. **The correct answer is (D).** The officers observed the suspects alighting from the roof by way of ladder.
3. **The correct answer is (D).** The two white males ran into an alleyway, and the black male and Hispanic male ran into a parking lot.
4. **The correct answer is (A).** This information is included in the description of the white male with long blond hair.
5. **The correct answer is (A).** This information is included in the description of the Hispanic male.
6. **The correct answer is (B).** This information is included in the description of the white male with short hair.
7. **The correct answer is (D).** This information is included in the description of the white male with short hair.
8. **The correct answer is (B).** This information is included in the description of the white male with long blond hair.
9. **The correct answer is (D).** This information is included in the description of the Hispanic male.
10. **The correct answer is (C).** This is the description of the vehicle in which the two white males fled.
11. **The correct answer is (D).** The description states only that the escape vehicles fled west on Seventh Street. There is no information as to what type of street Seventh Street is.
12. **The correct answer is (C).** Both the black male and Hispanic male entered the parking lot. However, it was the black male who was carrying what appeared to be a portable TV set.
13. **The correct answer is (B).** This information is included in the description of the black male.
14. **The correct answer is (A).** This information is included in the description of the black male.
15. **The correct answer is (C).** The description refers only to Officer Smith using a walkie-talkie and broadcasting information.
16. **The correct answer is (C).** Photographs form a permanent record of how the crime scene appeared when the police arrived. These pictures can be used at a criminal trial to show how the crime scene looked.
17. **The correct answer is (A).** There is no immediate danger to the officer or to the woman, since the gun is in the man's pocket. Therefore, it is not necessary or proper for the officer to fire a shot. The office should repeat his order before taking any further action.
18. **The correct answer is (B).** If the suspect observes that notes are being taken, he or she may freeze up or not talk as freely, because he knows that what he or she is saying will become part of the permanent record.
19. **The correct answer is (A).** The prisoner would either have to roll over or turn his head completely around to see the officer in order to shoot accurately. The time that is required for this type of movement would allow the officer to take cover or to fire the first shot.
20. **The correct answer is (B).** Ignoring the rumors or not supplying the true circumstances of the emergency as soon as they are available only increases the fear people may have and may result in a possible panic situation.
21. **The correct answer is (B).** If a child had been missing for an extended period of time, police headquarters usually would have received information concerning the child.
22. **The correct answer is (B).** If the plainclothes officer were to stop following the suspect now, the suspect would be difficult to locate again, since he is known to have changed residences frequently.
23. **The correct answer is (C).** If a police officer doesn't fully understand the instructions given by a supervisor, the officer should immediately ask for clarification from the person giving the instructions so that he or she can carry out the assignment properly.

24. **The correct answer is (A).** A police officer should always be alert and on guard until the nature of the situation in which he or she is involved is made completely clear.

25. **The correct answer is (B).** Police officers and police departments should never recommend a specific product or business. Endorsements tend to indicate favoritism, and police officers should always be impartial.

26. **The correct answer is (B).** Suspects and witnesses should always be questioned separately so that the description that one person gives does not influence the description given by any other persons at the scene.

27. **The correct answer is (A).** If there is the slightest chance that the object could be a bomb, all persons should be removed from the location for safety reasons.

28. **The correct answer is (A).** The call could be a set-up for robbing both the owner and his store. If there were a real emergency, the police would most likely be on the scene.

29. **The correct answer is (B).** In most cases, it takes a thorough search of the crime scene to uncover the clues left by the criminal. Most clues in and of themselves are not conclusive. However, when used collectively, they form the foundation for proving the guilt or innocence of the suspect.

30. **The correct answer is (A).** He was wrong. The principle here is that a police officer has a duty to protect the public at all times, even when off duty.

31. **The correct answer is (B).** A statement should be taken as soon as the suspect offers to make one. The suspect may feel an immediate need to tell someone what happened. A delay in taking the statement may cause the suspect to remain silent about the matter.

32. **The correct answer is (D).** The situation fits both the definitions of burglary (to enter a building to commit a crime) and of robbery (stealing by force—in this case, the punch in the face).

33. **The correct answer is (A).** John Brown can be charged with larceny only, because there was no intent to commit a crime when he entered the store, and there was no force used.

34. **The correct answer is (D).** The charges are sexual abuse (touching of the buttocks) and larceny (taking $10 from the pocketbook). No force was used to remove the money, thus eliminating the charge of robbery.

35. **The correct answer is (C).** To charge a person with burglary, it must only be shown that the building was entered with the intention of committing a crime therein. (In this case, the crime was sexual abuse.) Despite the fact that Saunders was not successful in committing the crime he intended, the intention was there.

36. **The correct answer is (C).** Taylor's intention for entering the apartment was to have sexual intercourse with his 16-year-old girlfriend, a crime because she is younger than 17 years of age. He could be charged with burglary (intent to commit a crime) and sexual misconduct (sexual intercourse with a female less than 17 years of age).

37. **The correct answer is (D).** Mary is 17 years old and gave her consent.

38. **The correct answer is (C).** There was neither any intention to commit a crime when Bill entered the building nor was there any injury incurred. For the charge to be assault, there must be some kind of injury.

39. **The correct answer is (A).** Joe had no intent to commit a crime before he entered the warehouse. He caused an injury to a fellow worker, a broken arm, by his actions; therefore, the charge of assault could be preferred. Emotional disturbance is not a valid excuse for such actions.

40. **The correct answer is (D).** The charges are burglary (entering the school with the intention of taking a movie projector), robbery (using force on the security guard to take the projector), and assault (causing an injury, the broken nose, to the security guard).

41. **The correct answer is (C).** Because Tom used force to touch Sue's private parts, he could be charged with sexual abuse. Since there was no intention to commit the crime prior to his entering her apartment, the possibility of a burglary charge is eliminated.

42. **The correct answer is (C).** Minor complaints, when properly investigated, can show a pattern of conduct that could lead to a major problem for the police.

43. **The correct answer is (D).** With the exception of a few narrowly defined situations, the courts demand that actual witnesses be examined under oath.

44. **The correct answer is (A).** A police officer does a multitude of things other than arrest people. The officer responds to sick, injured, and emotionally disturbed people calling for help. He or she handles vehicle accidents, family disputes, lost children, traffic problems, and so on. The officer's effectiveness should be based on how the officer handles the entire spectrum of his or her duties rather than on the number of arrests he or she makes in a given period of time.

45. **The correct answer is (C).** Fire destroys valuable clues that are usually found at a crime scene. Investigation is made considerably more difficult as a result.

46. **The correct answer is (C).** When the police observe potential delinquent-producing conditions, they can take immediate action to correct them.

47. **The correct answer is (A).** By questioning the man first, the officer may be able to ascertain who he is and where he lives and thereby return him to his home without any further delay.

48. **The correct answer is (D).** A suspect who broods silently may be feeling very humiliated and depressed and may indeed be suicidal.

49. **The correct answer is (B).** Police descriptions must be accurate in order to match the article to the complainant. For example, just listing the watch as a yellow, metal man's wristwatch would fit thousands of complaints of lost or stolen watches.

50. **The correct answer is (D).** Witnesses and suspects should always be separated when being questioned or giving statements so that the statement one makes does not influence what the others might say.

51. **The correct answer is (A).** This information is stated clearly in the quotation itself.

52. **The correct answer is (B).** Until a crime scene is properly searched and investigated, no one other than those assigned directly to the case should be allowed to enter the area because of the likelihood that valuable evidence will be destroyed.

53. **The correct answer is (A).** By stationing themselves in this manner, the two officers would be able to observe all four sides of the building.

54. **The correct answer is (A).** In order to function effectively, police departments have specific rules and regulations that must be followed. Individual police officers must follow the rules; they cannot change or disregard these rules because they think they are unwise or unnecessary. All changes are made by the chiefs of the respective departments.

55. **The correct answer is (B).** With the passage of time, accurate mental recall of an incident decreases. Written reports should always be prepared for future reference, especially if the case may go to court.

56. **The correct answer is (A).** Once the people in the neighborhood get to *know* the police officer who is regularly assigned, they are more likely to cooperate. People don't generally cooperate with strangers, even if the stranger is a police officer.

57. **The correct answer is (D).** All the letters in column 2 and all the numbers in column 3 are in sequence with the capital letters in column 1.

58. **The correct answer is (C).** When compared to column 1, the letters (column 2) *z, q, o,* and *a* and the numbers (column 3) *5* and *4* are out of sequence.

59. **The correct answer is (B).** When compared to column 1, all the letters in column 2 are in their proper sequence; however, the numbers *2* and *3* in column 3 are out of sequence.

60. **The correct answer is (A).** When compared to column 1, all the numbers in column 3 are in their proper sequence; however, the letters *a* and *o* in column 2 are out of sequence.

61. **The correct answer is (D).** When compared to column 1, all the letters in column 2 and all the numbers in column 3 are in proper sequence.

62. **The correct answer is (A).** When compared to column 1, all the numbers in column 3 are in proper sequence; however, the letters *r* and *a* in column 2 are out of sequence.

63. **The correct answer is (D).** The person is treated at a location other than his home. If he were treated at home, a report would not be required. The reporting officer is from the 2nd Precinct.

64. **The correct answer is (B).** The directions for box #9 state that the officer will enter the nature of the illness or injury to the best of his or her knowledge.

65. **The correct answer is (C).** Mr. Mandello was the victim of a robbery; therefore, a crime report is required. A street injury report is not required because he was not injured as a result of a defect in the sidewalk.

66. **The correct answer is (A).** As he was taking the information from the assistance report, Officer Whelan noticed that the corner streetlight was not working.

67. **The correct answer is (B).** An admission number is required only when a relative or friend can't be notified that a person was admitted to a hospital. This is true only in the case of Mr. Rodriguez.

68. **The correct answer is (A).** The directions for preparing the report state that the official diagnosis will be listed in box #17, "Remarks."

69. **The correct answer is (C).** Only a vehicle accident report is required. There was no crime involved, and the accident was not caused by a defect in the roadway, thus eliminating a street injury report.

70. **The correct answer is (A).** The witnesses state that the traffic light was not working; therefore, the Traffic Department should be notified.

71. **The correct answer is (D).** John Francis was the ambulance attendant who responded. The victims were not sick; they were injured. Mr. Serrano's brother, not his father, was notified as to his injury in an accident that occurred on Seventh Avenue and 82nd Street.

72. **The correct answer is (C).** Refer to the first sentence of the passage.

73. **The correct answer is (C).** Refer to the third sentence of the passage.

74. **The correct answer is (A).** It is stated in the fourth sentence that many of the situations in which police assistance is required involve emotionally disturbed persons.

75. **The correct answer is (D).** A police officer arrests; the courts sentence, indict, or call people before a grand jury.

76. **The correct answer is (B).** The passage talks exclusively about tire tracks. No mention is made of autos being used in the commission of crimes, of scientific police work, or of positive identification through cars.

77. **The correct answer is (D).** Refer to the third and fourth sentences of the passage.

78. **The correct answer is (C).** Refer to the second sentence of the passage.

79. **The correct answer is (C).** Refer to the last sentence of the passage.

80. **The correct answer is (D).** The paragraph doesn't state that the type of roadblock mentioned is escape-proof, but it does state that the roadblock described will force all approaching vehicles to reduce speed and make it extremely difficult for vehicles to crash out of the roadblock.

81. **The correct answer is (C).** Refer to the fourth sentence of the passage. If the car is parked in the right lane with its front facing the center line, the front is necessarily facing the left side of the road.

82. **The correct answer is (D).** Refer to the next-to-the-last sentence of the passage.

83. **The correct answer is (D).** Refer to the eighth sentence of the passage.

84. **The correct answer is (B).** Refer to the last sentence of the passage.

85. **The correct answer is (D).** Refer to the second sentence of the passage.

86. **The correct answer is (A).** Refer to the last sentence of the passage. The changing of color or the repairing of body damage could not be accomplished in a short period of time.

87. **The correct answer is (D).** Certain conditions that might go unnoticed by day are visible at night, especially lighting problems. Officers notice these on the night shift; building owners are thus alerted to make the corrections.

88. **The correct answer is (B).** Refer to the first sentence of the passage.

89. **The correct answer is (A).** The first sentence of the passage states that the patrol officer "should serve as eyes, ears, and legs for the detective division." No statement in the passage makes any mention of police officers being considered for assignment to the detective division, leaving the scene when detectives arrive, or performing detectives' duties.

90. **The correct answer is (D).** Refer to the second sentence of the passage.

91. **The correct answer is (D).** Refer to the last sentence of the passage.
92. **The correct answer is (B).** Refer to the third sentence of the passage.
93. **The correct answer is (A).** Refer to the first sentence of the paragraph. The medical examiner deals with dead human bodies, not with trying to identify arson suspects or with determining the causes of a fire.
94. **The correct answer is (D).** *Marilyn and he* is the compound subject of the plural verb *were*.
95. **The correct answer is (A).** The singular noun *teacher* is the subject of the sentence. The *students* represent additional information but are not part of the subject.
96. **The correct answer is (A).** The statement contrary to fact (the boy is not an airplane) correctly takes the subjunctive *were*.
97. **The correct answer is (D).** The correct tense of the verb to use in this sentence is the present perfect. *Costs* are plural. The construction here is "fuel costs have risen."
98. **The correct answer is (B).** The correct form is *different from*.
99. **The correct answer is (B).** Don't change persons midsentence. The sentence is about gardeners, not about you. Choice (C) does not change persons but is awkwardly stated.
100. **The correct answer is (C).** Who was wearing a blue and white bathing suit? Only this choice makes it clear.

MODEL EXAMINATION 5: ANSWER SHEET

1. Ⓐ Ⓑ Ⓒ Ⓓ Ⓔ   26. Ⓐ Ⓑ Ⓒ Ⓓ Ⓔ   51. Ⓐ Ⓑ Ⓒ Ⓓ Ⓔ   76. Ⓐ Ⓑ Ⓒ Ⓓ Ⓔ   101. Ⓐ Ⓑ Ⓒ Ⓓ Ⓔ
2. Ⓐ Ⓑ Ⓒ Ⓓ Ⓔ   27. Ⓐ Ⓑ Ⓒ Ⓓ Ⓔ   52. Ⓐ Ⓑ Ⓒ Ⓓ Ⓔ   77. Ⓐ Ⓑ Ⓒ Ⓓ Ⓔ   102. Ⓐ Ⓑ Ⓒ Ⓓ Ⓔ
3. Ⓐ Ⓑ Ⓒ Ⓓ Ⓔ   28. Ⓐ Ⓑ Ⓒ Ⓓ Ⓔ   53. Ⓐ Ⓑ Ⓒ Ⓓ Ⓔ   78. Ⓐ Ⓑ Ⓒ Ⓓ Ⓔ   103. Ⓐ Ⓑ Ⓒ Ⓓ Ⓔ
4. Ⓐ Ⓑ Ⓒ Ⓓ Ⓔ   29. Ⓐ Ⓑ Ⓒ Ⓓ Ⓔ   54. Ⓐ Ⓑ Ⓒ Ⓓ Ⓔ   79. Ⓐ Ⓑ Ⓒ Ⓓ Ⓔ   104. Ⓐ Ⓑ Ⓒ Ⓓ Ⓔ
5. Ⓐ Ⓑ Ⓒ Ⓓ Ⓔ   30. Ⓐ Ⓑ Ⓒ Ⓓ Ⓔ   55. Ⓐ Ⓑ Ⓒ Ⓓ Ⓔ   80. Ⓐ Ⓑ Ⓒ Ⓓ Ⓔ   105. Ⓐ Ⓑ Ⓒ Ⓓ Ⓔ
6. Ⓐ Ⓑ Ⓒ Ⓓ Ⓔ   31. Ⓐ Ⓑ Ⓒ Ⓓ Ⓔ   56. Ⓐ Ⓑ Ⓒ Ⓓ Ⓔ   81. Ⓐ Ⓑ Ⓒ Ⓓ Ⓔ   106. Ⓐ Ⓑ Ⓒ Ⓓ Ⓔ
7. Ⓐ Ⓑ Ⓒ Ⓓ Ⓔ   32. Ⓐ Ⓑ Ⓒ Ⓓ Ⓔ   57. Ⓐ Ⓑ Ⓒ Ⓓ Ⓔ   82. Ⓐ Ⓑ Ⓒ Ⓓ Ⓔ   107. Ⓐ Ⓑ Ⓒ Ⓓ Ⓔ
8. Ⓐ Ⓑ Ⓒ Ⓓ Ⓔ   33. Ⓐ Ⓑ Ⓒ Ⓓ Ⓔ   58. Ⓐ Ⓑ Ⓒ Ⓓ Ⓔ   83. Ⓐ Ⓑ Ⓒ Ⓓ Ⓔ   108. Ⓐ Ⓑ Ⓒ Ⓓ Ⓔ
9. Ⓐ Ⓑ Ⓒ Ⓓ Ⓔ   34. Ⓐ Ⓑ Ⓒ Ⓓ Ⓔ   59. Ⓐ Ⓑ Ⓒ Ⓓ Ⓔ   84. Ⓐ Ⓑ Ⓒ Ⓓ Ⓔ   109. Ⓐ Ⓑ Ⓒ Ⓓ Ⓔ
10. Ⓐ Ⓑ Ⓒ Ⓓ Ⓔ   35. Ⓐ Ⓑ Ⓒ Ⓓ Ⓔ   60. Ⓐ Ⓑ Ⓒ Ⓓ Ⓔ   85. Ⓐ Ⓑ Ⓒ Ⓓ Ⓔ   110. Ⓐ Ⓑ Ⓒ Ⓓ Ⓔ
11. Ⓐ Ⓑ Ⓒ Ⓓ Ⓔ   36. Ⓐ Ⓑ Ⓒ Ⓓ Ⓔ   61. Ⓐ Ⓑ Ⓒ Ⓓ Ⓔ   86. Ⓐ Ⓑ Ⓒ Ⓓ Ⓔ   111. Ⓐ Ⓑ Ⓒ Ⓓ Ⓔ
12. Ⓐ Ⓑ Ⓒ Ⓓ Ⓔ   37. Ⓐ Ⓑ Ⓒ Ⓓ Ⓔ   62. Ⓐ Ⓑ Ⓒ Ⓓ Ⓔ   87. Ⓐ Ⓑ Ⓒ Ⓓ Ⓔ   112. Ⓐ Ⓑ Ⓒ Ⓓ Ⓔ
13. Ⓐ Ⓑ Ⓒ Ⓓ Ⓔ   38. Ⓐ Ⓑ Ⓒ Ⓓ Ⓔ   63. Ⓐ Ⓑ Ⓒ Ⓓ Ⓔ   88. Ⓐ Ⓑ Ⓒ Ⓓ Ⓔ   113. Ⓐ Ⓑ Ⓒ Ⓓ Ⓔ
14. Ⓐ Ⓑ Ⓒ Ⓓ Ⓔ   39. Ⓐ Ⓑ Ⓒ Ⓓ Ⓔ   64. Ⓐ Ⓑ Ⓒ Ⓓ Ⓔ   89. Ⓐ Ⓑ Ⓒ Ⓓ Ⓔ   114. Ⓐ Ⓑ Ⓒ Ⓓ Ⓔ
15. Ⓐ Ⓑ Ⓒ Ⓓ Ⓔ   40. Ⓐ Ⓑ Ⓒ Ⓓ Ⓔ   65. Ⓐ Ⓑ Ⓒ Ⓓ Ⓔ   90. Ⓐ Ⓑ Ⓒ Ⓓ Ⓔ   115. Ⓐ Ⓑ Ⓒ Ⓓ Ⓔ
16. Ⓐ Ⓑ Ⓒ Ⓓ Ⓔ   41. Ⓐ Ⓑ Ⓒ Ⓓ Ⓔ   66. Ⓐ Ⓑ Ⓒ Ⓓ Ⓔ   91. Ⓐ Ⓑ Ⓒ Ⓓ Ⓔ   116. Ⓐ Ⓑ Ⓒ Ⓓ Ⓔ
17. Ⓐ Ⓑ Ⓒ Ⓓ Ⓔ   42. Ⓐ Ⓑ Ⓒ Ⓓ Ⓔ   67. Ⓐ Ⓑ Ⓒ Ⓓ Ⓔ   92. Ⓐ Ⓑ Ⓒ Ⓓ Ⓔ   117. Ⓐ Ⓑ Ⓒ Ⓓ Ⓔ
18. Ⓐ Ⓑ Ⓒ Ⓓ Ⓔ   43. Ⓐ Ⓑ Ⓒ Ⓓ Ⓔ   68. Ⓐ Ⓑ Ⓒ Ⓓ Ⓔ   93. Ⓐ Ⓑ Ⓒ Ⓓ Ⓔ   118. Ⓐ Ⓑ Ⓒ Ⓓ Ⓔ
19. Ⓐ Ⓑ Ⓒ Ⓓ Ⓔ   44. Ⓐ Ⓑ Ⓒ Ⓓ Ⓔ   69. Ⓐ Ⓑ Ⓒ Ⓓ Ⓔ   94. Ⓐ Ⓑ Ⓒ Ⓓ Ⓔ   119. Ⓐ Ⓑ Ⓒ Ⓓ Ⓔ
20. Ⓐ Ⓑ Ⓒ Ⓓ Ⓔ   45. Ⓐ Ⓑ Ⓒ Ⓓ Ⓔ   70. Ⓐ Ⓑ Ⓒ Ⓓ Ⓔ   95. Ⓐ Ⓑ Ⓒ Ⓓ Ⓔ   120. Ⓐ Ⓑ Ⓒ Ⓓ Ⓔ
21. Ⓐ Ⓑ Ⓒ Ⓓ Ⓔ   46. Ⓐ Ⓑ Ⓒ Ⓓ Ⓔ   71. Ⓐ Ⓑ Ⓒ Ⓓ Ⓔ   96. Ⓐ Ⓑ Ⓒ Ⓓ Ⓔ   121. Ⓐ Ⓑ Ⓒ Ⓓ Ⓔ
22. Ⓐ Ⓑ Ⓒ Ⓓ Ⓔ   47. Ⓐ Ⓑ Ⓒ Ⓓ Ⓔ   72. Ⓐ Ⓑ Ⓒ Ⓓ Ⓔ   97. Ⓐ Ⓑ Ⓒ Ⓓ Ⓔ   122. Ⓐ Ⓑ Ⓒ Ⓓ Ⓔ
23. Ⓐ Ⓑ Ⓒ Ⓓ Ⓔ   48. Ⓐ Ⓑ Ⓒ Ⓓ Ⓔ   73. Ⓐ Ⓑ Ⓒ Ⓓ Ⓔ   98. Ⓐ Ⓑ Ⓒ Ⓓ Ⓔ   123. Ⓐ Ⓑ Ⓒ Ⓓ Ⓔ
24. Ⓐ Ⓑ Ⓒ Ⓓ Ⓔ   49. Ⓐ Ⓑ Ⓒ Ⓓ Ⓔ   74. Ⓐ Ⓑ Ⓒ Ⓓ Ⓔ   99. Ⓐ Ⓑ Ⓒ Ⓓ Ⓔ   124. Ⓐ Ⓑ Ⓒ Ⓓ Ⓔ
25. Ⓐ Ⓑ Ⓒ Ⓓ Ⓔ   50. Ⓐ Ⓑ Ⓒ Ⓓ Ⓔ   75. Ⓐ Ⓑ Ⓒ Ⓓ Ⓔ   100. Ⓐ Ⓑ Ⓒ Ⓓ Ⓔ   125. Ⓐ Ⓑ Ⓒ Ⓓ Ⓔ

MODEL EXAMINATION 5

TIME: 3½ HOURS—125 QUESTIONS

> **Directions**: Each question numbered 1 through 81 has four possible choices lettered (A), (B), (C), and (D). You are to select the answer that you deem to be correct.

1. In addressing a class of recruits, an instructor remarked: "Carelessness and failure are twins." The one of the following that most nearly expresses the meaning of this statement is
   - (A) negligence seldom accompanies success
   - (B) incomplete work is careless work
   - (C) conscientious work is never attended by failure
   - (D) a conscientious person never makes mistakes

2. In lecturing on the law of arrest, an instructor remarked: "To go beyond is as bad as to fall short." The one of the following that most nearly expresses the meaning of this statement is
   - (A) never undertake the impossible.
   - (B) extremes are not desirable.
   - (C) look before you leap.
   - (D) too much success is dangerous.

3. In recent years, the age group 16 through 25 showed the greatest number of arrests for
   - (A) grand larceny from highways and vehicles.
   - (B) burglary.
   - (C) rape.
   - (D) homicide.

4. The two leading causes of traffic accidents involving pedestrians are
   - (A) crossing a street against the light and crossing past a parked car.
   - (B) crossing a street at a point other than the crossing and crossing against the light.
   - (C) crossing a street at a point other than the crossing and running off the sidewalk.
   - (D) crossing a street against the light and failing to observe whether cars are making right or left turns.

5. A "modus operandi" file will be most valuable to a new state trooper as a means of showing the
   - (A) method used by criminals.
   - (B) various bureaus and divisions of the police department.
   - (C) number and nature of vehicular accidents.
   - (D) forms used by the police department.

6. A state trooper is frequently advised to lie down before returning fire if a person is shooting at him or her. This is primarily because
   - (A) a smaller target will thus be presented to the assailant.
   - (B) he or she can return fire more quickly while in the prone position.
   - (C) the assailant will think the trooper has been struck and cease firing.
   - (D) it will indicate that the trooper is not the aggressor.

7. In making arrests during a large riot, it is the practice for troopers to take the ringleaders into custody as soon as possible. This is primarily because

   (A) the police can obtain valuable information from them.
   (B) they deserve punishment more than the other rioters.
   (C) rioters need leadership and, without it, will disperse more quickly.
   (D) arrests of wrongdoers should always be in order of their importance.

8. As you are patrolling your post, you observe two men running toward a parked automobile in which a driver is seated. You question the 3 men and you note the license number. You should

   (A) let them go if you see nothing suspicious.
   (B) warn them not to be caught loitering again.
   (C) arrest them because they have probably committed a crime.
   (D) take them back with you to the place from which the 2 men came.

9. Assume that you are a state trooper. A woman has complained to you about a man's indecent exposure in front of her house. As you approach the house, the man begins to run. You should

   (A) shoot to kill as the man may be a dangerous maniac.
   (B) shout at the man to halt.
   (C) summon other troopers in order to apprehend him.
   (D) question the woman regarding the man's identity.

10. You are patrolling a parkway in a radio car with another trooper. A maroon car coming from the opposite direction signals you to stop, and the driver informs you that he was robbed by 3 men speeding ahead of him in a black sedan. Your radio car cannot cross the center abutment. You should

    (A) request the driver to make a report to the nearest precinct as your car cannot cross over to the other side.
    (B) make a U-turn in your radio car and give chase on the wrong side of the parkway.
    (C) fire warning shots in the air to summon other troopers.
    (D) flash headquarters over your radio system.

11. On patrol, you notice that a man is limping hurriedly, leaving a trail of blood behind him. You question him and his explanation is that he was hurt accidentally while he was watching a man clean a gun. You should

    (A) let him go as you have no proof that his story is not true.
    (B) take him to the nearest hospital and question him again after treatment.
    (C) ask him whether the man had a license for his gun.
    (D) ask him to lead you to the man who cleaned his gun so that you may question him further about the accident.

12. Which of the following situations, if observed by you while on highway patrol, should you consider most suspicious and deserving of further investigation?

    (A) A shabbily dressed person is driving a new Mercedes Benz.
    (B) A 1987 Chrysler has been parked without lights outside an apartment house for several hours.
    (C) A light is on in the rear of a one-family luxurious residence.
    (D) Two well-dressed men are standing at a bus stop at 2 a.m. and arguing heatedly.

13. In addition to cases of submersion involving blocked breathing, artificial respiration is a recommended first aid procedure for

    (A) sunstroke.
    (B) chemical poisoning.
    (C) electrical shock.
    (D) apoplexy.

14. An injury to muscle or tendon brought about by severe exertion and resulting in pain and stiffness is called a

    (A) strain.
    (B) sprain.
    (C) bruise.
    (D) fracture.

15. The delivery of an arrested person, upon giving security for his appearance at the time and place designated to submit to the jurisdiction and judgment of the court, is known as

    (A) bail.
    (B) habeas corpus.
    (C) parole.
    (D) probation.

16. Jones was charged with the murder of Smith. Brown, Jones's landlord, testified at the trial that Jones had in his home a well-equipped laboratory that contained all the necessary chemicals for producing the poison that an autopsy showed caused Smith's death. Brown's testimony constitutes what is called

    (A) corroborative evidence.
    (B) opinion evidence.
    (C) hearsay evidence.
    (D) circumstantial evidence.

17. The procedure whereby a defendant is brought before a magistrate, informed of the charge against him, and asked how he pleads thereto, is called

    (A) arraignment.
    (B) indictment.
    (C) presentment.
    (D) inquisition.

18. It is customary for state police to keep records of lost or stolen automobile license plates. Of the following, the best reason for this practice is to

    (A) permit the prompt issuance of new plates.
    (B) keep a record of all outstanding license plates in use.
    (C) prevent cars from being stolen.
    (D) capture or detain any person found using or attempting to use any of these plates.

19. "A criminal will become a thief, an assailant, or a sexual offender, never an all-around criminal." Of the following, an important reason for these basic differences in criminal behavior is probably that

    (A) to be an all-around criminal requires more intelligence than the average criminal has.
    (B) crime syndicates have gained control over certain branches of crime and have made it difficult for a beginner to break in.
    (C) criminal acts are an expression of the criminal's whole personality.
    (D) most crimes are committed on the spur of the moment and without previous thought.

20. One of the chief reasons why fingerprints are of great value in helping to identify people is that
    (A) criminals always leave fingerprints at the scene of a crime, whether they know it or not.
    (B) no two persons have the same fingerprint pattern.
    (C) fingerprint patterns change as people grow older.
    (D) nationality, religion, and race can be determined by fingerprint patterns.

21. It is *least* accurate to state of fingerprints that:
    (A) It is possible to fingerprint even a dead person.
    (B) The value of fingerprints left at the scene of a crime does not vary with the distinctness of the fingerprint impressions.
    (C) No fingerprints of different persons have ever been found to be alike.
    (D) The prime value of fingerprints lies in their effectiveness in identifying people.

22. Of the following, the one that is least a purpose of fingerprinting procedure is the
    (A) identification of deceased persons.
    (B) identification of the guilty.
    (C) protection of the innocent.
    (D) recognition of first offenders.

23. It is suggested that a suspect should not be permitted to walk in or about the scene of a crime where fingerprints may be present until a thorough search has been made for such evidence. This suggested procedure is
    (A) good; the suspect, if permitted to walk about the scene, would smear all fingerprints that might be found by police investigators.
    (B) bad; the return of a suspect to the scene of a crime provides an opportunity to obtain additional fingerprints from the suspect.
    (C) good; if the suspect handled any objects at the scene, the value of any original fingerprints, as evidence, might be seriously impaired.
    (D) bad; the return of a suspect to the scene of a crime provides an opportunity to identify objects that had been handled during the commission of the crime.

24. According to a manual of procedure of a state police department, the delivery, for laboratory examination, of any article required as evidence must be made by the member of the force finding or coming into the possession of such evidence. Of the following, the most likely reason for this procedure is that it.
    (A) assists in the establishment of the authenticity of the evidence.
    (B) encourages a more careful search of the crime scene for all physical evidence that may be related to the crime.
    (C) ensures that the evidence will be properly marked or tagged for future identification.
    (D) prevents the undue delay that might result from a delivery through official channels.

25. A certain trooper brought a bullet to a scientific crime laboratory for examination. The officer produced the bullet from his pocket and with it money and a penknife that were his personal property. The officer had carried the bullet for several days in his pocket in this manner. His action in this case is
    (A) not proper, since the value of ballistics analysis of the bullet has probably been largely decreased.
    (B) intelligent, since his technique of preserving the bullet practically eliminates the possibility of losing the bullet.

(C) intelligent, since no harm has been done and the entire matter has been handled without the undue expenditure of time or effort.

(D) not proper, because evidence of this type necessarily decreases in value if carried on one's person for more than a maximum of 24 hours.

26. Of the following, the most accurate characterization of the value of the scientific laboratory to a police force is that the laboratory is

(A) a supplement to the work of the police officer.

(B) destined eventually to replace the police officer.

(C) a device, especially useful in detective work, without which police officers could hope to solve only a small percentage of crimes committed.

(D) useful as an instrument for the prevention of crime but likely to be grossly fallible as a device to help solve crimes actually committed.

27. The use of truth serum (scopolamine)

(A) is specifically authorized.

(B) is specifically outlawed.

(C) is regarded as a violation of the privilege against self-incrimination.

(D) needs no statutory sanction.

28. Poroscopy is

(A) the science of identification through the sweat pores.

(B) the science of microscopic hair analysis.

(C) a term applied to art or literature of an obscene nature.

(D) the science of determining the mineral content of soil.

29. Suppose you are checking an alphabetical card reference file to locate information about a "George Dyerly." After checking all the "Ds" you can find a card only for a "George Dyrely." Of the following the best action for you to take is to

(A) check the balance of the file to see if the card you are interested in has been misfiled.

(B) check the data on the card to see if it relates to the same person in whom you are interested.

(C) correct the spelling of the name on your records and reports to conform to the spelling on the card.

(D) reject this reference file as a source of information regarding this person.

30. A businessperson requests advice concerning good practice in the use of a safe in the office. The one of the following points that should be stressed most in the use of safes is that

(A) a safe should not be placed where it can be seen from the street.

(B) the combination should be written down and carefully hidden in the office.

(C) a safe located in a dark place is more tempting to a burglar than one that is located in a well-lit place.

(D) factors of size and weight alone determine the protection offered by a safe.

31. In general, a police officer dealing with teenagers should

(A) establish two-way communication with them.

(B) show them that he or she can solve their problems.

(C) force them to respect the law.

(D) avoid face-to-face contact.

Completion of Forms

Directions: Questions 32 through 36 test your ability to fill out forms correctly. An incident is described requiring that a police form be filled out. Read the questions that apply to the form. For each question, choose the one best answer (A), (B), (C), or (D), and circle the correct choice.

Answer questions 32 through 36 on the basis of the passage below and the Report of Aid Given form shown on the next page.

Troopers Margaret Firestone and Harry Davis are partners on patrol. They see a man lying on his back on the southwest corner of Capital Highway. Trooper Firestone leaves the patrol car to look at him more closely. The man is dressed in clean clothes and seems to have stopped breathing. Trooper Firestone bends over him, makes a quick inspection, and tells Trooper Davis to send for an ambulance. She begins to administer mouth-to-mouth resuscitation. At this point, the man becomes fully conscious and states that this has happened before. He insists that all he needs is a glass of water. He does not want to go to the hospital, nor does he want to be driven home. Trooper Davis gets a glass of water for the man from a nearby store. The man refuses to give his name and will not wait for the ambulance. He drinks the water, thanks the officers for their help, and walks north on Second, where he disappears from view.

32. Under *Identification*, the correct entry for Place is
    (A) Capital Highway.
    (B) Second and Seventh.
    (C) corner of Sixth Avenue and Second Street.
    (D) Second Avenue North, East Sixth Street.

33. Since the man refused to give his name, Trooper Firestone should check the box for
    (A) Other, under *Aid Given*.
    (B) Unknown, under *Identification*.
    (C) Other, under *Disposition of Case*.
    (D) Unknown, under *Nature of Illness or Injury*.

34. Under *Nature of Problem*, the correct box to check is
    (A) Injured.
    (B) Ill.
    (C) Neglected.
    (D) Destitute.

REPORT OF AID GIVEN

Identification

Date _____   Time _____   Place _____

Name of Person Aided _____   ☐ Unknown

Nature of Problem

☐ Abandoned   ☐ Destitute   ☐ Ill

☐ Neglected   ☐ Lost   ☐ Injured

Nature of Illness or Injury

☐ Mental   ☐ Physical   ☐ Unknown

Aid Given

☐ Artificial Respiration   ☐ Food or Water

☐ Control of Bleeding   ☐ Clothing or Blankets

☐ Temporary Splint   ☐ Other

Disposition of Case

☐ Taken Home   ☐ Left in Custody of Friend or Relative

☐ Removed to Hospital   ☐ Taken to Morgue

☐ Left at Place of Occurrence   ☐ Other

Name of Officer Reporting _____

35. The correct boxes to check under *Aid Given* are

    (A) Food or Water and Other.
    (B) Food or Water and Clothing or Blankets.
    (C) Artificial Respiration and Food or Water.
    (D) Artificial Respiration and Other.

36. Under *Disposition of Case*, Officer Firestone should check the box for

    (A) Removed to Hospital.
    (B) Left in Custody of Friend or Relative.
    (C) Other.
    (D) Left at Place of Occurrence.

Assume that you are a state trooper. A duty roster (see below) has been posted in the barracks. Answer the following questions, 37–46, only on the basis of this duty roster.

TROOPER'S NAME	MON.	TUES.	WED.	THURS.	FRI.	SAT.	SUN.
T. Adams	A	D	A	A	A	A	A
R. Brown	D	B	A	C	B	B	B
B. Carlos	C	C	C	C	C	C	D
R. Donaldson	A	C	D	A	C	C	C
A. Edwards	B	B	D	A	A	A	A
C. Frederickson	B	D	A	A	C	C	C
H. Galway	A	A	C	C	D	A	A
L. Isaacson	B	B	B	B	D	B	B
D. Jackson	A	A	A	D	C	A	A
R. Karlsen	C	C	D	A	A	A	A
M. Latimer	B	B	B	B	D	B	B
P. Goldberg	C	C	D	B	B	B	B
L. Mulvaney	A	D	A	A	A	A	A

CODE: A = 8:30 a.m.–4:30 p.m.
              B = 4:30 p.m.–12:30 a.m.
              C = 12:30 a.m.–8:30 a.m.
              D = Day Off

37. The troopers who have only one tour during the week are

    (A) Adams and Carlos.
    (B) Karlsen and Mulvaney.
    (C) Galway and Latimer.
    (D) Edwards and Galway.

38. The one of the following troopers who shifts from tour A to tour C is

    (A) Isaacson.
    (B) Jackson.
    (C) Karlsen.
    (D) Goldberg.

39. The troopers assigned exclusively to the B tour are

    (A) Isaacson and Latimer.
    (B) Brown and Edwards.
    (C) Goldberg and Brown.
    (D) Edwards and Frederickson.

40. The one of the following troopers who shifts only from tour C to tour B is

    (A) Latimer.
    (B) Brown.
    (C) Galway.
    (D) Goldberg.

41. The one of the following troopers who is assigned on all three tours during the week is

    (A) Donaldson.
    (B) Brown.
    (C) Karlsen.
    (D) Galway.

42. The one of the following troopers who is assigned exclusively to the A tour is

    (A) Galway.
    (B) Frederickson.
    (C) Mulvaney.
    (D) Latimer.

43. The following pairs of troopers who could be assigned as partners on highway patrol each day of the week are

    (A) Galway and Jackson.
    (B) Edwards and Frederickson.
    (C) Latimer and Goldberg.
    (D) Adams and Mulvaney.

44. The following pairs of troopers who could be assigned as partners on highway patrol each day of the week are

    (A) Carlos and Galway.
    (B) Isaacson and Latimer.
    (C) Donaldson and Jackson.
    (D) Latimer and Mulvaney.

45. The one of the following troopers who is assigned exclusively to the C tour is

    (A) Donaldson.
    (B) Carlos.
    (C) Goldberg.
    (D) Galway.

46. The one of the following who could have the least regular sleeping hours is

    (A) Karlsen.
    (B) Goldberg.
    (C) Brown.
    (D) Edwards.

Arithmetic Questions Based on Mileage

47. On a certain map a distance of 10 miles is represented by $\frac{1}{2}$ inch. If two towns are $3\frac{1}{2}$ inches apart on this map, then the actual distance in miles between the two towns is

    (A) 35 miles.
    (B) 65 miles.
    (C) 70 miles.
    (D) 80 miles.

48. If a highway patrol car averages 18 miles to a gallon of gasoline, how many gallons of gasoline will be needed on a trip of 369 miles?

(A) $20\frac{1}{2}$ gallons
(B) 28 gallons
(C) 15 gallons
(D) 12 gallons

49. A distance of 25 miles is represented by $2\frac{1}{2}$ inches. On the map, 1 inch is therefore

(A) 5 miles.
(B) 10 miles.
(C) 15 miles.
(D) 20 miles.

50. On a road map, $\frac{1}{4}$ inch represents 8 miles of actual road distance. How many miles apart are two towns that are represented by points $2\frac{1}{8}$ inches apart on the map?

(A) 32 miles
(B) 64 miles
(C) 68 miles
(D) 72 miles

51. A family is planning a trip of 4,000 miles. Later they increase the estimated mileage by 25%. They plan to average 250 miles per day. How many days will the trip take?

(A) 20 days
(B) 40 days
(C) 60 days
(D) None of these

Calendar/Procedure Questions

52. A state trooper, while completing his report of a multicar accident, should know that during a year when the first of November falls on a Saturday an accident that occurred on October 13th happened on

(A) Monday.
(B) Tuesday.
(C) Wednesday.
(D) Thursday.

53. If the last day of June occurs on a Sunday, June 1st will have fallen on

(A) Monday.
(B) Tuesday.
(C) Saturday.
(D) Thursday.

54. If during a given year Christmas was celebrated on a Thursday, the first of the month of December would have fallen on

(A) Monday.
(B) Tuesday.
(C) Wednesday.
(D) Thursday.

55. A state trooper, before testifying in court, notes from his memorandum book that he had made an arrest on November 6th. If he were asked to testify in court as to the day of the week that the arrest took place, he could do so by

    (A) determining the number of days from election day.
    (B) determining the number of days from the third Thursday in the month.
    (C) counting back from his last payday.
    (D) determining the day on which that month began.

56. During the year of 1985, one month contained all of the days of the week four times each. The month was

    (A) March.
    (B) September.
    (C) February.
    (D) October.

57. A highway has two lanes, one in each direction. The lanes are separated by a broken white line. Cars are permitted to pass when there is a broken line. On a solid line, passing is forbidden. Further on, the solid line occurs as the highway climbs a hill. The solid line is necessary to prevent

    (A) cars passing each other in the face of oncoming traffic that cannot be seen.
    (B) motorists attempting to pass slow-moving vehicles.
    (C) truck drivers crawling up a hill blocking traffic.
    (D) cars in the right lane being unable to drive onto the shoulder of the road in an emergency.

58. Many states have laws to control and penalize motorists who drive while intoxicated (DWI). Such laws are most effective in instances where

    (A) troopers stop and check all vehicles.
    (B) all DWI operators are given jail sentences.
    (C) traffic restrictions are enforced strictly.
    (D) enforcement is combined with publicity about the dangers of DWI.

59. A state trooper is patrolling a busy highway and passes a small pickup truck driven by a person who appears to be a young girl. The trooper is concerned because

    (A) the girl could get in trouble.
    (B) motor vehicles should not be driven by underage persons who may not be licensed operators.
    (C) drivers of other vehicles may be distracted by this pickup truck.
    (D) the truck could be involved in an accident.

60. Large, slow-moving vehicles, such as garbage collection or building material trucks, often cause passenger car drivers to become impatient and irritable. The best one of the following practices that a trooper should enforce to avoid trouble in these situations is

    (A) keep slow-moving vehicles in one right lane.
    (B) order all slow-moving vehicles off the highway onto side roads.
    (C) give slow-moving vehicle operators court summonses.
    (D) All of the above

61. Posted symbols used as highway signs are placed not only for the convenience of motorists but also for safety precautions. A double zigzag line near the top of a hill indicates

    (A) a steep, straight incline upon descent from the top.
    (B) a curve at descent from the hill with an obstructed view of oncoming traffic.
    (C) an intersecting road at the top of the hill.
    (D) an intersection at the bottom of the hill with an obstructed view of oncoming traffic.

62. At a certain highway intersection, left and right turns are permitted in any direction at all hours on the green signal light. Right turns are only permitted on the red signal light. In patrolling through this intersection, the highway patrol trooper should mainly be concerned with

    (A) left turns against the red signal light.
    (B) right turns on the green signal light.
    (C) traffic volume during the night hours.
    (D) traffic volume during daylight hours.

63. State troopers on highway patrol must stop to assist motorists involved in accidents that may have resulted in personal injury. The major concern of the highway patrol is to

    (A) keep traffic moving as efficiently as possible.
    (B) call for emergency medical assistance.
    (C) see that motorists involved have each other's license numbers and insurance companies' names.
    (D) All of the above

64. A state trooper assigned to highway patrol passes two motorists who appear to be arguing over some body damage to their vehicles. Traffic is restricted to one lane moving slowly past the scene. The most important action for the trooper to take is to

    (A) stop the argument.
    (B) direct traffic so motorists do not stop to observe the scene.
    (C) call for assistance to direct traffic and move the vehicles.
    (D) arrest the motorists.

65. Automobile accidents unfortunately often result in serious injury. The one of the following that is the primary duty of the state trooper is to

    (A) render first aid.
    (B) call for emergency medical service assistance immediately.
    (C) contact relatives of the injured.
    (D) direct traffic at the site of the accident.

66. A state trooper is on highway patrol on a median-barrier-divided highway and observes two cars that appear to be in a high-speed chase but are in the lanes going in the opposite direction. The trooper should

    (A) jump the barrier to follow the two cars.
    (B) speed in the same direction he has been following until he finds a legal crossing through the median barrier.
    (C) radio for other police vehicles to investigate.
    (D) ignore the situation.

Answer questions 67 through 76 on the basis of the diagram shown below.

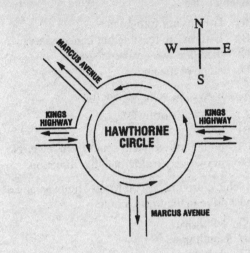

67. In the traffic circle illustrated above, vehicles traveling from east to west must

    (A)   drive north around the circle.

    (B)   drive south around the circle.

    (C)   cross Marcus Avenue south and proceed thereon.

    (D)   drive completely around the circle.

68. In the traffic circle illustrated above, Marcus Avenue

    (A)   flows from east to west.

    (B)   flows from north to south.

    (C)   flows south and northwest.

    (D)   is a dead-end road.

69. The traffic circle illustrated above provides a safe passage for vehicles chiefly because

    (A)   the circle separates traffic going in different directions thus avoiding left and right turns at a right-angle intersection.

    (B)   it provides a means of exit from Kings Highway.

    (C)   it can allow for maximum traffic speed.

    (D)   highway patrols can observe traffic from various stationary positions.

70. A disadvantage of the traffic circle illustrated above is that

    (A)   distance traveled is modified by time saved.

    (B)   traffic flow within the circle is one way.

    (C)   to get to Marcus Avenue south from Kings Highway going west, a vehicle would have to drive almost $\frac{3}{4}$ of the road around the circle.

    (D)   traffic volume can modify traffic patterns.

71. To go east along Kings Highway, vehicles coming from the west travel around the circle

    (A)   south and east.

    (B)   north and west.

    (C)   north and east.

    (D)   south and west.

72. In examining the above map, a vehicle driver could consider traveling around the circle to reverse direction on Kings Highway by driving

    (A)   clockwise.

    (B)   counterclockwise.

    (C)   either direction.

    (D)   None of the above

73. In examining the above map of the Hawthorne Traffic Circle, it is most reasonable to conclude that

(A) U-turns are forbidden.
(B) U-turns are feasible but unnecessary.
(C) there are two dead-end streets.
(D) None of the above

74. Marcus Avenue vehicles can travel

(A) one-way northwest.
(B) one-way south.
(C) both northwest and south from the circle.
(D) in two-way traffic in either direction.

75. A vehicle driving east on Kings Highway and desiring to enter Marcus Avenue South must drive in the traffic circle

(A) southeast.
(B) southwest.
(C) northeast.
(D) northwest.

76. Reversing traffic around the traffic circle would necessitate reversal of direction on

(A) Marcus Avenue.
(B) Kings Highway.
(C) Marcus Avenue north only.
(D) None of the above

For questions 77 through 81, refer to the direction indicator below.

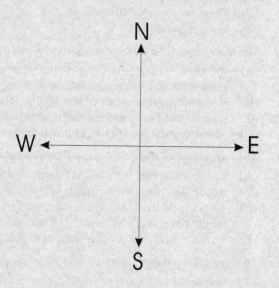

77. A vehicle proceeding diagonally north and veering right is said to be traveling

(A) northeast.
(B) northwest.
(C) southeast.
(D) None of the above

78. A vehicle proceeding diagonally northwest and veering right is said to be traveling

    (A) northwest.
    (B) north by northwest.
    (C) north by northeast.
    (D) north.

79. A vehicle proceeding east and veering right diagonally toward the southeast is said to be traveling

    (A) east by northeast.
    (B) east by southeast.
    (C) south by southeast.
    (D) north by northeast.

80. In describing a location as south and west of a right-angle intersection, a trooper would be required to indicate a

    (A) southbound road with a right turn at the closest intersection to the destination.
    (B) southbound road with a left turn at the closest intersection to the destination.
    (C) westbound road with a left turn at the closest intersection to the destination.
    (D) southwest path that is available only to pedestrians.

81. In describing a location as north and west of a right angle intersection a trooper would be required to indicate a

    (A) northbound road with a right turn at the closest intersection to the destination.
    (B) northbound road with a left turn at the closest intersection to the destination.
    (C) westbound road with a right turn at the closest intersection to the destination.
    (D) westbound road with an alternate northbound road in an easterly diagonal direction.

Directions: This part of the test consists of several reading passages, each followed by a number of statements. Analyze each statement on the basis of the material given. Then, mark your answer sheet (A), (B), (C), or (D).

Mark it (A) if the statement is entirely true.
Mark it (B) if the statement is entirely false.
Mark it (C) if the statement is partially false and partially true.
Mark it (D) if the statement cannot be judged on the basis of the facts given in the excerpt.

Questions 82 through 86 are to be answered based on the contents of the following paragraph.

A prisoner, who, being confined in a prison, or being in lawful custody of an officer or other person, escapes from such prison or custody, is guilty of a felony if such custody or confinement is upon a charge, arrest, commitment, or conviction for a felony, and of a misdemeanor if such custody or confinement is upon a charge, arrest, commitment, or conviction for a misdemeanor. A prisoner confined in a state prison for a term less than for life, who attempts, although unsuccessfully, to escape from such prison, is guilty of a felony.

82. An unsuccessful attempt at escape from custody is not generally punishable.

83. A captured state convict serving less than a life sentence is reimprisoned for life upon recapture.

84. A prisoner having been arrested on a misdemeanor charge is guilty of a felony if he makes a successful attempt at escape but is later recaptured.

85. A person charged with a misdemeanor being held in legal custody is guilty of a misdemeanor in the event of an escape from custody.

86. A prisoner not under a life sentence confined to a state prison is deemed guilty of a felony if he or she makes a successful attempt at escape and is subsequently recaptured; but if the attempt is unsuccessful, the prisoner is guilty of a misdemeanor.

Questions 87 through 91 are to be answered on the basis of the contents of the following paragraph.

A person, who, with intent to effect or facilitate the escape of a prisoner, whether the escape is effected or attempted or not, enters a prison, or conveys to a prisoner any information, or sends into a prison any disguise, instrument, weapon, or other thing, is guilty of a felony if the prisoner is held upon a charge, arrest, commitment, or conviction for a felony, and of a misdemeanor if the prisoner is held upon a charge, arrest, commitment, or conviction of a misdemeanor.

87. A person sending a misdemeanant a weapon with intent to effect that person's escape is liable to arrest under the charge of felony.

88. Entering a state prison for the sole purpose of conveying information to a prisoner is not legally punishable.

89. The attempt by a third party to effect the escape of a state prisoner is not punished as severely as an actual attempt by the prisoner.

90. Any attempt on the part of an outside person to facilitate the escape of a felon is punishable as a felony.

91. The act of conveying a disguise to a prisoner is in itself punishable as either a misdemeanor or a felony.

Questions 92 through 96 are to be answered on the basis of the following paragraph.

A sheriff, or other officer or person, who allows a prisoner, lawfully in his custody, in any action or proceedings, civil or criminal, or in any prison under his charge or control, to escape or go at large, except as permitted by law, or connives at or assists such escape, or omits an act or duty whereby such escape is occasioned, or contributed to, or assisted is: 1. If he corruptly and willfully allows, connives at, or assists the escape, guilty of a felony; 2. In any other case, guilty of a misdemeanor. Any officer who is convicted of the offense specified, forfeits his office and is forever disqualified to hold any office, or place of trust, honor, or profit, under the constitution or laws of this state.

92. If a prisoner escapes from a guard through no fault of the latter, the guard is not liable to any action.

93. A prison guard assisting the escape of a felon is himself open to a charge constituting felony.

94. A person having legal custody over a prisoner, who unlawfully permits his freedom, is liable to forfeiture of his office if the charge against the prisoner is criminal but is not so liable if civil.

95. A guard who through negligence in his duty permits a prisoner to escape is not open to a criminal charge.

96. A sheriff illegally permitting a prisoner in a civil action, not under a charge of felony, to go at large may be punished as a misdemeanant.

Questions 97 through 101 are to be answered on the basis of the following paragraph.

A person who gives or offers a bribe to any executive officer, or to a person elected or appointed to become an executive officer, of this state with intent to influence that person in respect to any act, decision, vote, opinion, or other proceedings as such officer, is punishable by imprisonment in a state prison not exceeding ten years or by a fine not exceeding five thousand dollars, or by both.

97. An elected executive officer may not generally be punished for accepting a small bribe.

98. An appointed executive officer convicted of accepting a bribe may be punished by either fine or imprisonment.

99. Bribing of an executive officer with intent to influence the officer's vote is deemed a criminal act and, in certain instances, may be punishable by life imprisonment.

100. The length of a sentence to which a person is liable upon conviction for offering a bribe to an executive officer is limited to ten years.

101. An executive officer accepting a bribe is equally guilty as the person offering the bribe, though the punishment is not as severe.

Questions 102 through 106 are to be answered on the basis of the following paragraph.

A Commissioner of Correction, warden, or other officer or prison guard, employed at any of the prisons, who: 1. Shall be directly or indirectly interested in any contract, purchase, or sale, for, by, or on account of such prison; or 2. Accepts a present from a contractor or contractor's agent, directly or indirectly, or employs the labor of a convict or another person employed in such prison on any work for the private benefit of such commissioner, warden, or guard, is guilty of a misdemeanor, except that the warden shall be entitled to employ prisoners for necessary household services.

102. A guard who employs the labor of prisoners in his or her own interests is guilty of a misdemeanor, except that such labor may be so employed indirectly.

103. Only a Commissioner of Correction may accept a small present from a contractor, and then only indirectly.

104. In no case may a prison guard be directly interested in a contract in which the prison is a party.

105. It is illegal to employ the labor of a convict in any case.

106. A warden may only indirectly be interested in the sale of merchandise on account of the prison at which he or she is employed.

Directions: This test of your ability to comprehend what you read consists of a number of different passages. One or more questions are based on each passage. Questions consist of incomplete statements about a passage. Each incomplete statement is followed by four choices lettered (A), (B), (C), and (D). Mark your answer sheet with the letter of that choice that best conveys the meaning of the passage and that best completes the statement.

Questions 107 through 114 are based on the following excerpt from an annual report of a police department. This material should be read first and then referred to in answering these questions, which are to be answered solely on the basis of the material herein contained.

Legal Bureau

One of the more important functions of this bureau is to analyze and furnish the department with pertinent information concerning federal and state statutes and local laws that affect the department, law enforcement, or crime prevention. In addition, all measures introduced in the state legislature and the city council, which may affect this department, are carefully reviewed by members of the Legal Bureau and, where necessary, opinions and recommendations thereon are prepared.

Another important function of this office is the prosecution of cases in the Criminal Court. This is accomplished by assignment of attorneys who are members of the Legal Bureau to appear in those cases that are deemed to raise issues of importance to the department or questions of law that require technical presentation to facilitate proper determination and also in the cases where request is made for such appearances by a magistrate, some other official of the city, or a member of the force. Attorneys are regularly assigned to prosecute all cases in the Supreme Court.

Proposed legislation was prepared and sponsored for introduction in the state legislature, and, at this writing, one of these proposals has already been enacted into law and five others are presently on the Governor's desk awaiting executive action. The new law prohibits the sale or possession of a hypodermic syringe or needle by an unauthorized person. The bureau's proposals awaiting executive action pertain to: an amendment to the Code of Criminal Procedure prohibiting desk officers from taking bail in gambling cases or in cases mentioned in Section 552, Code of Criminal Procedure, including confidence men and swindlers as jostlers in the Penal Law, and prohibiting the sale of switchblade knives of any size to children under 16 and bills extending the licensing period of gunsmiths.

The following is a report of the activities of the Bureau during Year 2 as compared with Year 1:

	Year 2	Year 1
Memoranda of law prepared	83	68
Legal matters forwarded to Corporation Counsel	122	144
Letters requesting legal information	756	807
Letters requesting departmental records	139	111
Matters for publication	26	17
Court appearances of members of bureau	4,678	4,621
Conferences	94	103
Lectures at Police Academy	30	33
Reports on proposed legislation	255	194
Deciphering of codes	79	27
Expert testimony	31	16
Notices to court witnesses	81	55
Briefs prepared	22	18
Court papers prepared	258	

107. One of the functions of the Legal Bureau is to

    (A) review and make recommendations on proposed federal laws affecting law enforcement.
    (B) prepare opinions on all measures introduced in the state legislature and the city council.
    (C) furnish the department with pertinent information concerning all new federal and state laws.
    (D) analyze all laws affecting the work of the department.

108. The one of the following that is not a function of the Legal Bureau is

    (A) law enforcement and crime prevention.
    (B) prosecution of all cases in Supreme Court.
    (C) prosecution of cases in Criminal Court.
    (D) lecturing at the Police Academy.

109. Members of the Legal Bureau frequently appear in Criminal Court for the purpose of

    (A) defending members of the department.
    (B) raising issues of importance to the department.
    (C) prosecuting all offenders arrested by the members of the department.
    (D) facilitating proper determination of questions of law requiring technical presentation.

110. The Legal Bureau sponsored a bill that would

    (A) extend the licenses of gunmen.
    (B) prohibit the sale of switchblade knives of any size to children.
    (C) place confidence men and swindlers in the same category as jostlers in the Penal Law.
    (D) prohibit desk officers from admitting gamblers, confidence men, and swindlers to bail.

111. From the report it is not reasonable to infer that

    (A) fewer briefs were prepared in Year 2.
    (B) the preparation of court papers was a new activity assumed in Year 2.
    (C) the Code of Criminal Procedure authorizes desk officers to accept bail in certain cases.
    (D) the penalty for jostling and swindling is the same.

112. According to the report, the activity showing the greatest increase in Year 2 as compared with Year 1 was

    (A) matters for publication.
    (B) reports on proposed legislation.
    (C) notices to court witnesses.
    (D) memoranda of law prepared.

113. According to the report, the activity showing the greatest percentage of increase in Year 2 as compared with Year 1 was

    (A) court appearances of members of the bureau.
    (B) giving expert testimony.
    (C) deciphering of codes.
    (D) letters requesting departmental records.

114. According to the report, the percentage of bills prepared and sponsored by the Legal Bureau that was passed by the State Legislature and sent to the Governor for approval was

    (A) approximately 3.1 percent.
    (B) approximately 2.6 percent.
    (C) approximately .5 percent.
    (D) Unable to determine from the data given

Answer questions 115 through 118 on the basis of the following statement.

Disorderly conduct, in the abstract, does not constitute any crime known to law; it is only when it tends to a breach of the peace, under the circumstances detailed in Section 1458 of the Consolidation Act, that it constitutes a minor offense cognizable by the judge, and when it in fact threatens to disturb the peace, it is a misdemeanor as well under Section 675 of the Penal Code as at common law, and not within the jurisdiction of the judge, but of the Criminal Court.

115. Of the following, the most accurate statement on the basis of the preceding paragraph is that

    (A) an act that merely threatens to disturb the peace is not a crime.
    (B) disorderly conduct, by itself, is not a crime.
    (C) some types of disorderly conduct are indictable.
    (D) a minor offense may or may not be cognizable.

116. Of the following, the least accurate statement on the basis of the preceding paragraph is that

    (A) disorderly conduct that threatens to disturb the peace is within the jurisdiction of the judge.
    (B) disorderly conduct that "tends to a breach of the peace" may constitute a minor offense.
    (C) Section 1458 of the Consolidation Act discusses a "breach of the peace."
    (D) disorderly conduct that "tends to a breach of the peace" is not the same as that which threatens to disturb the peace.

117. The preceding paragraph does not clarify the difference between

    (A) jurisdiction of a judge and jurisdiction of the Criminal Court.
    (B) disorderly conduct as a crime and disorderly conduct not as a crime.
    (C) what "tends to a breach of the peace" and what threatens to disturb the peace.
    (D) a minor offense and a misdemeanor.

118. Of the following generalizations, the one that is best illustrated by the preceding paragraph is that

    (A) acts that in themselves are not criminal may become criminal as a result of their effect.
    (B) abstract conduct may, in and of itself, be criminal.
    (C) criminal acts are determined by results rather than by intent.
    (D) an act that is criminal to begin with may not be criminal if it fails to have the desired effect.

Questions 119 and 120 pertain to the following section of the Penal Code.

Section 1942. A person who, after having been three times convicted within this state of felonies or attempts to commit felonies, or under the law of any other state, government, or country, of crimes which if committed within this state would become felonious, commits a felony, other than murder, first or second degree, or treason, within this state, shall be sentenced upon conviction of such fourth, or subsequent, offense to imprisonment in a state prison for an indeterminate term, the maximum term provided for first offenders for the crime for which the individual has been convicted, but, in any event, the minimum term upon conviction for a felony as the fourth or subsequent offense, shall not be less than fifteen years, and the maximum thereof shall be his natural life.

119. Under the terms of the quoted portion of Section 1942 of the Penal Law, a person must receive the increased punishment therein provided if

(A) he is convicted of a felony and has been three times previously convicted of felonies.

(B) he has been three times previously convicted of felonies, regardless of the nature of his present conviction.

(C) his fourth conviction is for murder, first or second degree, or treason.

(D) he has previously been convicted three times of murder, first or second degree, or treason.

120. Under the terms of the quoted portion of Section 1942 of the Penal Law, a person convicted of a felony for which the penalty is imprisonment for a term not to exceed ten years, and who has been three times previously convicted of felonies in this State, shall be sentenced to a term the minimum of which shall be

(A) ten years.

(B) fifteen years.

(C) indeterminate.

(D) his natural life.

In answering questions 121 to 125, the following definitions of crimes should be applied, bearing in mind that all elements contained in the definitions must be present in order to charge a person with that crime.

BURGLARY is the breaking and entering of a building with intent to commit some crime therein.

EXTORTION is the obtaining of property from another, with his consent, induced by a wrongful use of force or fear or under color of official right.

LARCENY is the taking and carrying away of the personal property of another with intent to deprive or defraud the owner of the use and benefit of such property.

ROBBERY is the unlawful taking of the personal property of another from his person or in his presence, by force or violence or by putting him in fear of injury, immediate or future, to his person or property.

121. If A entered B's store during business hours, tied B to a chair, and then helped himself to the contents of B's cash register, A should, upon arrest, be charged with

(A) burglary.

(B) extortion.

(C) larceny.

(D) robbery.

122. If A broke the panel of glass in the window of B's store, stepped in, and removed some merchandise from the window, he should, upon arrest, be charged with

    (A) burglary.
    (B) extortion.
    (C) larceny.
    (D) robbery.

123. If A, after B had left for the day, found the door of B's store open, walked in, took some merchandise, and then left through the same door, he should, upon arrest, be charged with

    (A) burglary.
    (B) extortion.
    (C) larceny.
    (D) robbery.

124. If A, by threatening to report B for failure to pay to the city the full amount of sales tax he had collected from various customers, induced B to give him the contents of his cash register, A should, upon arrest, be charged with

    (A) burglary.
    (B) extortion.
    (C) larceny.
    (D) robbery.

125. If A, on a crowded train, put his hand into B's pocket and removed B's wallet without his knowledge, A should, upon arrest, be charged with

    (A) burglary.
    (B) extortion.
    (C) larceny.
    (D) robbery.

MODEL EXAMINATION 5: ANSWERS AND EXPLANATIONS

ANSWERS

1.	A	26.	C	51.	A	76.	D	101.	D
2.	B	27.	D	52.	A	77.	A	102.	C
3.	B	28.	A	53.	C	78.	B	103.	B
4.	B	29.	B	54.	A	79.	B	104.	A
5.	A	30.	C	55.	D	80.	A	105.	B
6.	A	31.	A	56.	C	81.	B	106.	B
7.	A	32.	A	57.	A	82.	B	107.	D
8.	A	33.	B	58.	D	83.	D	108.	A
9.	B	34.	B	59.	B	84.	B	109.	D
10.	D	35.	C	60.	A	85.	A	110.	C
11.	B	36.	C	61.	B	86.	C	111.	D
12.	A	37.	A	62.	A	87.	B	112.	B
13.	C	38.	B	63.	B	88.	D	113.	C
14.	A	39.	A	64.	C	89.	B	114.	D
15.	A	40.	D	65.	B	90.	A	115.	B
16.	D	41.	B	66.	C	91.	B	116.	A
17.	A	42.	C	67.	A	92.	D	117.	D
18.	D	43.	D	68.	C	93.	A	118.	A
19.	C	44.	B	69.	A	94.	C	119.	A
20.	B	45.	B	70.	C	95.	B	120.	B
21.	B	46.	C	71.	A	96.	A	121.	D
22.	D	47.	C	72.	B	97.	D	122.	A
23.	C	48.	A	73.	A	98.	D	123.	C
24.	A	49.	B	74.	C	99.	B	124.	B
25.	A	50.	C	75.	A	100.	A	125.	C

EXPLANATIONS

1. **The correct answer is (A).** The preamble of the question states that carelessness leads to failure. Choice (A) says essentially the same thing, that being negligent seldom leads to success. Incomplete work is not necessarily careless work. Conscientious work, on the other hand, does not ensure success. Conscientious workers make errors, although they probably make fewer than workers who are not conscientious.

2. **The correct answer is (B).** The lecturer is saying that it is nearly always best to follow the required procedures and not go beyond. Very often doing too much causes as many difficulties as doing too little.

3. **The correct answer is (B).** This age group has a large number of drug addicts, and the need for money to acquire drugs leads to burglaries.

4. **The correct answer is (B).** These are the two leading causes of pedestrian involvement in traffic accidents.

5. **The correct answer is (A).** A "modus operandi" file classifies criminals by the methods they use to commit crimes, e.g., criminals who tend to burglarize homes of women living alone are filed together. When such a crime is committed, the police will look in that part of the file for likely suspects.

6. **The correct answer is (A).** This answer explains itself.

7. **The correct answer is (A).** The ringleaders started the riot, and knowing how it got started could help bring it to an end.

8. **The correct answer is (A).** Based on the facts presented in the question, there is nothing further for the trooper to do. The trooper's suspicion was aroused, an investigation was made, and nothing turned up.

9. **The correct answer is (B).** A shout to stop delivered in an authoritative manner could very well do the trick. This would be the first step to take, to be followed by a call for assistance to apprehend him if he does not respond favorably.

10. **The correct answer is (D).** This is an occasion when assistance is needed; call for it. The course of action in choice (A) would permit the car to get away. Choice (B) would create a dangerous situation, and choice (C) would only be effective if other troopers were in the area.

11. **The correct answer is (B).** Initially, medical treatment is most important. Further investigation should follow medical care.

12. **The correct answer is (A).** Of the four situations, only this one would seem to be suspicious. The other three situations are really quite ordinary.

13. **The correct answer is (C).** Artificial respiration is called for whenever breathing has stopped. This is often the case during electrical shock.

14. **The correct answer is (A).** A bruise is an abrasion. A sprain involves stretching or dislocating a joint unnaturally, and a fracture involves a broken bone.

15. **The correct answer is (A).** The preamble of the question states the legal definition of "bail."

16. **The correct answer is (D).** Purely circumstantial. No evidence has been brought forward that Jones committed the murder, only that Jones might have had the wherewithal to do so.

17. **The correct answer is (A).** The arraignment represents the first step in the trying of an accused.

18. **The correct answer is (D).** This procedure often leads to the location of stolen vehicles and the apprehension of wanted criminals. Many jurisdictions now use a computer to expedite the process.

19. **The correct answer is (C).** Criminals are essentially specialists. The type of crime that a criminal tends to commit is a manifestation of his or her personality. The criminal who tends to commit sexual crimes does not generally feel a compulsion to commit other types of crimes. The same for the burglar and the thief, etc. There are occasions when a rapist will commit a larceny at the same time as the rape, but the primary tendency will be towards rape, and that act is an expression of the personality of the perpetrator.

20. **The correct answer is (B).** A set of fingerprints is unique, and no two people have the same fingerprints. They are not subject to change or to being changed; therefore, they are an excellent means of identification.

21. **The correct answer is (B).** This is a negative question, and, therefore, you should select the choice that contains a statement that is the least accurate of the choices given. Many fingerprints left at the scene of a crime are not valuable because they are smudged, are too light to read accurately, etc.

22. **The correct answer is (D).** This is not the primary objective of a fingerprint system. All of the other choices contain objectives of a sophisticated fingerprint system. This, again, is a negative question requiring the choice of an item that is the least correct of the items given.

23. **The correct answer is (C).** Choice (C) is a much better reason for this procedure because there would be no positive way of saying that the fingerprints were made at the time of the commission of the crime and not at a later date.

24. **The correct answer is (A).** The officer will then be in a position to testify that what he or she found at the scene of the crime was brought to the laboratory for analysis.

25. **The correct answer is (A).** The surface of the bullet would probably be altered by the articles in the officer's pocket.

26. **The correct answer is (C).** Many crimes are solved in the police laboratory through scientific means that bring to light facts that cannot be determined by the naked eye.

27. **The correct answer is (D).** The law neither sanctions nor prohibits its use.

28. **The correct answer is (A).** The arrangement of the sweat pores on the skin's surface is unique and is not subject to change. However, the science of poroscopy is not used much today in police work because fingerprints are much more useful in the identification of criminals.

29. **The correct answer is (B).** There is the chance the name was misspelled either on the card or on your records.

30. **The correct answer is (C).** A thief will assume that the concealed safe contains more valuable items than the safe left out in the open. Also, a passerby may spot someone trying to break into a safe.

31. **The correct answer is (A).** Two-way communication should be established to show that the officer is there not only to enforce the laws but also to help people. The officer may not be able to solve a citizen's problems, but he/she should be able to refer them to sources where they may be able to receive help. Two-way communication is the most effective means of dealing with all persons.

Answers 32–36: no explanations necessary.

32. **The correct answer is (A).**
33. **The correct answer is (B).**
34. **The correct answer is (B).**
35. **The correct answer is (C).**
36. **The correct answer is (C).**
37. **The correct answer is (A).** Troopers Adams and Carlos are the only ones who have one tour listed next to their names. Therefore, choice (A) is the only answer. Karlsen, Galway, and Edwards each have two tours. Mulvaney and Latimer have one tour but are partners with others who have two tours; therefore, the other options would not be correct.

38. **The correct answer is (B).** Jackson shifts from tour A to tour C on Friday. Isaacson is entirely on tour B. Karlsen goes from C to A and Goldberg, from C to B.

39. **The correct answer is (A).** An inspection of the table shows only Isaacson and Latimer on the B tour during the entire week. Goldberg goes from C to B on Thursday. Brown shifts from B to A to C, and then to B. Edwards shifts from B to A on Thursday, and Frederickson shifts from B to A and C.

40. **The correct answer is (D).** Goldberg is the only trooper of those listed shifting from tour C to tour B. Latimer is only on tour B, Brown is on all three tours, and Galway goes from tour A to tour C.

41. **The correct answer is (B).** As noted in the explanation for question 39, Brown is assigned to all three tours. Donaldson, Karlsen, and Galway have two each.

42. **The correct answer is (C).** Of all of the choices given, Mulvaney is the only one assigned the A tour during the entire week. Galway is on the A and C tours. Frederickson is on all three, and Latimer is on the B tour for the entire week.

43. **The correct answer is (D).** Adams and Mulvaney are assigned to tour A each day of the week and therefore could be assigned as partners for the week. Galway, Jackson, Goldberg, Edwards, and Frederickson change tours. Latimer is on tour B.

44. **The correct answer is (B).** Isaacson and Latimer are both assigned to tour A each day of the week. Mulvaney and Latimer are on different tours, as are Carlos and Galway. Donaldson and Jackson shift tours during the week.

45. **The correct answer is (B).** Of those given, Carlos is the only one assigned to the C tour. Donaldson, Goldberg, and Galway shift tours during the week.

46. **The correct answer is (C).** Trooper Brown has all three tours during the week; therefore his sleeping hours change Tuesday, Wednesday, and Friday. Karlsen has only two duty tours with a day off between. The same with Goldberg and Edwards.

47. **The correct answer is (C).**
    10 miles = $\frac{1}{2}$ inch
    20 miles = 1 inch
    60 miles = 3 inches
    Therefore $3\frac{1}{2}$ inches = 70 miles

48. **The correct answer is (A).** Divide 369 by 18. Answer is $20\frac{1}{2}$ gallons.

49. **The correct answer is (B).**

$$\frac{25}{2\frac{1}{2}} = \frac{25}{\frac{5}{2}} = 25 \times \frac{2}{5} = \frac{50}{5} = 10$$

50. **The correct answer is (C).**
    $\frac{1}{4}$ inch = 8 miles
    1 inch = 8 x 4 = 32 miles
    2 inches = 32 x 2 = 64 miles
    $\frac{1}{8}$ inch = $\frac{1}{2}$ of $\frac{1}{4}$ inch
    Therefore $\frac{1}{8}$ inch = 4 miles
    Total for $2\frac{1}{8}$ inches = 68 miles

51. **The correct answer is (A).**
    25% of 4,000 = 1,000
    Total mileage is 5,000
    5,000 divided by 250 = 20 days

52. **The correct answer is (A).** October

S	M	T	W	Th	F	S
12	⑬					
19	20	21	22	23	24	25
26	27	28	29	30	31	①

53. **The correct answer is (C).**

S	M	T	W	Th	F	S
						①
2						
9						
16						
23	24	25	26	27	28	29
30						Ⓢ

54. **The correct answer is (A).**

      ①   2   3   4

                     11

                     18

                     25

      S Ⓜ T   W   Th   F   S

55. **The correct answer is (D).** Election Day date varies depending on which date falls on the first Tuesday after the first Monday in November. Choice (B), the third Thursday is far ahead of the 6th of November. Choice (C), back from his last payday, would be indeterminate depending on the day of the court testimony. Choice (D) is the current and logical calculation. If November 1st falls on a Saturday, the sixth day would be Thursday, i.e., six days thereafter.

56. **The correct answer is (C).** February has 28 days. Each week contains 7 days. 28 is evenly divisible by 4.

57. **The correct answer is (A).** The use of a solid line dividing a highway, with traffic in both directions, prevents cars from passing each other by driving in the lane for traffic going in the opposite direction. This avoids head-on collisions. Choices (B) and (C) are not relevant, and choice (D) is not affected by the lines.

58. **The correct answer is (D).** Publicity as a form of education is often used to aid law enforcement. **Choice (A) is incorrect because of the word "all."**

59. **The correct answer is (B).** All states have a minimum age for driving vehicles. Choices (A), (C), and (D) are speculative.

60. **The correct answer is (A).** This is the most common practice. Choice (B) would be impossible to enforce. There is no law against slow-moving vehicles, choice (C). For these reasons, choice (D) is inoperative.

61. **The correct answer is (B).** A zigzag line logically would mean a curve or curves. There would be no need for a zigzag line if the road were straight.

62. **The correct answer is (A).** Of the four options given, option (A) is the only one that is forbidden by the terms of the question and is a general prohibition to motorists.

63. **The correct answer is (B).** No explanation necessary.

64. **The correct answer is (C).** Two conditions are stated in the question, i.e., the motorists arguing and the slow-moving traffic. Since the trooper cannot handle both, he would be wise to call for assistance.

65. **The correct answer is (B).** The primary duty of the trooper is to ensure that victims get medical treatment as soon as possible. All the other choices, though important, are secondary considerations.

66. **The correct answer is (C).** The trooper cannot jump his vehicle over a median barrier without considerable risk to himself, his vehicle, and others. If he continues in the same direction, even at high speed, he would still lose time. Since he cannot ignore such an obvious suspicious occurrence, his best action is to use his radio.

67. **The correct answer is (A).** Note the arrows in the circle. If you enter the circle from the right of the map you will be going from east to west. See now that the arrow goes northerly to get around the circle.

68. **The correct answer is (C).** This can be determined from looking at the map. Marcus Avenue leaves the circle at the bottom of the map going south and at the top of the map going northwest.

69. **The correct answer is (A).** Choice (A) is clearly the answer as shown on the map by the arrows within the circle.

70. **The correct answer is (C).** Note the question asks for a disadvantage. If you look at the right of the map, you will see the arrow going from east to west. Upon entering the circle it can only go north, then west and southeast. Thus a vehicle would have to drive _ of the road around the circle.

71. **The correct answer is (A).** This question is the opposite of question 70. If you look at the left side of the map and at the cross compass, you will find Kings Highway going east. Upon entering the circle, a vehicle must "turn down south" and then "up east."

72. **The correct answer is (B).** This question is self-explanatory. If you imagine this map placed on a clock face, the arrows will go opposite to the direction of the minute hand.

73. **The correct answer is (A).** It is clearly the answer since traffic in the circle is only going one way. Since a dead-end street has no means of exit, choice (C) is false; all streets enter or leave this circle. Choice (B) is false, since the traffic goes in one direction around the circle.

74. **The correct answer is (C).** This question can be explained by referring to question 68 and its explanation.

75. **The correct answer is (A).** Looking at the map on the left side, you will see the arrow going east. Then the vehicle would enter the traffic circle southerly and go around for a short distance easterly to exit at Marcus Avenue South.

76. **The correct answer is (D).** This question is understandable when the map is placed on a clock; reversal of traffic would mean a clockwise direction. Since all streets are either two-way or exit from the circle, there is no need to change direction on any accessible street.

Explanation for Compass Direction Questions

In answering questions on compass directions, the reader should imagine that facing forward is north, the right hand is east, the left is west, and the rear is south. In a circular view, the compass may be depicted as shown here.

The directions in between the four points are stated in terms of the nearest quarter direction. Thus going from north to east the compass runs: north by northeast, northeast, east by northeast, east.

Diagonally opposite northeast is southwest.

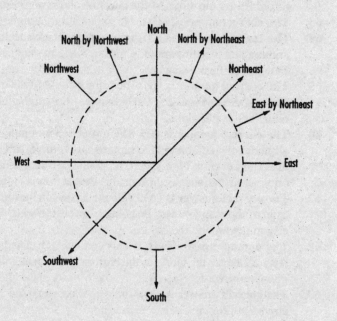

77. **The correct answer is (A).** Note introduction—veering right moves toward the east.

78. **The correct answer is (B).** See diagram—the right of northwest is north by northwest, as indicated.

79. **The correct answer is (B).** If you face north and then turn right, you will be facing east. Continuing to turn right, the direction is east by southeast.

80. **The correct answer is (A).** Following the circular diagram given above, the vehicle would go south and then make a right turn to go west.

81. **The correct answer is (B).** Northwest is shown on the above diagram as a leftward direction from north of the center of the circle.

82. **The correct answer is (B).** This statement is entirely false. The extent of the punishment is directly related to the crime for which the arrest was made. If the prisoner was arrested for a felony, an attempt to escape is a felony.

83. **The correct answer is (D).** No such statement is made in the paragraph.

84. **The correct answer is (B).** On the contrary. Refer to the last part of the first sentence in the paragraph.

85. **The correct answer is (A).** The last part of the first sentence in the paragraph conveys this thought.

86. **The correct answer is (C).** The statement is true as far as successful escape is concerned but is not true as far as an unsuccessful escape is concerned. In the case of an unsuccessful escape, the prisoner would be guilty of a felony.

87. **The correct answer is (B).** The statement is entirely false. Refer to the latter part of the paragraph.

88. **The correct answer is (D).** This paragraph in part concerns itself only with the conveyance of information that would assist the prisoner to escape.

89. **The correct answer is (B).** On the contrary, one who assists in the escape of a prisoner who is guilty of a felony is also guilty of a felony.

90. **The correct answer is (A).** This is a true statement according to the paragraph.

91. **The correct answer is (B).** Only if an attempt at escape is made. The act of conveying the disguise in itself is insufficient to be charged with a crime.

92. **The correct answer is (D).** This condition is not referred to in the paragraph at all.

93. **The correct answer is (A).** Refer to the fourth line of the paragraph.

94. **The correct answer is (C).** It is true if the charge against the prisoner is of a criminal nature. It is also true if the action is civil. Therefore the statement is partially true and partially false.

95. **The correct answer is (B).** Refer to that part of the paragraph that reads, "or omits an act of duty," etc.

96. **The correct answer is (A).** Refer to the sixth line of the paragraph, sentence numbered " 2."

97. **The correct answer is (D).** There is no reference in the paragraph to the acceptance of a bribe.

98. **The correct answer is (D).** Again, there is no reference in the paragraph to the acceptance of a bribe. The paragraph refers only to the offering of a bribe.

99. **The correct answer is (B).** The maximum time one may be sentenced to prison for the bribing of an executive officer is ten years.

100. **The correct answer is (A).** This is stated in the last line of the paragraph.

101. **The correct answer is (D).** There is no information in the paragraph concerning the punishment of an executive officer who accepts a bribe.

102. **The correct answer is (C).** The first half of the statement is true. The second part, which refers to indirect employment of prisoners, is false.

103. **The correct answer is (B).** No employee of the Department of Correction may accept a small present from a contractor. The paragraph does not differentiate one level of employment from the other. Top to bottom, all employees are prohibited from accepting gifts from contractors.

104. **The correct answer is (A).** This is the implication contained in the regulation.

105. **The correct answer is (B).** The regulation states that it is illegal to utilize the labor of a convict for private benefit only.

106. **The correct answer is (B).** A warden may not have an interest in the sale of merchandise produced or used in the prison, directly or indirectly.

107. **The correct answer is (D).** This is stated in the last sentence of the first paragraph.

108. **The correct answer is (A).** There is no implication in the reading that the Legal Bureau has any responsibility in law enforcement or crime prevention.

109. **The correct answer is (D).** This is stated in the second sentence of the second paragraph.

110. **The correct answer is (C).** Refer to the last part of the third paragraph.

111. **The correct answer is (D).** There is nothing in the question in support of this contention.

112. **The correct answer is (B).**
Matters for publication, 9.
Reports on proposed legislation, 61.
Notices to court witnesses, 26.
Memoranda of law prepared, 15.

113. **The correct answer is (C).**
Court appearances of members, 1.2 percent.
Giving expert testimony, 9.4 percent.
Deciphering codes, 19.3 percent.
Letters requesting departmental records, 2.5 percent.

114. **The correct answer is (D).** This information is not contained anywhere in the report.

115. **The correct answer is (B).** At the beginning of the paragraph.

116. **The correct answer is (A).** Disorderly conduct that threatens to disturb the peace is a misdemeanor and is within the jurisdiction of the Criminal Court.

117. **The correct answer is (D).** The paragraph gives examples of minor offense and misdemeanor but does not define either one.

118. **The correct answer is (A).** This inference is supported in the very beginning of the paragraph.

119. **The correct answer is (A).** This is true according to the paragraph, even though the convictions had taken place for crimes committed in other states.

120. **The correct answer is (B).** Refer to the last part of the paragraph.

121. **The correct answer is (D).** A took B's property in B's presence by force using violence (tying B to a chair).

122. **The correct answer is (A).** A broke into B's store taking B's property when B was not present.

123. **The correct answer is (C).** The act of "breaking and entering" was not involved.

124. **The correct answer is (B).** A obtained B's property with B's consent. However, the consent was forthcoming only because A instilled appropriate fear in B's mind.

125. **The correct answer is (C).** A took B's property without B's consent. A's intention was to deprive B of the use of B's property. A's plan for the use of the property is not an element in the crime.

MODEL EXAMINATION 6: ANSWER SHEET

1. Ⓐ Ⓑ Ⓒ Ⓓ
2. Ⓐ Ⓑ Ⓒ Ⓓ
3. Ⓐ Ⓑ Ⓒ Ⓓ
4. Ⓐ Ⓑ Ⓒ Ⓓ
5. Ⓐ Ⓑ Ⓒ Ⓓ
6. Ⓐ Ⓑ Ⓒ Ⓓ
7. Ⓐ Ⓑ Ⓒ Ⓓ
8. Ⓐ Ⓑ Ⓒ Ⓓ
9. Ⓐ Ⓑ Ⓒ Ⓓ
10. Ⓐ Ⓑ Ⓒ Ⓓ
11. Ⓐ Ⓑ Ⓒ Ⓓ
12. Ⓐ Ⓑ Ⓒ Ⓓ
13. Ⓐ Ⓑ Ⓒ Ⓓ
14. Ⓐ Ⓑ Ⓒ Ⓓ
15. Ⓐ Ⓑ Ⓒ Ⓓ
16. Ⓐ Ⓑ Ⓒ Ⓓ
17. Ⓐ Ⓑ Ⓒ Ⓓ
18. Ⓐ Ⓑ Ⓒ Ⓓ
19. Ⓐ Ⓑ Ⓒ Ⓓ
20. Ⓐ Ⓑ Ⓒ Ⓓ

21. Ⓐ Ⓑ Ⓒ Ⓓ
22. Ⓐ Ⓑ Ⓒ Ⓓ
23. Ⓐ Ⓑ Ⓒ Ⓓ
24. Ⓐ Ⓑ Ⓒ Ⓓ
25. Ⓐ Ⓑ Ⓒ Ⓓ
26. Ⓐ Ⓑ Ⓒ Ⓓ
27. Ⓐ Ⓑ Ⓒ Ⓓ
28. Ⓐ Ⓑ Ⓒ Ⓓ
29. Ⓐ Ⓑ Ⓒ Ⓓ
30. Ⓐ Ⓑ Ⓒ Ⓓ
31. Ⓐ Ⓑ Ⓒ Ⓓ
32. Ⓐ Ⓑ Ⓒ Ⓓ
33. Ⓐ Ⓑ Ⓒ Ⓓ
34. Ⓐ Ⓑ Ⓒ Ⓓ
35. Ⓐ Ⓑ Ⓒ Ⓓ
36. Ⓐ Ⓑ Ⓒ Ⓓ
37. Ⓐ Ⓑ Ⓒ Ⓓ
38. Ⓐ Ⓑ Ⓒ Ⓓ
39. Ⓐ Ⓑ Ⓒ Ⓓ
40. Ⓐ Ⓑ Ⓒ Ⓓ

41. Ⓐ Ⓑ Ⓒ Ⓓ
42. Ⓐ Ⓑ Ⓒ Ⓓ
43. Ⓐ Ⓑ Ⓒ Ⓓ
44. Ⓐ Ⓑ Ⓒ Ⓓ
45. Ⓐ Ⓑ Ⓒ Ⓓ
46. Ⓐ Ⓑ Ⓒ Ⓓ
47. Ⓐ Ⓑ Ⓒ Ⓓ
48. Ⓐ Ⓑ Ⓒ Ⓓ
49. Ⓐ Ⓑ Ⓒ Ⓓ
50. Ⓐ Ⓑ Ⓒ Ⓓ
51. Ⓐ Ⓑ Ⓒ Ⓓ
52. Ⓐ Ⓑ Ⓒ Ⓓ
53. Ⓐ Ⓑ Ⓒ Ⓓ
54. Ⓐ Ⓑ Ⓒ Ⓓ
55. Ⓐ Ⓑ Ⓒ Ⓓ
56. Ⓐ Ⓑ Ⓒ Ⓓ
57. Ⓐ Ⓑ Ⓒ Ⓓ
58. Ⓐ Ⓑ Ⓒ Ⓓ
59. Ⓐ Ⓑ Ⓒ Ⓓ
60. Ⓐ Ⓑ Ⓒ Ⓓ

61. Ⓐ Ⓑ Ⓒ Ⓓ
62. Ⓐ Ⓑ Ⓒ Ⓓ
63. Ⓐ Ⓑ Ⓒ Ⓓ
64. Ⓐ Ⓑ Ⓒ Ⓓ
65. Ⓐ Ⓑ Ⓒ Ⓓ
66. Ⓐ Ⓑ Ⓒ Ⓓ
67. Ⓐ Ⓑ Ⓒ Ⓓ
68. Ⓐ Ⓑ Ⓒ Ⓓ
69. Ⓐ Ⓑ Ⓒ Ⓓ
70. Ⓐ Ⓑ Ⓒ Ⓓ
71. Ⓐ Ⓑ Ⓒ Ⓓ
72. Ⓐ Ⓑ Ⓒ Ⓓ
73. Ⓐ Ⓑ Ⓒ Ⓓ
74. Ⓐ Ⓑ Ⓒ Ⓓ
75. Ⓐ Ⓑ Ⓒ Ⓓ
76. Ⓐ Ⓑ Ⓒ Ⓓ
77. Ⓐ Ⓑ Ⓒ Ⓓ
78. Ⓐ Ⓑ Ⓒ Ⓓ
79. Ⓐ Ⓑ Ⓒ Ⓓ
80. Ⓐ Ⓑ Ⓒ Ⓓ

81. Ⓐ Ⓑ Ⓒ Ⓓ
82. Ⓐ Ⓑ Ⓒ Ⓓ
83. Ⓐ Ⓑ Ⓒ Ⓓ
84. Ⓐ Ⓑ Ⓒ Ⓓ
85. Ⓐ Ⓑ Ⓒ Ⓓ
86. Ⓐ Ⓑ Ⓒ Ⓓ
87. Ⓐ Ⓑ Ⓒ Ⓓ
88. Ⓐ Ⓑ Ⓒ Ⓓ
89. Ⓐ Ⓑ Ⓒ Ⓓ
90. Ⓐ Ⓑ Ⓒ Ⓓ
91. Ⓐ Ⓑ Ⓒ Ⓓ
92. Ⓐ Ⓑ Ⓒ Ⓓ
93. Ⓐ Ⓑ Ⓒ Ⓓ
94. Ⓐ Ⓑ Ⓒ Ⓓ
95. Ⓐ Ⓑ Ⓒ Ⓓ
96. Ⓐ Ⓑ Ⓒ Ⓓ
97. Ⓐ Ⓑ Ⓒ Ⓓ
98. Ⓐ Ⓑ Ⓒ Ⓓ
99. Ⓐ Ⓑ Ⓒ Ⓓ
100. Ⓐ Ⓑ Ⓒ Ⓓ

MODEL EXAMINATION 6

TIME: 4 HOURS—100 QUESTIONS

MEMORY BOOKLET ONE

> **Directions**: You will be given 5 minutes to study the scene that follows. Try to notice and remember as many details as you can. You may not take any notes during this time.

TEST QUESTIONS

> **Directions**: Answer questions 1 through 10 on the basis of the sketch that you just studied. You will have 10 minutes to answer these questions.

1. The number of people clearly visible at street level in this scene is
   (A) 7.
   (B) 8.
   (C) 9.
   (D) 10.

2. From all appearances, the accident was caused by
   (A) a tow truck that cut off a taxi.
   (B) a taxi going the wrong way on a one-way street.
   (C) a motorcycle that distracted a driver.
   (D) a taxi that ran a red light.

3. The officer wearing a hat is
   (A) directing traffic.
   (B) standing near the garbage truck.
   (C) wearing a long-sleeved shirt.
   (D) standing beside a tow truck.

4. There is a manhole cover in the street in front of
   (A) #126 Washington Avenue.
   (B) #126 Washington Street.
   (C) #126 Lincoln Avenue.
   (D) #126 Lincoln Street.

5. The name of the private sanitation company that owns the sanitation truck is
   (A) Joe's.
   (B) John's.
   (C) Tony's.
   (D) Bob's.

6. The beauty parlor is above the store at number
   (A) 130.
   (B) 200.
   (C) 202.
   (D) 204.

7. The sign on the window of Tony's Pizza parlor says,
   (A) "Open."
   (B) "Pizza."
   (C) "Eats."
   (D) "Tony's."

8. In a window above the drug store can be seen
   (A) potted plants.
   (B) drying laundry.
   (C) a resting cat.
   (D) a little boy with a yo-yo.

9. At the front of the school can be seen

   (A) a fire hydrant.
   (B) an American flag.
   (C) a street light.
   (D) a wire trash can.

10. The person on a motorcycle is

   (A) traveling north on a one-way street.
   (B) traveling north on a two-way street.
   (C) traveling east on a one-way street.
   (D) traveling west on a two-way street.

MEMORY BOOKLET TWO

Directions: Use the next 10 minutes to study the six "Wanted" posters below. Be sure to concentrate on the faces and on the information provided. Try to remember as many details as you can. You may not take notes during this time.

WANTED FOR ASSAULT AND ARMED ROBBERY

Name: Pauline Chen
Age: 20
Height: 5'2"
Weight: 98 lbs.
Race: Native American
Hair color: black
Eye color: dark brown
Complexion: mottled
Identifying marks: badly scarred left forearm from severe scald in childhood
Suspect usually wears overalls with lots of pockets filled with plumbing tools; weapon of choice is heavy monkey wrench.

WANTED FOR RAPE

Name: Louis Joseph
Age: 43
Height: 6'1"
Weight: 240 lbs.
Race: African American
Hair color: black
Eye color: brown
Complexion: dark
Identifying marks: large scar over right eye; cauliflower ears; tattoo of rose on left buttock
Suspect is former boxer; not known to be armed; he intimidates with sheer bulk and strength

WANTED FOR INTERNATIONAL TERRORISM

Name: Mary Kiley
Age: 27
Height: 5'5"
Weight: 120 lbs.
Race: White
Hair color: red
Eye color: green
Complexion: very fair
Identifying marks: gold left front tooth
Suspect is very active with the IRA; often carries false ID and uses alias.
Known aliases: Joan Carey, Martha Riley, Meg O'Hara. Has been seen in company of Len Brown.

WANTED FOR INTERNATIONAL TERRORISM—GUN RUNNING

Name: Len Brown
Age: 31
Height: 5'11"
Weight: 180 lbs.
Race: White
Hair color: light brown
Eye color: blue
Complexion: very fair; freckled
Identifying marks: nearsighted; left-handed; missing last three fingers of right hand; tattoo on right arm is map of Ireland
Suspect is wanted for questioning about car bomb in front of British consulate; has evaded prosecution for smuggling arms to Ireland; has skill and expertise with explosives. Snappy dresser: favors tweed caps and turtleneck sweaters with tweed jackets. Often seen in company of Mary Kiley.

WANTED ESCAPEE FROM JUSTICE—CHARGE: KIDNAPPING

Name: Don Juan
Age: 24
Height: 5´7"
Weight: 145 lbs.
Race: Hispanic
Hair: dark brown
Eyes: brown
Complexion: swarthy
Identifying marks: missing two upper teeth on right side of mouth; heavy cigar smoker, always reeks of cigar smoke; slight limp from childhood polio
Suspect escaped from prison and now is wanted on charges of a second kidnapping. He is never without a firearm and must be considered extremely dangerous.

WANTED FOR BANK ROBBERY AND HOMICIDE

Name: Jane Jones
Age: 18
Height: 5'8"
Weight: 140 lbs.
Race: African
Hair: black
Eyes: dark
Complexion: black
Identifying marks: scar on right cheek, nose stud, pierced eyebrows and navel; African immigrant speaks French and heavily accented English.
Suspect is member of group that recently robbed Federal Bank. Is identified as person who shot and killed bank guard on retreat. User of cocaine. Likes to drive German luxury cars, and drives very fast. Desperate and dangerous.

Directions: Answer questions 11 through 20 on the basis of the information contained in the "Wanted Posters" you just studied.

11. Which of the following suspects has already served time in prison?

(A)

(B)

(C)

(D)

12. Which of the following might be positively identified in a strip search?

(A) Len Brown
(B) Pauline Chen
(C) Louis Joseph
(D) Don Juan

13. Which one of the following might be found carrying a forged ID? The suspect who

(A) is friendly with the gun runner.
(B) pretends to be a plumber.
(C) is always armed.
(D) speaks French.

14. Which of these suspects might be found at the wheel of a Mercedes Benz?

(A)

(B)

(C)

(D)

15. Which is an identifying mark of this suspect?

(A) Navel ring
(B) Scarred left forearm
(C) Limp
(D) Gold front tooth

16. Which one of the following uses drugs?

(A)

(B)

(C)

(D)

17. Which of these suspects might be recognized in a lineup on the basis of odor?

(A) The suspect who speaks with an accent
(B) The suspect who suffered a childhood accident
(C) The suspect who is missing teeth
(D) The suspect with the rose tattoo

18. An identifying characteristic of this suspect is

(A) a tattoo of the map of Ireland on his left arm.
(B) missing fingers on his night hand.
(C) a limp as legacy of polio.
(D) a long scar on his right thigh.

19. Which one of the suspects is easily recognized as a former boxer?

    (A) The suspect wanted for rape
    (B) The suspect who escaped from prison
    (C) The suspect who attacks victims with a monkey wrench
    (D) The suspect who drives very fast

20. Which of these suspects is wanted for armed robbery?

(A)

(B)

(C)

(D)

MEMORY BOOKLET THREE

Directions: Use the next 10 minutes to read the following account of a preying on the elderly. Focus on the details as well as on the story as a whole, and commit to memory as much information as possible. You may not take any notes during this time.

On Thursday, May 10, at 8:50 a.m., the doorbell rang at 169 Butler Road, home of Mr. and Mrs. Prince, an elderly couple. Mr. Prince had just gone out to walk the dog, Rover. Mrs. Prince opened the door to 2 men who appeared to be utility workmen. The men identified themselves as Matt French and Harry English of the sanitation department and asked to be admitted to the basement to check for possible sewage backup. Matt French, a blond white man, approximately 6 feet tall and quite thin, was wearing hip-high rubber boots. Harry English, a husky African-American man a little shorter than Matt French, wore boots that came only to his knees. Both men wore belts laden with tools and equipment that appeared to be meters of various kinds. Mrs. Prince pointed out the steps to the basement, and Matt French went down while Harry English maneuvered Mrs. Prince into the parlor where he attempted to answer her questions about how such backup could occur and what might be consequences in terms of cost and mess. While Harry English had Mrs. Prince engaged in conversation, Matt French quietly went upstairs and ransacked the bedrooms, taking jewelry and cash. French returned to the parlor and reported that there was no evidence of seepage in the Prince home. The two men departed just as Mr. Prince returned home with Rover. Mr. Prince noticed that the men drove away in a blue car with a license plate that began with the letters "MYP."

At 11:30 a.m. Mr. Prince went upstairs to take a nap and discovered that the bedroom had been heavily tossed. He immediately called the police, and Officers Rice and Rye responded. Mr. Prince reported that among the missing items were an emerald ring valued at $935, diamond earrings worth $2320, onyx cufflinks valued at $128, and a packet of five $100 bills. Officer Rice took down the information and assured Mr. and Mrs. Prince that their case would be investigated.

Officers Rice and Rye returned to their station house just as a call came in from Ms. Brenda Tracey of 287 Butler Road. Ms. Tracey had just discovered that her bedroom and study had been ransacked. The sergeant dispatched Officer Rye and Officer Backus to investigate and to take a report. Ms. Tracey related that her house cleaner, Leslie Jones, had just left to pick up some cleaning supplies at the nearby store at about 9:30 a.m. when the doorbell rang. At the door were two workmen who identified themselves as Tom Bridge and Frank Tunnel from the gas department. Tom Bridge was an African-American man, heavy set, about 30 years old. He wore knee-high rubber boots. Frank Tunnel was a tall, thin white man wearing boots that reached all the way to his hips. Both men wore an impressive array of tools on their belts. Frank Tunnel told Ms. Tracey that there was a gas leak in the neighborhood and that the connection to her home would have to be interrupted for a time. He asked for permission to shut off the gas. Ms. Tracey was unsure of the location of the gas service to the house, but showed Tunnel the entrance to the basement. She then asked Tom Bridge how long service would be out and how it would be restored. Bridge suggested they sit down while he explained, and Ms. Tracey led him to the front room. As Tom Bridge spoke with Ms. Tracey, Frank Tunnel crept upstairs and emptied dresser drawers in the bedroom. He pocketed a gold watch valued at $270, a string of cultured pearls worth $128, silver filigree earrings worth $89, and approximately $230 in assorted bills. Tunnel then returned to the front room and told Ms. Tracey that they would return to turn the gas on again when the repair work had been completed—probably within two hours. Leslie Jones returned with the cleaning supplies just as a blue car pulled away from the curb. Jones noticed that the license plate ended with the numbers "561."

At 11:45 a.m., Ms. Tracey went into the kitchen to prepare lunch. She turned on the range and suddenly realized that the gas was on even though the workmen had not returned. Ms. Tracey became suspicious and together with Leslie Jones walked through the house, including the upstairs. There they discovered the overturned dresser drawers and missing items and notified police.

Directions: Answer questions 21 through 30 on the basis of the story you just read. Do not look back at the story; you must answer from memory.

---

21. The intrusion on Ms. Tracey occurred on

    (A) Thursday, May 10.
    (B) Tuesday, May 16.
    (C) Thursday, May 11.
    (D) Monday, May 10.

22. The man who identified himself as Matt French was probably the same man who identified himself as

    (A) Tom Bridge.
    (B) Larry English.
    (C) Frank Tunnel.
    (D) Leslie Jones.

23. The bogus workmen always approached their target houses

    (A) when no one was at home.
    (B) after making certain that there was no dog that might bark.
    (C) under cover of darkness.
    (D) after seeing someone leave.

24. A pair of diamond earrings was stolen from

    (A) 187 Butler Road.
    (B) 169 Butler Road.
    (C) 269 Butler Road.
    (D) 287 Butler Road.

25. The license plate on the blue car read

    (A) NYP 651.
    (B) MYP 561.
    (C) NYD 165.
    (D) MYB 169.

26. The person who went into the basement at the Tracey household was

    (A) a tall African-American man.
    (B) shorter than Matt French.
    (C) blond.
    (D) about 30 years old.

27. The theft of a packet of five $100 bills was reported to

    (A) Officer Backus by Mr. Prince.
    (B) Officer Rice by Mrs. Prince.
    (C) Officer Rye by Ms. Tracey.
    (D) Officer Rice by Mr. Prince.

28. The items stolen from 287 Butler Road included

    (A) a gold watch.
    (B) a string of fresh-water pearls.
    (C) silver cufflinks.
    (D) a gold filigree brooch.

29. The ring stolen at the home of Mr. and Mrs. Prince was

    (A) a diamond ring worth $2320.
    (B) an emerald ring worth $935.
    (C) a gold ring worth $270.
    (D) a pearl ring worth $560.

30. Officer Rice

    (A) checked the Prince basement to make sure there was no sewage backup.
    (B) returned to the station house before responding to Ms. Tracey's call.
    (C) told Ms. Tracey that the gas had been turned back on.
    (D) promised that the Prince larceny would be investigated.

31. The officer responding to the alarm from the storage facility noted a blue van leaving the site. Investigation revealed that the storage facility had been vandalized, so the officer felt that the van should be mentioned in the response report. The most effective way for the officer to report this fact is with the following statement:

    (A) "I arrived at the storage facility just as a blue van was driving away from the site."
    (B) "A van that should not have been at the warehouse left as I arrived."
    (C) "The vandals escaped the scene in a blue van."
    (D) "I arrived at the storage facility and a vehicle sped away when I arrived."

32. At the training academy, the sergeant is explaining to the recruits their role in domestic disputes. Often a call comes from neighbors who are being disturbed by the noise of domestic conflict. The situation faced by the responding officers is that most often no crime has been committed. However, since a major objective of the police officer is to stop crime before it starts, the arrival of an officer on the scene of domestic quarrel may be very effective. The most effective way for the sergeant to sum up the police role in domestic conflicts is:

    (A) "If you are called to a domestic conflict and no crime has been committed, you don't have much to do."
    (B) "When you respond to a domestic conflict, you should restore order and prevent any crimes from occurring."
    (C) "Your goal in responding to domestic disputes is to protect the innocent."
    (D) "People involved in domestic conflicts may call upon you to serve as an objective authority to help them settle their disputes."

33. Officer Petrillo has taken notes at the scene of a traffic accident. The following five sentences will all be included in the accident report.

    1. The Hyundai struck the right rear fender of Dr. Denton's Mercury Marquis and continued on its way.
    2. Dr. Denton stated that she was making a left turn from Cranstoun Court onto Highland Boulevard.
    3. As the car passed, Dr. Denton noticed the dangling rear license plate, Montana #673-9X3.
    4. Dr. Denton complained to the officer of neck pains and was taken by Volunteer Ambulance #3 to People's Hospital.
    5. A battered black Hyundai traveling on Highland Boulevard failed to stop at the stop sign at the intersection of Highland Boulevard and Cranstoun Court.

    The most logical order for the above sentences to appear in the report is:
    (A) 1, 3, 2, 5, 4
    (B) 2, 5, 1, 3, 4
    (C) 4, 5, 1, 2, 3
    (D) 5, 3, 1, 2, 4

34. At 10:20 a.m. today, Officers Pipkin and D'Ortona reported to a crime scene that soon appeared to be a criminal homicide. The two officers spent much of the day interviewing and collecting evidence. Pipkin's notes include the following five sentences.

    1. I noticed that the cash register drawer was open and empty.
    2. We got a call reporting that the front door of the Carlton candy shop was open, but the owner was not in sight.
    3. We interviewed tenants of the apartments above the store.
    4. Upon arrival, we discovered the body of the shop's owner, apparently dead from a gunshot wound to the chest.
    5. Officer D'Ortona called an ambulance to pick up the victim.

    The most logical order for the above sentences to appear in the report is:
    (A) 2, 1, 4, 5, 3
    (B) 2, 4, 5, 1, 3
    (C) 2, 5, 1, 3, 4
    (D) 4, 5, 2, 3, 1

Answer questions 35 and 36 on the basis of the following scenario.

Officer Orton has been asked by her supervisor to analyze crime patterns in her patrol area. She has noticed that most assaults occur in the Redwood neighborhood, while auto theft is rampant in Greenville. She has further noticed that traffic accidents are heavily concentrated in the Whitestone area.

In keeping careful track of incidents, Officer Orton has written in her report that auto theft is most prevalent under cover of darkness between 3 a.m. and 7 a.m. and traffic accidents are most common either between 6:30 a.m. and 9 a.m. or between 5 p.m. and 8:30 .p.m., while assaults have been occurring between 7 p.m. and 9 p.m. or between 11 p.m. and 4 a.m.

Strangely, traffic accidents almost always occur on Mondays and Fridays while most assaults are confined to any day from Wednesday through Saturday. Auto theft seldom occurs on the weekend.

35. Officer Orton will be most effective in reducing crime if she concentrates her patrol as follows:

    (A) Monday through Wednesday in Redwood from 8 p.m. to midnight, Thursday and Friday in Greenville from 5 a.m. to 10 a.m., and Tuesday and Thursday in Whitestone from noon to 4 p.m.
    (B) Sunday, Monday, and Tuesday in Greenville from midnight to 4 Am, Friday and Saturday in Whitestone from 5 p.m. to 9 p.m., and Friday and Saturday in Redwood from 10 a.m. to 2 p.m.
    (C) Monday and Friday in Whitestone from 6 a.m. to 10 a.m. and Tuesday through Thursday in Redwood from 6 p.m. to 2 a.m.
    (D) Monday and Tuesday in Greenville from 1 a.m. to 8 a.m. and Thursday and Friday in Redwood from 8 p.m. to 4 a.m.

36. If Officer Orton is unable to work irregular hours, the single most effective regular 8-hour tour for purposes of crime reduction would be:

    (A) 6 p.m. to 2 a.m. Monday and Tuesday in Greenville, Wednesday through Friday in Redwood.
    (B) 4 p.m. to midnight Monday and Tuesday in Whitestone, Thursday through Saturday in Redwood.
    (C) 8 p.m. to 4 a.m. Sunday through Tuesday in Redwood, Thursday and Friday in Greenville.
    (D) 9 p.m. to 5 a.m. Monday and Tuesday in Greenville, Wednesday through Friday in Redwood.

37. Law enforcement officers carry radios that keep them in constant touch with the dispatcher. Often the radio crackles with reports of many situations that all demand some sort of attention. The officer must make a quick decision as to which of a number of incidents requires the most immediate attention. Of the following, which constitutes the greatest emergency?

    (A) An automobile alarm has been sounding for 30 minutes.
    (B) A cyclist and an in-line skater have collided. They are sitting at the edge of the roadway comparing their bruises.
    (C) A roofer has fallen from the roof of the house he is working on and is lying motionless in the yard.
    (D) An elderly woman fainted briefly and then vomited but is now sipping from a glass of water.

38. An alert officer must be aware of all that is going on in the vicinity. Some activities that are not in any way unlawful may still raise suspicions in the officer's mind. Of the following, which might be a suspicious activity?

    (A) A large van is driving in the area behind a warehouse at 2 a.m. without headlights.
    (B) A bedraggled man is standing by the side of the highway entrance ramp holding a sign that says, "Hungry with AIDS."
    (C) A woman standing in the bank lobby next to the ATM is looking furtively over her shoulder as she counts bills and puts them in her wallet.
    (D) Three teenagers are standing behind the high school smoking.

39. Upon their return from an evening at the movies, Mr. and Mrs. Avila discover their kitchen window broken, the house tossed and ransacked, and the back door open. Officer Tostanoski, responding to their call, takes down this list of missing property.

1	Television set	$580.00
2	Silver Candlesticks	@ $120.00
1	Mink Coat	$3900.00
6	Etchings, signed and numbered	@ $835.00
	Cash	$1763.29

The total value of the reported missing property is
(A) $13,163.29.
(B) $11,493.29.
(C) $11,466.29.
(D) $11,373.29.

40. If an officer who has responded to a 911 call that was placed because a person was unconscious finds that the person has regained consciousness, the officer must do the following in the order specified below.

1. Put in a call for emergency medical services.
2. Check the patient's pulse rate.
3. Ask patient for name, age, birthdate, address, and mother's maiden name.
4. Ask name of patient's physician and hospital affiliation.
5. If patient is 75 years or older, call for ambulance for mandatory transport to hospital.
6. Stand by to await arrival of emergency medical services.

Mrs. Stern, age 95, has fainted after eating a festive meal with her family. Her panicked son dials 911, and Officer Reilly responds within minutes. Even so, Mrs. Stern is conscious and alert by the time of Reilly's arrival. Reilly calls for emergency medical services, and checks Mrs. Stern's pulse rate, which he finds to be rapid but not alarmingly so. He asks all the requisite questions and receives satisfactory answers from Mrs. Stern. Then he tells Mrs. Stern that he is calling for an ambulance. Mrs. Stern argues that this has happened before and that she is okay now. She does not want to go to the hospital. Officer Reilly waits for emergency medical services to arrive, then leaves. Officer Reilly's actions have been

(A) appropriate; he followed all the steps in the prescribed order.
(B) inappropriate; Mrs. Stern is over 75 and is required to go to the hospital.
(C) appropriate; Mrs. Stern is no longer unconscious and can speak for herself.
(D) inappropriate; he should not have left until the ambulance arrived.

Answer questions 41 through 45 on the basis of the following passage.

At 4:15 p.m. on Saturday, July 13, the dispatcher received a call from Mrs. Perry of 9 Kings Highway. Mrs. Perry reported that she and her young son, Tim, had just returned from an out-of-town trip and discovered the back door open. The dispatcher ordered Mrs. Perry to leave the premises promptly and immediately ordered officers Bligh and Dewey to the scene. As Mrs. Perry and Tim stepped out onto the back porch, they heard a loud thud on the opposite side of the house, followed by the screech of a car leaving the area in a great hurry. They walked to the side of the house from which the thud had come and discovered an open suitcase on the lawn with clothing and jewelry scattered about.

Officers Bligh and Dewey arrived at 9 Kings Highway and began to search the house. The downstairs rooms did not appear to have been disturbed. Silver candlesticks and an antique silver tea service were immediately visible in their places on the buffet in the dining room. The Perry's collection of sculptures of monks from all over the world was untouched. However, they found that the master bedroom had been heavily tossed and two more open suitcases were on the floor. Also on the floor was a clipping torn from the local newspaper. The clipping described the foreign medical convention for which Dr. Perry had departed on the previous day.

Officer Dewey questioned Mrs. Perry about the family's movements in the past few days. Mrs. Perry stated that she had planned to travel abroad with Dr. Perry, but that her son had qualified as a semifinalist in an oratorical contest, so she delayed her trip abroad to accompany Tim to his competition. Since the family plans had changed rather suddenly, she had left her own suitcases ready to pack so that she could join her husband soon.

41. According to the preceding passage, when the Perrys arrived home during the afternoon of July 13th, they discovered that their house had been

    (A) ransacked, but nothing was stolen.
    (B) entered, and the silver candlesticks and antique tea set were stolen.
    (C) entered, and the intruders were still in the house.
    (D) entered, and the bedroom window was broken.

42. According to the preceding passage, the only statement that accurately reflects the information gathered is that

    (A) Officer Bligh found a newspaper clipping on the floor.
    (B) the intruders used Mrs. Perry's luggage to steal clothing and jewelry.
    (C) the oratorical contest was in Europe.
    (D) the intruders took one monk from the sculpture collection.

43. One can reasonably infer from the information in the preceding paragraphs that

    (A) the intruders expected the house to be unoccupied.
    (B) Officers Bligh and Dewey knew that the Perry family was out of town.
    (C) the intruders fled the scene in Mrs. Perry's car.
    (D) the intruders entered the house through an upstairs window.

44. Mrs. Perry was ordered to leave the house at once

    (A) because the intruders were still inside.
    (B) so that she could pick up the items on the lawn.
    (C) to direct the responding officers to the scene of the crime.
    (D) by the dispatcher.

45. According to the preceding passage, the intruders had entered the house by way of

    (A) an upstairs window.
    (B) the back door.
    (C) a stack of suitcases to climb up on.
    (D) newspaper information.

Answer questions 46 and 47 solely on the basis of the following definitions.

BURGLARY. The breaking and entering the house of another in the nighttime, with intent to commit a felony therein, whether the felony is actually committed or not.

BURGLARY IN THE FIRST DEGREE. Unlawful and intentional breaking and unlawful and intentional entry in nighttime into dwelling house presently occupied, with intent to commit felony.

LARCENY. Felonious taking and carrying away of personal goods of another.

ROBBERY. Felonious taking of personal property in the possession of another, from his person or immediate presence, and against his will, accomplished by means of force or fear.

THEFT. The fraudulent taking of corporeal personal property belonging to another, from his possession, or from the possession of some person holding the same for him, without his consent, with intent to deprive the owner of the value of the same, and to appropriate it to the use or benefit of the person taking.

46. At 2:25 a.m., Tom Jones, carrying a crowbar, entered the house at 18 Locust Avenue in which Margaret and Frank Moore were sound asleep. In attempting to disconnect the VCR, Jones knocked over a lamp. The noise awakened Frank Moore who shouted out, "Hey there!" When Tom heard Moore call out, he picked up his crowbar and fled from the premises. Tom Jones is guilty of

(A) robbery.
(B) burglary in the first degree.
(C) theft and burglary.
(D) larceny.

47. Which one of the following is guilty as charged?

(A) At 11:30 p.m., Pete Potter and Jane Jilly expertly pick the lock of the door in the back alley behind the Martin Paint Store. They load six cases of Moore's Exterior White into their van and drive off. Potter and Jilly are charged with burglary.

(B) Barbara Brooks enters the toy store carrying a large pocketbook, a tote bag, and a shopping bag. As she walks up and down the aisles, she surreptitiously slips a small stuffed animal into the tote bag and drops a number of finger puppets into the shopping bag, where they slide under the merchandise already wrapped and carried in that bag. Brooks then pays for a large box of crayons and two coloring books and leaves the store. She promptly goes to a group home for developmentally disabled children, leaves her purchases and the animal and puppets on the doorstep, rings the bell, and disappears. Barbara Brooks is charged with theft.

(C) Nancy Tomkins purchases a large bunch of bananas from a street vendor just as Jack Frost is approaching. As Frost passes Tomkins, he mumbles loudly, "I really want a banana." Tomkins thrusts the whole bunch of bananas into Frost's hand, turns, and runs. Jack Frost is charged with robbery.

(D) Terry Toon has just opened the car door in the parking lot at the mall. Suddenly, Leslie Link appears, shoves Toon aside, grabs the car keys from Toon, and drives away. Toon is charged with robbery.

48. In the course of a week's work, an officer encounters any number of people who behave in strange or even bizarre ways. Many of these evoke nothing more than a sad smile; eccentricity is not illegal. However, at times the behavior of disturbed individuals may constitute a danger to themselves or to the public. Which of the following requires active intervention?

(A) On a summer evening, a man clad only in a loincloth is standing at a street corner loudly urging all passersby to repent.

(B) A man with disheveled hair and reeking of beer is standing at the curb in a "No Standing at Any Time" zone blowing a whistle and waving away motorists who attempt to pull up.

(C) A woman is walking in a very straight line down the middle of the street, face upturned to the heavens, singing hymns.

(D) Two young people are seated at a table with a large container in front of them and are urging pedestrians to contribute to a fund toward immediate colonization of Mars.

49. Officer Dallas is interviewing witnesses to a hit and run accident in which a pedestrian was killed. The descriptions of the vehicle are as follows:

Witness 1 "The car was a mid-size four-door sedan being driven by a tall African-American man. The license plate was from out of state."

Witness 2 "The car was gray or dirty white, four doors, maybe a small wagon, with a tall driver and someone in the back seat. I didn't notice the license plate."

Witness 3 "The car was white, maybe a Camry, with four doors; the driver was very large and dark; the license plate was blue like Connecticut, but I couldn't read it."

Witness 4 "The car was a heavily rusted yellow hatch back with its license plate missing being driven by a blond woman with long flowing hair. There was no one else in the car."

Officer Dallas should suspect that there is a problem with the description given by witness

(A) 1.
(B) 2.
(C) 3.
(D) 4.

50. Officer Swift is interviewing witnesses to the armed robbery of a patron in an off-track betting establishment. The witnesses give the following descriptions of the robber:

Witness 1 "He was light-skinned with long black hair, mid-twenties, close to 6 feet tall, and very thin. He was wearing blue jeans and cowboy boots. He held a snub-nosed pistol to the victim's neck. The head of a snake was tattooed on the back of his hand and, the tattoo of the snake's body curled up his arm."

Witness 2 "He was medium height, white, with dark hair in a pony tail. He looked to be about 30 years old and about 150 pounds, actually pretty skinny. He had on dark pants and a baseball cap. He was very muscular for such a skinny guy, and the tattoo on his arm rippled as he pointed his gun."

Witness 3 "He was sort of short, probably Hispanic, with black hair, and very thin— my guess is somewhere in his twenties. He had on black pants and a black biker's jacket with a snake on the back. His pistol was small and black."

Witness 4 "He was about 5´10", about 160 pounds, about 28 or so, light-skinned black or dark-skinned white. He wore dark pants and a dark T-shirt and carried a small pistol."

Presented with these reports, Officer Swift should recognize that there is a problem with the description given by witness

(A) 1.
(B) 2.
(C) 3.
(D) 4.

51. Upon receiving report of a suspicious, possibly explosive, unidentified object, bomb squad officers must perform a specific set of steps in sequence. These steps are listed below but are NOT listed in the correct order.

   1. Clear the entire area of bystanders.
   2. Request specific information as to physical characteristics of the object.
   3. Don protective gear.
   4. Remove object to isolated area.
   5. Examine object.
   6. Request an ambulance to accompany bomb squad and stand by.

   The above steps should be performed in the following order:

   (A) 5, 1, 3, 6, 2, 4
   (B) 2, 6, 1, 4, 5, 3
   (C) 2, 5, 4, 6, 3, 1
   (D) 2, 6, 3, 1, 4, 5

52. If an officer observes a person attempting to jimmy open the door of an illegally parked motor vehicle, the officer must follow a specific order of procedure. The steps that the officer must take are listed below but are NOT listed in the correct order.

   1. Identify him- or herself as a police officer.
   2. Issue a parking ticket.
   3. Ask to see a driver's license and the vehicle's registration
   4. If the person can prove ownership, assist in opening the vehicle.
   5. Spread eagle the person facing the car with hands on the roof and pat for weapons.
   6. Order the person to drop the implement with which he or she is attempting to open the vehicle door.

   The above steps should be performed in the following order:
   (A) 1, 6, 5, 3, 2, 4
   (B) 2, 1, 3, 6, 5, 4
   (C) 1, 5, 6, 3, 4, 2
   (D) 2, 1, 6, 5, 3, 4

53. At the scene of a multiple traffic violation that leads to an accident in which there is no visible personal injury but in which vehicles show signs of damage, an officer should take these steps in the following order:

   1. Request driver's licenses, registration papers, and insurance card from all drivers involved.
   Note: Documented foreign diplomats are not required to carry registration or insurance cards nor are they subject to summons or arrest.
   2. Take a statement from each driver as to how that driver thinks the accident occurred.
   3. Visually inspect each vehicle, noting evident damage to each.
   4. Write license plate number on visible damage report.
   5. Enter one violation on each ticket.
   6. Issue a separate ticket for each violation.

   A black Cadillac fails to signal a turn, enters the intersection on a red light, and turns right from the left-hand lane striking a green Nissan broadside. Officer Larsen hears the crash and runs to the scene. Larsen first asks both drivers if they are injured, and both assure the officer that they are just fine. Larsen then requests and receives license, registration, and proof of insurance from the driver of the green Nissan. In response to the same request, the driver of the Cadillac produces driver's license and diplomatic papers showing that he is an official in the consulate of a foreign country. Next Officer Larsen asks each driver exactly what happened. The procedure being followed by Larsen is

(A) correct; the next step in the procedure is to ask how the accident occurred.

(B) incorrect; foreign diplomats are not subject to questioning.

(C) correct; Larsen did not ticket the diplomat.

(D) incorrect; Larsen should have asked for license, registration, and insurance cards before asking the drivers if they were injured.

54. Mrs. Miniver requests assistance in finding her 72-year-old father, an Alzheimer's Disease sufferer, who lives with her and who has wandered away from her home. She is too distraught to give a detailed description of her father, but tells officers that he is a quiet old man and a meticulous dresser. He is of average height and slight build, balding, and is often delusional, thinking he is a movie star. Officer Sved drives around the area in ever widening concentric circles and notices four elderly men who might be Mrs. Miniver's father. Of the following, which is most likely to be the man Officer Sved is seeking?

(A) A tall, thin, totally bald man with well-trimmed goatee wearing gray sweat pants and a blue windbreaker who gives him name as James Doe.

(B) A man who stands about 5'9" weighing about 160 pounds, wearing gray slacks, tweed sports jacket, and tweed cap who gives his name as Fred Astaire.

(C) A man with thin gray hair, about 5'8" and about 200 pounds, wearing plaid slacks with a striped button-down shirt, who gives his name as Mickey Mouse.

(D) A small man in a dirty, torn three-piece suit, with wispy hair, who refuses to give his name.

55. If a female prisoner is brought in to be booked at a time when there is no female officer present, the steps listed below must be followed to conduct a basic search. (These steps are NOT listed in the correct order.)

1. Starting at the neck, carefully pat down chest, stomach, and back.
2. Have the prisoner empty all pockets, pulling them inside out.
3. From behind, run a fine comb through prisoner's hair starting from the forehead and moving from left to right in even strokes.
4. Summon a matron to stand at your side and to witness the search.
5. Using both hands, pat down buttocks and both legs, one at a time, from crotch to floor.
6. Ask matron to search inside brassiere and panties.
7. Have the prisoner stand facing a wall, back to you, legs spread and arms extended straight out.

The above steps should be performed in the following order:

(A) 7, 2, 1, 3, 5, 4, 6

(B) 3, 1, 2, 7, 4, 5, 6

(C) 4, 3, 1, 7, 2, 6, 5

(D) 4, 2, 7, 3, 1, 5, 6

56. CRIMINAL RECKLESS ENDANGERMENT occurs when a person behaves in a manner so as to create a substantial risk of serious injury to another person with full awareness and understanding of the possibility of this risk.

Which of the following is an example of criminal reckless endangerment?

(A) Hiram, a Native-American construction worker, walks on a narrow catwalk on the superstructure of a suspension bridge knowing full well that a fall would be fatal to him.

(B) In the early morning, with some employees already on the premises, Barry, a security guard at a wholesale jeweler's shop, returns the fire of an armed robber.

(C) Sam watches to be sure that his hit really is a home run, then flings his bat into the crowd standing just behind the first base line before starting his circuit.

(D) Bob, a member of a house cleaning team cleaning behind furniture, loosens the plug to a respirator.

57. A SANCTUARY is a consecrated place (such as a church) to which special privileges are attached and to which offenders may resort for refuge because they can not be arrested there nor the laws executed.

Which of the following represents use of sanctuary as defined above?
(A) Martha, a homeless woman, moves out of a shelter and into a church.
(B) John breaks into a church and steals silver candlesticks to sell for funds to buy crack.
(C) Pedro and Carmen, illegal immigrants, hide in a church to elude the Border Patrol.
(D) Louise comes into a church to pray for forgiveness for lying to her parents.

58. Every police manual lists departmental guidelines and specific instructions for dealing with hostage situations. The following example is typical:

1. Establish early contact; try to determine most effective person to conduct negotiations.
2. Keep all outside operations quiet and calm. Do not use loudspeakers to communicate among police personnel.
3. Police presence should be visible, but not overwhelming. Do not mass vehicles.
4. Do not threaten. Try reasoning, bargaining, even bribery.
5. Accede to hostage-taker's demands so long as no one is endangered by so doing.
6. If storming premises seems to be the only way to break a stalemate, stay under cover.
7. Do not discharge firearms.

Given the above instructions, the most potentially dangerous mistake has been made in which of the following?

(A) Upon arrival at the house in which an unidentified man is holding a whole family hostage, Officer Blank shouts over his bullhorn, "Come out with your hands up or we'll smoke you out in a hurry."
(B) Upon learning that the woman holding her children hostage and threatening to kill them all has a respected grandmother who lives just over an hour away, Sergeant Yale maintains casual small talk while awaiting the grandmother's arrival.
(C) Officers bring sandwiches and fruit into the lobby of the bank in which an armed robber is holding tellers hostage in the vault.
(D) Officer Tuller asks a hostage taker, "Would you like us to broadcast your statement over the network radio station?"

59. The FOURTH AMENDMENT states that the right of the people to be secure in their persons, houses, papers, and effects, against unreasonable searches and seizures, shall not be violated, and no warrants shall issue, but upon probable cause, supported by oath or affirmation, and particularly describing the place to be searched, and the persons or things to be seized.

You will note from the language of this amendment that only unreasonable searches and seizures are prohibited. Searches with a legal warrant are always permissible, and there are many warrantless searches and seizures that are not unreasonable.

In a 1969 California case, the Supreme Court ruled that a search incident to a lawful arrest must be limited to a search of the following:

1. The person arrested.
2. Anything found on the arrested person.
3. The area into which the arrested person might reach in order to grab a weapon or an evidentiary item (the grabbable area). Items in the grabbable area might include pocketbooks, packages being carried, and so forth.

Consider the following situation:

Officers have received reliable information that a man who claims to be an antique fancier and a small-time buyer, restorer, and seller of antiques is actually concealing an active drug trade with his antique dealings. Officer Wall, in regular drive-bys on patrol, has been observing the man loading and unloading his van, polishing and rubbing old wood, and admiringly dusting off old china. In order to seize solid evidence of illicit drug traffic, Officer Wall may

(A) stop the van and search and seize in the grabbable area.
(B) walk into the driveway, put the man under arrest, and search him.
(C) follow the man's van to an antique sale and search the van when he leaves it.
(D) continue observing until he sees a suspicious transaction.

60. Officer Hanninen is interviewing bank patrons who witnessed a holdup at the bank at lunch hour. Four witnesses gave these descriptions of the lone holdup person.

Witness 1 "The bank robber was a medium-height woman wearing green leggings and a plaid shirt. She carried a large canvas tote bag and wore a ski mask. She said that she had a gun, but I didn't see it."

Witness 2 "The holdup man was of average height and weight. He wore tight black pants and a lumber jacket. His knit watch cap covered his hair, so I can't give a hair color or style. He didn't say a word, just held out his gun."

Witness 3 "It was really scary. This bank robber came in wearing a ski mask, dark pants, and a plaid, long-sleeved top. I didn't see a weapon, but there was a suspicious pocket bulge. The robber handed a note to the teller. I couldn't tell if the robber was a man or a woman."

Witness 4 "The bank robber pushed me out of line, so I got a pretty good look. He or she, probably she because of the voice, though I can't be positive, was wearing tight dark pants, a loose plaid shirt, and a nylon stocking that covered head and face. The robber handed a note to the teller with one hand, keeping the other in a pocket until the teller handed over a canvas bag with money. Then the robber ran out."

Officer Hanninen should recognize that there is a problem with the description given by

(A) Witness 1.
(B) Witness 2.
(C) Witness 3.
(D) Witness 4.

Answer questions 61 through 63 solely on the basis of the following map. The flow of traffic is indicated by the arrows. If there is only one arrow shown, then traffic flows only in the direction indicated by the arrow. If there are two arrows shown, then traffic flows in both directions. You must follow the flow of traffic.

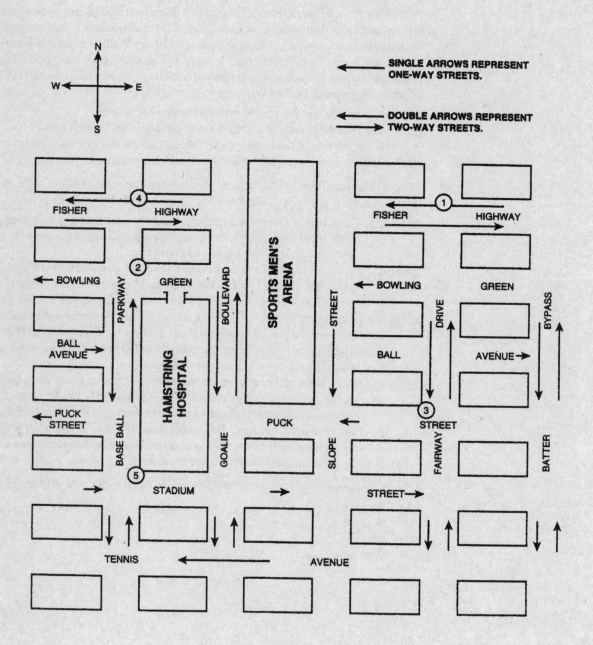

61. Officer Marlin is in car 66 patrolling the Athletic Acres neighborhood. Proceeding west from the intersection of Fairway Drive and Fisher Highway, Marlin drives one block, then turns and goes south for four blocks. Marlin then makes a left turn and then a right turn as soon as it is legal to do so. Marlin then makes another right turn, travels two blocks, makes a right turn, then takes the first left. After driving one block, Marlin is located at point

   (A) 2.
   (B) 3.
   (C) 4.
   (D) 5.

62. Later that same day, the dispatcher radios Marlin, who is located on Slope Street just where it intersects Stadium Street, that a hockey player has been hit square in the forehead by a hard-driven puck. The hockey game has been going on at the northeast corner of Sportsmen's Arena. Marlin must check on the injured hockey player as quickly as possible. The best route to take is

   (A) east on Stadium Street to Batter Bypass; north on Batter Bypass for four blocks; then west on Fisher Highway.
   (B) south on Slope Street to Tennis Avenue; east on Tennis Avenue to Fairway Drive; north on Fairway Drive five blocks to Bowling Green; west to the Arena.
   (C) east for one block on Stadium Street to Fairway Drive; left turn onto Fairway Drive to Fisher Highway; west on Fisher Highway.
   (D) straight up Slope Street to the northeast entrance to Sportsmen's Arena.

63. Officer Marlin recognizes that the hockey player's injury could be serious and calls for an ambulance. Upon learning that the nearest available ambulance is currently somewhere outside of Athletic Acres, Marlin decides to transport the hockey player to Hamstring Hospital in the patrol car. The emergency room entrance to Hamstring Hospital is on Bowling Green. The best route for Marlin to take is

   (A) south on Slope Street to Tennis Avenue; right onto Tennis Avenue to Baseball Parkway; Baseball Parkway to Bowling Green; right into emergency room entrance.
   (B) south on Slope Street to Puck; right and one block west on Puck Street to Goalie Boulevard; west off Goalie to Bowling Green.
   (C) Fisher Highway east to Batter Bypass; Batter Bypass south to Tennis Avenue; Tennis Avenue west to Baseball Parkway; Baseball Parkway north to Fisher Highway; Fisher Highway one block east to Goalie Boulevard; Goalie Boulevard south to Bowling Green, then right.
   (D) Slope Street south to Stadium Street; right onto Stadium Street to Baseball Parkway; Baseball Parkway to Bowling Green; east on Bowling Green to the hospital.

Answer questions 64 through 68 on the basis of the following passage.

It was New Year's Eve and celebrations were going on in homes, restaurants, and private halls around town. Celebrants were carousing in the streets as well. The air was filled with sounds of music, laughter, loud talk, and the occasional burst of illegal fire-crackers.

Jim Dandy was pleased that he had landed a good babysitting job at 148 Jane Street for this night. He would be paid triple wages for sitting on New Year's Eve, and the quiet night caring for sleeping children would pay for all the partying he had done in the previous week. Suddenly Jim started. The noise he heard was unlike the sound of fireworks. It sounded to him like gunshots. Oddly, the gunshots were followed by the sound of metal striking metal. Jim ran to the window but could see nothing, so he called the police.

Officer Manny Blank took Jim Dandy's call. Frankly, he was skeptical. New Year's Eve brings in so many crank calls about noise and so many false alarms. Still, the possibility of gun-toting drunks could not be ignored, so he dispatched Officers Pauline Diaz and Warren Lau to Jane Street to investigate. The officers were amazed to find Bob Doyle, Maria Hill, and Ned Swanson shooting the "For Sale" sign in front of 152 Jane Street with a single-barrel shotgun.

Officer Diaz demanded that the group stop shooting immediately, then asked what was going on. Ned Swanson, as spokesman for the group, told Officer Diaz that their very good friends, the Hashimotos, had put their house up for sale, but that he and his buddies did not want the Hashimotos to move away. They were shooting the sign to express their displeasure.

Officer Lau warned Doyle, Hill, and Swanson that their behavior was illegal, asked them to move on, and wished them a Happy New Year.

64. According to the preceding passage, Jim Dandy called the police.

(A) because he was babysitting and feared for the safety of the children.
(B) to report illegal fireworks.
(C) because he thought he heard gunfire.
(D) because the neighborhood had become so noisy with New Year's Eve revelers.

65. The *only* statement that accurately reflects information in the preceding passage is that

(A) the Hashimotos moved away on New Year's Eve.
(B) the gun belonged to Ned Swanson.
(C) Officer Diaz gave the shooting party a summons.
(D) Jim Dandy would be well paid for sitting on New Year's Eve.

66. Officer Manny Blank

(A) ignored Jim Dandy's first call because New Year's Eve brings out so many crank complaints.
(B) was aware that drunk people may act irresponsibly.
(C) dispatched Officer Pauline Diaz to bring in the "For Sale" sign.
(D) asked Maria Hill for her gun permit.

67. According to the preceding passage,

(A) the house at 152 Jane Street was for sale.
(B) three children lived in the house at 148 Jane Street.
(C) Warren Lau was behaving illegally.
(D) the officers found the "For Sale" sign riddled with bullet holes.

68. On the basis of the preceding passage, all of the following statements are true EXCEPT

(A) the "For Sale" sign was made of metal.
(B) the gun was not a single barrel shotgun.
(C) the Hashimoto family did not want to move.
(D) Bob Doyle and Maria Hill were friends.

Answer questions 69 and 70 on the basis of the following definitions.

ACCIDENTAL KILLING. One resulting from an act that is lawful and lawfully done under a reasonable belief that no harm is possible—distinguished from "involuntary manslaughter," which is the result of an unlawful act or of a lawful act done in an unlawful way.

HOMICIDE. The killing of any human creature.

MALICE. The intentional doing of a wrongful act without just cause or excuse, with an intent to inflict an injury or under circumstances that the law will imply an evil intent.

MANSLAUGHTER. The unlawful killing of another without malice, either express or implied, which may be either voluntarily, upon a sudden heat, or involuntarily, but in the commission of some unlawful act.

INVOLUNTARY MANSLAUGHTER. It exists where a person in committing an unlawful act not felonious or tending to great bodily harm, or in committing a lawful act without proper caution or requisite skill, unguardedly or undesignedly kills another.

VOLUNTARY MANSLAUGHTER. Manslaughter committed voluntarily upon a sudden heat of the passions; as if, upon a sudden quarrel, two persons fight, and one of them kills the other.

MURDER. The unlawful killing of a human being by another with malice aforethought, either express or implied.

69. Henry Field, age 16 and a brand new licensed driver, invites Joan Dawes, Betsy Hyde, Larry Dinks, Fred Smith, Warren Ehee, and Barbara Diaz to join him for a ride in his Honda Civic. The teenagers happily pile into the car, but soon find themselves cramped for space. Fred Smith climbs out of the car and onto the hood, and Field drives on. As Field takes a curve, Smith loses his grip and slides off the hood and under the front wheels of the car. Field stretches his foot for the brake, but hits the gas pedal and drives over Smith's body. Smith dies. Henry Field is guilty of

(A) involuntary manslaughter.
(B) accidental killing.
(C) malice and homicide.
(D) murder.

70. Which of the following is guilty of murder?

   (A) Bob Brooks has had three martinis and is arguing with his wife who constantly nags him about his drinking. In anger, Brooks grabs their infant daughter Tiffany, straps her carefully into her car seat, and slips behind the wheel of his 2001 Ford Taurus. He starts the car, puts it into reverse, and backs rapidly out of his driveway. He backs the car directly into the driver's seat of a passing car killing its driver instantly.

   (B) The neighbors' dog, Rover, barks and barks every night. Erica Young has called to complain and has even asked the police for help, but the barking continues. In desperation, Young purchases cyanide-based rat poison, laces a piece of fresh meat with it, and tosses the meat over the fence into the neighbors' yard. Rover takes the bait and dies a horrible death.

   (C) Todd Toole suspects that his wife has been two-timing him. Sure enough, he comes home one day at 3 p.m. and finds his wife in bed with Peter Cook. Toole confronts both his wife and Cook and warns them that he will kill them both if he ever catches them again. Some months pass, and Toole again becomes suspicious. He purchases a pistol and ammunition and again comes home in midafternoon. He enters the house, finds his wife in bed with a man who is not Peter Cook. Enraged, he shoots and kills his wife and her new lover.

   (D) It is just about dusk, and Jaime Ramos is driving at a speed of 15 mph in a designated school zone. Suddenly a ball rolls into the street. Ramos, fearing a child may be behind the ball, slams on his brakes. The child runs headlong into the hood of the car.

71. In response to a cell-phone call from a motorist, Officer Gentry drove to the major intersection of Main Street and Highway 1 at which all traffic lights were out of operation. Traffic was backing up in all directions. At the same time, some automobiles were pulling out of line and speeding through the intersection without stopping to look. Officer Gentry radioed for a repair crew and requested assistance in directing traffic. Gentry then jumped out of the patrol car and proceeded to direct traffic until the lights again became operational. The most effective way for Gentry to report this activity is:

   (A) "There was a big traffic jam at Main Street and Highway 1, so I directed traffic until it was repaired."

   (B) "I called on the cell phone for them to repair the signals at Main Street and Highway 1 that were out while I directed traffic."

   (C) "The lights weren't working at Main Street and Highway and there was a traffic jam and it was dangerous and so I called for a repair crew and directed traffic."

   (D) "I learned that the traffic signals were out at Main Street and Highway 1, so I radioed for a repair crew and directed traffic until the repair was made."

72. Officers Mutt and Jeffris report to Apartment 3-W at 91 Front Street with a search warrant directing them to search the apartment for bomb-making apparatus. The officers are admitted by Ms. Werkster, who tells them she is the housekeeper. A voice calls out from a back room, "Throw those cops out," and 3 very large, menacing men appear at the door of the room. Despite their search warrant, the officers feel outnumbered and do not press to search the back room. They look around the room to which they were admitted and notice neat piles of glassine envelopes containing white powder stacked on an end table. As Officer Jeffris reaches for an envelope, one of the men pulls out a gun. Mutt and Jeffris retreat empty handed. The most effective way for Officer Mutt to explain what happened and to request reinforcements is:

   (A) "We went to Apartment 3-W at 91 Front Street, but they wouldn't let us use our search warrant. We think we saw drugs, but one of them has a gun, and we need more people to go back."

(B) "Jeffris and I had a search warrant for 91 Front Street, 3-W, but Ms. Werkster is the nice housekeeper, and the 3 guys are big and have a gun. We didn't find bombs, but we saw drugs and left. We'll need reinforcements for the search"

(C) "Officer Jeffris and I attempted search at 91 Front Street, 3-W, but were outnumbered and outsized by armed inhabitants. Warrant is for bomb apparatus, possibility of drugs as well. Reinforcements needed to execute."

(D) "Me and Jeffris tried to search 3-W at 91 Front Street with a warrant but they wanted to throw us out, and they wouldn't let us look or take any drugs. Ms. Werkster let us in, but he pulled out his gun so we left without reinforcements."

73. Officer Miller was involved in a high-speed vehicle pursuit this evening. Upon return to the station house, Miller is writing a report about this evening's activity. The report will include the following five sentences.

1. I followed the Nissan for nearly a half mile and then motioned to the driver to pull over.
2. I informed the dispatcher that I was in a high-speed pursuit.
3. When the driver ignored me, I turned on my siren and flashing dome light; the driver increased his speed.
4. The Nissan hit a tree, and I promptly arrested the driver.
5. While patrolling in car #544, I observed a Nissan with a broken tail light that was driving erratically, drifting in and out of lane.

The most logical order for the above sentences to appear in the report is

(A) 5, 1, 3, 2, 4.
(B) 2, 5, 3, 1, 4.
(C) 5, 1, 2, 4, 3.
(D) 2, 1, 5, 4, 3.

74. Officer Roget has discharged his gun and has seriously wounded a suspect. He must now prepare a detailed report justifying his actions. The report will include the following five sentences.

1. I ran through the crowd of observers and saw a man pointing a gun at a taxi driver.
2. I shouted out, "I am a police officer, drop that gun and don't move."
3. I was on foot, patrolling on Walnut Street near the corner of Maple, when I heard a woman's voice cry out from a crowd, "He's got a gun."
4. The man turned around and rapidly fired three shots at me.
5. I responded by firing once, hitting the suspect in the right shoulder.

The most logical order for the above sentences to appear in the report is

(A) 1, 3, 4, 2, 5.
(B) 4, 5, 2, 1, 3.
(C) 3, 1, 2, 4, 5.
(D) 3, 1, 5, 2, 4.

Answer questions 75 and 76 on the basis of the following table.

Date	Day	Offense	Time	Location
3/2	Monday	Robbery	3:15 p.m.	1112 Grove Street
3/4	Wednesday	Rape	9:00 p.m.	1998 Clinton Street
3/4	Wednesday	Rape	4:10 p.m.	2360 Clinton Street
3/6	Friday	Robbery	1:45 p.m.	1365 Grove Street
3/6	Friday	Homicide	1:06 a.m.	1246 Barrow Street
3/7	Saturday	Robbery	9:00 p.m.	1814 Grove Street
3/7	Saturday	Robbery	9:21 p.m.	1930 Grove Street
3/7	Saturday	Robbery	10:01 p.m.	1986 Grove Street
3/8	Sunday	Homicide	12:42 a.m.	1010 Barrow Street
3/9	Monday	Homicide	3:09 a.m.	1318 Barrow Street
3/9	Monday	Rape	3:15 p.m.	1492 Clinton Street
3/11	Wednesday	Rape	8:09 p.m.	1622 Clinton Street
3/12	Thursday	Rape	9:45 p.m.	2011 Clinton Street
3/13	Friday	Homicide	1:04 a.m.	1700 Barrow Street
3/13	Friday	Robbery	3:10 p.m.	1776 Grove Street
3/14	Saturday	Robbery	2:10 p.m.	1812 Grove Street
3/15	Sunday	Homicide	2:10 a.m.	1936 Barrow Street
3/16	Monday	Rape	5:25 p.m.	2121 Clinton Street

75. The incidence of rape might best be cut down by concentrating patrols

   (A) on Grove Street from 1 p.m. to 4 p.m. on Fridays and on Clinton Street between 8 p.m. and midnight on Monday through Wednesday.

   (B) on Clinton Street from noon to 5 p.m. on Monday and Wednesday and from 4 p.m. to midnight on Thursday and Saturday.

   (C) on Clinton Street from 9 a.m. to 4 p.m. Monday through Friday.

   (D) on Barrow Street from midnight to 4 a.m. on Saturday and Sunday and on Clinton Street from 8 p.m. to 1 a.m. on Tuesday and Wednesday.

76. If patrols were beefed up between the hours of 3 p.m. and 11 p.m., they might effectively cut down incidence of the crimes of

   (A) rape and robbery.

   (B) rape and homicide.

   (C) robbery and homicide.

   (D) robbery only.

77. An officer should be courageous and independent, but sometimes it is prudent to ask for backup. Of the following situations, in which should the officer not act until backup arrives?

   (A) A shopper had fallen to the floor in a department store because of an apparent epileptic seizure.

   (B) A heavily armed man is holding a classroom of small children hostage and is shouting, "I dare you to come and get me."

   (C) A 6-year-old girl has fallen through thin ice in an area of a lake that is 4-feet deep.

   (D) A despondent man is standing on a wide window ledge on the 8th floor and is threatening to jump.

78. A man enters the First National Bank and hands a teller three plain canvas bags and a note reading, "I have a pistol in my pocket and friends outside with submachine guns. Do not press your alarm. Put all the bills in your drawer into these bags, and hurry." The teller fills the bag with six bundles of $100 bills, 100 bills to the bundle; eight bundles of $50 bills, 100 bills to the bundle; twenty-five bundles of $20 bills, 100 bills to the bundle; and forty-eight bundles of $10 bills, 100 bills to the bundle. At this point the robber gets nervous and says, "That's enough," and flees out the door. The robber leaves with a total of

(A) $188,000.
(B) $198,000.
(C) $1,980,000.
(D) $19,800,000.

79. On April 5, a group of fourth grade girls was approached by a blue van with white curtains at the windows and a farm scene painted on the back as the children were leaving the Harley Elementary School. The driver, a sandy-haired white male, asked directions to the mall. As the girls approached the van, the man flung open the door and exposed himself. The girls ran off, and the van drove away.

Officer Walter is comparing this incident with others recently reported.
Report 1 (March 15) Curtained blue van, white male driver, idled engine outside Martin Elementary School schoolyard 2:20 to 3:30 p.m. Cruised around neighborhood until 4:00 p.m. No contact.
Report 2 (March 22) Three 9-year-old boys report that they observed an African-American man relieving himself behind a blue van in the alley behind the Arcade strip mall at around 4:00 p.m.
Report 3 (March 26) White van with mountain scene painted on one side pulled up alongside teenage boys walking on Front Street, 11:00 a.m. White male driver offered to sell reefers.
Report 4 (April 2) Blue van, white gray-haired driver tossed candy and bubble gum to children in playground at Webster Elementary School during recess. Called to them that he would have better goodies for them after school.

Officer Walter should consider that the suspect in the most recent report may be the same as that in

(A) Reports 1 and 4.
(B) Reports 1, 3, and 4.
(C) Reports 1 and 2.
(D) Report 4 only.

80. Drive-by purse snatchings present a real problem for police officers because the victim is usually too stunned to notice anything about the perpetrators. Sometimes, however, witnesses do report what they have seen. Today has been a record day for drive-by purse snatchings. The day's activity has included:

Report 1(10:15 a.m.) Dented white four-door Chevrolet, white license plate, white female driver. African-American male in front passenger seat reached out for and grabbed purse of elderly African-American woman and sped away.

Report 2 (11:30 a.m.) Red sports car, white female driver. African-American male in front passenger seat reached out for and grabbed purse of elderly Chinese woman and sped away.

Report 3 (12:42 p.m.) White four-door American car, red license plate, white female driver. Black male in front passenger seat reached out for and grabbed purse of elderly woman.

Report 4 (1:50 p.m.) Black convertible, white male driver. White man in front passenger seat reached out for and grabbed shoulder bag of business man.

Report 5 (3:10 p.m.) Light-colored American car, blue license plate, white female driver. African-American male in rear seat reached out for and grabbed satchel of elderly man with cane.

At 5:18 p.m., Officer Osten in a patrol car observes a drive-by purse snatching. Osten gives chase and stops the dented white four-door Taurus and arrests a white woman driver and her African-American male passenger. These suspects should also be considered as suspects in which other purse snatching reports?

(A) None of these; all are different.
(B) Reports 1, 2, and 3
(C) Reports 1, 3, and 5
(D) Reports 1, 2, 3, and 5

81. The all-night convenience store has been the site of a series of muggings. The descriptions of the mugger as submitted by the victims appear below.

Mugger 1 (June 12) Male, Asian, about 30, 5' 11", about 180 pounds, black hair, cut-off jeans, pocket t-shirt.

Mugger 2 (June 16) Male, Asian or Hispanic, late teens, approximately 5' 8" and 150 pounds, black hair, gray pants, sweatshirt, earring in left ear.

Mugger 3 (June 24) Male, Hispanic, maybe 25, 5' 10", 210 pounds, black hair, jeans, t-shirt, heavy silver cross on chain around neck.

Mugger 4 (June 29) Male, light-skinned African-American, 30 to 35, 6' 1", 190 pounds, black hair, blue jeans, tank top, earrings in both ears, nose stud.

On July 2, a customer in the store notices a mugging in progress outside and alerts a cashier to dial 911. Officer Trooper arrives in time to give chase to the fleeing mugger and to apprehend him. The suspect Officer Trooper takes into custody is a 22-year-old Hispanic male, of average height and slightly built. He has black hair and is wearing black pants and a long-sleeved polo shirt. He has on no jewelry but has holes in both earlobes.

On the basis of the descriptions of the June muggers, the mugger arrested on July 2 should be considered the same person as mugger

(A) 1.
(B) 2.
(C) 3.
(D) 4.

82. An officer who observes smoke billowing from a car some distance ahead on a roadway must do the following in the specified order.

 1. Radio for fire fighting and emergency medical services.
 2. Call for backup patrol cars and police personnel.
 3. Drive to the scene of the car fire and park as close as is safe so as to avoid involvement of the patrol car in the fire.
 4. Check that all occupants are out of the car.
 5. Render emergency first aid if necessary.
 6. Stop all traffic in the direction in which the car was traveling.
 7. Block one lane in the opposite direction to hold it open for emergency vehicles.

 Officer Galamian, patrolling northbound on Shady Parkway, sees smoke rising from the roadway some distance ahead. Galamian radios the location and requests emergency response from firefighting and medical equipment and personnel. Then Galamian calls headquarters and asks for patrol car assistance. She then drives to within 50 feet of the car and jumps out. The heat is intense, and she is unable to see through the smoke, but a woman calls out from the shoulder that she and her dog are both out of the car and that no one is inside. The next action Galamian should take is to

 (A) find out if the woman needs first aid.
 (B) check that all occupants are really out of the car.
 (C) stop all traffic in both directions.
 (D) wait in the opposite roadway to direct emergency vehicles.

83. If there is good reason to suspect that certain premises are being used for processing and distribution of illegal substances, officers should search those premises. It is important that officers follow the following steps in the specified order.

 1. Collect information and evidence that substantiates suspicion.
 2. Organize information and present it to a judge; request search warrant.
 3. Carry search warrant to premises.
 4. Identify selves as law enforcement officers and request admittance.
 5. Show warrant and search.
 6. If no one is at premises, force entrance and search.

 Officers Ahmed and Moko have observed excessive activity at 31 Oak Avenue that has led them to suspect that illegal drug trade is occurring right under their noses. They compile their evidence and request and receive a search warrant from Justice Baroni. Officer Moko takes the warrant and together Ahmed and Moko go to 31 Oak Avenue. The next thing Ahmed and Moko should do is

 (A) identify themselves as law enforcement officers and force open the door.
 (B) search the premises.
 (C) show the warrant.
 (D) announce, "We are police officers with a warrant, please let us in."

84. A violent crime scene makes many demands on reporting officers. They must consider the needs of victims and witnesses along with necessity for preserving evidence. When arriving at the scene of a violent crime, officers should do the following in the order specified below.

1. Render first aid to any survivors in need of it.
2. Request ambulance.
3. Identify witnesses and take statements.
4. Reassure witnesses for their physical safety.
5. Assess need for emotional support for witnesses.
6. Secure area.
7. Request police photographer.

Officer Michaelis is first to respond to a scene of criminal violence. Michaelis finds a woman lying on the floor bleeding profusely from a stab wound to the stomach, a teenage girl cowering in a corner, and a 3-year-old boy crying hysterically. Michaelis attempts to control the woman's bleeding and calls for an immediate ambulance. Michaelis then turns to the teenager, ascertains that she is the victim's daughter and that the little boy is the victim's son. The teenager tells Michaelis that her uncle, her mother's brother, is a heroin addict who periodically comes to ask for money. This time her mother refused. Both youngsters are terrified of the uncle and apprehensive about their mother. Officer Michaelis assures the children that arrangements will be made for their safety while their mother is hospitalized. Michaelis notes that a social worker should be assigned to assist the children. Michaelis has acted

(A) properly; it is important to keep unauthorized persons away from a crime scene.
(B) improperly; there is no way to stop bleeding from a stomach wound.
(C) properly; Michaelis has done his best first for the mother and then for the children.
(D) improperly; Michaelis should have interviewed the boy as well.

Answer questions 85 through 87 solely on the basis of the following map. The flow of traffic is indicated by the arrows. If there is only one arrow shown, then traffic flows only in the direction indicated by the arrow. If there are two arrows shown, then traffic flows in both directions. You must follow the flow of traffic.

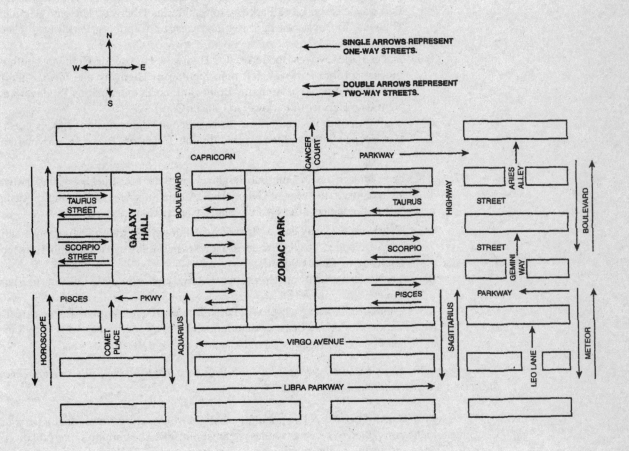

85. Officer Austin is taking lunch break seated on a bench in the northwest corner of Zodiac Park when the dispatcher broadcasts information of a mugging in progress on Comet Place. Austin jumps into the patrol car in hopes of arriving at the scene in time to catch the mugger. The best way to get there is

(A) west on Capricorn Parkway to Aquarius Boulevard; left onto Aquarius Boulevard to Pisces Parkway; right into Comet Place.

(B) east on Capricorn Parkway to Sagittarius Highway; south on Sagittarius Highway to Virgo Avenue; right onto Virgo Avenue; right into Comet Place.

(C) east on Capricorn Parkway to Sagittarius Highway; right onto Sagittarius Highway to Pisces Parkway; west on Pisces Parkway to Comet Place.

(D) west on Capricorn Parkway to Meteor Boulevard; south on Meteor Boulevard to Libra Parkway; Libra Parkway one short block to Leo Lane; Leo Lane west and left turn onto Virgo Avenue; Virgo Avenue to Comet Place.

86. The mugger has eluded Officer Austin who is suddenly alerted to a rape on Cancer Court.

Austin should get to Cancer Court by taking
(A) Pisces Parkway to Aquarius Boulevard, Aquarius Boulevard north to Capricorn Parkway, and Capricorn Parkway east to Cancer Court.
(B) Pisces Parkway to Horoscope Highway, left onto Horoscope Highway to Libra Parkway, east on Libra Parkway to Sagittarius Highway, left onto Sagittarius Highway to Capricorn Parkway, and west on Capricorn Parkway to Cancer Court.
(C) Pisces Parkway west to Horoscope Highway, Horoscope Highway south two blocks to Libra Parkway, left onto Sagittarius Highway one block, then left onto Virgo Avenue to Aquarius Boulevard, north on Aquarius Boulevard then right onto Capricorn Parkway to Cancer Court.
(D) a left turn onto Pisces Parkway to Horoscope Highway, three blocks north on Horoscope Highway, then a right turn onto Capricorn Parkway, and a left onto Cancer Court.

87. It has been a rough day in Celestial Heights. Now there is a street brawl underway on Taurus Street just to the west of Galaxy Hall. Austin must break up the fight. Austin's best route to the melee, after backing out of Cancer Court, is

(A) Capricorn Parkway east to Sagittarius Highway; Sagittarius Highway south to Virgo Avenue; Virgo Avenue to Horoscope Highway; right onto Horoscope Highway to Taurus Street.
(B) Capricorn Parkway to Horoscope Highway; Horoscope Highway to Taurus Street.
(C) Capricorn Parkway west to Aquarius Boulevard and south to Taurus Street.
(D) Capricorn Parkway east to Sagittarius Highway south, then west onto Taurus Street.

Answer questions 88 and 89 on the basis of the following excerpt from the Fifth Amendment and the accompanying explanation.

The FIFTH AMENDMENT is popularly thought of as stating simply that a person must not be compelled to serve as witness against himself. The common interpretation of "Taking the Fifth" is the making of a statement such as, "I refuse to answer on grounds that I might incriminate myself." In actual practice, the Fifth Amendment is far more complex. One aspect of the Fifth Amendment that impacts on the police is the Miranda Rule passed down by the Supreme Court in 1966. In brief the Miranda Rule states that: Before questioning of a person being held in custody begins, the person must be warned that:

1. He or she has a right to remain silent; and
2. Any statement he or she does make may be used as evidence against him or her; and
3. He or she has the right to the presence of an attorney; if he or she cannot afford an attorney, one will be provided.

Further, "Miranda" states that a defendant may waive these rights if he or she does so voluntarily, knowingly, and intelligently. The same defendant may change his or her mind at any time during questioning, in which case interrogation stops until an attorney is present. The fact that a defendant may have volunteered information before being taken into custody does not deprive him or her of the right to refuse answers to inquiries until he or she has consulted with an attorney.

88. Police officers usually give Miranda warnings automatically, fearing that if they neglect this step, a guilty person might go free on a technicality. However, there are instances in which Miranda warnings are not required. In which of the following situations would the officer not need to read a Miranda warning?

   (A) Officer Popper has just arrested a man he observed trying to hot-wire a parked automobile.
   (B) Officer Yarrow has stopped for questioning a woman he observed running hurriedly from a building carrying a portable television set with its cord trailing behind.
   (C) Officer Bender is about to question a suspect who is in custody in the station house with his personal attorney at his side.
   (D) Officer White is ready to question attorney, Jane Doe, who has been placed under arrest on a drug charge.

89. Officer Horti, on foot patrol in a neighborhood business area at 2:00 a.m., observes and follows a man carrying a heavy television set through the alley behind a small appliance and electronics shop toward a Subaru wagon. As the man attempts to open the tailgate while holding the television set, Officer Horti offers to give him a hand. The man shrugs off Horti's offer with, "I can do it myself; after all, I stole it myself." Horti arrests the man and brings him in. At which point in this process should Horti have given the suspect Miranda warnings?

   (A) At first sighting of the man carrying a TV set from a store in the middle of the night
   (B) When the man tried to put the television set into a car that might have been stolen
   (C) When the man said that he had stolen the set
   (D) At the station house immediately after booking

90. As the getaway car sped away from the jewelry store, a number of people on the crowded midday sidewalk attempted to memorize its license plate number. Officer Crum has recorded the following numbers as reported.

   Report #1 659 OTP
   Report #2 560 UZP
   Report #3 365 PTZ
   Report #4 650 OPT

   In broadcasting a description of the getaway vehicle, Officer Cram should include the license plate number in

   (A) Report 1.
   (B) Report 2.
   (C) Report 3.
   (D) Report 4.

91. Women's Health Services Clinic has recently added early abortion to the services it provides. Now antiabortion protesters arrive by 7:00 a.m. each day to prevent the clinic staff from entering and then to heckle and harass women coming into the clinic for any reason. Officers assigned to keep order and to protect staff members and patrons have been alerted to watch for suspicious activity that might alert to violence in the wings. Which of the following activities should prompt officers on duty to call for additional backup?

    (A) A curtained van with 2 men in the front seat has been slowly circling the area for the past 45 minutes.

    (B) A woman is gripping a young girl tightly by the arm and is pushing her toward the clinic door.

    (C) Three nuns are sitting with linked arms on the front steps of the clinic and are singing hymns.

    (D) A teenaged boy has dropped off a young girl at the clinic and is sitting in a parked car across the street.

92. Officer Spano was first to respond to what appeared to be a one-car accident followed by a vehicle pileup under a highway overpass. His report of his observations at the scene will include the following five sentences. (These sentences are NOT listed in the correct order.)

    1. A black pickup truck skidded into the left rear fender of the Honda.
    2. The driver of the Honda lost control and crashed into the center guardrail.
    3. A large rock thrown from above crashed into the windshield of the Honda Civic.
    4. The bus driver saw two preteen boys running westward off the overpass.
    5. A bus managed to stop just short of hitting the gray Buick Skylark that hit the pickup truck.

    The most logical order for the above sentences to appear in Spano's report is

    (A) 2, 3, 1, 5, 4.

    (B) 1, 3, 2, 4, 5.

    (C) 3, 4, 1, 2, 5.

    (D) 3, 2, 1, 5, 4.

93. When Officer Flanders responded to 80-year-old Mrs. Barber's call that she felt very ill, he discovered Mr. Barber, age 87, lying unconscious on the living room couch and a car with its motor running in the garage under the house. The most effective way for Officer Flanders to report these facts is with the following statement:

    (A) "Mrs. Barber was sick and Mr. Barber was unconscious and the car was still running."

    (B) "Maybe they were trying to commit suicide because the motor was running under the house making Mrs. Barber sick and Mr. Barber unconscious in the living room."

    (C) "Elderly Mr. Barber was rendered unconscious and his wife sickened by exhaust fumes from a car left running in their indoor garage."

    (D) "Mrs. Barber called to say that the car engine was running, she was sick, and Mr. Barber was unconscious on the living room couch."

Directions: Answer questions 94 through 98 on the basis of the allowing sketches. The first face is an artist's sketch of a suspect based on witnesses' descriptions. The sketches labeled (A), (B), (C), and (D) represent possible ways in which the suspect might have changed his or her appearance. Assuming that no surgery has been done on the suspect, select the face this is most likely that of the suspect in disguise.

94.

(A)

(B)

(C)

(D)

95.

(A)

(B)

(C)

(D)

96.

(A)

(B)

(C)

(D)

97.

(A)

(B)

(C)

(D)

98.

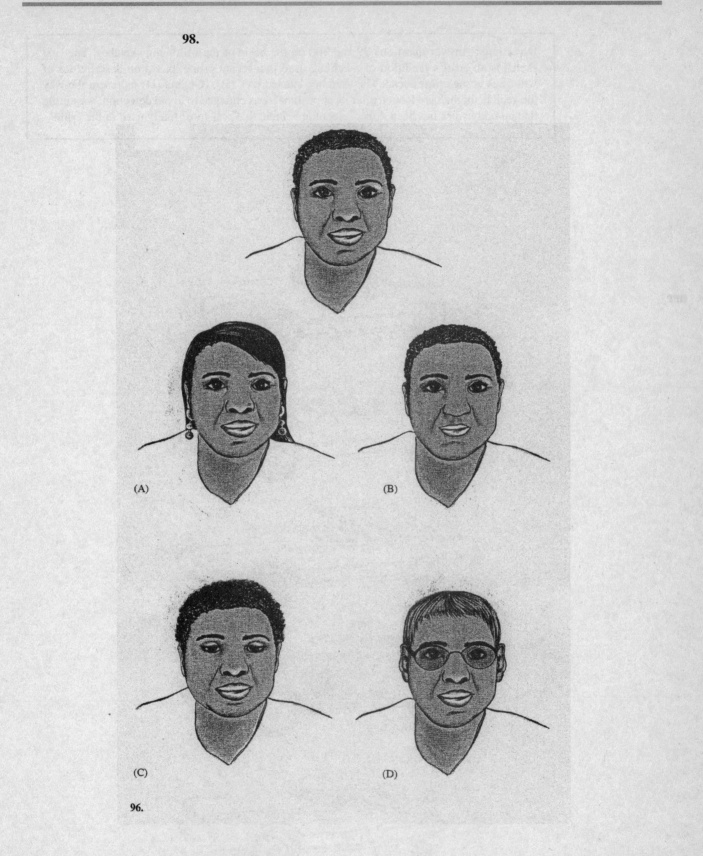

(A)

(B)

(C)

(D)

96.

Directions: Answer questions 99 and 100 on the basis of the following sketches. The first sketch is an artist's rendition of a vehicle used in a recent crime, based on descriptions of witnesses at the crime scene. The sketches labeled (A), (B), (C), and (D) represent the way the vehicle might have looked after its appearance was changed to avoid detection. Assuming that no body work has been done, select the vehicle that was most likely used in the crime.

99.

(A)

(B)

(C)

(D)

100.

(A)

(B)

(C)

(D)

MODEL EXAMINATION 6: ANSWERS AND EXPLANATIONS

ANSWERS

1.	C	21.	A	41.	C	61.	A	81.	B
2.	B	22.	C	42.	B	62.	C	82.	A
3.	D	23.	D	43.	A	63.	B	83.	D
4.	A	24.	B	44.	D	64.	C	84.	C
5.	A	25.	B	45.	B	65.	D	85.	B
6.	B	26.	C	46.	B	66.	B	86.	D
7.	D	27.	D	47.	D	67.	A	87.	A
8.	C	28.	A	48.	C	68.	C	88.	C
9.	B	29.	B	49.	D	69.	A	89.	C
10.	A	30.	D	50.	C	70.	C	90.	D
11.	B	31.	A	51.	D	71.	D	91.	A
12.	C	32.	B	52.	A	72.	C	92.	D
13.	A	33.	B	53.	A	73.	A	93.	C
14.	B	34.	B	54.	B	74.	C	94.	C
15.	D	35.	D	55.	D	75.	B	95.	A
16.	D	36.	D	56.	C	76.	A	96.	D
17.	C	37.	C	57.	C	77.	B	97.	B
18.	B	38.	A	58.	A	78.	B	98.	A
19.	A	39.	B	59.	D	79.	A	99.	C
20.	C	40.	B	60.	B	80.	C	100.	D

EXPLANATIONS

1.   **The correct answer is (C).** If you got this wrong, look again. Did you overlook the motorcyclist?
2.   **The correct answer is (B).** Washington Avenue is a one-way street, eastbound. The taxi is headed west.
3.   **The correct answer is (D).** The officer in the hat is near the tow truck and is wearing short sleeves.
4.   **The correct answer is (A).** It is important to notice street signs in this type of memory test.
5.   **The correct answer is (A).** The name is on the cab of the sanitation truck.
6.   **The correct answer is (B).** There is no number on the florist's door, but it is directly next door to number 202. Since the corner store on the previous block is number 128, it is clear that each block begins with a new hundred.
7.   **The correct answer is (D).** Tony has his name on the window as well as on the sign above the store.
8.   **The correct answer is (C).** That's the window with the cat. The potted plants and the hanging laundry are over the pizzeria.
9.   **The correct answer is (B).** There is a flag hanging from the front of the school.
10.   **The correct answer is (A).** The directional compass to the right of the scene indicates that the motorcyclist is traveling north. The street sign attached to the lamp post shows that Lincoln Street is a one-way street.
11.   **The correct answer is (B).** Don Juan escaped from prison.
12.   **The correct answer is (C).** Louis Joseph has a tattoo on his left buttock.
13.   **The correct answer is (A).** Mary Kiley uses aliases and carries forged identity. She is active with the IRA as is her gun-running friend, Len Brown.
14.   **The correct answer is (B).** Jane Jones likes to drive German luxury cars.
15.   **The correct answer is (D).** Mary Kiley has a gold front tooth.
16.   **The correct answer is (D).** Jane Jones is a cocaine user.
17.   **The correct answer is (C).** Don Juan, the heavy cigar smoker, is missing a couple of teeth. Jane Jones speaks with an accent, Pauline Chen suffered burns in a childhood accident, and Louis Joseph has the rose tattoo.
18.   **The correct answer is (B).** Len Brown is missing some fingers, likely from an accident with explosives. The tattoo of the map of Ireland is on his right arm, not his left.
19.   **The correct answer is (A).** Louis Joseph, the suspect wanted for rape, is easily recognized as a former boxer by his cauliflower ears.
20.   **The correct answer is (C).** Pauline Chen is wanted for armed robbery.
21.   **The correct answer is (A).** Thursday, May 10.
22.   **The correct answer is (C).** Matt French and Frank Tunnel both were tall, thin white men wearing hip boots.
23.   **The correct answer is (D).** In both cases, someone had just left the house when the workmen approached.
24.   **The correct answer is (B).** The diamond earrings were stolen from 169 Butler Road, the home of Mr. and Mrs. Prince.
25.   **The correct answer is (B).** Mr. Prince saw "MYP," and Leslie Jones noticed "561."
26.   **The correct answer is (C).** The same person went into the basement at both houses. Ms. Tracey estimated his age at about 30 years. He was a stocky African-American man and was the same person who identified himself to Mrs. Prince as Matt French.
27.   **The correct answer is (D).** Mr. Prince reported the theft of the $100 bills to Officer Rice.
28.   **The correct answer is (A).** A gold watch was stolen from Ms. Tracey at 287 Butler Road. Other items stolen from her included cultured pearls, not fresh water, and silver filigree earrings.
29.   **The correct answer is (B).** The emerald ring stolen from Mr. and Mrs. Prince was worth $935. The item worth $2320 was a pair of diamond earrings.

30. **The correct answer is (D).** Officer Rice told Mr. and Mrs. Prince that their case would be investigated. The officers had no reason to suspect a sewage backup. Rice did not go to Ms. Tracey's home at all.

31. **The correct answer is (A).** The officer must report only fact, not conjecture. The officer does not know that the van did not belong at the warehouse nor that the vandals were necessarily in that van. Choice (D) is inadequate in its description of the vehicle.

32. **The correct answer is (B).** This is a neat restatement of the next to last sentence. Choice (A) is not very helpful as a directive to trainees. Choices (C) and (D) bring in topics outside the scope of the paragraph.

33. **The correct answer is (B).** Of these five sentences, the logical lead-in to the description of the accident is the victim's statement of how it began, with her left turn. The sequence then continues with the ignored stop sign, the collision, the noting of the license plate, and, finally, the trip to the hospital.

34. **The correct answer is (B).** The report begins with the call that brought the officers to the candy shop. "Upon arrival" is the obvious next sentence. Since choice (B) is the only choice offering this sequence of sentences, you needn't look further. You can confirm your choice by reading the remaining sentences as ordered. It makes rˇûse.

35. **The correct answer is (D).** This constitutes 24 hours of high-crime time. Choice (A) includes only 6 high-crime hours; choice (B), 8 such hours; and choice (C), 15 high crime hours. Choice (C) offers quality hours in Whitestone, but auto accidents are not crimes.

36. **The correct answer is (D).** 19 "quality" hours here. Choice (A) encompasses 14 such hours; choice (B), 9; and choice (C), only 8.

37. **The correct answer is (C).** The roofer needs immediate medical attention. Call for an ambulance.

38. **The correct answer is (A).** What is that van doing there without its headlights? Investigate. The woman in the ATM is probably worried about being mugged.

39. **The correct answer is (B).**

1 Television set		$ 580.00
2 Silver Candlesticks	@ $120.00	$ 240.00
1 Mink Coat		$3900.00
+ 6 Etchings	@$835	$5010.00
Cash		<u>$1763.29</u>
		$11,493.29

40. **The correct answer is (B).** *Mandatory* means that no one has a choice in the matter. The officer must send for an ambulance, and the patient must go.

41. **The correct answer is (C).** The Perrys heard the intruders leave, so the intruders were obviously still in the house when the Perrys returned home.

42. **The correct answer is (B).** Clothing and jewelry spilled from Mrs. Perry's suitcase that was dropped in the yard. The passage does not say who noticed the newspaper clipping on the floor.

43. **The correct answer is (A).** The information in the newspaper led the intruders to believe that the family had departed for Europe on the previous day. There is no way to know whose car was used for the escape.

44. **The correct answer is (D).** We know for certain that the dispatcher ordered Mrs. Perry to go outside at once. The dispatcher's concern was for Mrs. Perry's and Tim's safety, but the dispatcher did not know for certain that the intruders were still inside.

45. **The correct answer is (B).** Since the back door was open, we can assume that the intruders used it to enter.

46. **The correct answer is (B).** Tom Jones entered an occupied house during the night. He was armed, but he did not use his crowbar to threaten, and he took nothing, so he did not commit robbery.

47. **The correct answer is (D).** Link shoved Toon, grabbed the car keys, and stole the car. Clearly Toon committed robbery. Choice (A) does not fit the definition of burglary be-

cause the paint store was not a dwelling. Choice (B) fulfills the condition of intent to deprive the owner of the value of the property being taken from him without his consent but fails to fulfill the condition that the person taking the property would use or benefit from it. In choice (C), Frost did not threaten or take. Tomkins was spooked and gave voluntarily.

48.   **The correct answer is (C).** Even though the woman is walking in a very straight line, she is not paying attention and is likely to be hit by a car. The pair collecting for the colonization of Mars are likely to be defrauding the public, but they do not constitute an immediate danger to themselves or to others.

49.   **The correct answer is (D).** The descriptions of the car vary, but all witnesses seem to agree that the car was neither of luxury size nor a subcompact and that it was light in color. Again, discrepancies as to the license plate are understandable. The car was undoubtedly speeding away. On the other hand, Witness 4's description of the driver presents a problem.

50.   **The correct answer is (C).** It is surprising that Witness 4 did not notice the tattoo on exposed arms, but the description otherwise is consistent with the observations of Witnesses 1 and 2. Witness 3's description is of a shorter man wearing a jacket.

51.   **The correct answer is (D).** Think about it. Of the choices offered to you, it makes sense to first know what the object that you are going after looks like and what makes it suspicious. Then on the assumption that explosion is a clear possibility, you want medical backup. Then you'll do what you can to protect yourself before you approach the object. You also must move away any bystanders who could interfere or be injured in case of explosion. Only then can you approach the object and remove it to an area in which detonation might be safe. Finally, you can examine the object and detonate it if warranted. The only possible variation here is that steps six and three could be reversed, but the reverse order is not offered to you in an answer choice.

52.   **The correct answer is (A).** An officer must always begin by identifying him- or herself. In this instance, no other person is in danger of life or limb, so you must turn to self protection. The person attempting to jimmy open the door has some sort of pointed object in hand, probably a screwdriver or a spike. Assuming that the person is up to no good, you must check for other weapons as well. Only then can you proceed to the routine ownership check. If it turns out that the person is the legitimate owner who has misplaced the car keys, issue the parking ticket before you assist the driver.

53.   **The correct answer is (A).** The lead-in to this question specifies that the procedure applies in an accident in which there are no personal injuries. Therefore, it is necessary to establish that there are none. Larsen is following the book. Larsen will not be able to charge the diplomat, even if the diplomat admits driving infractions, but Larsen certainly is correct in taking down statements from both drivers.

54.   **The correct answer is (B).** Unless some other part of the description were to contraindicate, the self-identification as Fred Astaire would be a dead giveaway. In this case, the other aspects of the description are consistent with the daughter's report.

55.   **The correct answer is (D).** If the matron is to witness the search, she must be called in before it begins. After that, the logical progression is to first have the pockets emptied, then get the prisoner's arms out of the way and search from top to bottom.

56.   **The correct answer is (C).** Sam watched the ball go; the bat did not fly out of his hands as follow through to his swing. A spectator could have been badly hurt. Hiram endangered himself, not others. Barry took a calculated risk; he might have accidentally hit another employee, but the armed robber might have taken aim at more than one. Bob's action was without awareness of possible risk.

57.   **The correct answer is (C).** Illegal immigrants have often used churches for sanctuary. In A, the woman is using the church as shelter, not as sanctuary; homelessness is not a legal offense. As for choice (B), crimes committed in a church are subject to prosecution outside the church.

58. **The correct answer is (A).** Making a threat upon arrival at a hostage situation, before learning the nature of the hostage holder or the reasons for taking of hostages, is potentially very dangerous to the hostages. Such a threat almost demands that the hostage taker harm the hostages in order to save face. Use of the bullhorn to communicate with those inside is acceptable; they must be able to hear. Choice (B) extends the time that the hostages are held, but the hope that the trusted grandmother can resolve the situation peacefully is well worth it. The action in choice (C) should reassure the hostage taker that officers are not planning to use force. The food might be used to sustain officers, hostages, and the hostage taker as well. Choice (D) represents a good move in line with rules 4 and 5.

59. **The correct answer is (D).** Until Officer Wall observes an illegal activity for which he might arrest the man, he cannot conduct a search incident to lawful arrest.

60. **The correct answer is (B).** Witness 2 saw a face. All the other witnesses said the bank robber wore some sort of mask that totally covered his or her face, and no other witness was certain that it was a man. All other discrepancies can be explained by witnesses' location in the bank.

61. **The correct answer is (A).** Officer Marlin's route is marked out on the map below.

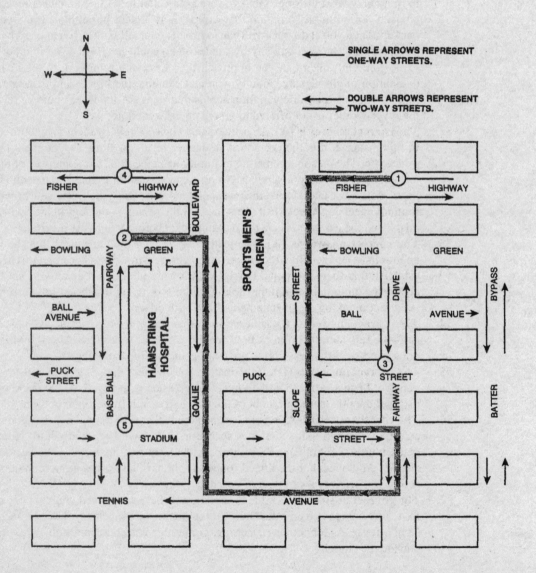

62. **The correct answer is (C).** Officer Marlin should follow the dotted-line route on the map. Choice (A) is unnecessarily long. Choice (B) involves going the wrong way on Tennis Avenue. As for choice (D), Slope Street is one way, southbound.

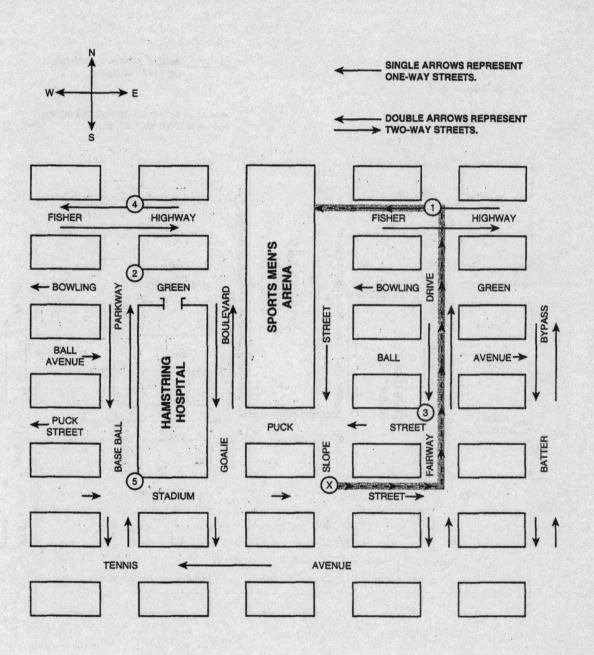

63.   **The correct answer is (B).** The dotted line shows the best route. Choice (A) is a long way round and ends up going the wrong way on Bowling Green. Choice (C) is entirely legal, but very long. Choice (D) goes the wrong way on Stadium Street.

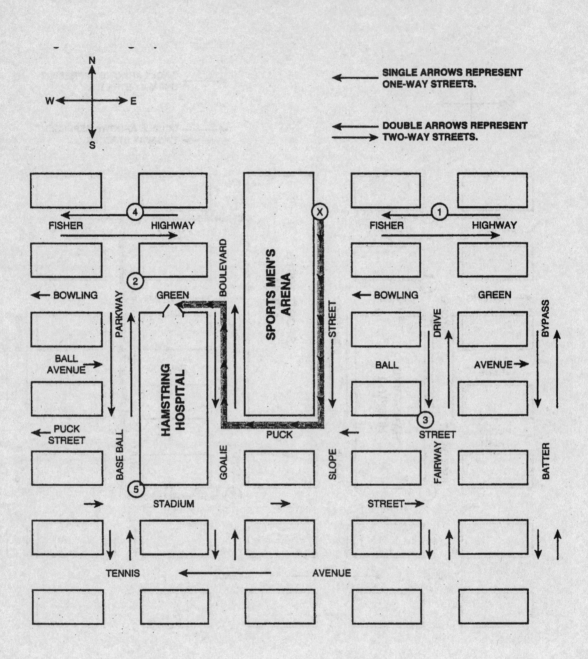

64.   **The correct answer is (C).** As a responsible baby sitter, Jim Dandy may well have feared for the safety of the children, but the immediate reason for his call to the police was that he thought he heard gunfire.

65.   **The correct answer is (D).** Jim Dandy was earning triple wages for sitting on New Year's Eve.

66. **The correct answer is (B).** The third paragraph tells us that Officer Blank worried about "gun-toting drunks."

67. **The correct answer is (A).** The "For Sale" sign was in front of 152 Jane Street. It probably was riddled with bullet holes, but the passage does not tell us this. Possibly the bullets ricocheted off.

68. **The correct answer is (C).** We know that their friends did not want the Hashimotos to move, but we haven't a clue as to the Hashimotos' own wishes.

69. **The correct answer is (A).** This sure looks like an accident, but in legal terms it is involuntary manslaughter because Field was committing a lawful act without proper caution or requisite skill.

70. **The correct answer is (C).** Despite the heat of passion, this is murder. Toole had made a previous threat, purchased the murder weapon, and set up the opportunity to act on his threat by coming home midday. Choice (A) is manslaughter because Brooks was committing an unlawful act (drunk driving). Choice (B) falls under none of these definitions because the victim was a dog, not a human. Choice (D) does not state whether or not the child was killed.

71. **The correct answer is (D).** Choice (A) reads as if the traffic jam needed repair; the lights are not mentioned. Choice (B) misstates how the officer relayed the message; and who is "them"?, choice (C), conveys all the information in a run-on sentence.

72. **The correct answer is (C).** Both choices (A) and (D) are unclear as to reference of pronouns. Choice (B) makes two unsubstantiated assumptions: that the housekeeper is nice and that the officers saw drugs.

73. **The correct answer is (A).** Something must attract the notice of an officer in a patrol car; in this case a car with a broken tail light being driven erratically. From that point on, events fall into place. Choice (C) represents the wrong sequence, because the officer would not have informed the dispatcher that he was in a high-speed chase until the driver picked up speed.

74. **The correct answer is (C).** The cry of "He's got a gun" sets the scene and begins Officer Roget's explanation. Then Roget verified the presence of the gun. If Roget had immediately fired, as in choice (D), he would have been acting out of order. The correct sequence is that he identified himself as an officer and drew first fire from the suspect.

75. **The correct answer is (B).** All of the rapes occurred on Clinton Street, three of these on Wednesday, two on Monday and one on Thursday. All the rapes were in the afternoon or evening between the hours of 3:15 and 9:45.

76. **The correct answer is (A).** Along with the rapes that all occurred within this time period, four of the six robberies reported also occurred between 3 and 11 p.m. The homicides all occurred after midnight.

77. **The correct answer is (B).** You don't want to alarm this heavily armed man. He might well harm any or all of the children or shoot you. You need the assistance of a well-trained hostage team and many reinforcements.

78. **The correct answer is (B).**

$$
\begin{aligned}
6 \times \$100 \times 100 &= \ \$\,60{,}000 \\
8 \times \$\,50 \times 100 &= \ \$\,40{,}000 \\
+\ 25 \times \$\,20 \times 100 &= \ \$\,50{,}000 \\
48 \times \$\,10 \times 100 &= \ \underline{48\,000} \\
&\quad\ \$198{,}000
\end{aligned}
$$

79. **The correct answer is (A).** The white man driving a blue van in Reports 1 and 4 seems to share with the April 5 suspect an interest in young children. It is relatively easy to repaint a vehicle, but most unlikely that anyone would undertake the chore from blue to white and back to blue within one month. The suspect in Report 3 is also a predator on young people, but not the same predator. Report 2 is inconsistent in terms of description of the driver and his activity, which was not directed at children.

80. **The correct answer is (C).** The suspects in the Report 4 incident are quite clearly different people from those in any other incident. It would be reasonable for Officer Osten to discount the Report 2 incident as well. While the perpetrators fit the descriptions of those

in 1, 3, and 5 and those in custody, it seems unlikely that they would use a different car only once during such a concentrated spree. On the other hand, switching license plates is quickly and easily done and is a common criminal practice. The variations in descriptions of the white car are to be expected from witnesses to a fast-moving crime.

81. **The correct answer is (B).** Your best clues are the size and age of the suspect. All the other muggers are older and larger. On different days, a suspect may wear different clothing, so clothing in itself is not identifying. However, a man who wears an earring on any day should have a hole to show for it on a day when he is not wearing an earring. (Women sometimes wear earrings that clip or screw on, leaving no hole; men almost universally wear their earrings through pierced ears.)

82. **The correct answer is (A).** It is impossible for Officer Galamian to get a closer look into the car, and it is reasonable to accept the woman's assurance that no one is inside. However, just because the woman is speaking coherently does not mean that she is not injured or in shock. Galamian must check the woman's physical condition and render first aid if necessary before dealing with the traffic.

83. **The correct answer is (D).** The officers must announce themselves and request admittance before barging in or searching. A little politeness is never out of order.

84. **The correct answer is (C).** Officer Michaelis has done everything right. The attempt to control bleeding from a stab wound to the stomach may well be futile, but he was right to try. As for interviewing a crying 3-year-old-a little common sense must enter answering of exam questions as well as once you get out into the field.

85. **The correct answer is (B).** Follow the broken line. Choices (A) and (D) start right out in the wrong direction on Capricorn Parkway. You can discount them without reading further. Choice (C) presents an impossible route because Pisces Parkway does go through Zodiac Park.

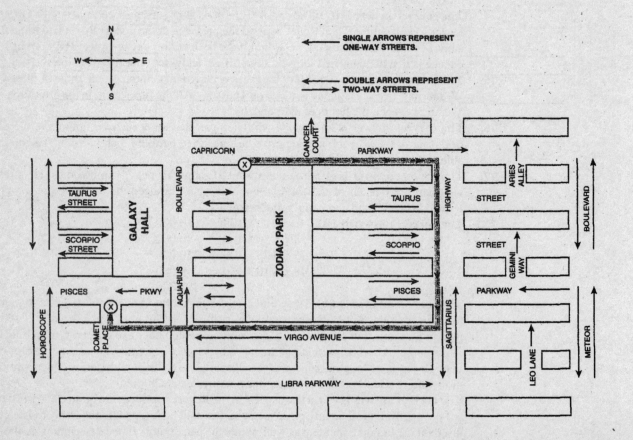

86. **The correct answer is (D).** Follow the route on the map below. Pisces Parkway is a one-way street, west bound in the two blocks surrounding Comet Place, so Choice (A) is impossible. Choice (B) sends Officer Austin the wrong way on Capricorn Parkway. Choice (C) is legal, but too long.

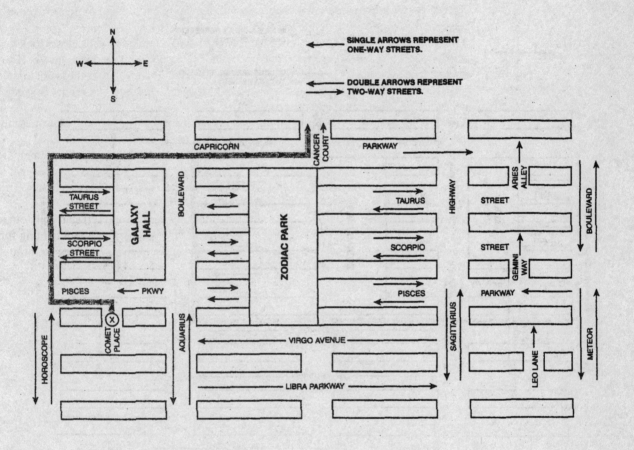

87.   The correct answer is (A). The route is long, but it skirts both Zodiac Park and Galaxy Hall and avoids going the wrong way on one-way streets. Choices (B) and (C) start out going against traffic on Capricorn Parkway. Choice (D) is impossible because Taurus Street does not go through Zodiac Park or through Galaxy Hall.

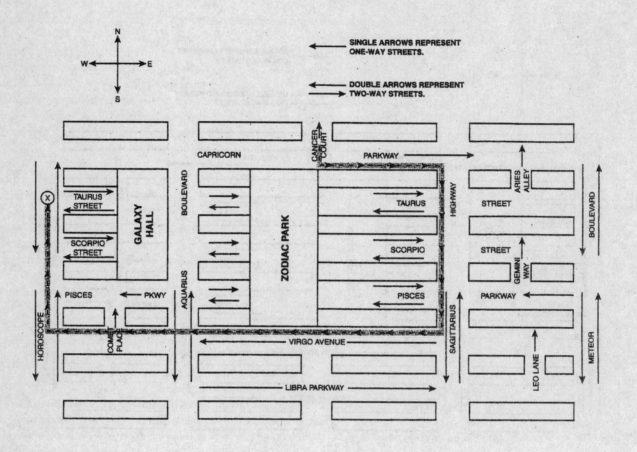

88.   **The correct answer is (C).** The suspect who is already represented and whose attorney is present does not need a Miranda warning. The alleged car thief who has just been arrested does need Miranda warnings. The woman who is giving probable cause for arrest on charge of absconding with stolen goods also needs to be warned. And the attorney, even though she is well aware of her right to representation, must nevertheless be read those rights.

89.   **The correct answer is (C).** When the man announced that he had stolen the television set, he gave probable cause for his arrest. Even though he had, in effect, already made a confession, he had to receive Miranda warnings and be advised that he need not answer questions without representation. Until the man stated that he had stolen the set, he might well have been an employee or the store's owner taking a set home in his own car. Horn could have asked the man for identification or purpose in carrying the TV without Miranda warnings because the man was not in custody and had not yet given probable cause for arrest.

90. **The correct answer is (D.)** Report #4 combines the most frequently appearing letters with the most frequently appearing numbers. Further, the numbers in the fourth report are the same as those in the second, and the letters are the same as those in the first report.

91. **The correct answer is (A).** Why is the van circling the clinic? Could its occupants be waiting for a good opportunity to do someone some harm? There is no way to know how many more people might be in the curtained van or whether or not anyone is armed. Officers need good backup before approaching the van. The nuns may or may not move if asked, but they are certainly not dangerous. The young girl being brought to the clinic against her will may be questioned, but this is probably not a police matter and surely poses no danger to officers on duty.

92. **The correct answer is (D).** If the rock hadn't crashed into the Honda's windshield, the accident would not have happened. If the Honda had not hit the guardrail and jutted into the roadway, it would not have been hit by the pickup truck. We never are told that the Buick hit the pickup truck, but logically that is the next step in the sequence because the bus didn't hit the Buick that did hit the pickup truck. Obviously, all these drivers had their eyes on the road. The bus driver who had stopped looked up and saw the boys running away. That must be the last sentence of this segment of the report.

93. **The correct answer is (C).** Choice (A) says nothing at all in a run-on sentence. Choice (B) makes an unsupported assumption. Choice (D) makes a statement that is not true; Mrs. Barber did not call about the car, in fact she probably was unaware that the car was the source of their problem.

94. **The correct answer is (C).** The man in choice (A) has a wider nose and a more pointed chin; the one in (D) has a fuller face and thinner lips. Choice (B) is incorrect because removal of the earring from his left ear should have revealed a hole. (B) also has larger, rounder eyes.

95. **The correct answer is (A) .** Choice (B) has thicker lips; (C) has a narrower face and more prominent chin; (D) has a fuller face and a dimple in her chin. Choice (A) has bleached and straightened her hair and plucked her eyebrows, but she is the same woman.

96. **The correct answer is (D).** Choice (A) has larger, lighter eyes; the chin on choice (B) is too pointed; the ears on (C) are smaller than the large and floppy ones on the original.

97. **The correct answer is (B).** The eyes on choice (A) are too small and round; choice (C) has the wrong ears; (D) is a larger man with a thicker neck.

98. **The correct answer is (A).** Choice (B) has an entirely different nose and thinner lips; choice (C) had a different shape face and sleepier eyes; choice (D) has different ears.

99. **The correct answer is (C).** Choice (A) has only two doors; choice (B) is not a convertible, and its back windows are a different shape; choice (D) is a four-door convertible, but is otherwise an altogether different car.

100. **The correct answer is (D).** Choice (A) is an upscale breed of jeep; choice (B) is real army surplus, not a trendy current jeep; choice (C) is even more upscale than choice (A), hardly a jeep at all.

PART FIVE

Civil Service Career Information Resources

HOW TO FIND A GOVERNMENT JOB

Very often finding a job is a matter of luck. However, we'd like to take some of the luck out of it and make it more directive. Below are a variety of sources you can contact in your search for employment. Keep in mind that as a State Trooper, Highway Patrol Officer, or State Traffic Officer, you will be working for the state. That's where the jobs are.

STATE EMPLOYMENT

Almost every state has its own Web site. In order to access the state systems via the Internet, there's a very simple way to find each state, although it may take some searching once you're on line.

To find the state Internet site, enter the following: www.state.___.us. In the blank, enter the two-letter code for that state. For Arizona, for example, you would enter www.state.az.us. For Wisconsin, enter www.state.wi.us. Here's a list of the latest URLs for the state sites. Be aware, however, that they change from time-to-time.

Alabama: www.state.al.us
Alaska: www.state.ak.us
Arizona: www.state.az.us
Arkansas: www.state.ar.us
California: www.state.ca.us
Colorado: www.state.co.us
Connecticut: www.state.ct.us
Delaware: www.state.de.us
District of Columbia: www.washingtondc.gov
Florida: www.state.fl.us
Georgia: www:state.ga.us
Hawaii: www.state.hi.us
Idaho: www.state.id.us
Illinois: www.state.il.us
Indiana: www.state.in.us
Iowa: www.state.ia.us
Kansas: www.state.ks.us
Kentucky: www.state.ky.us
Louisiana: www.state.la.us
Maine: www.state.me.us
Maryland: www.state.md.us
Massachusetts: www.state.ma.us
Michigan: www. state.mi.us
Minnesota: www.state.mn.us
Mississippi: www.state.ms.us
Missouri: www.state.mo.us

Montana: www.state.mt.gov
Nebraska: www.state.ne.us
Nevada: www.state.nv.us
New Hampshire: www.state.nh.us
New Jersey: www.state.nj.us
New Mexico: www.state.nm.us
New York: www.state.ny.us
North Carolina: www.state.nc.us
North Dakota: www.state.nd.us
Ohio: www.state.oh.us
Oklahoma: www.state.ok.us
Oregon: www.state.or.us
Pennsylvania: www.state.pa.us
Rhode Island: www.state.ri.us
South Carolina: www.state.sc.us
South Dakota: www.state.sd.us
Tennessee: www.state.tn.us
Texas: www.state.tx.us
Utah.: www.state.ut.us
Vermont: www.state.vt.us
Virginia: www.state.va.us
Washington: www.wa.gov
West Virginia: www.state.wv.us
Wisconsin: www.state.wi.us
Wyoming: www.state.wy.us

If that state also has a Job Bank, you can find that the same way. This time you would enter www.abj.org/___, and enter the state's two-letter code in the blank space.

There are, however, specific State Trooper Web sites. Here's a complete list of them, current as of this edition.

Alabama	www.dps.state.al.us
Alaska	www.dps.state.ak.us
Arizona	www.dps.state.az.us
Arkansas	www.state.ar/asp/asp.html
California	www.chp.ca.gov/index.html
Colorado	www.state.co.us/gov-dir/cdps/csp.htm
Connecticut	www.state.ct.us/dps/csp.htm
Delaware	www.state.de.us/dsp
Florida	www.fhp.state.fl.us/
Georgia	www.ganet.org/dps/index.html
Hawaii	www.hawaii.gov/icsd/psd/psd.html
Idaho	www.isp.state.id.us
Illinois	www.state.il.us/isp/index
Indiana	www.ai.org/isp/index
Iowa	www.state.ia.us/government/dps/isp/
Kansas	www.ink.org/public/khp
Kentucky	www.state.ky.us/agencies/ksp/ksphome.htm
Louisiana	www.lsp.org
Massachusetts	www.state.ma.us/msp/massachu.htm
Maryland	www.inform.umd.edu/ums+state/md_resources/mdsp/index.htm/
Maine	www.janus.state.me.us/dps/msp/homepage.htm
Michigan	www.msp.state.mi.us
Minnesota	www.dps.state.mn.us/patrol/index.htm
Missouri	www.mshp.state.mo.us/hp32p001.nsf
Mississippi	www.dps.state.ms.us/

Montana	www.doj.state.mt.us/mhp/index.htm
North Carolina	www.shp.state.nc.us/
North Dakota	www.state.nd.us/ndhp
Nebraska	www.nebraska-state-patrol.org
New Hampshire	www.state.nh.us/nhsp/index.html
New Jersey	www.state.nj.us/lps/njsp/index.html
New Mexico	www.nmsp.com
Nevada	www.state.nv.us/dmv_ps/nhphome.htm
New York	www.troopers.state.ny.us
Ohio	www.state.oh.us/ohiostatepatrol/
Oklahoma	www.dps.state.ok.us/
Oregon	www.osp.state.or.us/
Pennsylvania	www.state.pa.us/pa_exec/state_police/
Rhode Island	www.risp.state.ri.us/
South Carolina	www.schp.org
South Dakota	www.state.sd.us/state/executive/dcr/hp/page1sdh.htm
Tennessee	www.state.tn.us/safety/
Texas	www.txdps.state.tx.us/
Utah	www.uhp.state.ut.us/
Virginia	www.state.va.us/vsp/vsp.html
Vermont	www.dps.state.vt.us/vsp/index.html
Washington	www.wa.gov/wsp
Wisconsin	www.dot.state.wi.us/dsp/
West Virginia	www.wvstatepolice.com
Wyoming	www.wydotweb.state.wy.us/docs/patrol/patrol.html

If you're interested in more personal information, there is an excellent site that provides links to everything from Academies to Forensics to Mounted Police and SWAT Troops. It can be found at www.StateTroopersDirectory.com/troops.htm. The site also features individual personal Trooper pages, tributes to fallen officers, and so on.

You can also use some of the popular search vehicles, such as Yahoo.com, Ask.com, Altavista.com, and so on, to locate other job-related sites. Use search terms such as *jobs*, *employment*, *labor*, *business*, and *help-wanted* as well as *trooper*, *patrol officer*, and so on. Add that to the specific city or state, and you'll be surprised at the number of suggested sites you'll get. You might enter into the search box something like *Miami+trooper*. The plus sign (+) indicates that you want both Miami and jobs to be in the same suggested sites.

HOW TO GET A GOVERNMENT JOB

Now that you know where to look for a job, it's important to understand the procedure. The procedure you must follow to get a government job varies little from job to job and from one level of government to another. There are variations in details, of course, but certain steps are common to all.

Once you have found a *Notice of Examination* (it may be called an Announcement), read it very carefully. If you can get a copy for yourself—all the better. If not, take lots of time to take notes. Make sure you write down all of the details. The Notice of Examination gives a brief job description. It tells the title of the job and describes some of the job duties and responsibilities. On the basis of the job description, you decide whether or not you want to try for this job. If the job appeals to you, you must concentrate on:

■ **Education and experience requirements.** If you cannot meet these requirements, do not bother to apply. Government service is very popular; many people apply. The government has more than enough applicants from which to choose. It will not waive requirements for you.

■ **Age requirements.** Discrimination on the basis of age is illegal, but a number of jobs demand so much sustained physical effort that they require retirement at an early age. For these positions there is an entry age limit. If you are already beyond that age, do not apply. If you are still too young, inquire about the time lag until hiring. It may be that you will reach the minimum age by the time the position is to be filled.

■ **Citizenship requirements.** Many jobs are open to all people who are eligible to work in the United States, but all law enforcement jobs and most federal jobs are limited to citizens. If you are well along the way toward citizenship and expect to be naturalized soon, inquire as to your exact status with respect to the job.

■ **Residency requirements.** If there is a residency requirement, you must live within the prescribed limits or be willing to move. If you are not willing to live in the area, do not waste time applying.

■ **What forms must be filed.** The announcement of the position for which you are applying will specify the form of application requested. For most federal jobs, you may submit either the Optional Application for Federal Employment (OF 612) or a resume that fulfills the requirements set forth in the pamphlet, "Applying for a Federal Job (OF 510)." For other than federal jobs, the Notice of Examination may tell you where you must go or write to get the necessary form or forms. Be sure you secure them all. The application might be a simple form asking nothing more than name, address, citizenship, and social security number, or it may be a complex Experience Paper. An Experience Paper, as its title implies, asks a great deal about education, job training, job experience, and life experience. Typically, the Experience Paper permits no identification by name, sex, or race; the only identifying mark is your social security number. The purpose of this procedure is to avoid permitting bias of any sort to enter into the weighting of responses. The Experience Paper generally follows a short form of application that does include a name. When the rating process is completed, the forms are coordinated by means of the social security number

■ **Filing dates, place, and fee.** There is great variation in this area. For some positions, you can file your application at any time. Others have a first day and last day for filing. If you file too early or too late, your application will not be considered. Sometimes it is sufficient to have your application postmarked by the last day for filing. More often, your application must be received by the last date. If you are mailing your application, allow five full business days for it to get there on time. Place of filing is stated right on the notice. Get the address right! Most applications may be filed by mail, but occasionally in-person filing is specified. Follow directions. Federal and postal positions require no filing fee. Most other government jobs do charge a fee for processing your application. The fee is not always the same. Be sure to check this out. If the Notice specifies "money order only," purchase a money order. Be sure the money order is made out properly. If you send or present a personal check, your application will be rejected without consideration. Of course, you would never mail cash; but if the announcement specifies "money order only," you cannot submit cash, even in person.

■ **How to qualify.** This portion of the Notice of Examination tells you the basis on which the candidates are chosen. Some examination scores consist of a totaling up of weighted education and experience factors. This type of examination, called "an unassembled exam" because you do not come to one place to take the exam, is based upon your responses on the application and supplementary forms. Obviously these must be very complete for you to get full credit for all you have learned and accomplished. The notice may tell you of a qualifying exam, which is an exam that you must pass in addition to scoring high on an unassembled written or performance test, or the notice may tell you of a competitive exam—written, performance, or both. The competitive exam may be described in very general terms or may be described in detail. It is even possible that a few sample questions will be attached. If the date of the exam has been set, that date will appear on the notice. Write it down.

When you have the application forms in hand, photocopy them. Fill out the photocopies first. That way, you can correct mistakes, change the order of information, or add or delete information. You can work at fitting what you have to say into the space allowed. Do not exaggerate, but be sure to give yourself credit for responsibilities you've taken on, for cost-saving ideas you've given your prior employer, and for any other accomplishments. Be clear and thorough in telling what you have learned and what you can do.

When you are satisfied with your draft, copy over the application onto the form(s). Be sure to include any backup material that is requested; by the same token, do not send more "evidence" than is truly needed to support your claims of qualification. Your application must be complete according to the requirements of the announcement, but it must not be overwhelming. You want to command hiring attention by exactly conforming to the requirements.

Check over all forms for neatness and completeness. Sign wherever indicated. Attach the fee, if required. Then mail or personally file the application on time.

WARNING! If you are currently employed, do not give your notice now. Stay at your present job. If you are job hunting, continue your search. The time lag between application for a government job and actual employment is always many months; it may even be a year or two. You cannot afford to sit back and wait for the job.

If the Notice of Examination told you that there is a competitive exam and told you about subjects of the examination, you can begin to study now. If not, just continue working and await notice of next steps.

When the civil service commission or personnel office to which you submitted your application receives it, the office will date, stamp, log, and open your file. The office may acknowledge receipt with more forms, with sample exam questions, or with a simple receipt slip. Or, you may hear nothing at all for months.

Eventually you will receive a testing date or an interview appointment. Write it on your calendar in red so that you don't let the dates slip by. Write the address to which you are to report in the same place. If you receive an admission ticket for an exam, be sure to put it in a safe place; but keep it in sight so that you will not forget to take it with you to the exam. With an exam date, you should also receive information about the exam. Tine may be short. If you have not already done so, begin to study and prepare right away.

If the next step is an exam, that exam might be either a written exam or a performance exam. The type of exam depends on the nature of the job. The applicant for a locksmith's position might be asked to cut some complicated keys and to repair a broken lock; the track maintainer hopeful might have to replace ties or reset switches. The applicant for a position as a clerk-stenographer might have to take dictation and a typing test as well as a multiple-choice test of general clerical abilities. Applicants for most jobs take only a written test. The written test is most frequently a multiple-choice test, one in which the test-taker chooses the best of four or five answer choices and marks its number on a separate answer sheet. Multiple-choice tests are machine scored. Machine scoring insures accuracy and objectivity. No one can misinterpret your answers. Machine scoring also allows many applicants to be rated at the same time. It speeds up the process, but if you are waiting to hear about your job you may doubt this fact.

Occasionally, the written test consists of an essay portion along with the multiple-choice section or even of essays alone. Essays usually appear at levels above initial entry level, where there are fewer applicants and fewer papers to score. On an essay, the examiners are looking for indications that you can organize your thoughts and can express them effectively in writing.

If you are called for an exam, arrive promptly and dress appropriately. Neatness is always appropriate; however, you do not need to "dress up" for a performance exam or for a written exam. If you will do manual work for your performance exam, wear clean work clothes. For a written exam, neat and casual clothing is fine.

THE INTERVIEW

If there is no exam and you are called directly to an interview, what you wear is more important. Take special care to look businesslike and professional. You must not appear to be too casual, and you must certainly not look sloppy. Overdressing is also inappropriate. A neat dress or skirted suit is fine for women; men should wear a shirt and tie with a suit or slacks and a jacket. In addition, pay attention to your grooming.

Interviews take up an interviewer's time. If you are called for an interview, you are under serious consideration. There may still be competition for the job, someone else may be more suited than you, but you are qualified and your skills and background have appealed to someone in the hiring office. The interview may be aimed at getting information about:

- **Your knowledge.** The interviewer wants to know what you know about the area in which you will work. For instance, if you will be doing data entry in a budget office, what do you know about the budget process? Are you at all interested in this area of financial planning? You may also be asked questions probing your knowledge of the agency for which you are interviewing. Do you care enough to have educated yourself about the functions and role of the agency, whether it's child welfare, pollution control, or international trade?

- **Your judgment.** You may be faced with hypothetical situations, job-related or in interpersonal relations, and be asked, "What would you do if . . . ?" questions. Think carefully before answering. You must be decisive but diplomatic. There are no "right answers." The interviewer is aware that you are being put on the spot. How well you can handle this type of question is an indication of your flexibility and maturity

- **Your personality.** You will have to be trained and supervised. You will have to work with others. What is your attitude? How will you fit in? The interviewer will be trying to make judgments in these areas on the basis of general conversation with you and from your responses to specific lines of questioning. Be pleasant, polite, and open with your answers, but do not volunteer a great deal of extra information. Stick to the subjects introduced by the interviewer. Answer fully, but resist the temptation to ramble on.

- **Your attitude towards work conditions.** These are practical concerns: If the job will require frequent travel for extended periods, how do you feel about it? What is your family's attitude? If you will be very unhappy about the travel, you may leave the job and your training will have been a waste of the taxpayers' money. The interviewer also wants to know how you will react to overtime or irregular shifts.

Remember, working for the government is working for the people. Government revenues come from taxes. The hiring officers have a responsibility to put the right people into the right jobs so as to spend the taxpayers' money most effectively. And, as a government employee, you have a responsibility to give the people (including yourself) their money's worth.

Other steps along the hiring route may be a medical examination, physical performance testing, and psychological interviewing. If there is a written test, these steps do not occur until the written test is are scored and ranked. Steps that require the time of one examiner with one applicant are taken only when there is reasonable expectation of hiring.

THE MEDICAL EXAMINATION

The state police officer's route must be covered at all times. This means that the assigned officer must show up. Otherwise, the scheduling officer must find a substitute and must rearrange the work tours of many other officers. The candidate with a history of frequent illness or one with a chronic ailment that may periodically crop up and interfere with attendance is not an acceptable candidate. Likewise, the applicant with an underlying physical condition that presents no problems in everyday life but that might be aggravated under the stressful activity of a police officer must be rejected.

Every candidate under consideration must undergo a thorough medical examination. This examination always occurs after the applicant has passed the written exam and often before the test of physical fitness or physical performance. The reason many police examining boards conduct the medical examination before the physical test is so that candidates whose health might be jeopardized by the strenuous activity of the physical test are screened out ahead of time. The police department does not want its applicants collapsing on the floor of the physical testing arena. In the interest of cost-efficiency, however, you may be asked to take the physical performance test before your medical examination. Since applicants who cannot qualify on the physical performance test need not undergo the more expensive medical examination, the department saves money. If you are to take the physical performance test before taking your medical examination, you will probably be asked to bring a certificate of fitness in order to participate in the physical exam, which has been signed by your own doctor. Then, after you have qualified on the physical performance test, the police physician will conduct the departmental examination. Both the physical performance test and the medical exam are administered to one applicant at a time, but the medical exam needs a physician while the physical performance exam can be administered by a police department employee with a stopwatch. Disqualification on the basis of either the physical performance test or the medical exam stops the screening process and eliminates the candidate from further consideration.

The medical exam will resemble an army physical more than a visit to your personal physician. You will start by filling out a lengthy questionnaire relating to your medical history. This questionnaire will be used by the physician to single out special health areas for consideration. It may also be used by the personnel interviewer when you approach the final step of the screening process.

Do not lie on the medical questionnaire. Your medical history is a matter of record at school, in your service dossier, and in the hospital or clinic files. If you lie, you will be found out. If the medical condition does not disqualify you, the fact of your untruthfulness will. On the other hand, there is no need to tell more than is asked. You do not need to expand upon your aches and pains. You needn't make an illness or injury more dramatic than it was. Stick to the facts and do not raise any questions. If you have any current concerns, the police department's examining officer is not the person to ask.

Your medical examination almost certainly will include height and weight measurement, chest x-ray, eye test, hearing test, blood tests, urinalysis, cardiogram, blood pressure, and actual visual and physical examination by the doctor. If you have any doubts as to how you will fare with any of these examinations, you might want to consult your personal physician ahead of time. You may be able to correct a borderline situation before you appear for the exam.

Most police departments provide candidates with height-weight standards and with lists of medical requirements before their scheduled medical examinations. If you receive these, look them over carefully. If they present any problems to you, see your doctor. Your worry may be misplaced, or it may be real. Possibly you will have to change your career goals. Or, likely, you can correct the situation, pass the medical exam, and go on to serve on the police force.

Read over the medical specifications very carefully before you visit your personal physician. Some state police departments require nearly perfect uncorrected vision. Others permit glasses and/or contact lenses. Some departments welcome applicants who have had their vision surgically corrected. Others specify that applicants who have undergone Radial Keratotomy, Epikeratoplasty, or Ortho Keratology are not acceptable. If your own status cannot satisfy their requirements, you may have to move to another state or consider a city, town, or county force that has different requirements.

Not all state police departments have the same standards for medical conditions. Some will accept conditions that are absolutely disqualifying in others. The height-weight charts and the list of medical requirements on the following pages are illustrative. They are typical of those of many police departments. They should serve you as a general guide at this time. If your own medical position is way out of line, you may need to reconsider or embark on a major health reform campaign right away. Once you get your own department's official set of guidelines, follow those standards rather than the ones printed here.

HEIGHT AND WEIGHT FOR FEMALES

ACCEPTABLE: WEIGHT IN POUNDS ACCORDING TO FRAME

Height (in bare feet)		Small Frame	Medium Frame	Large Frame
Feet	Inches			
4	10	92–98	96–107	104–119
4	11	94–101	98–110	106–122
5	0	96–104	101–113	109–125
5	1	99–107	104–116	112–128
5	2	102–110	107–119	115–131
5	3	105–113	110–122	118–134
5	4	108–116	113–126	121–138
5	5	111–119	116–130	125–142
5	6	114–123	120–135	129–146
5	7	118–127	124–139	133–150
5	8	122–131	128–143	137–154
5	9	126–135	132–147	141–158
5	10	130–140	136–151	145–163
5	11	134–144	140–155	149–168
6	0	138–148	144–159	153–173
6	1	142–152	148–163	157–177

NOTE: Although the above table commences at a specified height, no minimum height requirement has been prescribed. This table of height and weight is adhered to in all instances except where the Civil Service examining physician certifies that weight in excess of that shown in the table (up to a maximum of twenty pounds) is lean body mass and not fat. Decision as to frame size of candidate is made by the examining physician. The following tests will be part of the medical examination:

- Vision

- Hearing

- Serology

- Urinalysis

- Chest X-Ray

- Blood Pressure

- Electrocardiogram

HEIGHT AND WEIGHT FOR MALES

ACCEPTABLE WEIGHT IN POUNDS ACCORDING TO FRAME

Height (in bare feet) Feet	Inches	Small Frame	Medium Frame	Large Frame
5	3	115–123	121–133	129–144
5	4	118–126	124–136	132–148
5	5	121–129	127–139	135–152
5	6	124–133	130–143	138–156
5	7	128–137	134–147	142–161
5	8	132–141	138–152	147–166
5	9	136–145	142–156	151–170
5	10	140–150	146–160	155–174
5	11	144–154	150–165	159–179
6	0	148–158	154–170	164–184
6	1	152–162	158–175	168–189
6	2	156–167	162–180	175–194
6	3	160–171	167–185	178–199
6	4	164–175	172–190	182–204
6	5	168–179	176–194	186–209
6	6	172–183	180–198	190–214

NOTE: Although the above table commences at a specified height, no minimum height requirement has been prescribed. This table of height and weight is adhered to in all instances except where the Civil Service examining physician certifies that weight in excess of that shown in the table (up to a maximum of twenty pounds) is lean body mass and not fat. Decision as to frame size of candidates is made by the examining physician.

The following tests will be part of the medical examination:

- Vision

- Hearing

- Serology

- Urinalysis

- Chest X-Ray

- Blood Pressure

- Electrocardiogram

Candidates are required to meet the physical and medical requirements stated below at the time of the medical examination, at the time of appointment, and at appropriate intervals thereafter.

1. **Weight.** Candidates should have weight commensurate to frame. Weight should not interfere with candidate's ability to perform the duties of the position of Police Officer.

2. **Vision.** Candidates must have binocular visual acuity not less than 20/20 with or without correction; if correction is required, binocular visual acuity not less than 20/40 without correction. Binocular peripheral vision should not be less than 150 degrees.

3. **Color Vision.** Candidates must be able to distinguish individual basic colors against a favorable background.

4. **Hearing.** Candidates must be able to pass an audiometric test of hearing acuity in each ear. A binaural hearing loss of greater than 15 percent in the frequency ranges of 500, 1000, 2000 Hz would be considered disqualifying. Hearing appliances should correct the deficiency so the binaural hearing loss in the combined frequency level of 500, 1000, 2000 Hz is not greater than 15 percent.

5. **Heart.** Candidates must be free of functionally limited heart disease and must have functional cardiac classification of no greater than Class 1. This determination is to be made clinically or by cardiac stress test.

6. **Lungs.** The respiratory system must be free of chronic disabling conditions that would interfere with the candidate's performance of required duties.

7. **Diabetes.** Candidates who are diabetic must not require insulin injections or oral hypoglycemic agents for control.

8. **Neurological Health.** Candidates must be free of neurological disorders that may affect job performance. Candidates with epilepsy or seizure disorders must provide evidence of one-year seizure-free history without drug control.

9. **Musculoskeletal Health.** Candidates must be free of musculosketetal defects, deformities, or disorders that may affect job performance. Functional use of the arms, hands, legs, feet, and back must be demonstrable at the examination. Candidates will be asked to demonstrate physical fitness through tests of strength, agility, flexibility, and endurance.

10. **Hernia.** Candidates must be free of abdominal and inguinal hernia that would interfere with job performance.

11. **Blood/Vascular Health.** Candidates must be free of blood or vascular disorders that would interfere with the performance of duties. Candidates with uncontrolled high blood pressure will be disqualified unless it is remediable.

12. **Mental Health.** Candidates must be free of mental illness, serious emotional disturbances or nervous disorders, alcoholism, and drug dependence or abuse.

13. **General Medical Statement.** Candidates must be free of any medical and/or nervous condition that would jeopardize the safety and health of others. Candidates with communicable diseases will be disqualified unless they are remediable.

FORMULATION OF MEDICAL REQUIREMENTS FROM ANOTHER STATE POLICE DEPARTMENT

The duties of these positions involve physical exertion under rigorous environmental conditions; irregular and protracted hours of work; patrol duties on foot, in motor vehicles, and in aircraft; and participation in physical training. Applicants must be in sound physical condition and of good muscular development.

Vision

■ Binocular vision is required and must test 20/40 (Snellen) without corrective lenses,

■ Uncorrected vision must test at least 20/70 in each eye, although some agencies limit this to 20/50,

■ Vision in each eye must be corrected to 20/20 (again, some agencies permit vision to be corrected to 20/30, using soft contact lenses),

■ Near vision, corrected or uncorrected, must be sufficient to read Jaeger Type 2 at 14 inches, and

■ Ability to distinguish basic colors by pseudoisochromatic plate test (missing no more than four plates) is required, as is normal peripheral vision.

Hearing

▨ Without using a hearing aid, the applicant must be able to hear the whispered voice at 15 feet with each ear; or

▨ Using an audiometer for measurement, there should be no loss of 30 or more decibels in each ear at the 500, 1000, and 2000 levels.

Speech

▨ Diseases or conditions resulting in indistinct speech are disqualifying.

Respiratory System

▨ Any chronic disease or condition affecting the respiratory system that would impair the full performance of duties of the position is disqualifying; e.g., conditions that result in reduced pulmonary function, shortness or breath, or painful respiration.

Cardiovascular System

The following conditions are disqualifying:

▨ Organic heart disease (compensated or not),

▨ Hypertension with repeated readings that exceed 150 systolic and 90 diastolic without medication, and

▨ Symptomatic peripheral vascular disease and severe varicose veins.

Gastrointestinal System

▨ Chronic symptomatic diseases or conditions of the gastrointestinal tract are disqualifying.

▨ Conditions requiring special diets or medications are disqualifying.

Endocrine System

▨ Any history of a systemic metabolic disease, such as diabetes or gout, is disqualifying.

Genitourinary Disorders

▨ Chronic symptomatic diseases or conditions of the genitourinary tract are disqualifying.

Hernias

▨ Inguinal and femoral hernias with or without the use of a truss are disqualifying. Other hernias are disqualifying if they interfere with performance of the duties of the position.

Nervous System

▨ Applicants must possess emotional and mental stability with no history of a basic personality disorder.

▨ Applicants with a history of epilepsy or convulsive disorder must have been seizure-free for the past two years without medication.

▨ Any neurological disorder with resulting decreased neurological or muscular function is disqualifying.

MISCELLANEOUS

Though not mentioned specifically above, any other disease or condition that interferes with the full performance of duties is also grounds for medical rejection. Before entrance on duty, all applicants must undergo a pre-employment medical examination and be medically suitable to perform the full duties of the position efficiently and without hazard to themselves and others. Failure to meet any one of the required medical qualifications will be disqualifying for appointment. These standards are considered minimum standards and will not be waived in any case. Applicants found to have a correctable condition may be restored to any existing list of eligibles for further consideration for appointment when the disqualifying condition has been satisfactorily corrected or eliminated.

PHYSICAL PERFORMANCE TESTS

The physical performance requirements for all police officers are very similar. All police officers must be able to jump in an instant, must be able to move very quickly, must be strong, must have the stamina to maintain speed and strength for a long time, and must be able to continue physically stressful activity at a high level while withstanding discomfort and pain. The ideal police officer is "Superman." The actual police officer does well to approach those qualities.

While police departments have similar physical performance requirements, they tend to measure fitness in many different ways. Three different police officer physical fitness tests follow. Read them through and note the variations. Try each out to the extent that you can without the actual testing course. See how you do. You may need to get yourself into a regular bodybuilding routine some time before you are called for examination. Strength and fitness cannot be it developed overnight. You will need to work yourself up to par over a long period. Set up a program and get started right away. You will not be called for a physical fitness test until after you have passed the written examination and until there is some possibility that your place on the list will soon be reached. The hiring process moves along slowly, but it does move. You have time, but not that much time. Start now.

A TYPICAL QUALIFYING PHYSICAL FITNESS TEST FOR POLICE OFFICER

Instructions for Candidates

These subtests are electronically timed by your stepping on the start mat and the finish mat.

Stair Climb/Restrain: (One Trial)
(Maximum Time Allowed: 2 Minutes)

In this subtest, you will be expected to run up 3 flights of stairs, down 1 flight, push and pull a box 5 times, and run 5 feet to the finish line.

- On the signal GO, step on the start mat, run up the stairs on your right, and continue up to the landing on the third floor.

- Both feet must be placed on the landing.

- Run quickly down one flight of stairs and into the lobby.

- Grab the box and pull it towards you until the front of the box reaches the tape on the floor.

- Now push it back to its starting position.

- Repeat 4 more times as the examiner announces the count.

- After the last trip, turn RIGHT and step on the finish mat.

Dummy Drag: (Two Trials)
(Maximum Time Allowed: 1 Minute)

In this subtest, you will be expected to drag a dummy 30 feet.

- Step on the start mat.

- Grab the dummy under the shoulders.

- Holding the dummy in this position, move backwards around the traffic cone set 15 feet away and return.

- Place the dummy EXACTLY as you found it in the starting position.

- Step on the finish mat.

Wall Climb/Obstacle Run: (Two Trials)
(Maximum Time Allowed: 1 Minute)

In this subtest, you will be expected to go over the 5-foot wall and continue through the obstacle run.

- Step on the start mat.

- Run to the wall and go over. You are NOT allowed to use the support bars.

- Follow the tape on the floor around the cones.

- If you miss a cone or go around it the wrong way, you must go back and go around the cone CORRECTLY.

- If you knock a cone over, you must STOP and set it up before you continue.

- Step on the finish mat.

ANOTHER PHYSICAL FITNESS TEST

Medical evidence to allow participation in the physical fitness test may be required, and the Department of Personnel reserves the right to exclude from the physical test any eligibles who, upon examination of such evidence, are apparently medically unfit. Eligibles will take the physical fitness test at their own risk of injury, although efforts will be made to safeguard them.

Candidates must complete the entire course consisting of seven events in not more than *65 seconds*.

Candidates who do not successfully complete events 3, 5, and 6 will fail the test.

Description of Events

1. Run up approximately 40 steps.

2. Run approximately 40 yards, following a designated path, including at least four 90-degree turns, to a sandbag.

3. Push the sandbag, weighing approximately 100 pounds, forward a distance of approximately 5 yards and then back to its original position. (Failure to meet all of the conditions for this event will result in failure of the test as a whole.)

4. Run approximately 10 yards to a dummy, weighing approximately 110 pounds, which is hanging with its lowest point approximately 3 feet above the floor.

5. Raise the dummy so as to lift the attached ring off the metal pipe. Allow the dummy to slide onto the floor or place it on the floor. *You must not drop it or throw it down.* (Failure to meet all of the conditions for this event will result in failure of the test as a whole.)

6. Step up approximately 18 inches and walk across a 12-foot beam by placing one foot in front of the other until you reach the other end. (You must be in control at all times, and falling off the beam will result in failure of the test as a whole.)

7. Run approximately 10 yards to the finish line.

Candidates who fail the test on their first trial will be allowed a second trial on the same date after a rest period.

Candidates who do not successfully complete all the events in their proper sequence will fail the test.

ONE MORE PHYSICAL FITNESS TEST, VERY DIFFERENT IN STYLE

The candidates who qualify on the medical examination will be required to pass the qualifying physical fitness test. A total score of twenty is required for passing this test; the scores attained on the five individual tests are added together to obtain your final score.

Test I: Trunk Flexion Test (Three Chances)

Candidates will assume a sitting position on the floor with the legs extended at right angles to a line drawn on the floor. The heels should touch the near edge of the line and be 5 inches apart. The candidate should slowly reach with both hands as far forward as possible on a yardstick that is placed between the legs with the 15-inch mark resting on the near edge of the heel line. The score is the most distant point (in inches) reached on the yardstick with fingertips.

Rating	Trunk Flexion (Inches)	Points
Excellent	22 and over	6
Good	20–21	5
Average	14–19	4
Fair	12–13	3
Poor	10–11	2
Very Poor	9 and under	1

Test II: Hand Grip Strength Test (Three Chances)

The candidate places the dynamometer (hand grip tester) at the side and, without touching the body with any part of the arm, hand, or the dynamometer, should grip the dynamometer as hard as possible in one quick movement. The best of the three tries will be recorded.

Rating	Hand Grip in Kg.	Points
Excellent	65 and above	6
Good	57–64	5
Average	45–56	4
Fair	37–44	3
Poor	30–36	2
Very Poor	29 and under	1

Test III: Standing Broad Jump (Three Chances)

Candidates will be permitted three chances in consecutive order, and the longest distance will be credited. Candidates will be required to jump from a standing position, both feet together. Distance of jump will be recorded from starting point to back of heels. It is each candidate's responsibility to have a nonskid surface on the soles of his or her sneakers.

Rating	Distance	Points
Excellent	7'10" or better	6
Good	7'0" to 7'9"	5
Average	6'1" to 6'11"	4
Fair	5'6" to 6'0"	3
Poor	5'0" to 5'5"	2
Very Poor	Less than 5' 1	1

Test IV: One-Minute Sit-Up Test

The candidate will start by lying on the back with the knees bent so that the heels are about 18 inches away from the buttocks. An examiner will hold the ankles to give support. The candidate will then perform as many correct sit-ups (elbows alternately touching the opposite knee) as possible within a 1-minute period. The candidate should return to the starting position (back to floor) between sit-ups.

Rating	Sit-Ups in 1 Minute	Points
Excellent	35	6
Good	30–34	5
Average	20–29	4
Fair	15–19	3
Poor	10–14	2
Very Poor	9 and under	1

Test V: Three-Minute Step Test

The candidate will step for 3 minutes on a 1-inch bench at a rate of twenty-four steps per minute. The time will be maintained by a metronome. Immediately after the 3 minutes of stepping, the subject will sit down and relax without talking. A 60-second heart rate count is taken starting 5 seconds after the completion of stepping.

Rating	Pulse	Points
Excellent	75–84	6
Good	85–94	5
Average	95–119	4
Fair	120–129	3
Poor	130–139	2
Very Poor	Over 140	1

SLIDING SCALE STANDARDS

The Americans with Disabilities Act requires that age not be a consideration in hiring except where youth, or maturity, is a bona fide qualification for performance of the job. The federal government has established 37 as the highest age at which persons can and may effectively enter certain federal law enforcement positions. In order to establish an age-based hiring limit, each jurisdiction must justify the age it has chosen. At this time, not all guidelines are clear. Each jurisdiction makes its own interpretation of the requirements of the Americans with Disabilities Act, and its interpretation remains in effect until challenged and overturned by a court of law. Some states have chosen to take the Act at face value and have done away with upper age limits altogether.

When states, or jurisdictions within those states, discard upper age limits, they open themselves to new complications. According to the U.S. Justice Department, physical fitness standards that are the same for everyone violate the Americans with Disabilities Act. In response to this determination, many states have relaxed the physical fitness requirements for state police officers. The following is a recently announced Physical Fitness Screening Test that takes into consideration both age and sex.

PHYSICAL FITNESS SCREENING TEST

Candidate will go from Stations I through IV in order. Each station is pass/fail. Candidate must pass each station in order to proceed to the next station. Candidate will be allowed up to 3 minutes' rest between stations. Once a station is started, it must be completed according to protocol. See the chart below:

Station I:

Sit-up—Candidate lies flat on the back, knees bent, heels flat on the floor, fingers interlaced behind the head. Monitor holds the feet down firmly. In the up position, candidate should touch elbows to knees and return with shoulder blades touching floor. To pass this component, candidate must complete the requisite number of correct sit-ups in one minute.

Station II:

Flex—Candidate removes shoes and places feet squarely against box with feet no wider than 8 inches apart. Toes are pointed directly toward ceiling, knees remain extended throughout test. With hands placed one on top of the other, candidate leans forward without lunging or bobbing and reaches as far down the yardstick as possible. The hands must stay together and the stretch must be held for one second. Three attempts are allowed with the best of three recorded to the nearest $\frac{1}{4}$ inch to determine whether the candidate passed/failed.

Station III:

Bench—Monitor loads weights to $\frac{1}{2}$ of candidate-required weight. Candidate is permitted to "press" this weight once. Monitor increases weight to $\frac{2}{3}$ of candidate-required weight. Candidate is permitted to "press" this weight once. The required test weight is then loaded. The candidate has up to four (4) attempts to "press" required (maximum) weight. In order to pass, <u>buttocks must remain on the bench</u>. Candidate will be allowed up to 2 minutes' rest between each "press." (Universal Bench Press Equipment)

Station IV:

1.5-Mile Run—Candidate must be successful on Stations I, II and III in order to participate in Station IV. It will be administered on a track. Candidate will be informed of his/her lap time during the test.

SCORING CHART

AGE/SEX		TEST		
MALE	SIT-UP	FLEX	BENCH	1.5 MI RUN
20–29	38	16.5	99	12.51
30–39	35	15.5	88	13.36
40–49	29	14.3	80	14.29
50–59	24	13.3	71	15.26
60+	19	12.5	66	16.43
FEMALE				
20–29	32	19.3	59	15.26
30–39	25	18.3	53	15.57
40–49	20	17.3	50	16.58
50–59	14	16.8	44	17.54
60+	6	15.5	43	18.44

THE BACKGROUND CHECK

The police officer is in a position of public trust. He or she must be deserving of that trust. The police department must feel very certain that the police officer will not use his or her position for personal gain, will not use it to harass individuals or groups that he or she dislikes, will not be easily corrupted, and will not take advantage of privileged knowledge. It is for this reason that the background check is such an important part of the police selection process. The background check is a time-consuming process. Therefore, the police personnel office will not initiate the background check until an applicant appears to be qualified in nearly every way; that is, the background check occurs after the written test, physical performance test, and full medical examination.

The standard predictor of future behavior is past behavior. The police department must find out how you have behaved in the past. It will do this by first having you fill out a questionnaire. As with the medical questionnaire, there is no point in lying or cheating. You will be found out and will be disqualified. State the facts clearly. Explain fully and factually.

If you have a totally clean record and face no problems in your personal or family life, then you need have no concern about the background check. Fill in the blanks. List references, and inform those people whose names you have given, so that they are not upset when they are contacted by the police.

Most people have something in their backgrounds that can spark more inquiry. The problem may be financial: If you are strapped for money, the police department may fear that you might be corruptible. The problem may be marital: The police department may worry that you will be distracted. The problem may be one of frequent job changes: The police department questions your stability and the value of investing in your training. The problem may be one of poor credit: Are you responsible and reliable? Or the problem may be one of a brush with the law, minor or major. Most minor infractions can be explained at an interview; reassure the interviewer that these were youthful indiscretions unlikely to recur. Arrests for felonies, and, worse still, convictions, present greater obstacles. It may be wise to consult an attorney who specializes in expunging criminal records to see what can be done to clear your name. Some offenses are absolutely disqualifying. You may as well know ahead of time and take all possible steps to make yourself employable by the police department.

A felony record needs the service of an attorney. So might multiple misdemeanor convictions. You can help yourself in many other situations. If you have a poor credit rating, pay up and have your rating upgraded. If you are behind on alimony payments, catch up. If you have an unanswered summons, go to court and answer it. Pay your parking tickets. Even if these past problems turn up in the background check, your positive attitude in clearing them up will be in your favor.

Be sure that you are able to document any claims you make with reference to diplomas, degrees, and honors. You may have to produce these at an interview. Likewise, be certain that you understand the nature and gravity of the problems in your background. Be prepared to admit that you misbehaved and to reassure the examiners that you have matured into a responsible citizen.

THE PSYCHOLOGICAL EVALUATION

THE PURPOSE OF THE PSYCHOLOGICAL EVALUATION

Some states subject all police officer candidates to a psychological evaluation before appointment; others, because of the expense involved, limit psychological evaluations to those cases where there are signs that one might be necessary. However, in all cases the sole purpose of a psychological evaluation is to determine the candidate's mental fitness for performing the specific duties of a police officer. The evaluation is not concerned with other aspects of mental well-being. In fact, because of this exclusive focus on police work, a candidate might be judged psychologically unfit to be a police officer even if he or she is perfectly suited for other types of employment.

What makes police work so different from other occupations? Soon after orientation and the usual training at the police academy, the police officer begins functioning more or less independently. Although the officer functions under supervision, that supervision is present only periodically, and although the officer should be guided by the department's rules of procedure, many times the officer will be thrust into situations where immediate action is required to save lives or protect property. For example, the officer who encounters a pregnant woman about to give birth must take decisive action at once. In such situations, there is no time to consult the rules of procedure. The officer must do whatever is necessary right away.

Another crucial difference is that the police officer carries a gun as part of the job. Prudent use of this weapon requires not only conformity to the rules of procedure but also a good sense of police judgment. The officer who must decide in an emergency whether to use that gun must have a very high degree of psychological stability.

Psychological evaluations of police officer candidates are usually conducted by a psychologist or psychiatrist who is trained to detect signs of deficiencies that could interfere with the proper performance of police work. The job is twofold: to look for signs of potential trouble and to evaluate the sincerity of the candidate. For example, consider the possible responses when the psychologist asks, "Why do you want to become a police officer?" A proper response would be: "I want a career in public service, and I feel that effective law enforcement will make for a better society for my children and eventually for my grandchildren." There is nothing wrong with this response. The only thing to be judged is the sincerity of the candidate. Now look at the following response to the same question: "I have always liked uniforms. They bring respect and admiration, and they permit you to perform your duties without interference." Something is wrong here. Or consider this response: "I hate criminals. They take advantage of the weak and elderly. They are cowards, and I want to do everything I can to eliminate them." This intense hatred may indicate the need for further investigation of this candidate's psychological stability.

TYPICAL EVALUATION QUESTIONS

The questions that you will be asked will, for the most part, be quite predictable. The majority of them will be based on your responses to application forms and other papers that you have been required to file. The psychologist will ask you to amplify or to explain the personal data that you listed on those papers. Sometimes you will be asked to describe your feelings about events that happened to you. Also, as a way of encouraging you to talk, you may be asked more open-ended questions about your personal likes, dislikes, or emotions.

You may also be asked your opinion about what you might do in a hypothetical police work situation, but such questions are unlikely to form the bulk of the evaluation. In this case, the psychologist is not testing your knowledge of police procedures but only your ability to make reasoned judgments and to avoid rash behavior. Because most of the questions you will be asked are predictable, it is relatively easy to prepare answers for them. Begin your preparation by looking over the application forms that you filled out and any other papers that you were required to file. You should be able to pick out the points that a psychologist will want to clarify or explain.

Typical questions you might encounter include the following:

- Why did you choose your area of concentration in school?

- What particularly interests you about that subject?

- Why did you transfer from school x to school y?

- How did you get the job with _____?

- Which of the duties described in your second job did you like best? Which least? Why?

- What did you do during the nine months between your second and third jobs?

- Explain the circumstances of your leaving a particular job.

- Please clarify: armed forces service, arrest record, hospitalization record, etc., as applicable.

Other questions are much like those asked at a routine job interview. They can be anticipated and prepared for as well.

- Why do you want to leave the kind of work you are doing now?

- Why do you want to be a state trooper?

- How does your family feel about your becoming a state police officer?

- What do you do in your leisure time?

- Do you have a hobby? What is it? What do you particularly like about your hobby?

- What is your favorite sport? Would you rather play or watch?

- How do you react to criticism? If you think the criticism is reasonable? If you consider the criticism unwarranted?

- What is your pet peeve?

■ What are your greatest strengths? Weaknesses?

■ What could make you lose your temper?

■ Of what accomplishment in your life are you most proud?

■ What act do you regret?

■ If you could start over, what would you do differently?

■ What traits do you value in a coworker? In a friend?

■ What makes you think you would make a good state police officer?

Still other questions may be more specific to police work. You should have prepared answers to:

■ How much sleep do you need?

■ Are you afraid of heights?

■ What is your attitude toward working irregular hours?

■ Do you prefer working alone or on a team?

■ Are you afraid of dying?

■ What would you do with the rest of your life if your legs were crippled in an injury?

■ How do you deal with panic? Your own? That of others?

■ What is your attitude toward smoking? Drinking? Playboy magazine? Gambling?

■ What is your favorite TV program? How do you feel about watching the news? Sports? Classical drama? Rock music? Opera? Game shows?

Now make a list of your own. The variety of evaluation questions is endless but most can be answered with ease. Preparation makes the whole process much more pleasant and less frightening.

There is one question that strikes terror into the heart of nearly every candidate for police officer or any other job. This question is likely to be the first and, unless you are prepared for it, may well throw you off guard. The question is "Tell me about yourself." For this question you should have a prepared script (in your head, not in your hand). Think well ahead of time about what you want to tell. What could the psychologist be interested in? This question is not seeking information about your birth weight nor about your food preferences. The psychologist wants you to tell about yourself with relation to your interest in and qualifications for police work. Think of how to describe yourself with this goal in mind. What information puts you into a good light with reference to the work for which you are applying? Organize your presentation. Then analyze what you plan to say. What is a psychologist likely to pick up on? To what questions will your answer lead? You must prepare to answer these questions to which you have opened yourself.

Toward the end of the evaluation, the psychologist will most likely ask if you have any questions. You undoubtedly will have had some before hand and should have come prepared to ask them. If all of your questions have been answered in the course of the evaluation, you may tell this to the psychologist. If not, or if the evaluation has raised new questions in your mind, by all means ask them. The evaluation should serve for your benefit; it is not just to serve the purposes of the Police Department.

The invitation of your questions tends to be the signal that the evaluation is nearly over. The psychologist is satisfied that he or she has gathered enough information. The time allotted to you is up. Be alert for the cues. Do not spoil the good impression you have made by trying to prolong the evaluation.

SHOULD YOU REVEAL PERSONAL OPINIONS AND FEELINGS?

The psychologist does not expect candidates to be devoid of personal feelings. After all, everyone has likes and dislikes. However, the mature, psychologically stable person is able to keep those feelings from interfering with the performance of job duties. The police office will encounter a very wide variety of people on the job. Some the officer may find personally likable; others may be unlikable, even downright unpleasant. However, whatever the officer's true feelings about the persons encountered, he or she must serve those individuals in an effective manner or serious repercussions—even loss of life—may result. This type of behavior takes mental maturity and stability, qualities every officer must possess. It is these qualities that the psychologist is looking for at the evaluation, not an absence of personal feelings. The successful candidate does not have to like everyone he or she meets. What is important is the ability to control personal feelings in order to function effectively.

Sometimes during an evaluation a candidate will express "extreme" views on certain subjects. Unlike typical opinions or feelings, these may indeed be cause for disqualification. An obvious example is a display of unreasonable dislike for people from a particular ethnic or religious background. To the psychologist, this is a sure sign of trouble. The candidate who says, "People from ethnic group X are always the ones who commit the violent crimes," will never be appointed a state police officer.

SHOULD YOU VOLUNTEER INFORMATION?

One very important point to remember at the evaluation is to limit your responses to what is asked. An evaluation session of this type is one of the very few opportunities most people have to reveal their true inner selves to others. The psychologist knows this and will often encourage the person being evaluated to talk freely and openly about personal matters and opinions. An unthinking candidate may use this opportunity to bring up matters that ordinarily he or she would never discuss. The talkative candidate might even know that he or she is getting in too deep but may be unable to refrain from continuing. The psychologist will encourage this type of individual to talk at length in order to reveal personal matters that will indicate the level of the candidate's psychological stability.

One device that psychologists use to make candidates keep talking is to assume a facial expression that indicates further explanation is expected. It is very important not to respond to this suggestion! If you do, you are likely to say things that can only be harmful to you. Try to be satisfied with your original response and have the maturity to stand by it no matter what expression you see on the psychologist's face. Display a sense of self-assurance that convinces the psychologist that you are satisfied with your answers.

HOW TO EXPLAIN PROBLEM INCIDENTS IN YOUR PAST

One concern of many police officer candidates is how to handle questions about problem incidents in their past. More than a few candidates have at some time—usually in their youth—gotten into trouble in some incident involving property damage or even personal injury to others. Such incidents almost always come to light during the candidate's background check, often through school, court, or military records. If you have such an incident in your past and are questioned about it by the psychologist, the wisest course is to accept full responsibility for it and to attribute it to your youthful immaturity at the time. Claiming that the record is false or giving excuses for your bad behavior is not likely to be regarded favorably. The psychologist is much more apt to respond positively if you accept responsibility and, just as importantly, if you attribute any such incident to an immature outlook that you have now outgrown. One mistake of this type will not necessarily disqualify you if you can convince the psychologist that you have become a fully responsible adult and will never do anything of the kind again.

"PENCIL-AND-PAPER" EVALUATIONS

As part of the psychological evaluation, some jurisdictions use standardized personality tests that you answer by marking a sheet of paper. These tests may contain a hundred or more questions. Your responses help the psychologist determine your specific personality traits. Your answer to any one question by itself usually means very little, but your answers to a group of questions, taken together, will have significance to the psychologist. Your wisest course when taking one of these written personality tests is to give honest, truthful answers. Any attempt to make yourself appear different from the way you really are is not likely to be successful.

KEEP A POSITIVE ATTITUDE

One final word of advice: It is important to approach all psychological evaluations with a positive attitude. Think of the evaluation not as an ordeal that you must endure but rather as an opportunity to prove that you are qualified to become a police officer. In truth, the psychologist will be looking for traits that qualify you, not ones that disqualify you. And if disqualifying evidence exists, it is the psychologist's responsibility to consider every factor before making a negative recommendation. So go into the evaluation with confidence and be prepared to "sell" yourself to the psychologist. You will be given every chance to prove your worth.

EVALUATION CHECKLIST

Here are some valuable points to remember as you prepare for the psychological evaluation.

1. Get a good night's sleep the night before the evaluation.

2. Do not take any medication beforehand to calm yourself. You may be tested for drugs before the evaluation.

3. Dress neatly and conservatively.

4. Be polite to the psychologist or psychiatrist.

5. Respond to all questions honestly and forthrightly.

6. Use as few words as possible to communicate your thoughts. When you have finished answering a question, do not let the psychologist's behavior lead you to think that you have not said enough.

7. Admit responsibility for any youthful indiscretions and attribute them to your immaturity at the time of the incident.

8. Do not permit any deep-seated prejudices to assert themselves. If you can control them during the evaluation, you will be able to control them while performing the duties of a police officer.

9. Most important, be yourself. You're bound to do better than if you pretend to be someone you're not.

APPEALS

A police officer candidate who is marked "not qualified" on the psychological evaluation will be afforded an opportunity to appeal. In most jurisdictions, a notice of disqualification will include information on appeal procedures and on any time limitations.

Because the official disqualification is made by a psychologist or psychiatrist, the best way for the candidate to appeal is to engage another psychologist or psychiatrist to testify on the candidate's behalf. To start preparing the appeal, the candidate should obtain the official notice of the examination, the medical standards on which the evaluation was based, and a document telling the precise reason for the disqualification. If these items are not furnished by the examining agency, the candidate should petition for them at once. If necessary, the candidate should be prepared to resort to the procedures specified in the Freedom of Information Act in order to find out the exact reasons for rejection. This information is crucial to preparing a proper appeal. Any psychological testimony on the candidate's behalf must respond to the reasons given for disqualification. It is not enough for a psychologist to simply assert that the candidate is generally mentally stable. The psychologist must show that the candidate is, in fact, psychologically competent to perform the specific duties of a state police officer.

If you are disqualified as a result of the psychological evaluation, you should certainly consider filing an appeal. Often this kind of show of determination has influenced a hiring jurisdiction to take a chance on a "borderline" candidate. You will find many psychologists and psychiatrists who specialize in helping rejected police officer candidates.

Reading all the applications and weeding out the unqualified ones takes time. Weighing education and experience factors takes time. Administering and scoring of exams takes time. Interviews, medical exams, and physical performance tests take time. Verifying references takes time. And, finally, the vacancies must occur, and the government agency must have the funds to fill the vacancies.

All of this clarifies why you must not leave a job or a job search at any step along the way. Wait until you are offered your government job before you cut other ties. But when you finally do get that job, you will have a good income, many benefits, and job security.

NCAA® MARCH MADNESS®

Cinderellas, Superstars, and Champions from the NCAA Men's Final Four

MARCH MADNESS

An Official NCAA Publication

Copyright © 2004 by Triumph Books

No part of this publication may be reproduced,
stored in a retrieval system, or transmitted,
in any form by any means, electronic, mechanical,
photocopying, or otherwise, without the prior
written permission of the publisher, Triumph Books,
601 S. LaSalle St., Suite 500, Chicago, Illinois 60605.

Library of Congress Control Number 2004109951

This book is available in quantity at special
discounts for your group or organization.

For further information, contact:

Triumph Books
601 South LaSalle Street
Suite 500
Chicago, Illinois 60605
(312) 939-3330
Fax (312) 663-3557

Printed in U.S.A.
ISBN 1-57243-665-4

Design by Rob Wyszkowski

All photos courtesy of Rich Clarkson/NCAA Photos except
where otherwise indicated. Rich Clarkson's photographs from
Final Fours have accounted for many of his 68 *Sports Illustrated* covers.
After photographing seven Olympics, many college and professional
football games, and numerous other sports, he is quick to say that the
Final Four is his favorite event. He now owns his own photography and
publishing company in Denver, Colorado.

CONTENTS

"I NEVER GREW
TIRED OF THE FINAL FOUR
. . . IT'S STILL THE BEST
EVENT THERE IS."

—John Wooden
Former UCLA coach and winner of 10 NCAA Championships

As he leaves the court at the end of his final game in 1971, senior Sidney Wicks thanks coach John Wooden.

THE FINAL FOUR

By John Wooden

THE FINAL FOUR NEVER GOT OLD FOR ME. ONE REASON, I suppose, is that I understood how hard it was to get there. Early in my career at UCLA, I told my old friend Indiana coach Branch McCracken that I was afraid I would never win a championship. The other reason was that every team, every season, was unique. So while I finally grew tired of coaching when I reached the age of 64, I never grew tired of the Final Four.

I'm often asked to name my favorite national championship team. While each of the 10 was special, I would have to say the first and the last. The first, in 1964, because, well, it was the first. Besides that, without any starter taller than 6´5´´, we were the shortest team to win the championship. Early in the year, that team was not expected to be a contender. But we played as well together as a team could play. Without much size, we had to use our quickness. We introduced the 2-2-1 fullcourt press to the nation, and, in Keith Erickson, we had the perfect player to play the No. 5, or safety position, in the press.

My last championship team, like the first one, was not expected to do well. We had lost four starters, including two superstars in Bill Walton and Keith Wilkes, from the 1974 team that had lost to North Carolina State in the national semifinals. David Meyers was the only returning starter. But we improved as the season went along. To do the unexpected is sometimes more exciting than doing the expected.

There were special moments between those first and last championships. At the end of our 68–62 win over Villanova in the 1971 championship game, a photographer, Rich Clarkson of *Sports Illustrated*, took a picture of Sidney Wicks and me that I particularly liked. It was taken at the end of the game. We had it won and we were shooting free throws. During a timeout, I told the players, "When the game's over, let's keep our cool and not be foolish." I wanted them to get the nets, but I didn't believe in any excessive exuberance.

When we broke the huddle, Wicks came over to shake my hand. In the Astrodome, the benches were below the floor, so I had to look up at him. He leaned over and said, "Coach, congratulations for another championship." Then he left, but he turned around and came back. Leaning down again, he said, "Coach, you're really sumpin'!" That brought tears to my eyes. Only a week earlier, I had disciplined him for something minor. But the way he said, "sumpin' " . . . I really liked that.

As I said, my final season was special because nobody expected us to do much. In the semifinals, we had a great game against Louisville, which was coached by Denny Crum, one of my former players and assistants. We won, 75–74, in overtime. Neither team deserved to lose, but the proper one did, at least from my standpoint. If a Louisville player hadn't missed a one-and-one at the end of regulation play, our chances would have been just about gone. I was unhappy for Denny because he was, and is, very dear to me.

My decision to retire was very much a spur-of-the-moment thing. Before the game, I would have said that I was going to coach two more years. With what we had coming back and what we had coming in, I knew we had the chance to have outstanding teams. I didn't want to leave the cupboard bare because that would have put extra pressure on whoever succeeded me.

After I visited with Denny following the semifinal, I felt good, but also sorry for him. I hadn't been feeling good at all—I was tired—and my wife, Nell, hadn't been well. "Now," I thought, "I've got to go meet the press." Then I thought, "If this is a bother to me, it's time to get out." So I just went in there and announced it.

That overshadowed our championship game against Kentucky. It turned out to be a hard-fought game, but we won, 92–85. Of all my teams, that one gave me as much pleasure as any. They were absolutely no trouble on or off the court, and that's a nice thing to be able to say about your last team.

In the years since that last game, I've often been asked if I think anybody will ever break our records of 10 titles in 12 years and 7 in a row. Well, if somebody had told you 10 years ago that Lou Gehrig's record of consecutive games played would be broken and that it would be done by a shortstop (Cal Ripken Jr.), you would have said it could never happen. But it did. That's sort of the way I feel about those records. It'll be very difficult, but most records are broken.

I pretty much stopped going to the Final Four after Nell died in 1985. It wasn't that I no longer enjoyed it, because I did. It's just that it wasn't the same without her. Although I returned in 1995, I've been content to watch from afar. It's still the best event there is. I'm just pleased that I was fortunate enough to be a part of it for so many years. ∎

"Early in my career at UCLA, I told my old friend Indiana coach Branch McCracken that I was afraid I would never win a championship."

—*John Wooden*

Introduction

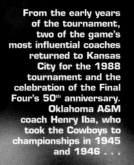

From the early years of the tournament, two of the game's most influential coaches returned to Kansas City for the 1988 tournament and the celebration of the Final Four's 50th anniversary. Oklahoma A&M coach Henry Iba, who took the Cowboys to championships in 1945 and 1946 . . .

. . . and Oregon's Howard Hobson, winner of the first tournament in 1939, were among those saluted. Both have since died.

THE GREAT AMERICAN DREAM

By Billy Reed

The walk from the locker room to the floor isn't a long one. Maybe 100 yards. But during that time, if you're a college basketball coach who has a team good enough to make it to the Final Four of the NCAA tournament, it's the walk of a lifetime.

YOUR PLAYERS GO AHEAD OF YOU, AND WHEN THEY leave the darkness of the tunnel and burst into the bright lights of the cavernous domed stadium, your fans go berserk with pride and excitement. You hear the school band strike up the fight song. And then here you are, moving as if on a cloud. Your fans roar and call your name. Maybe you smile and wave, maybe you don't. Later you won't remember. All you know is that you have arrived at the pinnacle of the sport that has been your life since you were a kid, shooting hoops in the driveway or on the playground. "The walk onto the floor," former Marquette coach Al McGuire once said. "Savor it. It's the best. You're there!"

It never gets old, this walk on the last Saturday of the college season. It doesn't make any difference how many times a coach makes it. That's because it's so doggoned hard to get there. As college basketball has expanded into a truly national game, parity has become as much a part of every season as the slam dunk and the three-point jumper.

Every year new programs jump up to challenge the perennial contenders—and every year the early tournament rounds are riddled with stunning upsets that have fans from coast-to-coast ripping up their office-pool bracket sheets. Since the end of the surreal UCLA dynasty (10 titles in 12 years) in 1975, only Duke, in 1991 and 1992, has achieved back-to-back championships.

Heading into the new millennium, no sport owns a month the way the NCAA basketball tournament owns March. It begins with the conference tournaments, which theoretically give almost every member of Division I a chance to play its way into the 65-team field. On what has become known as "Selection Sunday," the field, seedings, and pairings are announced on CBS, touching off a wild scramble for airline,

hotel, and rental-car reservations. In the tournament's formative years, teams were assigned to regions on a geographical basis. But as the tournament expanded, geographical considerations became virtually nonexistent. The committee's goal is to properly seed the teams based on performance, even if it means, say, sending UCLA to Orlando or Syracuse to San Jose.

After the first and second rounds, the 16 survivors advance to four regionals. One of the regionals usually is held at the site of the next year's Final Four, giving the NCAA staff and the local organizing committee an opportunity to hold a sort of "trial run." At this stage of the tournament, there's almost no such thing as an upset because everybody is a legitimate contender. With the Final Four so close, emotions elevate the quality of play. The best example came in the final of the 1992 East Regional, when Duke needed a last-second, miraculous turn-around jumper by Christian Laettner in overtime to subdue Kentucky, 104–103, in Philadelphia. Some veteran observers consider it to be the finest college game ever.

Then, finally, comes the Final Four.

When the quartet of regional champions arrive under the same roof with their pom-pom girls, cheerleaders, pep bands, fans, and mascots, the college game reaches its pinnacle. Everywhere you look, hopes and dreams and backgrounds and traditions are colliding in a riot of noise and color. For a few hours, America seems to grind to a halt, just as it used to do in the long-gone days when baseball's World Series was unchallenged as the nation's premier sporting event. Now, arguably, the Final Four has replaced the World Series. It has fans from every state, not to mention every social and economic class. To enable more fans to

It's a heart-breaking cycle, this thing we call college basketball. At the start of every season, there are a lot of coaches who talk the talk. But on the last Saturday, only the most fortunate get to walk that emotional walk.

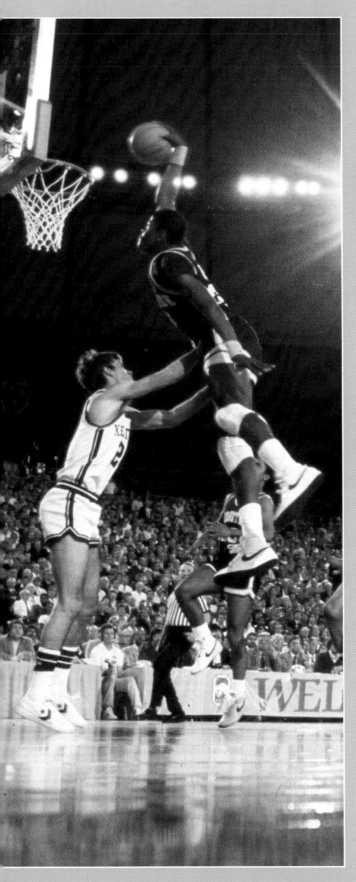

participate in the event, the tournament committee mandated that it would be held every year in a domed stadium. Nevertheless, year after year the NCAA receives far more requests for tickets than it can possibly fill.

"The Final Four is now, in my opinion, the major sporting event of the year," said former Kentucky Athletics Director C. M. Newton, who chaired the tournament committee from 1997 through 1999. "A lot of sports have one-day events such as the Kentucky Derby or the Super Bowl, but this is a national championship that runs over three weeks. For those of us who remember the days when the tournament was mainly a regional thing and didn't even have a national TV deal for the Final Four, the growth has been staggering."

Although college basketball had been around since Dr. James Naismith nailed up his peach basket at Springfield College before the turn of the 20th century, there was no recognized national championship until 1939, when the National Coaches Association staged the inaugural edition of what was to become the NCAA tournament. As early as March 1945, a whopping crowd of 18,035 pushed through the turnstiles at Madison Square Garden in New York City to see Oklahoma A&M and its 7´ center Bob "Foothills" Kurland defeat New York University for the NCAA title. By 1949, the tournament celebrated its 10th anniversary with 66,077 total attendance and a $60,848 net profit.

In 1951 the NCAA made what was to be a fateful decision, hiring Walter Byers, then only 29 years old, as its first executive director. Byers had attended Rice and Iowa before enlisting in World War II. After being discharged, he worked a few years for United Press International before being hired in 1947 to assist Kenneth L. "Tug" Wilson, then commissioner of the Big Ten and secretary-treasurer of the NCAA. When the NCAA broke away from the Big Ten and named Byers as its executive director, he moved headquarters to Kansas City. In his first year, the basketball tournament field was doubled to 16 teams.

Nevertheless, the NIT, held at Madison Square Garden, was regarded as a more prestigious postseason championship. But then came the shocking news that in the late forties a number of college games had been "fixed" by gamblers who paid certain players to see to it that their team failed to get above the gambling point spread in certain games. Since most of the tainted games had taken place in the Garden, the point-shaving scandal effectively killed the NIT and opened the way for the NCAA to become the postseason tournament of choice.

The tournament's growth was slow but steady. In 1954 the first telecast of a championship game found only a handful of East Coast stations showing Tom Gola's virtuoso performance in leading La Salle to victory over Bradley. Two

years later, 6´9´´ Bill Russell made "intimidation" a part of the game's vocabulary and established the black players' growing influence by leading San Francisco to its second consecutive title.

In the 1957 title game in Kansas City, unbeaten North Carolina's triple-overtime victory over Kansas and its 7´ sophomore, Wilt Chamberlain, focused unprecedented national attention on the college game. Considering the cast of characters and the stakes, this has to be regarded as the best game ever.

The game's greatest dynasty began in 1964 when guards Walt Hazzard and Gail Goodrich led UCLA to its first title. Under coach John Wooden, a former All-American at Purdue, the Bruins captured 10 titles in 12 years, including 7 in a row from 1967 to 1973. The run was broken only by Texas Western, which in 1966 became the first team with an all-black starting lineup to win the title, and N.C. State, which upset the Bruins in the 1974 semifinals.

The Final Four made its debut in a domed stadium, the Houston Astrodome, in 1971. It didn't return to a dome until 1982, which was especially unfortunate in 1979, the year that Earvin "Magic" Johnson led Michigan State against Larry Bird's unbeaten Indiana State team in the title game at the Salt Palace in Salt Lake City. Although neither the game (State won, 75–64) nor the matchup lived up to expectations, the excitement generated by Johnson and Bird set the tone for the tournament's popularity explosion in the eighties.

As the tournament committee expanded the field from 25 teams to 32, then 48, and finally to its current 65, fans everywhere began discovering what the folks in hoops hotbeds such as North Carolina, Kansas, Kentucky, and Indiana had known for years—namely, that college basketball was as colorful, exciting, beautiful, emotional, and rewarding as a game can get. The tournament turned out to be a ratings bonanza for CBS, the tournament's television partner since 1982. Analyst Billy Packer, who was the point guard for Wake Forest when the Demon Deacons played in the 1962 Final Four, developed into Mr. March for millions of television viewers. Also profiting enormously from the college hoops explosion was ESPN, a cable network that was founded in 1979. Where Packer became known for his cogent analysis of the game's Xs and Os, his counterpart on ESPN was a bald, one-eyed former coach (he took Detroit to the 1977 Mideast Regional) who shouted his love for the game incessantly, much to the delight—or consternation—of the viewing public. Or, as Dick Vitale himself might put it in that modest way of his, "When it comes to college hoops, I'm a P-T-P'er, ba-bee!"

Today the Final Four is a four-day carnival that features everything from banquets to conventions to a street fair for

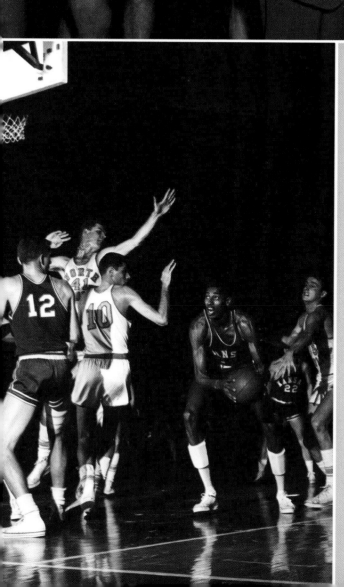

the fans. There are all sorts of ways to measure its popularity, one of the most oft-quoted being the $6 billion that CBS paid to retain television rights to the tournament through the 2012–2013 season. But beyond the glitz, crowds, and money, the event is still about basketball—and the people who play and coach it. The stage is bigger and brighter, but the court is still 94 feet long and the baskets still 10 feet off the floor. And victory usually goes to the team most able to do the little things that don't show up in the boxscore—come up with the loose balls, take the charge, deny easy shots, and find the open man.

For veteran sportswriters, the Final Four is always a sentimental journey—a time to honor the past while celebrating the present. It's impossible to attend a Final Four without remembering Bill Bradley's 58-point performance for Princeton against Wichita State in the 1965 consolation game; the 44-point effort by UCLA's Bill Walton against Memphis State in the 1973 title game; N.C. State coach Jim Valvano, running around the floor in Albuquerque, looking for somebody to hug after his team's upset of Houston in the 1983 title game; and Arizona's gripping overtime win over defending champ Kentucky in the 1997 final game.

Unlike other major sporting events, the Final Four never fails to deliver excitement and drama. Never. It probably has something to do with the unpredictable, improbable nature of college athletes and basketball itself. Some nights the best team doesn't get the bounces. Other nights a team will rise up far above its head, the way Villanova did in 1985 when it upset Georgetown during the title game in Lexington, Kentucky.

How tough is it to make the Final Four?

Well, consider Jim Calhoun of Connecticut. For more than a decade he produced one Top 10 team after another. But every year the Huskies came up short of the Final Four. However, just when it seemed as if Calhoun was destined to remain forever on the list of great coaches who never made it to the big show (Ralph Miller, Lefty Driesell, Uncle Ed Diddle, C. M. Newton, Clair Bee, Ray Mears, Peck Hickman, Bob Boyd, Press Maravich, and Pete Carril, to name a few), the Huskies broke through in 1999 and put Calhoun into the sport's most exclusive club by shocking heavily favored Duke to win the national title.

The walk isn't that long. But getting to it requires years of highs and lows, successes and failures, surprises and disappointments. How many potential championship teams have been ruined by an injury? Thwarted by a bad officiating call? Caught off guard by an opponent playing the game of its life? All a coach can do is suck it up and start over again. ∎

Billy Reed covered his first Final Four in 1967 when sophomore center Lew Alcindor began his three-year championship reign at UCLA. He has been a staff writer at Sports Illustrated, *sports editor of the* Louisville Courier-Journal, *and a columnist for the* Lexington Herald-Leader.

WAR AND PEACE AND THE BARON REIGNS

THE YEAR 1939 WAS HARDLY THE BEST TIME TO begin a new sporting endeavor. Even as America finally was pulling itself out of the throes of the Great Depression because of President Franklin D. Roosevelt's New Deal, war clouds were overtaking Europe. On December 7, 1941, the Japanese attacked Pearl Harbor to plunge the U.S. into World War II.

During the war years, the anxious nation was hungry for entertainment that would divert its attention from the battles in Europe and the Pacific. It was the Big Band era of Glenn Miller, Benny Goodman, and Tommy Dorsey, among others. The teens' heartthrob was a skinny young crooner named Sinatra, and Hollywood was in its heyday with sexy leading men such as Clark Gable and Humphrey Bogart starring with bombshells such as Betty Grable, Lana Turner, and Rita Hayworth.

The only big-time sport as we know it today was major league baseball, and even the national pastime was diluted when many of its stars, including Joe DiMaggio, Ted Williams, and Stan Musial, were called into service. The heavyweight boxing champion, Joe Louis, the renowned "Brown Bomber," also was a soldier who spent his tour of duty fighting exhibition bouts.

From the beginning, the college basketball tournament was truly national in scope. The first champion in 1939 was Oregon, coached by Howard Hobson. Nevertheless, most of the best coaches and teams were to be found either in the East or the Midwest, perhaps because the severe winters created a greater need for an exciting indoor game to help pass the long, cold nights.

When Oklahoma A&M won its back-to-back titles in 1945 and 1946, it was coached by Henry Iba, who tailored his ball-control offense and man-to-man defense to take advantage of 7´ Bob "Foothills" Kurland's size and dominance. But when Kurland graduated, the game came to be dominated by teams that employed a more up-tempo style that emphasized passing, shooting, and ballhandling.

The epitome of this style was found at Kentucky. Its coach, Adolph Rupp, had played for the great Forrest "Phog" Allen at Kansas in the twenties. Allen, in turn, had learned the game directly from its inventor, Dr. James Naismith. When Kentucky's so-called "Fabulous Five" won back-to-back titles in 1948 and 1949, it did so not with size—the tallest starter was 6´7´´—but with speed and skill.

Rupp was a clever, sarcastic individual who ruled through intimidation and fear. To this day, his former players love to tell stories about the man known as "the Baron." When guard Ralph Beard came to Rupp as a freshman and told him he was thinking of transferring to Louisville, Rupp snorted and said, "Well, Ralph, I don't know why you would want to go to that normal school, but I can promise you we don't plan on canceling our schedule." Beard stayed and became a two-time All-American.

At the end of the decade, after his 1949–1950 Kentucky team had suffered a 39-point trashing at the hands of the City College of New York in the final of the National Invitation Tournament, Rupp told his players, "Thanks, boys, you bring me up here and then you embarrass the hell out of me." A member of the Kentucky state legislature proposed that state flags fly at half-mast. ∎

Adolph Rupp

"The tempo of the game began to pick up in the forties. The center jump after every basket had been eliminated, which opened up fast-break opportunities, and the midcourt line and 10-second rule ushered in the press defense."

—Pete Newell

Oregon's Tall Firs returned to Eugene four days after the championship and were met by a crowd of several thousand fans. University President Donald Erb declared the day a school holiday.

1939

THE TALL FIRS

By Earl Luebker

THE TROPHY WAS SOMEWHAT BATTERED AND bruised, in two pieces, when it arrived in Eugene, Oregon, in the spring of 1939. As had happened to so many things that had come into contact with Bobby Anet, it had come out second-best.

The beat-up condition of the trophy, however, did nothing to detract from its significance. It became symbolic of the first NCAA basketball championship. (The first tournament was actually under the auspices of the National Association of Basketball Coaches, with the NCAA taking control the following year.)

Other teams, such as the UCLA Bruins, Kentucky Wildcats, and North Carolina Tar Heels, would come along later to earn their places in the basketball history book. But nobody else could ever lay claim to being the first.

That honor cannot be taken away from coach Howard Hobson and his Oregon Ducks, the "Tall Firs" who beat the Ohio State Buckeyes, 46–33, in Evanston, Illinois, on the night of March 27, 1939.

Just what kind of team was this to come out of the Pacific Northwest and cruise to three relatively easy victories—the smallest margin was the 13 points in the championship game—against college basketball's elite?

For one thing, it was big, at least according to 1939 standards. They might be dubbed the Elfin Elms today, but they were the Tall Firs in 1939.

Urgel "Slim" Wintermute was the giant at 6´8˝ when that was king-sized for centers, not point guards.

"Forwards Laddie Gale and John Dick measured in at around the 6´4˝ mark, maybe a little taller, so it was Wintermute, Gale, and Dick who put the Tall into the nickname. Most teams rarely had any one player with those Herculean dimensions, let alone three," wrote Ken Rappaport in his book, *The Classic: The History of the NCAA Basketball Championships*.

The two guards, Anet at 5´8˝ and Wallace Johansen, came closer to fitting the usual basketball mold of the era and did the job of making the Firs' fast break something special.

The fast break was a vital part of the Tall Firs' game plan. With Wintermute, Dick, and Gale dominating the backboards and Anet and Johansen keeping things under control, the Firs were in business.

"Our fast break was a little unusual in that we looked for it on every possession," Hobson said. "We used it all the time until the opportunity closed. It was a break that we always attempted after we gained possession, with the two guards handling the ball most of the time, the two forwards down ahead, and the center trailing and coming in on the rebound."

Gale explained it further to Rappaport. "I'd call it a controlled fast break," he said. "There was nothing reckless about it. We knew where we were going, and we knew where to expect our teammates to be. When the situation would present itself, we were there. Prior to that, many who used fast breaks would just have five men run down the floor, get a long pass or something, and just throw the ball up."

The Firs however were not just a free-wheeling offensive unit. Dick, in fact, thinks that defense was their strongest point.

Hobson was a bit of a con man when it came to defense. Deceit was part of his game.

Playing against Oklahoma in the Western playoff final in San Francisco, the Firs opened with a zone defense. After a few minutes, a shift to a man-to-man was signaled, but all the Firs continued to play with their hands held high so that Oklahoma continued to take it for a zone defense and worked for outside shots.

The same ploy worked in the title game against Ohio State.

(above) University of Oregon basketball coach Howard Hobson led his team to the first championship by defeating Ohio State in the 1939 final.

(right) The first national championship trophy was presented by Big Ten Commissioner John L. Griffith to Oregon captain Bobby Anet. The Ohio State captain, John Schick, watched with his second-place award. Played before a sellout of 5,500 fans in Northwestern's Patten Gymnasium, it would be the smallest championship crowd.

Ohio State's Schick goes up for two points in the first-ever NCAA championship game.

into the playoffs, they would have won the NCAA title because they were superior to the other teams in the playoffs."

One of Hobson's favorite stories concerning the championship game involves Anet, the sparkplug playmaking guard and captain.

"I talked to Bobby before the game," Hobson recalled. "He was a great team leader and led our fast break. I told Bobby to make Ohio State call the first timeout and not to call any until we were really tired. Ohio State called five timeouts, and we didn't call any.

The 1939 tournament was the start of something big, although there was little indication of such at the time.

"After the game I said to Bobby, 'Why didn't you call a timeout and take a little rest when the game was pretty well in hand?' He said to me, 'You told me not to call a timeout unless we were tired, and hell, we're not tired.' "

Anet was that type of guy, and it figures that he would be the Fir to go flying through the air and hit the trophy sitting on a courtside table. Anet went over the table and clipped off the figure of a basketball player that was on top of the trophy.

Dick said, "When they presented the trophy to us at the end, they had to hold the little figure on top. We had to bring the trophy back home in two pieces and get a jeweler to mend it."

While the Tall Firs played a special kind of basketball, they also had that special name. It was given to them by L. H. Gregory, longtime Portland Oregonian sports columnist.

"Greg had taken to calling the team the 'Alley Cats' when they lost and the 'Bear Cats' when they won," Hobson said. "Fortunately it was his later name that stuck. He used Tall Firs first in a column on March 5, 1938, and it remained with the team from then onward."

The 1939 tournament was the start of something big, although there was little indication of such at the time. That first tournament, sponsored by the NABC, lost $2,531. The NCAA agreed to pick up the tab in return for sponsorship of future tournaments.

"One of the great bargains in sports history," Hobson said. ∎

Hobson took particular pride in the fact that the Firs were home grown. He was a native Oregonian, as were the five starters. Wintermute had attended high school in Longview, Washington, but the other four were Oregon through and through.

Hobson attributed much of his team's success to a grueling 10-game, 22-day trip to New York and back by train. They learned the facts of basketball life on the road.

The Firs won 7 of those 10 games, and Hobson told Rappaport, "Because of playing all through the rest of the

country, we were ready for any kind of officiating on any kind of court." Hobson felt that the first NCAA Tournament was a relative piece of cake for his Tall Firs. They had to work harder against the Washington Huskies and California Bears en route to the Pacific Coast Conference championship than they did in any three of their tournament games—a 56–41 win over Texas, a 55–37 victory over Oklahoma, and the 46–33 triumph over Ohio State.

In his book, *Shooting Ducks: A History of University of Oregon Basketball*, Hobson wrote, "Had the Huskies gotten

Earl Luebker retired as associate editor of the Tacoma News-Tribune *after 37 years, covering Final Fours as sports editor for much of that time. He was a graduate of the University of Oklahoma.*

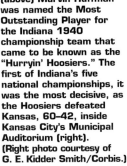

1940

HAIL THOSE HURRYIN' HOOSIERS

By Joe McGuff

THE ONLY THING SCORING A POINT A MINUTE would get you today in college basketball is a lot of one-sided losses. Not so in 1940. Like the dollar, a point went a lot further in those pre-inflationary times.

The Indiana team that defeated Kansas for the NCAA championship that year was considered something of a wonder team because of its offensive ability. Indiana was known as the Hurryin' Hoosiers because of its fiery fast break, and as the point-a-minute team because of its prolific scoring.

As the decade of the forties began, college basketball was just starting to take on the look of the game we know today, with rapid changes taking place on and off the court.

Indiana was one of the forerunners of a new wide-open style of play. The NCAA Tournament and other postseason events were steering the structure of the game in new directions.

The concept of college basketball as a tournament sport was starting to take hold. Ned Irish had established the National Invitation Tournament (NIT) in New York's Madison Square Garden, and Emil Liston had started a small-college tournament in Kansas City.

Surprisingly, the National Association of Basketball Coaches (NABC) was, for the most part, indifferent to starting a tournament, but a few progressive-minded members prevailed, and the first tournament was held on the Northwestern campus. When the 1939 event attracted only limited attention, the coaches asked the NCAA to assume responsibility for future tournaments.

The tournament was looking for both acceptance and financial stability in 1940. It found both in Kansas City. The championship game drew a standing-room-only crowd of ten thousand to the Municipal Auditorium. The tournament, which even turned a profit of $9,523, had taken its first steps toward becoming one of the nation's greatest sporting events.

The changes taking place on the court were equally dramatic. The championship game between Indiana and Kansas generated unusual interest because it matched a leading exponent of the newly developed run-and-shoot game with a team that believed in the fundamentals of the traditional ball-control game.

"All we care about is getting the ball in the enemy basket in the shortest possible time," Branch McCracken said in summing up his philosophy.

The running game suited McCracken's combative personality. He earned three varsity football letters at Indiana even though he supposedly had never seen a football game before arriving on campus. He was recruited as a basketball player from the farming community of Monrovia, Indiana.

Throughout his career, McCracken was an innovator. He was the first coach to break the color line in the Big Ten, he was a pioneer in using air travel, and he was one of the first coaches to recognize the value of television.

Another Hoosier coach, Bobby Knight, would recognize a kindred spirit in McCracken, who drove himself relentlessly, put his players through nonstop two-hour scrimmages, and battled with officials. On one occasion, he became so enraged at an officiating decision that he ran on the court to pursue the official. An assistant coach grabbed him by the coat to restrain him, and he dragged the assistant onto the court with him.

McCracken was especially fond of his 1940 team.

"They could really run and shoot," he said, recalling that championship season. "They were good on defense. All of 'em were real hustlers. They worked all the time and there was no selfishness. That was a team."

Indiana did not win the Big Ten title in 1940 but defeated Purdue, the league champion, twice and was named the conference representative for the NCAA Tournament.

The Hoosiers were not extended on their way to the final. They defeated Springfield (Massachusetts) College,

(above) Marvin Huffman was named the Most Outstanding Player for the Indiana 1940 championship team that came to be known as the "Hurryin' Hoosiers." The first of Indiana's five national championships, it was the most decisive, as the Hoosiers defeated Kansas, 60–42, inside Kansas City's Municipal Auditorium **(right)**. (Right photo courtesy of G. E. Kidder Smith/Corbis.)

Southern California and Everett Dean of Stanford, had an important bearing on the outcome of the title game.

Dean asked McCracken what kind of defense he was going to play, and McCracken told him shifting man-to-man. Barry asked McCracken if he had scouted Kansas, and McCracken said no. Barry recommended a switch to a pressing fullcourt defense, and Dean concurred.

"We pressed them from the moment the ball changed hands," McCracken said later. "It took stamina and condition. It meant high speed for 40 minutes. But it wrecked Kansas' set shots and let us play our fireball game." Indiana also had one other advantage, a canine mascot named Tootsie. The dog, a cross between a fox terrier and a spitz, was brought to Kansas City by 71-year-old Charles P. McNabb, who said the dog had been to seven games and Indiana had won all of them.

Tootsie's record would soon be 8–0. The game started with promise for Kansas, which took a 10–4 lead in the first seven minutes. The Hoosiers, who came into the game lighthearted and confident, called a timeout to reflect on what was going wrong. Guard Marv Huffman said the Hoosiers just looked at each other and didn't say a word.

"We just knew that we weren't playing ball," he said. "We weren't doing the job. We weren't blocking out good and we weren't running fast enough." Huffman said the Hoosiers were determined to go out and do the job right. They did just that, and for all practical purposes the outcome was decided by halftime.

The Kansas City Star recorded the Hoosiers' performance this way: "Scorching the floor with smooth speed and slicing the air with zipping passes, they moved through the Kansas defense for easy setups, dropped spectacular one-handed shots from all angles, and buried longshots from the outside while Allen's lads looked on, powerless to do anything about it."

Kansas was never able to get close in the second half, and Indiana won, 60–42. "We didn't know what to expect because we had never seen Indiana," Engleman recalled later. "The only scouting report we had was a letter from a KU alumnus back there. They hit us with a fast break a little different than anything we had seen." ■

48–24, in the quarterfinals and scored a 39–30 victory over Duquesne in the semifinals.

Kansas possessed good speed but played a more conservative possession game. The Jayhawks were known as the "Pony Express" team, a name that Allen gave them because they were small but fast. The Jayhawks also had exceptional outside shooters in Bill Hogben, Don Ebling, Howard Engleman, and Bob Allen, the coach's son. Dick Harp, who later coached the Jayhawks, played on the team as did Ralph Miller, who later enjoyed a long and distinguished coaching career.

Kansas lost its final conference game at Oklahoma and finished in a three-way tie for the Big Six championship with Oklahoma and Missouri. The three teams met in a playoff. Kansas drew a bye and Oklahoma defeated Missouri, 52–41. Kansas then defeated Oklahoma, 45–39. The Jayhawks gained the fifth district spot by defeating Oklahoma A&M (now Oklahoma State), 45–43, in overtime.

The Jayhawks eliminated Rice, 50–44, in the first round of the NCAA Tournament, but seemingly that was as far as the Jayhawks were going to go. Southern California was the Jayhawks' semifinal opponent and the Trojans were widely regarded as the best team in the country.

The tournament, which even turned a profit of $9,523, had taken its first steps toward becoming one of the nation's greatest sporting events.

"I told 'em USC was great but had a reputation of just playing hard enough to win," Allen noted. "Then I said if they had any ideas about things they wanted to try, go ahead and try 'em, don't look at the bench to see if the old man would approve."

Southern Cal led, 42–41, late in the game, but Engleman hit from the corner with 16 seconds left to put Kansas ahead. The Trojans called a timeout and planned their strategy.

They developed a wedge at the center circle and gave the ball to Jack Morrison, their best outside shooter. He got his shot off, but it hit the back of the rim and bounced away. Astonishingly, the Jayhawks were in the NCAA championship final.

The story is told that a late-night conversation among McCracken and two old coaching friends, Sam Barry of

Joe McGuff was sports editor of The Kansas City Star *for much of his career, which he ended as editor and vice president of the company. He was president of the Baseball Writers of America.*

University of Wisconsin's Charles Epperson (No. 38) and a Washington State player go for the basket during the 1941 NCAA Championship held in Kansas City, Missouri.

1941

"HELL, WE'VE FORGOTTEN HOW TO LOSE"

By Tom Butler

JOE DIMAGGIO AND TED WILLIAMS WERE REVVING up for monumental baseball exploits, and Pearl Harbor was a little more than eight months off when Wisconsin won its only NCAA basketball championship.

The Badgers capped a 20–3 season with a 39–34 victory over Washington State in the NCAA final at Kansas City on March 29, 1941. Basketball hadn't evolved into the free-wheeling game we know today, but Badger fans consistently jammed the Wisconsin Field House to its thirteen thousand capacity during that memorable season.

Wisconsin coach Bud Foster taught a methodical, disciplined brand of basketball that relied on deft passing, tight screens, and sharp cuts. The team was paced by All-American center Gene Englund and deadeye sophomore John Kotz, the first one-hand shooter of prominence in Wisconsin history.

"We played more ball control," Englund said. "We passed the ball and kept the ball because the other team couldn't score while we had the ball."

Kotz was taught to shoot with one hand by his Rhinelander (Wisconsin) High School coach, Russ Leksell, who theorized that everyone has one "dominant" hand and shooting with two hands on the ball resulted in less accuracy. It worked for Kotz. He led Rhinelander to a 20–0 record and the Wisconsin Class A state championship in 1939, scoring 467 of his team's 952 points. His total was just nine points fewer than all Rhinelander opponents combined.

Sophomores played a prominent role as the Badgers charged toward the national championship. Kotz and guard Fred Rehm teamed with seniors Englund and guard Ted Strain and junior forward Charley Epperson in the starting lineup. Reserves included giant center Don Timmerman, sparkplug guard Bob Alwin, and swingman Ed Scheiwe, along with Harlo Scott, Bob Sullivan, Warren Schrage, and Bob Roth.

The Badgers showed little of their championship caliber early that season when they lost three of their first eight games, including the Big Ten opener at Minnesota, 44–27.

"We got waxed, absolutely stomped," said Englund, recalling that opening loss at Minneapolis.

So inept were the Badgers that night that they failed to get a field goal in the second half. Foster expressed disgust afterward. When asked if his team had a chance to finish in

the Big Ten's first division, the coach replied, "Never! Not after that dismal exhibition."

There was little to cheer about. Wisconsin, which had finished with a 5–15 record the year before, ninth (3–9) in the conference, lost to Pittsburgh, 36–34, at Madison and to Marquette, 40–30, in Milwaukee during December.

The Badgers rekindled hope after returning home from Minnesota by defeating Iowa and Purdue, the latter 48–42 in overtime. That launched a 15-game winning streak that culminated with the victory at Kansas City.

"I really think the turning point was the overtime game with Purdue," said Englund, the Big Ten's most valuable player that year. "That's what turned the whole thing around as far as giving us the confidence we needed."

Kotz's three-point play in the waning moments of regulation sent the Purdue game into overtime with the teams deadlocked at 38–38. Baskets by Englund, Kotz, and Alwin in the first two minutes of the extra period sparked the Badgers to victory.

Wisconsin won another overtime game at Northwestern, 48–46, and avenged the loss at Minnesota by trouncing the Gophers, 42–32, at Madison in the final conference game of the season. It gave Foster his second of three Big Ten titles as Badgers coach.

Wisconsin then was chosen to host the NCAA Eastern Regional that included Dartmouth, Pittsburgh, and North Carolina. The tournament featured such standouts as North Carolina's George Glamack, Pitt's Ed Straloski, and Dartmouth's Gus Broberg.

Wisconsin shaded Dartmouth, 51–50, and Pitt knocked off the Tar Heels, 60–59, despite Glamack's 31 points in the opening round. The Badgers earned a trip to the final by avenging their earlier loss to the Panthers, 36–30, before a record crowd of fourteen thousand in the Field House.

The Badgers were cocky and confident heading for their showdown with Washington State. When the Wisconsin party arrived in Chicago on the way to Kansas City, some hometown friends met Scheiwe at the train station, and one hollered, "Good luck! I hope you win in Kansas City!"

The often brash reserve guard shrugged and replied, "Hell, we've forgotten how to lose."

It wasn't that easy, however, against the Cougars. The Badgers rallied from a 23–18 deficit early in the second half

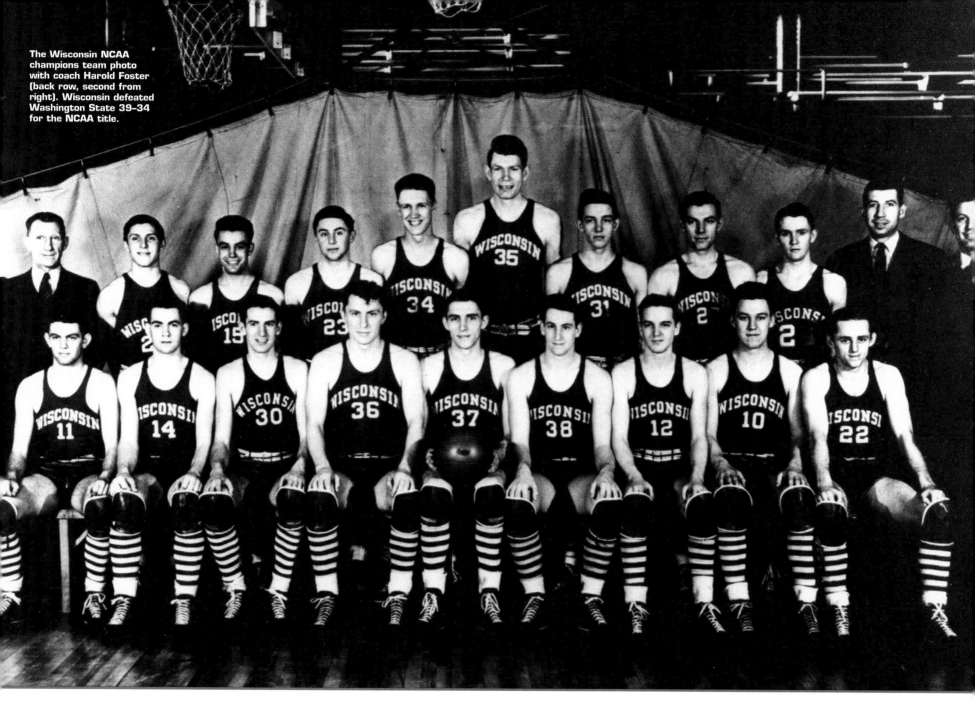

The Wisconsin NCAA champions team photo with coach Harold Foster (back row, second from right). Wisconsin defeated Washington State 39–34 for the NCAA title.

by running off 10 unanswered points, 6 by Kotz, to gain the upper hand.

Washington State featured 6´7˝, 230-pound center Paul Lindman, a big man in that era, who scored 40 points while leading them to victories over Creighton and Arkansas in the Western Regional. The Badgers stymied him without a field goal. He sank three free throws.

Englund contributed 13 points and Kotz 12 to Wisconsin's victory, and the Rhinelander sophomore, who was to earn All-America recognition the next year, was named the tournament's Most Outstanding Player.

Wisconsin relied on teamwork, tenacity, and a knack for working the ball inside consistently for good percentage shots. Cougar guard Kirk Gebert sank 10 field goals, but Wisconsin's persistent defense denied Lindeman the ball in good position—which proved instrumental in the victory.

The Badgers rallied from a 23–18 deficit early in the second half by running off 10 unanswered points, 6 by Kotz, to gain the upper hand.

"We had plays that set up all the guys and we mixed them up," Englund said. "In fact, I'd say that teams we played scouted us enough so they knew exactly what our plays were, but we ran them so well we were able to score anyway. There was no doubt everybody knew what we were going to do."

When the Badgers returned from Kansas City the next night, a crowd estimated by Madison police at between ten thousand and twenty thousand greeted them uproariously at the North Western depot and on the route back to the university campus.

Reflecting on what has transpired since that tournament, Englund said, "To tell you the truth, I don't think I could even play with those kids today. I don't think I have enough ability. I couldn't run fast enough, and playing under the basket, those guys would make mincemeat out of me."

But Englund and his teammates reigned supreme during that magical last season before World War II sent most of them into military service. ∎

Tom Butler covered the University of Wisconsin football and basketball teams for 34 years at the Wisconsin State Journal *before retiring in 1987.*

1942

THOSE LONG-LEGGED, GANGLY INDIANS

By Art Rosenbaum

IN 1942, BASKETBALL WAS A GROWTH INDUSTRY. When Stanford players alighted from the train in Kansas City for the fourth NCAA championship, they were greeted by gasps from a welcoming committee. How could one team have so many tall men—all agile, all coordinated, and all able to pass, rebound, and shoot?

Typically, newspaper accounts at the tournament site always included words like *tall*, *lanky*, *long-legged*, *angular*, and *gangly*, just as West Coast sportswriters had described Stanford all season. They were giants for their time. Center Ed Voss was all of 6´5˝, forward Jim Pollard 6´5˝, guard Howie Dallmar 6´4˝, forward Don Burness 6´3˝, and guard Bill Cowden 6´3˝. Nearly a half century later, they'd all be small guards.

To make the Final Four hardly meant megabucks in 1942. Coach Everett Dean, noted as an innovator of defenses, was also the holder of the exchequer. Stanford's

(above) Stanford's Bill Cowden. (Photo courtesy of AP/Wide World Photos.)

(right) Stanford coach Everett Dean, whose 1942 team beat Dartmouth for the NCAA title. (Photo courtesy of AP/Wide World Photos.)

winning net share was $93.75 and a trophy that honors the school's best all-time basketball team.

There were other differences in 1942. The NCAA Tournament was mushrooming but still less publicized than New York's prestigious National Invitation Tournament (NIT). While media applications in the nineties could fill an entire arena, even northern California newspapers used only wire service stories in those early years.

Additionally, there was a war going on. "We had a lot on our minds," recalled Dallmar. "We were only a few months beyond what President Roosevelt had called the 'Day of Infamy'—December 7, 1941. Should we enlist or wait to be drafted? What were we doing there playing games when guys our age were defending their country? Remember, too, our regional was held in Kansas City and in those days we didn't fly, so we stayed on that full week and had regular study periods to prepare for final exams as soon as we got home."

In 1942, before the term "Final Four" was coined, it was the Final Two. In one regional, Stanford muscled and sped past Colorado, 46–35, behind Pollard's 17 points. Meanwhile, in the regional at New Orleans, Dartmouth was trouncing Adolph Rupp's heavily favored Kentucky Wildcats, 47–28, and automatically became the favorite of the Final Two.

Some unknowing commentators guessed Stanford would benefit by remaining for a second weekend in Kansas City, with what amounted to a home court.

"Not so," said Dallmar. "We hated their new parquet floor. It had no give and was hard on the feet. We practiced at another gym."

Coach Dean was a master at devising defenses, but this Stanford team was special—it could run. One must remember the times. The fast break was something of a novelty. Nobody dunked. The one-handed jump shot, popularized by Stanford's Hank Luisetti only a few years earlier, was still experimental for many schools. Long shots were rarely taken. And scores, of course, were low.

"We were," said Dallmar, "the first big team that could move faster than our opponents. With our success, the basketball world began to realize a big team could not only rebound but also run a good fast break."

Pollard had starred in the semifinal, but he was sidelined by the flu and did not suit up for Dartmouth. Burness'

The starting five from Stanford's 1942 championship team. Pictured, from left, are Bill Cowden, Howie Dallmar, Ed Voss, Jim Pollard, and Don Burness. (Photo courtesy of AP/Wide World Photos.)

sprained ankle did not respond despite a week's rest, and though he started, he was out within two minutes. In their places came 6´4˝ Jack Dana and 5´9˝ Fred Linari with a different but just as effective style. Against Rice, Stanford had used a zone for a 53–47 win; against Colorado, a shifting man-for-man for a 46–35 victory; and against Dartmouth, a combination of both for the runaway 53–38 win.

With two first stringers gone, Dean decided on a different tempo: no setting up plays, fast break and shoot as often as possible, freelance all the way. It worked—eventually. Dartmouth led five minutes into the second half, 27–26, but suddenly the Indians of Dartmouth collapsed to the Indians of Stanford. Dallmar, Dana, Voss, and Linari all scored quickly, and in the end, Dartmouth had been held to a 19.3 percent shooting average, while

"With our success, the basketball world began to realize a big team could not only rebound but also run a good fast break."

—Howie Dallmar
Forward on Stanford's 1942 championship team

Stanford shot 38.7, outstanding for the type of basketball in that era.

In that tournament, much was made of Stanford's height, smoothness, and skills during an era of low scoring. The following paragraph from the Associated Press report of the finale captured the tremendous change in the game of basketball:

"In the closing 10-minute surge, Voss, Dana, and Linari collaborated for 15 points in one of the greatest sprees of point tabulating seen in this college basketball capital."

The talent of that Stanford team was re-emphasized later when both Pollard and Burness were named All-America; Dallmar was the NCAA Tournament's Most Outstanding Player and later Stanford coach. Pollard moved on to the pros for an illustrious career capped by his selection to the NBA Hall of Fame. ∎

Art Rosenbaum was the sports columnist of the San Francisco Chronicle for many years and was sports editor from 1954–1977. Eleven of his stories were selected for the anthology Best Sports Stories.

1943

WAR-TIME WYOMING TAKES THE PRIZE

By Dick Conner

THEY WEREN'T STRANGERS, EXACTLY. THEY HAD, after all, barnstormed the East a couple of times, the most recent trip only a few months earlier as the war deepened and America began to tighten itself for what it recognized would be a long and bloody siege.

It was the winter of 1942–1943, and the American public was looking for something, anything, to give it a few moments away from the gloomy news on Page One.

Maybe that's why Wyoming and its basketball Cowboys struck such a responsive chord. From the time in 1939, as freshmen, when they had challenged and beaten the varsity, they knew they were special. So did their coach, Everett Shelton. After that exhibition, he began scheduling his team into the big population centers of the East.

Or maybe it was Kenny Sailors, unleashing what would become the standard weapon for all basketball players of the future—the jump shot.

Perhaps it was the fluid, almost flamboyant style of these homegrown Westerners from the windy plains of the high country. In a time when the stationary, two-handed set shot was almost an act of faith, they all shot one-handed. Even free throws.

They ran the pick-and-roll, set screens as if they were blocks of granite on the ridges along the mountains next to Laramie, and they throttled that war-torn basketball season as few teams have ever managed, before or since. Consider this:

In the 1942–1943 season, they played 33 games and lost just 2. They beat Georgetown for the NCAA championship. Then they defeated St. John's, the NIT champions, in the Red Cross fundraiser that packed Madison Square Garden a couple of nights later. A little more than a week before, they had finished third in the AAU tournament against the best of the past.

"We should have won that," recalled Sailors. "We got beat in the semifinals by a team that wasn't as good as us, and we beat the eventual champions [Phillips 66] twice during the season."

A half century later, Sailors taught in Angoon and coached girls basketball. During summers and falls he was a fishing and hunting guide and outfitter. And he still played basketball in the city league. "I still shoot the jump shot. Not as often, and I don't jump as high, but I still shoot it."

Six decades ago, that shot and his dribbling wizardry took the blond kid from southeastern Wyoming to the Most Outstanding Player award of the 1943 NCAA championship.

No less an authority than Ray Meyer of DePaul credits Sailors with the creation of the modern shot. Many lean toward Hank Luisetti, but Sailors notes a critical difference:

"Hank never shot a jump shot. All the old-timers I have talked to credit him with starting the one-handed set shot, and I would agree. But he never shot a jump shot in his life."

Sailors did. "I had to start it as a kid. My older brother was 6´5˝, and it was the only way I could get the ball over him."

The rest of his Cowboy teammates—all but two of them homegrown Wyomingites—each featured the one-handed set shot, and few college teams came close to them until they reached the NCAA Western Division tournament in Kansas City in March. They had rolled over everybody in the Mountain States Conference, beaten Brigham Young in a special three-game title series, then came within a whisker of winning the AAU before heading for Kansas City.

There they faced Texas and Oklahoma.

This, remember, was not a normal season. Illinois, the scourge of the Midwest, and Notre Dame each passed up both the NIT and the NCAA. Washington arrived in Kansas City as the fourth member of the Western championships,

Wyoming coach Ev Shelton, pictured in the above photo, and at right with starters (left to right) Jim Weir, Don Waite, Milo Komenich, Floyd Volker, and Kenny Sailors.

It was the Cowboys, beaten just once, with 6´7´´ Milo Komenich and the clever Sailors, who were favored. After a 43–33 loss to Duquesne to open a six-game barnstorming tour of the East just after Christmas, Wyoming had not lost again until the semifinals of the AAU the week before.

The Cowboys would not lose another game, but none would be easy. As a wartime nation watched with fascination, Wyoming came from behind in four straight games to claim not only the NCAA but a special posttournament game against St. John's, the NIT champion.

"And he didn't come back until the end of the third quarter. By then, we had finally gone ahead."

Their 58–54 victory sent them back aboard the train for the East and a date in the old Garden against Georgetown in what the papers of the time called "the Big Game."

The Hoyas had beat George Mikan and DePaul and blistered New York University to qualify as the Eastern representative. Led by 6´8´´ freshman John Mahnken, who averaged 15.4 points a game, the Hoyas were a high-scoring, disciplined team that had beaten the best in the East.

It would be a fitting matchup of geography and style.

It was a one-game, championship setting, East vs. West, with the winner already scheduled to advance to meet the NIT champion later in the week for the Red Cross benefit.

As it had in its previous NCAA games, Wyoming fell behind early, then surged late on the strength of Sailors' floor work, Komenich's scoring, and the rebounding of Jim

"I had to start it as a kid. My older brother was 6´5´´, and it was the only way I could get the ball over him."

—Kenny Sailors
Guard on Wyoming's 1943 championship team, on introducing the modern jump shot

Against Oklahoma, they sent the mobile Komenich into a highly physical game that saw the Sooners' Tucker foul out before half-time. Komenich then rolled in 16 points in the second half, and the Cowboys won, 53–50.

Texas, meanwhile, saw Washington sprint out to a 21–8 lead before following John Hargis' 30 points to a 59–55 win to set up the title game.

For a while on that long ago Saturday night, it appeared Wyoming's one-handed magic had ended.

"I remember coming into the dressing room at halftime," said Sailors. "We were down 10 or 15 points, which were a lot of points in those days." Actually, they had trailed by 13 at one point, 26–13, and were still behind by 6, 33–27.

"Ev Shelton was our coach, and he was a master psychologist," Sailors said. "He walked in and never said a word, until he finally turned to us. 'Well, boys, it looks like this is it. We didn't go all the way like I thought we might. I'll just tell you what: I'll go back up to the hotel and start packing things up, and I'll see you toward the end of the game.'

Weir. But they also got a superb night from substitute Jimmy Collins, who got all eight of his points just when the Hoyas had taken a 28–24 lead and were threatening to break away.

Komenich and Mahnken had been expected to dominate. But they spent so much time neutralizing each other that it was Collins and Sailors who eventually decided the game, 46–34.

Sailors was named winner of the Chuck Taylor medal as the game's outstanding player with 16 points, high for either team. "And he deserved it," wrote Bob Considine. "He's one of the greatest dribblers the yellow Garden court ever saw. He ran through Georgetown's fine defense the other night like a good halfback skirting the steel uprights of the Third Avenue el."

"I learned to dribble, I guess, in grade school," Sailors recalled. "We'd get off the school bus in the morning and go into the gym before class started. We'd get a basketball. The rules were, if you could keep dribbling, you kept the ball."

In an otherwise bleak and somber year, Sailors and Wyoming never seemed to lose it. A month later, almost the whole lineup was wearing other uniforms. But the 1943 trophy remained in the lobby of the Cowboys' athletics building, a shiny memorial to a season as special as the mountains that framed it. ■

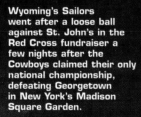

Wyoming's Sailors went after a loose ball against St. John's in the Red Cross fundraiser a few nights after the Cowboys claimed their only national championship, defeating Georgetown in New York's Madison Square Garden.

but it arrived sans its captain. Walk Leask had been called into service. Texas had a 17-year-old guard, 5´9´´ Roy Cox, as one of its key elements. Oklahoma had finished second in the Big Six that abbreviated season, but it had a legitimate star in 6´4´´ Gerald Tucker.

The late Dick Connor was a sports columnist of the Rocky Mountain News *and the* Denver Post *and was named Colorado Sportswriter of the Year 17 times. He was president of both the Pro Football Writers of America and the National Sportswriters and Sportscasters Association.*

1944

THE TEAM WITHOUT A HOME

By Lee Benson

IT WAS 2:00 IN THE MORNING AT THE BELVEDERE Hotel in Manhattan, and the nine players who made up the 1944 University of Utah basketball team weren't asleep.

Only hours before the Utes had lost their opening game in the NIT in Madison Square Garden, a 46–38 defeat to Kentucky, and now they had been rousted from their beds and summoned to the room of coach Vadal Peterson, who had an offer he thought they might want to refuse.

Officials from the NCAA Basketball Tournament had just called, he told his players, and they needed a last-minute replacement for Arkansas, whose team had cancelled because of an automobile accident that had killed an assistant coach and one of the players.

The problem was, the opening-round NCAA game against Missouri was scheduled two nights later in Kansas City. That meant the Utes would have to catch the first train out of New York the next morning. There would be no time for Broadway shows, visiting the Statue of Liberty, or riding to the top of the Empire State Building.

"We've made a good showing here, and we've made some money," Peterson told his players. "Now we have a chance to see New York. What do you think?"

The coach's tone implied that he thought it might be a good idea if they called it a season then and there.

In 1944 the Utah basketball team was hardly the most feared in the land and certainly not the best known. The Utes had been the last team invited to the eight-team NIT and now they were getting the last call to the NCAA Tournament. They had accumulated a 17–3 regular-season record, but as with most records during the war years, it was suspect.

The Utes didn't have a home gymnasium—their fieldhouse had been converted into an army barracks. They had played only three college teams all season long—Colorado, Weber State, and Idaho State. The rest of their games were against service teams. Their three losses were to Fort Warren, the Salt Lake Air Base, and Dow Chemical. Only because Keith Brown, the team's graduate manager, had sent clippings weekly to Ned Irish, president of Madison Square Garden, had they worked their way into the NIT's consciousness and wrangled that tournament's final bid.

When they arrived in New York, they were the epitome of gangly country kids with their hands in their pockets gaping open-mouthed at all them tall buildings.

If somebody had offered, they'd have all bought the Brooklyn Bridge.

This was the makeup of the team: nine players, seven freshmen, one sophomore, and one junior. Their average age was 18½. All were Utahns—the majority Mormons—who had grown up within 35 miles of the University of Utah campus.

They would have all been in the service except for the fact that the seven freshmen weren't 19 yet and therefore not eligible for the draft; the sophomore was center Fred Sheffield, who was in medical school; and the junior was Wat Misaka, a Japanese-American who, at that stage of the war, couldn't be drafted.

In a year, virtually every member of the team, including Misaka, would be off joining the war effort.

But in March of 1944 they had other fronts to conquer.

That's what they told Vadal Peterson, their coach, when he suggested they turn down the NCAA Tournament invitation in favor of a sightseeing tour of downtown Manhattan.

In their 2:00 A.M. meeting they voted unanimously to get right back on the train and accept the NCAA bid. If they got out of Kansas City alive, they could return to New York for the NCAA final game.

With the brashness of teenagers, they told the manager at the Belvedere as much when they asked him not to rent out their rooms because they'd be right back.

At Kansas City, they beat Missouri, 45–35, in their NCAA Western Regional opener and next faced an Iowa State team that had beaten Pepperdine, 44–39.

Iowa State, like all the teams Utah faced in its postseason play, was older and more experienced than the Utes. Utah did not have any armed services programs, like the navy's V-12 training program, in its curriculum, and consequently did not have servicemen on campus who were still free to play college basketball.

Iowa State was a heavy favorite in the Western Regional title game. So heavy, in fact, that Reaves Peters, the tournament director, came to Brown, the Utah manager, before the game and tactfully explained that the winner would have to catch a New York–bound train at midnight and he'd already checked Iowa State's players out of their

Utah coach Vadal Peterson led his Utes to a 22–4 season and the national championship in 1944.

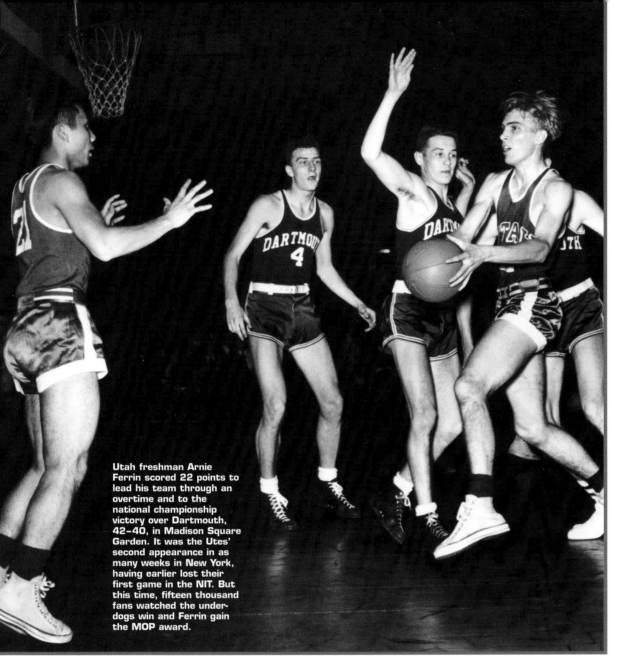

Utah freshman Arnie Ferrin scored 22 points to lead his team through an overtime and to the national championship victory over Dartmouth, 42–40, in Madison Square Garden. It was the Utes' second appearance in as many weeks in New York, having earlier lost their first game in the NIT. But this time, fifteen thousand fans watched the underdogs win and Ferrin gain the MOP award.

New Yorkers' penchant for siding with the underdog was an added plus.

Dartmouth could not break loose from the freshmen, and with a minute to play in regulation the Big Green found themselves down by four, 36–32. Gale got a field goal to cut the deficit to two, and then, with two seconds on the clock, McGuire made a set shot that sent the game into overtime.

Ferrin, who had scored 18 points in regulation and was on his way to the tourney's Most Outstanding Player award, took charge in the overtime, scoring four points as the teams drew to 40–40. He drove for the game-winner in the closing seconds, but the ball bounced loose near the free throw line, where Utah's Herb Wilkinson picked it up and made an off-balance shot that just beat the buzzer, and Dartmouth, 42–40. Now it was time to see the sights—almost.

A crowd 18,125 strong filled the Garden to raise $35,000 for the war effort. Ferrin scored 17 and Wilkinson 11 as the Utes, now known in New York newspapers as the "Blitz Kids," won going away, 43–36.

The New York newspapers had arranged for the Red Cross benefit game two nights later, also in Madison Square Garden, pitting the champion of the NCAA—Utah—against the NIT champion—St. John's of New York.

No one had to hype this game. A crowd 18,125 strong filled the Garden to raise $35,000 for the war effort. Ferrin scored 17 and Wilkinson 11 as the Utes, now known in New York newspapers as the "Blitz Kids," won going away, 43–36.

They were the toast of the town. Parties were held in their honor everywhere. Their money was no good in any of New York's finest restaurants and theaters. They saw *Finian's Rainbow* and the *Ice Follies*. They ate at the Copacabana. They were feted at the Waldorf-Astoria. They were on Kate Smith's CBS radio show and Senator Elbert Thomas invited them to Washington, D.C., to dine.

But that was one invitation they turned down. They caught the train going straight back to Salt Lake. There they were paraded through the city streets in convertibles as they told tales of their trip back East, where not only had they managed to see the sights, but they had been one. ∎

---

hotel rooms—and if it was all right with the Utes, they'd be leaving their luggage in Utah's rooms.

As it turned out, after Utah beat Iowa State, 40–31, the Cyclone players stayed that night in Utah's rooms, and the Utes slept in Pullmans—on their way back to the Empire State.

By now, Utah's players were losing their anonymity—in particular, a slender 6´4˝ blond-haired freshman named Arnie Ferrin. He had scored 12 points against Missouri and another 6 against Iowa State and was the heart of Utah's attack—especially so after Sheffield, the defending NCAA high jump champion and the Utes' starting center, sprained an ankle in practice in Kansas City and was rendered ineffective the rest of the way.

In the NCAA championship game in Madison Square Garden—the affair was a Final Two back then—Utah was up against Eastern Regional champ Dartmouth, yet another seasoned squad made up of soldier-athletes. Many of the Dartmouth players had been transferred by the military and

hadn't even been on campus at the beginning of the school year. Among the team's best players were Harry Leggat, a former New York University star sent to Dartmouth by the marines; Bob Gale, formerly at Cornell; and Dick McGuire, a proven star at St. John's now assigned to Dartmouth by the navy V-12 program.

The morning of the final, Pete Crouch, Utah's assistant coach, overheard a breakfast conversation among the Dartmouth players. They were suggesting that they should play an intrasquad scrimmage before the game—so the people could get their money's worth.

Thanks to Couch, this information found its way into the pregame locker room. Only a week had passed since their first experience in Madison Square Garden—when they lost to Kentucky in their NIT opener—but the Utes were now adjusted to life in the big city. The fifteen thousand fans who came to watch the title game—establishing a new single-game NCAA Tournament record—did not unnerve them. Indeed, the

---

Lee Benson wrote sports for the Salt Lake City Desert News, *covering every Final Four from 1978 to 1993, when he left the newspaper to write books. He returned to the* Desert News *in 1998, where he is a metro columnist.*

1945

THE BIG MAN ENTERS COLLEGE BASKETBALL

By Dan Foster

HANK IBA, WHOSE OKLAHOMA A&M TEAMS WON the seventh and eighth (1945 and 1946) NCAA Basketball Tournaments ever staged, looked back over four decades one day and concluded that 1945 was an especially significant year.

"Those were the years," he said, "which brought the big man into basketball."

And 1945 was special not only because it brought together Bob Kurland and George Mikan, both of whom would grow to legendary status as players, but it also became a reference point in the friendly duel between the NCAA and the NIT for recognition as the number one postseason basketball tournament.

Just as Kurland's 7´ frame and remarkable skills had helped his Oklahoma A&M team win the NCAA championship, Mikan's 6´10˝ frame and talent were the catalyst in DePaul's capturing the NIT title. Both would later be enshrined in the NBA Hall of Fame.

It was during the last winter of World War II that those two teams emerged as the best in the two college tournaments. In an added climax to the season, they were brought face-to-face in a benefit game for the Red Cross. It was labeled the "Champion of Champions" game.

As Ken Rappoport related it in his 1979 book, *The Classic*, early foul trouble for Mikan sent him out of their confrontation game with only nine points. Kurland had 14 in Oklahoma A&M's 52–44 triumph.

Given the unquestioned superiority of the NCAA Tournament's stature over the NIT in the eighties and nineties, it may be difficult to realize that until 1945, when the NCAA's champion was recognized as the "true" national champ, the NCAA had not overtaken the NIT in tournament prestige.

The 1945 NCAA triumph was the first of two in succession for Iba's Oklahoma A&M Aggies (later the Oklahoma State Cowboys).

(above) Seven-foot center Bob "Foothills" Kurland led the Oklahoma A&M Aggies to consecutive NCAA titles in 1945 and 1946. (Photo courtesy of AP/Wide World Photos.)

(right) Oklahoma A&M coach Henry Iba, with outside shooting specialist Cecil Hankins.

Kurland pulls down a rebound during a regular-season game against New York University. (Photo courtesy of AP/Wide World Photos.)

Although the rule against goaltending was in force by 1945, changing Kurland's earlier style, he was still a dominant figure—on both defense and offense.

With Kurland scoring 28 points in the first round, the Aggies routed Utah, 62–37. Cecil Hankins, described by Iba as "a great outside shooter," scored 22 points, Doyle Parrack 16, and Kurland 15 as the Aggies dispatched Arkansas 68–41 in the semifinals.

Kurland didn't have to wait until he faced Mikan to play against a future NBA Hall of Famer. While Kurland and Mikan would be enshrined there, so would Dolph Schayes, a member of the New York University Violets team in 1945.

Schayes, playing center, scored 13 points as NYU beat Tufts, 59–44, and 14 in NYU's 70–65 overtime conquest of Ohio State in the semifinals. Against the Aggies in the final, Schayes—younger, smaller, and less experienced than Kurland—scored 6 points to Kurland's 22, as Iba's team won the championship game, 49–45.

Although the rule against goaltending was in force by 1945, changing Kurland's earlier style, he was still a dominant figure—on both defense and offense.

Iba, whose 767 college coaching victories rank sixth, described in tones worthy of a pulpit the emphasis his teams place on controlling on offense and patrolling on defense.

"We ran our offense with set plays," he recalled. "There was no freelance. We'd run the set, and reset, and run it again."

Defensively, "we never did play anything but man-to-man," except for the season before he won the 1945 national title.

They played some zone then, Iba recalled, because Kurland could pin enemy shots to the backboard or sweep them away around the basket. But after the goaltending rule came in, it was back to man-to-man.

He said an outside shot then was "about where the three-point line is now, and we didn't take a whole lot of those. I imagine we were taking better shots. We had to get inside of the free throw line."

The emergence of big Bob Kurland, and the other big men in college basketball, made all that possible. ∎

His 1945 team, like the rest of the great teams in his 38 years as the Aggies coach, was characterized by a strict control offense and a physical man-to-man defense, where forwards sometimes turned into linebackers.

Having remained close to the sport since his last coaching season in 1970, it was Iba's opinion that, "in 1945 and 1946, we were playing much better defense than they are right now. There was more stress on defense and possession.

"Keeping possession of the ball was the strength of defense in the early days."

As the NCAA Tournament format operated from its inception in 1939 through 1951, the starting field included one team from each of the eight NCAA districts.

Dan Foster started with the Piedmont newspapers in 1948, was sports editor of the Greenville Piedmont *and the* Greenville News. *His coverage of Final Fours dates to 1966.*

1946

MISTER IBA'S PRIZE PUPIL, BOB KURLAND

By Bob Hurt

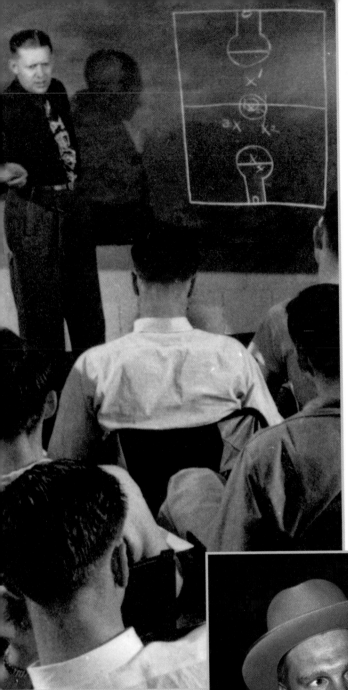

(right) Oklahoma A&M's Bob Kurland became a dominant player as the war years ended in the mid-forties, and America turned to a different style of competition. Kurland and George Mikan were the first big men whose style changed the game. And it was Kurland, the anchor of Henry Iba's (above) back-to-back national championship teams, who brought about the game's first goaltending rule.

SOME CALLED HIM HANK AND OTHERS CALLED him "the Iron Duke," but to those who best knew Henry P. Iba, he always was Mister Iba. It was Mister Iba this, Mister Iba that, as if Mister was his given name.

Maybe it was. Maybe Mister was given out of respect to a man who coached basketball for 41 years and won 767 games. Only five major college coaches have more wins.

Iba, who won so often, ironically is remembered for one he lost. He coached the 1972 U.S. Olympic team, "robbed" in the basketball final in Munich. A Yank victory celebration was interrupted when the secretary general of the basketball federation extended the game by three seconds—three seconds used by the Russians to win, 51–50.

More appropriately, Iba should be remembered for his 1946 Oklahoma A&M team, which became the first to win back-to-back NCAA titles by defeating North Carolina, 43–40, in Madison Square Garden. That team was pure Iba—disciplined, unselfish, deliberate.

It was built around seven-footer Bob "Foothills" Kurland, a basketball Pygmalion brought to life by Iba.

In Kurland's opinion, no Iba team, before or since, came as close to doing what the coach wanted as that one.

"And there were other teams we met that year with more talent," Kurland said. "North Carolina may have been one. I'm talking about physical speed and grace and so forth."

It was not a big Aggie team. The forwards were Weldon Kern, 5´10˝, and Sam Aubrey, 6´4˝, with A. L. Bennett, 6´0˝, as the first sub. The guards were J. L. Parks, 6´0˝, and Blake Williams, 6´2˝.

Kurland chuckled as he looked back on the motley crew.

"We had Sam, who had his butt shot off. We had Kern, who was barely 5´10˝. J. L. Parks had fingers about two inches long and actually hit the ball with his fist when he dribbled it. Blake had a bad heart. More than once, we had to stop a game because his heart

was fibrillating. Bennett was a great athlete, but not a great driver. He had been in the Battle of the Bulge. When the chips were down, he just didn't rattle."

Iba's raspy voice, which sounded as if he gargled with sandpaper, took on an edge as he talked about what Kurland had said. He contended he had great athletes, as good as any of that day. In Iba's mind, part of being great was following orders. These players did.

"I'd go to war with those guys," he said.

So would the U.S. of A. Four members of the team, including Aubrey and Bennett, had been in World War II.

They mixed well with Kurland, Kern, and Williams, who had been starters on the 1944–1945 team, which was 27–4 and a 49–45 victor over New York University in the NCAA final.

The soul of the team was to become Sam Aubrey, who in 1970 succeeded Iba as head coach at the school which was by then Oklahoma State.

"That team didn't have any griping," Aubrey said. "We knew what we wanted. The man told us what we wanted."

Aubrey left A&M in 1943 to go to war. In September 1944, Aubrey was shot in the hip while serving in Italy. He spent a year in a hospital, where a doctor warned him his condition would deteriorate and relegate him to a wheelchair at age 35.

In September 1945, Aubrey hobbled onto campus with a cane and vowed he would play.

"The poor guy; he couldn't make it the length of the floor at first," Iba said. "But he ended up starting every damn ballgame. He was a team player—not a lot of flash, but he did his job."

Kurland recalled Sam stumbling to the floor while trying to backpedal in a defensive crouch.

Ironic. Aubrey has a strong recollection of Kurland stumbling over the same Gallagher Hall planks.

Aubrey roomed with Kurland when the shy 17-year-old kid arrived in Stillwater from a St. Louis suburb in 1942. Aubrey recalled that Kurland was "awkward." Kurland called himself "clumsy."

Others were less kind. Phog Allen, the venerable Kansas coach, referred to Kurland as a "glandular, mezzanine-peeping goon."

Iba was infuriated at his old coaching friend. Later in Kurland's freshman year, Iba finished a game at Kansas with

four players on the floor rather than use his only remaining eligible player, Kurland.

"Hell, Kurland wasn't ready to play," Iba said. "There was no way we could help ourselves, the way the game was being called. I didn't want to embarrass the boy."

Kurland quickly developed from "goon" to "great"—a fact brought to Allen's attention in 1946 when the big redhead scored 28 points as the Aggies beat Kansas, 49–38, to win a playoff for a spot in the NCAA Tournament.

Kurland worked at scoring. He once spent an afternoon putting up 600 left-handed hooks as Iba watched. The first 100 did not draw iron. Then he started hitting.

Kurland, however, endeared himself to his coach by majoring in defense. He became so adept at swatting foes' shots out of nets that Oklahoma coach Bruce Drake built a platform behind the hoop in 1944 and talked a national rules authority into mounting it to observe Kurland's second-story work. That led to the establishment of goaltending rules.

Kurland's scoring average improved each season from 2.5 to 13.5 to 17.1 to 19.5. Only once did he cut loose. On February 22, 1946, he scored 58 against St. Louis and "Easy" Ed Macauley, then a freshman, to erase the national record of 53 set by DePaul's George Mikan.

Kurland vs. Mikan were classic confrontations of the day, hyped-up duels which largely were responsible for opening basketball doors to big men—a fact in which Kurland took pride.

> **Kurland vs. Mikan were classic confrontations of the day, hyped-up duels which largely were responsible for opening basketball doors to big men—a fact in which Kurland took pride.**

Kurland was sensitive. He always insisted he was 6´11˝ and ¾ of an inch—not 7´.

And he was emotional. Blake Williams said Kurland threw up before each of his games against Mikan. They were standoffs, each team winning twice.

Mikan went to the pros. Kurland went into AAU ball with the Phillips 66ers and wound up as the longtime national sales manager for the oil company.

The Aggies ended the 1945 season by beating DePaul, the NIT champ, 52–44, in a special Red Cross charity classic but lost to the Demons to start the 1946 season in Stillwater.

The Aggies were to lose only one other game. Among their 31 victories was one over DePaul in Chicago.

They breezed through the regional by beating Baylor, 44–29, and California, 52–35.

Ben Carnevale's North Carolina team posed more of a problem in the final in New York. The Tar Heels were led by 6´6˝ Horace "Bones" McKinney, who vowed to talk the Aggies out of the title if he couldn't beat them out of it.

His efforts to needle Kurland backfired. McKinney was held to five points. Not until John "Hook" Dillon moved into the pivot did the Tar Heels make a late and futile run at A&M.

Kurland scored 23 points and fed mates for three more buckets to earn the tournament's Most Outstanding Player award for the second straight year. He also forced what Carneavale called the biggest turnover of the game. Kurland had his back turned to the ball, which accidentally bounced off his hand to a teammate.

The unsung hero, however, was Bennett. The Tar Heel press, an unfamiliar weapon in those days, confused the Aggies until Bennett invented a new way to pass the ball into play.

"Not too many guys can play low to the floor," Aubrey said. "So A. L. just got down and rolled the ball in like a bowling ball and they just froze." ∎

Bob Hurt has been sports editor and columnist for The Daily Oklahoman, The Topeka (Kansas) Capital-Journal, *and the* Arizona Republic. *He was selected as his state's Sportswriter of the Year nine times. He's now retired and lives in Phoenix.*

1947

THE ORPHANS TAKE THEIR PLACE IN HISTORY

By Lesley Visser

IT WAS SIX MONTHS AFTER A RADICAL NEW BATHING suit had been modeled in Paris, named after the atomic bomb test on the island of Bikini. It was the year of *A Streetcar Named Desire*, and the year Chuck Yeager flew his experimental *Bell X-1* through the sonic barrier. It was the year an actor named Ronald Reagan testified before the House Un-American Activities Committee on what he knew about communism in Hollywood. It was 1947, the year Holy Cross won the NCAA championship.

They were called the "orphans," a team from a tiny Catholic school in Worcester, Massachusetts, that never played a home game. They practiced in a local barn, played some games at the Boston Garden, and a few more at the Boston Arena. The rest of the time they were away. No team from the East had ever won the NCAA championship, and Oklahoma A&M had won it two years in a row. But on March 25, 1947, more than eighteen thousand fans at Madison Square Garden saw Holy Cross beat the Oklahoma Sooners, 58–47, in the championship game.

It wasn't a big team (only one player was taller than 6´3˝) or a very experienced team (no seniors, two juniors, and a handful of sophomores). But it was, in a sense, a veteran team. Bob Currans had played for the navy in Chicago, Charles Graver had been a forward at the Victorville Army Air Base, and Andy Laka played in Greensboro, North Carolina, for one of the best service teams in the country.

Two more Crusader standouts had been service starts. Sophomore guard Joe Mullaney served three years as a *B-26 Marauder* pilot and was named MVP while playing at Turner Field in Georgia. Center Frank Oftring spent three years as an aviation machinist while leading the Quonset (Rhode Island) Naval Base to the First Service Command title in 1945, the same year Bob McMullan carried Fort Dix to the Second Service Command title.

They were serious players led by a serious coach named Alvin "Doggie" Julian. He was 46 years old, a basketball devotee from Reading, Pennsylvania. In the seventh grade, Julian used to watch the Boston Celtics when they came to play in the old Reading Armory. He studied the masters of the fast break and patterned his game after the Celtics' basic maneuvers. His nickname came from an incident in the 11th grade. While walking to school with some friends, Julian stepped aside to let a woman pass. His friends continued on, oblivious to Julian's good manners. When they discovered he was 20 yards behind them, one of them called out, "C'mon little doggie," and the appellation stuck.

In 1947 Julian was already a legend in college basketball. He put together a disciplined team known as the "Fancy Pants A. C." because of the intricate way they played. After losing three straight games early in the 1946–1947 season, Julian directed his team to 23 straight victories, including three in the NCAA Tournament. Because he had 10 good players, Julian platooned them. One team had Dermott O'Connell, George Kaftan, Joe Mullaney, Ken Haggerty, and either Frank Oftring or Bob Curran. The other had Bob McMullan, Charles Bollinger, Andy Laska, either Oftring or Curran, and a freshman named Bob Cousy.

> ## Kaftan, the 18-year-old forward, was named tournament Most Outstanding Player for his 63 points in three games, including 18 in the championship against Oklahoma.

Cousy had been the schoolboy star at Andrew Jackson High School in New York City. Even then, he was the stylish scoring guard who could pass quicker than a summer afternoon. In 1947, 30 years before Patrick Ewing, Cousy wore a T-shirt underneath his uniform. His college bio said he liked poetry and playing basketball—"365 days a year."

In March 1947, Holy Cross took the train to New York as the Cinderella squad of the ninth NCAA Tournament. In the quarterfinals against Navy, Joe Mullaney dazzled the fans with nine field goals and even some one-handed shooting. Defensively, he went to work on the Middies' scoring ace, Kenny Shugart. Sophomore George Kaftan, the "Great Greek," scored 15 points, and Holy Cross rebounded from a 23–16 deficit to win the game, 55–47.

In the semifinals against powerful City College of New York (CCNY), Kaftan scored 30 points, one shy of the Garden record for individual scoring set by George Glamack of North Carolina in 1941. Mullaney's hook shot gave the Crusaders a 27–25 lead, but CCNY evened the

A happy George Kaftan, captain of the 1947 Holy Cross team, was carried from the Madison Square Garden court after leading the Crusaders to a 58–47 victory over a talented Oklahoma team. By now, the NCAA Tournament had overtaken the NIT as America's most important basketball championship. Eight teams from their geographic region began the tournament with four regionals before advancing to the Final Four. It would be four more years before the field would expand to 16 teams.

score at 36–36. Holy Cross rallied to beat Nat Holman's Lavender, 60–45.

Kaftan, Oftring, and O'Connell led the charge against Oklahoma in the final. During the first 18 minutes, the lead changed hands 10 times and the score was tied on nine occasions. The Sooners looked to the great Gerry Tucker (who was called a "giant" at 6´6´´). Tucker scored 15 points in the first half and Oklahoma took a 31–28 lead, but Doggie Julian put Bob Curran on Tucker in the second half and the Sooner center scored only seven points.

Kaftan, the 18-year-old forward, was named tournament Most Outstanding Player for his 63 points in three games, including 18 in the championship against Oklahoma.

It was the first time anyone from Massachusetts had ever won the coveted honor and the only time a team from the

Bay State, where Dr. James Naismith invented the game, ever captured the title game.

Back in Worcester, more than fifteen thousand people jammed Main Street to sing and dance while Holy Cross' deep purple banner was raised to the top of the flagpole at City Hall. The orphans had won the crown.

It was 1947, before multiyear contracts, million-dollar endorsements, and high-powered agents. George Kaftan went on to become a dentist, and Bob Curran became a successful insurance salesman. Joe Mullaney made his name as a coach, Andy Laska became a respected athletic director, and Bob Cousy went to the Hall of Fame.

In the old *Boston Record*, sportswriter Dave Egan summed up their winter of 1947. "For Kaftan, Mullaney, Oftring, Cousy, and O'Connell, it will always be yesterday,"

Egan wrote. "We know them and hail them as champions; we place them in a special group of invincible underdogs who will never die as long as New England lives. Stallings and his Braves, Leahy and his Eagles, Julian and his Crusaders. There they will stand, side by side, men and teams of such resolve and character that they could not and would not lose." ■

Lesley Visser began her career in print journalism. She was a sportswriter for The Boston Globe *and then moved to television in the eighties, working for CBS Sports and ABC Sports. She covered and attended Final Fours over her career and she particularly enjoyed the 1985 Final Four championship won by Villanova.*

1948

FABULOUS FIVE: EVEN BETTER ON FILM

By Dave Kindred

ONE WINTER DAY IN 1975, THE GENERAL MANAGER of the ABA Kentucky Colonels, a tall and beefy man named Alex Groza, flicked on a movie projector and asked a sportswriter to sit down and have a look.

They would see film of a basketball game played in 1948 by the University of Kentucky's "Fabulous Five." Groza had been one of those Kentucky players. He was 6´7˝ and 220 pounds in his college days. Not as tall as Bob Kurland, not as wide as George Mikan, Alex Groza was a strongman whose bounding, running, shooting, and ballhandling foreshadowed the gifted giants of basketball's future.

Only he seemed not to believe that of himself. He said as much to the sportswriter that day in 1975. "We were good for our time," Groza said of his Kentucky teams, "but we couldn't play with these kids today."

He turned on the projector with the idea the movie would confirm his judgment. What Groza saw on the film was a team with one man taller than 6´4˝. He saw a team without a jump shooter. He saw the year 1948 from the perspective of 1975, and he looked at the "Fabulous Five" as a curiosity of an age long past, a dinosaur bone uncovered in a high-tech age.

The sportswriter saw something different. What the sportswriter saw he will never forget, for in the movie's images he saw the past made real. It had been one thing to hear old-timers speak of the "Fabulous Five." We learned their names by rote: Ralph Beard and Kenny Rollins at guards, Alex Groza at center, Wallace "Wah Wah" Jones and Cliff Barker at forwards. We would nod in deference to the old-timers who insisted on the greatness of those players.

But did we really believe it? Not likely. Young sportswriters think the world was invented five minutes ago. So the sportswriter was ready to agree with Alex Groza in 1975 that the "Fabulous Five" of 1948 wasn't all that good—until he saw the movie, and then he said to Groza,

"You're right, Alex. You weren't as good as people say. You were better."

The movie showed Kentucky on the run. It was breathtaking. Groza ripping off a rebound. An outlet pass to Barker on the right side. Quickly across midcourt to Rollins, who tipped it ahead to Jones. And Jones whipped the ball into the middle, there to Beard on the fly down the free throw lane. From end line to end line, Kentucky moved the ball from rebound to layup in five seconds, with each man handling the ball and the ball never touching the floor.

As the movie played out on Groza's office wall, Kentucky worked without mercy to win an NCAA Tournament game by 20 points. The unforgettable images were of Groza's quickness with a little hook shot and of Beard's magic on the fast break. However self-depreciatory Groza would be on that winter day in 1975, the movie images told the whole truth—the "Fabulous Five" could flat-out play some ball.

They were a kind of team never before seen. They won the NCAA without a giant in the middle. They didn't play offense in the standard style of walk-it-up-and-make-a-dozen-passes. In an era of cautious, plodding, defensive-minded teams, here came Kentucky on the run. The speed itself was unusual, but here speed was only part of the equation: running, always running, yet Kentucky was beautiful in its ballhandling precision. They were an eighties team in the forties. They were the future made real.

In Groza, Kentucky had the requisite strongman in the middle. Working the perimeter, running the break, talking the short jumper, Kentucky had a little guard who was All-American three times, who twice was college player of the year, and who would be All-NBA.

He was Ralph Beard, 5´10˝, 160 pounds, a competitor of such ferocity that he once awoke from a dream to find himself squeezing his pillow in a bear hug and calling out the name of a man he'd guard the next night, "I've got you, Jerrell, you son of a bitch."

Never had there been a better guard in college basketball than Ralph Beard. Not John Wooden in the twenties, not Bob Cousy in the forties. The great coach Clair Bee said in 1948, "Ralph Beard is what this game is all about." Phillips Oilers coach Bud Browning said, "Beard is absolutely the best." Adolph Rupp, Beard's coach, said, "Ralph's the greatest basketball player I ever saw." For Kentuckians who adored Beard, the photograph that best

Kentucky's Alex Groza (above) and Ralph Beard (at right) helped make up the heralded "Fabulous Five."

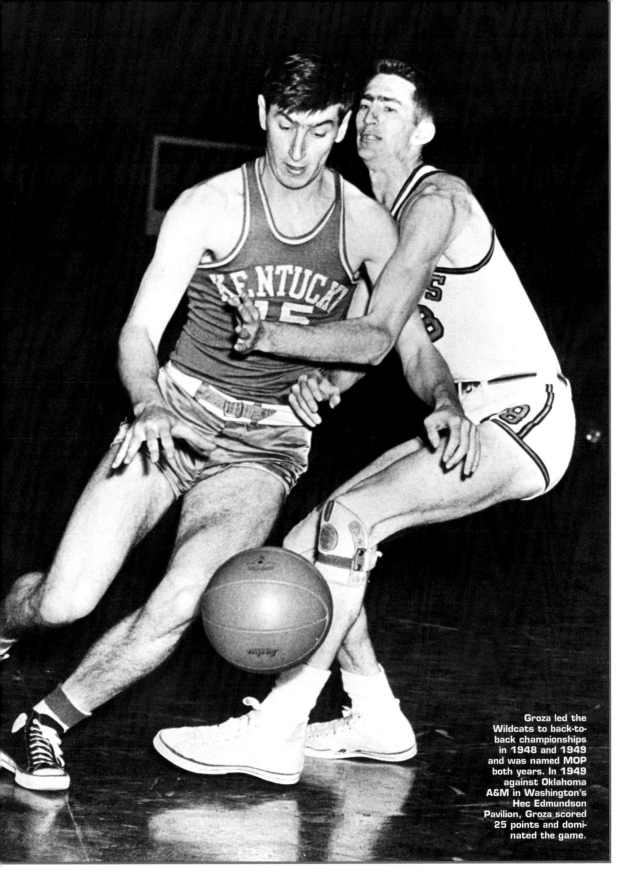

Groza led the Wildcats to back-to-back championships in 1948 and 1949 and was named MOP both years. In 1949 against Oklahoma A&M in Washington's Hec Edmundson Pavilion, Groza scored 25 points and dominated the game.

Beard took Rupp's word as gospel. "Some guys say they hated Rupp. Not me. He was it as far as I was concerned. If he told me to run through a brick wall, I'd have backed up as far as it would take. I wanted to show him I was the best basketball player who ever came down the pike."

With Beard at guard in 1948 was Rollins, a six-footer with good speed. "He was the catalyst, the unselfish one," Beard said. Rollins put his gifts to the ultimate test in the NCAA Tournament semifinal when Rupp assigned him to guard college basketball's newest phenomenon, the Holy Cross guard named Bob Cousy.

Cousy's exploits had prompted a banner-maker to hang a bedsheet in Madison Square Garden: COUSY—THE GREATEST. Going against Kentucky and Rollins, Cousy scored one point. After Kentucky won, 60–52, with Beard and Groza scoring 13 each, someone delivered the Cousy bedsheet to Kenny Rollins.

In an era of cautious, plodding, defensive-minded teams, here came Kentucky on the run. . . . They were an eighties team in the forties. They were the future made real.

Kentucky's championship victory over Baylor, 58–42, was anticlimactic. In it Groza scored 14, Beard 12. The 1948 championship was Kentucky's first, earned in a season when the Wildcats won 34 of 36 games. After the season, Rupp's team competed in the Olympic Trials and finished second to the Phillips Oilers. In the 1948 Games in London, the gold medal U.S. team included Rupp as assistant coach and all five Kentucky starters—Groza, Beard, Jones, Rollins, and Barker—as team members. Kentucky won the national championship again in 1949, Beard's senior season.

In that winter of 1975 when Alex Groza invited a sportswriter to see the past, the writer later told Ralph Beard about the movie. He told Beard he thought Groza was too modest, and he asked Beard how good the "Fabulous Five" had been.

"Of all our good years, we were best in 1948," Beard said. He smiled then, warmed by the memory. "You tell Alex to get suited up because I don't care if we're 50 years old or what, I think we can beat these kids today." ∎

---

identified the little guy showed him stern-visaged and hard-muscled, flying—always flying—for another layup at the end of a sudden sprint that left the enemy wondering where he went.

After his freshman year at Kentucky, Beard asked Rupp to write a letter detailing his weaknesses so he could work on them that summer. Rupp advised him to improve his free throw shooting, use his left hand more on the dribble, and develop a 15-foot jump shot. "If you can correct those few weaknesses," Rupp wrote to Beard, "you will not only be a greater basketball player, but you will be almost a perfect basketball player."

Dave Kindred is the back page columnist of The Sporting News *after a distinguished career as book writer and lead columnist for the Louisville* Courier-Journal, The National, The Washington Post, *and the* Atlanta Journal-Constitution.

1949

GROZA FOILED IBA'S STRATEGY

By Tev Laudeman

HANK IBA HAD A SURPRISE FOR HIS OKLAHOMA A&M basketball players when they went to Seattle to play Kentucky for the 1949 NCAA championship. The Aggies would not use their traditional sagging man-to-man defense, designed to take away the high-percentage shot.

Iba figured Adolph Rupp's Wildcats had too many long-range sharpshooters for the sagging defense to work. So Iba decided to take on Kentucky in a straight man-to-man.

He assigned J. L. Parks to stick with three-time All-American guard Ralph Beard, a deadly long shooter. Jack Shelton, a 6´6˝ forward, drew another Kentucky All-American, 6´4˝ Wallace "Wah Wah" Jones. Vernon Yates, a 6´4˝ forward, was to cover 6´2˝ Jim Line, a junior forward and the only Wildcat starter who was not a senior. Joe Bradley would guard Cliff Barker, Kentucky's ball-handling wizard.

Bob Harris, at 6´7˝, the same height as Kentucky center Alex Groza, was given the toughest task of all: stopping Groza, the Wildcats' third All-American and arguably the best center in the country.

The defense was 80 percent effective; four of Kentucky's starters were shut down. Beard, Jones, and Barker each had one field goal.

The other 20 percent of A&M's defense was fatally flawed. Harris, whom Iba had called "the best defensive center I've ever coached," couldn't handle Groza. The smooth, mobile center scored nine field goals and seven free throws for 25 points as Kentucky won, 46–36, before 12,500 spectators in the University of Washington Pavilion.

For the second straight year, Groza was named the NCAA Tournament's Most Outstanding Player.

Kentucky became only the second team to that time to win two NCAA championships. Ironically, Oklahoma A&M was the other, winning in 1946 and 1947 under Iba.

Yates, a senior in 1949 for A&M, remembered that final game vividly. He didn't doubt that the Wildcats had more talented players, but he wondered if the outcome might have been different, at least closer, if the Aggies had played their standard defense.

"What really won the game [for Kentucky] was the fact that we didn't sink back and help out," Yates said. "In my opinion, that was the key. I think we could have allowed a few more outside shots and sunk in there to help Bob Harris. That was the first time Mr. Iba had changed his defense that I know of. He never did cover strictly tight man-to-man. He always sank and helped. 'Fill the middle, fill the middle,' that's all we were ever told. That night he decided to go strictly tight man-for-man. He thought Harris could cover Groza; that's what he thought."

Yates recalled how, out of force of habit, he lapsed into his old defensive style of sagging inside. A&M was leading, 3–0.

"As soon as the ball came to Jim Line, he took that little left-handed pop shot from the corner and hit it," Yates recalled.

Yates said he was immediately pulled from the game "long enough to get chewed out."

Yates, later a high school teacher and successful coach in Ponca City, Oklahoma, said he and his teammates expected to defeat the Wildcats.

"We thought we could slow 'em down," he said. "That was our game, slowing people down and making them play our way." A&M was able to stop Kentucky's fast break, but Groza was so strong inside that the Wildcats' set offense was effective.

Kentucky (in dark jerseys, above) got the upper hand over coach Henry Iba's Oklahoma A&M squad (at right) to give the Wildcats and coach Adolph Rupp a second consecutive title.

But the deliberate offense had worked wonders for Iba and A&M. He wanted to get the good percentage shot and test the patience of the opposing defenses. Rupp and Iba were without question two of the best ever to coach the game.

Kentucky came to Seattle with a 31–2 record, having lost to St. Louis, 42–40, in the Sugar Bowl final and to Loyola of Chicago, 67–56, in the NIT's first round.

Oklahoma A&M was 23–4 with losses to St. Joseph's of Philadelphia, DePaul, Oklahoma, and Bradley. A&M had beaten Kentucky's Sugar Bowl conqueror, St. Louis, and had avenged all its losses but the one to St. Joseph's.

> ## "That night [coach Iba] decided to go strictly tight man-for-man. He thought Harris could cover Groza; that's what he thought."
>
> **—Vernon Yates**
> *Forward on Oklahoma A&M's 1949 team*

Kentucky was a six-point favorite against A&M. Rupp's basic strategy was to go to his top gun, Groza, as much as possible. To that end, Wah Jones was given the job of driving across the lane to draw attention away from Groza—then Jones was to pass off to Groza.

It worked beautifully, a perfect plan considering Iba's decision not to sag into the middle. Five of Groza's field goals were layups, the other four were hook shots.

Groza's most important layup was one he manufactured for himself. With the score tied 5–5, he intercepted a pass and scored to put Kentucky ahead for the first time. The Wildcats never trailed after that.

"We got behind, we had to play the uphill game, which is not our type of play," Iba said after the game.

Groza recalled that A&M "didn't have a lot of speed. We had a lot [of speed], and good outside shooting. With Wah's quickness and speed and ability, when he made his move, someone had to get him. It opened the inside for me."

Harris fouled out four minutes into the second half with the Wildcats leading, 31–21.

"I guess that's an answer to those guys who said Harris would stop him," Rupp said after Groza scored a tournament-record 82 points in three games. ■

Tev Laudeman covered Kentucky basketball for The Louisville Times *when Adolph Rupp was coach. He also wrote for the* Portsmouth (Ohio) Times *and* Indianapolis Times. *He wrote the book* The Rupp Years.

"You might say we beat the Aggies at their own game," Kentucky assistant coach Harry Lancaster said the next day. "We played as near a possession type of game as we have ever played."

The genesis of Iba's defensive planning may have come four nights earlier in New York's Madison Square Garden, when Kentucky gave a marvelous performance in whipping Big Ten champion Illinois by 29 points, 76–47, for the NCAA Eastern Regional title and a trip to Seattle. Illinois had gotten by Yale, 71–67, in the first round.

Groza scored 27 points against Illinois, but Iba may have been more impressed by the 15 points of Line, the 9 apiece by Jones and Beard, and 8 by Barker. Jones had spent a good part of the game on the bench.

Or, Iba could have been equally impressed by Kentucky's opening game of the Eastern playoffs, when Groza scored 30 and Barker 18 in an 85–72 victory over Villanova. The Wildcats' balance was vital in that one because Paul Arizin had also scored 30 to get an even break in a duel in which he and Groza guarded each other.

Kentucky had as much balance as any college coach could want. Groza and Beard had been named to the Associated Press All-America first team. Those two plus Jones had been picked on the United Press International first five.

The Wildcats had an easier time getting to the final game than Oklahoma A&M. The Aggies barely escaped being upset by Wyoming in the opening game of the four-team Western playoffs. Jack Shelton's layup with four seconds to play gave A&M the 40–39 triumph in Kansas City. Oregon State defeated Arkansas, 56–38, in the other Western game, then lost to A&M, 55–30.

No. 1–ranked Kentucky vs. No. 2 Oklahoma A&M. A study in contrasts.

Rupp was a firm believer in the fast break and a perfectionist set offense, based on slashing drives to the basket and taking the outside shot to open up the opposing defense. He also taught an aggressive man-to-man defense. No one ever doubted that Rupp was serious about defense. What he didn't believe in was what Iba taught: slow-down basketball.

RUSSELL, CHAMBERLAIN, BAYLOR, WEST, AND ROBERTSON

In the locker room of Washington's Hec Edmundson Pavilion, Kansas coach Dr. Forrest C. "Phog" Allen gave his final charge to the Jayhawks before they faced St. John's in the 1952 title game. Listening intently was Dean Smith (center), who would later join Allen as an influential coach.

BY THE MID-FIFTIES, AMERICA WAS IN THE MIDST of an unprecedented social and cultural revolution. The nation was hooked on the new one-eyed monster named television, which overnight changed tastes and habits forever. And while families from coast to coast were glued to the tube, they also had more leisure time and more money to indulge such fads as the Hula-Hoop, the Davy Crockett coonskin cap, and the 3-D movie. In music, the big-band sound of the forties had been replaced by something called rock 'n' roll, the leading practitioner of which was a snarling, pouting, swivel-hipped ex-truck driver from Memphis, Tennessee, by the name of Elvis Presley. He was considered so risque that when he appeared on the Ed Sullivan television program, he was shown only from the waist up.

Sports was enjoying its biggest boom since the so-called "Golden Era" of the twenties. Through the decade, the New York Yankees, Brooklyn Dodgers, and Milwaukee Braves battled for supremacy in major league baseball. Pro football began to gain credibility and support when TV allowed fans to see first the great Cleveland Browns teams, then the benchmark National Football League championship game between the Baltimore Colts and the New York Giants in 1958. A college football coach named Paul "Bear" Bryant moved from Kentucky to Texas A&M to Alabama on his way to building a legend.

As far as college basketball was concerned, the fifties will be remembered for the arrival of the black athlete as a dominant force. And surely it wasn't coincidental that as more teams came to have black players, the game's overall level of skill also improved dramatically.

The 1955 championship game boiled down to a duel between La Salle's Tom Gola, a gifted 6´7´´ white player of the sort who had dominated the game for the previous 10 years, and San Francisco's Bill Russell, a skinny 6´9´´ black center who became the greatest defensive force the game had ever seen. By either blocking shots or forcing players to alter their trajectory, Russell elevated defense to an art form as he led the Dons to back-to-back championships in 1955 and 1956.

The year after Russell departed the college scene for the Boston Celtics, Kansas seemed to have the next dominant center in 7´1´´ Wilt "the Stilt" Chamberlain. But proving that basketball still was a game where teamwork usually would prevail over a one-man show, North Carolina outlasted Kansas through three overtimes in the 1957 title game, a contest that many still regard as the greatest in NCAA history.

By the end of the decade, the game's dominant players were 6´6´´ Elgin Baylor of Seattle, 6´5´´ Oscar Robertson of Cincinnati, and 6´3´´ Jerry West of West Virginia. Those three probably would be on anybody's all-decade team, along with Chamberlain and Russell. Yet of those five, only Russell played on an NCAA championship team. ∎

> **"When Bill Russell came onto the scene, he changed the thinking about the importance of the big man, not just from an offensive standpoint, but from a defensive one as well. Russell could turn a game around with his defense."**
>
> **—Pete Newell**

In 1957 Kansas and North Carolina faced off in the epic Final Four game. The Carolina defense held Wilt Chamberlain, the Kansas sophomore, to 23 points and won the championship.

1950

"ALLAGAROO, GAROO, GARA"

By Malcolm Moran

THE INSTITUTION IS KNOWN AS THE CITY COLLEGE of New York, but for its students, alumni, and fans, there was no need for such formalities. For them, the place is simply known as "City." Anyone who was there around the time of the 12th NCAA basketball championship can remember the pride in going to City, as well as the emotional value of the following words:

"Allagaroo, garoo, gara;
Allagaroo, garoo, gara;
Ee-yah, ee-yah, sis-boom-ba;
Team, Team, Team."

During the brief, remarkable stretch in which the Beavers of City College made basketball history, the words were screamed in the old Madison Square Garden on 8th Avenue between 49th and 50th Streets; downtown at Times Square, uptown at the main campus building at 139th Street and Convent Avenue; really anyplace in a city where basketball had become a passion.

At that time, the Beavers were the passion. Decades later, the New York Knickerbockers would win an NBA championship with a game reminiscent of the City College style—a game that emphasized movement, the creation of opportunities, and the unselfish, never-ending search for the open man. In the last week of March in 1950, however,

the Knicks' involvement in the new league's playoffs was an afterthought. The Beavers were playing for a championship—their second of the month.

City had already defeated Bradley, 69–61, for the championship of the older National Invitation Tournament (NIT). The victory was part of an eight-game winning streak that sent the Beavers to a rematch with the Braves in the NCAA championship game on the same Garden floor.

In the eighties, credibility would be achieved with important victories in the presence of network television cameras. But in 1950, national attention was the result of a successful appearance before the eighteen thousand seats at the old Garden. Those seats were filled late on that Tuesday night, March 28—10 nights after the NIT final—with fans who had come to see if the Beavers could complete an achievement known as the Grand Slam (NIT and NCAA titles).

Midway through the second half, six Braves each had been charged with four fouls, and Bradley trailed by 11 points. But the Braves switched from their zone to a man-to-man defense, gambled with full-court pressure, and reduced the lead to five with two minutes to play. With the rules of the time awarding possession of the ball after a free throw attempt—regardless of whether the foul shot was made or missed—a 66–61 lead was usually considered safe.

The City lead was not. Bradley's Gene Melchiorre, the smallest player on the court, stole a pass, dribbled half the length of the floor, and made a layup to cut the lead to three.

The Beavers seemed to end the crisis when Norman Mager made a foul shot and Irwin Dambrot scored for a six-point lead with 57 seconds to play.

But City's continued mistakes frightened the New York crowd. After a foul shot by Bradley's Joe Stowell, Melchiorre made a layup, intercepted a pass, and scored again. Suddenly the Braves were within a point with 40 seconds to play.

A City timeout did not prevent the Beavers from making another mistake. Ten seconds later, the Braves had the ball and a chance to take the lead. Melchiorre drove the lane into an area occupied by three Beavers.

Years later, a slow-motion look at the films does not produce a clear answer to what happened. Melchiorre's drive took him into a triangle of dark CCNY shirts, where he was stripped of the ball. To the outrage of the Bradley fans, a foul was not called.

The fifties began in New York, and Madison Square Garden was home to the Beavers of City College of New York and their coach, Nat Holman.

After defeating Bradley University for the championship, Holman appeared before a campus rally, saying the victory belonged to the team "because of their cooperation and wonderful CCNY spirit."

Dambrot lifted a lead pass to Mager, downcourt at the other foul line. Mager went in alone for the layup that put the Beavers ahead by three points, 71–68—the final margin—with 10 seconds to play.

Nat Holman, in his 31st season as the coach at City College, proclaimed this Beaver team to be his greatest. Their Grand Slam seemed to be just a beginning. Just one starter was a senior, and four important parts of the team were sophomores. The Helsinki Olympic Games, two years away, could have been the final championship step for a history-making group.

Classes were suspended. The buildings on the main campus in upper Manhattan were emptied except for resourceful students who leaned out of windows for a view of the celebration rally.

The bell on the top of the main building was rung for five minutes. The moment was proclaimed as the proudest in the 102 years of the college. Harry N. Wright, the CCNY president, said, "I want to point out that they are given no scholarships to

> "The game was really undermined by the gambling and point-shaving scandal that involved, among other teams, CCNY. It was a serious black eye for the game."
>
> —*Pete Newell*
> *Hall of Fame coach*

play ball, and they have not been imported to play basketball. I am particularly proud of their high scholastic rating."

And then it was all over, and a new, sadder history was recorded.

Seven members of the championship team, and eleven from other colleges, were arrested in the game-fixing scandal that changed the game forever. The Board of Higher Education also reported that high school records of 14 players had been changed to make them eligible for admission to CCNY.

The Board determined that City would no longer play games at the Garden, and that the emphasis would be placed on an intramural program. Holman was suspended by the Board, but later won an appeal of the decision.

"I will not at any time say anything about it," he said. "That situation is dead. My heart bleeds for some of those youngsters who made a mistake. They say to err is human, to forgive divine. The thing is in the past. Those boys have all been on their feet. They're all fine citizens now, and the press will never get anything from me. They'll never get it from the coach." ∎

Malcolm Moran began covering the Final Four in 1979 in Salt Lake City and has been a regular since. He was the lead college writer for The New York Times *during many of those years before returning to the Midwest where he now has a similar assignment for* USA Today.

Kentucky center Bill Spivey goes for a layup in the Wildcats' tournament victory over Illinois en route to the 1951 crown. (Photo courtesy of AP/Wide World Photos.)

1951

THIRD TITLE'S CHARM . . . A CIGARETTE LIGHTER

By Earl Cox

WITH VOLATILE COACHES ADOLPH RUPP AND Paul "Bear" Bryant occupying offices just a few feet apart, the late forties and early fifties were super-charged times at the University of Kentucky.

Rupp's basketball teams won consecutive national championships in 1948 and 1949. Bryant's football Wildcats, after losing the 1950 Orange Bowl to Santa Clara, gained national recognition when he directed them to a tremendous upset victory over Bud Wilkinson's Oklahoma Sooners in the 1951 Sugar Bowl.

Yes, there was competition and rivalry between Rupp and Bryant.

After Bryant left Kentucky for Texas A&M and, eventually, Alabama, he got a lot of mileage by telling a story about basketball-mad Kentucky.

"When Adolph won those national championships, they gave him a Cadillac," said Bryant. "Here's what I got for stopping Oklahoma's winning streak in the Sugar Bowl and then winning the Cotton Bowl." He held up a cigarette lighter!

Three months after Bryant took Kentucky to its first major bowl (the Orange in 1950), Rupp's third-ranked basketball team was humiliated in the first round of the National Invitation Tournament by City College of New York, 89–50.

Despite the big loss to CCNY, Kentucky was an exciting place to be, recalled Cliff Hagan, who later became the director of athletics there.

"Kentucky was the first team to win more than one NCAA [championship] and also the NIT, and Bryant was winning all those games," said Hagan. "And everyone was excited in the spring of 1950 about moving into Memorial Coliseum, which was the Taj Mahal of on-campus basketball arenas."

Rupp was more than excited. He was so devastated by the NIT loss that for the second time in his career he scheduled a spring practice.

"The only other time he had done that was in 1948 when his starting team represented the USA in the London Olympics," said Hagan.

Rupp wanted to get an early start with his outstanding freshmen—two of whom were Hagan and Frank Ramsey, both future Hall of Famers.

Hagan, who had graduated from Owensboro, Kentucky, Senior High School at midsemester, would not be eligible until after the first semester of 1950–1951. Rupp said that he probably would not use Hagan at all, thus preserving three full seasons for the 6´4´´ forward-center.

After three weeks of spring practice (it was legal then) Rupp was itching to get started again. The 1950–1951 season was his 21st at Kentucky, and his record was 410–77. He had the new coliseum. His teams were 72–16 in major tournaments during his first 20 years. His sophomore-studded 1949–1950 team was 25–5 and he had all those promising freshmen.

Rupp said, as he began practice for what was to become his third championship season, "Potentially, we have one of the best teams in Kentucky history."

Only one senior starter, Capt. Walt Hirsch, was on the 1950–1951 Wildcats. Eight juniors returned, headed by 7´0´´ All-American center Bill Spivey, who had broken many of Alex Groza's Kentucky records.

Among other Wildcats were Lou Tsioropoulos, C. M. Newton, Guy Strong, Shelby Linville, Bobby Watson, and Lucian "Skippy" Whitaker. Rupp had quality and depth at all positions.

Kentucky defeated Purdue, 70–52, in the Memorial Coliseum dedication game, then blitzed Rupp's old coach, Phog Allen, and alma mater Kansas, 68–39, as Spivey outplayed Clyde Lovellette. The Cats took a 6–0 record to New Orleans for the Sugar Bowl Tournament, where they lost a 43–42 overtime game to St. Louis in the first round. Three days later, Bryant's football team ended Oklahoma's 47-game winning streak.

Whether that had anything to do with it or not, Rupp decided to play Hagan at the start of the second semester. Hirsch, having played varsity ball his freshman season, was ineligible for postseason play, and that may have been the reason Rupp decided to use Hagan.

The smooth hook-shooter played his first varsity game on his 19th birthday, January 26, 1951, scoring 13 points against Vanderbilt. He started for Spivey in this first game of the Southeastern Conference Tournament in Louisville and scored 20 points. Hagan scored 25 the next day against Alabama, and the Cats gained a spot in the final against Vanderbilt. The Commodores had lost to Kentucky by 32 points on February 24 in Lexington, but they turned the tables on the Cats in Louisville on March 3 by 61–57.

Two tournaments for Kentucky, two losses for Kentucky.

"We turned down a chance to play in the NIT," Hagan said, "but coach Rupp wasn't happy when the NCAA put him against in-state rival Louisville in a first-round game."

Rupp had other reasons to be crotchety besides having to play Louisville.

"Coach Rupp had a bad year with his health," said Hagan. "He had trouble with a cornea, a bad back, his leg was in a cast because of a bad knee, and he had a bad stomach."

To prepare for the NCAA, Rupp added a postseason game with Loyola, beating the Chicago team, 97–61. The Cats then beat Louisville, 79–68, at Raleigh, North Carolina, and it was on to the Eastern Regional at Madison Square Garden and a return engagement with St. John's. The Cats had beaten the Redmen, 43–37, on December 23 at New York City, and this time the Kentuckians again prevailed, 59–43. Rupp's team scored 16 in the last five minutes to pull away.

Rupp said, as he began practice for what was to become his third championship season, "Potentially, we have one of the best teams in Kentucky history."

Kentucky won the Eastern championship as Spivey scored 28 points and Linville got 14 to lead the Cats to a 76–74 squeaker over Illinois. Linville got free under the basket to score the decisive goal with 12 seconds left.

So it was on to Minneapolis to meet Western champion Kansas State, coached by Jack Gardner. Hagan had the flu, and Whitaker started in his place. Spivey was sick, too, suffering from a cold.

Kentucky trailed, 29–27, at halftime, but the second half was all Kentucky. The Cats took control early and went on to win Rupp's third national championship by a score of 68–58. Spivey more than lived up to his All-America billing with 22 points and 21 rebounds. Hagan scored 10 points. K-State center Lew Hitch was hot early, scoring 10 points in the first half. But Rupp got on Spivey's case, and the big man held Hitch to three the rest of the way.

Hagan turned the final game around. With the Cats trailing 20–13 midway through the first half, Rupp sent Hagan in. He tipped in a missed free throw, then led a Kentucky rally late in the first half, and continued to play well throughout. Linville was also an effective player for Kentucky, scoring eight points and rebounding well.

A crowd of 15,428 showed up for the game at Williams Arena on the campus of the University of Minnesota. There was no television. "The only Minneapolis station was not interested," said Hagan.

The Cats had a hard time getting back to Kentucky. Bad weather grounded their plane, and they had to take a train to Chicago, a plane to Cincinnati, and another on to Lexington.

At the victory banquet, Rupp praised Hagan: "We wouldn't be here if Hagan hadn't played this year." ∎

Adolph Rupp was back in the winner's circle in 1951, his third NCAA title for Kentucky in the past four seasons. (Photo courtesy of AP/Wide World Photos.)

Earl Cox was executive sports editor and columnist at
The Louisville Courier-Journal and Times.
He was founder of the Associated Press Sports Editors Association.
He is now retired.

1952

WHEN LOVELLETTE GOT CAUGHT IN THE PHOG

By Dick Snider

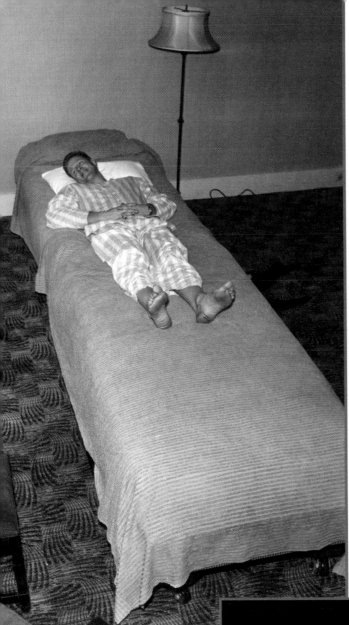

(above) The era of big men began in the forties and fifties. At the 1952 championship, 6´9˝ Clyde Lovellette led Kansas. When he requested a longer bed, the hotel manager put together two beds lengthwise.

(right) As the 1952 championship game wound down, coach Phog Allen took Lovellette from the game with a fond handshake as Kansas won, 80–63.

BY THE TIME THE GAME ENDED AND THE KANSAS Jayhawks had defeated St. John's of Brooklyn to win the 1952 NCAA basketball title, a sportswriter was standing on the court next to KU's legendary coach, Dr. Forrest C. "Phog" Allen.

The tournament was in Seattle, and it was well past deadline back at the writer's newspaper, the *Topeka (Kansas) Daily Capital.* He was in a hurry.

"Doc," the sportswriter yelled as the celebration started, "how about a quick quote for the folks back home?"

Allen, 66, who was in his 42nd year as a college head coach, and who had just won his first national championship, hesitated only a second.

"Tell them," he yelled back, "that we were just like Casey at the bat." With that Allen started to move into the crowd. The sportswriter grabbed his arm.

"But Doc," the writer yelled into his ear, "Casey struck out."

"Yeah," Allen thundered, "BUT WE DIDN'T."

That was that.

The sportswriter was hoping he would say something about Clyde Lovellette, his 6´9˝ senior center, who had played exceptionally well most of the season and who had been phenomenal in the final week and in the NCAA playoffs. The title was a personal triumph for the 245-pound Lovellette as much as it was for the controversial Allen.

In the last two games of the regular season, Clyde scored 33 points as Kansas defeated its top rival, Kansas State, to clinch a tie for the Big Seven title, and then scored 41 in a victory over Colorado that clinched both the title and the NCAA berth.

In regional play in Kansas City, he scored 31 in a 68–64 win over Texas Christian and 44 in a 74–55 bashing of St. Louis. Allen called the latter Clyde's best game ever.

In Seattle, he scored 33 as Kansas whipped Santa Clara, 74–55, in the Western final, and 33

more as the Jayhawks wiped out St. John's, 80–63, in the NCAA championship game.

And remember, folks, this was in the days when 30 points was a whole bunch, and 40 was a rare night to remember.

Kansas went on to play in the Olympic Trials and defeated Southwest Missouri State and La Salle before losing to the Peoria Caterpillars of the AAU in the final. Lovellette scored 91 points in the three games but somehow missed a layup that could have been one of the biggest buckets of his career.

With 50 seconds to go against Peoria and the score tied, Lovellette stole the ball and dribbled the length of the court, escorted by two teammates. It was a three-on-nothing break. Incredibly, Clyde missed the layup. Peoria got the rebound and scored with eight seconds left to win, 62–60.

Clyde and four other Jayhawks made the Olympic squad that went to Helsinki and defeated Russia in the final.

Despite all this, *Look* magazine, headquartered in New York and one of the major sports voices of the day, didn't name Lovellette to its All-America first team. This caused Allen to dust off his old observations that "New Yorkers are taller and fairer than the Chinese, but not nearly as progressive."

Allen had a lot to say and made his usual headlines as Kansas ran out the season. First, Phog ripped the NCAA playoff system, saying Kansas was going only because the players wanted to go, and calling NCAA Tournament officials "as big a bunch of promoters as the AAU's quadrennial transoceanic hitchhikers."

After Kansas won the NCAA title and faced the Olympic Trials in New York's Madison Square Garden, Allen threatened not to go unless he could have at least one Midwestern official work Jayhawk games. He didn't get the one he wanted, but he got one.

Phog had no reason to complain about the NCAA Final Four, particularly after St. John's upset Kentucky, which included the likes of Cliff Hagan and Frank Ramsey, in the Eastern final in Raleigh, North Carolina, and Santa Clara bounced UCLA in the Western final in Corvallis, Oregon.

Kansas won in Kansas City in a tournament that is memorable not only because of Lovellette, but also because a TCU player named George McLeod closed out a remarkable season there. In 24 games, he fouled out of 14 and had four fouls in 9 of the other 10 (in all probability, an NCAA record that still stands).

The semifinal game in 1952 pitted Santa Clara against Kansas, which won 74–55 to move to the championship game and the title. It was late in that game when a fiery little sub got in the game to steal the ball for the Jayhawks. Years later, that sub, Dean Smith, would have an even bigger impact on 11 Final Fours in which his North Carolina Tar Heels played.

campus didn't amount to much. There was no television, so the teams traveled directly from the regionals to Seattle, and settled it all by playing Tuesday and Wednesday nights.

A few radio stations covered the tournament, but there probably were no more than a dozen newspapers from outside the area represented. Because it was an Olympic year, the Associated Press sent star writer Will Grimsley out from New York to cover it. It was the first time the Associated Press had invested that heavily in Final Four coverage.

On the squad with Lovellette was a fellow named Dean Smith, who didn't play much but who obviously learned a lot.

Things were so slow that when the writers covering Santa Clara learned that Midwest writers called Lovellette "the Great White Whale," they looked over their roster and dubbed Kenny Sears, the lean, fair-skinned Santa Clara star, "the Wan Worm from Watsonville."

Members of the Kansas supporting cast also deserved mention. Allen's assistant was Dick Harp, who was said by many to do most of the coaching while Phog did all the talking. Harp never dignified that observation with a reply.

On the squad with Lovellette was a fellow named Dean Smith, who didn't play much but who obviously learned a lot. There was Charlie Hoag, who also played football well enough to be ranked right up there with contemporaries Billy Vessels of Oklahoma and Bobby Reynolds of Nebraska.

There were the Kelley brothers, Dean and Allen; B. H. Born, who would lead the Jayhawks to the 1953 Final Four; Al Squires, the first black player ever at Kansas; and the rest—Kenney, Lienhard, Hougland, Keller, Heitholt, and Davenport.

Allen died in 1974 at 88. Lovellette played professional basketball and was in law enforcement for a time before becoming a teacher at White's Institute in Wabash, Indiana. ∎

Big Ten champ Illinois won in Chicago to complete the Seattle field, and Lovellette took care of the rest. The toughest time Kansas had came the night before the tournament when Clyde went out for the evening and was missing all night.

It wasn't his fault, and Allen knew where he was, or at least thought he did. Lovellette laughed about it later but admitted it was a matter of some concern at the time. Here's what happened:

A Sigma Chi fraternity brother of Clyde's from KU had become an ensign in the coast guard and was stationed on a cutter anchored in Puget Sound. He invited Lovellette out for dinner, and things went fine until they tried to return to shore in a small boat.

A dense fog had set in, and the two couldn't make it. After wandering around for a while, they wound up back on the cutter, and Clyde didn't get back to the hotel until after dawn.

"Phog had something to say to me," Clyde recalled, "but not too much. I think he was as glad to see me as I was to be back on dry land."

An early-rising radio man from Topeka, Gerry Barker, saw Clyde enter the hotel upon his return, but he never said anything and neither did the Jayhawks, so the rest of the media missed the story.

Compared to current Final Fours, the 1952 affair in Edmundson Pavilion on the University of Washington

Dick Snider was the sports editor and later managing editor, of The Topeka Daily Capital *before joining Bud Wilkinson as assistant director of the President's Council for Physical Fitness in the Kennedy administration. Today, he is retired in Topeka, Kansas, where he still writes a weekly column for* The Topeka Capital-Journal.

1953

McCRACKEN'S SWEET REVENGE

By Ted O'Leary

INDIANA UNIVERSITY BASKETBALL COACH BRANCH McCracken's deliverance from three years of musing over what might have been came in 1953, appropriately at the expense of coach Forrest C. "Phog" Allen of Kansas.

In the late summer of 1948, one of the nation's most ardently recruited high school centers—Clyde Lovellette of Terre Haute, Indiana—was in Bloomington, having assured McCracken that he would enroll at Indiana. McCracken figured that a big center like Lovellette would provide the missing element that Indiana needed to win its second NCAA championship. The first had been won over Allen's Kansas team in 1940.

McCracken was not unduly alarmed when, just before enrolling, Lovellette said he was going home to pick up some belongings. He never returned.

By mid-September he had enrolled at Kansas. Asked how he had landed such a prize, Allen blandly told newsmen that Lovellette had decided to attend Kansas because he suffered from asthma. Although he was an osteopathic physician, Allen did not explain why asthma sufferers would find the Kansas climate more salubrious than that of Indiana.

Many years later, recalling notable recruiting coups, Allen, making no reference to asthma, with a wink told a writer, "There was nothing irregular in my recruiting of Wilt Chamberlain—I sold his mother on Kansas. But Clyde Lovellette—well, that's another story." He did not tell it.

In 1952 McCracken had been forced to watch as Lovellette, who had become one of the most dominant players in collegiate history, led Kansas to one of the most lopsided victories in an NCAA final, over St. John's of New York. Lovellette broke nine tournament records in the process.

Kansas' success with Lovellette substantiated McCracken's belief that college basketball had reached a stage where a big, good-shooting center, of which Lovellette was the prototype, was essential for national dominance.

Believing he had on his squad forwards and guards of national championship caliber, McCracken went prospecting for the missing ingredient. He found what he sought in Don Schlundt, 6´6´´ and still growing. He was playing for Washington-City Township High School in South Bend, Indiana. When Schlundt visited Bloomington in the summer of 1951, McCracken, recalling Lovellette's defection, promptly enrolled him in summer school.

Schlundt met expectations. Not only did he grow four inches, but as a sophomore he established a Big Ten season scoring record. His addition, plus the switching of excellent long shooter Bob Leonard from forward to guard after the 1951–1952 season, worked wonders. The Hoosiers went to the Final Four in Kansas City (where Indiana had won its 1940 championship) with a Big Ten title and a 21–3 record. The losses—to Notre Dame, Kansas State, and Minnesota—were by a total of five points. All three losses came on field goals in the last 30 seconds of play—a memory that returned to haunt some of the Indiana players as their championship game against Kansas reached its final 27 seconds with the result still agonizingly in doubt.

That the defending champion Jayhawks made it to the NCAA Tournament at all, let alone the championship game, was totally unexpected. Four starters from the 1952 championship team, including Lovellette, had been lost. Kansas was picked no higher than third in the Big Eight race, and Allen said he doubted Kansas would win more than five games in 1952–1953.

However, some factors were overlooked. B. H. Born, painfully thin but tall, 6´9´´, had been completely overshadowed by Lovellette as a sophomore. But two years of daily practice scrimmages against Lovellette had taught Born more than he would have learned as a starter matching up against lesser players. Allen added two superior athletes—football stars Harold Patterson and Gil Reich—to

(above) Indiana coach Branch McCracken joined the late-game debate at the scorer's table, where the number of B. H. Born fouls seemed crucial. The scorer signaled Born's fifth foul, but the Kansas bench and the press row showed only four—which became the argument's result. However, McCracken soon smiled as the team posed for its championship picture (right).

Kansas returned to defend its title in 1953, but Indiana, with Don Schlundt, Bobby Leonard, and Charley Kraak, defeated the Jayhawks for the championship. Indiana kept Kansas center Born (No. 25) out of position, which got him into foul trouble. Schlundt led the Hoosiers with 30 points.

his squad. Dean Kelleys brother Al became a starter, and the two 5´11´´ Kelleys became the leaders of a terrorizing full-court press.

Playing in Kansas City's Municipal Auditorium, 40 miles from the Kansas campus, was almost like playing at home for the Jayhawks. Pressing defenses tend to be inspired by noisy exhortations, and the Kelleys got them from the Kansas City crowd.

Kansas played its semifinal against tournament-favorite Washington, which came in at 29–2. The Huskies were led by Bob Houbregs, regarded by many as the top college player of the season. Although obviously outsized, Kansas rushed to an 8–0 lead. Rattled by the Kansas fullcourt press, which somebody said started when the Huskies came through their hotel door, Washington not only failed to score on its first six possessions, it didn't even get the ball to the keyhole area.

Kansas stole the ball 18 times. At the half, the Jayhawks were up by 11. If it wasn't all over then, it was when Houbregs, outscored by Born 25–18, fouled out in the third quarter (college games were played in quarters then). Kansas won, 79–53. Indiana players were apprehensive over what they had seen.

Kansas' success with Lovellette substantiated McCracken's belief that college basketball had reached a stage where a big, good-shooting center . . . was essential for national dominance.

Indiana's semifinal against Louisiana State, led by the great Bob Pettit, was a classic example of a basic basketball dilemma—how to defense a team that possesses both a strong inside and a strong outside offense. The Tigers began with a compact defense intended to hold Schlundt in check under the basket. Leonard, finding himself loosely guarded just behind the foul circle, promptly hit six field goals in a row. LSU was forced to go outside after him, thus freeing Schlundt inside. He and Pettit each scored 29, while Leonard added 22, as Indiana won, 80–53.

The pulsating Indiana-Kansas final was a welcome contrast to the two semifinal lulling blowouts. Indiana led by one at the end of the third quarter, which had been marked

by a bitter dispute. When a foul was called on Born, the scorers signaled that it was his fifth, disqualifying him and almost certainly dooming Kansas. The Kansas bench claimed its scorebook showed only four fouls on Born. Writers at the press table said their books bore that out. After rechecking, the official scorers agreed. That sent McCracken into a tirade. He charged that the scorers had eliminated one of Born's fouls. He also questioned their hospitality. "We came out here as your guests," he yelled, "and now you are robbing us."

Later came another eruption, this time by Indiana's Charley Kraak. Angered by a charging foul with 1:21 left to play and Indiana ahead by three, Kraak slammed the ball on the court so hard that, as he recalled years later, it almost bounced up and hit the ceiling. Presumably, McCracken almost did too, as he saw Kansas given three free throw opportunities—one on a technical—and possession of the ball under the rules then in effect. Patterson converted only one of his free throw chances, and Al Kelley missed on the technical. But on the ensuing possession, Dean Kelley hit a layup with 1:05 left. So the game was tied (for the 14th time) at 68–68. With 27 seconds left, Leonard made one of two free throw chances.

During a timeout, Allen instructed his players to hold the ball for 22 seconds, then get it to Al Kelley for a shot that might give Kansas its second straight NCAA championship. The possibility loomed that Indiana was fated to lose for the fourth time on a last half-minute field goal. When Kelley got the ball, he found he had no chance to get off a shot over a thicket of upstretched Indiana arms. He snapped the ball to little-used substitute Jerry Alberts deep in the corner on the baseline. His desperate shot appeared on line, but it banged against the rim, and an Indiana substitute, Dick White, snatched the key rebound of his career to preserve the 69–68 victory. Leonard later confessed he couldn't stand to look at Alberts' shot.

After the game ended, Indiana students hoisted their victorious players on their shoulders and carried them back to the hotel. The sight of young men carrying other young men, apparently wearing brightly colored long underwear, through a downtown city street near midnight may have startled the unknowing. But to those caught up in the near hysteria of the moment, nothing could have seemed more appropriate.

The Kansas team took the bus back to Lawrence, arriving after midnight to be greeted by more than 2,500 cheering supporters. Allen told the throng, "I have received more cheer from this team than any other in my 43 years of coaching." ■

Ted O'Leary was an All-American basketball player and Phi Beta Kappa at Kansas. He was a writer and book reviewer for 54 years at The Kansas City Star *and a regular contributing writer to* Sports Illustrated *for 25 years. He died in the autumn of 2000.*

1954

TOM GOLA AND THE EIGHT GARBAGE MEN

By Dick Weiss

TOM GOLA WAS THE MAGIC JOHNSON OF THE fifties, a gifted 6´7´´ junior All-American who put his personal signature on La Salle's national championship team. He was the son of a Philadelphia policeman who grew up in the Olney section of the city, just walking distance from the school's campus.

The brightest star in the rugged Catholic League when he played at La Salle High School, Gola was recruited by more than 60 schools. When he accepted a scholarship to play for Kenny Loeffler at La Salle, he only had to travel across the street.

Gola, a quiet neighborhood kid who learned how to play the game in the school yards at Incarnation Parish, gave the tiny Christian Brothers' school a national address during his brilliant career. Gola was the first freshman ever selected MVP in the NIT when he combined with Norm Greckin and Buddy Donnelly to lead La Salle to the 1952 championship.

Two years later, he was the dominant player in the game.

Gola could play all five positions. Loeffler used him at center, but did not limit him to the post in the Explorers' flash pivot offense. Gola was too valuable. He could pass. He could handle the ball. He could rebound. He could play great defense. He could score.

He could score at will, but never did, preferring to enhance the abilities of eight other, more anonymous players.

Gola averaged 22.8 points during the tournament and was an overwhelming choice for Most Outstanding Player when the Explorers defeated Bradley, 92–76, in the championship game in Kansas City.

Gola only scored 19 in the final, but that did not stop Bradley coach Forrdy Anderson from lauding him.

"Gola killed us," he told the writers afterward. "It wasn't his shooting that killed us. It was the way Gola controlled the ball by grabbing those rebounds off the backboards and the way he kept faking our defense out of position, opening up the middle so their other players could drive through for layups.

"Actually, Gola hurt us the most when he was just faking around out there, working without the ball."

In that respect, Gola might have been light years ahead of his time. He was La Salle's meal ticket throughout the season and did wonders for Loeffler, who had been hospitalized the previous summer for a severe case of ulcers.

Loeffler, who coached the NBA Providence Steamrollers before accepting the head coaching job at La Salle in 1949,

was a brilliant man who once served as a federal labor negotiator and was an accomplished pianist. He was a stern disciplinarian who had a reputation for squeezing the most out of his talent.

Loeffler thought he would open the season with talent to spare. But then Jack George, a 6´3´´ guard, signed to play pro basketball with the Philadelphia Warriors after he was discharged from the army. Jackie Moore, a 6´7´´ center who played a pivotal role on the Explorers' 1952 NIT championship team, was declared academically ineligible. Forward Bill Katheder entered the service, and guard

> ## "Gola killed us . . . Actually, Gola hurt us the most when he was just faking around out there, working without the ball."
>
> **—Fordy Anderson**
> *Coach of Bradley's 1954 team*

Eddie Altieri, the best ballhandler on the team, was a victim of the five-year eligibility rule.

"Our team this year is Tom Gola and eight garbage men," Loeffler reportedly told an audience of New York City writers before the Holiday Festival that year.

Loeffler molded his 26–4 team around Gola and senior lead guard Frank "Wacky" O'Hara and used them as the catalysts for a young team that also featured sophomores Fran O'Malley, Bobby Maples, Charlie Singley, Frank Blatcher, and Charley Greenberg.

O'Hara and Greenberg both played with Gola in high school. Singley, who played at West Catholic, also had a Catholic League background. Blatcher prepped at South Philadelphia High School and Navy. O'Malley was from St. Rose of Carbonville in upstate Pennsylvania. The 6´6´´ Maples was originally from Chicago but was spotted by Loeffler when he played for naval teams in Wilmington.

O'Hara was dependable. The sophomores were talented but erratic. Gola was simply great. The older college fans in Philly still talk in reverent tones about the time Gola overshadowed the great Frank Selvy when the Explorers defeated Furman, 100–93, before a record crowd of 9,164

La Salle's Tom Gola was carried off the court in Kansas City after he led the Explorers to the 1954 championship over Bradley.

Gola, leaping over an opponent en route to a basket during the regular season, was the Magic Johnson of his time: a 6´7´´ All-American who had the size and skills to play all five positions. (Photo courtesy of Hank Walker/ Time Life Pictures/Getty Images.)

at Philadelphia Convention Hall. Selvy scored 40, but Gola had 25 points and 27 rebounds in 32 minutes.

The Explorers, who were distinguishable by their short- sleeved jerseys, dominated the East and looked like a lock to return to the NIT, where they had been upset in the semifinals the year before.

But the Explorers created quite a stir locally when they chose to participate in the NCAA Tournament instead of going to the Garden for the NIT. It was no secret that players would have preferred to play in New York City, but the Middle Atlantic Conference, a loose organization of smaller colleges in the Philadelphia area that controlled scheduling, reportedly twisted the Explorers' arm to enter the 24-team NCAA Tournament.

La Salle, ironically, was almost eliminated in the opening round by Fordham. The Explorers won, 76–74, in overtime but needed a great pass from Gola to O'Malley for a layup to tie the game at 66–66 in the final second of regulation.

Gola got the ball at the foul line, surrounded by three frantic Fordham players. He spun and jumped, ready to take the shot. Then, at the last second, he spied O'Malley underneath the basket.

"Even when he's thinking, Gola can kill you," said a disappointed Fordham coach Johnny Bach after Gola, who finished with 28 points, destroyed the Rams in overtime.

Gola scored 26 in a more convincing 88–81 second-round win over North Carolina State. Gola dominated the Eastern regional final, scoring 22 points as the Explorers breezed to a 64–48 win over Navy. Charlie Singley added 16 as the Explorers prepared to head for Kansas City.

Before the team left, the Philadelphia Chamber of Commerce presented shamrocks, specially flown in from Ireland, to O'Hara for St. Patrick's Day.

As it turned out, La Salle did not need much luck. Gola and Blatcher, a protégé of NBA great Paul Arizin who learned to shoot in the South Philadelphia church leagues, each scored 19 points during a 69–54 win over upset-minded Penn State in the national semis.

Bradley succeeded in shutting Gola down to some degree in the final, but Blatcher broke loose again, this time scoring 23. Singley added another 23.

When La Salle arrived back in Philadelphia, the Explorers were greeted by more than ten thousand fans, who jammed the corridors and plane aprons at Philadelphia Airport.

The crowd knew just what to say when Gola deplaned.

They started the "Go Gola Go" chant that has since become a big part of La Salle folklore. ■

Dick Weiss, a Philadelphia native, has covered Final Fours since 1970, including Villanova's Final Four appearances in 1985, for the Philadelphia Daily News.

1955

EAST VS. WEST, GOLA VS. RUSSELL

By Ted O'Leary

IN HIS PREVIEW OF THE 1952–1953 BASKETBALL season for the *Official NCAA Basketball Guide*, Jim Enright, a knowledgeable Chicago sportswriter and respected basketball game official, asserted that the time had come to reverse Horace Greeley's famous advice, "Go West, young man."

Enright suggested that if Greeley were alive today and a basketball fan, sound judgment would compel him to proclaim, "Go East, young man, in your desire to find the 1955 national basketball champion." Enright turned out to have been disoriented.

Enright listed two dozen teams he said were the most likely to make it to the 1955 NCAA Tournament. He did not name San Francisco. The most likely candidates for national college player of the year, Enright declared, were Tom Gola, defending NCAA champion and La Salle's two-time All-American, and Sihugo Green of Duquesne, who Enright asserted had the best chance to dethrone La Salle.

This is not to fault Enright. Except for a few insiders on the West Coast, San Francisco was just another aspiring basketball team, and Bill Russell was a young guy who went to San Francisco because it was about the only college to offer him a scholarship. Ridiculed at Oakland's McClymonds High School for his awkwardness, Russell worked long hours to improve his play. As a 6´6˝ senior

center, he had played well enough to interest San Francisco, which at the time didn't even have its own court.

In Russell's first year on the varsity, the Dons went 14–7. By the beginning of the 1954–1955 season, Russell had reached an announced 6´10˝. Russell dissented, complaining. "I'm only 6´9˝ and ⅝ of an inch. Don't call me 6´10˝. I'm enough of a goon already!"

The skills that were to make him probably the best defensive player in basketball history, both college and professional, made Russell the ideal player for San Francisco coach Phil Woolpert. Woolpert was convinced that defense was the basis of basketball success, a belief mostly borne out by college results in the decade of the fifties. "We figure to have the ball only about half the time in a game," said Woolpert, "so in practice, we work on defense half the time."

San Francisco first began to attract national attention as a result of its performance in the All-College Invitational Tournament in Oklahoma City, one of the first and most prestigious of the Christmas holiday tournaments. San Francisco trounced tournament favorite Wichita State, 94–75, and the following week made the wire service Top 20 polls for the first time that season.

San Francisco had lost its third game of the season, to UCLA, but it never lost again that season, or the next either. No other team came closer than 10 points except Oregon State, which in the NCAA West Regional challenged the Dons to the end, losing 57–56 in the final.

Joining San Francisco (26–1) in the Final Four at Kansas City were La Salle (25–4), Iowa (19–5), and Colorado (18–5). Almost everyone predicted a final between San Francisco and La Salle. Few confrontations in college basketball history had been more eagerly awaited than that between Gola, who had recently been named to a five-man all-time college team, and Russell. A similar individual matchup would make headlines years later when Magic Johnson of Michigan State faced off against Larry Bird of Indiana State in 1979.

What happened in the semifinal games only whetted the interest of basketball followers everywhere. La Salle beat Iowa, 76–73, with Gola scoring 23 points, and San Francisco defeated Colorado, 65–50, as Russell scored 24 points. Wrote Bob Busby in the *Kansas City Times*:

It was Bill Russell's moment in 1955 as he jumped in the air and clicked his heels (photo on page 45). An almost unknown San Francisco team held off Tom Gola and La Salle for the championship in Kansas City. Russell, the Final Four MOP, and teammate K. C. Jones dominated the game. Russell scored 23 points and grabbed 25 rebounds.

Few basketball officials have ever entertained crowds like Chicago sportswriter Jim Enright in the fifties. He would run across the floor, sometimes jumping in the air, gesturing dramatically on almost every call. A crowd favorite, he was respected by coaches for calling a fair game.

congesting the middle, blocking La Salle drives for layups, and picking up rebounds.

The strategy proved inspired. Russell ended with 25 rebounds to go with 23 points. During one 21-minute period, Jones held Gola scoreless. His point total for the game was 16.

La Salle coach Ken Loeffler's scouting report on Jones proved only too accurate. On the locker room blackboard he had scribbled, "Jones, No. 4. Can hit from outside." So he did, adding 21 points to San Francisco's total in a 77–63 victory. The outcome was never really in doubt.

One of the most graphic descriptions of Russell's play was included in the report on the final in *Sports Illustrated*, then a fledgling magazine. After noting that La Salle was not able to deny Russell the ball, the report went on: "Particularly deadly were Russell's tap-ins. Timing his leaps perfectly, he would soar into the air just as a shot by a colleague floated in toward the basket and tip the ball in the basket while La Salle defenders impotently stretched and strained beneath. It was not Gola's night to give an ulcer to Phil Woolpert but Russell was no help for Ken Loeffler's duodenal condition."

It is a measure of how interest in the Final Four has increased through the years. *Sports Illustrated*, which would later cover the event like a World Series or Super Bowl, devoted only three columns to its report and did not give the author of its story a byline.

The 1955 Final Four set off repercussions that went beyond the crowning of one more NCAA champion. The performances of Russell and Jones, plus the presence of four other blacks on the San Francisco squad,

"A packed crowd of 10,500 at Municipal Auditorium probably never before saw such a display of talent as was presented by two centers in one evening. Gola was perfection personified in all departments, as usual.

"Russell showed great all-around ability. The 6´10˝ San Francisco junior swept rebounds from levels halfway up the backboard and he made one two-handed dunk shot over his head with his back to the basket."

Now the Gola-Russell matchup seemed assured. Russell downplayed the individual angle, saying, "I'm not worrying about Gola. I'm just going to try to help my team win." Russell granted, however, that "Gola could really give coach [Woolpert] an ulcer."

A startling strategic move by Woolpert turned the Gola versus Russell buildup into an excitement-dampening

The 1955 Final Four set off repercussions that went beyond the crowning of one more NCAA champion . . . By 1958, four of the five consensus All-American players were black.

letdown. To the astonishment of his players, Woolpert informed them at their pregame meal that he had decided to assign 6´1˝ K. C. Jones to guard Gola, who was 6 inches taller. Woolpert figured that with Jones dogging Gola wherever he went, Russell could lurk under the basket,

accelerated the liberation of black college basketball players from the restrictions that racial prejudice had imposed upon them for far too long. By 1958, four of the five consensus All-American players were black.

In March 1956, after Russell had led the Dons to their second consecutive NCAA championship, the basketball rules committee outlawed offensive goaltending. No longer would a player be allowed to do what Russell had elevated to a physical art form. After watching him guide and tap teammates' shots into the basket, voluble Kansas coach Phog Allen, who had campaigned for raising the height of the baskets from 10 to 12 feet, raised the ante to 20 feet!

Appropriately the new anti-goaltending rule was called "the Russell rule," part of Bill Russell's legacy to college basketball. ∎

1956

THE NCAA CROWNS FIRST UNDEFEATED CHAMPION

By Art Spander

BILL RUSSELL, GRAY IN MUSTACHE AND MELLOW in mood, squinted into a spotlight and attempted to peer into the past.

"Who are all those old people sitting next to me?" he asked in mock surprise. A muffled laugh carried through the hotel ballroom. Sweet nostalgia carries with it frightening realizations.

Thirty years had flown since that first championship season. Yesterday these men had carried the University of San Francisco to consecutive NCAA basketball titles. Now there were bald heads, pot bellies, and delicious memories.

Their accomplishments continued after graduation. "One judge and several lawyers," noted Phil Woolpert, who had coached those San Francisco teams. "These men have been successful."

No more successful than Woolpert himself. When great college basketball coaches are discussed, we hear the names of Wooden and Rupp, and Smith and Allen. But rarely Woolpert. Which is wrong.

He was a man ahead of his time. He was also a man who preferred remaining behind the scenes.

Woolpert died at age 71 in May 1987 in the deep forest of Washington's Olympic Peninsula, figuratively hiding from the spotlight and pressure of a sport he helped shape but in the end came to disparage. "The tail is wagging the dog," he contended, alluding to an imbalance between academics and athletics. His final job had been as a school bus driver over dirt roads. And that's the way his world ended . . . with a whimper.

The bang came earlier. NCAA championships in 1955 and 1956. Sixty consecutive victories. Coach of the Year awards. But if there's anything worse than losing all the time, it is winning all the time. He retired from San Francisco in 1959, talking about the strain on his nerves.

There would be other seasons on the floor—a brief period in control of the San Francisco Saints, a franchise in the American Basketball League, and then some time formulating a program at the University of San Diego.

In the early seventies, the man who brought together Bill Russell and K. C. Jones for the first time would flee from the ills of recruiting and the shouts of the fans by moving to Sequim, Washington. It was there he spent the final 15 years of his life, far from the madding crowd.

Once in a while he would return to the past. The journey was always pleasant. "Isn't it great to be back together on an occasion like this?" he asked those who had come to the 30th reunion. The response was thunderous applause, as he knew it would be.

"I may sound immodest," he said, "but I firmly believe those two teams were as great as any in college basketball. In 1956 we beat everyone by seven points or more."

Everyone. The Dons were the first undefeated team in history to win the NCAA Tournament. They went 29–0, extending the streak that had started the previous season to 55 straight victories. Five more would accrue the following season before that historic defeat.

Credit Russell, who revolutionized the game. Credit Jones, who could handle the ball and, as seen from his achievements coaching the Boston Celtics, could also handle men. Credit Phil Woolpert, who turned out to be a crusader for civil liberties as well as an instructor in zone defense.

Coach Phil Woolpert brought his San Francisco Dons to the Northwestern Fieldhouse in Evanston, Illinois, to defend their title in 1956, where they ended up facing Iowa's talented Carl "Sugar" Cain (No. 21, right) in the final. But the Hawkeyes would be no match for San Francisco's Bill Russell (No. 6, above) and his teammates, who won 83–71 after rolling over Southern Methodist in the semifinals. (Photo courtesy of AP/Wide World Photos.)

"Phil was so far ahead of other coaches in recruiting black players it was scary," said Pete Newell. "There were a lot of rednecks then."

Newell was the man who Woolpert replaced as San Francisco coach in 1949. Newell was the man who would coach the University of California to an NCAA championship in 1959—the last team without a black player to win the title.

America was different in the fifties. Phil Woolpert was different from many Americans. The only color he cared about was that of a man's uniform.

In later years, Bill Russell would complain of Woolpert's insensitivity toward blacks, and toward Bill Russell in particular. Eventually, those feelings were soothed.

"I have thrown down some of my psychological baggage," Russell said in what amounted to an apology. "Phil Woolpert saw something in me nobody else did. He gave me my chance."

We know what Russell did with the opportunity. NCAA championships at San Francisco in 1955 and 1956. An Olympic gold medal. And, as the Boston Celtics center, a domination of the NBA that would never exist again.

During the 1954 season, when Russell was a sophomore and awkward rather than arrogant, San Francisco started three whites and two blacks. The next season the lineup was the same, and the blacks were indignant. Russell and Jones knew Hal Perry belonged in the lineup instead of Carl Lawson.

> ## "Phil was so far ahead of other coaches in recruiting black players it was scary. There were a lot of rednecks then."
>
> **—Pete Newell**
> *Hall of Fame coach*

Tension was noticeable. "The Junior Globetrotters," someone wrote when the Dons went to three black players. Convention worked against Woolpert. Perception worked for him. The hell with the old ways. Perry would start. So would the winning streak. And many years in the future, Hal Perry, then an attorney, would confess, "I owe Phil Woolpert everything."

Woolpert would explain he owed his wife, Mary, everything. The day he was named San Francisco's coach in 1949, Phil sat down at a desk stacked with telegrams and letters and began to peruse the roster and the schedule. He couldn't balance one against the other.

"I went home," he recalled on more than one occasion, "and told Mary I was quitting, for the athletic director to get another guy. I wasn't going to coach USF. I wasn't ready for the job.

"She called me a coward and a quitter and names that are censored. What could I do? I put my hat back on, went back to the office, and dug into the debris. Mary was the inspiration for everything I have accomplished."

What Russell accomplished was literally to change the rules of basketball. After the Dons' first championship, in 1955, the rest of the college coaches, facing the specter of another year of Russell's greatness, widened the three-second lane from 6 feet to 12 feet.

Russell used everything he had against Iowa in the championship game at Northwestern University's fieldhouse. So did Woolpert.

Jones had played in one game two years earlier before an appendectomy ended his season. Although permitted to play the regular schedule in 1955–1956, K.C. was ruled ineligible for the tournament.

In the opening minutes of the final game, the Dons trailed, 15–4, their biggest deficit of the season. But Woolpert switched guard Gene Brown on Iowa's Carl Cain, who would have been K.C.'s man.

Cain stopped scoring. Russell started rebounding. The Dons beat the Hawkeyes, 83–71. "I can't say how much I contributed to our success," advised a humble Woolpert.

His contribution was enormous. Phil Woolpert was unique. ∎

Art Spander has all sides of the Bay Area covered, writing columns for the San Francisco Examiner, *the* Chronicle, *and the* Oakland Tribune, *as well as for an Internet site. A frequent award winner, he began his career at United Press International.*

1957

WHEN THE FINAL FOUR CAME OF AGE

By Frank Deford

THE 1957 CHAMPIONSHIP MARKED A WATERSHED year for the NCAA and was, indisputably, one of the two or three most important tournaments. It was not just that North Carolina won in perhaps the most exciting final—before or since—in triple overtime; North Carolina also won its semifinal in triple overtime. North Carolina finished undefeated and became the first team from the old Confederacy to take the title.

In a sense, that was the last step in making college basketball truly national, for before that champions had come from the East, West, Midwest, and Southwest. Perhaps even more significant was where the personnel came from. Carolina, an essentially regional university in a Protestant state, fielded a team of Irish Catholic Yankees (and a Jew), while the team it beat in the final, Kansas, a rural state of down-home whites, featured a black sophomore seven-footer from Philadelphia, the fabled Wilt Chamberlain. College basketball was never the same again.

In point of fact, though, the 1957 championship did not have the immediate effect all of the foregoing would suggest. For purposes of comparison, recall that about a year and a half later the National Football League finally went on the map with a similar equivalent showcase—the overtime championship between the Baltimore Colts and the New York Giants. That changed the stature of the NFL literally overnight. But the greatest game ever played in college basketball, Carolina's 54–53 win over Kansas in triple overtime, was only the beginning of the process which made college basketball big time.

There were simple reasons for this. In 1957, even though everyone in college basketball recognized that the NCAA Tournament had replaced the NIT as the official championship, the parochial New York Press—and its first cousin, the National Press

Carolina's Lenny Rosenbluth (right) fouled out, and a distraught Chamberlain (above) was consoled by coach Dick Harp. Chamberlain blamed himself for the loss, and Harp soon retired from coaching.

in New York—still looked down on the NCAA as a bush-town rival imitation. Even the presence of Chamberlain, who, it is safe to say, was the most ballyhooed athlete ever to enter college, wasn't enough to attract genuine national television coverage.

A few years ago, in searching for photographs to go with an article on the game, *Sports Illustrated* discovered, to its amazement, no more than three or four photographers on the floor. *Sports Illustrated* itself gave the game exactly one page—and no photograph—buried deep in the magazine back where there used to be bridge and food articles. Jerry Tax, who covered basketball for the magazine then, managed to get the article in only by pleading that it was, after all, three overtimes, Wilt the Stilt had been upset, and the kids who wore Carolina blue all came from New York.

Ironically, even though almost nobody saw the game—there was, evidently, only one television feed, back to North Carolina—the Kansas loss appears to be what is responsible for Chamberlain being tagged with a loser label. Chamberlain himself was convinced that was so. But in fact, he played a terrific game, and Carolina had to be almost picture-perfect to win by a point. In fact, in the last five seconds, Carolina botched defense on Chamberlain, and the teammate passing the ball to Chamberlain botched the pass. Chamberlain was the only one who did it right, but he didn't get the ball, and he got forever jacketed as a loser.

Actually, Carolina had no business even being in the final. Chamberlain had scored 32 to lead Kansas past San Francisco, 80–56, in its semi, but the only reason the Tar Heels got past Michigan State was because Bob Cunningham, the fifth man and a defensive specialist, scored a career-high 21 when the others went cold. Michigan State led, 64–62, and had Jumpin' Johnny Green on the free throw line with six seconds left in the first overtime. But Green missed, and Pete Brennan took the rebound, dribbled up the court, and fired up a 20-footer at the buzzer to stay alive. As Chamberlain told Tommy Kearns, the Carolina playmaker, years later after the old rivals became best friends, "Tommy, you were blessed."

Frank McGuire, the Tar Heels coach, sent Kearns to jump against Chamberlain at the tip-off. He wanted to rattle the giant; Kearns was the smallest Tar Heel, short of six feet. Chamberlain won the jump, of course, but Carolina

The game that seemed to go on forever pitted Wilt Chamberlain against a talented North Carolina team. Going into a third overtime, Chamberlain yelled from the bench before returning to play. Teammates Lew Johnson (foreground) and Bob Billings watched what many experts call the finest Final Four championship game, won, 54–53, by North Carolina.

time, got the ball at the top of the key. Quigg pump-faked and drove against Chamberlain, but Maurice King reached in as Quigg put up the shot, and the foul was called. Six seconds remained on the clock.

Carolina called timeout, not Kansas. McGuire was renowned for knowing when to call time. Quigg was a 72 percent free throw shooter on the year, but he had missed his only foul shot in this game, so McGuire wanted to reassure him. "Now, Joe," he said, "as soon as you make 'em . . ." and then McGuire went on to discuss the defense.

Quigg swished twice, 54–53.

When Kansas threw in to Chamberlain, Quigg was also the one who batted the ball. Kearns picked it up, dribbled once, and then heaved the ball high in the air. He had seen "Hot Rod" Hundley do that once. By the time the ball came back down, North Carolina was the undefeated NCAA champion.

McGuire threw a victory party that night for all the Carolina people in Kansas City. The tab was $1,500, which the athletic director considered far too excessive just for winning a national basketball championship. So he made McGuire spring for the $58 extra for the Roquefort dressing.

The Tar Heels were celebrated in North Carolina, and then most of them returned home to New York, where, they assumed, more glory awaited them. Pete Brennan rushed to his home in Brooklyn. The Brennans shared a two-family house, with the Cocoas next door. Mrs. Cocoa was coming out her side just as Brennan hurried up his steps. "Hey, Petey," Mrs. Cocoa said. "When did you get back from the soivice?" It would be a bit longer before what truly began in Kansas City in 1957 became the event it is today. ∎

won the rest of the half, going to the locker room on top, 29–22. Kansas coach Dick Harp elected to play a box-and-one, dogging the Carolina high scorer, Lennie Rosenbluth. It was not, it turned out, wise strategy. Carolina did better, sagging everybody onto Chamberlain.

But in the second half, Chamberlain brought Kansas back. Thirty-one minutes into the game, the Jayhawks finally took the lead, 36–35, and second-guessers still think they could have blown it open then—especially with two Carolina starters in deep foul trouble—but Harp elected to sit on the ball.

Still, it almost worked. Kansas led, 44–41, with 1:45 left, and when Chamberlain, moving up to high post, made a beautiful pass down into Gene Elstun, Rosenbluth had to foul Elstun—his fifth. When Elstun moved to the line, Chamberlain clearly remembers spotting a buddy in the stands and smiling at him, sure of victory. But Elstun missed and the moment was gone, and with seconds to go in regulation, Kearns tied it at 46–46 from the free throw line.

The Tar Heels especially were exhausted . . . They were entering their sixth overtime—110 minutes of action—in barely 24 hours.

In the first overtime, each team scored one basket. In the second, nobody scored at all. The Tar Heels especially were exhausted, for their bench was thin, their high scorer was out of the game, and they were entering their sixth overtime—110 minutes of action—in barely 24 hours.

Kearns made a basket and then a one-and-one, but Chamberlain came back with a three-point play, and when Elstun sank two free throws, Kansas was up, 53–52. There were 10 seconds left when Joe Quigg, the center who had been playing with four fouls for almost half an hour's playing

Frank Deford is a senior contributing writer to Sports Illustrated, *a book author, and regular commentator on NPR's* Morning Edition. *A repeat winner as National Sportswriter of the Year, he was founding editor of* The National, *the sports daily newspaper in the late eighties.*

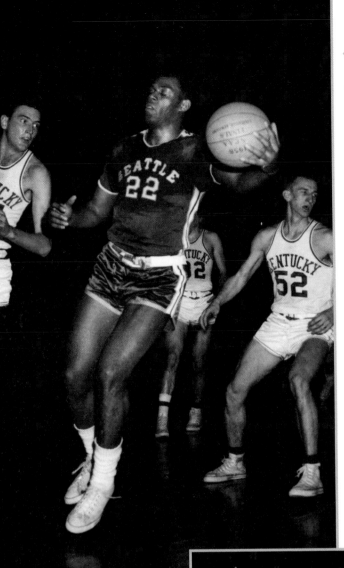

1958

THE FIDDLIN' FIVE

By Billy Reed

HIS PERPETUAL SCOWL ETCHED EVEN DEEPER THAN usual, Adolph Rupp didn't hear any sweet string music as he watched his team get ready for the 1957–1958 season. After a month of practice, the Kentucky maestro was heard to growl, "We've got fiddlers; that's all. They're pretty good fiddlers—be right entertaining at a barn dance. But I'll tell you, you need violinists to play at Carnegie Hall. We don't have any violinists."

This was a sad note to Wildcats fans, and not just because it had been six years since Rupp had won the last of his three NCAA titles. The 1958 Final Four was scheduled to be played at the new Carnegie Hall of college basketball—Freedom Hall in Louisville, just 80 miles from UK's campus in Lexington. With the Mideast Regional set in UK's Memorial Coliseum, the Wildcats had a chance to win the NCAA title without leaving the state.

But when Rupp looked at his talent, he didn't see any of the virtuosos that he saw at rival schools. Kansas had 7′1″ Wilt "the Stilt" Chamberlain back for his junior year. Fans at

Cincinnati and West Virginia were arguing about whether the Bearcats' Oscar Robertson or the Mountaineers' Jerry West was the best sophomore in the universe. Out in Seattle, there was a kid named Elgin Baylor who was a one-man symphony.

It was hardly surprising, then, that none of Rupp's fiddlers was named to any of the preseason All-America teams. The best players were Vernon Hatton, a bowlegged 6′3″ senior who loved to have his hands on the ball with the game on the line, and Johnny Cox, a skinny 6′4″ mountain kid from Hazard, Kentucky, who was shy except when it came to firing a one-hander from behind the circle or a sweeping hook from anywhere. But Rupp's center, Ed Beck, was only 6′7″ and a Methodist minister to boot, while his other starters, 6′4″ forward John Crigler and 5′10″ guard Adrian "Odie" Smith, were only role players.

As the season unfolded, the fiddlers didn't give Rupp much reason to believe they were capable of moving from the Grand Ole Opry to Carnegie Hall. In December, when Temple and slick guard Guy Rodgers came to Lexington, Hatton showed his clutch ability by hitting a pair of free throws to send the game into overtime, throwing in a 49-footer at the buzzer to create a third overtime, and then scoring six of the Wildcats' final eight points in an 83–81 victory. But that was one of few bright spots in a 19–6 season—Kentucky's worst regular-season record since 1940–1941.

In the Mideast Regional, the Wildcats easily whipped Miami of Ohio and its massive center, Wayne Embry, to set up a final with Notre Dame and its graceful forward, Tom Hawkins. A year earlier, on the same floor, the Wildcats had been upset by Michigan State. But this time, with a good team defense holding Hawkins to only 15 points, the Wildcats earned the 80-mile trip to the Final Four with an 89–56 win that was, as Rupp said, "as near perfect as I've seen."

So the fiddlers found themselves in Carnegie—uh, Freedom—Hall, but with a forbidding rematch against Temple in the national semifinals. Coach Harry Litwack's Owls brought a glittering 26–2 record into the game, their only defeat besides the triple-overtime loss in Lexington coming against Cincinnati and Oscar Robertson.

This time Temple had to figure that Kentucky had run out of miracles. Instead, in a memorable case of déja vu, Hatton once again came through in the clutch, his reverse

(above) Seattle's Elgin Baylor was among the nation's elite players in 1958 when the Final Four was played in the sparkling new Freedom Hall in Louisville. But it was Kentucky, with its many at-home fans, who faced Seattle in the final. Though Baylor had 25 points and 19 rebounds, a Kentucky team effort prevailed. The Wildcats were champions.

layup with 16 seconds left gave the Wildcats a 61–60 lead. Temple had one last chance to win, only to have guard Bill "Pickles" Kennedy bobble the ball out of bounds, much to the delight of the Wildcats fans who made up the large majority of a record Final Four crowd of 18,586.

That set up a championship game against surprising Seattle and Baylor, the 6´5´´ forward with the uncanny body control and satin moves. In the semifinals, Baylor had slashed his way to 23 points and 22 rebounds in leading Seattle to a stunning 73–51 victory over a tall, talented Kansas State team led by 6´9´´ Jack Parr and 6´8´´ Bob Boozer. "There's no way we can beat this team," Kentucky assistant coach Harry Lancaster told Rupp. "They're just too good."

On Saturday afternoon, as Rupp and Lancaster were in a room at the Brown Hotel forlornly trying to figure out a way to handle Baylor, there was a knock on the door. An obscure coach, John Grayson of Idaho, had come to offer the great Rupp a huge roll of film and advice on how to stop Baylor. "To beat Seattle," Grayson said, "you must convince your

> ## "To beat Seattle you must convince your kids that they can't stand there and watch Baylor play . . . He mesmerizes the other team."
>
> **—John Grayson**
> *Idaho coach, offering advice to legendary Kentucky coach Adolph Rupp*

kids that they can't stand there and watch Baylor play . . . He mesmerizes the other team."

He advised Rupp that Baylor tended to foul players who took the ball to the hoop against him. Rupp listened. "Wake up the kids 30 minutes early," he told Lancaster, "because we've got to give 'em a chalk talk on our new game plan."

The plan worked beautifully, much to the delight of the crowd of 18,803, another record. When Seattle coach John

Castellani put Baylor on Crigler, Rupp ordered his burly senior forward to drive on Baylor every time he got the ball. The result was three quick fouls on the Seattle star, which forced Castellani to put him on the Wildcats' low-scoring centers, Beck and backup Don Mills.

To counter, Rupp then ordered Hatton to drive the lane off picks set by Beck, which forced Baylor to either switch off and risk more foul trouble or else let Hatton score easy layups. After the frustrated Baylor picked up his fourth foul trying to block a Mills hook, it was over. Although Baylor had 25 points and 19 rebounds, Hatton scored 30 and Cox 24 as the Wildcats—violinists, finally—rolled to an 84–72 victory that gave Rupp his fourth championship, a record that stood until UCLA's John Wooden won number five in 1969.

"They weren't the greatest basketball players in the world," said Rupp of his team. "All they could do was win."

In Kentucky, where barn dances were popular even before basketball, the 1958 national champions always will be remembered fondly as the "Fiddlin' Five." ∎

1959

MY NAME'S DALTON. WHAT'S YOURS?

By Art Rosenbaum

THE FINAL FOUR OF 1959 INCLUDED THREE favorites and the no-star University of California. Two of those three favorites were led by future NBA Hall of Famers—two of the best players in the game's history.

High scoring Louisville, playing on its home court, was the hopeful choice, but there would be equal support for the two top gunners of the nation—the Cincinnati Bearcats' Oscar Robertson and the West Virginia Mountaineers' Jerry West—each able to dominate a game and lead their high-geared teams to victory after victory.

California excelled in clinging defense and an item called "winning," but no individual Bear even made the All-Coast five. In fact, no Bear would have been on the second team except that some merciful voters thought a conference champion should have one representative and gave a courtesy nod to Al Buch, who happened to be the team captain.

Cal coach Pete Newell had a basic idea about defensing the Big O and the Great West: one man guards the ball and four men help. The plan made a hero of Bob Dalton, whose assignment was Robertson one night and West the next.

As Cal and Cincinnati lined up for the semifinal tip-off, the nonglamorized but gritty Dalton extended his hand to Robertson and said, "My name's Dalton. What's yours?"

The next year when the U.S. Olympic squad gathered, Robertson told head coach Newell the story and asked with a tinge of annoyance, "Coach, who was that guy?"

That guy was a skinny, 6´4´´ forward often teased by teammates for his nonmuscular frame. He hounded Robertson, forcing the Big O to alter his driving patterns, and when he lost his man, he found a Darrall Imhoff or Bill McClintock or Buch sagging alongside to bring down Robertson's game-average of 35 points to 19 on only five field goals and nine free throws.

During the season Cincinnati was accustomed to scores in the eighties and nineties, and only once had been held to 57. Cal's shifting and frustrating defense, especially in the second half when the Bearcats went 8:43 without a point, could have lowered that mark. Leading by eight with seconds to play, Cal simply yielded the last bucket for the final count of 64–58.

Meantime, West Virginia was pounding Louisville, 94–79, as the lithe West scored 38.

In 1959 the Final Four was played two nights in a row—Friday and Saturday—with little time for coaches or players to create sophisticated schemes for the next game. Could Cal contain a big gunner again?

Newell, thinking back to that glorious weekend, wanted to distribute the praise.

"Some things," he mused, "can't be cataloged. Sure, we had a strong defense. Our [Western] style offense was ball control and patiently working the ball into the basket. More than that, our players had to believe. We really had team unity. You know, during the season seven nonvarsity players practiced and scrimmaged us with no credit whatsoever. We brought those seven with us to Louisville and they sat back of our bench all the way. I'm convinced their encouragement was worth inspirational points," Newell said.

"Then there was our famous Straw Hat band, those casual but energetic and excellent musicians. They played all over town and gathered a lot of support for us, especially

In the year of Jerry West and Oscar Robertson, premier players for that and many more years, the surprise champion was the University of California, which had no stars. The mastermind of the championship was Pete Newell, the Cal coach who figured the strategy to win.

(above) In the regular season, Cincinnati's Oscar Robertson dominated play throughout the Midwest. In the tournament, he led the Bearcats up to the semifinal game against eventual champion Cal. Cal's Bob Dalton held Robertson to 19 points in that game, well under his season average of 35. All Dalton had to do for two nights in a row was to contain the two finest players of the year, and he did.

The year 1959 marked the dominance of two exceptional players who were denied a championship trophy. West Virginia's magnificent Jerry West took the Mountaineers through the early rounds and into the championship game where he played much of the second half with four fouls. He kept West Virginia in the game until the very end.

sync again. On defense, they began penetrating the side court trap press that featured West. Dalton was tremendous, Grout picked up a quick six, and Cal's fine shooting guard, Denny Fizpatrick, started hitting middle distance jumpers, leading to an eventual 20 points.

"That Jerry West, was he something," Newell enthused. "He was carrying four fouls most of the second half yet managed 28 points despite our harassment. For us, that was like stopping him cold. Besides, Dalton had 15 himself to help level off that matchup. Three of Bobby's 16-footers came in the last eight minutes when West Virginia was slashing away at our lead."

> "None of my players made first-team All-Coast Conference, and none would have made second team but they voted an 11th player on the team to accomodate one of my players. Well, that was ridiculous. The coach doesn't get you there, it's the players who get you there. And I had some damn good players."
>
> **—Pete Newell**
> *Coach of California's 1959 championship team*

From 47–34, the Mountaineers began a dramatic comeback with a strong press that forced error after error. With eight minutes to go, it was only 61–57, but the inspired Dalton matched West, Akers, and Bob Clousson shot for shot. With a minute left, Ronnie Retton dropped two free throws and it was only 69–66. Next, Bucky Bolyard stole an inbound pass and flipped to West, who got two on Cal center Imhoff's goaltending.

Score: 69–68, truly clutch time. Now it was Imhoff's time for heroics. He missed under tremendous pressure, reached up, got the ball, and pumped in the rebound with 18 seconds left.

That bucket sealed the victory. With a three-point bulge and as many seconds to go, Cal again had the luxury of allowing Akers a final two. West Virginia never saw the ball again, and the Bears hung on, 71–70.

Writers voted West, Imhoff, Fitzpatrick, Robertson, and Don Goldstein of Louisville to the all-tournament team. This caused ripples around the Bay Area, where Dalton's feat of killing Robertson and West on successive nights was acclaimed as the basketball bonanza of Cal's greatest season. ■

after the hometown Cardinals had lost to the Mountaineers. So, when we had our team meal before the final, I invited the 40 band members to eat with us. Not only did I appreciate their effort, I felt our team needed to relax and enjoy after the furious and emotional experience against the Big O. This was no time for a quiet meal. I took a chance because we were on a tight budget, but after we became national champions and our athletic director got the dinner bill, I never heard a word."

Ten minutes before the tip-off, the Straw Hatters pranced into the pavilion playing an upbeat "My Old Kentucky

Home." The place went wild. As Newell was to observe, "That entrance also was worth inspirational points. We felt we had inherited the homecourt advantage."

The Bears needed every edge they could find. The Mountaineers raced ahead, 14–6, establishing a tempo too fast to suit Newell. "In a way," he reflected, "they were getting what we coaches call 'fool's goal'—their shots were too easy. We weren't working hard enough."

Newell rushed in three swingmen—Bernie Simpson, Dick Doty, and Jack Grout—with orders to slow the Cal offense. With one exchange of the ball, the Bears were in

THE OHIO CONNECTION AND LEW ALCINDOR

UCLA coach John Wooden (above) watched the final minutes of the 1964 championship when the Bruins defeated Duke for their first title. The year 1964 also marked the ninth and final championship played in Kansas City's Municipal Auditorium.

THE WORLD CHANGED ON NOVEMBER 22, 1963, never to be the same again. An assassin's bullet cut down John F. Kennedy, the charismatic young American president, during a motorcade in Dallas. It marked the end of the postwar era that had been relatively happy and carefree and the beginning of a long, dark, troublesome period in which the nation became involved in a faraway war it didn't understand.

Suddenly young people, more than in any previous generation, came to challenge and question all the old rules, standards, and values. As the decade unfolded, the nation seemed on the brink of being torn apart. In the magnolia-infested backwoods of the Deep South and the teeming asphalt jungles of the big city ghettos, blacks and their supporters fought for racial equality. On the college campuses, kids protested the Vietnam War by chanting, "Hell, no, we won't go." And in places such as Los Angeles, Memphis, Chicago, and Kent State, puddles of blood marked the death of our dreams, our hopes, our innocence.

But from all the turmoil, strife, and conflict came some bursts of creativity that were as frightening as they were exciting. In music, movies, and the arts, performers began probing the limits of their minds and their talents. The Beatles led a revolution in music, changing tastes forever. The decade also gave us actor Dustin Hoffman in *The Graduate*, a brilliant new TV show called *Sixty Minutes*, the shocking Broadway play *Hair*, and the scandalous female fashion known as the miniskirt.

Sports hardly lived in a vacuum during the sixties. A young black man named Cassius Clay won the heavyweight title, became a Muslim, changed his name to Muhammad Ali, and was stripped of the title for refusing to be drafted on religious grounds. Sports novels such as *The Long Season, Ball Four*, and *Instant Replay* revealed that our heroes often had feet of clay. In college sports, many athletes indicated sympathy with their fellow students by wearing longer hair, questioning their coaches more often, and speaking out on the issues of the day.

In college basketball, the decade's early years were dominated by Midwestern teams. For four straight years, from 1960–1963, at least one team from Ohio played in the final game every year. The torch was passed from center Jerry Lucas and Ohio State in 1960 to coach Ed Jucker and his Cincinnati champions of 1961 and 1962 to Loyola of Chicago in 1963. But when the greatest dynasty in the game's history arrived, it materialized on the West Coast, of all places.

Of the six NCAA Tournaments held from 1964–1969, the UCLA Bruins won five, enabling coach John Wooden to surpass Kentucky's Adolph Rupp as the coach with the most titles. His best player was Lew Alcindor, a 7´1˝ center from New York City who was so conscious of his roots that he eventually became a Muslim and changed his name to Kareem Abdul-Jabbar.

If Abdul-Jabbar was the dominant player in the decade, perhaps the most interesting was Bill Bradley, a cerebral kid from Princeton who was good enough to score 58 against Wichita in the 1965 NCAA consolation game. He went on to become a Rhodes Scholar, a pro star with the New York Knicks, a U.S. senator from New Jersey, and a presidential candidate. ■

> **"The success that we had with our full-court press led to a lot of teams going to the press. It showed it was possible to win a championship with smaller, quicker men."**
>
> **—John Wooden**

As Texas Western walked from the floor
of Maryland's Cole Fieldhouse,
a milestone in the evolution of the college
game was reached. An unknown
Southwestern school with a starting lineup
of all black players defeated the heavily
favored, all-white Kentucky Wildcats.

1960

HOMEGROWN AND OHIO PROUD

By Dick Fenlon

Center Jerry Lucas had his first of three straight All-American seasons for the 1960 champion Buckeyes.

T HEY HAD COME TO OHIO STATE FROM THE HAMLETS and cities of Ohio. That they all converged in Columbus at roughly the same time was nothing short of miraculous.

Center Jerry Lucas was from Middletown, near Cincinnati.

Forward John Havlicek was from Lansing, the eastern Ohio mill town where a buddy named Phil Niekro learned to throw a knuckleball.

Guard Larry Siegfried was from Shelby.

Reserve forward Bobby Knight was from Orrville, Mrs. Smuckers' place, famous for its jams and preserves.

Guard Mel Nowell and forwards Joe Roberts and Dick Furry were from cross-city Columbus.

They were all basketball players—two of such immense talent that it would land them in the Hall of Fame. And on the night of March 19, 1960, in the Cow Palace in San Francisco, they stood a victory away from bringing the school its first national title.

Defending champion California—coached by Pete Newell and led by All-American center Darrall Imhoff— barred the door. The night before, the Golden Bears, noted for their defense, had put the clamps on Oscar Robertson, holding him to four field goals, and beaten Cincinnati, 77–69. Playing one of his best games, the 6´10˝ Imhoff had scored 25 points, grabbed 11 rebounds, and clogged the middle on defense.

On the morning of the final, Fred Taylor, the young coach of the Buckeyes, happened into a *Sports Illustrated* reporter.

The magazine, the reporter said, had just completed a poll of coaches on who would win the final game.

"I've got news for you: you're not the favorite, by far," he said.

Fred Taylor wasn't surprised. When it's youth against experience, go with the experience. Cal (29–1) had been there before, and it would be playing before a home-state crowd. The 24–3 Buckeyes were on a roll, but they started three sophomores in their first year of varsity basketball.

But Taylor also had some news of his own.

"I think we may be a little bit better than anybody thinks," he said.

It was the understatement of the season. Taylor was only 34 and in his second season as a head coach. A sophomore, in effect, just as were starters Lucas, Havlicek, Nowell, and Knight, a substitute. But the coach knew what his team could do, and he knew what he was going to have his team do.

"We gambled on defense in a couple of areas," he remembered. "And it worked out. On offense, I suppose we thought we were good enough to take the ball to them. Everybody said you couldn't take it to Imhoff."

Wrong.

Ohio State worked the middle. Roberts scored on a driving layup, and Nowell on another. The Buckeyes led 11–6 before Lucas made his first basket. It was also a layup.

Ohio State ran when it could, and worked when it couldn't, and by halftime the Buckeyes led, 37–19. They had tried 19 shots, made 16, and were on their way to a 75–55 victory that would be regarded as one of the best final-game exhibitions ever given by an NCAA champion.

Fred Taylor, more than a quarter of a century later, would not argue with that, but he would dismiss the acclaim that Ohio State's 84 percent shooting in the first half received. "Everybody talks about the shooting percentage," he said. "Lord, only one shot came from outside the paint."

Ohio State in 1960 was that good.

Ohio State in 1960 could, when the time came to do it, do just about anything it wanted to.

It was a team of such diverse and exquisite talents, skillfully meshed, that it seemed to transcend eras and time warps. Four decades later, you could still suppose that this team, in its youth, could play any team from any time anywhere.

"I know they believe it," Taylor said.

"They believe it to this very day. Because they really could do a little bit of everything. They could run. They could set up. They could defend. And their passing was something to watch."

And, yes, that word: *chemistry*.

"Taking team goals and individual goals and seeing that they mesh toward a total winning season is one of the most difficult things in coaching," Taylor said.

"I'll guarantee you they didn't all like each other equally, but they sure as heck had respect for one another. And that was a very important facet. I kid them now. I say, 'You were playing roles when none of us were smart enough to call it role-playing.' "

It was a team conceived in confusion. Floyd Stahl had resigned as Ohio State coach in April 1958, just as Lucas,

Coach Fred Taylor wears the net around his neck as he celebrates the 1960 championship with team members. (Photo courtesy of Time Life Pictures/Getty Images.)

Havlicek, Nowell, and Knight were approaching graduation from high school. Taylor, his former assistant, remained, and did the recruiting.

Taylor wondered, under the circumstances, if he could convince the prize prospects to come. And if he could, would he be there to coach them? He was the last man to be interviewed for the head coaching job—on June 5, 1958. He was named the next day.

The Buckeyes went 11–11 his first season. The freshmen, ineligible for varsity, played six practice games with the upper classmen, losing the first four, winning the last two. Taylor, in the meantime, began to set up Ohio State's scheme with the next season in mind.

When it arrived, the Buckeyes rolled to six straight victories before losing, 97–92, at Utah. Two games later they were outscored at Kentucky, 96–93. They would lose only once more—99–83 at Indiana after they had wrapped up the Big Ten title and a tournament berth.

> **"Taking team goals and individual goals and seeing that they mesh toward a total winning season is one of the most difficult things in coaching."**
>
> **—Fred Taylor**
> *Coach of Ohio State's 1960 championship team*

"The biggest problem early was getting the idea over that we'd have to shut people down," Taylor said. "After the losses at Utah and Kentucky it became obvious to them that they had to do a better job on defense. That's when they really started to play."

Jerry Lucas was a consensus All-American for the first of three straight years.

John Havlicek played with the grit that would later make him an all-time NBA great with the Boston Celtics. "You had to tear the uniform off him to get him out of a game," Taylor said.

Knight came off the bench and hit two 20-foot baskets to help put away Western Kentucky in the regionals.

For him, enduring fame would come later as a coach.

But for Taylor—who beat Knight into the Hall of Fame as a coach—the best night of all would be that night in the Cow Palace when the homegrown Buckeyes answered not only the bell, but every question.

There was one question that Taylor never had.

"I always believed there was such good basketball played in this state that you didn't have to recruit the world," he said. ■

Dick Fenlon covered Final Fours first when at the Louisville Times *and later after joining the* Columbus Dispatch, *where he became the sports columnist. Today, he is retired and living in Columbus.*

1961

TEAM EFFORT COACHES DREAM ABOUT

By Pat Harmon

THE CHAMPIONSHIP GAME IN 1961 WAS THE 23ʳᵈ IN the NCAA series and the eighth played in Kansas City. It was supposed to be a routine demonstration by an all-time super team.

It didn't turn out that way.

One year earlier, the Ohio State Buckeyes had won the championship, and their margin over California, 20 points, was a record for the final game. The Buckeye starting lineup—three sophomores, one junior, one senior—had "dynasty" written all over it.

Ohio State started the season with four returning regulars—Jerry Lucas and John Havlicek (future all-pros), Larry Siegfried and Mel Nowell. They represented 74 percent of the Buckeye scoring power from the year before.

The fifth position on the team was taken by Richie Hoyt. And there was valuable sixth man Bobby Knight, who later would leave his imprint on the NCAA as the coach of three Indiana champions.

Cincinnati opened the season with two veteran starters —Paul Hogue and Carl Bouldin. The Bearcats had lost 63 percent of their point-makers to graduation—chiefly in the person of Oscar Robertson, who had led the nation in scoring for three straight years.

After some early experimenting, the Cincinnati lineup was completed with Bob Wiesenhahn, Tony Yates, and Tom Thacker.

At the start of the season Ohio State was magnificent. Cincinnati was awful. The Buckeyes went unbeaten in all their scheduled games, the first time a Big Ten team had done so since 1915. They won the games by an average margin of 22 points and reached the Final Four riding a 32-game winning streak.

Cincinnati lost early games by margins of 19, 17, and 8 points. Then the Bearcats won some close ones—by five points, three points, and one point. They had a 21-game winning streak of their own going into the championship.

If the result was a bombshell to most observers, it was no surprise to the winning coach. Ed Jucker had coached in the East, and his philosophy was formed around the concepts of Clair Bee, Joe Lapchick, and Bill Rinehart, three brainy basketball leaders. He had come to Cincinnati as assistant basketball coach and head coach for baseball. (In the latter job, he had Sandy Koufax as his pitcher for one year.)

This was Jucker's first year as Cincinnati's head coach. He told his players, "We have lost Oscar Robertson, the most complete basketball player of all time. But among you there are some who shoot well, some who pass well, some who play great defense. Put them all together, and the product will be an Oscar Robertson—as a team."

Jucker's formula for beating Ohio State had five points:

1. Match them in rebounds or close to it. (Cincinnati outrebounded Ohio State, 36–32.)

2. Put on defensive pressure to delay their fast break. (The Buckeyes made only one fast-break basket.)

3. Play Jerry Lucas loose; too often the other center fouls out against him. (Lucas scored 20 of Ohio State's first 41 points and 27 all told. But his counterpart, Hogue, stayed in the game.)

4. Play Havlicek tight. (Wiesenhahn held Havlicek to 4 points and scored 17 himself.)

5. Play our own game of short, sharp passes, working for the close-in shot. (Cincinnati committed only three turnovers, Ohio State had eight.)

The final was a match between Ohio State's run-and-shoot offense and Cincinnati's careful artistry. Rarely has there been a closer contest. (The score was tied 14 times.)

(above) Cincinnati's Paul Hogue and Ohio State's Jerry Lucas do battle during the 1961 title game.

(right) Cincinnati coach Ed Jucker was carried from the court after the Bearcats' victory in the 1961 championship— the first of Jucker's two championship titles.

Ohio State got off to a 20–13 lead, but Cincinnati caught up at 20–20. At the half Ohio State led, 39–38.

Early in the second half, Bouldin put in five jump shots as Cincinnati rolled to a 52–46 lead. Ohio State made 10 straight points—4 by Nowell, 2 each by Siegfried, Hoyt, and Lucas—to go up 56–52. Cincinnati got in front, 61–59. Then Knight made a layup, tying it 61–61 and sending the game into overtime.

Cincinnati got the tip in the extra period, worked the ball carefully, and passed to Hogue, who tried a layup. He was fouled by Lucas. Hogue made two free throws, Cincinnati went ahead, 63–61, and never trailed again. With Ohio State forced into foul trouble, Yates made three free throws in crucial spots, and Wiesenhahn socked in a layup. The Bearcats won, 70–65.

Lucas was the game's high scorer with 27 points, but Cincinnati showed balance. Wiesenhahn had 17 points, followed by Bouldin with 16, Thacker 15, Yates 13, and Hogue 9.

"But among you there are some who shoot well, some who pass well, some who play great defense. Put them all together, and the product will be an Oscar Robertson—as a team."

—Ed Jucker
Coach of Cincinnati's 1961 championship team

Jucker said in his postgame interview, "Not any All-American players, just an All-American team."

It was the first time two schools from the same state had met in the NCAA final. And it was an Ohio show in most ways. The Buckeyes' starting five plus their sixth man, Knight, were from Ohio high schools. The Bearcats had Hogue, the son of a Knoxville, Tennessee, school principal, but the other four kids were from Cincinnati. All four lived within 12 miles of the college campus.

Of the five Cincinnati starters, each had at least one game in which he led the team in scoring. Wiesenhahn was the season's leading scorer, Hogue the leader in free throw percentage, Bouldin the best in field goal percentage, Thacker tops in assists, and Yates the man with the fewest fouls.

Five departments—five leaders. A true team triumph. ∎

Pat Harmon covered Final Fours for newspapers in Champaign, Illinois; Cedar Rapids, Iowa; and Cincinnati, Ohio. He was sports editor of the Cincinnati Post *before becoming public relations director for the College Football Hall of Fame in South Bend, Indiana. Today, he serves as curator and historian for the Hall.*

Ohio State coach Fred Taylor talks strategy with his team during the 1962 championship game, the second straight year the Buckeyes would lose the final game to state rival Cincinnati.

1962

A BRAND-NEW BREED OF CAT

By Hubert Mizell

IN ONE OF ITS PERIODICAL PONTIFICATIONS, *SPORTS Illustrated* took a deep, frosty whiff of February 1961 air and editorially anointed Jerry Lucas, John Havlicek, a crewcut scrub named Bobby Knight, and their fellow Ohio State Buckeyes as "the best college basketball team of all time."

Lew Alcindor was 14, still playing junior high school basketball in New York, and UCLA did not romp among the NCAA elite. Ohio State had mutilated California, 75–55, in the 1960 national finals, and the redshirts from Columbus were lollygagging along on a 32-game winning streak.

But as America wondered if anybody could stand up to coach Fred Taylor's bullies, a threat was festering in the Bucks' own neighborhood. Downstate, a new-look team from the University of Cincinnati dared—amid the narrowmindedness of the early sixties—to start three, and eventually four, black players. The Bearcats were, in the Buckeye dictionary, about to become the meaning of the word *nemesis*.

Cincinnati had achieved the Final Fours of 1959 and 1960 but wilted in the national semifinals. And now Oscar Robertson, the Magic Johnson of the day, had gone off to the pros. If Cincinnati hadn't won it with Oscar, how could it…

But Ed Jucker, destined to be a short-lived colossus in the coaching profession, put a quick and disciplined team on the floor that could defense Ohio State into oblivion. It became an all-Ohio NCAA final in 1961, and the Bearcats strangled the giant, 70–65. Rather than an aberration, it would be a harbinger.

The 1962 Final Four was at Freedom Hall in Louisville. Ohio State made the championship game for a third consecutive time. Lucas, Havlicek, and their crowd were still around, and the Bucks (25–1) were ranked No. 1 in the polls. But, again, there stood Cincinnati.

At that time, newspapers weren't sold that the NCAA Final Four was that big of a deal. After all, it was only college basketball, and no major television network thought enough of the Final Four to put it on the air. Some sportswriters had to talk their newspapers into letting them cover it—at personal expense.

It was worth it.

Speaking of harbinger.

One of the 1962 national semifinalists was UCLA, the first time John Wooden coached the Bruins as far as the Final Four. UCLA was eliminated by Cincinnati and then dropped the third-place game to Wake Forest, both by two points, but it would be a Westwood preamble to a UCLA run of 10 NCAA championships in 12 seasons (1964–1975), a record that was not made to be broken.

That fourth-place Bruin squad, the tablesetter for the UCLA unstoppables of the Alcindor (Kareem Abdul-Jabbar) and Bill Walton eras, has become a trivia question that only the most devout Final Four disciple can handle. Just who were Wooden's five starters in 1962? You got it right if you said Fred Slaughter, 6´5˝, at center, Pete Blackman, 6´5˝, and Gary Cunningham, 6´6˝, at forward with John Green, 6´2˝, alongside Walt Hazzard, 6´2˝, at guard.

> **But as America wondered if anybody could stand up to coach Fred Taylor's bullies, a threat was festering in the Bucks' own neighborhood. . . . The Bearcats were, in the Buckeye dictionary, about to become the meaning of the word *nemesis*.**

Since Wake Forest did make that Final Four, the Deacons deserve at least some mention in this retrospection. Wake was a dying powerhouse breed, an all-white major college basketball squad. Horace "Bones" McKinney, an ordained Baptist minister, coached them to 12 straight victories to make it to Louisville. The Deacons (22–9) were led by a muscular 6´8˝ center, Len Chappell, and a 5´9˝ guard who, at the time, had a full head of hair and a killer jump shot—Billy Packer.

But it was the main event, the second coming of Cincinnati–Ohio State in the NCAA finals, that made 1962 one of the more glistening charms on a Final Four bracelet.

It takes a little less trivia expertise to recall the lineups of those Bucks and Bearcats. Ohio State's supporting cast for the 6´8˝ Doug McDonald at forward and 6´2˝ Mel Nowell and 6´0˝ Dick Reasback at guard. Knight, a senior,

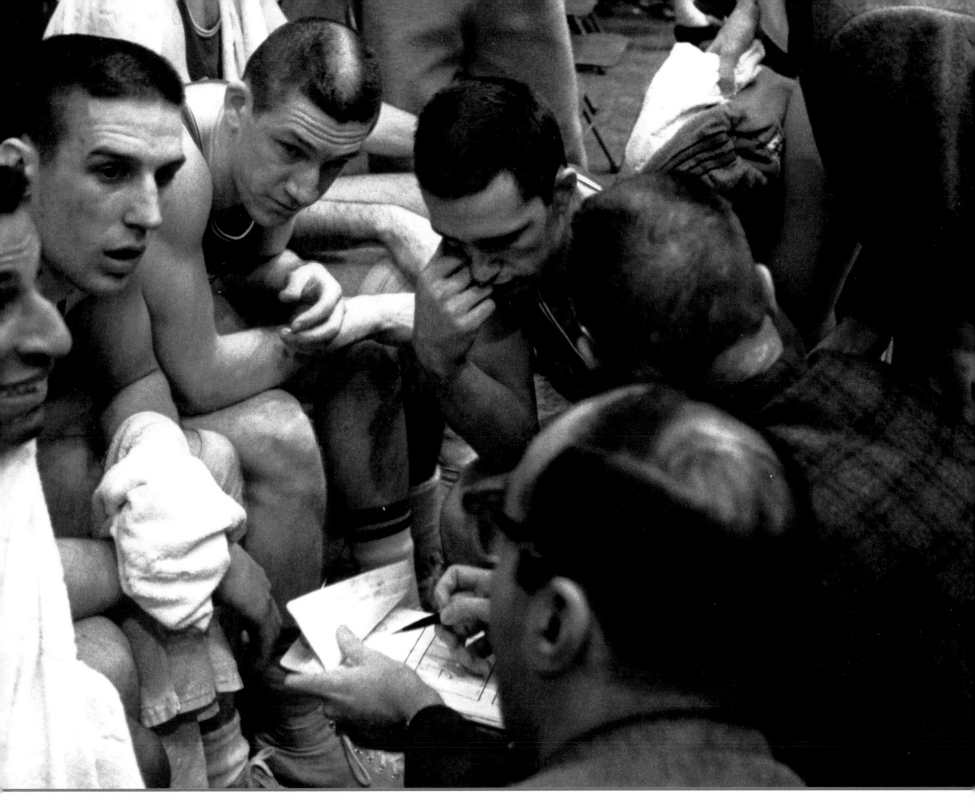

sat well down the Buckeye bench. Cincinnati's main men were 6´9˝ Paul Hogue, 6´8˝ George Wilson, 6´5˝ Ron Bonham, 6´2˝ Tom Thacker, and 6´1˝ Tony Yates.

Lucas was struggling on a gimpy knee. From the opening tip, he would be physically blitzed by the 235-pound Hogue.

Cincinnati's beating of Ohio State in the 1961 finals had been no fluke. That would become immediately and painfully evident to the Bucks.

Ohio State did lead, 23–22, but then the Bearcats ripped away on an 11–2 run. Cincinnati was ahead, 37–29, at halftime and was never threatened in the closing 20 minutes, coasting to a 71–59 win. Hogue outscored Lucas, 22–11, and Thacker buried Havlicek, 21–11.

Jucker, at 45, was finally acclaimed as one of the slickest minds in the coaching racket. Defense was the heart of his scheme, with the aggressive, quick-handed Yates as the Bearcat catalyst. Jucker called Yates "the best defensive player in the country." When the 1962 NCAA Tournament ended, nobody argued—especially nobody from a twice-thrashed Ohio State University.

The following season, Cincinnati threatened for an unprecedented third straight NCAA Championship. But Loyola of Chicago ended the dream in the 1963 final. ■

Hubert Mizell has covered Final Fours for 35 years for the Florida Times-Union, *the Associated Press, and most recently as a writer and columnist for the* St. Petersburg Times.

1963

THAWING THE CINCINNATI FREEZE

By Ron Rapoport

THE ALL-TOURNAMENT TEAM FOR THE 1963 NCAA basketball championships spoke volumes about the nature of the outcome.

The team contained Tom Thacker, George Wilson, and Ron Bonham of Cincinnati, whose team did not win the title, and the tournament's Most Outstanding Player, Art Heyman of Duke, whose team did not even play in the championship game.

Only Les Hunter was there to represent the team that did take home the trophy that year, which seemed to be proof enough that even when the final buzzer had sounded, nobody could really believe that Loyola of Chicago had actually pulled it off.

Maybe it's not fair to torment the selectors of the all-tournament team this way. They did, after all, have a perfect excuse for their embarrassment. In order for the squad to be announced immediately after the game was over, the balloting was conducted with about 10 minutes left. And with 10 minutes left, Cincinnati was murdering Loyola.

Cincinnati had also gone through the season undefeated and ranked a unanimous No. 1 in the polls. So what if Oscar Robertson wasn't in school anymore? If any team knew what it took to win a big basketball game, it was Cincinnati.

Loyola, on the other hand, had been a relatively unknown quantity when the season started. Sparked by the playmaking of scrappy, Chicago-born Johnny Egan, the Ramblers had been through a lot in the few years they had been together. Egan was the only white starter, and Loyola was the first nationally prominent college team to start four black players. Loyola had, in that era of heightened racial passions, undergone the indignities of hate mail, separate housing arrangements in the South, and even threats of arrest before a game in New Orleans.

But despite the fact that experiences like these had served to harden and bring the Loyola team together, nobody figured it to be a match for Cincinnati. And when Ed Jucker's squad stretched a 29–21 halftime lead to 45–30, the game seemed as good as over. Cincinnati was the top defensive team in the nation, after all, having allowed an average of only 52.6 points per game. Loyola, the national scoring leader with 92.9 points, seemed finally to have met a team that knew how to shut it down.

It might have been about this time, when Loyola's chances seemed so desperate, that one of the most famous photographs of that tournament was taken. It was of a Rambler cheerleader on her knees at courtside, praying for deliverance from the Cincinnati onslaught. The cheerleader was Kathy Ireland, daughter of the Loyola coach.

For his part, George Ireland was engaged with more worldly concerns. He was trying to figure out a way to stop the Bearcats and to get his own team's lagging offense to produce before it was too late. Fortunately for him, he was given some unexpected help from the Cincinnati side of the court.

Jucker sent his team into a stall, trying to burn some time off the clock by employing the understandable philosophy that if Loyola didn't have the ball, it couldn't score. Ireland responded by having his team press Cincinnati all over the court.

"I think they passed up too many good shots when they went into that freeze with 10 minutes to go," said Jerry Harkness, Loyola's scoring leader and a player many thought should have been named to the all-tournament team.

(above) As the 1963 game reached a last-minute climax, Loyola's Jerry Harkness hit a jumper from the baseline as Cincinnati's foul-plagued Ron Bonham held his position trying to avoid his fifth foul. The Ramblers designated Harkness for the final shot, but it was a rebound layup by Vic Rouse that iced the 60–58 upset.

(right) Loyola's John Egan drives past Cincinnati guard Larry Shingleton during the 1963 title game.

Loyola coach George Ireland took his Ramblers to the finals in Louisville's Freedom Hall, where he instructed players (from left) Vic Rouse, Johnny Egan, and Jerry Harkness before the tip-off. Their upset win ended Cincinnati's quest for a third championship in a row.

Given this reprieve, Loyola made the most of it. Playing with a poise that was supposed to be one of the chief assets of the tournament-hardened Bearcats, the Ramblers slowly began chipping away at their big deficit. Cincinnati, in the meantime, surprisingly and irretrievably began to fall apart.

Error followed error and foul followed foul as Loyola crept within striking distance. By the time the clock wound down to the final few moments, three Cincinnati starters—Wilson, Tony Yates, and Thacker—had four fouls, and the whole team seemed to be playing nervous, tentative basketball. With 12 seconds left, Loyola trailed by a single point and, frantic to get the ball back, Harkness fouled Cincinnati's Larry Shingleton.

Shingleton made the first free throw but missed the second. Hunter snatched the rebound and flung it to Harkness who drove for a layup that tied the game at 54–54. The buzzer sounded. Against all probability, Loyola had forced the game into overtime.

> **By the time the clock wound down to the final few moments, three Cincinnati starters had four fouls, and the whole team seemed to be playing nervous, tentative basketball.**

Both teams managed two baskets to tie the game at 58–58, and then, with barely two minutes remaining, it was Loyola's turn to gamble on a change of style and strategy. The hard-running, shoot-from-the-hip Ramblers slowed the game down and held onto the ball in an attempt to take the last shot.

The idea was to let Harkness, who was averaging 21.2 points during Loyola's five postseason games, take the last shot. And, indeed, the Ramblers got him the ball with a few seconds left. But Cincinnati's Bonham surrounded Harkness in a flurry of waving arms, and Harkness, unable to get a shot off, passed to Hunter.

Hunter shot; the ball rolled off the rim directly into the eager grasp of Rambler forward Vic Rouse. His rebound layup that ended the game with two seconds left may have been the easiest part of the Ramblers' long and improbable season. Loyola, with a stunning 60–58 upset, reigned as national champion. ■

Ron Rapoport has covered Final Fours for several newspapers throughout his career, which ended as a sports columnist at the Chicago Sun-Times. *He is known throughout the nation for his sports commentaries on National Public Radio's* Weekend Edition.

1964

A DYNASTY BEGINS

By Bob Hentzen

AS THE CELEBRATING UCLA BRUINS WERE CUTTING down the nets in Kansas City's Municipal Auditorium, Kansas State coach Tex Winter watched and observed to a writer, "I still think we could have beat 'em."

Shucks, Winter wasn't the only coach to express that opinion during the 1963–1964 season. How could any coach not believe there was a way to handle a ballclub with no starter standing taller than 6´5´´?

But UCLA was perfect, 30–0, after downing Kansas State, 90–84, in the semifinals and Duke, 98–83, in the final.

This was a memorable Final Four in that it was the start of UCLA's dynasty—the remarkable 12-year stretch in which John Wooden coached the Bruins to 10 national titles.

Wooden agreed that his first NCAA championship team didn't intimidate anybody. "They watch us warm up and can't see how we beat anyone," he said before the 1964 Final Four. "Teams don't get scared when they look at us, but we cause a little fright when we play. Our strength is real good quickness and unity."

UCLA didn't go into that season with much respect. *Sports Illustrated*'s preview called the Bruins "too short" and labeled 6´3´´ guard Walt Hazzard "the poorest defender on the coast."

But Hazzard, who came to Westwood from Philadelphia on a one-year, make-good basis, was to change some opinions. "He passes through holes you couldn't throw a golf ball [through]," *Sports Illustrated* later wrote.

Despite its unbeaten record, an average victory margin of 19.4 and the No. 1 national ranking, UCLA arrived in Kansas City for the national showdown as anything but an overwhelming favorite. No. 2 Michigan (22–4) also qualified, eliminating defending champion Loyola of Chicago, 84–80, en route in the Mideast semifinals. No. 3 Duke (25–4) also was present, scoring one-sided victories over Villanova and Connecticut in the East Regionals.

Kansas State (22–5) was unranked, but had plenty going for it. The Wildcats were fresh off a 94–86 upset of fifth-ranked Wichita State in Wichita in the Midwest final. They had come close to UCLA, losing 78–75, in a December neutral-court game. They would be playing on the Municipal Auditorium boards where they had won the Big Eight's Christmas tourney. They would be the crowd favorites.

UCLA didn't have a cakewalk in the West Regional, having to rally twice. After squeezing Seattle, 95–90, the Bruins fell behind San Francisco by 13 points in the first half before overhauling the Dons, 76–72, and breaking their 19-game winning streak.

Enthusiasm ran high for the 1964 Final Four, although it was tame by today's standards. For the Friday–Saturday night doubleheaders, all 10,800 seats were sold out a month in advance. Tickets cost $7 per session and scalpers were asking $50 by game night. A 16-station television network had been established.

The first semifinal matched Michigan against Duke. They were not strangers when they met because of a December game won by the Wolverines, 83–67, on their home court.

Dave Strack's team was respected for both beef—it averaged 201 pounds—and talent. Guard Cazzie Russell, 6´5´´ and 218, was the star with a 24.6 scoring average, but he came to Kansas City with a bad ankle. The supporting cast included 6´7´´ center Bill Buntin and forwards Oliver Darden, 6´7´´, and Larry Tregoning, 6´5´´.

Vic Bubas' Blue Devils had the reputation of being a brainy team—four players were on the dean's list—and featured 6´4´´ Jeff Mullins with a 24.4 average. Big guys Jay Buckley and Hack Tison, both 6´10´´, also were double-figure scorers.

In the game itself, the strategies of coaches John Wooden of UCLA (above) and Vic Bubas of the Blue Devils (right) formed the texture of the championship.

A contemplative Hazzard held the championship trophy in the locker room after the game.

Walt Hazzard cut and drove through the Duke defense to lead UCLA to its first of 11 Final Four championships. Making two key steals in the second half, Hazzard was named MOP.

Erickson, averaging 10.1 points, tallied 28 in the semifinals, while Hazzard contributed 19 points and nine assists. The 6´3˝ Washington came off the pines to score a career-high 13. But Washington was just getting warmed up as Duke found out less than 24 hours later in the championship game.

Washington, who came to Kansas City with a five-point average, scored 26 and hauled down 12 rebounds as UCLA blew away the Blue Devils, 98–83. The result was all but determined when the Bruins rattled off 16 straight points—8 by Goodrich—in a two-minute, 34-second blitz late in the first half to open a 43–30 lead.

> "This team has come as close to reaching maximum potential as any team I've ever had. It's most unlikely that I or anyone else will have it [a perfect season] again."
>
> **—John Wooden**
> *Coach of UCLA's 1964 championship team*

Duke missed 10 straight shots and committed three turnovers (two on steals by Hazzard) against UCLA's vaunted full-court press in that fatal span. The only problem the Bruins experienced in the second half was spark-plug Hazzard fouling out for the first time all season with 6:04 left. No sweat—UCLA led, 86–70, at the time and coasted in.

Goodrich, the southpaw who led the Bruins in scoring that season, finished with 25 while Mullins paced Duke with 22.

The all-tourney team consisted of Hazzard, the Most Outstanding Player, and Goodrich, Mullins, Murrell, and Buntin. The latter was a stallion—33 points and 14 rebounds in Michigan's 100–90 win over Kansas State in the third-place contest.

"This team has come as close to reaching maximum potential as any team I've ever had," Wooden said when it was over, adding, "It's most unlikely that I or anyone else will have it [a perfect season] again."

Wooden was wrong on the last part. Three more of his championship teams (1967, 1972, 1973) were unbeaten, and Indiana duplicated the feat in 1976. ■

Bob Hentzen came to the Topeka (Kansas) Capital-Journal *from the* Daily Oklahoman *and was named sports editor and columnist in 1968. He covered Final Fours regularly until his retirement in 1997. He was the former president of the U.S. Basketball Writers Association. He died in 2000.*

Duke's chartered plane had swerved into the mud while braking on landing in Kansas City. Nobody was hurt, and the Blue Devils proceeded to put the hurt on Michigan in a 91–80 triumph. Buzzy Harrison's four long jumpers in the first half lit Duke's fire, and Buckley finished with 25 points and Mullins 24 to more than offset Russell's 31 for Michigan.

Then Kansas State, led by 6´6˝ senior Willie Murrell and with 7´0˝ Roger Suttner in the lineup, took on Wooden's diminutive but quick-as-a-hiccup Bruins. Their "big man" was 6´5˝ Fred Slaughter from nearby Topeka, who had gone unrecruited by the area teams coming out of high school.

UCLA had started the same five every game—the 6´3˝ Hazzard and 6´1˝ scoring machine Gail Goodrich at guards, Slaughter at center, and 6´5˝ Keith Erickson and 6´3˝ Jack Hirsch at forwards. The first subs off the bench were Kenny Washington and Doug McIntosh.

Despite the lack of size, the Bruins seldom were outrebounded, averaging eight more per game than their opponents.

The partisan crowd was roaring as the Wildcats inched ahead, 75–70, with 7:28 left, but poised UCLA never blinked (K-State did, hitting but 10 of 21 free throws) in pulling out a 90–84 victory.

1965

THE BEST SECOND FIDDLE EVER

By Mark Purdy

(above) Against a beefy and physical Michigan team, UCLA's Gail Goodrich set a school scoring record of 42 points in the 1965 championship game. Three Wolverines fouled out trying to stop the diminutive senior, who played the game of his Bruins career.

(right) Princeton's Bill Bradley (No. 42) scored a record 58 points in the consolation game against Wichita State during the 1965 championships, held in Portland, Oregon. Princeton defeated Wichita State 118–82 to win third place.

THERE ARE TRIVIA QUESTIONS, AND THERE ARE TRIVIA questions. And then there is Gail Goodrich, UCLA Class of 1965. He shouldn't be the subject of a trivia question. But he is.

In fact, Goodrich may be the most famous trivia question —or at least the most famous name to be a famous answer to a famous Final Four trivia question—in history.

The Question: Which player scored 42 points in the NCAA championship game while leading his team to the Final Four title, but was not named the tournament's most outstanding player?

The Answer: You already know the answer.

In the long-playing record album of UCLA Basketball's Greatest Hits, Goodrich always is the guy who gets the last cut on side two—the 90-second outtake thrown in as an afterthought. His is the forgotten song on an album of blockbusters by Hazzard and Alcindor and Walton and the rest. Always.

In much the same way, when the 1965 Final Four is remembered, Goodrich often is considered more of a back-up singer than a headliner.

It's hardly fair. When you examine the evidence, you will find that Goodrich was one of the NCAA Tournament's most spectacular performers. He averaged 35 points per game in the West Regional at Provo. He then did the same thing in Portland while orchestrating UCLA's rush to its second straight championship.

So what about the most outstanding player award, then? What happened?

Bill Bradley. That's what happened.

Among the four teams competing that year at the Portland Memorial Coliseum—UCLA, Michigan, Wichita State, and Princeton—there were basically three players who the average American basketball lover knew by reputation.

There was Cazzie Russell of Michigan, who was powerful but stylish.

There was Goodrich of UCLA, who was gritty but quick.

And there was Bradley of Princeton, who was perfect.

Before he even set foot in Oregon, Bradley had been all but canonized by the nation's sports press. It wasn't his fault. The guy truly did seem to leap off a Wheaties box onto a basketball floor. Bradley, a native of the Missouri heartland, was a two-time All-American. He had served as captain of the 1964 U.S. Olympic Team in Tokyo. Plus, as a quintessential Ivy Leaguer, he had earned a Rhodes Scholarship to Oxford University in England.

If the world really were a Wheaties box, Bradley would have swept Princeton to glorious victory. Instead, in the semifinal against Michigan, Bradley picked up his fourth foul one minute into the second half. That smothered his game like a wet blanket. Princeton lost, 83–76. Russell had 28 points for Michigan.

Meanwhile, in the other semifinal, UCLA quickly vaporized Wichita State, 108–89. Goodrich played barely two-thirds of the game but still scored 28 points. Compared to Bradley's lean Ivy style, however, Goodrich was a blue-collar runt. As a 5´2˝ high school freshman, he plaintively had said to his mother, "I don't understand why God gave me all this ability and not the height to go with it." As a 6´1˝ college senior, he still felt like the picked-on underdog.

"When coach Wooden made me play forward during my sophomore year, I couldn't understand it," Goodrich said once of his UCLA experience. "But looking back, it gave me the confidence to go to the basket against bigger men."

This would come in handy the following night, against the beefy Wolverines of Michigan. Little did Goodrich realize that he would be following the toughest act in college basketball.

It was Bradley, of course. In the consolation game, with absolutely no marbles at stake, Princeton coach Butch van Breda Kolff turned loose his Oxford scholar. Bradley wound up with 58 points, a Final Four record.

"He didn't want to shoot," said van Breda Kolff. "But I told him to."

With Princeton's Tigers on their way to scoring 118 points in a 36-point rout of Wichita State, there was no reason for Bradley to worry about being selfish—although there were eyewitnesses who insist Bradley could have had 70 points that night if he had been less altruistic and had taken more of his classic 20-foot jump shots instead of passing the ball inside to teammates.

UCLA coach John Wooden and two players are presented with the national championship trophy following their 91–80 victory over the Michigan Wolverines on March 20, 1965, in Portland, Oregon.

As it was, Bradley made 22 of 29 field goal attempts and 14 of 15 free throws. When he left the game with 35 seconds remaining, he was given a standing ovation from the thirteen thousand customers. It lasted a full minute.

"I didn't realize I had a personal record," Bradley said. "I thought they were telling me to shoot because we had a chance at the team scoring record."

Minutes later, Goodrich and UCLA jogged onto the floor for warm-ups. It was a little like being on *The Ed Sullivan Show* and following the Beatles. The crowd already had made up its mind that the best part of the show was over.

Wrong. The smallest Bruins were about to give Michigan's bruisers a lesson in finesse. Goodrich was about to play what he later would call "his best game" at UCLA.

It didn't begin auspiciously, however. The Wolverines went ahead, 20–13, with Russell continually driving past the Bruins' Keith Erickson, who had pulled a leg muscle the previous night. Wooden fixed the glitch in a flash. He substituted Kenny Washington for Erickson, made an adjustment in the UCLA press to cut off a passing lane to Russell, and told Goodrich to start taking the ball to the basket.

The results were immediate. The Bruins outscored Michigan, 34–14, to take a 47–34 halftime lead. In the second

The smallest Bruins were about to give Michigan's bruisers a lesson in finesse. Goodrich was about to play what he later would call "his best game" at UCLA.

half, Goodrich put on a clinic. He alternately dribbled away time on the clock, double-pumped in the air to draw fouls, and sailed past the Michigan men to the basket. Three Wolverine starters—Bill Buntin, Larry Tregoning, and Oliver Darden—committed their fifth fouls trying to stop Goodrich. During the last 10 minutes of the game, he seemed to set up camp at the free throw line.

Final score: UCLA 91, Michigan 80.

"It gave me the satisfaction," he said, "that a little man can win in a big man's game."

His 42 points also gave UCLA a new school scoring record. Goodrich was 18 of 20 from the free throw line, 12 of

22 from the field. Russell of Michigan had 28 points, but was not a factor after the first 15 minutes.

And shortly after the final buzzer, Bradley was given the Most Outstanding Player trophy. Goodrich professed then— and professes now—not to care, figuring his team got the trophy that mattered.

And all three of them know who the real Most Outstanding Player in 1965 was. There was a lot of bad information floating around Portland that year. The hottest tournament rumor, for example, concerned a 7´1˝ high school senior from New York named Lew Alcindor. Supposedly, after sizing up 100 scholarship offers, the kid had decided he would enroll at Boston College to play for its legendary coach, Bob Cousy.

That's another good trivia question. ∎

Mark Purdy has been a sports columnist for the San Jose Mercury-News *since 1984, after stints at the* Dayton Journal-Herald, *he* Cincinnati Enquirer, *the* Chicago Tribune, *and the* Los Angeles Times. *Winner of many awards, he has covered 22 Final Fours.*

1966

A CASE OF BLACK AND WHITE

By Dave Kindred

I N HIS CLASSIC HISTORY OF COLLEGE BASKETBALL, *ALL the Moves*, Neil D. Isaacs returns to the twenties to remember the New York Rens, a touring team of black players whose success begot the Harlem Globetrotters. These great pro teams, working in a separate and unequal milieu, were the foundation stones of black development in basketball through the mid-forties. "When Don Barksdale was an All-American at UCLA in 1947," Isaacs wrote, "he was as much of a freak as Kurland and Mikan had been in 1944."

In 1950 the Boston Celtics of the NBA drafted the league's first black player, Chuck Cooper of Duquesne. Washington followed by choosing Earl Lloyd of West Virginia State. The New York Knicks went to the Globetrotters to acquire Nat "Sweetwater" Clifton. Those events opened the line of ascension for blacks all the way to the top levels of the game.

Or did they? After having won the 1956 NCAA championship at San Francisco as a teammate of K. C. Jones, the great center Bill Russell declared that the NBA had a "quota system" that limited the number of blacks on each team. The NBA's use of blacks seemed limited to those who could be stars. Seldom did a team use five black players even though the All-America lists of the mid-fifties were dominated by Wilt Chamberlain, Elgin Baylor, Willie Naulls, Sihugo Green, and Oscar Robertson. America's black colleges were largely untapped sources of basketball talent.

As late as 1962, Southeastern Conference champion Mississippi State refused an invitation to the NCAA Tournament because it would have to play integrated teams. This was eight years after the U.S. Supreme Court's ruling in *Brown vs. Board of Education* where the court denied legal segregation of public schools.

This Mississippi State boycott of 1962 was the dying breath of segregation in college basketball. Cincinnati won the NCAA title that year using four black starters. In 1963, with the governor's de facto approval, Mississippi State coach Babe McCarthy spirited his team out of Mississippi to play in the NCAA Tournament. Mississippi State lost in the first round to the eventual champions, Loyola of Chicago, a team with four black starters.

The game was changing in the early sixties, thanks to the influence of black players. Russell's shot-blocking ability showed the possibilities of defense. Baylor's magical body control and Robertson's mastery of the ball expanded the boundaries of offense. It wouldn't be long before an event came along that said the game belonged as much to black players as to whites. There would come a time when the issue was settled on a basketball court.

That time was March of 1966. The game: Texas Western against Kentucky. Out of the farthest reaches of Texas, coach Don Haskins created as unlikely a basketball team as ever had won the NCAA championship. "Haskins had brought more blacks to El Paso than they were used to seeing in the whole student body," Isaacs wrote, "including Dave 'Big Daddy' Lattin, Bobby Joe Hill, Willie Cager, Orsten Artis, Neville Shed, and Willie Worsley."

Texas Western began the season little-known, but entered the NCAA Tournament ranked third in the country with a 23–1 record. Lattin was the biggest Texas Western player, only 6´7´´ at that. Haskins' team won not because of overwhelming athletic ability; it won with pure, fundamental basketball. It could run and shoot, and the Miners played an unnerving man-to-man defense that allowed no breathing room.

(above) When the final scoreboard read 72–65, the Miners' Willie Worsley had an elevated seat to cut the championship nets.

(right) As Kentucky players scrambled to stop the Miners' attack, Texas Western's Willie Cager drove for a second-half basket. Failing to stop Cager were Kentucky stalwarts Pat Riley (42), Louie Dampier (10), and Cliff Berger (45).

Texas Western's Bobby Joe Hill broke open the game in the second half with two steals and full court drives to score key baskets.

Texas Western coach Don Haskins hugged players in an emotional celebration on the Cole Fieldhouse court. A one-time player at Oklahoma A&M, Haskins used the lessons he learned from mentor-coach Henry Iba; his Miners team was well-versed in the fundamentals of the game.

Texas Western had a matching 27–1 record and had survived successive games against seventh-ranked Cincinnati, fourth-ranked Kansas, and, in the semifinal, a Utah team that hadn't been pressed in the tournament. Still, who do you expect to win an NCAA championship game—the lords of basketball from the Bluegrass or the upstart commoners from a forlorn corner of football country?

The question was answered quickly. The game's signature moments came barely five minutes into play. Kentucky, perhaps drained by the Duke game, perhaps hurried by good defenders, shot poorly.

It wouldn't be long before an event came along that said the game belonged as much to black players as to whites. There would come a time when the issue was settled on a basketball court.

Then Bobby Joe Hill made successive midcourt steals from Dampier and Tommy Kron for easy layups. Suddenly, in contrast to Texas Western's quickness, Kentucky was seen as slow afoot.

Don Haskins' five black starters would defeat Kentucky's all-white team, 72–65, and nothing would be the same after that. Rupp would recruit his first black player three years later. All black players would be recruited by all schools, not only the primarily black universities. The Southeastern Conference and Atlantic Coast Conference became powerful leagues built on black talent. George Wallace once promised that the University of Alabama would never accept black students. A decade later, five black players started for Alabama's basketball team and played in a beautiful fifteen thousand–seat arena on campus.

Texas Western's victory over Kentucky was a landmark.

Sportswriter David Israel recognized the significance of the game. Writing about the game a decade later, Israel called it "the *Brown vs. Board of Education* of college basketball." ∎

Still, No. 1–ranked Kentucky was the overwhelming favorite in the championship game. These were "Rupp's Runts," the old coach's favorite team, no man taller than 6´5´´, a team like all of Rupp's: unselfish, good ballhandlers, good shooters, good on the run—the very model of great Kentucky teams, beaten only once in 28 games. The Kentucky stars were Louie Dampier, an All-American guard, and forward Pat Riley, later a successful NBA coach.

Kentucky's semifinal victory over second-ranked Duke, 83–79, seemed to wrap up Rupp's fifth NCAA championship.

1967

LET THE ALCINDOR ERA BEGIN

By Gary Nuhn

(above) This scene was to become a familiar one: UCLA players celebrating with the player of the decade, Lew Alcindor.

(right) UCLA guard Mike Warren dribbles upcourt during the 1967 championship game, in which UCLA defeated Dayton 79–64.

THIS WAS THE START OF AN AGE—THE UCLA AGE—as surely as the first flake of snow 3.5 million years ago signaled the start of the Ice Age. What was it, anyway? November 16, 3.498 million B.C.?

The UCLA titles in 1964 and 1965 were nice, but they weren't harbingers. Without the import of a King Kong center, UCLA would have become, like San Francisco in 1955–1956 and Cincinnati in 1961–1962, just a good program that won back-to-back titles, not one that was primed to dominate college basketball for a decade.

UCLA didn't get Kong—he was under contract to RKO studios and was thus considered a professional—but it did get a towering center: Ferdinand Lewis Alcindor Jr.

In the absence of Kong, Lew would do just fine.

The recruitment of Alcindor is an interesting story, especially viewed from 30 years later when recruiting is sometimes cloaked in used-car-lot, hard-sell hypocrisy.

As UCLA coach John Wooden told it, Alcindor, the nation's most prized recruit that year, just sort of fell onto the UCLA campus.

Wooden said Alcindor's coach at Power Memorial Academy, Jack Donohue, notified Wooden that UCLA was one of fiveschools Alcindor was considering, but that Donohue didn't want UCLA bothering Alcindor or his parents.

UCLA alumnus Dr. Ralph Bunche, the diplomat, stood in for Wooden at an awards ceremony in New York. Later, when Wooden sent Bunche a thank-you note, he mentioned that UCLA had a chance to land Alcindor and asked if he could help in any way.

Bunche dropped Alcindor's parents a note. Several days later Wooden received a call that Alcindor would like to visit.

Alcindor visited UCLA, not unlike a mail-order bride.

Then Wooden returned the visit to Alcindor's parents.

And Lewie was a Bruin. No huffing, no puffing, no begging and pleading. No dozen trips back and forth across the continent. It was just "Sign here, please, and let's see if we have a uniform to fit you."

It wasn't enough just to have Alcindor, however.

There had been teams in the past with giants—good giants, able giants, athletic giants—that didn't win NCAA titles: DePaul with George Mikan; Kansas with Wilt Chamberlain.

Wooden surrounded Alcindor with brilliant players. It was like the first cast of *Saturday Night Live*, a stunning array of talent, each of the pieces making the others better. The other members of Alcindor's freshman class were shooting forward Lynn Shackelford, defensive forward Ken Heitz, and guard Lucius Allen, who with junior Mike Warren (later of *Hill Street Blues* fame), reminded Bruin fans of the Gail Goodrich–Walt Hazzard tag team.

Wooden took that unit and went 26–0 in the regular season. UCLA was scared only once, in the third meeting with Southern Cal, which put on an Ice Age freeze that took the Bruins into overtime before UCLA won, 40–35.

UCLA swept through the West Regional, 109–60 over Wyoming and 80-64 over Pacific, and came to Louisville 28–0 but curiously, not complacently, not bigheadedly, not ripe for the upsetting.

The teams waiting for the Bruins in The 'Ville were Houston (26–3), North Carolina (26–4), and Dayton (24–5), the first two expected, the latter an unranked surprise.

Houston, ranked No. 7, was the first. The Cougars of coach Guy Lewis were a team of excesses—led in points, rebounding, and verbiage by Elvin Hayes, "the Big E," and led in fact by guard Don Chaney. Hayes billed the game as a matchup between him and Alcindor. "I don't think Lew can stay with me when he's on defense," the Big E crowed.

Replied Alcindor, "We play a team. We don't play one man."

Houston collapsed a three-man sewing circle around Alcindor, so the Bruin sharp-shooters took over. Shackelford zapped in 22, Allen 17, and Warren 14. The Big E was the high-scorer with 25 and the high-rebounder with 24, but he couldn't carry the Cougars alone. UCLA won, 73–58, after which Hayes accused his teammates of choking and bellowed how Alcindor (19 points, 20 rebounds) wasn't such hot stuff after all. He said Jimmy Walker of Providence was the best player in the country.

Alcindor puts up a shot despite the efforts of Dayton's Dan Sadlier during the championship game.

You can count the number of minutes Dayton was in the game on one hand. The Flyers missed their first 8 shots and 16 of their first 18. It was quickly 20–4, UCLA, and things got worse from there. It was like a forest fire after the wind comes up. Dayton spent the night searching for trenches that weren't there.

Wooden could have named his score, and he did. He pulled his horses early, then watched quietly as a 76–47 lead was reduced to a 79–64 final.

"Wooden was a man of tremendous class," said Dayton guard Bobby Joe Hooper. "We'll never forget him for it."

Alcindor led the Bruins with 20 points; Allen added 19, Warren 17, and Shackelford 10. May's 21 topped the Flyers.

Wooden still forbade player interviews in those days, but an enterprising Dayton reporter grabbed a ball, stuck it under his arm, and walked into the UCLA dressing room past the guard, posing as a UCLA manager. The reporter told Alcindor he didn't seem very excited for someone who had

> "We had four sophomores—and at that time freshmen weren't allowed to play varsity—and one junior in our starting lineup. But they were a talented bunch, led by Lew Alcindor. He showed the tremendous value of a big man."
>
> —*John Wooden*
> *Coach of UCLA's 1967 championship team*

just won a national championship. "I've always been that way," the big man said. "People think I don't care. I guess I just don't show my feelings like others do."

On the way home, a Dayton fan told Flyer assistant coach Chuck Grigsby that Alcindor didn't impress him very much. "Yeah," said Grigsby, "all he did was take us out of our offense and take us out of our defense. Other than that, he didn't impress us much."

Three days after the finals, the NCAA rules committee, in honor of Alcindor, outlawed the dunk. If it was supposed to end the UCLA Age, it fell a bit short. Ferdinand Lewis Alcindor Jr. just kept getting better. ∎

In the other semifinal, No. 4 Carolina was supposed to slide past Dayton without drawing a deep breath. This was the first of coach Dean Smith's Final Four teams, and it seemed perfectly balanced with bookend forwards Larry Miller and Bob Lewis, and a good big man in 6´10˝ Rusty Clark. The game plan: take off the warm-ups, run up and down a couple of times, get a lead, go "four corners," and start planning for UCLA. That's what most people thought.

But the Tar Heels ran into a little team of overachievers in Dayton, and they ran into a player, Don May, having the game of his dreams (except even he wouldn't have dreamed he could make 13 straight shots in his own personal game of Around the World). When May was finished, he had 16 baskets in all, 34 points, and the Flyers had won, 76–62.

The championship game, though, went according to the book.

Dayton and UCLA were staying in the same hotel, The Kentucky. One of the Flyer managers, Dave Borchers, remembers seeing Alcindor in the lobby before the game. "He sank down into a chair and all you could see were these knees," Borchers said.

As the teams warmed up, Dayton was further psyched. "He walked past our bench," said Dayton assistant manager Joe Emmrich, "and he was the biggest SOB I ever saw. I thought to myself, 'God, he's 7´13˝!' "

The Flyers' single moment of glory came early. Center Dan Obrovac won the tip. That was one of Alcindor's few weak areas—he had difficulty with his timing on jump balls.

Gary Nuhn is a sports columnist at the Dayton Daily News. *A graduate of Ohio State, he specialized in covering golf and basketball before becoming a columnist. He is a past president of the U.S. Basketball Writers Association.*

1968

PAYBACK FOR THE BRUINS

By Joe Jares

ANTICIPATION OF THE UCLA–HOUSTON/LEW Alcindor–Elvin Hayes rematch in March of 1968 was so delicious, and the game itself so startling, that even those who were there tend to remember it incorrectly as the grand finale of the season.

It wasn't. It was merely the NCAA semifinal—if "merely" can be associated with a UCLA performance that Houston coach Guy V. Lewis described afterward as "the greatest exhibition of basketball I've ever seen."

The Bruins and Cougars had battled at the Houston Astrodome earlier in the season before 52,693 people, the largest crowd ever to see a basketball game in the U.S. up to that time.

In that historic game, forward Hayes, "the Big E," had hit 68 percent of his shots, scored 39 points, taken down 15 rebounds, and made two deciding free throws in a 71–69 victory that stopped UCLA's winning streak at 47. The Astrodome scoreboard had flashed a gigantic *E* over and over again at game's end.

Alcindor, later called by UCLA coach John Wooden "the finest truly big man ever to play basketball up to his time," had made only 4 of 18 shots and finished with 15 points and 12 rebounds. His relatively poor performance probably had been caused by a scratched eyeball suffered three games earlier.

"Alcindor was just half of himself because of his injured eye," Wooden recalled. "He had been in a dark room and had not practiced in over a week."

The subsequent *Sports Illustrated* cover showed Hayes shooting a jumper over Alcindor. The 7´1˝ UCLA junior pinned up that cover in his locker, where he had to see it before and after every practice. Kentucky coach Adolph Rupp called the Bruins "complacent kids." Wooden pinned that quote up in his memory.

The rematch was in the Los Angeles Memorial Sports Arena, which had loaned its floor to the Astrodome for the earlier meeting. Almost nothing but the floor was the same the second time around. Certainly the crowd was smaller: 15,742 plus closed-circuit television audiences in six L.A. locations.

The event started inauspiciously for Houston—the Cougar's student manager was arrested outside the arena and booked on charges of scalping tickets. Things didn't get much better after that. Whoever was wearing Hayes' uniform should have been arrested for imitating the man who had been voted college player of the year.

Wooden and assistant coach Jerry Norman were determined not to let Hayes kill the Bruins again, so they devised a diamond-and-one defense—basically a four-man, diamond-shaped zone, plus the "one," forward Lynn Shackelford, whose job was to adhere to "the Big E" like tape.

"We worked all week on the diamond-and-one," said Shackelford. "This was the one time I felt Wooden and Norman were really trying to get me up for a game. Even during the game, they were screaming and yelling at me not to let Hayes get the ball. When he finally did hit a basket— and we were way ahead—I thought Wooden and Norman were gonna just go crazy. I thought they were gonna come out there on the court and kill me for letting him score."

UCLA got off to a 12–4 lead but saw it slip to 20–19. Then, as *Sports Illustrated* recalled the shift in momentum, "In the next four minutes and 17 seconds, UCLA outscored

(above) As the substitutes played out the remaining minutes of the championship game, UCLA guard Mike Warren cheered his teammates on as the Bruins took the 1968 crown. Years later, Warren became a star of the TV series, *Hill Street Blues*.

(right) North Carolina's Dean Smith raised his hands in frustration as UCLA dominated the Tar Heels by 23 points to win the 1968 championship. The Tar Heels used their famed four-corner offense in the final to no avail.

In a Final Four rematch of the famed Houston Astrodome game in mid-season, UCLA faced a Houston team with Elvin Hayes. However, this time, Alcindor out-rebounded and out-shot Hayes, and UCLA stunned everyone with a 101–69 thrashing.

Houston 17–5 and generally behaved as if it were playing against five blindfolded Campfire Girls."

Wooden was to remember it as "probably the greatest blitz any of my teams has ever put together." The Bruins led by 22 at halftime.

Lewis' halftime talk to his undefeated team concerned "pride, not quitting, hanging tough—those good ol' American principles we'll need if we ever fight the Russians or the Chinese or some of those folks." It did no good. UCLA's lead reached 44 before Wooden sent in his subs. The Bruins won, 101–69.

Hayes finished with 10 points and planted himself on the Houston bench with a towel over his head.

"That was the night Lynn Shackelford rose to the occasion," Wooden said. "It was a tremendous individual defensive

Carolina coach Dean Smith had his team, which had beaten Ohio State, 80–66, in the semis, play a four-corner, slow-down defense. Neither worked well, especially the man defense. Alcindor scored 34 points. Larry Miller of the Tar Heels could manage just 14.

Afterward, Smith called UCLA "the best college basketball team ever."

"This game counted a whole lot," said Alcindor, "but the win over Houston was our most satisfying victory. They'd had a lot to say about us. I don't think they were correct. We wanted to teach those people some manners."

"Our victory over Houston in the semifinals was one of the most gratifying I've ever had as a coach," Wooden said. "But our play against North Carolina in the finals was superior from a technical point of view. I have always felt that neither the excellent North Carolina team nor our

> ## "The UCLA-Houston game at the Astrodome, witnessed by more TV viewers than any other sporting event up to that time, brought a lot of attention to the sport. Houston won that one, but in the semifinals of the Final Four we ran away from them."
> **—John Wooden**
> *Coach of UCLA's 1968 championship team*

effort by a player who was not normally a good defender."

Alcindor, Lucious Allen, and Mike Lynn had 19 apiece, Shackelford 17, and never-off-balance guard Mike Warren had 14.

Wooden said the margin of victory perhaps could be attributed to a feeling that, "We knew we were better than some of the Houston players thought we were, and not as complacent as some coaching peers of mine thought we were."

"We haven't really said anything publicly, but we're a vindictive team," said Warren. "We've been looking forward to this game for a long time and we're not looking past North Carolina. We'll run them back down South, too."

Which the Bruins did 24 hours later, beating the Tar Heels by 23 points, 78–55, then the biggest margin in NCAA championship game history.

fine execution against them in the championship game received proper attention or due credit because of the factors that made it anticlimactic in the eyes of so many."

The subcapacity crowd of 14,438 for the final game reflected that anticlimactic feeling.

Carolina's Miller made the all-tournament team. The other four were Bruins: Alcindor, Allen, Shackelford, and Warren. To demonstrate how strong that UCLA team was, the starter who didn't make the all-tourney team, Mike Lynn, made 8 of 10 shots against Houston. ■

Joe Jares is a sports columnist for the Los Angeles Daily News *after spending many years as a staff writer for* Sports Illustrated, *where he covered Final Fours, among other sports.*

1969

EXIT OF A CHAMPION

By Bill Brill

THE 1969 FINAL WAS HELD IN LOUISVILLE'S FREEDOM Hall, the sixth time in a dozen years that the event had been there, and, coincidentally, the last time.

There was no question who would win. After all, UCLA not only was going for its fifth championship in six years and third in a row, but it was to be the finale for the greatest collegiate player ever, Lew Alcindor.

Since UCLA had begun what would be its decade of domination in 1964 at Kansas City, the Bruins had been virtually without challenge. This time the road to the Final Four was easier than ever.

UCLA never had to leave home. In the 25-team field, the Bruins were an overwhelming favorite. They would have been so under any other circumstances, but in 1969, the West Regional was played in Pauley Pavilion.

The Bruins entered the tournament with a losing streak—one game. It was the only one Alcindor ever lost in Pauley and one of only two defeats for UCLA during the career of the 7'1" center who was to become Kareem Abdul-Jabbar. UCLA was 90–2 during the Alcindor era. The first loss had been at Houston, where Alcindor's eye problems proved beneficial to the Cougars in a 71–69 upset rchestrated by "the Big E," Elvin Hayes.

Later, in the 1968 Final Four at Los Angeles, the Bruins proved that was a legitimate fluke: UCLA 101, Houston 69.

They never were challenged again until the final two games of the regular season. Then, in back-to-back meetings with crosstown rival Southern California, UCLA had to go two overtimes on Southern Cal's court before falling to the Trojans' slowdown, 46–44, at Pauley.

That stunning upset snapped a 41-game winning streak for the Bruins, who also had 52 straight at Pauley. John Wooden was not concerned after the Trojan stall and a collapsing defense limited Alcindor to 10 points. "We haven't been as hungry lately," he said. "Maybe this will wake us up."

The Bruins handled New Mexico State's version of the stall effectively, 53–38. But in the West Regional final, UCLA demonstrated the difference between first and everybody else. Santa Clara, once-beaten and ranked No. 3, was dismantled, 90–52. It was the greatest rout in NCAA West Regional history.

So the Bruins were headed to Louisville, where they were greeted by North Carolina, Purdue, and Drake. The Tar Heels were rated No. 4 in their third straight Final Four. Purdue was No. 6; Drake, in its first NCAA appearance, was No. 11.

It was supposed to be a rematch of 1968, with UCLA playing North Carolina. The Bruins had breezed in that first meeting, 78–55.

But there were warning signs that the Tar Heels weren't on top of their game. They had struggled in the ACC Tournament final against Duke. They had rallied to win both East Regional games. For too long they had depended on Charlie Scott. He bailed them out in the ACC final, and in the East championship game, it was his jumper with two seconds left that beat Davidson, 87–85. That would be as close as Lefty Driesell, then the Wildcats' coach, would come to the Final Four.

The Tar Heels showed up in Louisville without star guard Dick Grubar. The 6'4" senior injured a knee in the ACC finals and was lost for the season. It was a sign of things to come for Dean Smith, who, over the years, had more players missing at Final Four time than any other coach.

(above) Alcindor was joined by his father for the postgame celebration. After a narrow win over a surprising Drake team in the semis, the Bruins easily beat Purdue in the championship.

(right) An Indiana schoolboy hero who went up the road to Purdue, Rick Mount was the most important part of the Boilermakers' game. However, even his driving layups were not enough to win.

Alcindor closed out his sensational career with a sensational game in the 1969 final: 37 points and 20 rebounds against Purdue.

Alcindor scored 25 points and grabbed 21 rebounds, but he played only in spurts, even to the point of appearing somewhat disinterested. Meanwhile, the underdogs were scrapping and hustling, and beating UCLA to every loose ball.

It took 56 percent shooting by UCLA to survive, 85–82. By dint of their desire, the Bulldogs forced 22 turnovers and wound up with 33 more shots (83–50). "That's never happened to one of my teams before," Wooden said, " and I've been coaching a long time."

The Bruins had survived, but barely. One scare was enough for UCLA. Alcindor wasn't about to lose the final game of his career. He had 37 points, 20 rebounds, and numerous intimidations. Purdue, which needed to shoot well to stand a chance, misfired often. The Boilermakers were 12 of 51 in the first half, with Mount going 3 for 18. They finished at 29.3 percent.

> ## "Our history has been that teams don't shoot well against us. Alcindor forces them to do things differently."
>
> **—John Wooden**
> *Coach of UCLA's 1969 championship team*

UCLA breezed, 92–72.

Mount made his first 2, then missed his next 14. "I haven't been that bad since a game I played against Wisconsin my sophomore year," said the senior guard. "UCLA has a way of making everybody miss."

"A lot of teams have said after playing us that it might have been different had they shot better," Wooden said. "But our history has been that they don't shoot well against us. Alcindor forces them to do things differently."

Alcindor admitted he was ready, especially after two Louisville writers picked Purdue to win. "This is my greatest thrill," he said. "Nobody has ever won three straight before. That makes this something special."

What was special, of course, was Lew Alcindor. Twenty years later, Kareem Abdul-Jabbar (he became a Muslim and changed his name) was still scoring points playing basketball. Nobody—ever—has played so long and so well.

"I don't think I'd go through it again," he said that evening in Louisville. "There have been many times when I wondered if it was worth it. But perhaps it would have been the same no matter where I'd been."

Perhaps. ■

Without Grubar, the Tar Heels were without anybody to guard the opposing shooting guard, and Purdue, winners in the Mideast, had All-American Rick Mount. "He's the greatest shooter in college basketball," gushed Purdue coach George King.

King expected Scott, a 6´5´´ forward, to guard Mount in Grubar's absence. "If Scott can stop him, he'll have done some defensive job," he said.

Dean Smith didn't put his All-American against the Purdue star. Instead, he called upon senior Gerald Tuttle, a native of London, Kentucky, who got the rare start because of Grubar's injury.

Tuttle wasn't the answer. Neither was anybody else.

Following the opening basket, Mount and guard running mate Billy Keller scored 24 consecutive points for the Boilermakers. Purdue never looked back, running away from a four-point halftime lead to a shocking 92–65 thumping.

Mount (14–28, 36 points) and Keller made life miserable for the Tar Heels. They outscored the Carolina guards 56–6. Keller wasn't bothered by the press, and while Tuttle and Eddie Fogler couldn't shoot, they couldn't pass, either. North Carolina finished with 22 turnovers, a dozen by its starting guards.

"The boys are embarrassed, and I'm embarrassed for them and the conference," Smith said.

"I don't think there's any fella like my man Keller," said a delighted King.

Then he went courtside for the anticipated slaughter as UCLA went against a Drake team that was 6´8´´, 6´5´´, and 6´5´´ up front. Nobody, obviously, could guard Alcindor, and the Bruins had plenty of help with Lynn Shackelford, Curtis Rowe, and junior college transfer John Vallely.

Drake wasn't impressed with UCLA's press or its media hype, for that matter.

Bill Brill was the executive sports editor of the Roanoke (Virginia) Times & World-News *and retired in 1991. A former president of the U.S. Basketball Writers Association and the author of the book* The History of Duke Basketball, *he continues to write, from time-to-time, for* Basketball America.

1970

With a wink and a nod to the seventies, Bill Walton moved into the key where Lew Alcindor had stood, and the **UCLA** streak continued. In an era when American youth protested a war, experimented with drugs, and grew long hair, Walton put aside some of those thoughts to subscribe to the discipline of team as taught by coach John Wooden.

BILL WALTON, AL McGUIRE, MAGIC, AND BIRD

AFTER THE TURBULENT SIXTIES, THE NEXT DECADE was a time that tested America's national resolve and fiber. The end of the Vietnam War was followed closely by the agonies of Watergate. There was an oil crisis early in the decade, a hostage crisis at the end of it, and an identity crisis throughout.

But it wasn't all gloom and doom. History will remember the seventies as the decade that gave the world such oddities as Billy Carter, the leisure suit, the designated hitter, Clifford Irving, and serial movies with Roman numerals in their titles (*The Godfather*, *Jaws*, *Rocky*, etc.).

With the end of the draft and the country finally at peace, young people stepped back from the horrors of the sixties and became so introspective as to become selfish. The "Me" generation, it was called. As the divorce rate soared, the traditional family became almost as outmoded as high-button shoes. But even as almost everyone seemed to be redefining their roles and values in this changing society, the sports and entertainment industries continued to grow—and no sport experienced quite the explosion in popularity that belonged to college basketball.

As crowds grew, television ratings soared, new arenas were opened everywhere, and the UCLA dynasty reached its peak before finally fading away. When Lew Alcindor left UCLA in 1969, a collective sigh of relief passed through the sport. So all coach John Wooden did was win the 1970 and 1971 championships with teams lacking a dominant center. Then, in 1972, came the word that Wooden had found a big man as dominant as Alcindor, maybe even more so. Nobody could believe it at first, yet 6´11˝ Bill Walton proved to be every bit as good as his advance billing.

After UCLA's title string was stopped at seven in a row in Walton's senior year, Wooden finally was written off. But the man known as "the Wizard" had one more title left in him before he strolled off into the Hollywood sunset. His legacy to college basketball was a record of achievement that figures to still be standing in 2039, when the championship celebrates its 100th birthday.

Perhaps the decade's most compelling figure was Al McGuire, the flamboyant, controversial, streetwise refugee from New York City who built a minidynasty at Marquette. He retired tearfully after his 1977 team won the championship, then reappeared as the color man on an NBC announcing team that also included Dick Enberg and Billy Packer.

So good that it often tended to overshadow the games it called, the McGuire-Packer-Enberg triumvirate was at mikeside in 1979 for perhaps the greatest individual confrontation in championship game history—Michigan State's 6´8˝ Earvin "Magic" Johnson against Indiana State's 6´9˝ Larry Bird. Never had the game seen a big man who could pass and handle the ball like Johnson. Even so, he wasn't as complete a player as Bird, who could beat a team with his outside shooting, rebounding, passing, or great court sense.

It was a perfect way to end the dramatic seventies and lead into a glorious future in which the game's popularity became so huge that arenas such as Salt Lake City's seventeen thousand– seat Salt Palace would be deemed too small for the Final Four. ■

"When we won 10 championships in 12 years, we played a different team in each final. There was a great balance throughout the nation, but we stayed on top for a long time. Our 88-game winning streak is one of the most remarkable records in college basketball."
—*John Wooden*

1979

Earvin Johnson was truly magic, and the classic game of the decade came when Michigan State played Indiana State and Larry Bird for the title. The game lived up to its advance billing for a while, but in the end Michigan State won decisively, 75–64.

1970

WHO FILLED LEW'S SHOES? EVERYBODY

By Dwight Chapin

THE OTHER TEAMS IN COLLEGE BASKETBALL WERE supposed to have a chance again in the 1969–1970 season. Lew Alcindor—yes, he was still called that then—was gone after three seasons of incredible domination, and a mere mortal named Steve Patterson was in his place.

"No one is going to fill Lew's shoes," said Patterson, a sagacious young man. "It's going to take all of us, working together, to do that."

Work together they did, directed by Wizard of Westwood John Wooden at his most wizardly. Nearly all of the load, as usual with Wooden teams, was carried by an iron-man five: Sidney Wicks and Curtis Rowe, the brilliant forwards; guards Henry Bibby and John Vallely; and Patterson, who never got the credit he deserved because of the stature of the man who came before him and the man (Bill Walton) who came after him.

There had been one loss in the regular season to Oregon on the road, but it seemed to weld the Bruins together, and they had no trouble in the West Regional, beating Jerry Tarkanian's Long Beach State team by 23 points and Utah State by 22.

It looked as if things might be different in the NCAA semifinals at College Park, Maryland, where New Mexico State was waiting. The Aggies, who had lost to UCLA in the regionals in both of the preceding seasons, saw it as a grudge match they could win. "I feel we've got the momentum going now," said Jimmy Collins, the Aggies' fine guard.

Collins did. He scored 28 points. But his teammates couldn't match the Bruins' quickness, and New Mexico State exited a one-sided loser, 93–77.

That set the Cole Field House stage for one of the most intriguing matchups in NCAA history: a clash of cultures and lifestyles as much as basketball teams. UCLA and Jacksonville; the Establishment vs. the Age of Aquarius; an old, tested coach against one 23 years his junior.

Early in the tournament week, Wooden took his Bruins on a three-hour tour of Washington, D.C.'s, historical sites. Attendance was not optional.

In contrast, Jacksonville's Joe Williams, who wore a lucky suit the color of vanilla ice cream, took his players on a White House tour, but there were no restrictions. "They do what they want to do," Williams said.

> ## "I don't anticipate a letdown. I think we will always have pride in ourselves, and when you have that, you are going to be all right."
>
> **—John Wooden**
> *Coach of UCLA's 1970 championship team*

Jacksonville was a team that had come out of nowhere to post a 23–1 record, had beaten Western Kentucky, Iowa, and Kentucky in the regionals, and then topped a St. Bonaventure squad that was without injured Bob Lanier in the semifinals. If the Dolphins were nervous about facing UCLA for the championship, it didn't show. They put on a Harlem Globetrotters-style routine at one practice, while the Bruins watched in quiet amusement, and star center Artis Gilmore fell asleep in a motel armchair before another workout.

Jacksonville not only had "Batman" (Gilmore) and "Robin" (guard Rex Morgan) but two other huge front liners, 6´10´´ Rod McIntyre and 7´0´´ Pembrook Burrows III, who, when asked about his name, said, "It's not

(above) Artis Gilmore was the heart of the Jacksonville offense, and his aggressive play moved the Dolphins into an early lead in the 1970 NCAA Final. That was before UCLA coach Wooden moved Sidney Wicks into the way.

(right) The UCLA machine caught fire, and their team effort dominated Jacksonville. Henry Bibby (No. 45) scored as Steve Patterson (No. 32) waited, should a putback shot be needed.

UCLA forward Curtis Rowe tries to shoot over Gilmore during the 1970 championship game, held at the Cole Fieldhouse in College Park, Maryland.

unusual; my father was named that and so was my grandfather."

For the first few minutes of the final, the Dolphins played as big as they stood, taking a 14–6 lead as Gilmore got free for three easy baskets inside off Wicks, who had been surprised just before game time to learn that he was going to guard the giant. But UCLA called a timeout, and Wooden and Wicks, who many thought was then the most intimidating player in college basketball (at only 6´8´´), took over.

Wicks, who had been playing to the side of Gilmore, moved behind him, with Patterson and other Bruins sagging in to help out when they could. Wicks didn't require much assistance. The next time Gilmore went up for what he thought would be an easy shot, Wicks rose above him, whacking the ball away. It was one of those classic NCAA moments now frozen in time. It changed the course of the game, and saved a dynasty.

While Wicks—who acquired the nickname Super Sidney after this performance—was eliminating Gilmore, Rowe and Vallely shot UCLA into a 41–36 halftime advantage. It wasn't much of a cushion, but it was enough, the Bruins figured, if they could make a run in the first few minutes of the second half, which they did as Gilmore missed five straight shots. The lead went from 8 to 11 to 16 points, and Jacksonville could do little about it. With just under two minutes to play, Gilmore fouled out, and Jacksonville fans began taking off their "J.U. Can Do" badges. UCLA won with relative ease, 80–69.

"Everybody was looking forward to playing without Lew," Rowe said in the locker room "Right now, if Alcindor was on the team, who would the reporters be talking to? Look around you. The reporters are with five people, and that's beautiful. Every time somebody mentions three titles in a row, they say Lew did it. Now we just proved that four other men on the team could play basketball—with the best of them."

In the background, John Wooden, who had always seen basketball as a team game, was beaming.

He was already looking ahead to the next season. "I don't anticipate a letdown," he said. "I think we will always have pride in ourselves, and when you have that, you are going to be all right."

And it didn't hurt that the only starter he would lose was Vallely. ∎

Dwight Chapin is a senior sportswriter at the San Francisco Chronicle. *He previously was a sports columnist at the* San Francisco Examiner. *He covered UCLA basketball during the Wooden years for the* Los Angeles Times.

1971

PATTERSON GRABS THE SPOTLIGHT

By Dwight Chapin

THE BLUE-AND-GOLD UNIFORMS WERE THE SAME and so was the aura of invincibility, but this wasn't the same ol' UCLA team that showed up at the Houston Astrodome for the 1971 NCAA Tournament.

Of all the teams in the Bruins' amazing 10-time championship run, this one was the shakiest. Maybe it was the chemistry. Several players clashed with coach John Wooden and bickered among themselves. Or maybe it was the fact that teams were lying in wait for the sometimes-arrogant Bruins, particularly on the road. UCLA lost to Notre Dame and Austin Carr in South Bend, and had close calls all along the way—none closer than in the West Regional against Long Beach State.

The Bruins trailed by 11 points in the second half, All-American forward Sidney Wicks was on the bench with four fouls, and Wooden was thinking, "Maybe my wife and I can leave for Houston a day early next week and just have a good time as spectators at the national tournament."

But UCLA came back, escaped with a two-point win on a pair of Wicks free throws, and prepared to meet bullish Kansas in the NCAA semifinals. Not before a bit more testing of authority, however, in an era in which authority was being tested everywhere. As the Bruins got off their plane, a reporter noticed that Wicks had a stubble of beard,

and asked him if he planned to keep it for the game. "Yep," Wicks said.

The beard was gone by game time. The coach was still in control.

UCLA hadn't shot well against zone defenses all season, but it blistered the Jayhawk zone in the first half, with the clean-shaven Wicks doing most of the damage. As usual, Wicks played intimidator. In the first half, he yelled at Kansas' ace forward Dave Robisch, "Look out, here I come!" and later he screamed "Halt!" at Robisch, who knew better than to argue with a man whose glare was so intense it probably could have cut diamonds.

Kansas made things interesting for awhile in the second half, getting a tie at 39–39, but then the Bruin defense took the Jayhawks out of what they were trying to do. The result was something that could have been plucked from Wooden's "Pyramid of Success." The Bruins bolted to a 68–53 lead, called in the reserves, and won with more ease than the 68–60 final score indicated.

In the process, they survived a brouhaha on the bench. Early in the game, assistant coach Denny Crum—who would move on to the head job at Louisville the next season—told Terry Schofield to go in at guard for Kenny Booker. Wooden ordered Schofield to stay put. Schofield eventually did enter the game, but not before Wooden had railed at Crum, "I'm the coach of this team, and don't tell me how to coach my team!" Guard Henry Bibby had to step in as a peacemaker.

The sidelines were calmer in the title game against Villanova, but the game turned out to be tense.

Villanova had six losses, but it also had destroyed Pennsylvania by 43 points in the East Regional and had beaten a good Western Kentucky team in double overtime in the semifinals. It was coached by university division coach of the year Jack Kraft, and featured marvelous forward Howard Porter and underrated Hank Siemiontkowski, who had burned Jim McDaniels for 31 points in the semis.

Opening in a 2-3 zone defense much like the one that Long Beach State had

Opposing coaches who faced Wooden's Bruins (above) found the task frustrating. In the semifinal game, a talented Kansas team (right) watched the game get away in the second half. Guard Tom Kivisto (from left), coach Ted Owens, and assistants Sam Miranda and Bob Hill all showed the strain.

Bruin Sidney Wicks could be an intimidating player, but so could Villanova's Howard Porter. Their contest became an amazing sidebar to the 1971 championship game. Porter scored 25 points and was named Most Outstanding Player, but Wicks played for the championship team.

used so effectively against UCLA in the regionals, the Wildcats shackled Wicks and Rowe. But that left Steve Patterson free, outside first and then inside, and he broke a long shooting slump with 20 first-half points.

It was the most dramatic half of Patterson's career, and it might never have happened, because early in the season he'd had a disagreement with Wooden over the length of his sideburns and almost quit the team. But he decided not to, saying later, "I've never been a famous entity, but if I'd quit and UCLA lost a championship, I'd have been infamous."

Late in the first half against Villanova, UCLA went into a stall, hoping to bring the Wildcats out of their zone. Wooden opted to continue that strategy in the second half. That enraged a good portion of the vast Astrodome crowd, along with the Villanova players, who jeered, "You're the national champions. Play ball!"

"I've never been a famous entity, but if I'd quit and UCLA lost a championship, I'd have been infamous."

—Steve Patterson
Guard on UCLA's 1971 championship team

Wooden would admit that the slow-down was at least partially motivated by his desire to convince rulemakers that college basketball needed a time clock. But his move nearly backfired. The Bruins lost their momentum when they held the ball, and the Wildcats proved surprisingly adept with a man-to-man defense when they came out of their zone. Playing brilliantly down the stretch, they cut UCLA's lead to four points

with just under five minutes left, as Porter intimidated Wicks with fadeaway jump shots. With 2:38 remaining, the Bruins' lead was down to three, 61–58. But Bibby, one of UCLA's best tournament players, and Patterson held steady, and when Patterson hit a lay-in with 38 seconds left, UCLA was ahead by six and stayed there, winning 68–62.

Porter, who scored 25 points, was voted Most Outstanding Player, an honor that would lose its luster when it was revealed he had signed a professional contract before the tournament, forcing Villanova to forfeit its season's accomplishments.

But Patterson, who had scored 29, was the man of the moment, and somebody wanted to know what was responsible for his remarkable performance. Maybe, he said, it was the trout he'd had at dinner with his parents the night before at a Houston restaurant. Or maybe—and he looked over at teetotaler Wooden—it was that glass or two of vin rose. ■

1972

WALTON GANG

By Joe Jares

BEING A PASSIONATE TEAM MAN, UCLA COACH John Wooden didn't particularly care for the "Walton Gang" nickname dreamed up by the media. Being a conservative Hoosier by upbringing, he didn't care for some of the gang's student-revolutionary dietary attitudes. (Bob Hope kidded Wooden a few years later, "Who else would grow alfalfa in his garden so Bill Walton could have a decent lunch?")

But he certainly liked the gang's performance on the court in 1971–1972, when four of its members—Walton, Keith Wilkes, Greg Lee, and Tommy Curtis—were mere sophomores. Wooden was to remember that first Walton Gang as "probably the most versatile of all my teams."

Those Bruins could run in the finest, fleetest Wooden fast-break tradition or, with the 6´11˝ Walton dominating the middle, play a set offense. They could press or play a set defense. They could shoot—senior guard Henry Bibby had games when he could regularly have tossed a tennis ball into a drainpipe at 20 paces. They could pass and rebound.

And they had a fine bench—so fine that second-string center Swen Nater, who never started a game for them, became a first-round NBA draft choice. So fine that two dazzling, if sometimes erratic, guards—Curtis and Larry Hollyfield—were always ready to spell Bibby and Lee.

Wooden also felt the 1971–1972 Bruins "had more academic brilliance than any team I have ever had."

The team surprised Wooden by entering the NCAA Tournament undefeated. Each year he predicted the Bruins' regular-season record and sealed it in an envelope kept in his desk. That year the talent level might have warranted a forecast of perfection, but his pick, because of "their extreme youth, their inexperience," was 24–2.

The first Walton Gang reached the NCAA Final Four with no losses, but it did come burdened with some controversy. In the final of the West Regional at Provo, Utah, UCLA beat Long Beach State, 73–57. It was a game that sometimes resembled a rumble on the docks.

"Every year we play Long Beach, we get slugged," said Bibby.

"There wasn't much basketball being played out there," said Wooden. "What there was, we played it."

Long Beach players complained that Walton was a "crybaby" and that UCLA got the majority of the calls.

Some of this spilled over into the semifinals of the Final Four at the Los Angeles Sports Arena, when UCLA (28–0) played Louisville (24–3), coached by ex-Bruin assistant coach and player Denny Crum.

It was an easy victory. No Cardinal or combination of Cardinals could handle the young, red-haired giant from La Mesa, California. Walton, who scored eight straight points in an early three-minute stretch to put his team ahead, 20–14, finished with 33 points, 21 rebounds, and six blocked shots.

"Walton is strong, but you can't touch him," said Cardinal center Al Vilchek afterward (he had fouled out with 12 minutes left). "The officials put him in a cage. He cries a lot. I just don't think a man of his ability should cry so much. He wasn't hurt when he went to the floor in the first half. He was just resting."

"We lost and I'll make no excuses," said Louisville guard Jim Price, who had 30 points. "UCLA played better and it won, so it is the better team."

"I think this is the best UCLA team I've seen," said Crum.

(above) Walton at 6´11˝ could see more of the game and used his height to pass outside, here to Henry Bibby (No. 45). Florida State gave UCLA its toughest battle of the season, but Wooden earned his seventh NCAA title.

(right) Florida State forward Rowland Garrett (No. 23) goes up and over North Carolina guard George Karl (No. 22) during their 1972 semifinal game in Los Angeles, California.

Walton's domination of the game began in 1972, and the crowd in the Los Angeles Sports Arena watched the Bruins' new center lead UCLA to an 81–76 championship game victory over Florida State.

37–31, but it wasn't enough. Wooden sent Lee in for the last five minutes to run a keep-away, slow-down game.

Costly turnovers prevented Florida State from catching up, and UCLA won, 81–76.

King was high-point man with 27. Walton led UCLA with 24, followed by the silky Wilkes with 23, and 18 for Bibby, who made up for his lousy shooting versus Louisville.

"I'm not that elated because we didn't play that well," Walton said. "Florida State is an excellent team, but we didn't dominate the game the way we know we can. If we had played our game the way we can, it would have been different.

"No excuses, but I don't like to back into things. I like to win convincingly."

Bibby, the senior, wasn't so fussy. "We made mistakes we shouldn't have made, but any team would like to be in our position right now."

Wooden, a tough taskmaster and a severe critic, also didn't agree with Walton.

> ## "Very few championship games I've seen or been in have been exceptionally well played. There's too much emotion and too much at stake for that."
> **—John Wooden**
> *Coach of UCLA's 1972 championship team*

"I understand why Walton and some others aren't satisfied," he said. "Bill, for example, sets high standards for himself and is displeased when he doesn't reach them. But I don't think we played as poorly as the players do. Very few championship games I've seen or been in have been exceptionally well played. There's too much emotion and too much at stake for that," Wooden said.

"I was especially pleased when we fell behind but didn't lose our poise. I was not so pleased when we got cautious and started to stand around near the finish, which is why I went to a slower game, to protect our advantage.

"I'm satisfied."

One would hope the Wizard of Westwood was satisfied. UCLA had its sixth straight NCAA title, its eighth overall, 45 wins in a row (the third-longest streak in college basketball annals), and a 30–0 season.

But the dissatisfaction of that stellar sophomore class only served to motivate the Bruins toward their goal of perfection. And as Walton would prove one year later, perfection was an attainable goal. ■

UCLA's opponent in the final, Florida State, arrived in L.A. with the same sort of outlaw reputation that had been stuck on Texas Western back in 1966. The Seminoles, coached by Hugh Durham, had just gotten off three years of probation for recruiting violations, and some coaches (not including Wooden) were outraged by their presence.

"We've paid the price," said Durham. "We accepted it. We didn't debate it in the press or in public."

Florida State had beaten North Carolina, 79–75, in the semis, a surprise. Seminole guard Otto Perry thought his team was ready.

"No one knew us before. Now they know. We can play with anyone. They have the greatest coach in the world in Wooden and the greatest player in the world with Walton, but we just might upset them."

They almost did. Florida State gave the young Bruins their closest and toughest game of the season. It had a good outside shooter in Ron King and a good inside man in 6´11˝ Lawrence McCray.

The Seminoles broke ahead, 21–14, but, young or not, UCLA refused to crack and regained the lead, even spurting ahead by 11 at halftime. Florida State won the second half,

1973

BILL WALTON'S NEAR-PERFECT PERFORMANCE

By George Lapides

GOLD WAS STRUCK AT ST. LOUIS IN 1973. THIS was the first NCAA Final Four that was sold out in advance.

Before 1973, the tournament played before sellout crowds, but only because of the game day walk-up at the ticket booths. After 1973, the NCAA went to a lottery system to determine who could buy Final Four tickets.

The 1973 ticket demand was intense because followers from two of the participating teams—Indiana and Memphis State—lived within convenient driving distance of St. Louis.

Indiana loyalists were growing enchanted with their 32-year-old, second-year coach—brash Bobby Knight. About three thousand of them went to St. Louis to see if Knight and his Hoosiers could deliver a championship.

Memphis State fans created traffic jams on Interstate 55 as they flocked to St. Louis to pull for the Tigers. Almost six thousand of them—ecstatic over the way Memphis State pounded its opponents in the Midwest Regional and just plain wild about head coach Gene Bartow—made the 275-mile trip.

Otherwise, it was business as usual.

Providence was the East Regional representative and, as usual, UCLA arrived from the West.

By now, the event had become known as the "UCLA Invitational." The Bruins seemed to own the sport. When they arrived in St. Louis, they were winners of 73 consecutive games over a three-season span and seven of the past eight NCAA championships, including six in a row.

This also was the first Final Four split over a weekend, with the semifinal games on Saturday and the championship on Monday night.

An individual performance that many observers still consider the most extraordinary of all time would be seen in this Final Four.

A hint of Bobby Knight's genius also would be seen in the first semifinal game, even though his Hoosiers would lose, 70–59, to UCLA.

"Anytime you go into a basketball game, you don't know what your team is going to do over the course of the entire game," he said the day before the semifinals. "I think you have to wait and see what you can do."

But Knight understood what had to be done. He knew that in order to whip the Bruins, he'd have to figure a way to stop Bill Walton, UCLA's 6´11´´ junior center and already the Associated Press Player of the Year.

Knight's strategy was simple. He put his strongest player—6´8´´, 231-pound Steve Downing—on Walton. Downing would lean on Walton, use his muscles, push and shove, try to intimidate —do whatever it would take to get Walton in foul trouble.

Knight's strategy worked . . . sort of.

Downing got Walton into foul trouble.

But Downing got Downing into foul trouble, too.

Midway through the second half, Indiana had chopped a big Bruin lead to 54–51. The Hoosiers seemed to have the momentum. Walton, already saddled with four fouls, took a pass in heavy traffic inside, wheeled, and drove for the basket. Downing appeared to cut him off. Both tumbled to the floor.

The whistles blew and when they did it became so quiet in the jam-packed arena that you almost could hear John Wooden's scorecard hit the floor.

The refs said foul—on Downing. It was his fourth. Only 97 seconds later he was whistled for his fifth. The Indiana rally abruptly ended.

Knight was more understanding then of the call than he might have been later in his career.

"What the hell difference does one individual make?" he said. "UCLA had what it took to come back and win the game. Anything I could say about it wouldn't make any difference anyway. All that counts is that UCLA won the game by 11 points."

The second game that Saturday matched Dave Gavitt's Providence Friars against Bartow's unheralded Memphis State team.

(above) Bill Walton sat on the UCLA bench with an injured ankle and accepted congratulations from celebrating players and coaches in St. Louis. Two impressed Memphis State players helped carry him to the bench after the injury.

Walton takes one to the hoop during the national semifinals in the St. Louis Checkerdome, where he would return to dominate the championship game with a near-perfect night.

There were a few Providence fans in the seats behind the South goal. Other than that, it seemed like the entire arena was a sea of Memphis blue.

In the opening minutes, Ernie DiGregorio threw dazzling, halfcourt, behind-the-back passes to the Friars' big men—especially to Marvin Barnes—and Providence jumped to an early lead. Memphis State floundered.

A Providence zone kept the Tigers playing around the perimeter, although their best game was to jam it in the middle to either Ronnie Robinson or Larry Kenon.

The Friars led, 18–12, and then 22–14. But Barnes was felled by a knee injury, and the complexion suddenly changed. Larry Finch began hitting from outside, Providence extended its zone, and Memphis State then countered by going inside.

Ernie D. scored 32 points, but Kenon had 28, Robinson 24, and Finch 21. Barnes

It wasn't.

Bill Walton wouldn't allow it.

He missed only one of his field goal attempts in the first half but improved to perfection in the second. For the night he was an astonishing 21 of 22 from the field. He scored 44 points, still a record in a championship game.

His coach would joke after it was over that he would speak with Walton about that lone miss at the first practice the following autumn.

The last time the Tigers were close was at 49–47 with 13:48 remaining. Walton scored the next eight points. UCLA connected on 21 of its 30 second-half field goal attempts. The Bruins won the backboard battle, 40–21.

It ended 87–66, but the margin was somewhat misleading. It would have been a little closer if Memphis State had allowed

"I've never had a greater team both offensively and defensively."

—John Wooden
Coach of UCLA's 1973 championship team

limped back into the game in the second half, but it didn't matter. Memphis State won going away, 98–85.

It would be just another championship game for the Bruins, but in Memphis, the basketball Tigers were bigger heroes than Elvis. Even more fans poured up I-55 on Sunday and Monday, hopeful of acquiring tickets from departing Indiana and Providence followers. Some were fortunate; others milled around the parking lot hoping to join the postgame victory celebration.

But UCLA would rule again. The Bruin's victory party was a quiet one. Their players went for dessert at the Chase Park Plaza Hotel.

Oh, it was interesting and close for a while. Memphis State led early at 12–10, kept within striking distance most of the first half, and went to the intermission even at 39–39.

The huge Memphis State following in the crowd of 19,301 was practically hysterical. The largest national television audience ever to watch a championship game—42 million—may have wondered if this finally would be the time the Bruins would lose.

the clock to run out instead of fouling late in a vain attempt to catch up.

Walton injured his ankle in the game's waning moments. Two Memphis State players, Finch and Billy Buford, carried him to the Bruin bench. You could see the respect in their eyes. The crowd—including the Memphis State throng—gave the UCLA redhead a rousing standing ovation. They realized they had just witnessed one of the greatest championship performances ever in any sport.

Wooden admitted after it was over that this was his best UCLA team ever. "I've never had a greater team both offensively and defensively," said the Wizard of Westwood.

There was no argument from the Memphis State camp. ■

George Lapides was the sports editor of the Memphis Press-Scimitar. *He once was president of a Memphis class-AA baseball team, and he has been a longtime sports broadcaster and radio-show host.*

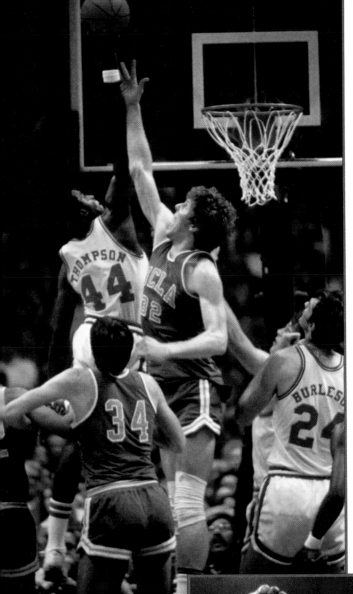

1974

THE HORIZON OF A NEW ERA

By Smith Barrier

THE END OF THE 1974 SEASON MARKED THE BEGINning of a new era in college basketball. Coach John Wooden and the absolutely amazing UCLA Bruins did not win. That in itself was a phenomenon. UCLA had 38 consecutive NCAA Tournament victories, leading to an unprecedented seven straight national championships. But coach Norm Sloan's N. C. State Wolfpack ended UCLA's run in the national semifinals and then defeated coach Al McGuire's Marquette Warriors for the title.

All of this excitement and novelty took place in a basketball-crazed section of the U.S. that had never hosted the NCAA Final Four. Louisville, Kentucky, and College Park, Maryland, had staged the finals in its formative years, before it was called the Final Four, but that is border South. The civic leaders of Greensboro, North Carolina, had sold the NCAA basketball committee on coming to "real basketball country" . . . to North Carolina, to Greensboro, not a populous metropolis.

It was the first sale of Final Four tickets a year in advance. Louisville and St. Louis had been sellouts several months in advance, but April 1, 1973, was the deadline for ordering tickets in Greensboro. Of Greensboro's 15,400 tickets, 8,800 went to public sale. There were 15,840 pieces of mail with the April 1 postmark, a total of 42,500 orders within two days, averaging 3.2 tickets per order, or 136,000.

Also, it was the first year for pairings rotation, eliminating the previous East-West finals and making it possible for top-ranked N. C. State to play No. 2 UCLA in the semifinals, one of the most eagerly awaited showdowns in tournament history.

When the Bruins stubbed their toes during a late-season swing through the Pac-8, N. C. State replaced the perennial champions atop the polls. The Wolfpack's star player was the splendid 6´4˝ leaper, David Thompson, also known as TWA

(Teeny Weeny Afro) because of a brush with disaster that shall be mentioned momentarily.

In the final of the Atlantic Coast Conference tournament, playing on the same Greensboro floor that was to be home of the Final Four, N.C. State outlasted Maryland, 103–100, in what some veteran ACC observers ranked as the greatest game they had ever seen. This was still the era, remember, when only the league champion went to the NCAA, meaning poor Lefty Driesell had to take his Maryland team home.

For the East Regional, the Wolfpack had only to move from Greensboro to its homecourt, Reynolds Coliseum on the campus in Raleigh. The Wolfpack whipped Providence and Pittsburgh to earn a return trip to Greensboro, but got a huge scare when Thompson fell from the sky and landed right on his head. When physicians severely cropped his Afro, Thompson became known as TWA.

When UCLA arrived in Greensboro, its star, 6´11˝ center Bill Walton, two-time college player of the year, was carrying a paper bag full of California oranges as he got off the transcontinental charter. While UCLA and the other semifinalists—Kansas and Marquette—worked out privately on Thursday, a cheering crowd of five thousand watched the Wolfpack go through their final drills, then sent TWA & Co. off on the two-hour bus ride to Greensboro with a pep rally at which 2,500 fans heard every player say a few words.

Until 1974, only some of the coaches, skipping clinics at the coaches convention, and a few diehard fans turned out for the Friday afternoon practice sessions at the Final Four site. But with tickets so scarce in Greensboro—N.C. State allotted only one hundred for students out of its one thousand, and 2,740 students applied—the only chance to see the teams was in the Friday afternoon practice. Unofficially, since it was free, six thousand fans attended.

Finally all the hoopla ended and it was time for the big one—UCLA and N.C. State. They met the opening Saturday afternoon, right after Marquette beat Kansas, 64–51. Nobody needed to be reminded that UCLA had soundly defeated the Wolfpack, 84–66, in a made-for-television matchup in St. Louis in December.

For most of the early going, it looked as if the Bruins were destined to win again. In the second half, UCLA was up by as many as 11. But the Wolfpack kept chipping until it gained a tie and had a chance to win in regulation, only to

(above) North Carolina State's David Thompson took the ball repeatedly to the basket over a towering Bill Walton. In one of the greatest games in Final Four history, the Wolfpack defeated UCLA 80–77 in double-overtime en route to its first championship.

(right) Most people expected a UCLA celebration in 1974, but North Carolina State, with Thompson (No. 44) at the helm, got to wear the nets. Upsetting UCLA in the semifinals, the Wolfpack went on to defeat Marquette, 76–64, in the final.

Marquette center Maurice Lucas takes it to the hole past North Carolina State's Tommy Burleson (No. 24) and David Thompson (No. 44) during the 1974 championship game in Greensboro, North Carolina.

have Tim Stoddard, later a major league baseball pitcher, bounce a side shot off the rim.

The same thing happened in the first overtime, when N.C. State's chance to win ended with 7′4″ Tom Burleson bumping a close shot off the back rim.

In the second overtime, UCLA went up seven behind the strength of Walton and Keith Wilkes. Then Thompson put the Wolfpack ahead to stay, 76–75, and he and Monte Towe converted free throws for the 80–77 final.

Wooden has reviewed that afternoon many times since, and he said, "I thought we had the game in hand two times. In the second half, up 11, we took three shots you just don't take when you have the lead. Then in

first half and helped Sloan's team to a 39–30 halftime lead. "The technicals sure gave us a lift," Thompson would say later, while McGuire manfully admitted that his strategy had backfired. That would haunt McGuire until he won his own national title three years later.

When it came time to hand out awards, Thompson was the Most Outstanding Player, and Burleson and Towe also made the all-tournament team, along with Maurice Lucas of Marquette and Walton.

The Wolfpack, in their tournament run, had beaten teams ranked Nos. 2, 3, 4, and 6 in the country. Sloan, years later, reviewed "Those Three Weeks," as they became known in his household.

"What happened in 1974 is almost like you're half awake and half asleep. When you get to this point, everything moves so quickly.

> ## "I thought we had the [semifinal] game in hand two times . . . In overtime we made a crucial mistake or two, but that's to the credit of North Carolina State."
>
> **—John Wooden**
> *Coach of UCLA's 1974 championship team*

overtime, up seven, we made a crucial mistake or two, but, that's to the credit of North Carolina State."

But, the Wolfpack still had Marquette to play.

North Carolina Governor James Holshouser, writing a daily "guest" column in the *Greensboro Daily News* for the tournament, spoke for everybody: "It somehow seems a shame that Saturday's N.C.State–UCLA game had to be the semifinals. The way it turned out, it would have been a perfect finale. When the No. 1 team in the nation defeats the No. 2 team in two overtimes, it's sort of hard to imagine a fitting encore."

But all of the 15,829 ticket-holders showed up Monday night, along with 27 million or so television watchers. The Wolfpack, as predicted, outscored Marquette, 76–64, with Thompson getting 21 points and Burleson 11 rebounds. Two technical fouls on McGuire provided the impetus for the Wolfpack's working margin late in the

You have so many things to take care of, there's no such thing as pressure. I never felt one bit of pressure, we were too busy.

"The enthusiasm of the basketball fans in North Carolina, no question about that . . . I don't know that we could have won the thing if we played anywhere else. We were good, don't misunderstand, but shoot, if we had been playing out in Los Angeles, I don't know that we could have beaten UCLA. They won three of theirs at home. It makes a difference.

"Everybody you bump into on the street . . . the intensity is greater . . . more people able to be at the game, more for us than for UCLA. Of course, UCLA had won so much. They had put themselves in that unenviable position. Everybody wanted to see them fall." ∎

Smith Barrier was publisher of Greensboro Publications and former executive sports editor of the Greensboro News & Record. *He is a member of the North Carolina Sports Hall of Fame.*

The 1975 title game was John Wooden's final appearance. After surviving against Louisville in overtime in the semifinals, the Bruins faced a talented and formidable Kentucky team for the title. Wooden fought for every call in the final (top). A charging Wildcat team saw Kevin Grevey (bottom above) dance down the press tables for a loose ball.

1975

ONE LAST HURRAH FOR THE WIZARD

By Mike Sullivan

THE 1974–1975 COLLEGE BASKETBALL SEASON WAS A good one for coaches quips. But it was an even better season for tradition.

Asked in a preseason interview if he thought UCLA could come back, John Wooden, the Bruins' 64-year-old coach, replied puckishly that he "didn't know we had been gone."

The man had a point. Only a double-overtime semifinal loss to 1974 champion N.C. State had kept UCLA from making an eighth straight appearance in the title game.

With the 1975 championship encounter less that 24 hours away, Joe B. Hall, Kentucky's third-year head coach and the successor to Adolph Rupp, joined in the speculation about a replacement for Wooden, who had just announced his retirement.

"I'm the obvious choice," Hall cracked. "Why ruin two lives?"

No lives were ruined in the San Diego Sports Arena on March 31, 1975, when UCLA used quickness and poise to befuddle Kentucky's bruisers, 92–85, and send Wooden into retirement with what is arguably the greatest coaching achievement in team sports—10 national championships in a span of 12 years.

But if lives were spared, nerves were liberally abused.

In the semifinals two days earlier, Louisville had played the Bruins off their feet, leading most of the way by five to nine points under Wooden's protégé, Denny Crum.

UCLA won, 75–74, in overtime —its only lead during the extra period—on Richard Washington's seven-footer with two seconds left. With 20 seconds to go and the Bruins trailing, 74–73, Washington had rebounded the missed first attempt in a one-and-one free throw situation by Louisville guard Terry Howard, who had stepped to the line with a 28 for 28 mark on the season.

In the other semi, Hall's Wildcats—who had come rumbling back from the ruins of a 13–13 record the year before—pummeled Syracuse, 95–79, getting 24 points and 11 rebounds from freshman reserve Jack Givens. Kentucky used 14 players in a game in which 61 fouls were called.

Columnist Dave Kindred, comparing the two contests, likened the Louisville-UCLA thriller to a Michaelangelo. On that basis he said Kentucky vs. Syracuse was "a Roto-Rooter sign on a panel truck."

Still, many observers in San Diego felt that Kentucky would keep on truckin' past UCLA, despite the inspiration generated by Wooden's locker room retirement announcement.

The Wildcats had four NCAA titles, a total that Wooden had matched in 1968 and surpassed in 1969. They had been runners-up to Texas Western in 1966, one of only two years since 1963 that UCLA did not appear in the championship game.

Kentucky had depth, size, and strength to go with its tradition. And it was on a ferocious roll, having stunned top-ranked and previously unbeaten Indiana, 92–90, in a rock-'em, sock-'em Mideast Regional final that avenged a 98–74 loss at Indiana in December.

Looking back, forward Kevin Grevey, who exploded for 34 points in the loss to UCLA, felt that Kentucky left some of its hunger on the floor at Dayton after the triumph over the Hoosiers.

"I think we kind of showed up in San Diego with our chest stuck out because we had beaten No. 1," Grevey said. "It was a case of being satisfied to get there. That experience helped Kentucky win the title in 1978, when the freshmen from our San Diego team were seniors. I still believe we were better than UCLA, but we gave a flat performance."

Wooden, meanwhile, did his part to flatten the opposition by surprising his players again, this time with a secret, walk-through practice on the morning of the game. He installed a trap play to free guard Pete Trgovich, whose five baskets late in the first half helped turn the game around, and he ran a brief refresher course of high-post plays for center Washington after relying more on low-post series throughout the season. Washington, the tournament's Most Outstanding Player, scored 28 points.

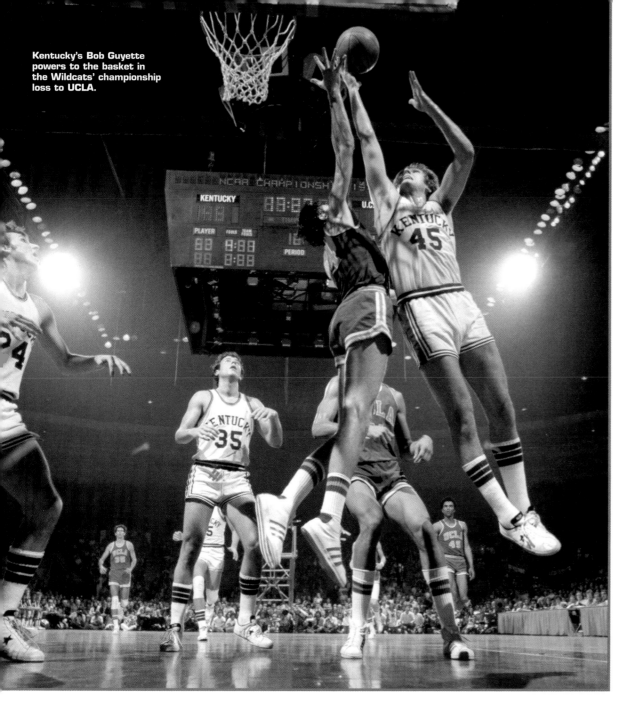

Kentucky's Bob Guyette powers to the basket in the Wildcats' championship loss to UCLA.

Emotion wasn't a problem. Not for a team that Wooden freely described as one of his favorites, a team without a superstar.

"We were at the right emotional level," Trgovich said. "We were ready to win for The Man, not emotionally yelling and screaming, but feeling it inside. I knew we were ready for the big one."

When it came time to prove it, though, emotions were spread all over the court, along with the thrashing bodies of Grevey and David Meyers, and the crowd of 15,513 was wilder than it had been during the UCLA-Louisville classic, if that was possible.

As the game moved inside the 6:30 mark, Grevey's 20-footer capped a Kentucky run that chopped a 66–56 UCLA lead to 76–75. Then Grevey bellied up to Meyers as the Bruin forward misfired on one of his patented leaning-

forward jump shots. Both players went down in a heap. Meyers, slapping the floor with his hand when he was called for a charging foul, drew a technical.

"As an offensive-minded player, I always believed there wasn't any such thing as a charging foul," Grevey said. "Even 12 years later, in a YMCA game, I got mad if a guy doesn't let me come down after I take a shot. There's no question I moved under Dave."

With the one-and-one, the technical shot, and an inbounds play, Kentucky had a chance to score five points before the Bruins saw the ball again. But Grevey drew a blank at the free throw line, and freshman James Lee committed a player control foul on the baseline.

Two free throws by Meyers, who scored 24 points, made it 78–75. A bank shot by Bob Guyette, who scored 14 of his 16 points in the second half, drew Kentucky within a single

point one final time. But the Bruins, who got 14 assists from Trgovich's backcourt mate Andre McCarter, were in total control down the stretch.

"I was 8 for 10 on free throws in that game and I'd take that any time," Grevey said.

But Hall wasn't used to taking 38 percent shooting from the field, and he was even less accustomed to being outplayed from buzzer to buzzer by a club that employed only six players.

The lone substitute Wooden inserted, 7´1˝ Ralph Drollinger, delivered 10 points and a game-high 13 rebounds in 16 minutes. UCLA, outrebounded 49–36 by Louisville, beat Kentucky on the boards, 55–49.

"Drollinger's baskets off the offensive board in the first half really killed us," said Hall, whose 6´10˝ freshman centers, Rick Robey and Mike Phillips, combined for only six points.

It was a magnificent last hurrah for the man they called the Wizard of Westwood. The victory gave Wooden's final UCLA team a 28–3 record and fixed his career mark at the school at 620–147 for 27 seasons. After an uncharacteristic

> **"We won the championship with only one returning starter, David Meyers. Bill Walton, Keith Wilkes, and Greg Lee were gone. That showed talent could overcome experience, because we had no real experience on that ballclub."**
>
> **—John Wooden**
> *Coach of UCLA's 1975 championship team*

tantrum when the technical was called on Meyers, he was, in the afterglow, his calm, professorial self.

"This was a team victory in the strictest sense of the word," Wooden said. "When I had a Jabbar or a Walton, I approached this tournament with a little more confidence. This team didn't have anyone like that."

What it had was John Wooden. As the records show, no other school ever had anyone like him. ■

The late Mike Sullivan covered many Final Fours, first as an Associated Press writer in the Louisville bureau, later on the staff of the Louisville Courier-Journal. He closed his career at the Columbus Dispatch.

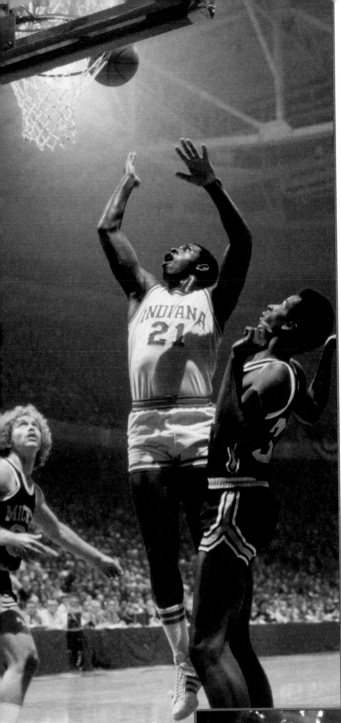

1976

A LAST LOOK AT PERFECTION

By Bob Hammel

IT WAS A SPECIAL TEAM THAT CAME ALONG SO SUD-denly in the Indiana coaching era of young Bobby Knight—a team so special, in fact, that their effort has yet to be duplicated.

It was a haughtiness that said, "You won't beat us," and a ferocity that backed up the words. It had muscle and strength, more of both than the sinewy quickness usually associated with great basketball teams. All five starters weighed 200 pounds or more. Those five begrudged every opponent every basket.

Knight, as intense a coach as the game has seen, always sent out teams that played in reflection of his demands, his teachings, and his refusal to accept less than the best. But in the 1975–1976 season, he was given the perfect personnel match for his insistences, a team as smart and full of basketball savvy as it was physically powerful. It was a team with an offense called "the Passing Game," and five better passers may never have played together on a college team.

The result was a perfect year—the last of those college basketball has seen.

Much went into the forging of the steel-tough Indiana team that completed a 32–0 season by pulling away from Big Ten rival Michigan, 86–68, in a historic championship game at The Spectrum in Philadelphia, in the nation's bicen-tennial year.

With no disrespect to John Wooden—or to the psychological magic generated by his Final Four retirement announcement, or to the outstanding team that won him his 10th and final NCAA championship at UCLA—the 1975 title, too, probably should have been Indiana's.

Knight put together a powerful blend of shooters and defenders and laid waste to the Big Ten as no team had before. The 1974–1975 Hoosiers won their 18 league games by a record average of 22.5 points per game, and they were an unchallenged No. 1 nationally until the late February day when they lost first-team All-American forward Scott May to a broken arm. Exactly one month later, the 31–0 Hoosiers were beaten in the NCAA Mideast Regional final at Dayton, 92–90, by the Kentucky team that ultimately lost to UCLA in the national championship game.

From the 1975 team, Knight lost shooters Steve Green and "super sub" John Laskowski, and they were missed. He gained on defense, fitting Tom Abernethy into the forward spot that Green left.

Not enough offense, appraisers said in looking at a lineup that suddenly had three players considered "nonshooters"—guards Quinn Buckner and Bobby Wilkerson, plus Abernethy.

They weren't especially wrong. There was a day when the three combined to shoot 2 for 22, and the opponent was the Michigan team the Hoosiers met in the national final. Still, Indiana found a way to win.

"We call it offense without the ball," Knight said.

Abernethy paired with May to give the Hoosiers two 6′7″ forwards who could play defense almost as well as the devastating guard combination that keyed everything: Buckner and Wilkerson.

Buckner, the 6′3″ floor general, was a two-year starter at Indiana as a football safety as well as a basketball star—rugged, strong, quick, street-tough, and classroom-smart—the consummate basketball leader.

Wilkerson, at 6′7″, was remarkably athletic, quicker than Buckner and such a jumper that he—not 6′10″ All-American center Kent Benson—handled tipoffs. "You think it isn't intimidating for a guard who's going to be playing against him to see him jumping center?" Minnesota coach Bill Musselman said. "He really complements Buckner. Those two take a team right out of its offense."

The 1976 NCAA Tournament marked the second year in which the field was opened to non-champions of major conferences, but there were restrictions. Only the runner-up

(above) Indiana's Quinn Buckner was the floor general of the 1976 team that defeated Michigan for the title.

(right) Mixed emotions overflowed at the game's end for coach Bobby Knight, who stood drained and misty-eyed on the victory stand with Kent Benson, Buckner, and Scott May.

Center Kent Benson scored 25 points to lead the Hoosiers' second-half charge to the 1976 championship. Indiana, which trailed Michigan by six at half-time, became the last team to complete a perfect season.

President Gerald Ford hosted the winning team at the White House, and Buckner got to sit in the presidential chair in the Oval Office.

Wilkerson but All-Americans May and Benson and captain Buckner doing the heavy work, Indiana was flawless. May scored a game-high 26 points, 20 in the second half, and fouled out stout-hearted Waymon Britt, a 6´2´´ forward whose defensive tenacity was crucial to coach Johnny Orr's team.

Benson scored 25 points (15 in the second half) and—for the third straight time—fouled out Michigan's freshman star, Phil Hubbard (the only college freshman to make the gold medal U.S. Olympic team that year).

Buckner, whose career average was slightly under 10 points per game, scored 16 points (12 in the second half) and took over Wilkerson's scheduled defensive assignment on swift Michigan standout Rickey Green. A devotee of basketball statistics wrote to *Sports Illustrated* to say in the second half of the game Indiana had the best "OER" (offensive efficiency rating) he had ever charted: more than 1.5 points per possession—with the national championship at stake.

> ## "Bob Knight refined the concept of the passing game, using the screen rule—where you just had to leave daylight between you and the player you were screening—to perfection."
>
> **—Pete Newell**
> *Hall of Fame coach*

was eligible; no team was sent more than one geographical region away. For extra teams in the East (that is, the ACC—the Big East hadn't formed yet), that meant an assignment in the Mideast, already clogged with powerful teams.

So No. 1 Indiana looked at a regional that included No. 2 Marquette, No. 6 Alabama, and No. 8 North Carolina. It was a circumstance that changed the tournament forever. The very next year, seeding was introduced.

But on they came, like Ruth, Gehrig, Foxx, Simmons, and Cronin for Carl Hubbell in all-star baseball lore: St. John's (90–70), Alabama (74–69), Marquette (65–56), UCLA (65–51), and Michigan (86–68).

Coach C. M. Newton's Alabama team led in the regional semifinals, 69–68, with two minutes to go when May—college basketball's player of the year—came off a typical Indiana pick and sank a 17-footer that wasn't an especially high percentage shot. "May's got a little more latitude than the other guys," Knight said.

Indiana vs. Marquette pitted No. 1 vs. No. 2, Knight vs. Al McGuire, in the Mideast Regional final at Baton Rouge, Louisiana. McGuire later referred to it as the game that matched two lineups in which all five starters on both teams went on to the NBA.

And so it was, just as the next one was: Indiana vs. UCLA in a rematch of the season opener. All 15 Indiana, Marquette, and UCLA starters became pros. Indeed, 19 months after the night in Philadelphia when their quest reached the national championship goal, all five Indiana starters were in starting lineups of pro teams on opening night of the NBA season.

Michigan did not have five future pros, but the Wolverines had fought their way through the Midwest Regional, past Adrian Dantley and Notre Dame (80–76), and Missouri with a hot hand named Willie Smith (95–88, despite 43 points by Smith). In the Final Four, the Wolverines took on another unbeaten team, Rutgers, and ran to an 86–70 victory.

And the Wolverines had a 35–29 lead at halftime of the final game. Indiana was wobbling. Wilkerson hit his head on the floor during a play in the first two minutes of the game and went to a hospital with a concussion. The backcourt demolition team was broken up. Memories of the 1975 title that got away with May's injury inevitably floated through Hoosier heads.

The game went into its last 10 minutes tied, 51–51. Down the stretch, with sophomore Jimmy Wisman filling in for

By then, they had been well-schooled in defense of their right to that championship. That stamp of No. 1 they wore all year long, most of the time by unanimous vote, had trained them well.

Minnesota coach Jim Dutcher said, "I don't think they're as overpowering as they were last year. I said at the time that was the best college team I'd ever seen."

Down deep, Knight agreed, and he felt for the seniors of that 1975 team who had joined him in the opening days of his coaching era and done so much to carry the program to the top—with no national championship ring to testify to their role.

On the steps of The Spectrum, heading out into the night that was his own hour of crowning achievement, Knight fielded one more handshake of congratulations and said wistfully, "Thanks. But it should have been two." ■

Bob Hammel covered Indiana basketball for some 30 years and has authored several books on Indiana sports. He was longtime sports editor of the Bloomington (Indiana) Herald-Times *and remains on the editorial management staff there. He currently is writing a new book about the Bobby Knight years.*

1977

SEASHELLS, BALLOONS, AND AL McGUIRE'S MOMENT

By Edgar Allen

H E STOOD AMID THE DEAFENING ROAR OF ATLANTA'S Omni, his ecstatic followers hoarsely shouting their appreciation and approval. This was it for Al McGuire, the moment wrapping up a colorful career in coaching. Something special for the New York City kid who grew up helping his mom and dad run a corner bar, who captained a good St. John's team in 1951, and who spent some time playing with the Knicks in the NBA.

It was one of the sport's more dramatic moments.

The 1977 NCAA championship only a few clock-ticks away, McGuire pulled away from a hug by longtime assistant Hank Raymonds, stood up, and with tears coursing down his cheeks, left the bench and made his way to the silence of the Marquette locker room.

"I want to be alone," he said as he entered the empty room, a towel to his eyes. "I'm not afraid to cry."

Seashells and balloons, as Al liked to call such occasions in his Big Apple terminology. College basketball 1977 had a fitting climax in the Al McGuire Story. It was in midseason that he had announced he would join Medalist Industries in Milwaukee as vice president. The 67–59

tingler over North Carolina in the final at Atlanta made for the perfect ending.

Emotions more under control as he met the press 30 minutes later, McGuire said huskily, "I feel washed out, but I'm very pleased. Normally, street fighters like me don't end up like this; but the numbers came up, and it's nice."

Thus did one of basketball's most absorbing figures wrap up a 20-year career, the last 13 at Marquette, where he was 295–80 and went to 11 consecutive postseason tournaments. Twenty years of haranguing officials. Taunting hostile crowds. Kicking tables. Knocking over chairs. Throwing towels. But still a favorite of fellow coaches and a tremendous contributor to the game. One who continued in the limelight as a network college basketball analyst.

"All I could think about at the end was—why me?" McGuire told writer Steve Guback later. "After all the jocks and socks, driving the car at Belmont Abbey, freshman coach at Dartmouth, all the PALs [Police Athletic League] and CYOs [Catholic Youth Organization]. And to have it end like this . . ." The reminiscing trailed off.

Soap opera television couldn't have done it up better than the Final Four in Atlanta.

Downcourt from the Warriors' bench was Dean Smith. Smith was already in "the big time" at Chapel Hill when McGuire was toiling at nearby Belmont Abbey, beating the bushes for Atlantic Coast Conference hand-me-down prospects and busing over rural North Carolina roads for games on homey little campuses.

Smith had won a world championship with his 1976 U.S. Olympic team but never the NCAA's top prize.

It would elude him again this time.

Perfecter of the four-corners offense, Smith may have used it once too often against Marquette—or at least too soon. Fiercely battling back with an 18–4 rampage after trailing, 39–27, at halftime, Carolina electrified its supporters, predominant in the close-to-home Omni, by taking a 45–43 lead. Shortly after, with more than 12 minutes still left to play, Smith opted for the spread pattern. The Tar Heels had won all season with the four-corners, but this time it led to their downfall.

"We were glad to see it," said Warrior Butch Lee, who scored 19 points and was voted the tournament's Most Outstanding Player. "They had a good streak going. It gave us a chance to catch our breath."

Marquette's colorful coach, Al McGuire (above), had taken his team to the NCAA final two years before and had been involved in several important regional games. But 1977 was the year he ascended to earn a long-awaited championship.

Maurice "Bo" Ellis fired a jumper over Carolina's Mike O'Koren as Marquette fought off a second-half surge by the Tar Heels. Ellis and Butch Lee led Marquette to the 1977 title in coach Al McGuire's final game.

The celebratory net was worn by Marquette forward Bernard Toone (above) as the team received its trophy at mid-court. The emotionally drained coach, Al McGuire, had retired to the locker room to compose himself and wipe away the tears.

Joined there by upstarts North Carolina–Charlotte, Nevada–Las Vegas (UNLV), and perennial contender North Carolina, it made for one of the more memorable NCAA windups.

If possible, the semifinals were more intensely fought than the final. Only three points separated the two victors, the closest NCAA semifinals on record. Marquette tipped UNC-Charlotte, 51–49, on Jerome Whitehead's last-second basket after taking a court-length pass off Cornbread Maxwell's fingertips and dropping in an almost-aborted dunk. Run-and-gun UNLV fell before Carolina in a barn-burner, 84–83, to set up the dramatic finale.

The Tar Heels, with Mike O'Koren pouring in 31 points, overcame a 10-point second-half deficit with 14 unanswered tallies, then hung on the final 14 minutes with their four-corners offense. They shot 70 percent the second half in a preview of the finals—in reverse.

> **McGuire pulled away from a hug by longtime assistant Hank Raymonds, stood up, and with tears coursing down his cheeks, left the bench and made his way to the silence of the Marquette locker room.**

Whitehead's winning shot was decided only after coaches, officials, and players surrounded timekeeper Larry Carpenter, clamoring to clarify the call. Television replays of the final seconds, with a clock superimposed on the screen, showed the basket in time, inflicting a heart-breaking loss on UNC-Charlotte.

Prior to Atlanta, upsets took their toll during the 1977 tournament series. Michigan, No.1 in both final wire-service polls, went down before inspired UNC-Charlotte in the Mideast Regional at Lexington, 75–68. San Francisco, No. 1 most of the season and undefeated until toppled by Notre Dame in the regular-season finale, was rudely upended by UNLV, 121–95. Potent but unknown Idaho State stunned mighty UCLA, 76–75.

It was that kind of tournament. And Al McGuire's scratchers and clawers gave it the storybook finish. ∎

The break came when Bo Ellis blocked Bruce Buckley's attempted shot with just under 10 minutes left. Marquette scored on Jim Boylan's reverse layup and never trailed again.

The 67–59 final score was somewhat deceiving. It was 51–49 with 1:56 to play, but the Warriors expanded the margin on free throws. Willis, Boylan, and Gary Rosenberger each hit four-of-four from the line to wrap it up.

"They went into their own delay game and killed us by making all their free throws," said Smith.

Walter Davis, playing with a broken finger sustained during the regular season, led the Tar Heels with 20 points,

but Phil Ford, recovering from a hyperextended elbow, was noticeably slowed and managed only 6. The ACC champs also played without Tom LaGarde, who went out late in the season with a knee injury.

Carolina fought doggedly to reach the Final Four after winning the ACC regular season and tournament titles. The Tar Heels squeaked by Purdue (69–66), Notre Dame (79–77), and Kentucky (79–72) to qualify for the Omni trip.

In Atlanta, after Midwest Regional wins over Cincinnati (66–51), Kansas State (67–66), and Wake Forest (82–68), the Warriors still had the worst record of any in the Final Four.

Edgar Allen, longtime sports editor of the Nashville Banner *and past president of the U.S. Basketball Writers Association, became director of media relations for Churchill Downs in 1979.*

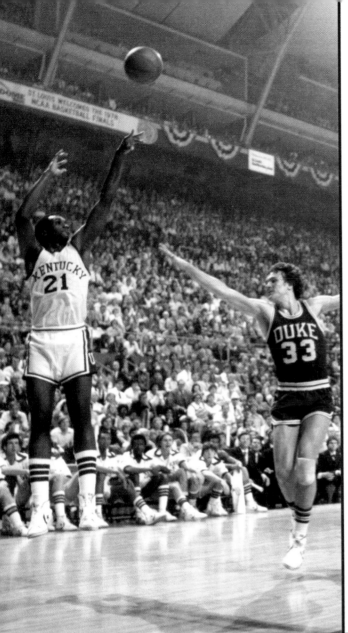

1978

THE SEASON WITHOUT A CELEBRATION

By John McGill

AT HALFTIME OF THE 1978 NCAA CHAMPIONSHIP game, Kentucky led Duke by seven points. To commemorate this comfortable turn of events, Kentucky's players lost their temper. In the locker room, emotions sizzled and accusations flew: not enough teamwork, not enough effort, they yelled. Joe Hall, the coach, thought he'd detected a smile on the face of center Mike Phillips and admonished him. "Dammit," Phillips snapped. "Do you think I'm happy?"

At Kentucky, happy was the ultimate sin. Happy meant complacent. Happy meant content. Until a title was secured—until its fans were sated and its coach could lift an aging albatross from his neck—Kentucky had no room for contentment.

This was a team of grim purpose, born of the Kentucky tradition which begot four national titles under Adolph Rupp but had come up empty for 20 years.

Nobody felt this pressure to produce more than Hall. This was his sixth season as successor to Rupp, who had died in December but whose presence as the standard for Wildcat basketball excellence was very much alive.

As a kid in Cynthiana, Kentucky, Hall had grown up listening to Wildcat games on the radio. But his relationship with Rupp—his idol—was to prove uneasy. A reserve on Kentucky's 1951 title team, Hall transferred to Sewanee. And

after he returned to Kentucky as an assistant, Hall succeeded Rupp only after the legendary coach had lost a bitter fight against mandatory retirement.

Hall knew that Kentucky's fanatical following would gauge this team as the true test of whether he deserved to follow in Rupp's footsteps. Mix that with a coach whose personality was inherently intense ("Perfection is an attainable goal," Hall once said), and the tone for a season was set.

From the outset, Kentucky was awesome. With King (6´10˝ Rick Robey) and Kong (6´10˝ Phillips) joining silky-smooth Jack Givens on the front line and muscular junkmaster James Lee developing into the nation's best sixth man, the Wildcats were a fright inside.

To that, Kentucky added the cerebral control and seamless shot of guard Kyle Macy, a transfer from Purdue, and the quickness of guard Truman Claytor.

Through all of December and most of January, things ran smoothly as Kentucky won its first 14 games. But the Wildcats then lost two of the next five. And with the second loss, "the Season Without Celebration"—as Hall would later term it during a Final Four press conference—began. Kentucky, which had beaten Louisiana State by 20 points at home, lost the road game rematch, 95–94, in overtime, despite all five LSU starters having fouled out in regulation.

In its NCAA Tournament opening game against Florida State, Hall took the biggest and boldest risk of his career. Trailing 37–27 with 3:30 left in the first half, he benched Givens, Robey, and Claytor and replaced them not with top reserves like Lee but with the seldom-used Dwane Casey, LaVon Williams, and Fred Cowan. The banished starters didn't return until 10 minutes remained in the game. When they did, Kentucky scored 14 straight points to turn a 53–48 deficit into a 62–53 lead. The Wildcats won, 85–76. Had they lost, Hall said he expected to be fired. The team was 26–2 at the time.

Trailing Michigan State and a freshman named Magic Johnson, 31–22, in the Mideast Regional final, Kentucky survived another serious threat with an improvised offense.

Macy wound up with a game-high 18 points and hit seven straight free throws in the final two and a half minutes. Kentucky won, 52–49.

When the Final Four opened in St. Louis, Kentucky faced a semifinal Arkansas team that boasted a three-guard offense

(above) Kentucky's Jack Givens drains a shot in the 1978 title game against Duke.

(right) Following the legendary Adolph Rupp had been difficult for Kentucky coach Joe B. Hall. As he talked to the team in the locker room before the championship game, Hall knew he was expected to win. With the pressure gone, the net-cutting was especially joyful.

Mike Gminski of Duke looks for help as Notre Dame's Gilbert Salinas closes in during the Blue Devils' Final Four semifinal victory.

He was the brunt of similar verbal attacks throughout his senior year. Givens, a bright and soft-spoken man, was perceptive enough not to take it personally, but moved enough to respond where Hall wanted him to—on the court.

In the title game, no such prompting was necessary. Givens was already primed. Because the back line of Duke's 2-3 zone tended to stretch from corner to corner, Hall suspected that Givens would be free in the key for good shots.

As Duke's weakness became evident in the first half, Givens began to flash toward the free throw line more and more. He hit 9 of 12 shots in the half and had 23 points by intermission, including Kentucky's last 16 points of the half. The Wildcats led, 45–38.

> **Givens, meanwhile, never let up. Duke adjusted its defense to cut off much of the lane, but now Givens was hitting from everywhere. He scored 18 in the final 20 minutes and finished with 41 points—the third highest total ever in a championship game.**

Duke—which again got balanced scoring from Banks (22), Spanarkel (21), and Gminski (20)—drew within three points on two occasions early in the second half, but Claytor drilled a long shot, and Macy hit two free throws and then set up Robey for a dunk. The Wildcats led by nine and never wavered.

Givens, meanwhile, never let up. Duke adjusted its defense to cut off much of the lane, but now Givens was hitting from everywhere. He scored 18 in the final 20 minutes and finished with 41 points—the third highest total ever in a championship game. Kentucky, leading 91–80, went to reserves in the final minute and saw the lead whittled down—making the final margin, 94–88, deceptive.

Givens wound up with 64 points and 17 rebounds in his two Final Four games. He was the runaway choice as the tournament's Most Outstanding Player. And Kentucky—grim Kentucky—had won 30 of 32 games and given the school its fifth national title. "Your names have been immortalized," Hall said as the team gathered in the locker room.

He wasn't finished. Maintaining a straight face, Hall looked at his championship team. "Fellas," he said, "curfew will be at 10:00 tonight."

At that, Kentucky's players did something strange. They laughed. ∎

headed by Sidney Moncrief and coached by Eddie Sutton, who in 1985 would become Hall's successor at Kentucky.

Those sensing an Arkansas upset envisioned Razorback quickness overcoming Wildcat size. But to its physical play, Kentucky added Givens, the 6´4˝ forward whose soft, left-handed jumper was an added dimension to the Wildcats' attack. Givens hit 10 of 16 floor shots and scored 23 points. Kentucky won, 64–59.

In the final, Kentucky faced Duke, a 90–86 winner over Notre Dame in a game that saw center Mike Gminski score 29 points, freshman Gene Banks 22, and guard Jim Spanarkel 20. The contrast between the two teams fairly screamed. Expected to win, Kentucky shouldered that responsibility soberly. Duke, on the other hand, had every reason to regard its entire tournament experience as a trip to

Disneyland. The Blue Devils—who started two freshmen, two sophomores, and a junior—were on a joyride of unexpected success.

Their glee, of course, made all the more glaring Kentucky's solemn mission. For the media, the scenario was easy to set: the Glad versus the Mad.

Of all the players who were subjected to Hall's tongue-lashings, Givens was the most frequent target. Givens would wind up the number two scorer in Kentucky history with 2,038 points. But Givens had a tendency to disappear in crucial moments, often reluctant to shoot, and Hall reacted with rage—calculated rage, perhaps, but brutal nonetheless.

On one such occasion in the previous season, Hall had called Givens "gutless" at halftime of a game against Alabama, and Givens had responded with 18 points in the second half.

John McGill covered many Final Fours while writing for the Lexington *(Kentucky)* Herald-Leader. *Now retired, he still writes an occasional column for the* Herald-Leader.

1979

MAGIC'S MOMENT

By Lee Benson

I T'S HARD TO IMAGINE NOW—AFTER ALL THEIR Biggest Game Ever showdowns; after more sequels than *Rocky*; after never playing together to a single empty seat—that there ever was a time when Magic Johnson and Larry Bird weren't coauthoring the history of basketball.

But it wasn't until the 1979 Final Four that they met.

It was in Salt Lake City. Bird was a 6´9´´ senior forward for the Indiana State Sycamores; Magic was a 6´8´´ sophomore guard for the Michigan State Spartans. Their schools, along with DePaul and Pennsylvania, made up the Final Four teams.

As surely as the fates conspired to get James Naismith to hang his peach basket, so did they conspire to get Bird's Sycamores past DePaul (and Mark Aguirre) and Magic's Spartans past Pennsylvania in the semifinal games at the University of Utah's Special Events Center.

That naturally set up the Big Two for the Big One—and set up America in its TV rooms.

If anyone ever needed a reason to justify the invention of television, this was it. Only 15,220 people could attend the confrontation live, leaving millions of Americans on the outside looking in. Literally.

At no time in the history of basketball or television had so many watched a single game, a record still unbroken today. Even as Bird and Magic went on to meet in the NBA Finals on almost annual occasions in the eighties, even as the NCAA game became a Monday night television ritual, even after Villanova upset Georgetown in the NCAA title game in 1985 and sets from coast to coast were clicking on in waves in the second half (the game finished with a 23.1 rating for number two on the all-time list)—no single game in history attracted as much attention as Magic-Bird I.

They were captivating.

They were as different as they were alike. They were both from middle America and had elected to attend colleges near their hometowns. They had each elevated an almost forgotten art—passing the basketball—into the favorite part of their respective games. They were both consummate team players and, as time would tell, they were not only the straw that stirred the drink, but the whole drink. (The following season, after Bird and Johnson had gone on to the NBA, neither Michigan State nor Indiana State made the NCAA Tournament field.) In other ways, they were as different as their skin colors. Earvin Johnson, a.k.a. Magic, was the extrovert, a point guard by way of a disc jockey —he was called "EJ the DJ" because of his hobby of announcing records at discos in East Lansing—and the quintessential finesse player who looked like he never even broke a sweat except on those occasions when he would flash the widest smile in Michigan, which was often.

On a basketball court, Bird looked like a plodder in the Kentucky Derby. He was slow-footed and had no discernible jumping ability. His deft passing and Houdini-like abilities to get open were never appreciated until later—like a subtle plot in a mystery novel. Off the court he was an introvert. He had left Indiana University in Bloomington as a freshman recruit because the size of the school didn't suit him as well as the small town atmosphere at Indiana State in Terre Haute, a town closer in both proximity and lifestyle to his native French Lick.

Bird's Sycamores were 32–0 coming into the Final Four. This was significant not only because the record was perfect but because:

(above) It was the matchup of the year—Larry Bird against Magic Johnson. Despite Bird's best efforts (guarded here by Michigan State's Greg Kelser), the Spartans rolled to a 75-64 victory before the largest television audience to watch a Final Four game.

(right) With a decisive lead, Magic cheered the substitutes from his seat on the bench.

A second-half slam dunk by Johnson was the exclamation point in the Michigan State victory.

a) Indiana State had a first-year coach in Bill Hodges, and b) the Sycamores had no history of grandeur. They had never before been to an NCAA Tournament, period, and now they were the No. 1–ranked team in the country and had made it to the Final Four.

Bird was the heart and soul of everything, averaging 29 points, 14.8 rebounds, six assists, and 2.4 steals a game. Where he went, others followed. Guard Carl Nicks—who would go on to a brief NBA career—was the hustle leader, forward-center Alex Gilbert was the leaper, forward Brad Miley was the defensive specialist, point guard Steve Reed was the floor director, and sixthman Bob Heaton was the designated keeper-of-the-streak. It was Heaton who hit a 50-foot shot at the regulation buzzer in the 19th game of the season to tie New Mexico State

Lake and see what the deal was with this Larry Bird.

Meanwhile, out of the East and West Regionals, Pennsylvania and DePaul had arrived at the Final Four in rather miraculous fashion.

Without the shadows of Bird and Magic to contend with, they'd have been the talk of Salt Lake. Here was Penn, an Ivy League team with a GPA almost higher than its scoring average and no athletic scholarships, playing like a Cinderella possessed.

And here was DePaul, an independent school from Chicago that had lost the heart of its team the year before (starters Dave Corzine and Joe Ponsetto both were drafted by the NBA) and was supposed to be rebuilding. Coach Ray Meyer hadn't been to a Final Four since 1943, and his main offensive weapon was a 6´7˝ freshman from Chicago—who hadn't yet shed his baby fat—named Mark Aguirre.

At no time in the history of basketball or television had so many watched a single game, a record still unbroken today . . . no single game in history attracted as much attention as Magic-Bird I.

and send the game into overtime, which Indiana State won. Against Arkansas, he hit the shot that won the game, 71–69, and kept the Sycamores on course for their date with Magic Johnson.

Michigan State's record was less lofty than Indiana State's. The Spartans came into the Final Four at 24–6. More impressive was their 13–1 mark since a midseason loss to Northwestern, 83–65. It was after that loss that coach Jud Heathcote and his players had a meeting. "It's not how good you are; it's how good you play," Heathcote told his players, after which they developed a locker room ritual. They would spell out the word *potential* after every game.

Despite being a mere 19-year-old sopho-more, Magic had developed into the world's biggest and best point guard. He averaged 8.8 assists, 16.9 points, and 7.3 rebounds a game, and made everyone else look better, particularly forward Greg Kelser—also a future NBA player—who was Magic's favorite target.

By the time the Spartans got to the NCAA Tournament, they had come close enough to their potential that Dale Carnegie wanted to adopt them. They beat Lamar in their Mideast Regional opener, 95–64. They beat Louisiana State, 87–61, and Notre Dame, 80–68, for the right to advance to Salt

But at the Final Four, DePaul had to face Larry Bird, and Penn had to face Magic Johnson, and neither team had enough momentum to contend with all of that.

Michigan State beat Penn, 101–67, and Indiana State beat DePaul, 76–74—and America started popping popcorn.

This was like being tipped off in advance about the landing at Normandy, or that something was going to happen at noon at the OK Corral.

As is often the case with epic showdowns that are advanced as such, the actual confrontation took a dive.

There was little suspense in Michigan State's wire-to-wire 75–64 win over Indiana State. Magic had a marvelous game. EJ the DJ played all requests. He led all scorers with 24 points. Kelser had 19 points, and guard Terry Donnelly 15 on a perfect five-of-five from the field. In the meantime, a modi-fied Spartan zone defense that kept 1 ½ men on Bird the entire game throttled Indiana State. Bird scored just 19 points on 7 of 21 shooting from the field.

And that was that. Magic and Bird had met for the first time. But it certainly wasn't for the last time; not with those kind of TV ratings. They had brought new meaning to the phrase *prime time*, both as it applied to television sports and to the game of basketball. ■

THE DECADE OF THE COACH

WHEN A FORMER HOLLYWOOD MOVIE ACTOR was elected U.S. president in 1980, cynics sneered. Yet in the next eight years, Ronald Reagan at least managed to restore some of the country's sense of pride, confidence, and well-being, while generally managing to avoid the traumatic, divisive conflicts of the previous two decades.

The eighties were a sentimental, nostalgic decade in which some rather amazing things made comebacks, including crewcuts, fifties music (in commercials, mostly), Tina Turner, miniskirts, the stock market, the institution of marriage, Bill Cosby, patriotism, and *Life* magazine. After decades of confusion, many young people became upwardly mobile again, earning them the tag of yuppies.

The computer age, born in the seventies, became a way of life. Many Americans did their writing and kept their books on home computers, and the proliferation of VCRs opened a mushrooming new industry for videotapes. The top rock stars of the decade were Bruce Springsteen, a throwback to the nitty-gritty days of the fifties, and Michael Jackson, a vision of the future whose frenetic dancing and androgynous sex appeal made him perfect for the new art form of music videos.

In a decade where style was more important than substance, the stars of the college game were the gifted athletes who could glide, soar, and stuff. Some of the prime examples were Darrell Griffith of Louisville, James Worthy and Michael Jordan of North Carolina, and Isiah Thomas of Indiana. Even the decade's best big man, Patrick Ewing of

Georgetown, was an agile giant whose timing and shotblocking brought visions of Bill Russell to mind.

The game came to be dominated more by coaches than by the players, sometimes much to the chagrin of the paying customers. Eventually, to eliminate such ploys as the stall offense and the pack-in zone, the rules committee attempted to speed up the game to its tempo of the late fifties and the sixties by installing first a shot clock, then a three-point field goal from 19´9˝. Still, it will be remembered as a coach's decade, and there were four who appeared on almost everybody's top five list—Bobby Knight of Indiana, Denny Crum of Louisville, John Thompson of Georgetown, and Dean Smith of North Carolina.

Each won at least one NCAA title in the eighties, and each made at least two trips to the Final Four. But as much as their results were alike, their styles and personalities differed.

Crum was laid-back and cool, much like Wooden, his mentor at UCLA. Smith was the innovator whose ideas were copied by almost every coach in the nation. Knight was the moody genius whose brilliant teaching tended to be over-shadowed by his tantrums and altercations. And Thompson was the stern authoritarian who trusted almost nobody outside his family of players and staff.

Not since Iba, Rupp, Allen, and McCracken had four coaches had so much impact on the game. And by defining it and refining it with such distinction, they created a legacy of excellence that will be part of the game for at least the next 50 years. ■

A dominant coach and player took Georgetown to three championship games in the eighties, winning it all in 1984. Coach John Thompson and center Patrick Ewing consulted during a timeout in 1984.

> **"The three-point shot made a huge impact on the game. It opened it up and caused transition defenses to focus not just on the ball, but on the wing players who were coming down, stepping in, then stepping back behind the three-point line."**
>
> **—Pete Newell**

The longest pauses are in a quiet locker room, each person with his own thoughts, awaiting the start of a championship game. Indiana waited at Philadelphia's Spectrum, soon to face North Carolina for the 1981 crown.

Denny Crum (above) once an assistant to John Wooden, guided his Louisville team to the championship for the first time, in 1980.

1980

DARRELL GRIFFITH AND THE DOCTORS OF DUNK

By Mike Sullivan

RESERVE PONCHO WRIGHT PROVIDED A COLORFUL slogan for Louisville's championship run after a preseason scrimmage in November of 1979. "The Ville," Wright declared, "is going to the Nap."

His reference was to Indianapolis and Market Square Arena, where the Cardinals captured their first NCAA championship in their third Final Four appearance by outnerving UCLA, 59–54, on March 24, 1980.

By the time Darrell Griffith had wrapped up player-of-the-year honors, scoring 23 points against UCLA to go with his 34 in an 80–72 semifinal win over Iowa, Louisville's achievement had acquired a false aura of inevitability.

There was that final 33–3 record, after all. There was Griffith, labeled "Dr. Dunkenstein" and "Louisville's Living Legend," the crowd favorite with the 48-inch vertical leap. And there was never a shortage of folklore. Remember Wiley Brown, the forward who left his artificial thumb on the table at the pregame meal? It was retrieved from a dumpster in time for the title game.

What may be harder to retrieve as the years go by is a firm grasp on the underdog status that coach Denny Crum's Cardinals actually carried into that season and, to an extent, into the tournament itself.

After failing to make the NCAA field in 1976, Louisville bombed out in three straight appearances. In Griffith's junior season, he had appeared lost in a nationally televised shellacking at Duke, then was badly out-shone by Sidney Moncrief in a Midwest Regional semifinal defeat against Arkansas.

Still trying to master the transition from forward to guard, Griffith entered the 1979–1980 campaign with much to prove in the eyes of the national media. The 6´3˝ senior's supporting cast had all but vanished. Forward Bobby Turner, his teammate from Louisville's Male High School, had career-ending academic problems. Sophomore Scooter McCray, the returning starter at center, was lost to a knee injury in the first week of the season. Senior Tony Branch, the previous year's floor leader, lost his job to sophomore Jerry Eaves and became a seldom-used reserve.

Louisville added a lack of height to its lack of experience, with Brown the tallest player at 6´8˝. Into the pivot went Rodney McCray, Scooter's younger brother, a 6´7˝ freshman who had been Crum's only recruiting signee. The forward opposite Brown, 6´6˝ Derek Smith, had been tried at guard late in the previous season. Griffith, Branch, and reserve guard Roger Burkman, a junior, were the only upperclassmen in the bunch.

"I don't think there's any question that team surprised a lot of people, including myself," Crum said. "I don't think anybody expected us to be very good. Even when we kept winning, I didn't think about the postseason much. There were so many teams with more experience than us that it wasn't realistic."

It also wasn't considered realistic, 16 years after UCLA's pressing dervishes of 1964, to employ a full-court press for every minute of every game. But Crum, in what may have been the most radical coaching decision of his tenure at Louisville, did just that, reasoning that his club could avoid having its size and youth exploited in half-court defense.

"The benefits we derived from the press didn't always surface until late in a game, when the general pace and our conditioning suddenly took a toll," he recalled.

There was more than a touch of irony in the fact that UCLA provided the opposition in the title game. Crum, after all, had played and coached at UCLA under John Wooden and had lost to his alma mater in three previous NCAA trips as the Louisville coach—in the national semifinals in 1972 and 1975 and in the first round in 1977.

The matchup itself was something else again. UCLA, like Louisville, made up in quickness for what it lacked in size and had upset its way through the tournament under coach Larry Brown after a fourth-place finish in the Pac-10. Senior forward Kiki Vandeweghe was the star, abetted by frisky freshmen guards Rod Foster and Michael Holton.

Using the same ferocious defense that had carried them past Purdue and 7´1˝ Joe Barry Carroll, 67–62, in the

> "I don't think there's any question that team surprised a lot of people, including myself. There were so many teams with more experience than us that it wasn't realistic."
>
> **—Denny Crum**
> *Coach of Louisville's 1980 championship team*

The Cardinals were led by player of the year Darrell Griffith, who was carried from the floor of Indianapolis' Market Square Arena

semifinal, the Bruins put Louisville in a 50–45 hole on Mike Sanders' layup with 6:28 left in the game.

Vandeweghe made a running interception and steamed toward the basket with a chance to all but finish the Cardinals. Eaves, in a hustling recovery, crossed in front of him at the last second and his altered shot was rebounded by Brown.

The rest of the game was a 14–4 parade to the championship by Louisville, which scored the last nine points. Griffith's soaring three-point play on a pass from Brown made it 50–48, and Griffith trimmed a 52–48 deficit to 52–50 with an 18-foot baseline jumper. Two clutch baskets by Eaves—a 17-footer and a driving layup in traffic—cut a 54–50 deficit in half and finally tied the score, 54–54, with 2:54 remaining.

McCray, the seasoned freshman, collared his game-high 11th rebound when a corner jumper by Holton rattled in and out of the basket, and Griffith struck from the top of the key to break the tie with 2:21 to go. Smith's two bonus free throws made it 58–54 with only 52 ticks left.

Afterward, Crum revealed that he had accused his players of choking at halftime when they trailed, 28–26. "Then I apologized and told them I loved them," Crum said. "I realized they had been trying as hard as they could. I told them to loosen up and give it their best shot."

It was just a hint at how much emotion and dramatics had gone into that glossy 33–3 record. The NCAA opener had been an overtime test against Kansas State, decided when Branch replaced Griffith, who had fouled out, and banged in a 16-footer at the buzzer. Texas

A&M also had fallen in overtime in the Midwest Regional semifinal.

"We had a rare chemistry," Crum said. "Darrell seemed to come through with a basket, a rebound, or a pass whenever we needed it most, and all of our younger players seemed to draw strength from Griff and also from Tony Branch, who never gave up his leadership role."

"It wasn't the Darrell Griffith Show, it was the University of Louisville Show," said Griffith, who had appeared on a televised insert before the tipoff to dedicate the final game to his lifelong friend Jerry Stringer.

The day after the game, Stringer, who was dying of cancer, had strands of the net draped around his head as he lay in bed in his home, surrounded by Louisville players.

Maybe it was inevitable, after all. ■

1981

KNIGHT GETS HIS WAY AND HOOSIERS WIN

By Bill Millsaps

VARIATIONS OF PRIMAL SCREAM THERAPY DEVEL-oped by the renowned Indiana University psychologist, professor Robert Knight, quite likely played a major role in the Hoosiers' capture of their fourth national basketball championship, in 1981.

In an effort to firmly establish early control of his young team, Knight twice took unusual actions with his best player in December of 1980. These actions were calculated to get the undivided attention of that player and his teammates.

There was the day that Knight, bereft of patience, tossed Isiah Thomas, his precocious point guard, right out of practice in Bloomington.

Then there was the day, later in the same month, that Knight became angry with Thomas for throwing a couple of careless passes in a game with North Carolina in Chapel Hill.

Knight summarily removed Thomas from the game and kept him on the bench long enough in the second half so that it was almost inevitable North Carolina would win by nine points. Some who watched that game still wonder if Knight didn't lose it on purpose in order to teach Thomas a lesson.

On the last day of 1980, Knight and North Carolina coach Dean Smith met again. This time, the setting was the airport in Kansas City.

North Carolina, having just lost by 16 points to Minnesota in a holiday tournament in Los Angeles, was on its way back to a game at Kansas. Indiana, having lost two straight to Clemson and Pan American at a tournament in Hawaii, was changing planes on its way home to Bloomington with a so-what 7–5 record.

The two famed coaches exchanged lists of woes. North Carolina had lost four starters from the previous year, and Smith wondered if his team, as inexperienced as it was talented, could pick up the subtleties of his system. Knight, with only one senior in his starting lineup, wondered out loud if his Hoosiers could pick up the simplicities of his system.

Almost four months later, their wonderings were at an end. The Hoosiers and the Tar Heels had made it to the Final Four along with two teams that had few down moments in their run to Philadelphia.

In the first semifinal at the Spectrum, Indiana played Louisiana State, which had won 26 straight games during the season and boasted a 31–3 record.

In the second semifinal, North Carolina played Virginia, which had won its first 23 games en route to a 28–3 record and had beaten the Tar Heels twice during the regular season.

Ralph Sampson, a 7´4˝ sophomore center bound for a college basketball career that received a grade of "incomplete," had scored 46 points and collected 24 rebounds in the two Virginia victories over Carolina. Each was a bitter pill for the Tar Heels to swallow, for on the first occasion the Cavaliers came from 13 points behind in the second half, and on the second, they came from 16 back in the last 20 minutes in Chapel Hill.

In those first two meetings, almost nobody had noticed that UNC's Al Wood had scored 51 points. Few failed to notice Wood when the Tar Heels and Cavaliers played for the third time.

Wood scored 39 points, 25 in a brilliant second half in which he missed only 1 of 10 shots from the floor. "Every time Al shot," said Tar Heel forward Matt Doherty, "I got in position for rebounds that never came off. After a while, I knew he was never going to miss."

"I wanted to break his arm," said Virginia forward Terry Gates.

(above) The celebration by the Hoosiers was joyous in Philadelphia, but things were to change before Indiana had a chance to defend its title the next year. Isiah Thomas (opposite inset) would leave school to begin his NBA career and Landon Turner (above) would be seriously injured in a car accident, ending his basketball career.

(right) The Tar Heels' Sam Perkins dove for a loose ball in what was a very physical game.

Returning to Philadelphia's Spectrum, site of an earlier championship, Indiana scrambled against North Carolina. However, it was Isiah Thomas in the second half who dominated, scoring 19 of his 23 points and earning MOP honors. Indiana won, 63–50.

Virginia coach Terry Holland tried five different defenders on Wood, and he charbroiled them all. "You almost had to stand up and cheer," said Holland, "even if you're on the opposite bench."

North Carolina won, 78–65, and, considering the setting and the stakes, took the season series with Virginia, 1–2.

The Indiana team that took on LSU had lost nine times, but the lineup Knight started against the Tigers had a perfect record. From February 21, 1981, when Knight put 6´10´´ sophomore Landon Turner into his starting five, the Hoosiers were unbeaten.

Against LSU, Turner scored 20 points and held Durand Macklin, the Tigers' leading scorer, to a career-low 4 points. LSU had a 3-point halftime lead, but Indiana scored the

23 points and earning Most Outstanding Player honors.

North Carolina got no closer than seven points down the stretch and wound up falling, 63–50. The Tar Heels' only consolation was that it was Indiana's closest game en route to the championship. The Hoosiers had won four previous tournament battles by 35, 15, 32, and 18 points.

"Ours is a game," said Knight, "of doing what we want to do the whole game. If we can do that, our ultimate objective is to break down a team over the whole 40 minutes. If we can stay with our defense and pressure the ball, and stay with our offense and be patient, we're going into the last part of the game and we've gotten control."

Knight thought that the best days were still ahead for his team. He was wrong. Thomas left

> ## "If we can stay with our defense and pressure the ball and stay with our offense and be patient, we're going into the last part of the game and we've gotten control."
> ### —Bobby Knight
> *Coach of Indiana's 1981 championship team*

first 11 points of the second half and cruised to a 67–49 victory.

That evening, Knight made some more headlines by getting into a physical confrontation with an LSU fan who, Knight said, had become verbally abusive.

Trying to explain himself the next day, Knight said, at first, that "If it happens tomorrow, I'd do exactly the same thing."

Later that day, Knight defined discipline as "doing what has to be done, doing it when it has to be done, doing it as well as it can be done, and doing it that way all the time." Asked how he squared those words with his actions of the night before, Knight said, "I'm human, and I failed in this situation in reaching the ultimate discipline."

Some six hours before the 1981 championship game, President Ronald Reagan was shot and wounded by a would-be assassin in Washington. The NCAA went ahead with the consolation game, but did not make a decision to play the title match until about 30 minutes before the scheduled tip-off.

This time, Knight didn't have Thomas on the bench in the second half. In the last 20 minutes, Thomas was merely wondrous at both ends of the floor, scoring 19 of his

school for the NBA after the 1981 season, and Turner was terribly injured in an auto accident.

Knight did not get back to the Final Four for six years, but his 1987 Hoosiers gave him his third NCAA title, in New Orleans.

There was also a certain symmetry to the stories of the other coaches in that 1981 Final Four.

Holland never returned to another Final Four with Sampson, but he reached the national semifinals the year after his three-time national player of the year graduated.

Dale Brown also returned in 1986, taking an LSU team that was dead in the water in midseason and somehow contriving a way to get it to Dallas.

In his seventh Final Four, Smith won his first NCAA title in 1982 in New Orleans.

The 1981 Final Four also reflected the tone of the decade—as coaches took center stage. ∎

Bill Millsaps joined the sports staff of the Richmond Times-Dispatch *in 1966, became sports editor in 1973, managing editor in 1992, and executive editor in 1994. A longtime fixture at Final Fours, he now watches the games on television.*

1982

THE CITY CARE FORGOT REMEMBERS DEAN SMITH

By Curry Kirkpatrick

SHORTLY AFTER NORTH CAROLINA FINALLY WON its elusive national championship in New Orleans, a photograph made the rounds in Chapel Hill that defined the emotions swirling around Dean Smith's one and only NCAA title better than words or numbers possibly could.

The classic, raw-thrills 63–62 victory over Georgetown was over; the momentary ecstasy had passed. As James Worthy, the shreds of net still clinging around his neck, and Jimmy Black sat vacantly, their bodies exhausted, their senses virtually paralyzed, Smith grimly stared at the floor while Tar Heel publicist Rick Brewer, cognizant there might still be life left on the planet, checked his watch. What time was it?

It was about time; 25 years since the last time Carolina had won the NCAA. It was relief time.

"The feeling was whew! What did we just go through?" Matt Doherty would say. "And thank God it was—finally—over." It was a very special time.

The wonder was that such a compelling year as 1981–1982 could be outdazzled by its own watershed Final Four. But the nouveau celebrity schools that showed up in the cavernous Louisiana Superdome to challenge old-money Carolina made sure that the colossal record crowds of over 122,000 (61,000 and change both Saturday and Monday) got their strained eyesight's worth. This was the first year college basketball went one-on-one against itself (NBC and CBS having hooked up with competitive weekend games during the regular season) and the last year it went backdoor on the shot clock.

The early rounds of the tournament featured: 1) a famous game that never happened—Louisville vs. Kentucky (Middle Tennessee State upset the Wildcats); 2) a famous team that never advanced—for the third year in a row DePaul, ranked first in somebody's poll, lost in the first round to a nobody; and 3) a famous player who just, well, never—Virginia's Ralph Sampson who was denied again, this time by Alabama-Birmingham.

As a result, the dregs New Orleans wound up with included Louisville, with four starters off its 1980 championship team and making its second appearance in three Final Fours in a four-year run; Houston, starting the first of a three-straight Final Fours streak; Georgetown, debuting in its own three-in-four-years roll, which would include the 1984 title over Houston; and Carolina, whose victory would culminate in three championship games in a six-year stretch.

In other words, the dynasties of the decade—that's all. In the eighties, these teams have combined for 11 Final Four appearances and four titles. Such a legacy left in 1982! Louisville's Derek Smith and the McCray brothers, Houston's Akeem Olajuwon and Clyde Drexler, Georgetown's Patrick Ewing, Carolina's Worthy, Sam Perkins, and Michael Jordan.

The star-touched Tar Heels traversed that bewitching season, emboldened from their final loss to Indiana the previous March. They were reinvigorated as No. 1 for most of the winter, rampagers of the Atlantic Coast Conference, slayers of pretender-dragons, Kentucky and Sampson. They were a nifty, resourceful, multidimensional and sometimes spectacular crew whose ability to play both fast and slow not only won games (32 of 34) but was to actually change the rules of the game.

(above) North Carolina came to New Orleans with an amazing lineup of raw talent, not the least of which was freshman Michael Jordan, shooting here against Houston in the semifinals.

James Worthy (right) claimed the baseline to move for a layup, as both Georgetown and Carolina traded baskets and the lead. As the game ended, most assumed Worthy or Sam Perkins would take the last shot. Instead, freshman Michael Jordan shot the winning goal.

Two nights later, Jordan's shot with 16 seconds left, lifted the Tar Heels to the championship over Georgetown and Patrick Ewing.

For the Final Four, the Hoyas stayed in that charming French Quarter suburb of Biloxi, Mississippi. After Georgetown eliminated Louisville in a brutal defensive semifinal, 50–46—Ewing had only 8 points and one block but several intimidations—to make Thompson the first black coach to reach the championship game, he bristled, "I don't want to be the first black nothing."

And the Hoyas' Eric Smith, asked if he missed staying in New Orleans, said, "I don't know what I missed. Can't you see? I ain't here."

Carolina's Worthy, meanwhile, was here, there, and everywhere when the Tar Heels took a two-touchdown lead, 14–0, over Houston in the other semifinal.

Georgetown maintained an edge midway through the second half until Sleepy Floyd got too cute on a breakaway that would have given the Hoyas a 6 point lead at 49–43. As it was, Worthy started swoop-jamming again, the Heels stiffened on defense—"I always felt like the hunted, and Georgetown was the hunter," Smith said—and Ewing picked up his third and fourth fouls.

Momentum swayed. Intensity increased. From the spread delay, Jordan made a preposterous switch-hands, rainbow scoop drive over Ewing, and Carolina led, 61–58. But Ewing (23 points, 11 rebounds) scored a turn-around, and Floyd coaxed in a jumper from the lane. The Tar Heels were behind for the 12th time in the game when Smith called timeout with 32 seconds left.

Most everybody assumed the ball would go to either Worthy or Perkins in the seams of the Georgetown zone. But Smith, knowing the Hoyas would deny his big men, instructed the Heels to take the first good shot. He also guessed that shot would be given to Jordan—the freshman, the rookie, the kid who had fantasized about this moment on the bus ride to the Superdome. As his team broke from the

"I always felt like the hunted, and Georgetown was the hunter."
—Dean Smith
Coach of North Carolina's 1982 championship team

Black was to shut out Cougar leading scorer Rob Williams, and by the time the infant Olajuwon came on—he scratched for one basket and six boards in as inauspicious a Final Four debut as any future legend ever suffered—it was all over, 68–63, to Carolina.

"Choke, Dean, Choke," the kindly Georgetown section roared at Smith on Monday night prior to the championship game. But

huddle, Smith took one step toward Jordan, patted him on the rump, and said, "Knock it in, Michael."

Of such are geniuses made, monkeys shot off backs, and titles won. At 0:16 Jordan's shot from the left side, smack on a line between his coach and his coach's holy grail, kissed only twine—63–62, Carolina.

After Georgetown raced downcourt without calling timeout, after Fred Brown froze and threw the ball directly into the hands of Worthy, after Worthy stole away like a phantom from Mardi Gras, even after Thompson embraced the crestfallen Brown on the sideline afterward, the image that lingers clearest from that hazy Louisiana evening is Dean Smith watching Jordan's shot: still seated, hands clasped, jaw set, totally in control.

Just Easin' Off here in the Big Easy. Would it were so. But on the same night Henry Fonda finally won his Oscar, Smith finally won his NCAA. The City Care Forgot ultimately took care of a coach the college game will always remember. ∎

After their stallball defeat of Virginia in the ACC Tournament forced the final blueprint for a shot clock, who could deny they were something extraordinary? Who could stop them from fulfilling Dean—"I've handled it well; I don't feel the emptiness," he said of his zero-for-six trips to the finals—and his dream?

Well, Georgetown seemed a prime candidate. The lean, mean Hoyas, with Ewing premiering his old gray mare of a T-shirt, had absolutely devastated the West Regional, limiting the States, Fresno and Oregon, to 41 and 39 percent shooting while they themselves hit a tournament-record 74.4 percent against the Beavers. No less did Georgetown coach John Thompson have his nasties on, housing his troops far from the playing sites, cutting off the outside world, and intimidating referees and the media in kind.

Deano was loose, even bantering with writers about his depleted cigarette pack. "Fewer [smokes] than for Duke at Duke," he laughed.

It was a full eight minutes after tip-off before Ewing ceased smoking and the Tar Heels finally saw one of their shots actually go down. The Hoyas' monster-child had been that dominating, swatting everything back to Bourbon Street and significantly altering Carolina strategy. To cut the court and challenge the freshman giant would be folly. Eventually, Smith had to take the cuffs off his 6´9˝ junior, Worthy (who would shoot 13 of 17 and explode for 28 points), and simply let him rush down the floor and tomahawk the ball before Ewing, a human Pac-Man, swallowed all the Tar Heels alive.

Worthy's rebound slam (which turned out to be *Sports Illustrated*'s cover shot) got Carolina a tie at 20–20. But

Curry Kirkpatrick was a staff writer at Sports Illustrated *covering the Final Fours during the UCLA years of the seventies. He has since worked as a special writer for* USA Today *and done commentaries for CBS Sports. Today he is a senior writer for* ESPN The Magazine.

1983

THE NINE LIVES OF N.C. STATE

By Bill Millsaps

NOBODY'S THAT LUCKY. NOBODY'S SUDDENLY THAT good. More than 20 years later, you still wonder how the entire college basketball melodrama—"The Nine Lives of N.C. State"—could've taken place. It was a blessed, heroic stretch that was roughly the antithesis of Murphy's Law: everything that needed to happen for the Wolfpack did.

North Carolina State winning the 1983 NCAA championship does not rank in the global/political/patriotic league with the United States' hockey upset of the Soviet Union at the 1980 Olympics. It is not as memorialized in sports history as New York's dual, wholly unanticipated 1969 triumphs of the baseball Mets and football Jets.

But for pure, athletic, never-say-die, long-running achievement by an underdog, North Carolina State might've outdone them all. It was far more than the national finals, where N.C. State used one last stroke of fortune/skill to overturn Houston, 54–52. It was the entire, unbelievable, nine-game Wolfpack package that led to the championship moment in Albuquerque.

Consider the elements:

• N.C. State's record at the end of the regular season was 17–10, leaving the Wolfpack unranked, unrespected; a team bettered in its own Atlantic Coast Conference neighborhood by North Carolina, Virginia, and Maryland. To even have a chance at an NCAA Tournament bid, State had to find a way to make the ACC Tournament final in Atlanta.

• One miracle makes few impressions, but the Wolfpack did come from behind in the second half to survive its ACC playoff opener against Wake Forest, 71–70.

• Against favored North Carolina in the league's semifinal game, N.C. State trailed, 80–74, with 2:13 left in overtime. Wolfpack coach Jim Valvano ordered his players to intentionally foul. The Tar Heels flunked at the free throw line, and the Wolfpack never missed a critical shot. North Carolina was outgunned 17–4 down the stretch and became little more than a blue puddle left on the Omni court. N.C. State won, 91–84.

• Virginia had beaten N.C. State twice during the regular season, but in the ACC Tournament final, Ralph Sampson and several shorter fellows wilted, and N.C. State rallied in the second half to succeed, 81–78.

• By now, Valvano and his sleight-of-hand artists were getting national attention. The New York coach with the Prince Valiant hair was an All-American quote machine. But, in the first round of the NCAA Tournament, the party seemed about over. Pepperdine took the Wolfpack into overtime and led by six points with 0:59 on the clock. Valvano went into his fouling, daredevil scheme and, in the end, State won, 69–67, in two overtimes.

• State had no geographical edge being assigned to the West Regional. It would play no NCAA Tournament game east of The Pit, on the University of New Mexico's campus in Albuquerque. On the night of its regional semifinal in Ogden, Utah, the little team in red seemed, one more time, to be on the verge of a crash. Nevada–Las Vegas led the Wolfpack by 12 points with 11 minutes to go. But lighting kept striking the same place, and State hit a shot at 0:04 to win 71–70.

• That gets us to the seventh of N.C. State's "nine lives"—the West Regional finals against a most familiar opponent, the Virginia Cavaliers. "I think we owe them one," said Virginia coach Terry Holland, referring to the ACC final his Cavs blew back in Atlanta. N.C. State again

(right, inset) As the clock ticked off the last five seconds with the score tied, Dereck Whittenburg (No. 25) took a 30-foot jumper, which fell short.

(right) In one stunning second, Lorenzo Charles (No. 43) grabbed the ball in mid-air for the stuff and the title. Afterward Wolfpack players fashioned a victory celebration from on high (above).

Houston's Akeem Olajuwon grabbed this shot from the hands of Thurl Bailey early in the game, but State stayed in the game and won at the buzzer.

trailed in the second half, but, in the end, the Pack did it again. Sampson's last chance for an NCAA championship perished in a 63–62 game.

• Luck, no matter how good, usually runs out. Even with a stacked deck, nobody deals himself eight or nine straight aces. Nobody but the 1983 North Carolina State basketball team. But, in the national semifinal at Albuquerque, the Wolfpack had to use little of its magic. In comparison, things went rather methodically in a 67–60 conquest of Georgia.

OK, it's now Monday night. The NCAA final. Even with all that had gone before, N.C. State remained a lopsided underdog against a No. 1–ranked Houston team that was 31–2 with 26 straight victories. In their semifinal, the Cougars took basketball into the 21st century with their so-called Phi Slamma Jamma offense, strangling a talented Louisville team, 94–81.

Houston had howitzers to fire against the blessed pop-guns of N.C. State. "We'll try to stay alive," Valvano said, "to keep it close and see if there's another stroke of magic in a very overused wand." But Houston had so much size, so much athletic ability, and so many killer nicknames in Akeem "the Dream" Olajuwon, Clyde "the Glide" Drexler, Michael "Mr. Clutch" Young, and Larry "Mr. Clean" Micheaux.

Overtime seemed all but assured when Whittenburg heaved a prayer from beyond 30 feet. It was well short, a pitiful game-winning attempt.

During pregame warmups, Houston dunked itself into a frenzy. It was like basketball batting practice where every hitter puts every pitch over the wall. Nevertheless, N.C. State did decide to show up.

N.C. State's cast of characters included husky, 6´7˝ Lorenzo Charles and skinny, 6´11˝ Cozell McQueen. The best NBA prospect on the Wolfpack end was 6´11˝ Thurl Bailey, who looked slack-jawed at Houston's high-flying warmup acrobatics. One of the great strengths of the Wolfpack was its guards, a rotation that included Sidney Lowe, Dereck Whittenburg, Ernie Myers, and Terry Gannon.

Once the game began, Valvano had some effective defensive ideas that worked against the ungodly giants from Houston. The Cougars weren't gliding and dunking like they

did in the semifinal against Louisville. N.C. State stayed close, just as Valvano had hoped. The game reached the final minute. Remarkably, it was 52–52. N.C. State had the basketball. "One shot!" Valvano yelled.

Lowe whipped the ball to Whittenburg. Time ticked below 15 seconds. The grand try was in motion. But at 0:05, the basketball was too far outside, leaving little chance to work for a high percentage shot, or to get the ball inside and perhaps draw a foul.

Overtime seemed all but assured when Whittenburg heaved a prayer from beyond 30 feet. It was well short, a pitiful game-winning attempt. But, no—the muscular hands of Lorenzo Charles reached above the seemingly stunned Cougars, taking the "air ball" two feet from the hoop and then dunking it as the buzzer went off.

State had won, 54-52.

In the 65 NCAA Tournaments, there have been extraordinary upsets. Remember 1963, when Loyola of Chicago upset 1961–1962 champion Cincinnati, 60–58, in overtime? Or 1966, when Texas Western flailed a giant, beating Kentucky, 72–65?

But when you count them all from top to bottom, nothing compares with the "nine lives of N.C. State." ∎

1984

DOMINATION AND INTIMIDATION

By Michael Wilbon

JUST A FEW MINUTES AFTER HIS PROUD KENTUCKY Wildcats had been obliterated, whipped, and humiliated like nobody's business, coach Joe B. Hall was still a might befuddled when he tried to describe the phenomena of his team's defeat and soon-to-be-crowned NCAA champion Georgetown.

Hall stammered and paused and finally said, "It was some kind of extraterrestrial." Georgetown's 53–40 victory over Kentucky that Saturday afternoon in Seattle's Kingdome and the Hoyas' run to the 1984 national championship certainly were not normal earthly stuff.

Two nights later, in an 84–75 victory over Houston, Georgetown and coach John Thompson finished a most impressive season. Houston's Akeem Olajuwon, who had played in the Final Four three times without going home happy, put his finger on just what it was that separated Georgetown from the other final three teams, besides Patrick Ewing and one of the best teams ever assembled:

"Georgetown—they don't care who scores, who takes the shots. That's the difference. They aren't a selfish team. The unselfish team won."

The previous two Final Fours had been characterized by the bizarre, the surreal: Georgetown's loss to North Carolina in 1982; Houston getting Phi Slamma Jamma'd by North Carolina State in 1983.

The 1984 Final Four wasn't one of a moment, or even a game. But the Seattle tournament involving Georgetown, Houston, Kentucky, and Virginia, will be remembered for Georgetown's everlasting dominance, and yes, intimidation.

Thompson hated, in fact still hates, the word *intimidate*. Used as many people did that year, it conjured up all the wrong images, many of them racial. But Georgetown did intimidate its opponents, through talent, smarts, unselfishness, relentlessness, and toughness. And, yes, Georgetown intimidated physically. From the time the Big East season started, right through the Final Four, teams grew more frightened of the Georgetown Hoyas because there didn't seem to be any way to beat them. In an early round NCAA Tournament game against Nevada–Las Vegas, Georgetown couldn't score for 10 minutes and 35 seconds and still beat the Runnin' Rebels by 14 points.

Kentucky and Houston—which was lucky to beat scrappy Virginia in overtime of the first semifinal—would find that out soon enough. Kentucky, after taking a seven-point lead at halftime, made only 3 of 33 shots the second half. The starters, including Sam Bowie and Melvin Turpin, went 0 for 21 in that second half. Georgetown's Gene Smith, one of the best defensive guards who ever lived, chased Kentucky's Dicky Beal and Jim Master like the Chicago Bears' Richard Dent chased quarterbacks.

That is the memory of the 1984 Final Four, even though Georgetown wasn't officially crowned until Monday night following the 84–75 victory over Houston. And Thompson, an all-world worrier, could finally enjoy it.

"The only time a team is special is at the end of the season," he said in reflection. "I'm so conservative with my opinions about the team during the season that it's difficult to assess until afterward. But it's not what they gave up that made it a special team."

David Wingate and Reggie Williams, the versatile youngsters who played two and three positions every night, had to sacrifice some of their offensive skills, as did point guard Michael Jackson, who was probably the most underrated player on the team. Bill Martin, the elegant power forward,

(above) A great from the 1955 and 1956 tournaments, Bill Russell, celebrated with John Thompson, whose Hoyas had just dominated to win the 1984 title. Thompson celebrated not with champagne but with swigs of milk.

(right) One of the great meetings of big men matched Houston's Akeem Olajuwon against Georgetown's Patrick Ewing in the 1984 Final Four in Seattle's Kingdome. The Hoyas destroyed Kentucky and Houston to win the championship.

Olajuwon defends
Georgetown forward
Michael Graham
during Georgetown's
84–75 victory in the
1984 championship game
in Seattle's Kingdome.

knew his job could change from day to day, depending on the opponent.

Fred Brown and Gene Smith were the quarterbacks—the players who knew Thompson so well they could relay his messages to the team before Thompson opened his mouth. And the centerpiece, of course, was Patrick Ewing, simply the most dependable player in the college game since Bill Walton.

And there were substitutes, including guard Horace Broadnax and center-forward Ralph Dalton, who could have started for other Top 20 teams but did what Thompson asked. It was a team that even an adversary such as Olajuwon could admire.

Also, unforgettably, there was Michael Graham, a 6´9˝ power forward and the source of much of the criticism aimed at Georgetown. During the regular season, Graham averaged three points and three rebounds per game and was largely an afterthought. In the Final Four, he sparkled: seven field goals in nine

pressure was there and do what is expected of you is one of the toughest things in any sport. Of course, Patrick was special. His attitude was as important as his ability, which of course was enormous.

"They were tough damn kids, competitive athletes. Michael Graham was the only one not mature enough to realize the total responsibility. Those kids fulfilled the whole responsibility."

Ewing, Martin, Wingate, Williams, and Jackson—all five starters—have played in the NBA. Everyone from that team except Graham graduated, and at least four have done postgraduate work.

Thompson is often asked if he carries a special game or a special moment from that championship season. Those who know Thompson well can anticipate the answer, and the moment has no rival.

Georgetown, flat and struggling—"I still can't, to this day, figure out why," Thompson says—was tied at 34–34 with Southern

"One of the great things about the team was that the kids were so secure in their abilities. To play that way when the pressure was there and do what is expected of you is one of the toughest things in any sport."

—John Thompson
Coach of Georgetown's 1984 championship team

attempts, with five rebounds against Houston; four field goals in six attempts, six rebounds, and a team-high 33 minutes against Kentucky. Number of bodies slammed: impossible to calculate.

"It shows you the enormous exposure the Final Four gets," Thompson said. "You'd have thought he was a superstar from the attention he got as a result of the NCAA Tournament, and specifically the Final Four. He contributed enormously at the right time."

In its own way, the Hoyas were a glamorous team: fast, smart, powerful—and kept away from the television lights just enough to add a dash of mystery. We could never get enough of the Hoyas. It never got boring because we never knew too much about them. And there was so much outsiders didn't know.

"One of the great things about the team was that the kids were so secure in their abilities," Thompson said. "To play that way when the

Methodist in a second-round tournament game at Pullman, Washington. Gene Smith was at the foul line in the waning seconds when Ewing ran over to Thompson on the bench.

"Patrick was supposed to go back on defense [and stand under the basket]," Thompson said. "But he asked me if he could stay up on the foul line in case Gene missed the free throw. I just looked at him, then told him, 'OK.' "

Smith did miss the foul shot; Ewing put it in. The Hoyas got another free throw and won, 37–36. Thompson says that in every season, even championship seasons, there is a game like that, a play like that. Only this time, it was a special player helping his team complete a special season. ∎

Michael Wilbon joined the staff of the Washington Post *in 1980 and has covered 17 Final Fours during that time. Today, he is a writer and a columnist for the* Post.

1985

THE PERFECT GAME

"There are only two great plays," an uncomplicated old coach used to say. "Put the ball in the basket and *South Pacific*."

By Tom Callahan

HOW WELL A TEAM REBOUNDS LOSES SOME SIG-nificance when there are no rebounds. This was the simplest moral of 1985, when the only team with 10 losses met the team with only 2, and for the first time in a long time, the early edition newspaper columnists felt they could safely write about dynasties again, being at least as certain of Patrick Ewing as the *Chicago Tribune* was of Thomas Dewey.

Georgetown University was going to be just the sixth college to repeat a national championship, and Ewing's Hoyas were already being measured beside the splendid San Francisco and UCLA teams of Bill Russell and Lew Alcindor. After losing one final to North Carolina, and winning another from Houston, the 7´ Ewing, and his mountainous coach John Thompson, brought a mood of graduation, if not coronation, to Lexington's Final Four.

Since two of the supporting actors, St. John's and Villanova, were Big East associates twice beaten by Georgetown, the Hoyas' preeminence was a matter of record as well as opinion.

Surrounded by all these city Catholics, country coach Dana Kirk cheerfully declared Memphis State the secular national champion, then genuflected to Villanova, 52–45. (The untidiness of the game obscured his parting prophesy: "If they're a Cinderella team, Cinderella wears boots.")

Meanwhile, Georgetown terrorized St. John's a third time, 77–59, terribly disabusing the city of New York. This was a nostalgic season for college basketball in Manhattan. The local papers clutched elfin coach Lou Carnesecca adoringly to their collective breast, and by a clever course of reasoning concluded that freckle-faced guard Chris Mullin was the finest player in the country. Mullin won the John Wooden Player of the Year award emphatically over Ewing, though it would probably be best if nobody asks the old coach's opinion.

Quietly, almost invisibly, another New Yorker remained—an agile, angular fellow named Ed Pinckney. A child of the Bronx, Villanova's 6´9½˝ center grew up, and up, in the natural way of the neighborhood, dribbling from borough to borough, studying various playground styles like a linguist sampling accents. Uptown, he learned power. In Queens, finesse. Brooklyn showed him flair, but it was unlike him to display any.

In the hours before the Monday night final, coach Rollie Massimino—coach Mass—urged the Wildcat players to think in terms of "the perfect game." Pinckney, in particular, was fascinated. "On a one-shot deal," the coach said, "we can beat anyone in the United States."

The scale of their task was evident from the tip-off: Villanova made seven of its first eight shots and still was behind, 20–14. Shot clocks were on order in college basketball, so this was something of a closing night for slow dancing. The custodian of the ball was a sharp little gizmo named Gary McLain, whose patience was equal to his caution. Without yet signaling much of an alarm, he steered Pinckney, Dwayne McClain, Harold Pressley, and Harold Jensen (this team was more Harolded than we thought) back to all-even at 20–20. On a follow-up shot by Pressley at the close of the first half, Villanova actually took a quaint 29–28 lead.

(above) Driving the baseline between Georgetown defenders, Villanova's Harold Pressley scored as the possibility of the upset began to form. The Hoyas were on track to repeat their national championship, but Rollie Massimino's Wildcats shocked the nation with a 66–64 title-game victory.

(right) Ed Pinckney became the Final Four Most Outstanding Player as he scored 16 points. Dwayne McClain scored 17 for the Wildcats. And Villanova, fourth place in the Big East Conference, finished the game with an unlikely 66–64 championship win over Georgetown.

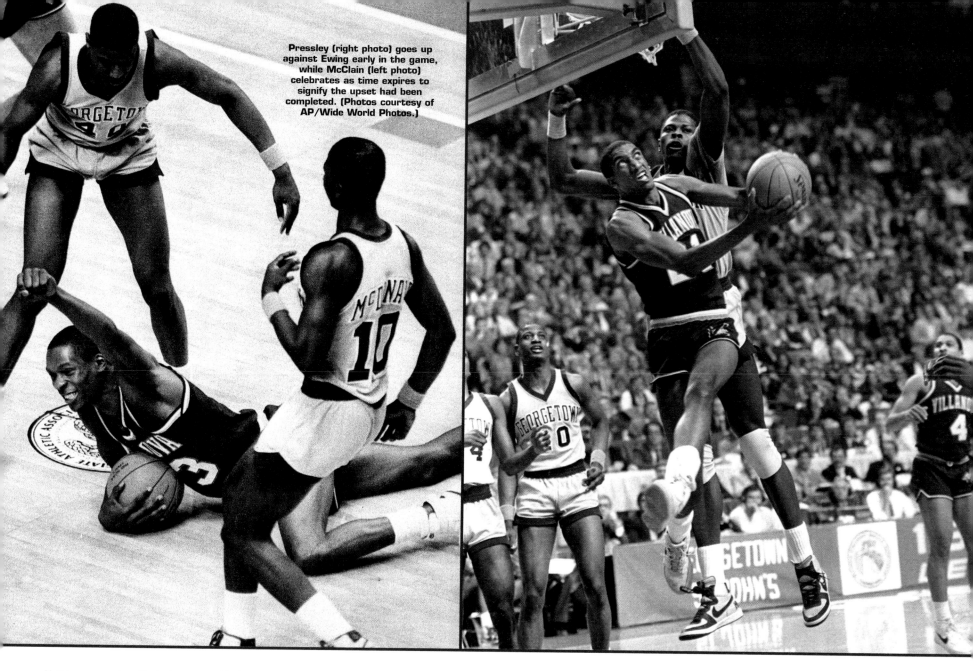

Pressley (right photo) goes up against Ewing early in the game, while McClain (left photo) celebrates as time expires to signify the upset had been completed. (Photos courtesy of AP/Wide World Photos.)

Nothing seemed particularly wrong with the Hoyas, though their spindly young forward, Reggie Williams, was slightly hobbled by a tender ankle. Beyond that, he looked spent from the 35–2 season and a 17-game winning streak. Used to dominating whole teams, Ewing was so utterly occupied by Pinckney, that at no time in the first half did he get to the free throw line. (Ewing didn't know it yet, but he would never go there again as a collegian.)

Come the second half, it was Villanova that spurted ahead a couple of times, and the full extent of Georgetown's emergency was perfectly plain by the time David Wingate's banked basket reclaimed a scarce 54–53 lead. After Villanova fumbled the ball out of bounds, coach Thompson ordered the Hoyas to delay. About three and a half minutes remained.

It is probably too easy, then, to say that the championship bounced off somebody's foot and into the arms of Harold Jensen, but in a manner of speaking, it did. Jensen tried his fifth shot of the game and made his fifth field goal. Villanova

"Really and truly, I don't know if we thought this would ever come true, but we did dream it."

—Ed Pinckney
Center on Villanova's 1985 championship team

did the rest of its uncanny shooting from the foul line. As soon as Pinckney and Jensen each made a pair, the score was 59–54. The 24–10 Wildcats, fourth-best in their conference, eighth-seeded in their region, 23-point losers to Pittsburgh on the last day of the regular season, became the champions of the world, 66–64.

Missing just 1 of 10 attempts in the second half, they shot 78.6 percent for the game. With 16 points, six rebounds, and five assists (to Ewing's 14, five, and two),

Pinckney was named the tournament's Most Outstanding Player. "Really and truly, I don't know if we thought this would ever come true," Pinckney said, "but we did dream it." In 40 minutes Gary McLain turned the ball over only twice. On the eve of the final, the expressive eyes of coach Mass had filled with water as he heard McLain describe him as "a brother, a friend, a father, your boss, your coach." Massimino murmured, "I've screamed at this group more than any other, not because they are such good players, but because they are such good kids. They could take it."

So could Georgetown. Through all their many glories, the Hoyas never looked as becoming as they did that night in Lexington standing at their bench applauding Villanova. ∎

Tom Callahan covered Final Fours in the eighties for Time magazine. Today, he lives in Charlottesville, Virginia, writes for The New York Times, and authors books.

1986

BIG D STANDS FOR DENNY

By Billy Reed

AS THE TOURNAMENT UNFOLDED, IT HAD SO MANY plots and subplots that at times it seemed a prime-time soap opera, which was rather fitting considering the Final Four was to be held in Dallas, known to millions of television viewers as the home of J. R. Ewing and his fellow wheeler-dealers in the oil business.

Was the Big East really dead or was it just a dream? Was Michigan only tired or too big-headed for even a 10-gallon hat? And while North Carolina was the answer to one question—Who got J. R. (Reid, the nation's best high school prospect?)—it also had everyone wondering how a team that was No. 1 so much of the season could be so flat at tournament time.

While the experts pondered these and other mysteries, they also agreed that the city known as "Big D" would be where classy Duke and its rowdy fans finally would claim the title. But they forgot that in the eighties, the "Big D" of college basketball was Denny, as in Crum, the laid-back coach at Louisville. When the Cardinals arrived in Dallas, it marked their third trip to the Final Four in five years, their fourth in the seven years of the decade, and their sixth in Crum's 15 seasons since leaving John Wooden's side at UCLA. In the age of parity, this was about as close to a, uh, dynasty as anybody could get without hiring Joan Collins as pom-pom coach.

Before the season, Crum's team looked to be just another big player. The previous season's 18–17 record had been: (a) the worst of Crum's career, (b) the first time he failed to win 20 games, and (c) unworthy of even an NCAA bid. But Cardinal fans had some reasons to expect improvement. The guard corps would be helped by the return of 6´5˝ Milt "Ice" Wagner, a cool veteran of two Final Fours who had been redshirted as a senior because of a foot injury. In Pervis Ellison, a 6´9˝ freshman from Savannah, Georgia, Crum had found a center precocious enough to invite comparisons with North Carolina's Sam Perkins because of his physique (all legs and arms) and ability to clean the boards ("Windex," he was promptly dubbed by Wagner).

> **But like the Louisville native Muhammad Ali taking punches from Joe Frazier, the Cards managed to stay on their feet, hang tough, and remain within striking distance.**

Invited to play in the inaugural preseason NIT, Crum's team played well enough to join Kansas, Duke, and St. John's for the final rounds in New York's Madison Square Garden. Although the Cards dropped tough losses to Kansas and local favorite St. John's, Crum was typically undismayed. "Those teams are as good as any in the country," he said. "This would have been a good Final Four."

That proved to be prophetic. The survivors who arrived in Dallas did, indeed, include Louisville, Duke, and Kansas. The fourth member was, surprisingly, Louisiana State, which lost to Kentucky three times during the season but beat the Wildcats when it mattered the most, in the final of the Southeast Regional.

While the season proved that Wagner's foot (and his shooting touch) were as good as ever and that Ellison was

(above) Reunion Arena in Dallas hosted the 1986 tournament, where Duke and Louisville eliminated Louisiana State and Kansas to play for the championship. Duke's David Henderson drives for the basket while teammate Johnny Dawkins (right) takes the same route later in the game.

In the second half of the 1986 championship at Reunion Arena in Dallas, Louisville's Herbert Crook (No. 41), Mark McSwain (No. 10), and Pervis Ellison (No. 43) had position for the rebound and shot. Ellison became the first freshman since 1944 to win the Most Outstanding Player award.

And ending LSU's fairy tale run to glory with an 88–77 victory, the Cardinals watched top-ranked Duke get a last-second basket by freshman forward Danny Ferry to pull out a 71–67 win for coach Mike Krzyzewski, who had played and coached for Bobby Knight at Army.

More than one writer saw the final game as a matter of students (Duke) vs. jocks (Louisville), an unfortunate and unfair stereotype. If Crum's program deserved more credit for its academic successes, then it also was true that Duke's players were hardly just a bunch of eggheads.

Preppy though he looked, forward Mark Alarie would trade elbows with anybody. In Johnny Dawkins, the Blue Devils had a flame so quick and deadly that Wagner, befuddled, was forced to the bench in the first half of the title game.

In retrospect, it's difficult to figure out how Louisville won. Twice, once in each half, Dawkins took the game into his own hands and burned the Cards so severely that the game teetered on the brink of dissolving into a Duke rout. But like the Louisville native Muhammad Ali taking punches from Joe Frazier, the Cards managed to stay on their feet, hang tough, and remain within striking distance.

With only 48 seconds left in the game and 11 on the shot clock in Reunion Arena, Louisville was clinging to a 66–65 lead when Crum called a timeout to set up a play. The idea was to get the ball to either Wagner or the other senior shooter, Jeff Hall, and let them go one-on-one in the hope of either a basket or a foul. Under heavy pressure, Hall threw up an off-balanced air ball. But suddenly, Ellison arose from the pack under the basket to wrap his hands around the ball and drop it in.

Cards 68, Devils 65.

Then, after rebounding a wild miss by Duke's David Henderson, Pervis showed why he was known as "Never Nervous," dropping in a couple of free throws for a 70–65 lead with 0:27 remaining. The Blue Devils quickly got four straight points, but finally were buried when "Ice" Wagner coolly swished two free throws with only two seconds to go to clinch the 72–69 win.

While Ellison became the first freshman since Arnie Ferrin of Utah in 1944 to be named the tournament Most Outstanding Player, Thompson was the catalyst. In six tournament games, he averaged 18.3 points and 7.8 rebounds while hitting 69 percent from the floor.

But it was the coach who drew the biggest hand from the jubilant Cardinal fans. On a night that "Big D" stood not for Dallas or Duke, but for Denny (and dynasty), Crum smiled and said, "I'm really going to enjoy this one . . . it kinds of puts you in select company." ∎

the best freshman center in the nation, the Cards didn't really begin to look like champions until 6´7˝ senior forward Billy Thompson finally began showing the consistency and leadership that Crum had been patiently awaiting for three and a half years, or since he came to Louisville from Camden New Jersey) High School ballyhooed as the best prospect in the nation. Booed at home after key mistakes in tough losses at Kansas and Memphis State, Thompson got his multidimensional act together just in time to help the Cards to a 26–7 season that included an 11-game winning streak heading into the NCAAs.

Named the No. 1 seed in the West, Crum's team rolled to easy wins over Drexel and Bradley to advance to Houston. Omen-watchers noted what this team and Louisville's 1980 champions had in common were freshman centers (Rodney McCray in 1980), their final loss to teams coached by Jim Valvano (Iona in 1980, N.C. State in 1986), and a regional played in Houston. Finding the Summit as much to his liking in 1986 as he had in 1980, Crum watched his team finally put North Carolina out of its misery, 94–79, before withstanding a fine individual effort by Auburn's Chuck Person to beat the Tigers, 84–76, and earn (ho-hum) another trip to the Final Four.

1987

HOLLYWOOD SCRIPT COMES TO LIFE

By Bob Hammel

I N HOLLYWOOD, NCAA TOURNAMENT CHAMPIONSHIP night was also Oscar Night. Writer Angelo Pizzo's first movie, *Hoosiers*, was nominated in two categories. It was the story of an Indiana high school team's improbable championship, won on a last-second basket. Pizzo, who grew up in Bloomington, Indiana, had his Oscar tickets, his tuxedo, his limousine . . . "but it just killed me that I wasn't in New Orleans," he said. He stayed home and watched the NCAA final on television. "You go back to your roots in times of stress," he said.

In New Orleans, Keith Smart was back to his roots. Ten years earlier, as a Boy Scout from nearby Baton Rouge, Smart had worked Sunday afternoons as a volunteer usher at New Orleans Saints football games in the Superdome— "so far up you needed television just to watch the game."

When Smart returned, television watched him. With five seconds to go in the championship game, Smart's 16-foot jump shot from the side swished through and made Indiana a 74–73 winner over Syracuse.

It was Indiana's fifth NCAA basketball championship in a glorious tradition that stretches to Everett Dean and Branch McCracken, decades and generations ago. In all that Hoosier history, there never was a single shot to rival Smart's.

And, of course, it worked the other way as well. Syracuse, which had felled a giant, North Carolina, to get to New Orleans, had its first championship in its grip, until:

- After hitting a free throw to put his team up 73–70, Howard Triche missed a free throw (0:38);
- Smart, lined up third on the right side of the lane, picked off the rebound and drove to a basket that cut the lead to 73–72 (0:30);
- After a timeout and an inbounds pass, Smart fouled freshman Derrick Coleman (0:28);
- Coleman missed a one-and-one free throw; Daryl Thomas rebounded for Indiana (0:27);
- Smart got the ball in the post to Thomas, who was covered by Coleman (0:08);
- So the ball went back to Smart . . . and into history.

"What do I remember most?" Smart said months later. "How quiet the arena got when the ball left my hand.

"And all of a sudden it went in."

It was an improbable finish, if only because Indiana's vast preference would have been to get the ball in the hands of its other guard for such a vital shot. Steve Alford had been taking those for Indiana for four years, and hitting most of them.

Four weeks earlier, in a game crucial to Indiana's Big Ten championship hopes, Alford felt the burden of last-second leadership and tried to create a shot with his team two points down at Illinois. He tried to get free for a three-point try but couldn't; he worked his way into the deep corner, then out just far enough to force up a two-point try that missed, and Illinois won.

Back home, it didn't take exacting film study to show that Alford's best play would have been to give the ball up because defensive concentration understandably had swarmed around him. The Illinois game was the 118th of Alford's Indiana career, but not too late for him to learn. With the national championship game on the line, Alford moved to the far side of the court—available if the defense ignored him; maneuvering room opened for the others if it didn't.

Smart had been using any room left open to him for the entire last 12 minutes of a breathless game. In the final minutes of the biggest game of the year, the fifth-leading scorer on Indiana's team put together his own highlight

Syracuse coach Jim Boeheim (inset) had brought his team to the tournament nine consecutive years. His 1987 team was best positioned for a championship, but it was Indiana that celebrated that night in the Superdome. Steve Alford, Dean Garrett, Tony Freeman, and Daryl Thomas (above) rejoice in the moment.

As players and coach Bobby Knight waited for the trophy celebration at game's end, Knight and senior point guard Steve Alford (right) shared the moment. Alford, son of a coach and a student of the game for his four Knight years, put into practice those lessons as an accomplished head coach.

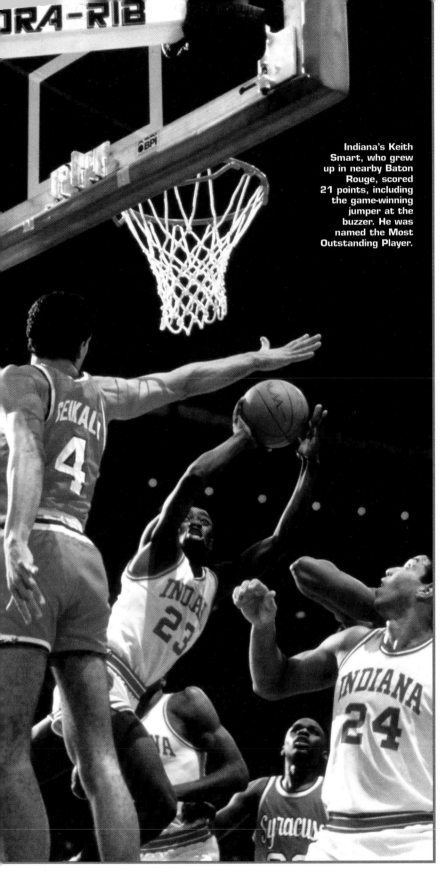

Indiana's Keith Smart, who grew up in nearby Baton Rouge, scored 21 points, including the game-winning jumper at the buzzer. He was named the Most Outstanding Player.

Why "Knight, of all people"?

That's a question Knight himself asks, though he knows the answer involves a collision of images more universal than absolutely accurate —his own, for a rigidity in all things, including recruiting; that of the "jucos," for turning out borderline students.

His change from a previous disinclination to recruit in the junior colleges came simply because the regional high school talent pool that fueled his program for its first 14 years went unexpectedly dry.

At the time, Indiana was halfway down its tournament road— Fairfield, Auburn, and Duke hurdled, Louisiana State up next.

The first two games had come in friendly environs for the Hoosiers: at the Hoosier Dome in Indianapolis, where tournament-record crowds watched home-state hero Alford lead the way over Fairfield and then score 31 points to rally the Hoosiers from a 24–10 deficit to a 107–90 win over Auburn.

The Duke game was the first to match Knight against a team coached by one of his former players. Mike Krzyzewski, who took Duke to the 1986 final game, was captain of a Knight team at Army. This game was a rousing matchup of friendly philosophies, and Indiana survived it, 88–82.

It all seemed over for the

Calloway, playing in his hometown, pulled teammate Daryl Thomas' missed shot out of the air and banked it in for the game-winner at 0:06.

From early February on, the nation's No. 1–ranked team was Nevada–Las Vegas. Jerry Tarkanian's Runnin' Rebels entered the tournament 33–1, the loss by a point at Oklahoma. Indiana went into the tourney 24–4, ranked No. 3 behind North Carolina.

Despite 38 points by UNLV guard Freddie Bands and 32 points by center Armon Gilliam, Indiana sped to a 97–93 victory.

Syracuse had its own three-point concerns in the semifinal round. Its Big East partner, Providence, had used the shot freely and well in leaving a shocking trail of higher-ranked victims, most notably No. 9 Alabama (103–82) and

"A lot of coaches didn't like the three-point rule, and some ignored it as if it weren't there. But Bob Knight adjusted with players like Alford and Smart, and Indiana won another title."

—Pete Newell
Hall of Fame coach

No. 4 Georgetown (88–73). The Friars, with Billy Donovan leading the way, took 78 three-point shots and hit 40 in the four victories that sent them to New Orleans. Unimpressed, Syracuse used guard Sherman Douglas to cool Donovan, and the Orangemen maintained their dominance (15 straight victories) over Providence, 77–63.

Syracuse went after Indiana with a variety of defenses but basically two: man-to-man, with Greg Monroe on Alford most of the time, or a box-and-one—a four-man zone defense with Douglas assigned to Alford. Alford got his points (23, including 7 for 10 from the three-point range), but Syracuse—never a finalist before and a Final Four team only once in its 14 previous NCAA Tournament trips—got 20 of them back from Douglas himself, 19 from center Rony Seikaly, and backboard domination from the game's only freshman starter, Derrick Coleman. The 6´9˝ forward from Big Ten country (Detroit) had 19 rebounds, 9 more than anyone else in the game.

Syracuse was in the box-and-one, and Douglas was dogging Alford, when Smart—who had 21 points (15 in the last 12 minutes) to win the Most Outstanding Player award—found the opening that won for Indiana.

When it was over, the Hoosier story seemed almost scripted. Alford had led the way through Indianapolis; the game-winning basket at Cincinnati was by Cincinnatian Calloway; the game-winning basket at New Orleans was by Louisianian Smart.

And in Hollywood, *Hoosiers* scriptwriter Angelo Pizzo smiled. ■

film. "It was just all Keith down the stretch," said Dean Garrett, who will have everlasting trivia fame standing alongside Smart as answers to the questions:

Who were the two junior college players who Knight, of all people, recruited and made starters on a national championship team?

Hoosiers, however, when LSU opened a 12-point second-half lead and was up 75–66 with four and a half minutes to go when Indiana's Rick Calloway drove to dunk and missed—spectacularly. The ball ricocheted off the rim and out of bounds. Indiana took a timeout, and somehow the Hoosiers found the answers for a 77–76 win.

1988

KANSAS CAPS STORYBOOK FINISH

By Bob Hentzen

UNIVERSITY OF KANSAS FANS HAD THE SCRIPT FOR April of 1988 in their minds months, even years, in advance. There were two givens: (1) the 1988 Final Four would be in Kansas City's Kemper Arena, 40 miles down I-70 from Lawrence, and (2) 1988 would be Danny Manning's senior season as a Jayhawk. What better place for Manning to end his brilliant college career than a Final Four "at home"?

But it did not happen the way that Kansas fans had first envisioned. Heck, even the most ardent supporter had given up on the script midway through the 1987–1988 campaign.

Kansas was leading the nation only in adversity—with injuries, ineligibilities, and suspensions decimating Manning's supporting cast. At one point the troubled Jayhawks were a so-so 12–8, and there was genuine doubt that they would even finish with a record good enough to qualify for the NCAA's 64-team starting field.

They made it safely, finishing the regular season 21–11. But they hardly came into the tourney with momentum, having been drilled by Kansas State 69–54 in the Big Eight Tourney semifinals in Kemper Arena.

History, along with common sense, said they would not be celebrating a national championship there 23 days later; no team with that many losses had ever won it all.

First stop on the tourney trail was Lincoln, Nebraska—not a particularly good omen because Kansas had blown a 16-point lead and lost to Nebraska there during the regular season. But in somewhat of an upset—Xavier was ranked No. 17—the Jayhawks won decisively, 85–72. They were fortunate to escape Lincoln alive, though. Murray State missed a potential go-ahead bucket at the end and Manning hit two free throws with one second left for a 61–58 victory.

Then it was on to the Silverdome in Pontiac, Michigan, and Kansans were busy resurrecting the Jayhawks' script and also writing one for another state Cinderella, Kansas State.

Doggone, it worked out that Kansans could not lose in the regional finals—they were going to have a team in Kansas City after KU rode Manning's 38 points to a 77–64 win over Vanderbilt and K-State stunned third-ranked Purdue 73–70.

Kansas had lost two of three previous confrontations with the Wildcats, but at the end the KU pep band was playing "Goin' to Kansas City." Coach Larry Brown was high-fiving Manning and congratulating other seniors Chris Piper and (the injured, but inspirational leader) Archie Marshall. Athletic director Bob Frederick was picking up the black bag with 1,625 Final Four tickets. The Jayhawks had prevailed, 71–58.

The field for the 50th anniversary NCAA championship could not have turned out to be more attractive for folks in the host city. There was fifth-ranked Duke (24–6), which had knocked off No. 1 Temple in the regional finals. There was second-ranked Arizona (31–2). And there was fourth-ranked Oklahoma (30–3).

Kansas City had been preparing for this Final Four for three years. It was the 10th time the city had hosted the championship, but the first time since 1964 and the first time in Kemper Arena.

The first semifinal matched Kansas against Duke, a nemesis to the Jayhawks and an albatross that Manning had carried for two years. In the Final Four of Dallas, remember, Mike Krzyzewski's Blue Devils knocked off Kansas, 71–67, when Manning experienced a nightmarish four-point game.

Larry Brown was not thinking so much about that before the tip-off, but of the season he had spent yelling at

For Kansas coach Larry Brown, high-five time arrived with seconds remaining as Danny Manning came from the game.

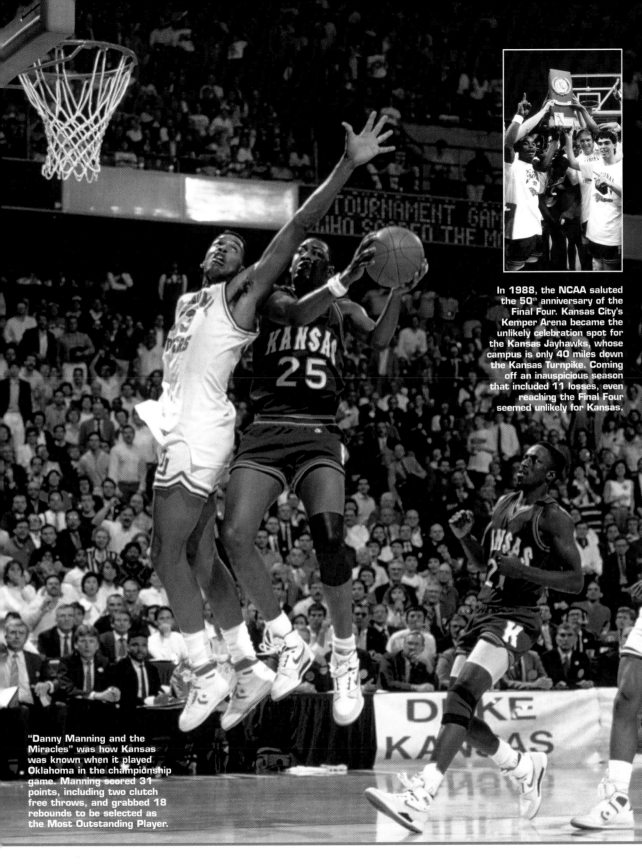

In 1988, the NCAA saluted the 50th anniversary of the Final Four. Kansas City's Kemper Arena became the unlikely celebration spot for the Kansas Jayhawks, whose campus is only 40 miles down the Kansas Turnpike. Coming off an inauspicious season that included 11 losses, even reaching the Final Four seemed unlikely for Kansas.

"Danny Manning and the Miracles" was how Kansas was known when it played Oklahoma in the championship game. Manning scored 31 points, including two clutch free throws, and grabbed 18 rebounds to be selected as the Most Outstanding Player.

Oklahoma had beaten Kansas twice during the season, 73–65 and 97–85, but the Sooners—like the rest of the basketball world—were realizing that the Jayhawks were on an amazing roll. "They're on a high right now; they know they can beat anyone," said Sooner guard Ricky Grace.

On Easter Sunday, the off day, Billy Tubbs' runnin', pressin' Sooners were being tabbed by coaches and media to win the championship. Kansas' only chance, most agreed, hinged on being able to slow the tempo as North Carolina State and Villanova had done (in preshot clock days) in scoring memorable upsets in the finals.

> ## "We wouldn't be sitting here talking to you right now if it wasn't for the rest of the kids. We got an unbelievable performance from a lot of kids."
>
> **—Larry Brown**
> *Coach of Kansas' 1988 championship team*

The first half ended 50–50—perhaps the most furious, exciting 20 minutes in college basketball history.

"I remember looking at the referees and seeing them shaking their heads and grinning," said Brown afterward. "I think they thought it was an excellent game, too."

No way could the two teams keep up that pace in the second half, and they did not—especially since Kansas did not want to. But the excitement, the drama, the electricity, lingered until the end.

Manning, appropriately, salted away the 83–79 victory with two free throws with five seconds left. He finished with 31 points and 18 rebounds, numbers that probably were in the original script when he first put on a Jayhawk uniform.

This NCAA championship was the Danny Manning Show, but as Brown said to the media later, "We wouldn't be sitting here talking to you right now if it wasn't for the rest of the kids. We got an unbelievable performance from a lot of kids."

In the title game, undersized 6´4˝ forward Milt Newton hit all six shots from the field, scoring 15 points. Guard Kevin Prichard hit six of seven shots from the floor and turned in a great floor game down the stretch. Piper, a rock throughout the season, capped his basketball career with eight points and seven boards.

The celebration, of course, started in Kemper Arena. It soon extended to the streets outside and then to the suburbs, lasting until the wee hours. The Jayhawks were back atop the basketball world. ∎

and criticizing his troops. He decided in his pregame pep talk that it was time for him to tell them they were doggone good.

"I thought our kids thought they could win, but I thought they needed to hear it from me," Brown said.

Kansas bolted in front 9–0, then 14–0, and, unbelievably, 18–2. It held on for a 66–59 victory to even the score with the Blue Devils. "This is like a dream season," said Manning

after a dream game—25 points, 10 rebounds, six blocked shots, and four steals.

Then Oklahoma made another dream, an all–Big Eight final, a reality by dispatching Arizona with surprising ease, 86–78. Lute Olson's Wildcats got 31 points from Sean Elliott, but were done in by the Sooners' inside combination of Harvey Grant and Stacey King, who both scored 21.

1989

FISHER AND COMPANY GRAB NCAA GOLD

By Bill Halls

THE NEWS HIT THE MICHIGAN CAMPUS LIKE A BOMB-shell. On March 15, four days after the regular season had ended and two days before the Wolverine basketball team was to play its first NCAA Tournament game, coach Bill Frieder resigned.

"We were shocked," said center Loy Vaught. "He never let on he was leaving."

Frieder made the announcement at a hastily arranged press conference in Tempe, Arizona. He was leaving Michigan following nine seasons and 191 victories to become head coach at Arizona State. Frieder said he planned to coach Michigan in the tournament.

Back in Ann Arbor, Bo Schembechler, the football coach and recently appointed athletic director, made a decision of his own. "A Michigan man will coach Michigan," he announced and immediately named Steve Fisher, Frieder's top assistant, interim head coach.

There had been high expectations among Michigan's basketball followers all summer. Michigan was coming off a 26–8 season and had a lineup overflowing with talented players, led by Glenn Rice, a 6´7˝ senior with exceptional shooting range. Rice and Mark Hughes, a senior backup center, were named cocaptains. The 6´10˝ Mills, who had never lived up to his high school rave notices, started at the other forward with Vaught in the pivot. The guards were Rumeal Robinson, a physically powerful and aggressive playmaker, and 6´6˝ Mike Griffin, a solid all-around player who specialized in defense.

Hughes and Sean Higgins, a 6´9˝ sophomore who was a taller version of Rice, were the primary reserves. Backing up Robinson at the point were juniors Demetrius Calip and Kirk Taylor. Michigan finished third in the conference but its 24–7 record earned the team an NCAA Tournament bid.

Fisher hardly had time to gather his thoughts. Michigan was scheduled to play Xavier (Ohio) in the first round of the Southeast regional in Atlanta. Fisher, a low-key, soft-spoken man, had never been a head coach at the collegiate level. Schembechler hastily made arrangements to attend the game. He gave the players a rousing pep talk.

The Wolverines struggled through most of the game but took an 84–82 lead on a three-point field goal by Rice with 3:32 remaining and held on down the stretch for a 92–87 victory. Rice and Robinson each scored 23 points. Mills added 18.

"I'm probably no different than anyone else cast in this situation," Fisher said. "I was scared to death prior to walking from the locker room onto the floor, but after the ball was thrown up, I think I settled into a routine that was business as usual."

After the Xavier game, Michigan seemed to settle down. Rice scored 36 points and Mills added 24 as Michigan eliminated South Alabama, 91–82. The Wolverines headed for Lexington, Kentucky, for a regional semifinal date with powerful North Carolina.

Dean Smith's Tar Heels had eliminated Michigan from the NCAA championship two years running. But Rice would not let it happen again. The talented senior scored 34 points, making 13 of 19 floor shots, including eight three-point field goals as Michigan prevailed, 92–87.

"I'm just going to hang on for the ride as long as I can," said a smiling Fisher.

In the Southeast regional final, Michigan crushed a solid Virginia team, 102–65, as Rice scored 32 points and Higgins added 31. Michigan was on its way to the Final Four in Seattle.

Physical Michigan arrived in Seattle for the Final Four, facing a team it knew well—Illinois. Michigan forward Mike Griffin dove for a loose ball (right) and, with the score tied, the game came down to a last-second shot by Sean Higgins. The shot went in, and the Wolverines were ready to face Seton Hall for the championship Monday night.

Seton Hall, putting together a Cinderella story with coach P. J. Carlisimo writing the script, faced Duke in the semis, where forward John Smith (inset) leaped high attempting to block a shot from Anthony Advent (No. 32). But the glass slipper broke as Michigan made two free throws with three seconds remaining to claim the crown, 80–79. The Wolverine bench cleared as the celebration began.

in a soft six-footer to give Michigan the victory with two seconds left on the clock.

"If this is a dream," Fisher said, "don't wake me up until Tuesday morning."

Now the stage was set for the championship game. Seton Hall, completing a Cinderella story of its own under P. J. Carlesimo, was making its first appearance in the final. And what a final it was.

Michigan led 37–32 at halftime and built a 12-point bulge early in the second half. Seton Hall, behind some miraculous shooting by John Morton, battled back and sent the game into overtime on Morton's three-pointer.

Morton nailed another three-pointer to give Seton Hall a 79–76 lead with 2:50 remaining in overtime. He finished the game with 35 points, but it was his last gasp in the championship.

> **"I was scared to death prior to walking from the locker room onto the floor, but after the ball was thrown up, I think I settled into a routine that was business as usual."**
>
> **—Steve Fisher**
> *Coach of Michigan's 1989 championship team*

Michigan trailed by a point when Rice's defense forced Morton to toss up an airball. Rice grabbed the rebound and fed a pass to Robinson, who was fouled with three seconds to play. Robinson calmly sank both free throws to give Michigan an 80–79 victory and the school's first NCAA basketball championship.

"You have to believe you're going to make them," said Robinson. "Because if you don't, you won't."

Rice finished the game with 31 points and 11 rebounds and was named the championship's Most Outstanding Player. Fisher had coached his team to six-straight victories under incredible pressure. "Don't pinch me," he said. Days later, Fisher was hired by Schembechler as Michigan's coach.

"It seems like a story," said Mills. "It seems like something someone would make up. But it came true for Michigan. You couldn't tell this story to anyone else. They wouldn't believe it." ∎

"We're playing with a lot more confidence," said Mills, who raised his game to a new level during the championship. "Coach Fisher found the right chemistry and the right combinations. It doesn't matter to us anymore who scores. We just want to win."

Lou Henson's Illinois team was awaiting the Wolverines in the Emerald City. But Fisher was becoming a Wizard of Oz for his Tin Man (Vaught), Cowardly Lion (Mills), and Scarecrow (Robinson). Vaught had been mired in a tourney-long slump, but his coach stood by him. Fisher quietly told Mills that he had not come close to scratching the surface of his talent. And Robinson needed to play under a bit more control and, for crying out loud, watch the silly fouls.

Each of the three players rose up to play their best basketball against Illinois. The smaller, quicker Illini raced in

front, 16–8, in the early going. But Michigan closed behind the heart of Vaught (16 rebounds, 10 points), the courage of Mills (9 rebounds, 8 points) and the heady play of Robinson (14 points, 12 assists) to take a one-point halftime lead.

Rice continued to pop rainbow jumpers through the nets with amazing regularity (28 points on 12 for 24 shooting). But it was left to Higgins to wear the hero's halo.

Michigan had taken an 81–79 lead on a three-point play by Hughes with 1:09 remaining. Ken Battle, who led the Illini with 29 points, tied the score with a 12-foot jumper with 50 seconds left on the clock.

Fisher set up a final play, but the Illini defense thwarted the Wolverines, and Mills was forced to fire up a wild 18-footer with the 45-second clock running out. The ball caromed off the rim and landed in Higgins' hands. He tossed

Bill Halls covered eight Final Fours throughout his 30-year career at the Detroit News. *After his last Final Four in 1981, he covered professional basketball. He has won numerous awards from the U.S. Basketball Writers Association and the Professional Basketball Association. He is currently retired and living in Michigan.*

1990

THE EMPIRE STRIKES BACK

IN THE FINAL DECADE OF THE 20ᵀᴴ CENTURY, AMERICA fought a high-tech war in the Persian Gulf, witnessed the crumbling of the Soviet Union, and rode the soaring stock market to a new level of prosperity. Actor Tom Hanks emerged as the Jimmy Stewart of his generation, starring in such movies as *Forrest Gump*, *Philadelphia*, *Sleepless in Seattle*, and *Saving Private Ryan*. In the record industry, compact discs rendered 33 rpm albums obsolete, and youngsters embraced a new kind of music known as "rap" that many of their elders insisted wasn't music at all.

In the burgeoning computer world, along came the Internet, which provided unprecedented access to an incredible amount of information. In addition to e-mail, cable TV grew and proliferated to the point that around-the-clock coverage was available for major news events such as the deaths of Princess Di and John F. Kennedy Jr.

Among the more stunning developments in the sports world were the inclusion of NBA players on the U.S. Olympic basketball team, the cancellation of the 1994 World Series because of a dispute between players and owners, and boxer Mike Tyson twice biting Evander Holyfield's ears during a heavyweight championship fight in Las Vegas. A couple of erstwhile bush-league sports—stock-car racing and professional wrestling—experienced surges in popularity that challenged the traditional "ball" sports for TV time and the entertainment dollar. Early in the decade, Michigan's "Fab Five" adopted long, baggy shorts, and it began a trend that swept throughout the basketball world and the nation's playgrounds.

From 1992 through the end of the decade, the White House was occupied by Bill Clinton, a native of Arkansas who presided over a tumultuous and controversial presidency. For college basketball, the most important thing about Clinton was that he was an avid and knowledgeable fan. He frequently watched games and he annually invited the men's and women's champions to the White House to be honored. When his favorite team, the Arkansas Razorbacks, won the 1993 NCAA title, Clinton attended the championship game in Charlotte, North Carolina.

Yet with all due respect to Arkansas and three other first-time champions—UNLV (1990), Arizona (1997), and Connecticut (1999)—the decade will be remembered as one dominated by the traditional powers. In 1991 and 1992 Duke became the first back-to-back champ since UCLA won its seventh consecutive title in 1973. In 1993 the Blue Devils' arch-enemy, North Carolina, won its third title, and in 1995 UCLA won its first title since the John Wooden era.

But the team of the decade may well have been Kentucky, the college game's all-time winningest program. When Rick Pitino became the Wildcats' coach in 1989, the program was at its lowest ebb due to NCAA sanctions stemming from rules violations. In only four years, Pitino had the Wildcats back in the Final Four. Then from 1996–1998, Kentucky went to three consecutive championship games. The Cats beat Syracuse for the title in 1996, lost to Arizona in 1997, and then won again in 1998, their first season under Tubby Smith, who became the third African-American coach to win a national title. (Others were John Thompson of Georgetown and Nolan Richardson of Arkansas.)

Entering the new millennium, no sport was more popular or healthy than college basketball. ∎

Corey Beck of Arkansas expresses his joy after his team defeated Duke 76–72 to earn the 1994 title in Charlotte, North Carolina.

> **"The nineties saw a big transformation with players like Kevin Garnett, Kobe Bryant, and Tracy McGrady jumping straight from high school to the NBA. Many collegiate underclassmen joined them, and suddenly you had stars who bypassed college altogether or who used it as a brief pit stop on the way to the NBA."**
>
> **—Pete Newell**

1999

Duke came to the finals five times in the nineties, winning twice and always contending.

1990

RUN, RUN, RUN, RUN AWAY

By Bob Sands

IT WAS 1:30 IN THE MORNING AND TWO OL' GUYS short of hair but long of basketball savvy were walking down the corridor of the Denver Sheraton Tech Center.

Smoke from an El Ropo victory cigar billowed toward the ceiling. Blush wine lapped at the glass with each step of Nevada–Las Vegas coach Jerry Tarkanian. James Madison coach Lefty Driesell, Tark's longtime buddy, was waving his arms like a band conductor gone mad. The two coaches stopped, Driesell offered more congratulations, and they parted.

Tarkanian took a drag on the cigar and let out a puff of smoke. He liked that. So he did it again. Then a Cheshire Cat grin and another drag.

This was a happy man.

The coach of the 1990 NCAA championship team certainly had reason to be. The Rebels had buried the Duke Blue Devils, 103–73, in the title game four hours earlier at McNichols Arena.

A 30-point victory—the widest margin in a championship game. The Rebels registered three 30-point victories during the NCAA championship, but this one . . . oh so superb. And Driesell, a Duke graduate, had stopped by to offer his congratulations.

Tark, indeed, was in a euphoric, reflective mood in these wee hours. National champions—what an awesome statement. Only 28 other universities had won the title since the NCAA championship started in 1939. At the beginning of last season, 293 schools had an opportunity to win the trophy. Nevada–Las Vegas became the one, the only.

But a 30-point margin . . . what in the world? Tark explained that the Rebels were able to get a good start on the Blue Devils.

Tarkanian was surprised that slight-of-build Duke point guard Bobby Hurley started defensively on bigger, stronger Greg Anthony. With the physical advantage, Anthony could penetrate and either dish it off or shoot the jumper.

The anatomy of an impending blowout. Oh, it didn't take long for Duke coach Mike Krzyzewski to change his scheme. But it was too late.

The foundation was in place. The Rebels were off and running—for 103 points.

But in analyzing the Rebels, you must first address the defense. The Rebels could play a hangman's-noose-choking-pressure defense. They also could play a quick-hands-and-feet-in-the-passing-lanes zone defense, which Tarkanian called the Amoeba. The Amoeba globbed on the Blue Devils in the first five minutes of the second half as the Rebels went on an 18–0 tear in three minutes to forge a 75–47 lead at 13:38.

Anderson Hunt, the championship's Most Outstanding Player, scored 12 of those 18 points on the way to a 29-point game.

Still, it was that early situation between Hurley and Anthony that launched the Rebels.

And, please, do not forget the defense. The Blue Devils had 14 of their 23 turnovers in the first half and they averaged 17 for the entire game during the season.

Anthony scored 10 of his 13 points in the first half and had five steals for the game.

(above) As the nation's basketball attention turned to Denver in 1990, UNLV's Larry Johnson went to the basket in the semifinal game against Georgia Tech. The Runnin' Rebels raced to a 101–91 victory to advance to the finals.

(right) As the game wound down, the UNLV bench began its celebration with Jerry Tarkanian still coaching his players.

Anderson Hunt rose above the Duke defenders. Hunt led UNLV with 29 points, was named MOP, and, in the epic blowout of all the tournament years, helped defeat Duke, 103–73. For Duke, the stunning defeat may have provided special resolve. For the next two years, the Blue Devils won back-to-back championships.

Hurley, who logged only two free throws and three assists, was not the only Devil in the doldrums. His guard running mate, Phil Henderson, made just one of eight three-point attempts, committed six turnovers, and had no assists.

The Rebels had been through a lot to get to the championship—all sorts of off-court battles. But this victory cushioned the blows.

But on the court, they ruled—supremely, majestically. Larry Johnson and Stacey Augmon became all-Americans. Anthony and Hunt became highly complementary guards.

Tark did not have a set lineup in the regular season because of eligibility and sickness problems. The Rebels lost five

national semifinals. The Rebels overcame a 53–46 halftime deficit to win, 90–81.

It was another shootout. But the Rebels overcame everything thrown at them. Georgia Tech's Dennis Scott was launching bombs, scoring 20 of his 29 points in the first half. But at the half, the Rebels regrouped and came out with defense on their minds.

Georgia Tech did not score the first six minutes of the second half as Tarkanian reverted to his hangman's-noose man-to-man defense.

Yellow Jacket coach Bobby Cremins said, "The turning point came in the first five minutes [of the second half], when we seemed to lose our composure. They really

It didn't take long for Duke coach Mike Krzyzewski to change his scheme. But it was too late. The foundation was in place. The Rebels were off and running.

regular-season games, but down the stretch, they meshed, winning the Big West Conference regular-season and tournament titles.

Their NCAA championship trail began with a 102–72 romp over Arkansas–Little Rock in Salt Lake City. Yes, the first of the three 30-point blowouts. The Rebels then beat Ohio State, 76–65.

On to Oakland, California. And wouldn't you know it, the Rebels found trouble where they least expected. Ball State of Muncie, Indiana.

The Rebels missed the front end of three one-and-one free throws, the back end of a one-and-one, and the second of a two-shot intentional foul in the last two minutes, but still managed to win, 69–67. The Cardinals had a chance to win it, but Rebel center David Butler intercepted a weak pass inside just before the buzzer sounded.

Then came the awaited classic: two teams not afraid to run and gun, Nevada–Las Vegas and Loyola Marymount. But wouldn't Nevada–Las Vegas' defense be the difference here? Yes, it would. The Rebels won, 131–101 —the second of their 30-point victories.

After Loyola Marymount, it was on to the Final Four to face Georgia Tech in the

played defense on us. They got into our jocks and really got after us."

The pressure defense triggered the explosive offense. The Rebels put five players in double figures and they were in the finals.

Duke beat Arkansas, 97–83, to gain the other championship berth. Arkansas had made it to the Final Four with a defense the Razorbacks called "40 Minutes of Hell." Heck, that was just fine for the Devils. They shredded the Razorbacks with 54 percent shooting as Henderson scored a heavenly 28 points.

So it was Duke and Nevada–Las Vegas. And, once again, Duke was the runnerup. Four times the runnerup. And the first NCAA championship title for the 30–5 Rebels.

It was Johnson who said, "You can call us bad. You can call us thugs. You can call us hoodlums. But at the end of that, please, call us national champions, too." ∎

Bob Sands covered seven Final Fours while writing for the Kansas City Star, *the* Las Vegas Review-Journal, *the* Manhattan (Kansas) Mercury *and the* Evansville (Indiana) Courier and Press. *Sands is now retired from newspapers and is living in Las Vegas.*

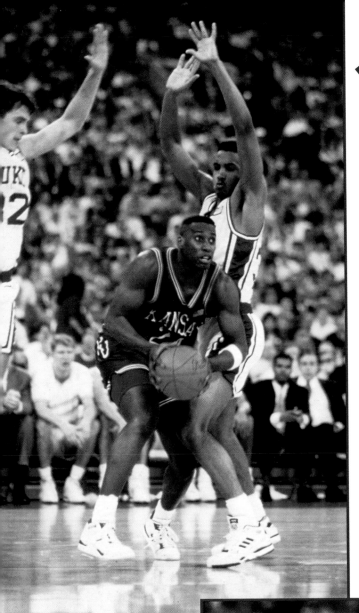

1991

DUKE IS KING

By Caulton Tudor

IT WAS ON THE NIGHT OF APRIL 1, 1991, THAT DUKE, having overthrown Nevada–Las Vegas two days earlier, finally was able to declare itself the king of collegiate basketball.

But was the NCAA championship clinched on that cool, windy night in Indianapolis, or did it actually occur way back on a humid afternoon in June of 1990?

Many Blue Devils, and virtually all of their fans, say the answer to that question is "both."

Certainly, the tangible evidence did not surface until the 72–65 win against Kansas in the Hoosier Dome was complete. That is what the official record will show—the win, and Grant Hill's antenna jam off a Bobby Hurley feed, and leg-dead Christian Laettner's 12 straight free throws, and Bill McCaffrey's 16 points off the bench, and Brian Davis' defense, and a dozen other things.

What the official Final Four record book will not show is that perhaps none of it would have happened if Mike Krzyzewski had not withdrawn his name from consideration for the Boston Celtics' coach search almost a year earlier.

"We wouldn't have been here without him," Laettner, the Final Four's Most Outstanding Player, said of Krzyzewski that night in Indianapolis. "What kind of team we would have been, I don't know. But we wouldn't have been anything like this, I know that."

In truth, the Blue Devils were not entirely anything like that as late as a week before the NCAA run began against Northeast Louisiana, Iowa, Connecticut, St. John's, and Nevada–Las Vegas, and culminated with Kansas.

Duke won those six games by an average margin of 14 points. But in its last game prior to the NCAA championship, the Blue Devils were reduced to shambles by archrival North Carolina, 96–74, in the championship game of the Atlantic Coast Conference Tournament in Charlotte, North Carolina.

"The low point of the season," Hurley recalled, a piece of one of the Hoosier Dome nets in one hand. "That was the lowest. You can't get lower than that."

On January 5, Duke began its Atlantic Coast Conference season with an 81–64 loss at Virginia. Eventually, the loss at Virginia and the ACC championship defeat to North Carolina brewed powerful incentive within the Blue Devils.

Following Virginia, Krzyzewski convened a practice session that ended with star freshman Grant Hill nursing a broken jaw and the remainder of the players united in a new mission.

"One of the things we learned that day was it's not good enough just to have some talent," Hurley said. "Talent's no good without the right kind of incentive."

Duke then won 12 of its next 13 games by an average margin of 20 points.

"During that stretch we saw our potential," Krzyzewski said. "The way the guys responded to that loss at Virginia made me feel very positive about what they could accomplish."

The storm ended with narrow losses at Wake Forest and Arizona. After three more wins, the complete collapse against North Carolina hit. Historically, the losing team in the ACC title game does not fare well in the NCAA championship, particularly teams that lose by an unsettling margin of 22 points.

But Duke was different.

(above) After disposing of **UNLV** in the semis, Duke faced Kansas in the championship game. The Jayhawks' Alonzo Jamison found himself boxed in the passing lanes as Grant Hill applied pressure. Duke took an early lead and kept control throughout for the 72–65 win.

(right) Duke's Grant Hill flies upcourt past Kansas guard Steve Woodberry during the title game in Indianapolis, Indiana.

"Losing that game like that didn't depress us," Hurley said. "It made us mad at ourselves. But it didn't depress us because we knew we'd been just that low before and had bounced back. We thought back to Virginia."

For the second time in one season, Duke recovered from a one-sided loss to play a brilliant stretch of basketball —one that would end three decades of Final Four frustrations.

"The ninth time's the charm," Laettner said, jokingly referring to eight previous Duke trips to the Final Four.

It was obvious from the opening tip in Saturday's semifinal against the Rebels that the Devils had no trouble forgetting the 103–73 humiliation they suffered a year earlier in Denver against Nevada–Las Vegas in the championship game.

Hurley was the most glaring difference. Older, tougher, and stronger, he did not wilt under the defensive heat that came from Nevada–Las Vegas' Anderson Hunt and Greg Anthony. Just the opposite, in fact. He flourished—12 points, nine assists, and only two turnovers.

And poetically, it was also Hurley who hit the biggest shot of the game, perhaps the biggest single shot in Duke

"We wouldn't have been here without him. What kind of team we would have been, I don't know. But we wouldn't have been anything like this, I know that."

—Christian Laettner
Center on Duke's 1991 championship team, on coach Mike Krzyzewski's impact

history to that point. Duke was behind 76–71 with less than three minutes to play when Hurley found himself with the ball and shooting room. His three-pointer put the outcome back in doubt, and maybe created some in the Rebels.

Whatever, Duke forced a turnover. Davis then drove the lane, hit a shot, was fouled, and converted the free throw. A free throw by Larry Johnson tied it at 77–77. Duke, on its last possession, went to Laettner. He was fouled with 12.7 seconds left, converted both chances, and after a long miss

by Hunt, Nevada–Las Vegas' undefeated season ended one game short of its target.

Duke celebrated in the most serious sort of way. But above the cheers and hugs, Krzyzewski could be heard screaming, "Our work's not finished! It's not finished!"

For artistic purposes, the Monday victory against Kansas paled. "I think players on both sides played a lot on guts," Krzyzewski said.

The Jayhawks, long-shots to go so far, were coming off an equally emotional semifinal win against North Carolina. "They had a little more left than we did," said Kansas star Mark Randall. "Not much, but a little." ■

Caulton Tudor has covered 22 Final Fours for the Raleigh News & Observer, *both as a basketball writer and a columnist. Selected to the National Basketball Writers Association Hall of Fame, he wrote a book about North Carolina State's 1983 championship team.*

1992

TWICE IS NICE

By Eddy Landreth

ONE YEAR LATER, MANY OF THE SAME DUKE players who had won the 1991 title sat in the locker room at the Minneapolis Metrodome, visibly exhausted, worn from a pressure-packed season of being No. 1, relieved their quest for a second title had come to an end.

"It took me a week to get over it," guard Thomas Hill said several months later.

No team since John Wooden's UCLA clubs (1967–1973) had won back-to-back titles. And when Duke completed its run, the Blue Devils understood why.

"I know how hard it is to win even one national championship," Hill said after Duke beat Michigan (71–51) for the title. "Then to win it back-to-back, that is incredible. I'm just sitting here in awe of our team and what we've gone through."

When the season began, the Blue Devils made it look easy. They rolled over most of their opponents in December and January by 20 or more points.

Their fastbreak resembled a high-wire act, with point guard Bobby Hurley tossing long, high lobs to Grant Hill. Except for reserve Greg Koubek and transfer Billy McCaffrey, Duke had returned all the key actors from the previous year. The experience showed. So did the confidence. The Blue Devils expected to win. They knew they would win.

Losing never entered their minds.

Then Hurley suffered a stress fracture in his foot during the Blue Devils' first game against North Carolina. Duke not only lost its first game of the season, but one of the two most important parts to its machine.

Then bad luck struck again. On the night Hurley returned to the lineup, Grant Hill missed the first of several games with a sprained ankle.

Somehow the Blue Devils persevered. They finished the regular season atop the Atlantic Coast Conference standings and headed to Charlotte for the Atlantic Coast Conference tournament to make their latest title official.

The ACC's recognized champion is the tournament winner. And for all seniors Christian Laettner and Brian Davis had accomplished, this one achievement had eluded them.

In addition, they had been embarrassed by archrival North Carolina the year before (96–74).

This time Duke breezed through with little resistance, resembling the team that had rolled across everyone at the beginning of the season as it beat North Carolina 94–74 to win the ACC championship.

"We played intelligently, aggressively," coach Mike Krzyzewski said.

With the preliminaries aside, Duke could now move on to the business of winning another national title.

"We're excited about the opportunity of doing something that's special, that's unique," said Krzyzewski. "I don't see where that should ever be perceived as pressure. What a fantastic opportunity for us. If we get beat, I hope somebody plays a great, great basketball game against us and we haven't defeated ourselves."

Kentucky almost made a prophet of Krzyzewski in the East regional final in Philadelphia. Just when it appeared Duke would run away with the game, the Wildcats found the resolve to come back.

They erased a 12-point Duke lead with a swarming full-court press, the kind of press that had been ineffective against the Blue Devils before.

With 2.2 seconds left in overtime, Kentucky's Sean Woods drove into the lane and flipped the ball over Laettner, off the glass and into the basket.

Timeout Duke.

With 2.1 seconds left, Kentucky led 103–102. History, it seemed, would have to wait for a repeat champion.

As his team gathered around, Krzyzewski assured his players they were going to win. Although the Blue Devils had great faith in their coach, Krzyzewski pushed the limits a bit on this occasion.

"Coach told us we were going to win," Hurley said. "I doubted him a little."

Grant Hill inbounded the ball. He threw a perfect, three-quarter court pass to Laettner. Kentucky coach Rick Pitino had stationed Deron Feldhaus behind Laettner and John Pelphrey as a rover at the free throw line. Pelphrey was supposed to break for the ball like a defensive back. Instead he allowed Laettner to catch it.

(above) A seemingly stoic Christian Laettner held aloft the victory net matter-of-factly. The senior had two championship rings, a place in the Blue Devils record book, and a video clip from a regional victory over Kentucky. That clip will be replayed at Final Fours for many years to come.

In Minneapolis' Hubert H. Humphrey Metrodome in 1992, Duke dominated Michigan for its second straight title. Bobby Hurley (No. 11) fired from three-point territory, but Christian Laettner, Grant Hill, and Thomas Hill shared in the scoring load.

of its first 16 field goals and led 29–21 at the outset. By the half, the margin stood at 42–37.

Perhaps Kentucky had beaten Duke after all.

Laettner, the savior against the Wildcats, went 1 of 6 from the field in the first half. He finished with just eight points.

Hurley, however, looked more like himself than he had since returning from his broken foot. He scored 26 points on 7 of 12 shooting.

As he had the year before, when he played all 80 minutes in the Final Four, Hurley made the difference.

The Hoosiers pulled to within 78–75 with 24.6 seconds left, but the Blue Devils hung on to advance to their third-straight championship game.

Michigan and its "Fab Five" freshmen had almost beaten Duke in a December game. The Blue Devils escaped with an 88–85 win. The memory of that game remained fresh in the minds of both teams.

"I think that served as a bit of a wake-up call," Hurley said. "We had some easy games and all of the sudden we were in a situation where we could have lost."

The two teams played the first half of the title game the way they had the waning moments of their December encounter. They were rarely separated by more than a point. But Laettner's poor play carried over from the Indiana game. He committed a career-high seven turnovers, went 2 of 8 from the field, and scored five points—in the first half.

Hurley exploded with a rare emotional outburst at halftime, ripping Laettner for his uninspired performance.

"Bobby doesn't speak out all that often," Lang said. "It sent chills down my spine to see Bobby do something like that. He said, 'I'm out there giving 110 percent. Why can't you give 110 percent?' "

Laettner responded as soon as the second half began. He scored on a driving layup—on an assist from Hurley—and sank a three-pointer on Duke's next possession.

The Blue Devils gradually pulled away, turning a close game into a rout. Their final game reflected their season, a hard-fought but successful struggle.

"This is the greatest year I've ever had as a coach," Krzyzewski said. "To beat such an outstanding team for the national championship, and Indiana, Seton Hall, and Kentucky in these last four games, makes it feel even better—like we deserve it." ■

With his back to the basket, Laettner faked to his right, dribbled once, spun left and released the ball with four-tenths of a second left in the game.

Woods lay face-down on the court, stunned as the scoreboard told the improbable story—Duke 104, Kentucky 103.

"All I could say for 10 minutes after the game was: 'This is unbelievable. This is unbelievable,' " Hurley said. "I asked (Duke associate coach) Pete Gaudet if I was alive or in a dream. He smacked me upside my head and said: 'You're alive.' "

So were the Blue Devils, thanks to Laettner.

Laettner finished 10 of 10 from the field, with one three-pointer, and 10 of 10 from the free throw line for 31 points.

"It was totally incredible," Laettner said. "I just thank God for giving me the opportunity to take the shot and win the game."

With just two games left, Krzyzewski decided his team needed a refresher course on defense. Unlike the previous season, when the Blue Devils played defense with a passion, the 1992 team had been offensive-minded. So with Indiana waiting ahead, Krzyzewski declared war in practice. The Blue Devils must play defense again.

"I asked (Duke associate coach) Pete Gaudet if I was alive or in a dream. He smacked me upside my head and said: 'You're alive.' "

—Bobby Hurley
Guard on Duke's 1992 championship team

"They were really rugged," Grant Hill said of the workouts. "Coach had to stop practice early because they were becoming too physical. People got bruised. Tony [Lang] got stitches [in his head]. Christian elbowed me in the mouth. I went up in the air for a dunk over Cherokee [Parks], and he undercut me and I landed on my butt.

"The Kentucky game showed us if we don't play defense, if we don't play tough, we can lose. So we just went out there and played hard."

Yet for all their desire and effort, the Blue Devils could not get going in the first half against Indiana. Indiana hit 12

Eddy Landreth is the sports editor of the Chapel Hill News *and a columnist for* ACC Today. *Covering ACC sports since 1987, he has covered Duke for the* Durham Herald-Sun *and college basketball for the* Charlotte Observer *and the* Winston-Salem Journal. *He also has written for* The Sporting News, Basketball Digest, *and* Basketball Weekly.

1993

A PICTURE OF PERFECTION

By Gary McCann

BEFORE THE SEASON BEGAN, NORTH Carolina coach Dean Smith gave each player a photo of the Superdome. It said, "North Carolina, 1993 NCAA Champions." It was taped in lockers and other places, never very far from sight and never out of mind.

"It's on the wall over my bed," said 7´0˝ center Eric Montross. "I was always looking at it, because throughout the season [getting to New Orleans] was our goal."

It was such a thrill that Montross, when the Tar Heels played a regular-season game in January against Louisiana State in the Superdome, got chills when the bus rolled past the mound of metal on Poydras Street.

"I'm going to carry that memory with me for a long time," Montross said.

Smith's photo was, if you will, a kind of paint-by-numbers blueprint for the Tar Heel season. Smith's goal each season was to have his team be a national contender.

But with archrival Duke winning back-to-back titles in 1991 and 1992, there was added incentive.

"By Duke being able to accomplish that," senior George Lynch said, "it has driven us. There is a lot of pride. If you are a player at Carolina, people expect you to win a national title."

From Montross in the middle, Donald Williams on the wing, Derrick Phelps on the point, and Henrik Rödl on the bench, there was only one goal.

"It would have been a disappointment not to get there," Lynch said. "We only had one dream. Get to New Orleans."

The trip wasn't without its bumps, bruises, and disappointments. Or its amazing performances. Down 21 to Florida State with 11:48 to play at home and behind 19 with 9:01 to play, North Carolina rallied for an 82–77 win.

The next time out, the Tar Heels went to Wake Forest and reached a turning point on their road to New Orleans. The Deacons ended an 11-game losing streak to the Tar Heels with an 88–62 blowout.

"That," Dean Smith said, "was our wake-up call."

Duke beat the Tar Heels three days later, giving them their longest losing streak of the season.

But Smith was pleased with the effort at Duke. His team was coming on. The offense began to click in February. And as was his custom, Smith met with each player at midseason to talk about his play.

One key conversation was between Smith and Rödl, the senior guard. The talk was about giving up the starting slot to Williams.

"It hurt not to start," Rödl said, "but Donald was coming on and the chemistry was working."

Phelps was a walking injury most of the season. Along the way he injured an ankle, elbow, foot, and back. He bruised his tailbone on a hard fall in the ACC Tournament semifinals and didn't play in the title game. North Carolina lost to Georgia Tech—it was the only goal the Tar Heels didn't reach.

Phelps played with pain throughout the NCAA championship, but when it came time to play hard, he somehow found the strength.

Williams' shooting ran hot and cold, until he got his act together in March and April when it mattered. Montross started slowly and peaked at the end. Forward Brian Reese limped around through half of the season, too, then played the best basketball of his career in the last 15 games.

Still, the Tar Heels were almost an afterthought when they joined blazing Kentucky, steady Kansas, and high-flying Michigan for the Final Four.

> ## "It would have been a disappointment not to get there. We only had one dream. Get to New Orleans."
>
> **—George Lynch**
> *Forward on North Carolina's 1993 championship team*

Kentucky ran through the regionals without a real test. Kansas, playing spectacular defense and getting excellent guard play from Adonis Jordan and Rex Walters, reached the Final Four for the second time in three seasons.And Michigan, riding those fabulous sophomores, moved to the Final Four for the second-straight season determined to complete the job it had failed to do against Duke in 1992.

North Carolina reached the regional semifinals after routs of East Carolina and Rhode Island. While the routs gave Phelps time to get healthier, they did not give the Tar Heels a test.

North Carolina erased an 11-point deficit in the first half of the East regional semifinal to beat Arkansas, 80–74. Williams scored North Carolina's final nine points to set the tone for what was to come in the next three games.

Cincinnati led by 15 in the first half of the regional final, with Nick Van Exel scoring 21 first-half points on 6 of 10 three-pointers.

But at halftime the Tar Heels made a switch. Phelps took Van Exel head to head without help.

He told his teammates, "He's mine."

Phelps, despite a sore tailbone and blisters, dogged Van Exel. Van Exel hit 1 of 11 shots in the second half, and North Carolina survived, 75–68,

(top) A memorable moment came when Smith's players insisted he cut the last strand of the net after the Tar Heels' championship win over Michigan.

(inset) But the game became notable for a moment when, with 11 seconds left, the Wolverines' Chris Webber (inset) called a timeout when Michigan had none left. Coach Steve Fisher asked him why, but it was too late—two technical shots by Donald Williams wrapped up the Carolina victory.

North Carolina's George Lynch slam-dunked in the first half of the championship game against Michigan. The game see-sawed with bench strategies providing intrigue to go with spectacular plays.

the Jayhawks were still hanging around despite 40 percent shooting. North Carolina led, 68–65.

At a time when it appeared the Tar Heels might be content to run some clock, Phelps lofted a looping pass to Williams running down the right wing.

He pulled up and swished a three-pointer from the right of the key.

"Every player has to know his role," Williams said. "Coach has told me that's the best time to take a three. The other team is trapping and we can usually get good rebounding position. I wanted to take it."

Williams finished with 25 points, making 7 of 11 shots, including 5 of 7 threes.

While the Tar Heels were getting past Kansas, Michigan was beating Kentucky, 81–78, in overtime. Like the Tar Heels, the Wolverines, who had lost to Duke in the 1992 finals, had pointed toward the Superdome all season. Anything less than a title, they said, would not be worth the trip.

The Wolverines had won the Rainbow Classic in December, beating North Carolina in the second round, 79–78, on a follow shot by Jalen Rose at the buzzer. The Wolverines played that game without Ray Jackson, who had injured a shoulder.

"I just hope it's a close game like it was in Hawaii," Smith said.

It was close and more. It was a game of runs early. It was physical inside with Montross, Lynch, and Reese battling Chris Webber, Juwan Howard, and Jackson.

North Carolina led early, but the Wolverines put together a spurt to take a 23–13 lead. North Carolina fought back to tie it at 25 and took a 42–36 halftime lead.

With 4:12 to play, Jimmy King hit a perimeter jumper to put Michigan ahead, 67–63. But the Tar Heels had gone to an effective zone defense, and Smith liberally went to his deep bench, using 37 subs in the final 20 minutes.

And Donald Williams continued his remarkable string of bailing out the Tar Heels, hitting his fifth three-pointer of the night with 3:50 left to cut the lead to one.

On his way to another 25-point night and the Final Four Most Outstanding Player award, Williams had 12 points in the last seven minutes.

Two quick missed three-point shots by Michigan opened the door, and North Carolina barged in. Phelps scored on a drive, Lynch hit a difficult shot over Howard, and the Tar Heels led 70–67. When Rose tried to drive into the teeth of North Carolina's defense, Montross knocked the ball away to Williams.

After a timeout and two Michigan fouls to get North Carolina into the one-and-one, Montross slipped behind the Michigan defense, took a pass from Lynch, and slammed home a five-point lead.

The Tar Heels had run off nine unanswered points.

"Basketball is a game of runs," Williams said. "We were playing good on offense and told each other to concentrate on stopping them on defense."

It almost backfired.

A basket by Jackson, a North Carolina turnover, and a follow shot by Webber cut the lead to 72–71 with 30 seconds left.

But the game's turning point came with 46 seconds left, although Michigan didn't know it at the time. Coach Steve Fisher had used his last timeout.

With 20 seconds left, North Carolina's Pat Sullivan made the front end of a one-and-one. Webber rebounded the second shot and headed up court. He dribbled hard to the corner where Lynch and Phelps turned him into a defensive sandwich right in front of the Michigan bench.

With nowhere to go, no shot to take, and no passing angle, Webber called time.

"I just called timeout," Webber said. "It was one we didn't have. It probably cost our team the game."

It was a bizarre ending to a superb game.

"Chris said he heard someone holler to call timeout," Fisher said. "We talked about not having any timeouts [during the timeout with 46 seconds left], but apparently we didn't make it clear."

With 11 seconds left, it was up to Williams to finish off the title. Standing there with no other players around him in the cavernous Superdome, he hit both shots of the technical.

Fouled with eight seconds to go, Williams made two more free throws.

"I never could have imagined this," Williams said. "Every kid dreams about making the game-winning shot, but last year [during an up and down freshman year] this didn't seem possible."

North Carolina won its second NCAA title in the Superdome, the other coming in 1982. And like that 1982 game, when Georgetown's Fred Brown threw a pass to James Worthy in the final six seconds, the ending left some people wondering about what might have happened if Webber hadn't called time.

"Say we're lucky, yes," Smith said. "I've always said you have to be lucky to win the NCAA championship. Say we're fortunate. But it still says we're national champions." ■

in overtime. Williams, finishing with 20 points, had two crucial three-pointers in the extra period.

"We're where we want to be," Montross said, "but we're not finished yet."

The national semifinal matchup against Kansas sent Smith against his former assistant coach, Roy Williams. Both quickly defused thoughts that the game was Dean versus Roy or that the teams were mirror images of each other.

While the two were almost evenly matched in New Orleans, North Carolina won, 78–68, thanks to superior size in the middle.

And Donald Williams.

For the third-straight game, the 6´3˝ sophomore knocked down a crucial three-point shot. With 2:48 left,

Gary McCann was a writer at the Greensboro News & Record *when he covered the 1993 tournament.*

1994

DUKE PROVES NO HAZARD TO HOGS' TITLE RUN

By Bob Holt

AFTER THE ARKANSAS RAZORBACKS BEAT Michigan, 76–68, in Dallas to win the 1994 NCAA Midwest Regional, exchanged high-fives with President Clinton, and cut down the nets, their Reunion Arena locker room seemed strangely subdued.

No one threw a bucket of ice water on coach Nolan Richardson. There were smiles, but no whooping or hollering. If you had walked in and didn't know better, you might have thought the Hogs had just beaten Alabama or LSU or another one of their Southeastern Conference foes.

"We've still got something to prove," sophomore forward Scotty Thurman said. "We want to play the last game of the season—and win it."

The Razorbacks did, thanks to Thurman's last-second heroics. His three-point basket with 50 seconds remaining in the game broke a 70–70 tie and propelled Arkansas to a 76–72 victory over Duke for the Hogs' first NCAA basketball championship.

Thurman now has a place in Final Four history, along with players such as Michael Jordan and Keith Smart, whose last-second shots lifted North Carolina (1982) and Indiana (1987) to national titles.

The Hogs followed presidential orders in putting the ball in Thurman's hands.

"I kept screaming to get the ball to Thurman," said Clinton, the former Arkansas governor and unabashed Razorback fan, who watched the game from a Charlotte Coliseum skybox. "He's a tremendous clutch player."

Thurman, who during the season hit game-winning three-pointers at Tennessee and LSU, saw the 35-second shot clock tick down to three seconds as junior point guard Corey Beck passed the ball to junior center Dwight Stewart.

Stewart, who hit 11 of 20 three-pointers in the NCAA tournament but was 0 of 5 against Duke, was looking for a game-winning three of his own when he caught Beck's pass at the top of the key. But Stewart fumbled the ball, so he passed it to Thurman on the wing.

"When the ball came to me," Thurman said, "I felt like the shot clock was going to run out. I had no choice but to put up the shot."

And Thurman figured he was due, considering he had missed his previous two attempts from the field.

"In practice, I hate it when I miss three in a row," he said. "I knew in the game I had missed my last two, so it was time to hit one."

Thurman's shot barely got over Duke forward Antonio Lang.

"His whole body was in my face," Thurman said.

Replays showed Lang's outstretched arm missed the ball by an inch or two.

"I still don't know how it went in," Lang said. "I was right there and I thought I could tip it. Obviously, I didn't get a hand on it. We've made big shots to win games. I guess it was just Arkansas' turn to make a big shot."

The Blue Devils still had a chance to win their third NCAA championship in four years, but sophomore guard Chris Collins missed a three-pointer with 37 seconds left. The Razorbacks then clinched the victory with free throws by junior guards Clint McDaniel and Alex Dillard.

Arkansas overcame a 13–0 Duke run that put the Blue Devils ahead, 48–38, with 17 minutes to play. Richardson called timeout to rally the Razorbacks.

"Our guys know the fat lady hasn't sung with 17 minutes to play," Richardson said. "It's all about being on a mission."

Richardson told his players three things: "One, we were taking too many early shots; two, I wanted Big Nasty [all-American sophomore forward Corliss Williamson] to touch the ball before we took a shot; and three—most important—I told them they'd better get their butts after it on defense. We did all three."

The Razorbacks, who were led by Williamson's 23 points, tied the game at 52 and moved ahead, 62–57, but Duke came back to tie the game, 70–70, on All-American senior forward Grant Hill's three-point basket with 1:29 to play.

"That was a heavyweight championship bout," Richardson said. "My turn, your turn. My turn, your turn. My turn."

(above) Corey Beck took a rebound, leaped high, and passed back outside to restart the offense. Arkansas had been rated No. 1 in the nation for nine weeks during the regular season, but proof came in Charlotte, North Carolina, with the Razorbacks' number one fan in attendance: President Bill Clinton.

(right) Duke senior Grant Hill kept his team alive, tying the game with less than two minutes to go on a three-point play. Hill ended his Duke career as an all-time great in college basketball.

Arkansas coach Nolan Richardson yelled instructions from the bench.

Arkansas' Corliss Williamson went up for a close-up jumper as Duke's Cherokee Parks fell backward to the floor in a key second-half run by the Razorbacks. Williamson's 34 points and commanding play earned him the Most Outstanding Player award as Arkansas claimed the national title.

Duke coach Mike Krzyzewski said it was hard to be disappointed.

"It was a great game," he said. "Everybody won and nobody lost."

The Hogs held Hill to 12 points on 4 of 11 shooting from the field.

"Hill is their workhorse, and we tried to keep pestering him," Richardson said. "I think fatigue set in."

Several Razorbacks alternated guarding Hill.

"Every time I looked up," he said, "they had a different guy on me."

Arkansas was ranked No. 1 for nine weeks during the regular season, twice as long as any other team, and finished 31–3, including 14–2 in the Southeastern Conference to win its second regular-season conference title in three years.

Williamson was voted the Final Four's Most Outstanding Player by the media and was joined on the all–Final Four team by teammates Beck and Thurman, and the Blue Devils' Lang and Hill.

Arkansas advanced to the championship game for the first time in five Final Four appearances with a 91–82 victory over Arizona in the semifinals.

The Wildcats led 67–62 with 8:02 to play, but the Razorbacks then applied their full-court pressure defense and went on a 12–0 run in a 2:04 span to move ahead 74–67 to take control of the game.

"That wasn't 40 minutes of hell," said Richardson, referring to his catch phrase to describe Arkansas' intense style. "That was eight minutes of torture. We had to go for the jugular at that point. We had no choice."

Williamson finished with 29 points, 13 rebounds, and five assists.

"My teammates challenged me to take over," Williamson said, "and I love it when somebody makes a challenge to me."

When Williamson was double-teamed, he was able to find his teammates for baskets.

"He did a good job of finding the open people," Arizona coach Lute Olson said. "Most players lose their poise when they're doubled, but he didn't."

"That was eight minutes of torture. We had to go for the jugular at that point. We had no choice."

—Nolan Richardson
Coach of Arkansas' 1994 championship team

North Carolina A&T made things interesting in the Hogs' first-round game at Oklahoma City, but the Razorbacks used a late 18–2 run to pull away for a 94–79 victory.

Arkansas then literally fought off Georgetown— Thurman was ejected in the first half when he went on the court to try to break up a scuffle that broke out—85–73 by hitting 61.4 percent from the field, a season-high by a Hoyas' opponent.

The Razorbacks advanced to familiar territory in Dallas, where they used to dominate the Southwest Conference tournament and also where they had won the 1990 Midwest regional to advance to the Final Four in Denver.

Tulsa took Arkansas to overtime in a regular-season matchup before the Hogs won, 93–91, on Williamson's short jumper. At Reunion Arena, however, the Golden Hurricane was no match for the Razorbacks, who won, 103–84, with Thurman and Williamson scoring 21 points each.

Arkansas then denied Michigan a third consecutive Final Four trip by making all the key plays in the last five minutes to win, 76–68. Williamson was held to 12 points but served as a decoy much of the game, allowing Thurman and McDaniel to combine to hit 7 of 14 three-point attempts and Robinson to score on the inside. The 6´11˝ freshman center tallied 14 points and was named to the Midwest Regional all-championship team.

It was a big day for Richardson, who before the game was named the Naismith National Coach of the Year and after the victory gave Clinton a high-five and then hugged the president. ∎

Bob Holt covers Arkansas from Fayetteville for the Arkansas Democrat-Gazette *and has written of the Razorbacks' trips to the Final Four in 1990, 1994, and 1995.*

1995

BRUINS ADD AN 11ᵀᴴ TITLE TO LEGACY

By Bud Withers

IT HAS HAPPENED BEFORE, AND IT HAPPENED TO UCLA and its coach, Jim Harrick. The winning of an NCAA basketball championship confers a glory onto its perpetrators far beyond the simple acts that may decide it—a missed shot, a fluky rebound, a hairline call on a foul.

So, too, with UCLA in 1995. This had been a team and a coach that couldn't seem to fulfill reasonable expectations, let alone the ones attached to the Bruins' outlandish 10 national championships in the sixties and seventies under John Wooden.

UCLA had bottomed out of the tournament just a year before, giving up 112 points to Tulsa to lose in the first round. In 1991, again in the first, a 13ᵗʰ-seeded Penn State team dropped the Bruins.

Meanwhile, Harrick had made an intemperate remark in 1992, to the effect that if people wanted big-time results, he needed to be paid like Lute Olson or Denny Crum.

But all that seemed to wash away with UCLA's ascent to the championship. In coaching his first Final Four team, Harrick gracefully handled the press inquiries about being a successor to Wooden. And his team got not only extraordinary play, but leadership from three seniors—Ed O'Bannon, Tyus Edney, and George Zidek—plus contributions from some freshmen like J. R. Henderson and Toby Bailey who were just happy to be a part of things.

UCLA's first-round opponent, Florida International, had made the tournament, despite an 11–18 record, by winning the Trans America Athletic Conference tournament. Its coach, former Mississippi and Texas coach Bob Weltlich, had already announced his resignation.

UCLA put to rest any notions of a Cinderella run by the Golden Panthers, breaking to a 20-point half-time lead and coasting to a 92–56 victory. Henderson had 16 points and Charles O'Bannon 14, but the game was more notable for every Bruin playing at least six minutes and the postgame jocularity of Weltlich, who said, "If anybody knows of any jobs out there, my number is . . ."

There was little to suggest UCLA would have any serious difficulty negotiating Missouri and thereby move on to Oakland, where it would have a big following in the regional.

What evolved was a game for the ages. Missouri took the fight straight to the Bruins, leading 42–34 at halftime, UCLA's largest deficit at the break all season. A familiar Bruin run in the second half seemed to make them comfortable, up six, but with Tiger guard Paul O'Liney having an unconscious shooting afternoon (9 of 13, 5 of 6 treys for 23 points), Missouri scratched ahead, 74–73, with 4.8 seconds left. The go-ahead basket came on guard Kendrick Moore's dish to Julian Winfield under the hoop.

All that remained were 4.8 of the most riveting seconds in NCAA history. Cameron Dollar, the UCLA guard, inbounded to Tyus Edney and could only watch and implore silently, "Go, Tyus, go."

Edney wound a behind-the-back dribble that redirected him to the right. Ed O'Bannon, the All-American forward, shoved Winfield to clear space for himself. Still, Edney kept motoring.

"When I got around the free-throw line, I saw an opening," he said. "No guys were coming to take me."

Finally, Edney encountered Missouri forward Derek Grimm as he hurtled toward the goal from the right. Grimm raised his arms dead vertical, intent on not fouling. Edney cast up sort of a half-hook, half-layup, half-prayer from five feet away. It kissed the backboard and hit net just about the time the horn sounded.

After UCLA mobbed Edney and fell into delirium, the little guard remembered having seen Danny Ainge's five-second court-length drive to beat Notre Dame by one in a regional semifinal game in 1981.

"I've seen clips of that," said Edney. "I knew it could be done."

In Oakland, they simply dismantled a good Mississippi State team that had won both at Arkansas and Kentucky. The Bulldogs couldn't match the Bruins' athleticism and facility for the running game, and UCLA won, 86–67, after having a 65–29 lead midway through the second half.

(above) Ed O'Bannon took control of the game in the second half, driving past Arkansas' Corliss Williamson on the way to the basket and to the Most Outstanding Player award.

(right) Arkansas center Dwight Stewart tries to get around O'Bannon during first-half action in Seattle's Kingdome.

O'Bannon works both sides of the camera following his team's national championship victory over Arkansas. O'Bannon's 30-point, 17-rebound effort led the Bruins to the 89–78 victory.

For coach Jim Harrick, the hugs on the bench at game's end were special.

That gave the Bruins a berth in the regional final against Connecticut, a team that earlier had been No. 1–ranked, and one seen as being as good—perhaps even better—at the running game.

But UCLA thought it detected a flaw in the Huskies' defense against the break, and the Bruins continually took advantage with edges in numbers. At the finish, it was 102–96, UCLA, and the Bruins had made their deepest push into the tournament since their runnerup finish to Louisville in 1980.

The national semifinal game featured two programs of extreme contrast. It was the Bruins, most of them from frenetic Los Angeles or nearby, against Oklahoma State's 7´ Bryant "Big Country" Reeves, pride of Gans, Oklahoma. It was UCLA's preference for the fast pace against the Cowboys' grinding, half-court approach.

"We've played that tempo before," insisted Dollar, the UCLA back-up point guard. "We know how."

It was 37–37 at halftime, and the Cowboys were playing at their speed. UCLA edged out by eight in the second half,

Harrick had asked the bus driver returning them to the hotel from a practice to detour to the Kingdome, just to send a little message.

but midway through it, Reeves led Oklahoma State back to within 50–49.

Soon, it became Edney's game again. He drove for a layup around Reeves for a 64–61 UCLA lead with a little more than two minutes left, and the Bruins sealed an uneasy 74–61 victory with 10 free throws down the stretch.

Edney finished with 21 points and five assists. Little did the Bruins—and those anticipating a drag-race Arkansas-UCLA final game—know that his work in the tournament was done.

On a hell-bent drive to the basket against the Cowboys, Edney had fallen hard after an Oklahoma State foul. He played

effectively the rest of the day, but that night, his right wrist swelled up, and while his Bruin teammates attended press conferences on Sunday, he was at the University of Washington, getting treatment for a sprain.

Belatedly, Edney was on the floor Monday night for warmups, but it was obvious he could not use the wrist. As if Arkansas, the defending national champion with the breakneck speed and the wilting pressure, needed any favors.

Edney started the game, but it was a courtesy. He played three minutes, and it was apparent he could not go. Dollar replaced him and was immediately stripped of the ball for a layup by the Hogs' Clint McDaniel.

"When I first came out there," admitted Dollar, "I was a little tense."

After an early 10–0 Arkansas blitz led to a 12–5 lead, Dollar and the Bruins—now only six deep in proven players—began warming to the game. UCLA beat the Razorbacks downcourt for points, and Dollar was increasingly pressure-proof.

UCLA led 40–39 at halftime and quickly assumed control after the break. Ed O'Bannon, who had a dynamite game, powered in a rebound basket, and with 16 minutes left, the Bruins led by eight.

There was one frail moment, when UCLA led only 67–63 with eight minutes left and Scotty Thurman, hero of the 1994 championship, cast up a long trey attempt for Arkansas. It bounded in and out, and UCLA nursed the lead back to eight with 4:06 left.

Whereas Bailey, the UCLA freshman guard, had been frustrated by the methodic Oklahoma State game, he was unshackled against Arkansas, scoring 26 points, including one emphatic, stratospheric slam that found its way to sports pages across the nation.

Ed O'Bannon was magnificent, with 30 points and 17 rebounds. The other component was UCLA's defense—center Zidek and no small amount of help—on Arkansas' 6´7˝, 250-pound All-American Corliss Williamson, held to a 3 of 16 shooting night.

The Bruins thus completed circles. Edney had done so much to get them here, and now they finished his labor. Ed O'Bannon, the Final Four Most Outstanding Player, had begun his college career with a significant knee injury, and he ended it by kneeling to kiss the Kingdome court.

And there was Harrick, once considered too small a coach for this job. He now seemed much larger, his place in history, and his team's, cemented. ■

Bud Withers has covered Northwest college sports for many years, first on the staff of the Eugene (Oregon) Register-Guard *and most recently at the* Seattle Times.

1996

KENTUCKY CATS REACH PINNACLE WITH SIXTH TITLE

By Rick Bozich

THIS IS WHAT THEY WERE SAYING ABOUT THE University of Kentucky basketball team before the Wildcats touched down in the 1996 NCAA Final Four at Continental Airlines Arena: Can't win the big one. Haven't done anything remarkable in the Final Four since Jack "Goose" Givens was golden and Kyle Macy was wiping his socks at the free throw line in 1978. You can depend upon the Wildcats to turn in one performance that gets them beat.

This is what they were saying about Kentucky coach Rick Pitino before he took a team into the Final Four for the third time since 1987: Can't win the big one. Didn't do anything remarkable in the Final Four with Providence in 1987 or with the Wildcats in 1993. Makes you wonder if you can win a championship playing his trademark shoot-the-three, press, press, press style.

This is what they were saying about a Kentucky team that started the season ranked first in the nation and carried that No. 1 ranking for part of the season: the preseason favorite rarely wins the title anymore. Too much pressure. Too many worry lines caused by all the expectations. Better to slip through a side door and get the job done when nobody is expecting perfection. Anything but that preseason kiss-of-death No. 1 ranking, please.

Then the Kentucky basketball team, the seventh team Pitino put together in Lexington, went to East Rutherford, New Jersey. They dispatched Massachusetts, one of two teams to defeat them during the regular season, 81–74, in the national semifinals. Then they outlasted, outplayed, and outfought Syracuse, 76–67, in the championship game.

They won Kentucky's sixth national title and Pitino's first. They answered all the questions, all the skeptics, and all troubles.

A great team that had a great time—beginning in August 1995, when this Kentucky team was put together during a preseason trip to Italy. That's where the Wildcats learned that Anthony Epps would emerge as the team's point guard, that senior guard Tony Delk would be unstoppable on the perimeter, that sophomore forward Antoine Walker would emerge as Pitino's go-to guy, that senior Walter McCarty could play forward or center, that center Mark Pope, the team's third senior, would step forward as a dependable leader, and that all the other important pieces would fit together.

It was in Italy, where the Wildcats won four of five games, that Pitino experimented with a variety of lineups. It was also in Italy where Pitino showed the valuable ability to deflect the expectations that had started building upon his team moments after the Wildcats had been upset by North Carolina in the championship game of the 1995 Southeast regional in Birmingham, Alabama.

They started the year in mid-November holding the nation's No. 1 ranking and then rallying from an 11-point deficit to defeat Maryland, 96–84, at the Hall of Fame Tip-Off Classic in Springfield, Massachusetts.

So much for perfection. The Wildcats lost the top ranking the next time they played. All-American center Marcus Camby stopped them with a 32-point, nine-rebound performance, leading Massachusetts to a 92–82 upset victory in Auburn Hills, Michigan. What was surely a jarring moment for Kentucky fans turned out to be the best thing Pitino could have written into the Wildcats' script. Just ask him if the defeat helped him get the attention of his players.

"If we win that game, we don't win the national championship," Pitino said after the season. "That loss taught us more about our team than any win on our schedule."

They would not be beaten again until they faced Mississippi State in the championship game of the SEC tournament at the Louisiana Superdome. That 84–73 Mississippi State victory reminded the nation of two things—that Mississippi State was supremely talented, which the Bulldogs proved by winning the Southeast regional and making the Final Four; and that Kentucky was guaranteed nothing when the 64-team tournament field was finally announced.

The Wildcats began their tournament run at Reunion Arena in Dallas. Getting 24 points from McCarty, 22 from Delk, and non-stop applause from mega-fan actress and Kentucky alum Ashley Judd, the Wildcats inflated a 47–41 halftime lead into a 110–72 victory over San Jose State. It

(above) Kentucky guard Anthony Epps passes back outside with Syracuse forward Jason Cipolla defending during the 1996 championship game in the Meadowlands Arena in East Rutherford, New Jersey. Kentucky defeated Syracuse, 76–67.

(right) As the Wildcat team circled around, Rick Pitino (second from right) accepted the 1996 trophy

Kentucky guard Tony Delk puts one up over University of Massachusetts guard Edgar Padilla during their semifinal game won by the Wildcats, 81–74.

was Walker, with 21 points and 11 rebounds, who carried the Wildcats past Virginia Tech, 84–60, in the second round, providing clues that every night there would be another hero.

In Minneapolis, where the Wildcats met Utah and All-American forward Keith Van Horn in the semifinals of the Midwest regional at the Metrodome, it was time for Epps to prove precisely how underrated he was. Epps drilled three three-point field goals, and Derek Anderson added 18 points as the Wildcats spurted away from the Utes for a 56–34 halftime lead and a 101–70 victory. "If we played them 90 more games, we would probably lose 89 more times," Utah coach Rick Majerus said.

Now the world wondered if Wake Forest, which had edged Louisville in the Midwest semifinals, was the team that could stop Kentucky. The Demon Deacons were led by All-American center Tim Duncan. Camby had destroyed the Wildcats around the basket in November. Maybe Duncan could do the same thing in March.

Wrong. Wrong. Wrong.

Duncan shook loose for only three field-goal attempts in the first half. He made only 2 of 7 shots all afternoon. Kentucky raced to a 38–19 lead and cruised over the ACC tournament champs, 83–63. This time it was Delk's turn to blaze, and he

"If we win that game, we don't win the national championship. That loss taught us more about our team than any win on our schedule."

—Rick Pitino
Coach of Kentucky's 1996 championship team

torched the Demon Deacons with 25 points. For that he was named the Most Outstanding Player in the regional.

Finally, the Final Four. As fate scripted it, another crack at Massachusetts, which met Kentucky in the second national semifinal game after Syracuse defeated Mississippi State.

This time Kentucky showed it had learned how to defend Camby. He scored only eight points in the first half, making only 3 of 9 shots. Camby finished with 25, but many of them came after the Wildcats surged to a 15-point lead in the second half.

Massachusetts cut Kentucky's lead to 63–60, but the Wildcats pushed their lead back to 68–60. Minuteman guard Edgar Padilla hit a 22-foot jumper to pull Massachusetts within

73–70 in the final minute and a half. But two free throws by Pope and a slam by Walker gave Kentucky an 81–74 victory—and its date with destiny. Once again it was Delk delivering a team-high 20 points, even though he missed more than two minutes with leg cramps.

"We made a couple of turnovers down the stretch that I wish we wouldn't have made, but we maintained our composure," Epps said. "The key was that we had confidence in each other that we would win the game."

In the championship game, it was something old and something new that carried the Wildcats to their first national title in 18 years. Something old was Delk. The veteran guard from Brownsville, Tennessee, delivered six three-point shots in the first half, pushing Kentucky to a 42–33 halftime lead. Something new was Ron Mercer, a freshman forward from Nashville. He came off the bench to score a career-high 20 points and help Kentucky withstand a furious rally by Syracuse, which rode the 29 points and 10 rebounds of rugged senior forward John Wallace.

In fact, the Orangemen cut Kentucky's lead to 64–62 with 4:46 to play. But McCarty came through with a follow-up, and Anderson drained a three.

Although the Wildcats shot only 38 percent from the field, they made 12 of 27 three-point shots, getting seven from Delk and three from Mercer.

"Not that many players get that many open looks," said Delk, who was also named the Most Outstanding Player of the Final Four. "If I wasn't penetrating and looking for them, it wouldn't have been possible. But when you shoot so many threes in practice and you're open, you take them. That's the way we play."

"We won our last two games in an untypical Kentucky style," Pitino said. "We just bumped and grinded it out."

Kentucky's average victory margin in six NCAA games was 21.5 points, fourth-best in NCAA history. Their 89.17 scoring average ranked as the sixth-best in tournament history. And the 34–2 record reigned as the school's best since the 1953–1954 squad finished 25–0.

"There was an incredible amount of pressure on us, but that just made it even sweeter to win it all," reserve guard Jeff Sheppard said. "Everyone expected us to win it, and we did." ■

Rick Bozich has covered Final Fours since his days as a student and writer for the Indiana student newspaper. At the Louisville Courier-Journal, *he has covered many sports and is now a sports columnist.*

1997

ARIZONA CATS CRADLE FIRST NCAA TITLE

By Corky Simpson

FAITH SLAM-DUNKED THE SKEPTICS AT THE 1997 NCAA Division I Men's Basketball Championship. Not once, mind you, but three times.

Arizona, perhaps the most unlikely champion ever, became the first team to defeat three No. 1 seeds when it upset tradition-rich Kentucky, 84–79 in overtime at the RCA Dome in Indianapolis.

It gave Arizona a national championship in its third advance to the Final Four under coach Lute Olson. The others were in 1988 and 1994.

Nobody could have predicted it.

Nothing about the Wildcats' trip to the tournament gave the slightest hint they would proceed through the championship. But like a fierce summer wind burning across the Sonoran Desert, Olson's kids made believers of a nation of basketball fanatics.

Kansas, the No. 1–ranked team in the nation, fell to these Wildcats on March 21 at the Birmingham-Jefferson Civic Center in Alabama. Clawing their way to the Final Four, the Wildcats then toppled North Carolina. And in the title game, they beat their more illustrious Wildcat opponent, Kentucky, in overtime. Just like that! Three top seeds fell to a bunch of sprouts.

Arizona started a freshman point guard (Mike Bibby), a sophomore center (A. J. Bramlett), and three juniors (shooting guard Miles Simon, wingman Michael Dickerson, and power forward Bennett Davison).

"This is one tough group of Cats," said Olson, his famous silver thatch of hair hidden by a "National Champions" ball cap slightly askew. "All along, we tried to impress upon them that the strongest will survive, that the toughest group of players out there would get the job done."

The final game was a microcosm of the season.

(above) Arizona guard Mike Bibby shoots a jumper over Kentucky center Nazr Mohammed as two teams of Wildcats clawed for the championship.

(right) The moment of celebration was sweet for junior guard Miles Simon, who left the court with the game ball—not officially awarded—and the Most Outstanding Player award, which was official.

There was a point when it looked as if the Arizona bubble might burst. Kentucky had forced overtime when Anthony Epps hit a three-pointer with 13 seconds left. Shots by Simon and Bibby had rimmed out.

"When Kentucky tied it up, though, I looked in everybody's eyes and I knew we'd come up with a victory," said Arizona guard Jason Terry, one of the best sixth men in America.

"Coach Olson told us that the strong would survive."

Only three and a half weeks earlier, though, there were those who wondered if Arizona would even be invited to the championship. The Wildcats were 19–9 and had just lost both games on a trip to the San Francisco Bay Area, 81–80 at Stanford and 79–77 at California. But Olson saw things differently.

"Those are two very tough teams, extremely hard to beat on their home courts," he said. "We had chances to win both games, and I think that's a 'positive' we can take into the postseason."

Just the same, the losses dropped Arizona to fifth place in the Pacific-10 Conference, with an 11–7 record. Ahead of the Wildcats in the final standings were champion UCLA (15–3) and three schools who tied for second place with 12–6 records, Stanford, California, and Southern California.

Simon, the soul if not the heart of the team, had sat out the first 11 games, on academic suspension. When the team rolled up an 8–3 record during that time, at least one media critic, wandering down an unpaved side road, speculated that the Wildcats might be better off without Simon. Olson laughed out loud at the suggestion. Simon went on to become the NCAA championship's Most Outstanding Player.

For Arizona in 1997, the way to the NCAA Tournament was nowhere near as amazing as the stay there. The "toughness" Olson spoke of was never more evident than in the opening round, against a splendid South Alabama team. With less than four minutes left in that first-round game, Arizona trailed South Alabama by 10 points. Somehow, the Wildcats rallied to win, 65–57.

From that point on, there was no stopping Olson's version of the "Desert Swarm" a nickname given to a particularly rugged Arizona football team earlier in the decade.

College of Charleston, a fearsome bunch of outstanding athletes, followed South Alabama. But Arizona won again at The Pyramid in Memphis, 73–69.

Kentucky center Jamaal Magloire has his shot blocked by Arizona forward Michael Dickerson during the first half of Arizona's 84–79 overtime win.

Then came the upset that stunned the nation: Arizona's 85–82 victory over top-ranked Kansas. If it wasn't the biggest win in the history of Arizona basketball, it was the greatest effort.

Kansas trailed by 13 with 3:28 remaining but put on a finishing kick that cut Arizona's lead to a single point, 83–82, with 21 seconds left. But a pair of free throws by Bibby, the coolest and probably best Wildcat freshman since Sean Elliott, clinched the shocking upset.

"This wasn't the biggest win," Olson said, perhaps prophetically. "The biggest win is the one that gets you to the Final Four."

Two nights later, Arizona toppled a rugged, physical Providence team, 96–92, and advanced to the Final Four. North Carolina fell on March 29, 66–58, setting up the national championship game against the Kentucky Wildcats.

"It is Lute's vision that has built the program," Thompson said.

"I went with him from Iowa, and when we first got to Tucson, honestly, I could not believe a program could be so terrible. I remember going with Lute to dormitories and fraternities, trying to get support from the students. When we first got there, people looked at us like we were crazy when we told them what our goals were. They told us they took recruits to hockey games rather than basketball games, because there was some excitement at hockey. The Arizona baseball team always drew more fans than basketball. The first season, at our games, there couldn't have been more than three thousand people in an arena that seats nearly fifteen thousand.

"Lute and I looked at each other like, 'What did we get ourselves into?' Now look at it: national champions!"

> ## "When we talk with the team on what makes champions, the first thing we discuss is family. Trust is the second, and team-support is right there, too."
> **—Lute Olson**
> *Coach of Arizona's 1997 championship team*

Cornell coach Scott Thompson, a long-time assistant to Olson, said he thought Arizona's national championship began one cold, dismal night 14 years earlier, in Kansas City. Olson was coaching Iowa at the time and Thompson was on his staff.

The Hawkeyes had just lost a heartbreaker to Villanova, 55–54, in the Sweet 16 at Kemper Arena in Kansas City. Into the Iowa locker room came a fellow named Cedric Dempsey. He said he was from Arizona and wanted to talk to Lute Olson.

Dempsey, later the president of the NCAA, was at the time Arizona's athletic director. He was looking for a basketball coach, a man to take over a team that had just gone 4–24 for the season, 1–17 in the tough Pacific-10 Conference.

Thompson said when Olson strolled into the Iowa basketball offices a week or so later and announced he had decided to accept the offer at Arizona, "I thought he had lost his marbles."

Seven Pacific-10 championships and three trips to the Final Four later, Olson was on top of the basketball world with an NCAA championship. His decision was validated.

Olson's family approach to his program had a lot to do with winning the NCAA title.

"When we talk with the team on what makes champions, the first thing we discuss is family," Olson said. "Trust is the second, and team-support is right there, too.

"The first thing I do each day is check to see how Kenny Lofton [New York Yankees outfielder and former Arizona basketball player] did in baseball . . . how all our past stars did that night in the National Basketball Association. They are still Wildcats. That never ends."

Kentucky coach Rick Pitino said Arizona's victory was no fluke. "This is a great basketball team," he said "Arizona just got better and better as the season and the tournament wore on."

It was a six-game winning streak in the NCAA, of course, that launched the Wildcats into the winner's circle. But interestingly enough, that was the longest winning streak of the season for Arizona. ■

Corky Simpson began covering Final Fours in the fifties as a sportswriter at the Carthage (Missouri) Evening Press. *For the past 26 years, he has covered college sports at Arizona and many NCAA events as the sports columnist for the* Tucson Citizen.

1998

KENTUCKY GRABS SEVENTH TITLE

By Janet Graham

THE FIRST TIME SCOTT PADGETT HEARD THAT HIS University of Kentucky team wasn't going to win the 1998 national title was in the summer of 1997. Padgett was at the USA Basketball tryout camp when Maryland's Laron Profit strolled by and delivered the challenge to Padgett and Nazr Mohammed.

"What are you going do next year when your two best players are gone, Ron Mercer and coach Pitino?" Profit said, taunting the two Kentucky players.

The usually loquacious Padgett didn't have much of a comeback. He and the Wildcats saved all those for later. But to himself, he thought, "We'll just see about that."

It's hard to think of Kentucky in underdog terms. With six players on the roster who had not played the previous season, they did not have the embarrassment of future NBA riches they had the previous two seasons, and they had to break in new coach Tubby Smith.

In the most endearing way possible, the "Comeback Cats" made a scintillating run to the national championship, capturing each game in heart-stopping fashion in an NCAA Tournament filled with a number of intriguing games.

"I think the way we did it was so special," Smith said. "That's what I always think about when the subject of the championship comes up."

When the season began, there was much consternation in Kentucky. It had taken a while for Rick Pitino and his brash New York style to work their way into the hearts of the fans, but eventually they couldn't get enough of the frenetic, high-powered basketball his teams created. Pitino capped his storybook run by leading the Wildcats to their first national title in 17 years in 1996, then returning the Wildcats to the title game the following season.

Then, the event many fans considered inevitable happened. Pitino departed for a return to the NBA and the East Coast. With

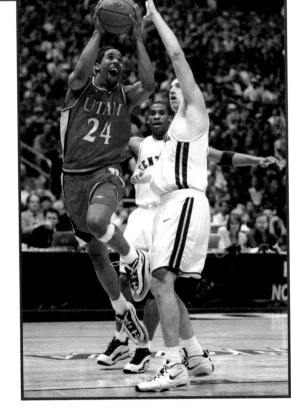

(above) Kentucky bench players leap to their feet at the end of the 1996 championship game in San Antonio, Texas. The Wildcats defeated Utah 78–69 for the title.

(right) Utah forward Andre Miller goes to the hoop in the losing cause against Kentucky.

Pitino gone to the Boston Celtics and a new coach in Smith, fans figured it might be a few seasons before the Wildcats would be holding a national championship trophy above their heads again.

Although Smith had been a Pitino assistant and liked some of the principles of Pitino's coaching, a transition period was inevitable because Smith definitely had his own style.

On the court, Smith implemented the ball-line defense, a more conservative style than Pitino's full-court press. Although Pitino's teams were characterized by a deep bench, there was more of a star system bolstered by role players. Smith liked a balanced attack and always told his players to make the extra pass. At practice and off the court, Smith's personality was less high-octane than that of the excitable Pitino. But Smith was more hands-on when it came to checking up on the players' classwork and whether or not they were making his strict curfew times.

There were adjustments, but the players eventually bought into what Smith was preaching.

Before the season began, the Wildcats would hear nothing of the term *rebuilding year*.

This was a group of players unaccustomed to anything but a Final Four appearance. But an early season blowout loss (89–74) to Arizona in the Maui Invitational was a wake-up call for the Wildcats.

Kentucky followed the Arizona loss with eight straight wins, and it appeared Smith and his staff were making headway with installing their own variations on the schemes that had worked so well for Pitino.

But a shocking December loss in Rupp Arena to unranked Louisville proved just how far the Wildcats had to go. That loss shook up the team and its coach. Smith started making some drastic changes. He shuffled the starting lineup by replacing sophomore center Jamaal Magloire with Mohammed, a 6´10˝ junior, and the team began to come together.

As the SEC season opened, Kentucky was still a heavy favorite and eventually proved it by going unbeaten on the road in the league. That included some compelling victories, such as Smith's first trip back to Athens, Georgia, since he left the head coaching post and his eldest son, G.G., Georgia's starting point guard, behind for the position at Kentucky.

In an incredibly emotional night for Tubby; his wife Donna, who wore the colors of both schools; G.G.; and

Kentucky guard Jeff Sheppard finds an open lane to the basket in the second half of the title game. Later, Jamaal Magloire (inset) embraces Heshimu Evans as the clock winds down on Kentucky's seventh NCAA crown.

it would be coming right back to Atlanta and the Georgia Dome to play its first two rounds of the NCAA Tournament. Undefeated in the building with a 7–0 record, including two SEC titles, the Wildcats were ecstatic at their draw, even as a No. 2 seed.

Kentucky continued on its roll, powering past South Carolina State, 82–67, in the first round and Saint Louis, 88–61, in the second round.

Then it was on to St. Petersburg and Tropicana Field, the baseball stadium turned basketball arena. In a matchup of two of college basketball's perennial power programs, Kentucky dominated UCLA, 94–68, in the South regional semifinals. But it was nearly overlooked in the race to hype the final—Kentucky-Duke.

6:00 A.M. conditioning drills paid off in the final five minutes as the Utes failed to make a field goal, missing 11 consecutive attempts. Kentucky held on for the 78–69 victory and the school's seventh national championship.

This ice-water-in-their-veins performance had become almost routine during the second half of the season. In games decided by 10 points or less, Kentucky was 10–3 on the season. In games decided by three points or less, the Wildcats were 7–1.

The most memorable sight in the Alamodome after the game was the impromptu celebration by the Wildcats as they hoisted their first-year coach onto their shoulders and carried him off the court. It was as good a piece of evidence as any of the continuity of the Big Blue dynasty. This wasn't about a coach or a player leading the team where they wanted to go. It was about a program where winning transcends the change of power.

Nearly every major player on the 1997–1998 team had been through some sort of crisis in his Kentucky career. Sheppard was forced to redshirt in 1996–1997 because of

> ## "I think the way we did it was so special. That's what I always think about when the subject of the championship comes up."
>
> **—Tubby Smith**
> *Coach of Kentucky's 1998 championship team*

It lived up to every expectation as the Wildcats came back from a 17-point deficit with just over nine minutes left, thanks to three-pointers by Kentucky natives Mills and Padgett. Again the game came down to the final play, with Duke having the chance to win it with 4.5 seconds left. Smith elected not to guard the inbounds pass, just as Pitino hadn't in 1992. This time, however, it worked as William Avery's shot bounced harmlessly off the backboard. Kentucky was headed back to the Final Four for the third straight year with an 86–84 win.

In San Antonio, the Comeback Cats lived up to their now widely known reputation for heart-pounding escapes. Against Stanford in the national semifinals, the game was tied at 73–73 at the end of regulation. Kentucky scored the first five points of the extra period and held off the Cardinals to win, 86–85, in overtime and become the first team since UCLA in 1973 to reach its third straight championship game.

Again in the national final, Kentucky fell behind, 41–31, at halftime against a valiant effort by Utah. But midseason

the overload of talent. Mills, a walk-on, endured almost three seasons of sitting on the bench. Turner sat on the bench the entire 1996 national championship game against Syracuse. Mohammed was put through Pitino's version of Weight Watchers, dropping 70 pounds while Pitino forced him to play on the junior varsity team as a freshman. Magloire lost his starting job to Mohammed at the start of the season. Allen Edwards lost his mother to breast cancer right before the SEC tournament. Heshimu Evans, who had been a star at Manhattan before transferring to Kentucky, was relegated to the role of sixth man. Saul Smith had to endure the chants of "Daddy's boy" from opponents' fans and the insults of the talk-show callers around the Commonwealth.

Smith made them believe that the team was the bond that could not be broken. As Turner said, Smith was the "MVP" of the team. ∎

Janet Graham covered four Final Fours and two championship Kentucky teams in 1993, 1996, 1997, and 1998 for the Cincinnati/Kentucky Post. As a sportswriter she has covered a variety of sports, including tennis and the 1990 baseball playoffs. She is also a backup Bengals beat reporter. Today she writes primarily feature stories for the Cincinnati/Kentucky Post.

middle brother Saul, Kentucky's backup point guard, Kentucky won, 90–79.

Kentucky breezed through the SEC tournament, beating Georgia, Arkansas, and South Carolina by an average of 18 points per game. It was the Wildcats' sixth SEC tournament title in seven years.

A few hours after the SEC championship game, when the NCAA Tournament draw was announced, Kentucky found out

1999

CONNECTICUT PERSISTENCE PAYS OFF

By Ken Davis

WE SHOCKED THE WORLD!" THAT'S WHAT POINT guard Khalid El-Amin screamed at a national television audience as the buzzer sounded on Connecticut's 77–74 victory over Duke in the national championship game at Tropicana Field in St. Petersburg, Florida. That was the delirious emotion as the Huskies won one of the most intensely fought championship games.

But before the Huskies could reach that plateau, they had to wind through a maze of obstacles that began a year earlier. Along the way they encountered disappointment, flirted with perfection, confronted self doubts, lifted an enormous monkey off their coach's back, and finally held off a rival who was responsible for so much of their heartache.

"To beat someone like Mike Krzyzewski and the Duke basketball team, I couldn't be prouder," Connecticut coach Jim Calhoun said. "Our kids had done so much for us, the only thing we needed to tell them was what they needed to do to beat a great team. They did it to perfection."

It was that type of year for the Huskies, who finished the season 34–2. In this unsettled age of college basketball, Connecticut kept together all the basic ingredients for a winner—and just barely missed perfection. Richard Hamilton, the Big East Player of the Year, was a pure scorer and clutch performer. There was Ricky Moore, a senior playing the defensive specialist role that is so important to Calhoun's system. El-Amin was the ball-handler and the engine that made things run. Jake Voskuhl played center like a goalie protecting the net. Kevin Freeman quietly pounded away at power forward, doing the dirty work that was part of Connecticut's blue-collar work ethic.

Calhoun recruited and planned this team with the Final Four in mind. There was no doubt when it came time to take aim on the final destination.

The process had started a year earlier, in the losing locker room at the East regional final at the Greensboro (North Carolina) Coliseum. It was March 21, 1998, and the Huskies had lost to North Carolina, 75–64, ending a 32–5 season, just shy of the Final Four—again.

This was the third time in the decade the journey for Calhoun and Connecticut ended one step from the Final Four. Calhoun was gaining the reputation as "Greatest Coach Never to Reach the Final Four," but that thought didn't enter his mind in Greensboro. He looked around the locker room and saw a young and talented team that could return all of its starters and would add some needed depth the following year.

"I want you to remember the hurt," Calhoun told his team. "Remember the pain. Keep it. Remember how it feels. You don't want to feel that way again."

The Huskies held on to Calhoun's words throughout the summer and cherished them all season long.

(above) Connecticut's Ricky Moore leaves the court after the final tick.

(right) In 1999, Connecticut reached high to achieve its championship goal. Jake Voskuhl (right) soared for this rebound as UConn took the 61ˢᵗ title, 77–74.

Coach Jim Calhoun (inset) cradled the trophy moments later. The celebration was one of the tournament's most enthusiastic.

"I think they're the best team, probably, in the country," Penn said.

Even though the Huskies had spent more weeks at No. 1 than Duke during the regular season, there weren't many who shared Penn's feelings. Calhoun didn't mind. This is when he could turn the underdog role to his favor.

Instead of a grueling two-hour workout the day before the game, the Huskies held a walk-through and the coaches handed over a game plan.

The first key was doubling down defensively on Blue Devils center Elton Brand. Voskuhl and Freeman had been playing this type of defense together for so long, they knew exactly what each other was going to do. Connecticut kept it simple. Brand, the national Player of the Year, was held to 15 points on eight shots.

> "Our kids had done
> so much for us, the only thing
> we needed to tell them was
> what they needed to do
> to beat a great team.
> They did it to perfection."
>
> **—Jim Calhoun**
> *Coach of Connecticut's 1999 championship team*

The Huskies never had an offensive lull. At the end of the game, it was Duke that was panicking, rushing shots, turning the ball over, and playing like the challenger instead of the champion.

Connecticut's final key was to keep pressure on guard William Avery and make Trajan Langdon handle the ball. Moore did that to perfection, especially on the final two possessions of the game—both of which resulted in Langdon turnovers.

When Moore forced Langdon to travel with Connecticut leading, 75–74, the Huskies could taste victory.

"It came down to crunch time, him against me," Moore said. "He tried a spin move and I was right there."

El-Amin was quickly fouled and hit two free throws to make it 77–74. Duke raced up the floor, but Langdon fell down and lost his dribble as the buzzer sounded.

After 14 ties and eight lead changes, Connecticut became the first team since Texas Western in 1966 to win the championship in its first Final Four appearance. And the Huskies did it against a Duke team that had blocked their path three times in the NCAA Tournament—including twice in the nineties.

"You really can't describe the feeling," Hamilton said. ■

The Huskies were rewarded with the No. 1 seed in the West region and what seemed to be a favorable draw.

In Denver, the Huskies posted easy victories over Texas–San Antonio, 91–66, and New Mexico, 78–56, and advanced to the Sweet 16 for the seventh time since 1990.

Two games away from the Final Four, Connecticut moved on to Phoenix along with No. 5 seed Iowa, No. 6 Florida, and No. 10 Gonzaga. The pressure intensified.

But the motivation was there, and so was the opportunity. Connecticut handled Iowa, 78–68, in Tom Davis' final appearance as coach of the Hawkeyes. That left Gonzaga, Cinderella of the tournament.

Hamilton scored 21 points as the Huskies defeated Gonzaga, 67–62. As the buzzer sounded, El-Amin embraced Calhoun and kissed him on the cheek.

Finally Four. There were tears all around as the Huskies cut down the nets in Phoenix. Cocaptain Rashamel Jones snuck up on his coach and emptied a cooler of ice water on Calhoun's head and back.

The Connecticut coach, who for years said it didn't matter if he ever reached the Final Four, broke down and cried with his team before the Huskies left Phoenix. A mellow smile broke across his face.

The Huskies, comfortable with their success, turned to the usually reliable components for a 64–58 victory over Ohio State. Hamilton scored a game-high 24 points; El-Amin had 18 points and six assists. Moore, Connecticut's defensive specialist all season, held Ohio State's All-American guard Scoonie Penn to 3 for 13 shooting from the field.

*Ken Davis covers Connecticut sports
for the* Hartford Courant.

THE EAST SHALL RISE AGAIN

AS THE YEAR 2000 APPROACHED, MANY PEOPLE GAVE in to Y2K hysteria, with doomsayers predicting everything from the shutdown of computers and the collapse of banking systems to the end of the world. People stored up water, dried goods, and canned food in preparation for the chaos that some predicted could happen. But none of the fears proved true, and the new year—and new millennium—were ushered in peacefully.

The peace was short-lived. On September 11, 2001, terrorists crashed two planes into the Twin Towers of New York City's World Trade Center and a third plane into the Pentagon in Washington, D.C. A fourth plane was downed in Pennsylvania, apparently headed for the White House. About 2,800 were killed, including the nearly 20 terrorists directly involved. The attacks triggered an economic tailspin. George W. Bush defined his presidency by declaring war on terrorism, with his sights set on al-Qaeda, the international terrorist network headed by Osama bin Laden. The United States went to war in Afghanistan, bent on destroying al-Qaeda's bases there and overthrowing the Taliban, the country's Muslim fundamentalist rulers who harbored bin Laden and his followers. In 2003 the U.S. declared war on Iraq, claiming that country had weapons of mass destruction and was in cahoots with al-Qaeda and other terrorist organizations. The initial stages of the war were won decisively and quickly by the U.S. and its allies, chiefly Great Britain. Months after his regime was overthrown, Iraqi president Saddam Hussein was captured.

Technology continued to flourish, especially in communications and computers. More than 1 billion people were using the Internet, and palm and pocket computers made computing ever more transportable. More and more viruses were hatched by hackers, attacking computers and networks. Junk e-mail proliferated, and legislation was passed to regulate it. Digital was all the rage,

with MP3 players for music and digital video recorders and cameras to record digital images. Major lawsuits were filed against people allegedly downloading music illegally from the Internet.

The space shuttle Columbia disintegrated over Texas in February 2003, killing the seven crew members aboard. In 2004 NASA sent two rovers to Mars to explore the red planet.

Back on planet Earth, Tiger Woods became the first golfer to win nine PGA titles in one year since Sam Snead won 11 in 1950; Woods was also the youngest, at age 24, to complete a career Grand Slam. Bobby Knight's long and sometimes rocky tenure as Indiana basketball coach came to an end in the fall of 2000, and he later landed at Texas Tech. The Yankees won their third straight World Series in 2000, then lost in 2001 to the Arizona Diamondbacks. Alex Rodriguez signed a 10-year, $252 million deal with the Texas Rangers, but the Rangers continued to flounder and A-Rod was dealt to the Yankees in 2004. Lance Armstrong won his fifth consecutive Tour de France in 2003.

Athletes were showing up in court, too: hours after Super Bowl XXXIV, Ray Lewis was arrested in the stabbing deaths of two men and later plea-bargained to a charge of misdemeanor obstruction of justice; youth hockey father Thomas Junta was charged with the fatal beating of a fellow hockey father; and Kobe Bryant, the Los Angeles Lakers' star guard, was charged with sexual assault.

In college basketball, the East dominated the action. The ACC took two NCAA championships in a row, with Duke beating Arizona to win it all in 2001, followed by Maryland's victory in the 2002 title game over a resurgent Indiana. The Big East's Syracuse topped Kansas to win the 2003 title, and Connecticut added the 2004 crown to its 1999 title. As a whole, the East, long a powerhouse in college hoops, flexed its muscles as the new decade unfolded. ∎

Maryland coach Gary Williams celebrates the Terrapins' title in 2002, but it was Emeka Okafor (photo at right) and Connecticut's turn in 2004.

"There's far more individual play today. Team play has not progressed from my time, but the individual play and athleticism has. There's so much more showmanship, with fancy dunks and slick ballhandling. I don't like it. If I want to see showmanship, I'll go see the Globetrotters."
—*John Wooden*

2000

IT'S ALL ABOUT PLACEMATS

By Billy Reed

T HE ROAD TO THE 2000 NATIONAL CHAMPIONSHIP began with placemats. It ended with the typical cutting of the nets and hoisting of the trophy at the RCA Dome in Indianapolis, but the table was first set nearly five years earlier.

In 1996, when second-year Michigan State head coach Tom Izzo was trying to convince Mateen Cleaves, Morris Peterson, and A. J. Granger to cast their lots with the Spartans, he always had special placemats at each recruiting dinner.

Each mat was tailored to a specific player's personality. They included photos, fictitious career stats, and predictions of stardom in East Lansing. For example, Granger's placemat included a headline: "Granger Makes Buzzer-Beater Against Kentucky as Michigan State Wins NCAA Crown."

But as Granger told writer Steve Grinczel of the *Saginaw News*, he thought the mats were rather cheesy. "Yeah, right," Granger remembers telling himself. "What can this Tom Izzo possibly know?"

Yet Granger, a power forward, signed with the Spartans, as did two products of the bleak industrial city of Flint—Cleaves, a highly recruited point guard, and Peterson, a late-blooming small forward.

Their careers didn't exactly get off to the start they envisioned. As freshmen, they belonged to a Spartan team that was eliminated in the second round. Of the NIT, that is.

Said Cleaves, "That was the lowest point of my career. There's nothing wrong with the tournament [NIT], but it was tough to sit in front of the television and watch the teams in the NCAA Tournament. All the media attention they get and how much fun it is and the smiles on the players' faces. And I said to myself, 'I'm going to play in the NCAA Tournament. I'm not going to the NIT anymore.'"

And he kept his promise. Before Cleaves' sophomore year, the Spartans added another product of Flint, shooting guard Charlie Bell.

The media dubbed Cleaves, Peterson, and Bell the "Flintstones," but they really were the cornerstones of a team that brought the Spartans their greatest glory since Earvin "Magic" Johnson led Michigan State to the 1979 national title.

In their final three years, Cleaves, Peterson, and Granger led the Spartans to victory in more than 80 percent of their games. They won three Big Ten regular-season titles and two Big Ten tournament championships.

Then, after being eliminated by Duke in the 1999 national semifinals, they all came back as seniors to lead the Spartans to the university's second NCAA title.

"The night we lost to Duke, we were down," Cleaves said, "but we still had some guys who felt that we had accomplished something just by getting to the Final Four. But Antonio stood up and said, 'Hey, learn from this. Don't feel like you've accomplished something until you've won it all.' And I talked to the guys and said we've got to get hungry. We can't just want to get to the Final Four."

The aforementioned Antonio, last name Smith, was the beginning of Izzo's pipeline to Flint. He exhausted his eligibility without fulfilling his dream, but he kept in constant contact with his former teammates during the 1999–2000 season, helping them cope with adversity.

Early in the season, for example, Cleaves, who had turned down an opportunity to be a cinch NBA first-round draft pick, missed 13 games with a stress fracture in his right foot, forcing Bell to move to the point. The Spartans lost some games, including a memorable one to Kentucky on the road in December, but they held themselves together until Cleaves returned.

During the regular season, the Spartans defeated Wisconsin twice. Then they eliminated coach Dick Bennett's ball-control, defensive-minded Badgers again during the Big Ten tournament. So they weren't exactly thrilled when they learned that their Final Four semifinal opponent would be—you guessed it—Wisconsin, which was making its first Final Four appearance since winning the third NCAA Tournament in 1941.

"You think you're finally finished with a team like that," said Cleaves, "and the next thing you know, you're playing them again. It's like, 'Oh, my God.'"

And that was pretty much the feeling of the RCA Dome crowed of 43,116 and everyone who watched the telecast of the Wisconsin–Michigan State game.

(above) Forward A. J. Granger of the Spartans finished this dunk, two of his 19 points, as Michigan State moved into the lead and won the championship.

(right) Michigan State coach Tom Izzo encouraged his team in the 2000 final as he faced off with Florida coach Billy Donovan, both enthusiastic and sometimes volatile bench coaches. The game was controlled by Michigan State even though Mateen Cleaves was out of the lineup briefly with an ankle injury.

Michigan State's Cleaves brought the ball down the court and passed it off to start play against Wisconsin in the semifinal game. The Spartans defeated the Badgers and then Florida for their first title since 1979.

Magic Johnson clapped and cheered as he watched his Spartans duplicate his team's feat of 21 years earlier.

In 1987, Donovan had been the point guard for Pitino's Providence team that made it to the Final Four in New Orleans. Later, when Pitino took the job at Kentucky, Donovan was one of his assistants.

Like Pitino, he believed in uptempo basketball—full-court pressure on defense, running and gunning on offense. After clawing their way to a 43–32 halftime lead, the Spartans appeared to suffer a fatal blow when, with 16:18 remaining, Cleaves was shoved out of bounds and came down hard on his right ankle, forcing him to hobble to the locker room.

But Bell, drawing on the experience he gained during his fellow Flintstone's 13-game absence, moved to the point and held things together until Cleaves returned with 11:51 remaining. Perhaps inspired by their fellow senior, Peterson and Granger combined for MSU's next 16 points to give the Spartans a 71–58 advantage with 7:36 remaining.

The Spartans lost some games, including a memorable one to Kentucky on the road in December, but they held themselves together until Cleaves returned.

At the end of the Spartans' 89–76 victory, Peterson had 21 points, Granger 19, and Cleaves 18. The three seniors also combined for 13 of Michigan State's 32 rebounds and contributed 10 of the Spartans' 19 assists.

Peterson said he was playing for his grandmother, Clara Mae Spencer, who had died the previous week in Mississippi, and Cleaves said he realized his dream of winning the NCAA title while CBS played the song, "One Shining Moment," in its postgame montage.

And naturally, both, along with Bell, said they were happy to give the citizens of Flint something to be proud of.

But the enduring lesson of the Spartans will be the value of staying in school.

Many of their rivals were decimated by early defections to the pros. Indeed, State was one of the few senior-dominated teams in the nation.

Yet because Peterson, Granger, and especially Cleaves, had a unique commitment to education, to a school, and to a coach, the Spartans prevailed. If it was a great triumph for Michigan State, and it surely was, it was just as great a triumph for college basketball.

In only his fifth year since replacing the popular Jud Heathcote, who coached the Magic-led Spartans to their 1979 title, Izzo had Michigan State back atop the college basketball world. ∎

At halftime, the Spartans led, 19–17. At the end, their margin was 41–33. For fans who think the game revolves around the slam dunk and the three-point shot, it wasn't exactly state-of-the-art basketball.

Despite a subpar performance by Cleaves, who made only one of his seven shots from the floor and committed four turnovers to only one assist, the Spartans won with rebounding (a 42–20 advantage) and superior defense. They also were blessed with an outstanding second half by the 6'7" Peterson, who scored 11 of his game-high 20 points during a 13–3 MSU run in the second half.

Still, it was such an unsatisfactory game that the Spartans' locker room was subdued. Then again, that might have had more to do with the team slogan that was rooted in Antonio Smith's comments after the loss to Duke the previous year:

"We haven't won anything yet."

As Izzo put it, "They really are excited about what they've accomplished, but they have a dream. Everybody has dreams, but few of us ever get to live them. And it's here. They get to live it."

The Spartans' championship-game opponent was a team about as different from Wisconsin as salsa music from the waltz. Under young coach Billy Donovan, the Florida Gators had mastered the uptempo style that Donovan had learned under Rick Pitino.

2001

DUKE DOES IT AGAIN

By Tom Hanlon

DUKE HAD WON A RECORD 22 CONSECUTIVE ACC road games, but on January 27 that streak was in jeopardy. Tenth-ranked Maryland led the Blue Devils 90–80 with 54 seconds remaining, and Cole Field House was ready to erupt once the victory was in the books.

Enter Jason Williams, one of Duke's two first-team All-Americans. One layup and two three-pointers later, and Duke was down only 90–88 with 40 seconds to go. Two Nate James free throws tied the game at 90–90 with 21 seconds to go. Maryland's Drew Nicholas missed from the corner at the buzzer. Overtime. Shane Battier, Duke's other first-team All-American, hit a three-pointer to give Duke its first lead since early in the first half. Duke went on to win 98–96.

Now fast-forward to February 27, the second meeting between the two ACC rivals. Maryland turned the tables on Duke, beating them in Durham 91–80. Adding injury to insult, Duke center Carlos Boozer broke his foot in the loss. Many fans and pundits—perhaps guilty of wishful thinking—began to write Duke off. "There were a lot of people who were happy; they thought that was it," Duke coach Mike Krzyzewski said. "It wasn't. It was the beginning of us becoming a great basketball team."

They were a pretty good team already: though their ACC road victory streak was broken with a loss at Virginia on February 14, they were 25–4 when Boozer went down. In their first game after Boozer's departure, the Blue Devils handed North Carolina a 14-point loss in Chapel Hill. They won the ACC tournament, beating North Carolina State by 15, Maryland by 2 in the semifinals (after being down by 11), and thoroughly dominating North Carolina in the final, 79–53.

With Boozer still on the sidelines, Duke rolled over Monmouth 95–52 in the first round of the NCAA Tournament. They dispatched Missouri 94–81 in the second round. Boozer made his return in the next game, a 76–63 win against UCLA. A 79–69 win against Southern Cal landed Duke in a familiar place—the Final Four—against a familiar opponent: Maryland. Having beaten Maryland two of three times during the season, Duke would have to make it three of four to have a chance at its third national title in 11 years.

Williams had engineered the electrifying, last-minute comeback on January 27 against Maryland, scoring eight points in 14 seconds. But in the semifinal game, he scored four points in the first half on just 1 for 7 shooting.

With 6:57 to play in the first half, the Terrapins opened up a 39–17 lead. Krzyzewski called a timeout and, in the huddle, looked each of his players in the eye. "You're losing by so much, you can't play any worse," he said. "So what are you worried about, losing by 40? We're already losing by 20, so will you just play?"

Duke freshman guard Chris Duhon, who scored 10 points and had six assists in the game, said, "It's a 40-minute game and they beat us for 12 minutes. If you're going to beat us, you've got to do it for 40."

Maryland, stung by two Duke double-digit comebacks in losses earlier in the year, knew the math. But Williams revved it up in the second half, scoring 19 points to finish with 23, and Battier scored 25 and snagged eight rebounds. It was Williams' three-pointer with 6:52 to play that gave the Blue Devils their first lead of the game, 73–72. "Well, nobody's 22 points better than Duke," said Maryland head coach Gary Williams. "I knew they'd make a run. I thought we had enough to sustain it."

They didn't. Maryland, vanquished by a superior team, ended its season 25–11, with four hard-fought games against the Blue Devils. Duke took its 95–84 victory into

(above) Duke's Mike Dunleavy goes airborne past Arizona guard Jason Gardner while looking to pass the ball to an open teammate during the Blue Devils' championship-game victory.

(right) Gardner and Duke guard Jason Williams went stride for stride in the second half, but in the end the Wildcats came up a step short.

Dunleavy, the championship game's MOP, makes his third straight three-pointer during the second half at the Hubert H. Humphrey Metrodome in Minneapolis, Minnesota.

scored 18 of his 20 points in the second half, it was not enough as Arizona broke from a 32–30 halftime lead to an 80–61 win, outscoring the Spartans 21–3 to begin the second half. Arenas picked off six passes, a Final Four semifinal game record, and all five Arizona starters scored in double figures, led by Gardner's 21. "We just did some things out there that were un-Spartanlike," Michigan State coach Tom Izzo said after the game.

Four future first-round NBA picks suited up for the title game: Duke's Battier, Williams, and Mike Dunleavy Jr., and Arizona's Jefferson. It was Duke's seventh title game under Krzyzewski, who tied legendary Kentucky coach Adolph Rupp with his ninth Final Four victory in beating Maryland in the semifinals. Krzyzewski had guided Duke to nine Final Fours in the past 16 seasons.

The Blue Devils weren't concerned about press clippings and history. They weren't thinking about their positioning in future drafts. They were focused on the here and now.

> ## "There were a lot of people who were happy; they thought that was it. It wasn't. It was the beginning of us becoming a great basketball team."
>
> —*Mike Krzyzewski*
> *Coach of Duke's 2001 championship team, on the Blue Devils' regular-season loss to Maryland*

The game, as expected, was tight. Duke led 35–33 at the half, and, with Dunleavy scoring 18 of his 21 points in the second half on the strength of five three-pointers, threatened to break away. A Dunleavy trey put Duke up 50–39 four minutes into the second half. But Arizona came storming back, going on a 9–0 run to cut the lead to 50–48.

In a game of swings, Duke ran the lead back to 10, 61–51, but the Cats kept clawing their way back into it. Four times Arizona cut the lead to within three. Three of those four times, Battier responded with buckets. Williams hit a three-pointer with 1:45 left to give Duke an eight-point margin. Duke's stifling defense, which held Arizona to 39 percent from the floor, maintained the margin, and Duke won its third title under Krzyzewski, 82–72.

"It's tough," Olson said after the game. "Someone's got to lose it. Duke is deserving. We gave them a good run and couldn't get it done." ∎

the championship game, winning its sixth straight semifinal game since 1990 under coach K. They had given themselves a shot at winning the title on the same floor that they won it on in 1992, at the Metrodome in Minneapolis.

Krzyzewski had spoken of Boozer's injury as the beginning of Duke becoming a great team. But Loren Woods, the Arizona Wildcats' center, believed in Arizona's greatness from the beginning of the season, proclaiming the Wildcats as perhaps "the greatest college team ever."

Indeed, all five Cats starters—Woods, Richard Jefferson, Michael Wright, Jason Gardner, and Gilbert Arenas—were preseason nominations for the John Wooden award for player of the year. Arizona was ranked No. 1 in several preseason polls, and the Cats were deep and strong. Coach Lute Olson, with a career record of 422–127 at Arizona (and 614–219 overall), had assembled an arsenal that could run, shoot, and wreak havoc on defense.

But the season was not picture-perfect. Woods and Jefferson were suspended early in the season for NCAA violations. Senior Eugene Edgerson, who played on Arizona's 1997 national championship team, was sent home for a few days in January after complaining about his role on the team. Arizona began the season 6–5 and fell to No. 10 in the AP

poll on December 16. Olson then took a leave of absence in late December to be with his sick wife, Bobbi. On January 1, Bobbi, Olson's wife of 47 years, died of ovarian cancer. The team, coached by assistant coach Jim Rosborough during Olson's leave, dropped to No. 21 in the polls. This was not how things were supposed to go.

But Olson returned on January 16, and the Cats kicked it into gear, winning 11 straight games through the end of the regular season, including a 76–75 victory over then–No. 1 Stanford, and on their march through the NCAA Tournament. They rolled early in the tournament, trouncing Eastern Illinois and handily beating Butler, then beating No. 3 seed Mississippi 66–56 and No. 1 seed Illinois 87–81. The latter win vaulted the Wildcats into the Final Four.

Arizona went up against a formidable opponent in its semifinal game: Michigan State, which had become just the ninth team to make it to three straight Final Fours. The Spartans had won their fourth straight Big Ten title and were a physical team that pounded the boards, created turnovers, and had great leadership in Jason Richardson, Charlie Bell, and Andre Hutson.

But Richardson and Bell were shut down by the Cats, combining for 3 for 21 from the floor. And though Hutson

---

Tom Hanlon is a freelance writer who has written 30 books, including a wide assortment of sports, coaching, and health and fitness titles. He lives in Champaign, Illinois, with his wife and two children.

2002

TAKING CARE OF UNFINISHED BUSINESS

By Tom Hanlon

THE FINAL FOUR IS FAMILIAR TERRITORY FOR THE Maryland Terrapins. The up-and-down 2001 team lost 95–84 to Duke in a Final Four semifinal game in Minneapolis after leading their Atlantic Coast Conference rivals by 22 points. The loss left a bad taste in their mouths and a hunger in their bellies.

In 2002, in Atlanta, they had unfinished business to take care of.

And they had the personnel to take care of it. They had senior leadership, four returning starters, arguably the country's best backcourt in All-American Juan Dixon and junior Steve Blake, and a deep and balanced frontcourt anchored by agile center Lonny Baxter.

Gary Williams, in his 13th year as Maryland coach, liked the Terps' chances. "I think we have the character that will allow us to get back to the Final Four," he said before the season began. Maryland was a consensus top-five pick in everyone's preseason polls.

Of course, any road to Atlanta must go through Durham, North Carolina, and the Duke Blue Devils. Maryland was No. 2 in the AP preseason poll. No. 1 belonged to 2001 NCAA champion Duke.

Maryland lost its first game of the season to Arizona, the 2001 NCAA runner-ups. But in early January the Terps extended the nation's longest home winning streak (84) against nonconference opponents with a 92–69 win over Norfolk State (the Terps' final nonconference game ever to be played at Cole Field House). Six days later they pummeled North Carolina, 112–79, Maryland's most lopsided victory against the Tar Heels in their 79-year-old rivalry. The win vaulted Maryland to No. 3 in the country.

Then came No. 1 Duke. The reigning champs ended up running away with a 99–78 victory over the Terps in a game that had 30 lead changes in the opening 23 minutes.

But Maryland was undeterred. They were 8–1 in the ACC by early February, and on February 17 they exacted their revenge on Duke, vanquishing the No. 1 Blue Devils 87–73. Maryland jumped to No. 2 with the win; Duke dropped to No. 3.

Maryland went on to win the ACC crown, and their entire lineup earned All-ACC honors. Dixon collected first-team All-American, first-team All-ACC, and ACC All-Defense awards. The Terps were upset by N.C. State in the ACC semifinals, 86–82, but earned the No. 1 seed in the NCAA East Region.

A few days before their first tournament game, Dixon was named the ACC Player of the Year and Williams was honored as the ACC Coach of the Year. The Terps cruised past Siena 85–70 in their opening round of the East regional, with Dixon scoring 29 points. Two days later they crushed Wisconsin 87–57, reaching the Sweet 16 for the sixth time in nine years. They took care of Kentucky 78–68 in the East regional semifinals, and found themselves one victory away from their second Final Four in a row.

Maryland indeed appeared to be on its way to the big dance in Atlanta. While a return trip to the Final Four for the Terps would not have surprised anyone, there was a Cinderella team out there that—to the great astonishment of all but their most diehard fans—was also mowing down its NCAA opponents.

The Indiana Hoosiers were no newcomers to the NCAA Tournament, having won five championships and being

(above) Juan Dixon of Maryland cuts down the net following the Terrapins' title-game victory over Indiana.

(right) Maryland's Tahj Holden tries to get a pass past Jared Jeffries of Indiana during the 2002 championship game at the Georgia Dome in Atlanta, Georgia.

Dixon jumps on top of Lonnie Baxter to celebrate Maryland's 64–52 victory over Indiana to claim the 2002 crown.

among the all-time leaders in tournament appearances and Final Four games and wins. But dust was gathering on their last championship, won in 1987 under Bobby Knight, and the Knight era was over at Indiana. Mike Davis was in his second season as coach of the Hoosiers, and they entered the NCAA Tournament with 11 losses and little chance to advance past the early rounds. But they played inspired ball, mowing down Utah 75–56 and UNC–Wilmington 76–67. Then came mighty Duke, No. 1 seed in the South Region.

> ### "It took us a good 25 minutes before we really ran our offense. It was a thrill for me to watch these guys work hard and get their reward."
>
> **—Gary Williams**
> *Coach of Maryland's*
> *2002 championship team*

Indiana—hot from the outside for most of the tournament—derailed the Blue Devils 74–73. "You don't have to be the best team; you only have to be the best team that day," Davis said.

The Hoosiers hit 15 of 19 three-point shots against Kent State to win the South Region and earn their trip to Atlanta. After their 90–82 victory over Connecticut, Maryland advanced to the Final Four. Kansas and Oklahoma advanced as well, and the Final Four was set: Indiana vs. Oklahoma, Maryland vs. Kansas.

Indiana continued its David-versus-Goliath ways in knocking off No. 2 seed Oklahoma 73–64. In a meeting of No. 1 seeds, Maryland overcame an early 13–2 deficit and outlasted Kansas 97–88 behind Dixon's 33 points. Kansas cut a 20-point deficit to 5 with a little over a minute to go, but this time Maryland didn't wither down the stretch and vaulted to the championship game, where they would be an 8-point favorite against Indiana.

The Hoosiers, who hit 23 of 32 three-pointers against Kent State and Oklahoma, started out 8 of 12 from behind the arc. But their big men, Jared Jeffries and Jeff Newton, struggled against Maryland's frontcourt of Baxter, Byron Moulton, Chris Wilcox, and reserve Tahj Holden. Jeffries and Newton combined for 14 points and 12 rebounds, and Dixon's three-pointer gave Maryland the lead for good at 45–44 with 9:42 left. Dixon wound up with 18 points, Baxter chipped in 15 to go with 14 rebounds, and the Terps and Williams came away with their first national championship by a score of 64–52, capping off a 32–4 season.

"We had to really grind it," Williams said. "It took us a good 25 minutes before we really ran our offense. It was a thrill for me to watch these guys work hard and get their reward." ∎

2003

THIRD TIME'S THE CHARM

By Tom Hanlon

JIM BOEHEIM HAD SEEN A LOT IN HIS 27 YEARS AS head coach of the Syracuse Orangemen. A relentless reviewer of tapes, he had seen most of Syracuse's games more than once—with one exception.

He had never reviewed the 1987 NCAA championship game, played in the Superdome in New Orleans. He didn't need to. He could still see Keith Smart's baseline jumper going in with four seconds to go, lifting Indiana to a 74–73 win over his Orangemen.

In 1996 Boeheim again led Syracuse to the title game, this time against Kentucky. No last-second drama here, but the results were the same: another Syracuse loss, 76–67.

Heading into the 2002–2003 season, no one expected much out of Syracuse. They were young, untested, and unrated at the beginning of the season. This was fine with Boeheim. He knew his team's potential. Young and untested? Yes. But *very* talented.

Syracuse lost to Memphis to begin the season, but then reeled off 11 victories in a row. The young team—led by sensational freshman Carmelo Anthony and fellow frosh standouts Gerry McNamara and Billy Edelin, and backed by sophomores Hakim Warrick and Josh Pace as well as

senior Kueth Duany—were playing like seasoned veterans. *Talented* seasoned veterans.

Most of these guys were in diapers when Smart drilled his baseline jumper in 1987. But they weren't interested in ancient history. They were focused on the *now*.

Fans around the nation began to take notice as the Orangemen continued to pile up wins. With a victory on February 26 against West Virginia, they stood 20–4 on the season. It marked the 25th time in Boeheim's career that Syracuse had notched at least 20 victories. Heading into the NCAA Tournament, Syracuse was 24–5. They were the third seed in the powerful East Region, which included Oklahoma (No. 1) and Wake Forest (No. 2).

Boeheim's young guns would be tested. They got there on the strength of their balance, athleticism, shooting, rebounding, and their stifling 2-3 zone. How far they would go was anyone's guess.

Manhattan, 14th seed in the East, gave Syracuse plenty to handle in the opening round. Early in the second half Syracuse clung to a 39–38 lead, but the Orangemen ground out a 76–65 victory behind Anthony's 17 points (including 10 in the second half) and Edelin's 15.

Up next was sixth seed Oklahoma State. The Cowboys jumped out to a 25–8 lead, but Syracuse, spurred by Edelin's 10 points, went on a 15–4 run to close to within 31–25 at halftime. Anthony's three-pointer gave the Orangemen the lead for good at 45–43, and Syracuse went on to win 68–56 as Edelin scored 20. All of Anthony's 12 points came in the second half.

Anthony followed up that game with another strong second-half performance, this time against Auburn. Scoreless in the first half, Anthony pumped in 18 in the final stanza and the Orangemen withstood four three-pointers by the Tigers in the final 80 seconds to hang on for a 79–78 win. Two days later Syracuse earned a trip to the Final Four—held in the Superdome, on the same court where Indiana had beaten them 16 years earlier—by easily handling No. 1 seed Oklahoma. The Orangemen held the Sooners to 31 percent shooting and forced 19 turnovers as Anthony notched his 20th double-double of the season, scoring 20 points and grabbing 10 rebounds.

Rounding out the Final Four were Marquette, which upset No. 1 seed Kentucky in the Midwest; Kansas, the

(above) Syracuse guard Josh Pace goes in for an uncontested layup against Kansas in the two teams' national title showdown at the Louisiana Superdome in New Orleans.

(right) Later, Syracuse players and fans celebrate the Orangemen's first national championship after the clock runs out on Kansas.

Syracuse forward Hakim Warrick and Texas center James Thomas battle for control of the ball during their semifinal matchup in New Orleans, Louisiana.

No. 2 seed in the West, which beat No. 1 seed Arizona 78–75 in the regional finals; and Texas, the No. 1 seed in the South, which advanced to New Orleans on the strength of its 85–76 victory over Michigan State in the regional finals.

Kansas shredded Marquette 94–61 in one semifinal game. Syracuse, behind Anthony's career-high 33 points and 14 rebounds, held on to oust Texas 95–84. Texas led briefly in the second half, with its last lead at 61–59, but Anthony proved too much for the Longhorns, and the Orangemen prepared to meet the Jayhawks in the championship game.

Boeheim entered the title game with 652 wins, good enough for 22nd on the all-time list. His .742 winning percentage was third among active Division I coaches. But none of that mattered to him on championship night.

What did matter was the next 40 minutes. Not 39 minutes, 56 seconds, as happened against Indiana. A full 40 this time.

It turned out he needed the full 40. The game went down to the final second.

> ## "Both teams gave it everything they had for 40 minutes. We were fortunate that we still had the lead at the end of the game."
>
> **—Jim Boeheim**
> *Coach of Syracuse's 2003 championship team*

The Orangemen led by 18 in the first half, but coach Roy Williams and his Jayhawks weren't accustomed to panicking. Kansas cut the lead to 11 by halftime, 53–42. The Jayhawks began the second half with a 10–2 run, slicing the lead to 55–52.

Anthony led Syracuse on a run of its own, pushing the lead back up to 12 with 7:32 to go, but the resilient Jayhawks manufactured a 14–4 run to pull within 2 (80–78) with 40 seconds remaining. No one said this was going to be easy.

Duany hit one of two free throws with 24 seconds to go; back to a three-point lead. Hakim Warrick missed two free throws, opening the door for a tie if Kansas could sink a three.

Warrick made up for his misses by swatting Michael Lee's three-point attempt out of bounds with 1.5 seconds to go. Kansas had a final chance to tie, but All-American Kirk Hinrich missed a desperation three and this time the close one went Boeheim's way.

Anthony once again led the way with 20 points and 10 rebounds, and McNamara nailed six three-pointers in the first half. With the win, Syracuse became the first team since Villanova in 1985 to win the title despite not being ranked in the AP preseason poll.

"I guess maybe this building owed us one game," said a jubilant Boeheim afterward. "Both teams gave it everything they had for 40 minutes. We were fortunate that we still had the lead at the end of the game." ∎

2004

REMEMBER THE ALAMODOME

By Tom Hanlon

CONNECTICUT COACH JIM CALHOUN AND HIS Huskies had been to San Antonio before. Calhoun had a picture of his players on a riverboat on the San Antonio River, taken in March 2003, shortly before they were knocked out of that year's NCAA Tournament by Texas. Before the Huskies returned home, Calhoun told them they'd be back in the Alamodome, where they had just lost. The Alamodome was the site of the 2004 Final Four.

It would be no sneak attack. UConn was ranked No. 1 going into the 2003–2004 season. No team since Kentucky in 1996 had begun the season as No. 1 and ended as NCAA champion. But Calhoun wasn't worried about going wire to wire. He had top guns Emeka Okafor and Ben Gordon returning, along with a stellar supporting cast including Rashad Anderson, Taliek Brown, and Denham Brown. He had signed freshmen Charlie Villanueva and Josh Boone to add depth. But lots of teams were loaded, including Pittsburgh in their own conference, the Big East. The road back to San Antonio would be neither easy nor short.

The stay at the top would not last long, either. In their fourth game of the season, playing in the preseason NIT

tournament, the Huskies were soundly beaten by Georgia Tech, 77–61, as Okafor's back problems flared up. After consecutive losses at Notre Dame and Pittsburgh in February, the Huskies had a 19–5 record, a No. 8 ranking, and an identity crisis. They then reeled off five wins in a row before losing the regular-season finale at Syracuse. Would the real Huskies please stand up?

They stood up in the Big East tournament, beating Notre Dame and Villanova without Okafor, who was stuck on the bench with back problems. They then beat Pittsburgh 61–58 with Okafor playing to win the Big East tournament.

UConn entered the NCAA Tournament a No. 2 seed in the Phoenix Region. They chalked up 17-point wins against Vermont and DePaul in the first two rounds, then ran over Vanderbilt, 73–53, in the Sweet 16, with Okafor hitting double-doubles in all three games. UConn easily handled Alabama in the Elite 8, 87–71, despite Okafor playing a painful 19 minutes and scoring only two points. The Huskies would be playing in their second-ever Final Four, their first being in 1999, when they won the national title over Duke, the team they would face in the semifinals.

Duke, the No. 1 seed in the Atlanta Region, was making its 10th Final Four appearance. The Blue Devils had been impressive in reaching the 2004 Final Four, notching wins against Alabama State (96–61), Seton Hall (90–62), Illinois (72–62), and Xavier (66–63). The game promised to be highly competitive—a duel between two top powers.

And it did not disappoint.

Both teams shot poorly in the first half, and, with Okafor spending most of the half on the bench with foul trouble, Duke took a 41–34 lead into the locker room. But UConn came out firing in the second half, and kept chipping away at the Blue Devil lead, three times getting within one point, the last at 63–62 with 7:31 left. Then Duke took off. Daniel Ewing hit a layup, J. J. Redick hit a three, and Chris Duhon hit a two. When Duhon sank two free throws at the 3:28 mark, the Blue Devils led 75–67.

(above) UConn head coach Jim Calhoun hoists the championship trophy following the Huskies' 82–73 victory over Georgia Tech in the 2004 championship game.

(right) UConn forward Rashad Anderson (left) celebrates with team-mate guard Taliek Brown as the final seconds tick off the clock during the championship game at the Alamodome in San Antonio, Texas.

From then on, it was all UConn. Anderson drilled a three-pointer, Gordon drained two free throws, and Okafor—who scored all 18 of his points after halftime—hit a jumper to cut the Duke lead to 75–74 with 1:18 to go. Okafor scored again with 0:25 to go, giving Connecticut its first lead since the first half, 76–75. Anderson then stole the ball from Redick and made two free throws with 0:12 to go, pushing the margin to 78–75. Following another errant Duke shot, Okafor rebounded and made one foul shot. Duhon hit a long three as time expired but Connecticut prevailed, 79–78, thanks to a 12–0 run in the final few minutes.

It would be no sneak attack. UConn was ranked No. 1 going into the 2003–2004 season. No team since Kentucky in 1996 had begun the season as No. 1 and ended as NCAA champion.

Meanwhile, Georgia Tech, the No. 3 seed in the St. Louis Region and 27–9 overall, had advanced to the Final Four by beating Kansas in overtime, 79–71. In the other semifinal game, Tech beat Oklahoma State 67–65 on Will Bynum's driving layup with 1.5 seconds to play. The Yellow Jackets were led by B. J. Elder (16 points per game), Jarret Jack (12.7), Marvin Lewis (11.6), and Bynum (10.1). Center Luke Schenscher led the teams in rebounds (6.2 per game) and blocks (47 on the season). Still, the upstart Yellow Jackets were the decided underdogs going into the championship game.

Both teams were cold in the opening minutes, and Georgia Tech took its first and only lead of the game at 12–11 with 13:41 to play in the first half on a layup by Clarence Moore. The rest of the half belonged to the Huskies, who led 41–26 at the intermission. Any thoughts of a comeback were immediately crushed by the Huskies at the beginning of the second half, as they quickly expanded their lead to 21 and then, by the 14:11 mark, to 25, at 56–31. A late flurry by the Yellow Jackets cut into that margin, but the game was never in doubt, ending at 82–73. UConn had its second national championship in six years. Okafor scored 24 points and grabbed 15 rebounds—his 24th double-double of the season—and Gordon and Anderson chipped in with 21 and 18 points, respectively.

UConn had gone wire to wire, claiming the title by beating the team that first knocked them out of the No. 1 spot early in the season. "Going wire to wire is one of the hardest things you can do," said Calhoun, who joined Bobby Knight and Mike Krzyzewski as the only active coaches with multiple NCAA titles. And the Huskies did it in the Alamodome, where Calhoun had told his players they would return.

They did more than return. ■